First Edition copyright © 2013

All rights reserved. permission in writing must be obtained from the writer before any part of this publication may be reproduced or transmitted in any form or by any means, electronic or mechanical. including photocopy, recording or any information storage or retrievel system.

CONTENTS

Part 1 – Algebra

1.1 Types of numbers..5
1.2 Interval notation..10
1.3 Rationalization..13
1.4 Exponents and Logarithms...14
1.5 Equations..33
1.6 Equations with absolute value..45
1.7 Polynomials..50
1.8 Binomial Theorem..58
1.9 Sequences and Series..63
1.10 Complex numbers...84
1.11 Mathematical induction..104

Part 2 – Functions

2.1 Introduction to functions..111
2.2 Linear functions..120
2.3 Quadratic Functions..141
2.4 Transformations..173
2.5 Absolute value functions..188
2.6 Simple Rational functions..208
2.7 Exponential functions...223
2.8 Logarithmic functions...240
2.9 Radical functions..261
2.10 Piecewise functions..272
2.11 Composite functions...305
2.12 Inverse functions..307

Part 3 – Trigonometry

3.1 Degrees and Radians..310
3.2 Definition of the Trigonometric functions.............................315
3.3 Trigonometric Identities...328
3.4 Trigonometric functions...331
3.5 Sine and Cosine Rule..345
3.6 Trigonometric Ratios..351
3.7 Inverse Trigonometric functions..355
3.8 Trigonometric equations...360
3.9 3D geometry...366

ANSWER KEY

PART 1 – ALGEBRA

1.2	Types of numbers	374
1.2	Interval notation	378
1.3	Rationalization	381
1.4	Exponents and Logarithms	382
1.5	Equations	392
1.6	Equations with absolute value	400
1.7	Polynomials	401
1.8	Binomial Theorem	406
1.9	Sequences and Series	409
1.10	Complex numbers	423
1.11	Mathematical induction	432

PART 2 – FUNCTIONS

2.1	Introduction to functions	435
2.2	Linear functions	440
2.3	Quadratic Functions	452
2.4	Transformations	478
2.5	Absolute value functions	483
2.6	Simple Rational functions	497
2.7	Exponential functions	511
2.8	Logarithmic functions	521
2.9	Radical functions	535
2.10	Piecewise functions	544
2.11	Composite functions	560
2.12	Inverse functions	561

PART 3 – TRIGONOMETRY

3.1	Degrees and Radians	563
3.2	Definition of the Trigonometric functions	566
3.3	Trigonometric Identities	570
3.4	Trigonometric functions	573
3.5	Sine and Cosine Rule	581
3.6	Trigonometric Ratios	586
3.7	Inverse Trigonometric functions	588
3.8	Trigonometric equations	589
3.9	3D geometry	593

CHAPTER 1 – ALGEBRA

1.1. – TYPES OF NUMBERS

Natural Numbers (N):   N = {_, __, __, __, __ ...}

Integers (Z):   Z = {..., __, __, __, __, __, 0, __, __, __, __, __ ...}

Rational Numbers (Q): $Q = \{\frac{a}{b}, a, b \in Z\}$

Numbers that **can** be written as _____ being both the

numerator and the denominator _____.

Examples: $\frac{1}{1}, \frac{2}{3}, \frac{-7}{3}, \frac{4}{-1}, \frac{\_\_}{\_\_}, \_\_\_\_\_, \_\_\_\_\_$ ...

Irrational Numbers (Q'): $Q' \neq \{\frac{a}{b}, a, b \in Z\}$ Numbers that _____ be written as

fractions, being both the _____ and _____ Integers.

Examples: __, __, __ ...

Real Numbers (R):   R = Q + Q' (Rationals and Irrationals)

Represented in a Venn diagram:

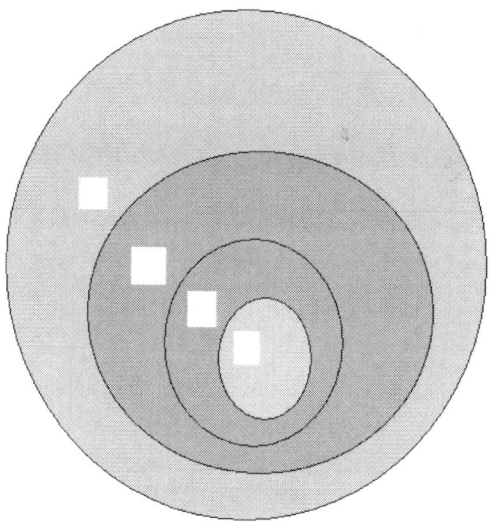

Exercises

1. Natural numbers are contained in the _____ numbers.

2. Integer numbers are contained in the _____ numbers

3. Rational numbers are contained in the _____ numbers.

4. Irrational numbers are located _____.

5. Shade the area in which the irrational numbers are located:

6. True or False:

    a. All Natural numbers are Integers: ____

    b. All Real numbers are Natural: ____

    c. All Rational numbers are Real: ____

    d. All Real numbers are Rational: ____

    e. All Integer numbers are Rational: ____

    f. All Real numbers are Irrational: ____

    g. Some Irrational numbers are Real and some are not: ____

    h. Some Irrational numbers are Integers: ____

    i. Some integers are negative: ____

    j. Some Irrationals are negative: ____

    k. Some Natural numbers are negative: ____

7. Fill the chart with yes or no (follow the example):

Number	Natural	Integer	Rational	Real
-2	no	yes	yes	yes
π				
$-3.121212...$				
-15.16				
$\sqrt{3}$				
$-2\frac{2}{5}$				
$\sqrt[3]{8}$				

6

8. Fill the numbers column with appropriate numbers and yes or no. Follow the example.

Number	Natural	Integer	Rational	Real
	no	yes		
		no	yes	yes
	yes	yes	yes	
			no	yes
		no	yes	yes
			yes	
	no			
		yes	no	

4. Convert the following numbers into the form: $\dfrac{n}{m}$

1. $0.333\ldots =$

2. $1.111\ldots =$

3. $5.3 =$

4. $5.2828\ldots =$

5. $-2.3535\ldots =$

6. $42.67 =$

7. $12.355355\ldots =$

8. $-31.44 =$

9. 0.125125… =

10. 3.22332233… =

11. 1115.36 =

12. 122.53 =

13. 1.123123… =

14. 1.22565656… =

15. 1.5696969… =

16. 5.540404040… =

5. Given the following diagram:

Write the following numbers in the appropriate location in the diagram:

a. 2.2
b. −5
c. 3
d. $\dfrac{1}{3}$
e. 5
f. −3.3
g. 1.111…
h. $\dfrac{1}{\sqrt{3}}$
i. 2π
j. $1+2\pi$
k. $\sqrt{2}+3$
l. $\dfrac{4}{2}$

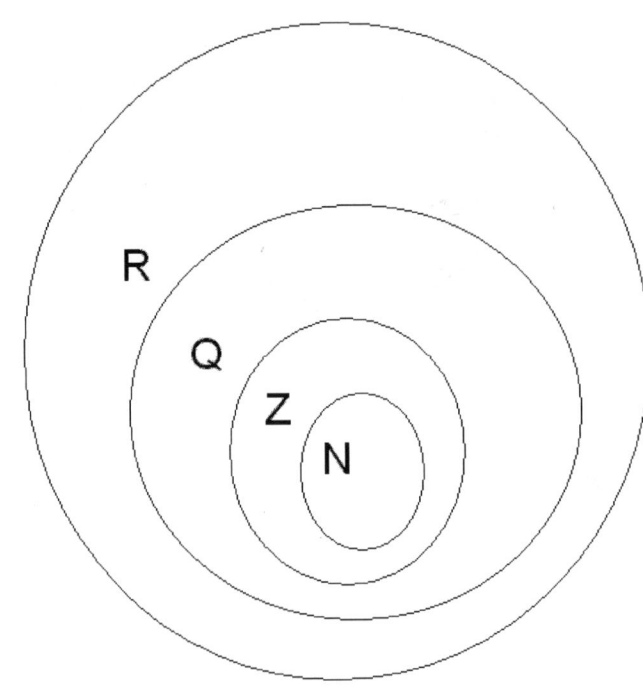

6. Circle the right option. The number –2 is:

    a. Integer and Natural.
    b. Positive
    c. Integer and Rational
    d. Natural and Real
    e. Natural and Rational
    f. None of the above

7. Circle the right option. The number 3.41414141..... is:

    a. Integer and Natural.
    b. Natural
    c. Integer and Real
    d. Rational and Integer
    e. Rational
    f. None of the above

8. Circle the right option. The number 3.41 is:

    a. Integer and Natural.
    b. Integer
    c. Rational and Real
    d. Integer and Real
    e. Rational and negative
    f. None of the above

9. Circle the right option. The number $\sqrt{31}$ is:

    a. Integer and Natural.
    b. Integer
    c. Decimal
    d. Integer and Real
    e. Rational
    f. Irrational

10. Circle the right option. The number 5 is:

    a. Natural.
    b. Integer
    c. Real
    d. Integer and Natural
    e. Rational and Natural
    f. All of the above

1.2. – INTERVAL NOTATION

x ∋ (a, b] or {x| a < x ≤ b} means x is between a and b, not including a and including b.

Exercises

1. Represent the following Intervals on the real line:

   a. x ∋ (2, 5]

   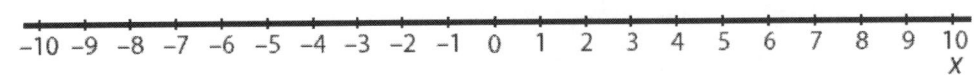

   b. x ∋ (3,6)

   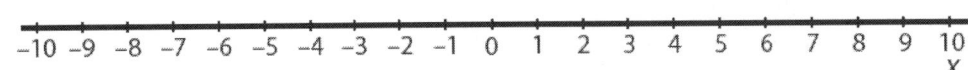

   c. x ∋ [–5,9]

   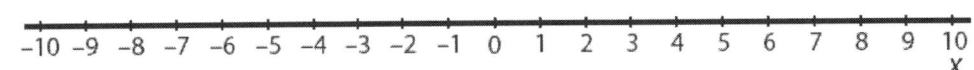

   d. x ∋ [–8,–1)

   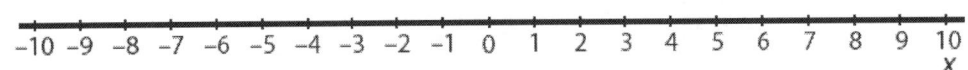

   e. x ∋ [–∞,–1)

   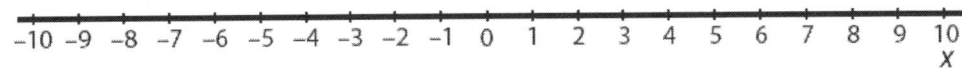

   f. x ∋ [–∞,6]

   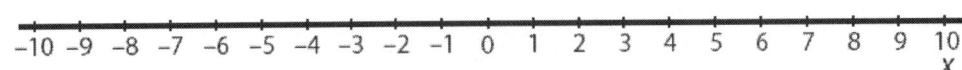

   g. x ∋ (6, ∞]

   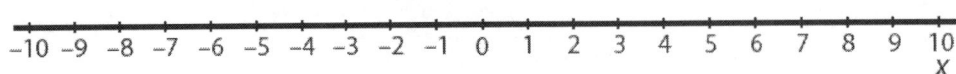

   h. {x| 7 < x < 9}

   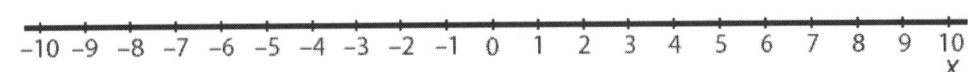

   i. {x| –7 < x < –2}

   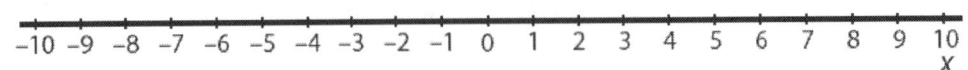

j. {x| 1 < x < 2}

```
-10 -9 -8 -7 -6 -5 -4 -3 -2 -1  0  1  2  3  4  5  6  7  8  9  10
                                                                x
```

k. {x| ∞ < x < 2}

```
-10 -9 -8 -7 -6 -5 -4 -3 -2 -1  0  1  2  3  4  5  6  7  8  9  10
                                                                x
```

l. {x| 1 < x < ∞ }

```
-10 -9 -8 -7 -6 -5 -4 -3 -2 -1  0  1  2  3  4  5  6  7  8  9  10
                                                                x
```

2. Write each one of the Intervals using all types of notations:

a. x ∋ (4, 5)

```
-10 -9 -8 -7 -6 -5 -4 -3 -2 -1  0  1  2  3  4  5  6  7  8  9  10
                                                                x
```

b. x ∋ (–∞, 5)

```
-10 -9 -8 -7 -6 -5 -4 -3 -2 -1  0  1  2  3  4  5  6  7  8  9  10
                                                                x
```

c. x ∋ (4, 5)

```
-10 -9 -8 -7 -6 -5 -4 -3 -2 -1  0  1  2  3  4  5  6  7  8  9  10
                                                                x
```

d. x ∋ (3, ∞]

```
-10 -9 -8 -7 -6 -5 -4 -3 -2 -1  0  1  2  3  4  5  6  7  8  9  10
                                                                x
```

e. x ∋]–5,9]

```
-10 -9 -8 -7 -6 -5 -4 -3 -2 -1  0  1  2  3  4  5  6  7  8  9  10
                                                                x
```

f. x ∋ [–8,–1[

```
-10 -9 -8 -7 -6 -5 -4 -3 -2 -1  0  1  2  3  4  5  6  7  8  9  10
                                                                x
```

g. {x| 7 < x < 9}

```
-10 -9 -8 -7 -6 -5 -4 -3 -2 -1  0  1  2  3  4  5  6  7  8  9  10
                                                                x
```

h. {x| –7 < x < –2}

```
-10 -9 -8 -7 -6 -5 -4 -3 -2 -1  0  1  2  3  4  5  6  7  8  9  10
                                                                x
```

3.
   a. Solve the inequality $3x - 7 \leq 2$

   b. Solve the inequality $-x < -2$.

   c. Represent both solutions on the real line:

   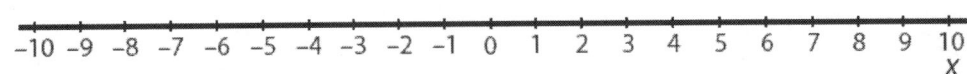

   d. State their intersection: _____.

4.
   a. Solve the inequality $5x - 2 \leq 2$

   b. Solve the inequality $-2x + 1 > -2$.

   c. Represent both solutions on the real line:

   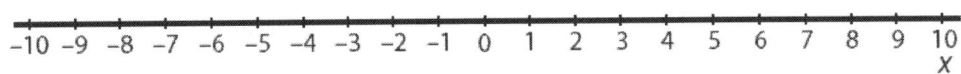

   d. State their intersection: _____.

5.
   a. Solve the inequality $5x - 2 \leq -12$

   b. Solve the inequality $-2x - 3 \leq -2$.

   c. Represent both solutions on the real line:

   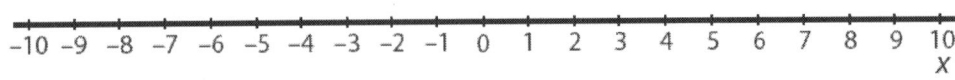

   d. State their intersection: _____

1.3. – RATIONALIZATION

1. Rationalize the denominator:

   a. $\dfrac{2}{\sqrt{5}} =$

   b. $\dfrac{3}{\sqrt{5}+1} =$

   c. $\dfrac{-7}{\sqrt{5}-2} =$

   d. $\dfrac{\sqrt{2}+3}{-5} =$

   e. $\dfrac{\sqrt{2}+3}{\sqrt{6}-5} =$

   f. $\dfrac{\sqrt{2}}{\sqrt{6}+\sqrt{3}} =$

   g. $\dfrac{\sqrt{2}-1}{2\sqrt{5}-\sqrt{3}} =$

   h. $\dfrac{-1}{2\sqrt{a}+b} =$

2. Rationalize the numerator:

   a. $\dfrac{\sqrt{4}}{\sqrt{5}} =$

   b. $\dfrac{3-\sqrt{2}}{\sqrt{5}+1} =$

   c. $\dfrac{-7}{\sqrt{5}-2} =$

   d. $\dfrac{\sqrt{2}+3}{\sqrt{6}-5} =$

   e. $\dfrac{\sqrt{2}}{\sqrt{x}+\sqrt{3}} =$

   f. $\dfrac{\sqrt{b}-a}{2\sqrt{a}-\sqrt{3}} =$

   g. $\dfrac{-3\sqrt{7}+8}{2\sqrt{5}+7} =$

1.4. – EXPONENTS & LOGARITHMS

Product:

$a^0 = \_\_$
$a^1 = \_\_$
$a^2 = \_\_ \times \_\_$
$a^3 = \_\_ \times \_\_ \times \_\_$
...
$a^3 a^2 = _____ = \_\_$

$$a^m a^n = _____$$

Division:

$$\frac{a^5}{a^3} = \frac{_____}{_____} = \frac{_____}{\_\_\_\_} = \_\_$$

$$\frac{a^2}{a^5} = \frac{_____}{_____} = \frac{_____}{\_\_\_\_} = \_\_$$

$$\frac{a^m}{a^n} = \underline{a^{m-n}}$$

Power:

$(a^2)^3 = _____ = \_\_$

$$\left(\frac{a^2}{b}\right)^3 = \frac{_____}{_____} = \frac{\_\_\_\_}{\_\_}$$

$$(a^m)^n = \_\_$$

$$\left(\frac{a^m}{b^k}\right)^n = \frac{\_\_\_}{\_\_\_}$$

Radicals:

$(a^3)^{\frac{1}{2}} = \_\_ = \_\_$

$(a^4)^{\frac{1}{7}} = \_\_ = \_\_$

$$(a^m)^{\frac{1}{n}} = \_\_ = \_\_$$

Exercises

Write in all possible forms and evaluate without using a calculator (follow example):

1. $4^{-1} = \dfrac{1}{4} = 0.25$
2. $10^0 =$
3. $10^1 =$
4. $10^3 =$
5. $10^{-1} =$
6. $10^{-2} =$
7. $10^{-3} =$
8. $10^{-4} =$
9. $2^0 =$
10. $2^1 =$
11. $2^{-1} =$
12. $2^{-2} =$
13. $2^{-3} =$
14. $2^{-4} =$
15. $(-1)^0 =$
16. $-1^0 =$
17. $(-1)^1 =$
18. $-1^1 =$
19. $(-1)^{-1} =$
20. $-1^2 =$
21. $(-1)^2 =$
22. $-1^2 =$
23. $(-1)^{-2} =$
24. $-1^{-2} =$
25. $(-3)^0 =$
26. $(-3)^1 =$
27. $-3^1 =$
28. $(-3)^2 =$
29. $-3^2 =$
30. $(-3)^{-1} =$

15

31. $-3^{-1} =$

32. $(-3)^{-2} =$

33. $-3^{-2} =$

34. $9^{\frac{1}{2}} =$

35. $16^{\frac{3}{4}} =$

36. $(3^{-1})^2 =$

37. $(-8^{-3})^{\frac{1}{2}} =$

38. $\left(\dfrac{1}{2}\right)^0 =$

39. $\left(\dfrac{1}{2}\right)^1 =$

40. $\left(\dfrac{1}{2}\right)^{-1} =$

41. $\left(\dfrac{1}{2}\right)^2 =$

42. $\left(\dfrac{1}{2}\right)^{-2} =$

43. $\left(\dfrac{3}{5}\right)^0 =$

44. $\left(\dfrac{3}{4}\right)^1 =$

45. $\left(\dfrac{2}{5}\right)^{-1} =$

46. $\left(\dfrac{5}{11}\right)^2 =$

47. $\left(\dfrac{-11}{2}\right)^{-2} =$

48. $\left(\dfrac{3}{-2}\right)^1 =$

49. $\left(\dfrac{-12}{\sqrt{2}}\right)^{-1} =$

50. $\left(\dfrac{5\sqrt{2}}{11}\right)^{2} =$

51. $\left(\dfrac{-2\sqrt{5}}{2}\right)^{-2} =$

52. $\left(\dfrac{3+5\sqrt{2}}{-2}\right)^{2} =$

53. $\left(\dfrac{-12}{2-\sqrt{2}}\right)^{-2} =$

54. $\left(\dfrac{5+\sqrt{2}}{11}\right)^{2} =$

55. $\left(\dfrac{-2-\sqrt{5}}{2+\sqrt{2}}\right)^{-2} =$

56. $\left(\dfrac{-27}{8}\right)^{\frac{2}{3}} =$

57. $\left(\dfrac{16}{9}\right)^{\frac{3}{4}} =$

58. $5^{27} 5^{-29} =$

59. $4^{27} 2^{-49} =$

60. $9^{12} 3^{-20} =$

61. $(-125)^{\frac{2}{3}} =$

62. $\dfrac{5^{10}}{5^{2}} =$

63. $\dfrac{3^{10}}{9^{2}} 3^{-2} =$

64. $\left(\dfrac{2}{5}\right)^{3} \times \left(\dfrac{5}{3}\right)^{3} =$

65. $\left(\dfrac{4}{7}\right)^2 \div \left(\dfrac{9}{7}\right)^2 =$

66. $\left(\dfrac{2}{5}\right)^3 \cdot \left(\dfrac{3}{5}\right)^{-4} =$

67. $\left(\dfrac{3}{4}\right)^5 \div \left(\dfrac{9}{64}\right)^2 =$

68. $\left(\dfrac{7}{5}\right)^7 \div \left(\dfrac{49}{125}\right)^3 =$

69. $\left(\dfrac{2^{-3}}{3^{-2}}\right)^3 \cdot \left(\dfrac{4}{27}\right)^2 =$

70. $\left(\dfrac{4^2}{5^{-1}}\right)^3 \cdot \left(\dfrac{25^{-1}}{64}\right)^2 =$

71. $\left(\dfrac{3^{-5}}{4^2}\right)^2 \div \left(\dfrac{9^{-2}}{2^3}\right)^3 =$

72. $\left(\dfrac{5^4}{7^{-3}}\right)^2 \div \left(\dfrac{25^{-1}}{49}\right)^{-3} =$

73. $\dfrac{3^{-2}}{9^{\frac{2}{3}}} 27^{\frac{5}{4}} =$

74. $\dfrac{4^{-4}\sqrt{2}}{8^{\frac{2}{3}}} 16^{\frac{3}{4}} =$

75. $\sqrt{5}\,\dfrac{25^2 5^{-1}}{25^{\frac{4}{3}}} 5^{\frac{1}{4}} \sqrt[3]{5} =$

76. $\dfrac{4^{-2}2^{-4}}{16^2(\sqrt[6]{16^4})}8^{\frac{1}{4}}2^{-1} =$

77. $x\sqrt{x}\sqrt{3} =$

78. $x\sqrt{x}+\sqrt{2x} =$

79. $\dfrac{1}{x\sqrt{x}} =$

80. $\dfrac{x\sqrt[3]{x}}{\sqrt{x}} =$

81. $s^n s^{2n} s^2 =$

82. $a^{2k}ba^3 b^{2k}a =$

83. $\dfrac{3^n}{9^n}27^n =$

84. $\dfrac{2^n}{8^{n+1}}16^{n-2} =$

85. $\dfrac{5^{-n}}{125^{2n-2}}5^{-n+2} =$

86. $\dfrac{x^{-n}}{x^{2n-2}}x^{-n+5} =$

87. $\dfrac{2x^{-n+1}}{2^2 x^{3n+2}}x^{n+5} =$

19

88. $\dfrac{2yx^{-2n+3}}{2^5 y^{-1} x^{-4n+2}} x^{-2n+1} =$

89. $\dfrac{4^2 y^2 x^{-3} z}{2^2 xz^2 y^{-1} x} x^{-2} z^2 =$

90. $\dfrac{4^2 y^2 (x^{-2} z^2)^{-2}}{(2^2 x)^3 z^2 y^{-1} x} x^{-2} z^2 =$

91. $\dfrac{4^{-2} y^3 (x^{-2} z^3)^{-1}}{(2^{-3} x)^{-3} z^{-2} y^{-1} x} xz^2 =$

92. $\left(\dfrac{a}{b^2}\right)^2 \div \left(\dfrac{a^{-1}}{b^3}\right)^{-3} \cdot \left(\dfrac{1}{b}\right)^3 =$

93. $\left(\dfrac{ab}{b^2}\right)^{-2} \div \left(\dfrac{(2ba)^{-1}}{b^3}\right)^{-3} \cdot \left(\dfrac{2}{b}\right)^3 =$

94. $\dfrac{a^{-2} b^n (a^{-2n} b^3)^{-1}}{(b^{-3n} a)^3 \sqrt{ab^{-1}}} =$

95. $\dfrac{a^{-2} b^n (a^{-2n} b^2)^n}{(b^{-3n} a)^n a^{-2n} b^n} =$

96. $\dfrac{3^n a^{-2} b^n (a^{-2n} b^3)^{n+1}}{(9^n b^{-2n} a)^n a^{-2n} b^{n+2}} =$

97. $\dfrac{3^n + 3^{n+1}}{3^{n-1}} =$

98. $\dfrac{4^n + 4^{n-1}}{2^{n-2}} =$

99. $\dfrac{7^{2n}+7^{2n-1}}{7^{2n-2}}=$

100. $\dfrac{7^{3n-1}-7^{3n}}{7^{2n-2}}=$

101. $2^{-1}+2=$

102. $3^{-1}-3^{-2}=$

103. $5^{-1}-5^{-2}=$

104. $3^{-3}+2^{-2}=$

105. $3^{-2}+4^{-2}=$

106. $7^{-2}+2^{-2}=$

107. $8^{-2}-3^{-2}=$

108. $7^{-2}-2^{-3}=$

109. $a^{-1}+a^{-1}=$

110. $ba^{-1}+a^{-1}=$

111. $a^{-1}-ba^{-1}=$

112. $(ba)^{-1}+a^{-1}=$

113. $ba^{-1}+(ba)^{-1}=$

LOGARITHMS

Definition of logarithms: $b^c = a \Leftrightarrow \log_b a = c \quad 1 \neq b > 0$

1. Complete the table and find x if possible:

Exponential Form	Logarithmic Form
$5^3 = 125$	
	$\log_6 36 = 2$
	$\log_x 64 = 2$
$x^3 = 27$	
	$\log_3(x+1) = 2$
$e^x = 9$	
	$\ln x = \log_e x = 2$
$e^{2x-1} = 17$	
	$\ln(3x+2) = \log_e(3x+2) = 2$
$4^x = 9$	
	$\log_6 x = 2$
$2^x = e$	
	$\ln(x^2) = \log_e(x^2) = 4$
	$\log 0.001 = x$
$10^x = 200$	
	$\log_3 \dfrac{1}{9} = -2$
	$\log_2 0.5 = x$

Logarithms were "invented" in order to solve equations in which: _____

Properties of logarithms

I. **Product Rule:** $Log_b(MN) = Log_b(M) + Log_b(N)$, M, N, b positive, b≠1

II. **Quotient Rule:** $Log_b(\frac{M}{N}) = Log_b(M) - Log_b(N)$, M, N, b positive, b≠1

III. **Power Rule:** $Log_b(M^p) = pLog_b(M)$, M, b positive, b≠1

IV. $a^{\log_a(x)} = x$

Evaluate

1. $Log_2(32) =$ 5
2. $Log_5(25) =$
3. $Log_5(125) =$
4. $Log_5(625) =$
5. $Log_3(3) =$
6. $Log_5(0) =$
7. $Log_5(1) =$
8. $Log_a(1) =$ 0
9. $Log_2(-3) =$
10. $Log_2(\frac{1}{8}) =$
11. $Log_7(\frac{1}{49}) =$
12. $Log_4(32) =$
13. $Log_8(32) =$
14. $Log_{\frac{1}{2}}(4) =$
15. $Log_{\frac{1}{2}}(16) =$ −4
16. $Log_{\frac{1}{3}}(81) =$
17. $Log_{\frac{1}{2}}(8) =$
18. $Log_{\frac{1}{2}}(-8) =$

19. $Log_{\frac{1}{3}}(\frac{1}{9}) =$

20. $Log_{\frac{1}{5}}(\frac{1}{125}) =$

21. $Log_1(8) =$

22. $Log_2(\frac{1}{\sqrt{8}}) =$

23. $Log_2(\sqrt[3]{32}) =$

24. $Log_3(\sqrt[3]{81}) =$

25. $Log_{\sqrt[5]{8}}(\sqrt[5]{8}) =$

26. $Log_{\frac{1}{2}}(\sqrt[5]{16}) =$

27. $Log_{17}(\frac{17}{17^{\frac{1}{3}}}\sqrt[5]{17}) =$

28. $Log(\sqrt{10}) =$

29. $Log(\sqrt[3]{10}) =$

30. $Log(\sqrt[7]{100}) =$

31. $Log(\sqrt[3]{10000}) =$

32. $Log(10^{-19}) =$

33. $Log(50) - Log(5) =$

34. $Log(25) + Log(4) =$

35. $Log_3(45) - Log_3(5) =$

36. $Log_6(18) + Log_6(2) =$

37. $Log_a(a^x) - Log_a(a^{2x}) =$

38. $Log_a(a^{2x-3}) =$

39. $Log_e(e) =$

40. $Ln(e) =$

41. $Ln(e^2) =$

42. $Ln(e^{\frac{1}{2}}) =$

24

43. $Ln(e^{\frac{2}{5}}) =$

44. $Ln(e\sqrt[3]{e^4}) =$

45. $\dfrac{Ln(e^{-1})}{Log_{12}(\sqrt{12})} =$

46. $Ln(1) =$

47. $Ln(0) =$

48. $Ln(e^0) =$

49. $Ln(e^n) =$

50. $Ln(\dfrac{1}{\sqrt{e}}) =$

51. $Ln(\dfrac{1}{\sqrt[3]{e^2}}) =$

52. $Log_\pi(\dfrac{1}{\pi^4}) =$

53. $Log_\pi(\dfrac{1}{\sqrt{\pi^5}}) =$

54. $Log_a(\dfrac{1}{\sqrt[3]{a^2}}) =$

55. $10^{Log(100)} =$

56. $3^{Log_3(9)} =$

57. $3^{Log_3(\frac{1}{27})} =$

58. $\dfrac{Ln(2e^{-1}) - Ln(2)}{Log_{12}(2\sqrt{12}) + Log_{12}(6\sqrt{12})} =$

59. $\dfrac{2Ln(3e^2) + Ln\left(\dfrac{e}{3}\right)}{Log_2(640) - Log_2(10)} =$

True or False

1. $Log(2x) - Log(3) = Log(2x+3)$

2. $Log(x) - Log(9) = 2 \Leftrightarrow \frac{x}{9} = 100$

3. $Log(12) + Log(x) = 1 \Leftrightarrow 12x = 10$

4. $Log(2) + Log(5) = Log(7)$

5. $Log(10) - Log(5) = Log(2)$

6. $Log(20) + Log(2) = Log(22)$

7. $Log(15) - Log(3) = Log(5)$

8. $Log(A+B) = Log(A) + Log(B)$

Simplify

1. $Log_2(2^x 2^{x+y}) =$

2. $5^{Log_5(x+y)} =$

3. $Log_7(49^{xy}) =$

4. $Log_2(xy) - \frac{1}{3} Log_2(x^2) =$

5. $Log_2(\frac{8x^2}{y}) - 2Log_2(2x^2 y) =$

6. $\frac{1}{2} Log_3(\frac{9xy^2}{y}) - Log_3(27xy) =$

7. $3Log_4((xy)^3) - Log_4(xy) =$

8. $Log(2A) + Log(B) - 2Log(AB) =$

9. $Ln(ab^t) - Ln((ab)^t) - 2Ln(a) =$

26

10. If $Log_{10}(8) = x$ and $Log_{10}(3) = y$ express the following in terms of x and y only:

   a. $Log_{10}(24) =$

   b. $Log_{10}(\frac{8}{3}) =$

   c. $Log_{10}(72) =$

   d. $Log_{10}(\frac{9}{8}) =$

   e. $Log_{10}(720) =$

CHANGE OF BASE

$$Log_b(M) = \frac{Log_c(M)}{Log_c(b)}$$

Change the following logarithms into a different base:

1. $Log_2(5) = \dfrac{\ln 5}{\ln 2}$

2. $Log_3(-12) =$

3. $Log_{22}(51) =$

4. $Log_{2.3}(1) =$

5. $Log_{2.9}(2.9) =$

6. $Log_3(-5) =$

7. $Log_a(5) =$

8. $Log_{12}(5y) =$

9. $Log_e(2) =$

10. $Log(5) =$

11. $Ln(15) =$

12. $Log_{\sqrt{2}}(5) =$

13. $Log_3(\frac{2}{3}) =$

14. $Log_5(\frac{2}{\sqrt{5}}) =$

15. Simplify:

   a. $\log_x b \cdot \log_b x =$ ___

   b. $\log_x q \cdot \log_q r \cdot \log_r x =$ ___

Logarithmic Equations

1. $Log_4(x) = 2$

2. $Log_{\frac{1}{3}}(x) = 4$

3. $Log_{10}(2x+1) = 2$

4. $Log_2(64) = x$

5. $Ln(x) = 2.7$

6. $Ln(x+1) = 1.86$

7. $e^x = 6.27$

28

8. $Log_b(81) = 4$

9. $e^{-2x} = 4.12$

10. $Log_3(x) = Log_3(7) + Log_3(3)$

11. $5 \times 9^x = 10$
$9^x = 2$
$log_9 2 = x$

12. $10e^{4x+1} = 20$

13. $3^t = 2 \cdot 5^{2t}$

14. $3^{t+1} = 4 \cdot 6^{2t-3}$

15. $3 \cdot 2^t = 5 \cdot 6^{2t-3}$

16. $2 \cdot e^t = 8 \cdot 7^{2t-3}$

17. $b^t = c \cdot d^{2t}$

18. $a \cdot b^t = c \cdot d^{2t}$

19. $e^t + e^t = 2$

20. $e^{2t} + e^{2t} = 3$

21. $Ln(x) = 2$

22. $Ln(x^2) = 2$

23. $Ln(x^2 - 1) = 2$

24. $Ln(x+1) - Ln(2x) = -1$

25. $Ln(x^2 + 1) = 1$

26. $Log_{10}(x^2 + 2) = 2$

27. $Ln(x-2) + Ln(x+1) = 0$

28. $Log_2(x) + Log_3(x) = 1$

29. $Log_2(x) - Log_3(x) = 1$

30. $Log_2(x) - 2Log_3(x) = 2$

31. $3Log_2(x) - 2Log_3(x) = 1$

32. $Log_2(x) - Log_3(x) = Log_3(x)$

33. $Log_2(x) - 2Log_x(2) = 0$

34. $Log_2(x) - 2Log_x(2) = 1$

35. $Log_2(x) - Log_x(3) = 0$

36. $Log_2(x) - 2Log_x(3) = 0$

1.5. – EQUATIONS

1st Degree

1. $\dfrac{x}{12} = 5$

2. $\dfrac{x}{7} + 2 = 5$

3. $\dfrac{2x}{7} + 2 = 5 - 3x$

4. $\dfrac{2x}{7} + \dfrac{2}{5} = -2x + 1$

5. $\dfrac{2x-1}{x} = 3$

6. $\dfrac{x+2}{2x} = 5$

7. $\dfrac{x-2}{2x-1} = 6$

8. $\dfrac{2x-2}{x+1} = -2$

9. $\dfrac{2x}{7} + 1 = \dfrac{-5x}{7}$

10. $\dfrac{2x}{7} + 4 = \dfrac{3x}{2}$

11. $\dfrac{2}{x} - 3 = \dfrac{3}{2x}$

12. $\dfrac{2}{x-2} - 3 = \dfrac{3}{x-2}$

13. $\dfrac{-2}{x} = \dfrac{3}{x-2}$

14. $\dfrac{4}{x+1} = \dfrac{4}{x+2}$

15. $\dfrac{2}{x+1} = \dfrac{4}{x+2}$

16. $-\dfrac{2}{2x+1} - 2 = \dfrac{4}{2x+1}$

33

Isolate x

1. $\dfrac{4}{x} = \dfrac{a}{x+6}$

2. $\dfrac{14}{x+2} = \dfrac{a}{x+2} - a$

3. $\dfrac{2}{x+3} - a = \dfrac{a+b}{x+3}$

4. $\dfrac{5}{2x+1} - 3a = \dfrac{b}{2x+1}$

5. $\dfrac{-2x}{a+3} = \dfrac{x+2}{2a-1}$

6. $\dfrac{-5x+1}{2a} = \dfrac{bx}{3a+2}$

7. $\dfrac{a}{x+2} = \dfrac{b}{x+2} - b + 1$

8. $\dfrac{b}{2x-4} - 3 = \dfrac{b}{2x-4} - b + 1$

9. $\dfrac{1}{ax+2} = \dfrac{b}{x+a}$

10. $\dfrac{1}{ax+2} = \dfrac{b}{ax+2} - 3$

11. $3\dfrac{x}{ax+2} = 3$

12. $-3\dfrac{2x}{ax+3} = b$

13. $\dfrac{2x-3}{2ax+5} = -3b$

14. $\dfrac{x}{ax+2} = \dfrac{2}{a} - 3$

34

Quadratic equations

a. Solve the following equations using the "complete the square method".
b. Check your answers using the quadratic formula.
c. Write the factorized expression.

1. $x^2 - 4x + 1 = 3$

2. $x^2 - 4x + 1 = -3$

3. $x^2 - 4x + 1 = -13$

4. $x^2 + 6x + 2 = 2$

5. $x^2 + 6x + 2 = -10$

6. $x^2 - 3x - 5 = 3$

7. $x^2 - 3x - 3 = -3$

8. $x^2 - 3x - 4 = -1$

9. $x^2 - 7x - 5 = 3$

10. $x^2 + x - 3 = 2$

11. $x^2 - 2x + 4 = 5$

12. $x^2 + 3x - 1 = 3$

13. $x^2 + 7x - 3 = 2$

14. $x^2 + 12x - 4 = -1$

Rational equations 2nd degree

1. $\dfrac{3}{x^2-4}=2$

2. $\dfrac{2}{x^2-2x+1}=1$

3. $-\dfrac{2}{x^2-2x+3}=1$

4. $\dfrac{x}{x^2-4}=2$

5. $\dfrac{x}{x-4}=5$

6. $\dfrac{x^2}{x^2-4x}=2$

7. $\dfrac{x^2-1}{x-5}=2$

8. $\dfrac{x}{x-4}+\dfrac{2}{x-4}=5$

9. $\dfrac{x}{x-4}+\dfrac{2}{x+3}=-2$

10. $\dfrac{x-1}{2x-2}-\dfrac{2x-1}{x+3}=3$

11. $\dfrac{x}{3x+2}-\dfrac{2x-1}{2x+3}=7$

12. $\dfrac{1}{x}+\dfrac{2}{x^2}=3$

13. $\dfrac{1}{x-1}+\dfrac{2}{x^2-1}=2$

14. $\dfrac{1}{x-3}-\dfrac{2}{x^2-9}=4$

Radical Equations

1. $\sqrt{8x+2} = 0$

2. $\sqrt{5x-2} = 6$

3. $\sqrt{5x^2-2} = 3$

4. $\sqrt{x^2+1} = -2$

5. $\sqrt{x^2-2} + 4 = -2$

6. $\sqrt{2x^2-2} + 4x = -2$

7. $\sqrt{2x-2} + 3x + 2 = -2$

8. $\sqrt{x+1} + \sqrt{x+3} = 2$

9. $\sqrt{x-1} + \sqrt{x+3} = 2$

10. $\sqrt{x-3} + \sqrt{x+3} = 3$

11. $\sqrt{5x+1} - \sqrt{3x-3} = 2$

12. $\sqrt{8x+2} - \sqrt{3x-3} = 0$

13. $\sqrt{x-1} + \sqrt{x+2} = -2$

14. $\dfrac{1}{\sqrt{-3x-1}} = \sqrt{-2+x}$

15. $-4\dfrac{1}{\sqrt{6x-2}} = \sqrt{2-5x}$

Higher degree simple equations

1. $x^4 - 2x^2 = 0$

2. $(2x - 3)(x^2 - 3)(x + 5)(x^3 + 2) = 0$

3. $(2x - 3)(x - 3) = 1$

4. $(6x - 7)(3x^2 - 5)(2x + 7)(2x^5 - 64)(4x^4 + 5) = 0$

5. $3x^5 - x^2 = 0$

6. $x^6 - 32x = 0$

7. $x^6 - 2x^5 + x^4 = 0$

8. $x^3 - 4x^2 + 3x = 0$

9. $2x^3 - 5x = 0$

10. $2x^3 - x^2 = 0$

11. $ax^4 - 3x = 0$

12. $ax^5 - x^2 = 0$

13. $x^4 - 5x^2 + 3 = -1$

14. $x^4 - 10x^2 + 3 = -6$

15. $x^6 + 3x^3 - 10 = 0$

16. $x^8 = -2x^4 - 1$

17. $x^4 - 13x^2 + 36 = 0$

18. $x^5 - 15x^3 + 54x = 0$

19. $x^5 + x^3 - 6x = 0$

20. $x^4 = 6x^2 - 5$

Rational exponent equations

1. $x^{\frac{1}{2}} = 2$

2. $2x^{\frac{2}{3}} = 3$

3. $3x^{-\frac{1}{2}} = 2$

4. $x + x^{\frac{1}{2}} = 0$

5. $2x - x^{\frac{2}{5}} = 0$

6. $x^{\frac{1}{3}} + 1 = 0$

7. $3x^{\frac{1}{2}} - x^2 = 0$

8. $5x^{\frac{4}{3}} = -1$

9. $3x^{-\frac{3}{4}} = -2$

10. $x - 2x^{\frac{2}{3}} = 0$

11. $2x^2 - x^{-\frac{3}{2}} = 0$

12. $x^{\frac{1}{2}} - 2x^{\frac{1}{6}} = 0$

Exponential equations

1. $2^x = 2$

2. $2^{x+2} = 2^2$

3. $\left(\dfrac{1}{32}\right)2^{3x+4} = 4$

4. $2^{-4x+1} = 8$

5. $3^{-5x+3} = 9$

6. $\left(\dfrac{1}{4}\right)^{x+2} = \dfrac{1}{16}$

7. $2^{x+2} = \dfrac{-1}{16}$

8. $2^{-2x+1} = 8^x$

9. $\left(\dfrac{1}{3}\right)^{4x^2-1} = 9^{2x}$

10. $\left(\dfrac{1}{125}\right)5^{x-1} = 1$

11. $3^{2x-5} = \dfrac{1}{3}$

12. $3^{2x^2-5} = \dfrac{1}{27}$

13. $\left(\dfrac{1}{5}\right)^{x-1} = -1$

14. $5^{x-1} = 5^{x(x-1)}$

15. $6^{x^2-8} = 6$

16. $5^{x-1} = \dfrac{1}{125}$

17. $\left(\dfrac{1}{36}\right)^{2x-3} = \dfrac{1}{6}$

18. $6^{2x-3} = -\dfrac{3}{4}$

19. $2^x = 3$

20. $5^x = 3$

21. $1^x = 2$

22. $2^x = -2$

23. $\dfrac{1}{5^x - 4} = 1$

24. $\dfrac{1}{5^x - 24} = 1$

25. $\dfrac{1}{5^{3x} - 24} = 1$

26. $\dfrac{2}{2^x - 7} = 2$

27. $\dfrac{125}{2^{\frac{x}{3}} - 7} = 5$

28. $6^x + 6^{x+1} = \dfrac{7}{6}$

29. $5^x + 5^{x+1} + 5^{x-1} = \dfrac{31}{5}$

30. $7^{x-1} + 7^{x-2} = \dfrac{8}{49}$

31. $7^{x-1} + 7^{x-2} = \dfrac{8}{7}$

32. $2^x + 2^{x-1} + 2^{x+2} = 11$

33. $2^x + 2^{x-1} + 2^{x+2} = 22$

34. $5^{2x} - 6 \times 5^x = -5$

35. $3^{2x} - 4 \times 3^x - 2 = -5$

36. $5^{2x} + 4 \times 5^x - 10 = -5$

37. $8^{2x} - 9 \times 8^x + 8 = 0$

38. $2 \times 8^{2x} - 18 \times 8^x + 10 = -6$

39. $3^{2x+1} - 3^{x+2} + 81 = 0$

40. $5^{2x-1} - 6 \times 5^{x-1} = -1$

41. $3^{2x+2} - 4 \times 3^{x+2} + 27 = 0$

Systems of equations

1. $\begin{array}{l} 5x+1=2y \\ 4y+x-3=0 \end{array}$

2. $\begin{array}{l} 5x+3y=2-2y \\ -y+2x-5=0 \end{array}$

3. $\begin{array}{l} 5x=2y \\ -y+2x=0 \end{array}$

4. $\begin{array}{l} x=2y-7 \\ 4y-2x=0 \end{array}$

5. $\begin{array}{l} -5x+1=2y \\ -4y+x-3=x \end{array}$

6. $\begin{array}{l} 5x+1=2y \\ 10y-25x=10 \end{array}$

7. $\begin{array}{l} 2x+1=2y \\ -4y+4x+2=0 \end{array}$

8. $\begin{array}{l} x=2y \\ -y+x^2-5=0 \end{array}$

9. $\begin{array}{l} x=1-y \\ -y+x^2-5=0 \end{array}$

10. $\begin{array}{l} x=1-y^2 \\ -y^2+x^2-5=0 \end{array}$

1.6. – EQUATIONS/INEQUALITIES WITH ABSOLUTE VALUE

I. $|x| = a$ $x = a$ OR $x = -a$
II. $|x| > a$ $x > a$ OR $x < -a$
III. $|x| < a$ $-a < x < a$;($x > -a$ and $x < a$) ;($x \in (-a, a)$)

1. $|x| = 5$

2. $|x| = -5$

3. $|x| = 0$

4. $|x| = -1$

5. $|x| < 3$

6. $|x| > 2$

7. $|x| > -5$

8. $|x| < -5$

9. $|2x| = 1$

10. $|x| \geq 0$

11. $|x| \leq 0$

12. $|2x| = 1$

13. $|2x + 1| = 5$

14. $|7x + 21| - 5 = -5$

15. $2 - |5 - 8x| = 15$

16. $|4x + 2| = -5$

17. $|8x + 12| = 100$

18. $|2x + 1| < 2$

19. $|8 - 2x + 1| > 6$

20. $|5x - 21| > 0$

21. $|5x - 21| \geq 0$

22. $|8x + 11| > -2$

23. $|91x + 61| < -2$

24. $|8 - 3x| > 8$

25. $|18 - 6x| > 3$

26. $|1 - 6x| < 7$

27. $|8 - 5x| \leq 0$

28. $|5x - 21| > 1$

29. $|x + 11| = 5$

30. $|x + 3| \leq 5$

31. $|x + 11| = -15$

32. $|2x + 11| + 2 < 15$

33. $|3x + 11| = x$

34. $|x + 2| = 5 - x$

35. $|3x + 1| < 5x$

36. $|x - 4| = 3x$

37. $|2x - 6| \leq 5 + 2x$

38. $|2x + 4| < 2 - 3x$

39. $|2x - 2| > 11 - 2x$

40. $|7x - 16| = 5 + 12x$

41. $|2x - 6| = 21$

42. $|2x - 6| \geq 4$

43. $|3x - 6| + 1 > -4$

44. $|4x - 6| - 4 < -4x$

45. $|\frac{1}{2}x - 4| \leq 1+x$

46. $|2x + \frac{1}{2}| > 2-3x$

47. $|2x - \frac{1}{2}| = 1-2x$

48. $|\frac{3}{2}x - 7| \leq 3+2x$

49. $|5x - 2| = 1 - x$

1.7. – POLYNOMIALS

Sum, subtraction, multiplication

1. Given the polynomials: $A = 3x + 5x^3 - 7x^{12} - 1$, $B = -3x^2 + 2x^5 - 2x^3$, $C = x^2 + x^3$
   $D = -x + 5 + 5x^4 - 4x^4 + 2x^2 - 4x^5$. Evaluate:

   a. $A + B + C + D =$

   b. $A - 2B + 3D =$

   c. $2AC =$

   d. $-3CB =$

Division

2. Divide $3x^3 + 1$ by x

3. Divide $-2x^3 - 5$ by $x + 1$

4. Divide $2x^4 + x$ by x

5. Divide $-2x - 5x^3 + 1$ by x

6. Divide $4 - x^4$ by $x - 1$

7. Divide $2x^3 + 3x - 5$ by $x - 3$

8. Divide $4x^4 + x - 5$ by $2x - 3$

9. Divide $2x^3 + 4x - 7$ by $x^2 - 1$

10. Divide $5x^4 + x^3 + 2x^2 - 5$ by $-2x + 1$

11. Divide $6x^5 + 2x^4 + 2x - 5$ by $x^3 + x$

12. Divide $5x^3 + x^4 + 2x^2 - 5$ by $x^4 + 1$

13. When $x^3 - 2x + k$ is divided by $x - 2$ it leaves a remainder of 5, find k.

14. When $x^3 - 2x + k$ is divided by $x + 1$ it leaves a remainder of 0, find k.

15. When $2x^3 - x^2 + kx - 4$ is divided by $x + 2$ it leaves a remainder of 0, find k.

16. When $x^3 - x^2 + kx - 4$ is divided by $x - 1$ it leaves a remainder of 2, find k.

The Remainder Theorem

If we divide 13 by 5:

$$\frac{13}{5} = \frac{10+3}{5} = \frac{10}{5} + \frac{3}{5} = 2 + \frac{3}{5} \qquad \text{OR} \qquad 13 = 2 \times 5 + 3$$

The same idea applies for polynomials:

$$\frac{P(Polynomial)}{D(Divisor)} = Q(quotient) + \frac{R(Remainder)}{D(Divisor)} \qquad \text{OR} \qquad P = QD + R$$

Example: If we want to divide $2x^3 - 8x^2 - 6x - 36$ by x – 1 and we are only interested in the remainder:

$$\frac{2x^3 - 8x^2 - 6x - 36}{x-1} = Q + \frac{R}{x-1} \qquad \text{OR} \qquad 2x^3 - 8x^2 - 6x - 36 = Q(x-1) + R$$

Since in an equation we can do "whatever we want" as long as we do it on both sides we can substitute x = 1 on both sides and obtain:

$$2 \times 1^3 - 8 \times 1^2 - 6 \times 1 - 36 = Q(1-1) + R$$

$$-48 = R$$

The Factor Theorem

In case we obtain R = 0 we conclude that the divisor is a factor of the polynomial

In each one of the following cases write the corresponding expression and use the Remainder theorem to find the remainder:

1. $2x^3 + 2x - 15$ is divided by x – 1

    $2x^3 + 2x - 15 = Q(x - 1) + R$ Substituting x = _____ on _____ sides:

    R =

2. $-4x^4 + 3x^3 - 5x + 1$ is divided by x + 2

3. $3x^3 + 2x - 4$ is divided by x + 3

4. $3x^4 + 6x^3 - 33x^2 - 36x + 108$ is divided by x – 2

5. $-2x^4 + x^3 + x^2 - 4x - 5$ is divided by $x - 2$

6. $9x^3 + 2x - 4$ is divided by $2x - 3$

7. $x^{44} + x - 5$ is divided by $x - 1$

8. $7x^4 + 14x^3 + 14x^2 + 14x + 7$ is divided by $x + 1$

9. $4x^{4455} + x^3 - x - 5$ is divided by $x + 1$

10. $2x^3 + 3x^2 - 4x - 3$ is divided by $3x - 4$

11. In which one of the questions 1 to 10 the divisor is Also a factor of the polynomial?

Factor the following polynomials and solve the equations (real solutions only):

12. $2x^3 + 2x^2 - 2x - 2 = 0$

13. $2x^3 + 4x^2 + 2x + 4 = 0$

14. $6x + 6 + 3x^3 + 3x^2 = 0$

15. $-4x + 12 + 2x^3 - 6x^2 = 0$

16. $x^3 - 4x^2 + 4x - 1 = 0$

17. $2x^3 - x^2 - 8x + 4 = 0$

18. $5x^3 - 8x^2 - 27x + 18 = 0$

19. $-11x^2 - x + 6 + 6x^3 = 0$

20. $4x^3 - 39x + 35 = 0$

21. $5x^3 - 8x^2 - 27x + 18 = 0$

22. $9x^3 + 18x^2 - 16x - 32 = 0$

23. $x^3 - 13x - 12 = 0$

24. $9x^3 - 32 + 18x^2 - 16x = 0$

25. $3x^3 + 6x^2 - 4x - 8 = 0$

26. $x^4 - x^3 - 12x^2 - 4x + 16 = 0$

27. $x^4 + 3x^3 - 6x - 4 = 0$

28. $6x^4 + 17x^3 + 7x^2 - 8x - 4 = 0$

29. Find the values of a and b if $6x^3 + 7x^2 + ax + b$ is divisible by $(2x - 1)$ and $(x + 1)$

30. $x^3 + ax^2 - 2x + b$ has $(x + 1)$ as a factor, and leaves a remainder of 4 when divided by $(x - 3)$. Find a and b.

31. Given that $(x - 1)$ and $(x - 2)$ are factors of $6x^4 + ax^3 - 17x^2 + bx - 4 = 0$, find a and b, and any remaining factors.

Solutions of polynomials

1. In the equation $x^2 + 3x - 10 = 0 = (x + 5)(x - 2)$ Find:

   $x_1 + x_2 =$ _____ $x_1 \cdot x_2 =$ _____ $-\dfrac{b}{a} =$ _____ $\dfrac{c}{a} =$ _____

2. In the equation $2x^2 - 5x - 3 = 0 = (2x + 1)(x - 3)$ Find:

   $x_1 + x_2 =$ _____ $x_1 \cdot x_2 =$ _____ $-\dfrac{b}{a} =$ _____ $\dfrac{c}{a} =$ _____

3. In the equation $6x^2 - 5x - 6 = 0 = (2x + 3)(2x - 3)$ Find:

   $x_1 + x_2 =$ _____ $x_1 \cdot x_2 =$ _____ $-\dfrac{b}{a} =$ _____ $\dfrac{c}{a} =$ _____

4. In the equation $x^3 - 5x^2 - 2x + 24 = 0 = (x+2)(x-3)(x-4)$ Find:

$x_1 + x_2 + x_3 =$ _____ $x_1 \cdot x_2 \cdot x_3 =$ _____ $-\dfrac{b}{a} =$ _____ $-\dfrac{d}{a} =$ _____

5. In the equation $12x^3 - 4x^2 - 3x + 1 = 0 = (2x+1)(2x-1)(3x-1)$ Find:

$x_1 + x_2 + x_3 =$ _____ $x_1 \cdot x_2 \cdot x_3 =$ _____ $-\dfrac{b}{a} =$ _____ $-\dfrac{d}{a} =$ _____

6. In the equation $x^4 - 2x^3 - 3x^2 + 8x - 4 = 0 = (x-1)^2(x-2)(x+2)$ Find:

$x_1 + x_2 + x_3 + x_4 =$ _____ $x_1 \cdot x_2 \cdot x_3 \cdot x_4 =$ _____ $-\dfrac{b}{a} =$ _____ $-\dfrac{e}{a} =$ _____

7. In the equation:

$2x^5 + 13x^4 + 27x^3 + 17x^2 - 5x - 6 = 0 = (2x-1)(x+1)^2(x+2)(x+3)$ Find:

$x_1 \cdot x_2 \cdot x_3 \cdot x_4 \cdot x_5 =$ _____ $x_1 + x_2 + x_3 + x_4 + x_5 =$ _____ $-\dfrac{b}{a} =$ _____ $-\dfrac{f}{a} =$ _____

8. Conclusion:

1.8. – BINOMIAL THEOREM

1. $0! =$ ___ $1! =$ ___ $2! =$ ___ $3! =$ ___ $n! =$ _____

2. Definition: $${}^nC_k = \binom{n}{k} = \underline{}$$

3. Evaluate: $\binom{6}{2} =$ $\binom{9}{6} =$

    $\binom{4}{0} =$ $\binom{7}{1} =$

4. Show that ${}^5C_2 = {}^5C_3$

5. Prove that ${}^nC_k = {}^nC_{n-k}$

6. $(a+b)^2 =$

7. $(a+b)^3 =$

8. $(a-b)^4 =$

9. $(a-b)^5 =$

10. $(a+b)^6 =$

11. Complete the _____ :

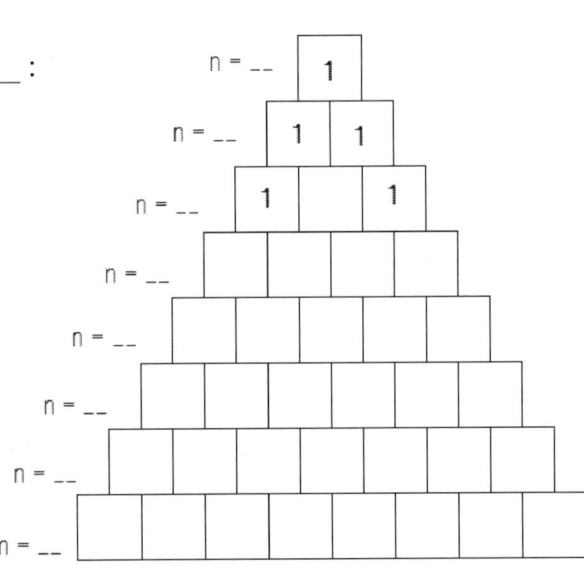

    n = __   1
    n = __   1 1
    n = __   1 1
    n = __
    n = __
    n = __
    n = __
    n = __

12. In conclusion: The coefficients of the binomial $(a+b)^n$ are given by the numbers in _____. The same numbers can be obtained by _____.

13. The binomial theorem can be summarized by:

$$(a+b)^n = \sum_{k=0}^{n} \binom{n}{k} a^{n-k} b^k$$

$$t_{k+1} = \binom{n}{k} a^{n-k} b^k$$

14. $(2x+3)^5 =$

15. $(2x+3y)^4 =$

16. $(a+\dfrac{1}{a^2})^6 =$

17. $(\dfrac{a}{b} - \dfrac{b}{a})^7 =$

18. In each one of the questions 14 to 17 state the number of terms.

   14. ___   15. ___   16. ___   17. ___

19. Complete the sentence: a binomial of degree n has _____ terms.

20. Find and simplify the 8th term of the binomial $(3a^2 + \frac{2}{a})^{13}$

21. Find and simplify the 7th term of the binomial $(3x - 5y)^{11}$

22. Find and simplify the 5th term of the binomial $(3a^2 + y^4)^7$

23. Given the binomial $(\frac{x^2}{2} - \frac{3}{x^3})^{10}$

   a. Write the first 3 terms and identify the pattern.

   b. Find the coefficient of x^5.

   c. Find the independent term.

   d. Find the middle term; draw a conclusion about the existence of a middle term and how to find it.

24. Write a binomial for which the first term of the expansion is $16x^{12}$.

25. Find the constant (independent of x) term in the following cases (identify the pattern first):

   a. $(2x - \dfrac{3}{x^2})^9$

   b. $(2x + \dfrac{1}{x^2})^4$

26. Given the binomial $(\dfrac{x}{2} - \dfrac{1}{x^2})^8$

   a. Write the first 3 terms and identify the pattern.
   b. Find the coefficient of x^3.
   c. Find the independent term.
   d. Find the middle term.

61

27. Given the binomial $(\frac{a}{x} - \frac{x^2}{a})^8$, it is known that the coefficient of the term in x^4 is 70. Find the possible values of a.

28. Given that in the expansion of $(ax+2)(2x+1)^4$ the coefficient of the term in x^4 is 16 find the value of a.

29. Given the expression $(x-1)^{n+1} - (x-1)^n$.

   a. Write it in the form $(x-1)^n(x+a)$. Write down the value of a.

   b. Find the independent term of the expression as a function of n.

1.9. – SEQUENCES AND SERIES

Given The following sequences, write the first 3 terms and the term in the 20th position. If possible identify the pattern using text (follow example):

1. $a_n = 3n$ $a_1 = 3$ $a_2 = 6$ $a_3 = 9$ $a_{20} = 60$ Pattern: __add 3__

2. $a_n = 3n + 1$ $a_1 =$ $a_2 =$ $a_3 =$ $a_{20} =$ Pattern: _____

3. $a_n = 3n - 5$ $a_1 =$ $a_2 =$ $a_3 =$ $a_{20} =$ Pattern: _____

4. $a_n = 2n + 1$ $a_1 =$ $a_2 =$ $a_3 =$ $a_{20} =$ Pattern: _____

5. $a_n = 2n$ $a_1 =$ $a_2 =$ $a_3 =$ $a_{20} =$ Pattern: _____

6. $a_n = 2n - 4$ $a_1 =$ $a_2 =$ $a_3 =$ $a_{20} =$ Pattern: _____

7. $a_n = -4n$ $a_1 =$ $a_2 =$ $a_3 =$ $a_{20} =$ Pattern: _____

8. $a_n = -4n + 10$ $a_1 =$ $a_2 =$ $a_3 =$ $a_{20} =$ Pattern: _____

9. $a_n = -4n - 6$ $a_1 =$ $a_2 =$ $a_3 =$ $a_{20} =$ Pattern: _____

10. $a_n = \dfrac{n}{3}$ $a_1 =$ $a_2 =$ $a_3 =$ $a_{20} =$ Pattern: _____

11. $a_n = \dfrac{n}{2}$ $a_1 =$ $a_2 =$ $a_3 =$ $a_{20} =$ Pattern: _____

12. $a_n = \dfrac{2n}{5} + 1$ $a_1 =$ $a_2 =$ $a_3 =$ $a_{20} =$ Pattern: _____

13. $a_n = \dfrac{-3n}{7} + 5$ $a_1 =$ $a_2 =$ $a_3 =$ $a_{20} =$ Pattern: _____

14. $a_n = \dfrac{n}{9} - 5$ $a_1 =$ $a_2 =$ $a_3 =$ $a_{20} =$ Pattern: _____

15. $a_n = \dfrac{n}{10} - 1$ $a_1 =$ $a_2 =$ $a_3 =$ $a_{20} =$ Pattern: _____

16. $a_n = \dfrac{3n}{4} + 2$ $a_1 =$ $a_2 =$ $a_3 =$ $a_{20} =$ Pattern: _____

17. $a_n = n^2$ $a_1 =$ $a_2 =$ $a_3 =$ $a_{20} =$ Pattern: _____

18. $a_n = n^3$ $a_1 =$ $a_2 =$ $a_3 =$ $a_{20} =$ Pattern: _____

19. $a_n = 2^n$ $a_1 =$ $a_2 =$ $a_3 =$ $a_{20} =$ Pattern: _____

20. $a_n = -2^n$ $a_1 =$ $a_2 =$ $a_3 =$ $a_{20} =$ Pattern: _____

21. $a_n = 2^{-n}$ $a_1 =$ $a_2 =$ $a_3 =$ $a_{20} =$ Pattern: _____

22. $a_n = -2^{-n}$ $a_1=$ $a_2=$ $a_3=$ $a_{20}=$ Pattern: _____

23. $a_n = (-2)^n$ $a_1=$ $a_2=$ $a_3=$ $a_{20}=$ Pattern: _____

24. $a_n = 2^{n-1}$ $a_1=$ $a_2=$ $a_3=$ $a_{20}=$ Pattern: _____

25. $a_n = 2^{n+2}$ $a_1=$ $a_2=$ $a_3=$ $a_{20}=$ Pattern: _____

26. $a_n = 3 \times 2^n$ $a_1=$ $a_2=$ $a_3=$ $a_{20}=$ Pattern: _____

27. $a_n = -5 \times 2^{n-1}$ $a_1=$ $a_2=$ $a_3=$ $a_{20}=$ Pattern: _____

28. $a_n = 5 \times 2^{1-n}$ $a_1=$ $a_2=$ $a_3=$ $a_{20}=$ Pattern: _____

29. $a_n = (-3)^{2-n}$ $a_1=$ $a_2=$ $a_3=$ $a_{20}=$ Pattern: _____

30. $a_n = 2 \times (-3)^n$ $a_1=$ $a_2=$ $a_3=$ $a_{20}=$ Pattern: _____

31. $a_n = 2 \times (-5)^{n-1}$ $a_1=$ $a_2=$ $a_3=$ $a_{20}=$ Pattern: _____

32. $a_n = (-3)^{n+1}$ $a_1=$ $a_2=$ $a_3=$ $a_{20}=$ Pattern: _____

33. $a_n = 1 + 5^{n-2}$ $a_1=$ $a_2=$ $a_3=$ $a_{20}=$ Pattern: _____

34. $a_n = 3 \times 2^n$ $a_1=$ $a_2=$ $a_3=$ $a_{20}=$ Pattern: _____

35. $a_n = -5 \times 2^{n-1}$ $a_1=$ $a_2=$ $a_3=$ $a_{20}=$ Pattern: _____

36. $a_n = 2 \times 3^n$ $a_1=$ $a_2=$ $a_3=$ $a_{20}=$ Pattern: _____

37. $a_n = 5^{n-2} + 3$ $a_1=$ $a_2=$ $a_3=$ $a_{20}=$ Pattern: _____

38. $a_n = (-3)^n$ $a_1=$ $a_2=$ $a_3=$ $a_{20}=$ Pattern: _____

39. $a_n = 2 \times (-3)^n$ $a_1=$ $a_2=$ $a_3=$ $a_{20}=$ Pattern: _____

40. $a_n = 2 \times (-5)^{n-1}$ $a_1=$ $a_2=$ $a_3=$ $a_{20}=$ Pattern: _____

41. $a_n = (-3)^{n+1}$ $a_1=$ $a_2=$ $a_3=$ $a_{20}=$ Pattern: _____

42. $a_n = 1 + 5^{n-2}$ $a_1=$ $a_2=$ $a_3=$ $a_{20}=$ Pattern: _____

43. The sequences in which the pattern is add/subtract a number are called _____

44. The sequences in which the pattern is multiply/divide (pay attention that dividing by a is the same as multiplying by ____) a number are called _____

45. $a_n = 2a_{n-1}$ $a_1=1$ $a_2=$ $a_3=$ $a_{20}=$ Pattern: _____

46. $a_{n+2} = a_n + a_{n+1}$ $a_1=1$ $a_2=1$ $a_3=$ $a_{20}=$ Pattern: _____

47. In the last 2 sequences the terms are given in terms of _____

48. (T/F) Arithmetic and Geometric sequences are most of the sequences that exist.

49. The terms in a convergent geometric sequence tend to _____, in a none–convergent sequence the terms tend to _____ or _____.

50. Give an example of a convergent geometric sequence:

51. Give an example of a divergent geometric sequence:

52. Give an example of a alternating convergent geometric sequence:

53. Give an example of a none alternating divergent geometric sequence:

54. A convergent geometric sequence is a sequence in which r is _____.

Arithmetic sequence (Pattern – Add a constant):

General term: $a_n = a_1 + (n-1)d$

Sum: $S_n = \frac{n}{2}(2a_1 + (n-1)d)$

Geometric Sequence (Pattern – multiply by a constant):

General term: $a_n = a_1 r^{n-1}$

Sum: $S_n = \frac{a(r^n - 1)}{r - 1}$

Convergent geometric sequence ($-1 < r < 1$): $S_\infty = \frac{a_1}{1-r}$

Example:

3, 7, 11, 15…
Arithmetic sequence.
Pattern: add 4.
General term: $a_n = 3 + (n-1)4$
General term can be written also like this: $a_n = -1 + 4n = 4n - 1$

Given the following sequences:

a. For each one write: arithmetic, geometric convergent, geometric divergent or neither, the <u>next term</u> and their <u>general term</u> (in case they are geometric or arithmetic only).

b. Try to write the general term of the other sequences as well.

65

55. 1, 2, 3, 4, ___ …

56. 1, 2, 4, 8, ___ …

57. 1, 3, 5, 7, ___ …

58. 1, 3, 9, 27, ___ …

59. 4, 6, 9, 13,5, ___ …

60. 4, 1, –2, –5, ___ …

61. 5, 0, –4, –7, ___ …

62. 10, 1000, 100000, ___ …

63. 30, 10, $\dfrac{10}{3}$, $\dfrac{10}{9}$, ___ …

64. 2, 10, 50, 250, ___ …

65. 2, 102, 202, 302, ___ …

66. 1, –1, 1, –1, ____

67. –2, 2, –2, 2, ___ ...

68. 3, –6, 12, –24, ___ ...

69. –8, 4, –2, 1, ___ ...

70. 5, 1, $\frac{1}{5}$, $\frac{1}{25}$, ___ ...

71. 100, 10, 1, $\frac{1}{10}$, ___ ...

72. $\frac{3}{4}$, $\frac{3}{8}$, $\frac{3}{16}$, ___ ...

73. 12, 11, 10, 9, ___ ...

74. $\frac{4}{9}$, $\frac{5}{9}$, $\frac{6}{9}$, ___ ...

75. 9, 8, 6, 5, 3, 2, ___ ...

76. 5, 9, 13, ___ ...

77. 1, $\frac{3}{2}$, $\frac{9}{4}$, $\frac{27}{8}$, ___ ...

78. 5, $-\frac{5}{3}$, $\frac{5}{9}$, $-\frac{5}{27}$, ___ ...

79. –1, –2, –3, ___ ...

80. –2, 4, –8, ___ ...

81. 70, 20, $\dfrac{40}{7}$, ___...

82. 100, 10, 1, ___...

83. 100, –10, 1, $\dfrac{-1}{10}$, ___...

84. 3, 24, 192, ___...

85. 90, 9, $\dfrac{9}{10}$, ___...

86. $\dfrac{3}{2}$, $\dfrac{4}{3}$, $\dfrac{5}{4}$, ___...

87. $\dfrac{40}{3}$, $\dfrac{20}{6}$, $\dfrac{10}{12}$, $\dfrac{5}{24}$, ___...

88. $\dfrac{2}{3}$, $-\dfrac{4}{9}$, $\dfrac{8}{27}$, $-\dfrac{16}{81}$, ___...

89. $-\dfrac{1}{2}$, $-\dfrac{1}{4}$, $-\dfrac{1}{8}$, $-\dfrac{1}{16}$, ___...

90. $\dfrac{1}{7}$, $-\dfrac{1}{14}$, $\dfrac{1}{21}$, $-\dfrac{1}{28}$, ___...

91. 8, 5, 3, 0, ___...

92. 3, $\dfrac{3}{4}$, $\dfrac{3}{16}$, ___...

93. 81, –9, 1, $-\dfrac{1}{9}$, ___...

94. 2, –10, 50, ___...

In each one of the following sequences find the term indicated:

95. $1, 4, 7 \ldots (a_{31})$

96. $-8, -5, -2 \ldots (a_{37})$

97. $4, -8, 16 \ldots (a_{15})$

98. $32, -8, 2 \ldots (a_{11})$

99. $68, -34, 17 \ldots (a_9)$

100. $3, 14, 25 \ldots (a_9)$

101. $-4000, 1000, -250, \ldots (a_7)$

102. The 4th term of a geometric sequence is 3, the 6th term is $\dfrac{27}{4}$.

   a. Find the ratio of the sequence.
   b. Is this sequence convergent? Explain
   c. Find a_1
   d. Find a_{12}
   e. Sum the first 15 terms.

103. The 2nd term of a arithmetic sequence is –2, the 6th term is –4.

   a. Find the difference of the sequence.
   b. Find a_1
   c. Find a_{12}
   d. Sum the first 50 terms.

104. The 10th term of a geometric sequence is 5, the 14th term is $\frac{80}{81}$

   a. Find the ratio of the sequence.
   b. Is this sequence convergent? Explain
   c. Find a$_1$
   d. Find a$_7$
   e. Sum the first 10 terms.
   f. Sum all the terms of the sequence.

105. The 7th term of a arithmetic sequence is 120, the 16th term is 201.

   a. Find the difference of the sequence.
   b. Find a$_1$
   c. Find a$_{12}$
   d. Sum the first 50 terms.

106. All the terms in a geometric sequence are positive. The first term is 7 and the 3rd term is 28.

   a. Find the common ratio.
   b. Find the sum of the first 14 terms.

107. The fifth term of an arithmetic sequence is –20 and the twelfth term is –44.

   a. Find the common difference.
   b. Find the first term of the sequence.
   c. Calculate the eighty–seventh term.
   d. Calculate the sum of the first 150 terms.

108. Sum the following sequences:

   a. $3 + 6 + 9 + 12 + \ldots + 69 =$

   b. $6 + 14 + 22 + 30 + \ldots + 54 =$

   c. $5 + \dfrac{5}{3} + \dfrac{5}{9} + \ldots =$

   d. $1 + 2 + 3 + 4 + \ldots + 158 =$

   e. $9 + 18 + 27 + 36 + \ldots + 900 =$

   f. $80 + 20 + 5 + \ldots$

109. Consider the arithmetic series $-6 + 1 + 8 + 15 + \ldots$

   Find the least number of terms so that the sum of the series is greater than 10000.

110. In a theatre there are 20 seats in the first row, 23 in the 2nd, 26 in the 3rd etc. There are 40 rows in the theatre. Find the total number of seats available.

111. A ball bounces on the floor. It is released from a height of 160 cm. After the 1st bounce it reaches a height of 120 cm and 90 cm after the 2nd. If the patterns continue find:

   a. The height the ball will reach after the 6th bounce.
   b. The total distance the ball passed after a long period o time.

112. In a certain forest the current population of rabbits is 200 objects. It is known that the population increases by 20% every year.

   a. Find the population of rabbits after a year.
   b. Find the population of rabbits after 2 years.
   c. What kind of a sequence is it? State the expression for the population after n years.
   d. Find the total number of rabbits after 10 years (assuming none has died).

113. In a research it was observed that 5% of the products produced by a machine are defective. This percentage decreases by 10% every year (due to technological improvements). In a certain year the machine made 300 products.

   a. Find the number of defective products produced a year later.
   b. Find the number of defective products produced 2 years later.
   c. What kind of a sequence is it? State the expression for the number of errors committed after n years.
   d. Find the total number of bad products produced in the first 8 years.

114. In a certain company the pay scale follows a pattern of an arithmetic sequence (every year). This means:

   a. The salary increases by a certain % every year (True/False), explain.

   b. The salary increases by a certain amount every year (True/False), explain

COMPOUND INTEREST

1. 1200$ are put in account that gives 2% per year. Calculate the amount of money in the account after:

    a. 1 year.

    b. 2 years.

2. To increase an amount A by 5% it should be multiplied by _____.

3. To increase an amount A by 56% it should be multiplied by _____.

4. To decrease an amount A by 5% it should be multiplied by _____.

5. To increase an amount A by 15% it should be multiplied by _____.

6. To decrease an amount A by 12% it should be multiplied by _____.

7. To increase an amount A by 230% it should be multiplied by _____.

8. 1000$ are put in account that takes 5% commission per year. Calculate the amount of money in the account after:

    a. 1 year.

    b. 2 years.

9. 2000$ are being put in a deposit that pays 5% (per year).

   a. Fill the table:

Number of Years	Interest earned at the end of the year	Amount in deposit ($)
0		2000
1	$\frac{5}{100} 2000 = 100$	2100
2	$\frac{5}{100} 2100 = 105$	2205
3	$\frac{5}{100} 2205 = 110.25$	
4		
5		

   b. Observe the numbers in the compound interest column: 2000, 2100, 2205… What kind of a sequence is that? Write its general term.

   c. How much money will be in the account after 20 years?

   d. Discuss the meaning of writing $a_n = a_1 r^{n-1}$ or writing $a_n = a_0 r^n$. Use the exercise as an example.

78

10. A loan of 1200$ is made at 12% per year compounded semiannually, over 5 years the debt will grow to:

   a. $1200(1 + 0.12)^5$
   b. $1200(1 + 0.06)^{10}$
   c. $1200(1 + 0.6)^{10}$
   d. $1200(1 + 0.06)^5$
   e. $1200(1 + 0.12)^{10}$

11. A loan of 23200$ is made at 8% per year compounded quarterly, over 6 years the debt will grow to:

   a. $23200(1 + 0.2)^{24}$
   b. $23200(1 + 0.08)^6$
   c. $23200(1 + 0.02)^{24}$
   d. $23200(1 + 0.08)^{24}$
   e. $23200(1 + 0.02)^6$

12. A loan of 20$ is made at 12% per year compounded monthly, over 8 years the debt will grow to:

   a. $20(1 + 0.12)^{80}$
   b. $20(1 + 0.01)^8$
   c. $20(1 + 0.012)^{96}$
   d. $20(1 + 0.01)^{96}$
   e. $20(1 + 0.06)^{12}$

13. A loan of X$ is made at 12% per year compounded every 4 months, over 5 years the debt will grow to:

   a. $X(1 + 0.12)^4$
   b. $X(1 + 0.4)^5$
   c. $X(1 + 0.4)^{15}$
   d. $X(1 + 0.04)^{15}$
   e. $X(1 + 0.012)^{15}$

14. A loan of X$ is made at i% per year compounded every m months, over n years the debt will grow to:

$$Debt = \underline{}(1 + \underline{})^{\underline{}}$$

15. Calculate the total amount owing after two years on a loan of 1500$ if the interest rate is 11% compounded

    a. Annually

    b. Semiannually

    c. Quarterly

    d. Monthly

16. How much will a client have to repay on a loan of 800$ after 2 years, if the 12% interest is compounded annually.

17. Find the compound interest **earned** by the deposit. Round to the nearest dollar. $3000 at 12% compounded semiannually for 10 years

18. How many years will it take to a 100$ to double assuming interest rate is 6%. Compounded semiannually.

19. How many years will it take to a X$ to triple assuming interest rate is 7%. Compounded quarterly

20. Find the interest rate given to a certain person in case he made a deposit of 1000$ and obtained 1200$ after 3 years, compounded monthly.

21. Find the interest rate given to a certain person in case he made a deposit of 2500$ and obtained 3000$ after 10 years, compounded yearly.

SIGMA NOTATION

1. The sum $\sum_{k=2}^{4} 2^k$ is equal to which of the following?
    a. $2^1 + 2^2 + 2^3 + 2^4$
    b. $2^2 + 2^4$
    c. $2^2 + 3^3 + 4^4$
    d. $2^2 + 2^3 + 2^4$

2. The sum $\dfrac{1}{4}\sum_{m=2}^{4} x_m$ is equal to which of the following?
    a. $\dfrac{1}{4}x_2 + \dfrac{1}{4}x_3 + \dfrac{1}{4}x_4$
    b. $\dfrac{1}{4}x_2 + x_3 + x_4$
    c. $\dfrac{1}{2}x_2 + \dfrac{1}{3}x_3 + \dfrac{1}{4}x_4$
    d. $\dfrac{1}{4}(2+3+4)$

3. The sum $\sum_{j=4}^{n} \dfrac{j}{j+1}$ is equal to which of the following?
    a. $\dfrac{1}{2} + \dfrac{3}{4} + \dfrac{5}{6} + \ldots + \dfrac{n}{n+1}$
    b. $\dfrac{1}{2} + \dfrac{2}{3} + \dfrac{3}{4} + \ldots + \dfrac{n}{n+1}$
    c. $\dfrac{4}{5} + \dfrac{5}{6} + \dfrac{6}{7} + \ldots + \dfrac{n}{n+1}$
    d. $\dfrac{4}{5} + \dfrac{5}{6} + \dfrac{6}{7} + \ldots + \dfrac{n+4}{n+5}$

4. Write out fully what is meant by
    a. $\sum_{i=4}^{i=6} 2i - 1 =$
    b. $\sum_{i=2}^{i=5} \dfrac{i}{i^2+1} =$
    c. $\sum_{i=4}^{i=6} (2i-3)^2 =$
    d. $\sum_{k=3}^{i=7} (2^k + \sqrt{k}) =$
    e. $\sum_{i=1}^{i=4} (-1)^i \times 3^{2i}$

82

5. Write each series using sigma notation:

   a. $4 + 9 + 16 + 25 + 36 + 49 + 64 + 81 = \sum_{i=\_}^{i=\_}$ _____

   b. $5 + 9 + 13 + 17 + 21 + 25 + 29 + 33... = \sum_{i=\_}^{i=\_}$ _____

   c. $1 - \dfrac{1}{3} + \dfrac{1}{9} - \dfrac{1}{27} + \dfrac{1}{81} - \dfrac{1}{243} = \sum_{i=\_}^{i=\_}$ _____

6. Use sigma notation to represent $3 + 6 + 9 + 12 + ...$ for 28 terms. Sum the terms.

   $\sum_{i=\_}^{i=\_}$ _____

7. Use sigma notation to represent $-3 + 6 - 12 + 24 - 48 + ...$ for 35 terms. Sum the terms.

   $\sum_{i=\_}^{i=\_}$ _____

8. Use sigma notation to represent: $8.3 + 8.1 + 7.9 + 7.7 + ...$ for 100 terms. Sum the terms

   $\sum_{i=\_}^{i=\_}$ _____

9. An infinite geometric series is given by $\sum_{i=1}^{\infty} 2(1-x)^i$

   a. Find the value of x for which the series has a finite sum

   b. When x=0.5, find the minimum number of terms needed to give a sum which is greater than 1.9

83

1.10. – COMPLEX NUMBERS

1. A complex number z is a number of the form $a+bi$ where a, b are _____ numbers and $i =$ ___ or $i^2 =$ ___ .

2. a is called the _____ part of z, $a = \text{Re}(z)$, and b is called the _____ part of z, $b = \text{Im}(z)$

3. z is said to be purely imaginary if and only if $\text{Re}(z) =$ ___ and $\text{Im}(z) \neq$ ___ .

4. When $\text{Im}(z) =$ ___ , the complex number z is real.

5. Practice:

$i^2 = i \cdot i =$ _____　　　　　　$i^{65} =$ _____

$i^3 = i^2 \cdot i =$ _____　　　　　$i^{176} =$ _____

$i^4 = i^3 \cdot i =$ _____　　　　　$i^{26} =$ _____

$i^5 = i^4 \cdot i =$ _____ .　　　　$i^{99} =$ _____

$i^6 = i^5 \cdot i =$ _____　　　　　$i^{100} =$ _____

$i^7 = i^6 \cdot i =$ _____　　　　　$i^{133} =$ _____

$i^8 = i^7 \cdot i =$ _____　　　　　$i^{88} =$ _____

6. Solve in terms of i:

   a. $x^2 + x + 1 = 0$

   b. $2x^2 + 3x + 6 = 0$

Operations on Complex Numbers

Let $z_1 = a + bi$ and $z_2 = c + di$. Then

7. $z_1 + z_2 = (\underline{\hspace{1cm}}) + (\underline{\hspace{1cm}})i$

8. $z_1 - z_2 = (\underline{\hspace{1cm}}) + (\underline{\hspace{1cm}})i$

9. $z_1 z_2 = (a+bi)(c+di) = \underline{\hspace{6cm}}$

10. $\dfrac{z_1}{z_2} = \left(\dfrac{a+bi}{c+di}\right) \cdot \left(\dfrac{c-di}{c-di}\right) = \underline{\hspace{4cm}}$, where $z_2 \neq 0$.

11. $\dfrac{1}{i} =$

12. $\dfrac{i}{z_2} =$

13. Given $z_1 = -4 - 3i$ and $z_2 = 1 - 5i$, find

    a. $z_1 + 2z_2 =$

    b. $-3z_1 - 2z_2 =$

    c. $z_2 - iz_1 =$

    d. $z_1 z_2 =$

    e. $z_1 z_2 z_2 =$

    f. $\dfrac{z_1}{z_2} =$

    g. $\dfrac{z_2}{iz_1} =$

14. The conjugate number of $z = x + iy$ is $z^* = \underline{\hspace{3cm}}$ (it can also be

    written as $\underline{\hspace{1cm}}$)

15. Given that z = x + iy, answer:

   a. $\frac{1}{2}(z + z^*) =$

   b. $\frac{1}{2i}(z - z^*) =$

   c. $zz^* =$

   d. z is real if and only if $\bar{z} = z$ (True/False)

   e. $\bar{\bar{z}} = z$ (True/False)

   f. $z\bar{z} =$ _____ $= |z|^2$

Let $z_1 = x + iy$ and $z_2 = a + ib$ be two complex numbers. Answer:

   g. $\overline{z_1 + z_2} = \overline{z_1} + \overline{z_2}$ (True/False)

   h. $\overline{z_1 z_2} = \overline{z_1} \cdot \overline{z_2}$ (True/False)

   i. $\overline{\left(\dfrac{z_1}{z_2}\right)} = \dfrac{\overline{z_1}}{\overline{z_2}}$ $(z_2 \neq 0)$ (True/False)

16. Find the square roots of the complex numbers (using algebra, later we will see how it can be done using DeMoivre's Theorem)

   a. $5 - 12i$

   b. $24 + 10i$

Geometrical Representation of a Complex Number

1. Complex numbers can be represented graphically on a diagram called _____ diagram. The real part is represented as the x coordinate and the imaginary part as the y coordinate.

2. On this plane, a number represented by points on x axis will be _____.

   For example: Sketch the number 4 on the Argand diagram:

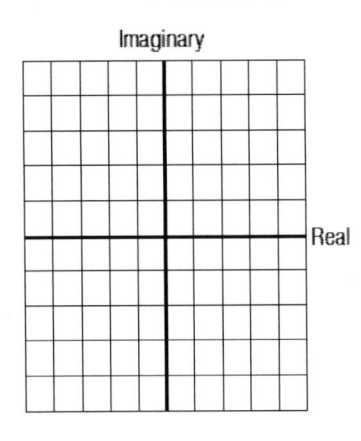

3. Imaginary numbers are represented by points on the _____.

   For example: Sketch the number 2i on the Argand diagram:

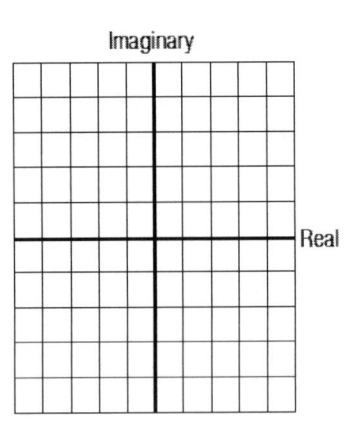

4. The number 0 is represented by the origin **O**.

5. z_1, z_2, z_3 are represented on the Argand diagram. Write down the 3 numbers:

   $z_1 = $ _____

   $z_2 = $ _____

   $z_3 = $ _____

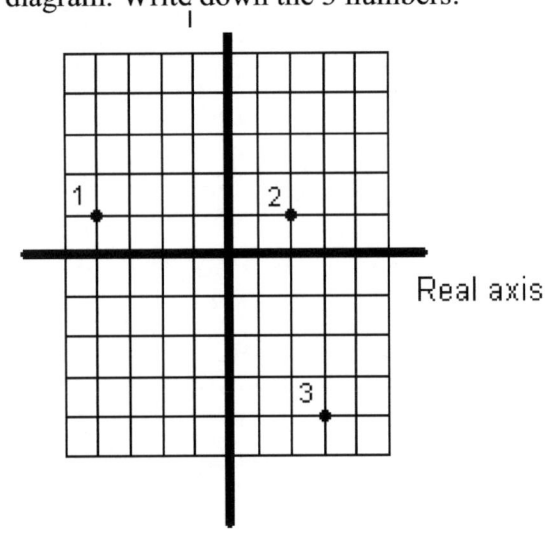

Polar Form of a Complex Number

A complex number $z = a + bi$ can be represented by a vector $\overrightarrow{OA}$ as shown in Figure:

1. The length of the vector $\overrightarrow{OA}$, $r = |\overrightarrow{OA}|$, is called the _____ (or _____) of the complex number z, and it is denoted by $|z|$.

2. The angle between the vector $\overrightarrow{OA}$ and the positive real axis is defined to be the _____ (or amplitude) of z and is denoted by $\arg(z)$ or $\text{amp}(z)$.

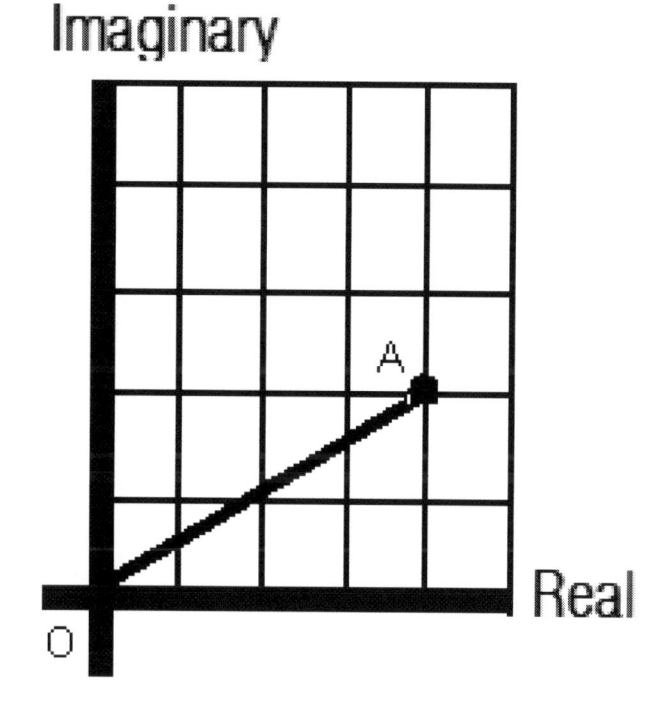

3. Show a, b, r and θ on the diagram.

4. In this case r = _____ and arg(z) = _____.

5. $A\text{rg}(z)$ has an infinite number of possible values: $\arg(z) = \theta + 2k\pi, k \in Z$.

6. In this case possible values of arg(z) are: _____.

7. If arg(z) lies in the interval $-\pi < \theta \leq \pi$, we call this value the ***principal value***.

8. In this case: z = $a + ib$ = _____ = rcis(_____)

9. In general z = $a + ib$ = _____ = rcis(_____)

10. Sketch the following complex numbers on an Argand diagram and write them in the polar form:

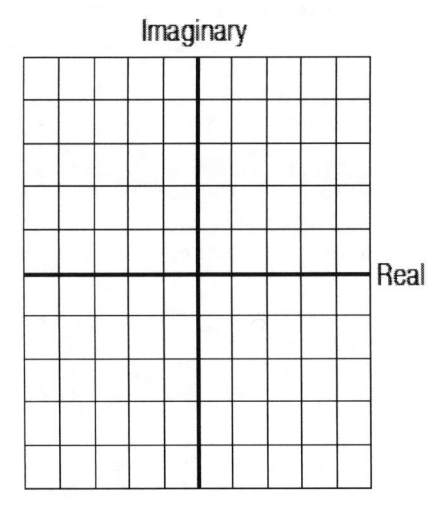

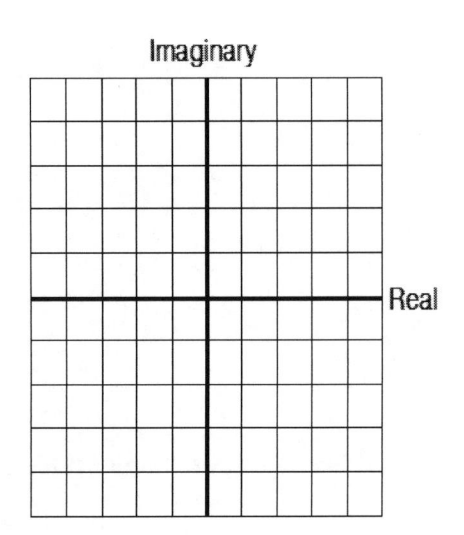

   a. $2 = \underline{} \text{Cis}(\underline{}) = \underline{} e^{i\underline{}}$

   b. $-5 = \underline{} \text{Cis}(\underline{}) = \underline{} e^{i\underline{}}$

   c. $i = \underline{} \text{Cis}(\underline{}) = \underline{} e^{i\underline{}}$

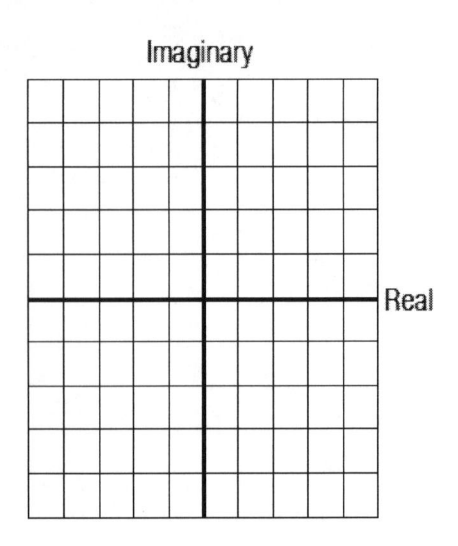

d. $-3i =$ ___Cis(___) = ___$e^{i\_\_}$

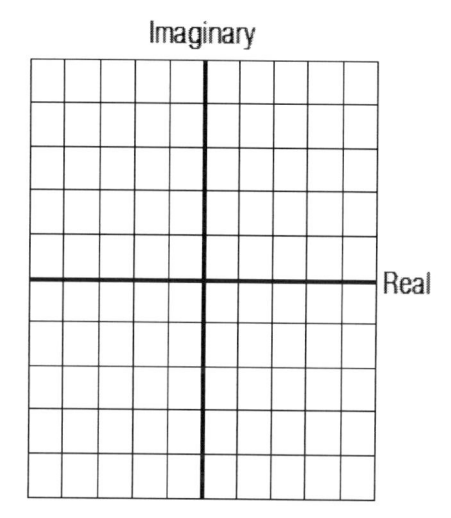

e. $1+i =$ ___Cis(___) = ___$e^{i\_\_}$

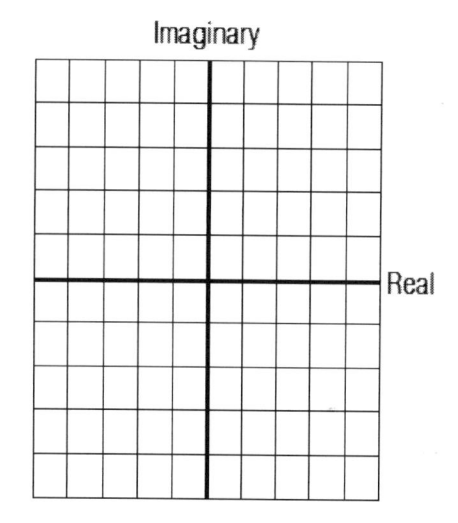

f. $-5+12i =$ ___Cis(___) = ___$e^{i\_\_}$

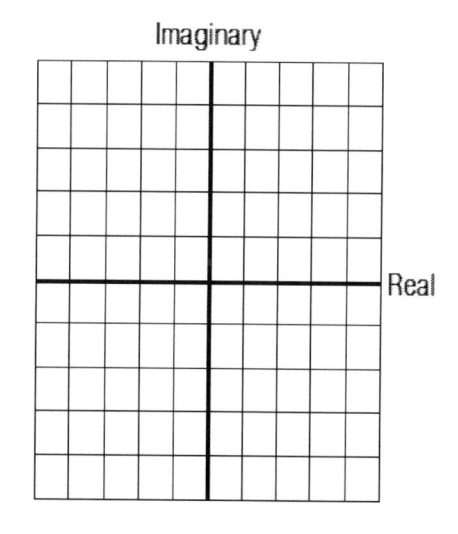

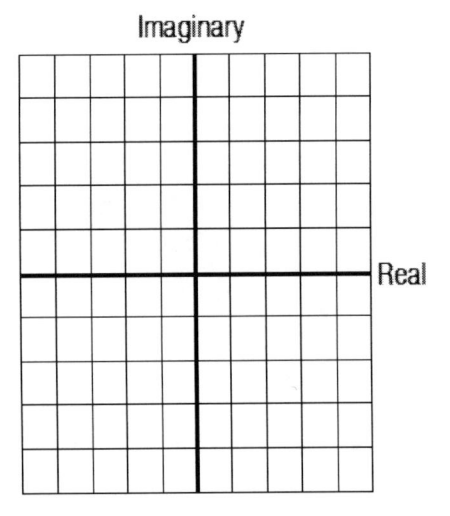

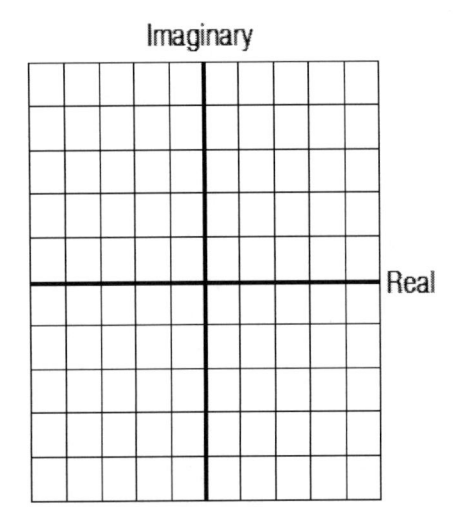

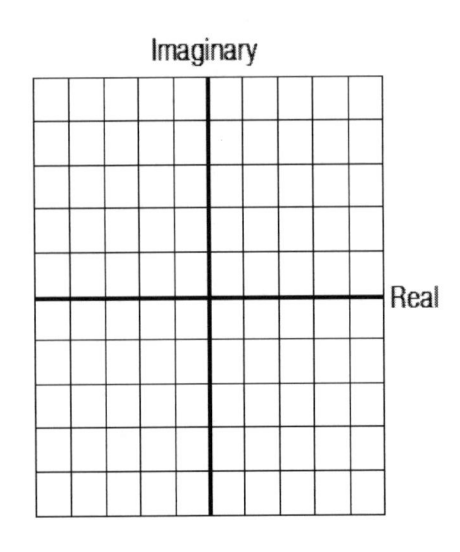

g. $3 - 3\sqrt{3}i = \underline{}\operatorname{Cis}(\underline{}) = \underline{}e^{i\underline{}}$

h. $-1 - i = \underline{}\operatorname{Cis}(\underline{}) = \underline{}e^{i\underline{}}$

i. $-1 + \sqrt{2}i = \underline{}\operatorname{Cis}(\underline{}) = \underline{}e^{i\underline{}}$

j. $-\sqrt{2}i = \_\_\text{Cis}(\_\_) = \_\_e^{i\_\_}$

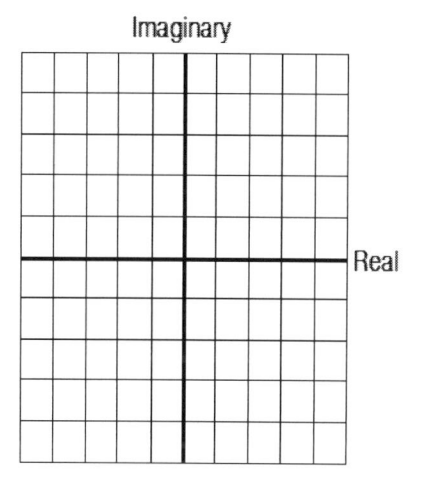

k. $(1-\sqrt{3}i)^2 = \_\_\text{Cis}(\_\_) = \_\_e^{i\_\_}$

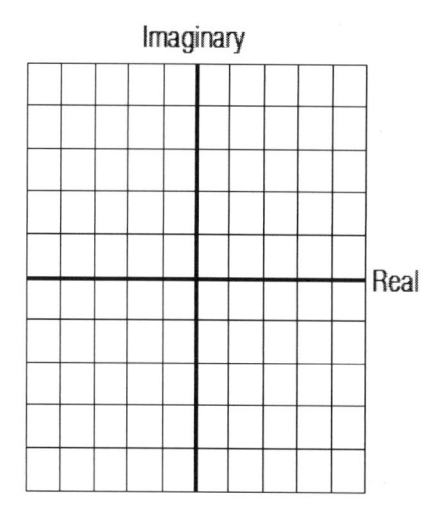

l. $\dfrac{1}{i-2} = \_\_\text{Cis}(\_\_) = \_\_e^{i\_\_}$

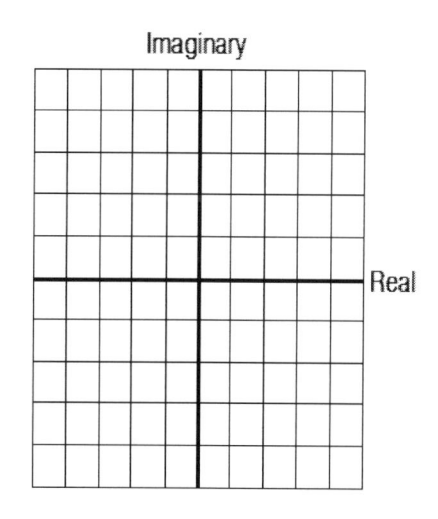

Use of Polar Form in Multiplication and Division

Let $z_1 = r_1(\cos\theta_1 + i\sin\theta_1)$, $z_2 = r_2(\cos\theta_2 + i\sin\theta_2)$, it follows that:

11. $|z_1 z_2| = |z_1||z_2|$

12. $\left|\dfrac{z_1}{z_2}\right| = \dfrac{|z_1|}{|z_2|}$

13. $\arg(z_1 z_2) = \arg(z_1) + \arg(z_2)$ or $z_1 z_2 = r_1 r_2[\cos(\theta_1 + \theta_2) + i\sin(\theta_1 + \theta_2)]$

14. $\arg\left(\dfrac{z_1}{z_2}\right) = \arg(z_1) - \arg(z_2)$ or $\dfrac{z_1}{z_2} = \dfrac{r_1}{r_2}[\cos(\theta_1 - \theta_2) + i\sin(\theta_1 - \theta_2)]$

15. $|\bar{z}| = |z|$ (True/False) (Sketch a diagram to show your answer)

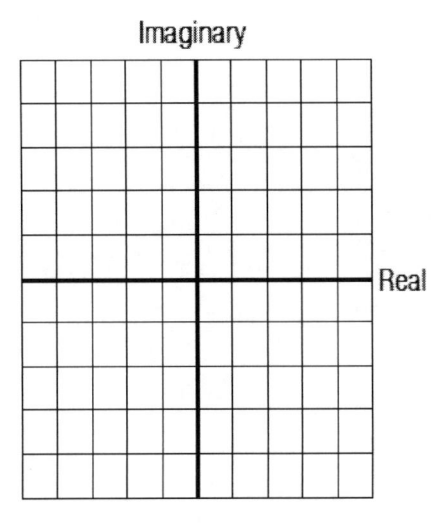

16. $\arg\bar{z} = -\arg z$ (True/False) (Sketch a diagram to show your answer)

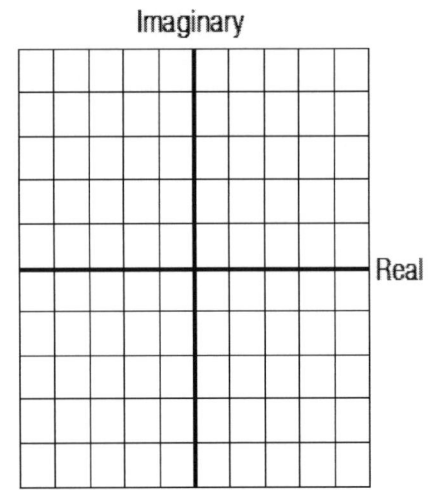

17. Let $z_1 = 1 + \sqrt{3}i$ and $z_2 = 3 - \sqrt{3}i$. Express z_1 and z_2 in polar form

$z_1 =$

$z_2 =$

Find and write in all forms:

a. $z_1 z_2 =$

b. $z_1(z_2)^2 =$

c. $iz_2 =$

d. $\dfrac{z_1}{z_2} =$

e. $\dfrac{z_1}{iz_2} =$

f. $\left(\dfrac{iz_2}{z_1}\right)^2$

DeMoivre's Theorem and nth Roots of a Complex Number

DeMoivre's Theorem: $z^n = [r(\cos(\theta) + i\sin(\theta))]^n = r^n(\cos(n\theta) + i\sin(n\theta))$

18. Calculate:

   a. $(1+i)^{10} =$

   b. $(1-\sqrt{3}i)^4 =$

   c. $i^{13} =$

   d. $(-2-\sqrt{3}i)^6 =$

   e. $\sqrt{(2-2\sqrt{3}i)} =$

   f. $i^{\frac{1}{3}} =$

   g. $(1-\sqrt{3}i)^{\frac{3}{2}} =$

19. Solve the equations and sketch the solutions on the Argand diagram:

   a. $z^2 = -1$

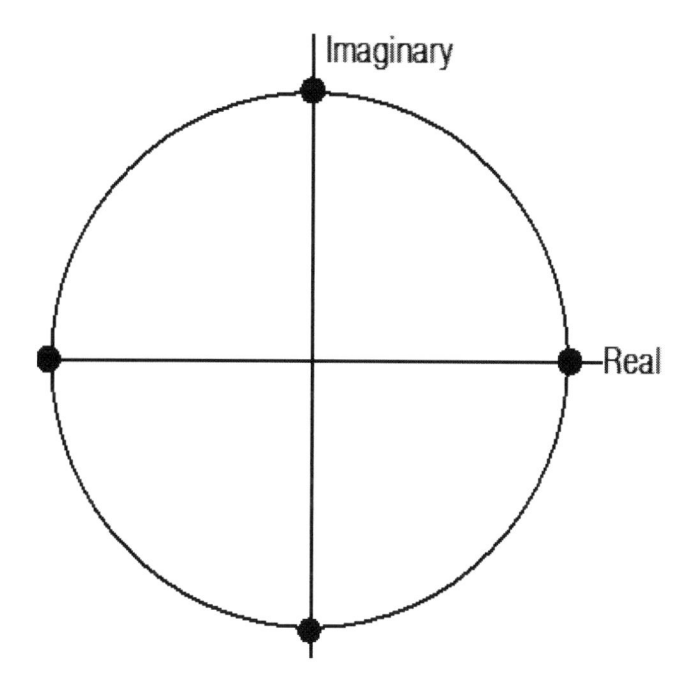

   b. $z^3 = -1$

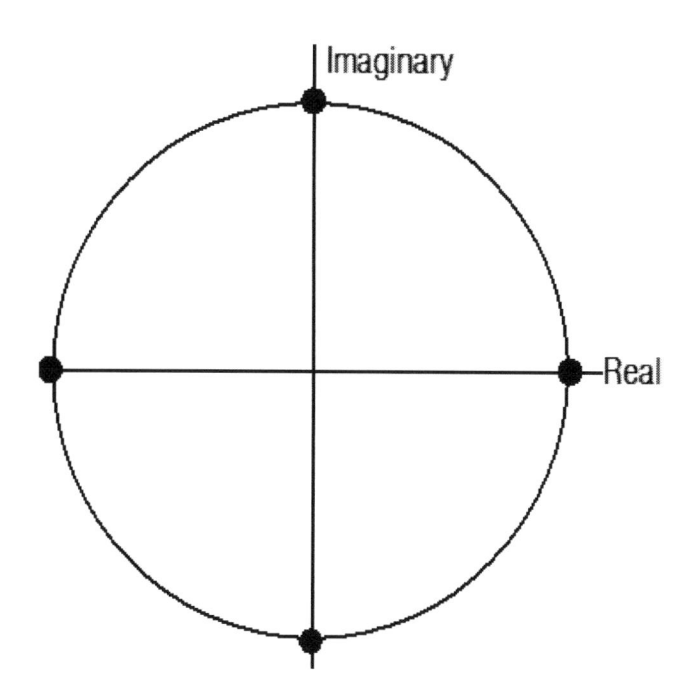

97

c. $z^4 = -1$

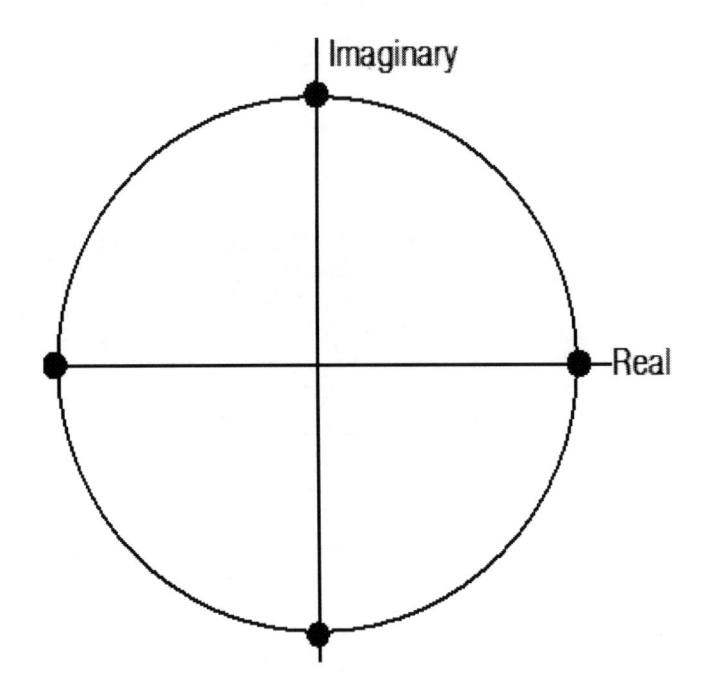

d. $z^5 = -1$

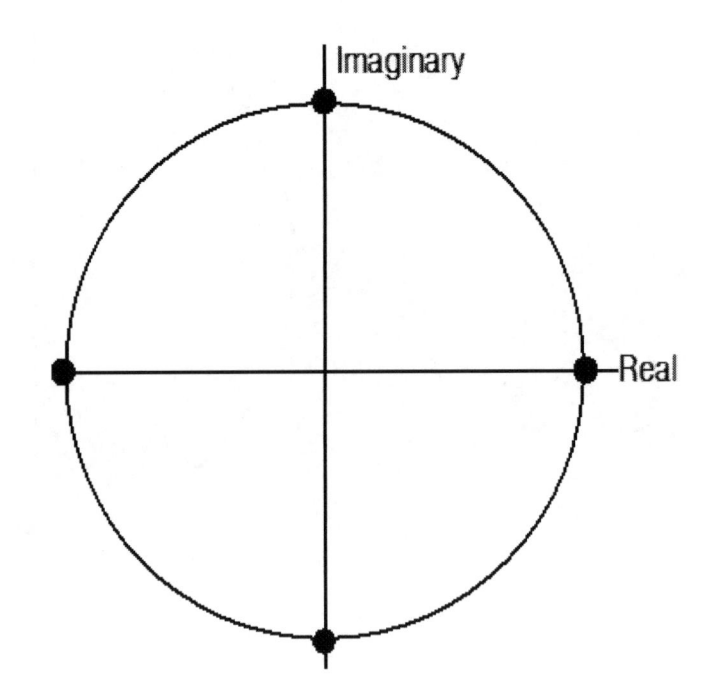

Solve the equations:

e. $z^4 = 16$

f. $z^3 = 8i$

g. Find the 4th roots of $1 + \sqrt{3}i$

h. Find the square roots of $6 + 8i$

Polynomials with Real Coefficients

If $f(x) = a_n x^n + a_{n-1} x^{n-1} + \cdots + a_1 x + a_0 = 0$ is a polynomial with _____ coefficients and degree $n \geq 2$ then if $z = a + bi$ is a root of this polynomial, then $\bar{z} = $ _____ is also a root.

20. Given that a certain polynomial equation with real coefficients of the 3rd degree has -2 and $3 - 2i$ as solutions.

    a. The 3rd solution is: _____

    b. The equation, factorized is: _____

    c. Expand the equation written in b.

21. Given that a certain polynomial equation with real coefficients of the 3rd degree has 2 and $1 + i$ as solutions.

    a. The 3rd solution is: _____

    b. The equation, factorized is: _____

    c. Expand the equation written in b.

22. Given that a certain polynomial equation with real coefficients of the 3rd degree has -5, and i as solutions.

    a. The 3rd solution is: _____

    b. The equation, factorized is: _____

    c. Expand the equation written in b.

23. Solve the equation $x^2 + 2x + 2 = 0$. Write the factorized equation.

24. Solve the equation $x^2 - 2x + 5 = 0$. Write the factorized equation.

25. Solve the equation $(z^2 + 2)(x + 5) = 0$. Write the factorized equation.

26. Solve the equation $x^3 - 3x^2 + 7x - 5 = 0$. Write the factorized equation.

27. Solve the equation $x^3 - 6x^2 + 13x - 10 = 0$. Write the factorized equation.

28. Given that $3 + i$ a solution to the equation $x^3 - 5x^2 + 4x + 10 = 0$, find the other solutions.

29. Given that i is a solution of the equation $x^4 - 2x^3 + 6x^2 - 2x + 5 = 0$, find all the other solutions.

30. **Remainder theorem:** If a polynomial is _____ by a first degree

   Polynomial of the form (x – a) then the remainder is _____. In case the

   Remainder obtained is _____ we say that the divisor is _____.

31. Find the remainder on dividing $x^{10} - x^9 + 2x + 1$ by $x - i$

32. Find the remainder on dividing $x^3 - x + 1$ by $x - i - 1$.

1.11. – MATHEMATICAL INDUCTION

1. Mathematical induction is used to prove mathematical conjectures. After a conjecture is proved we take it as a _____ and use it in other proofs.

2. The process takes place in ____ steps.

Example: Prove by induction that $1 + 2 + 4 + 8 + \ldots + 2^{n-1} = 2^n - 1$

Step 1: <u>Check</u> that the statement is true for *n = 1*.

$$1 = 2^1 - 1$$
$$1 = 1$$

(If this is not true no need to continue, we would conclude the statement false)

Step 2: <u>Assume</u> that the statement is true for *n = k*.

$$1 + 2 + 4 + 8 + \ldots + 2^{k-1} = 2^k - 1$$

Step 3: <u>Check</u> that the statement is true for *n = k + 1* using the assumption that it is true for n = k.

$$1 + 2 + 4 + 8 + \ldots + 2^{k-1} + 2^{(k+1)-1} = 2^{k+1} - 1$$

Using step 2, we substitute on the LHS:

$$2^k - 1 + 2^{(k+1)-1} = 2^{k+1} - 1$$

Simplifying the LHS:

$$2^k - 1 + 2^k = 2^{k+1} - 1$$

$$2 \cdot 2^k - 1 = 2^{k+1} - 1$$

$$2^{k+1} - 1 = 2^{k+1} - 1$$

We can conclude that the LHS is equal to RHS.

Step 4: <u>Conclude</u> that since the conjecture is true for *n = 1* and since it is true for *n = k + 1* assuming it is true for *n = k* it therefore must be true always.

104

Prove by induction:

1. $1 + 2 + 3 + \ldots + n = \dfrac{n(n+1)}{2}$

Step 1: Check that _____

Step 2: Assume that _____

Step 3: Check that _____

Step 4: Conclude that _____

2. $1^2 + 2^2 + 3^2 + \ldots + n^2 = \dfrac{n(n+1)(2n+1)}{6}$

Step 1: Check that _____

Step 2: Assume that _____

Step 3: Check that _____

Step 4: Conclude that _____

3. $1\cdot 2 + 2\cdot 3 + 3\cdot 4 + \ldots + n(n+1) = \dfrac{n(n+1)(n+2)}{3}$

Step 1: Check that _____

Step 2: Assume that _____

Step 3: Check that _____

Step 4: Conclude that _____

107

4. $n^3 + 1 > n^2$

Step 1: Check that _____

Step 2: Assume that _____

Step 3: Check that _____

Step 4: Conclude that _____

5. $5^n - 3^n$ is divisible by 2 for any positive n.

Step 1: Check that _____

Step 2: Assume that _____

Step 3: Check that _____

Step 4: Conclude that _____

6. $7^n - 2^n$ is divisible by 5 for any positive n.

Step 1: Check that _____

Step 2: Assume that _____

Step 3: Check that _____

Step 4: Conclude that _____

CHAPTER 2 – FUNCTIONS

2.1. – INTRODUCTION

1. Write the definition of a function in your own words:

2. Write 2 examples of relations that <u>are</u> functions:

3. Draw a sketch of the functions that describe those relations. Can you write the mathematical expression to describe them?

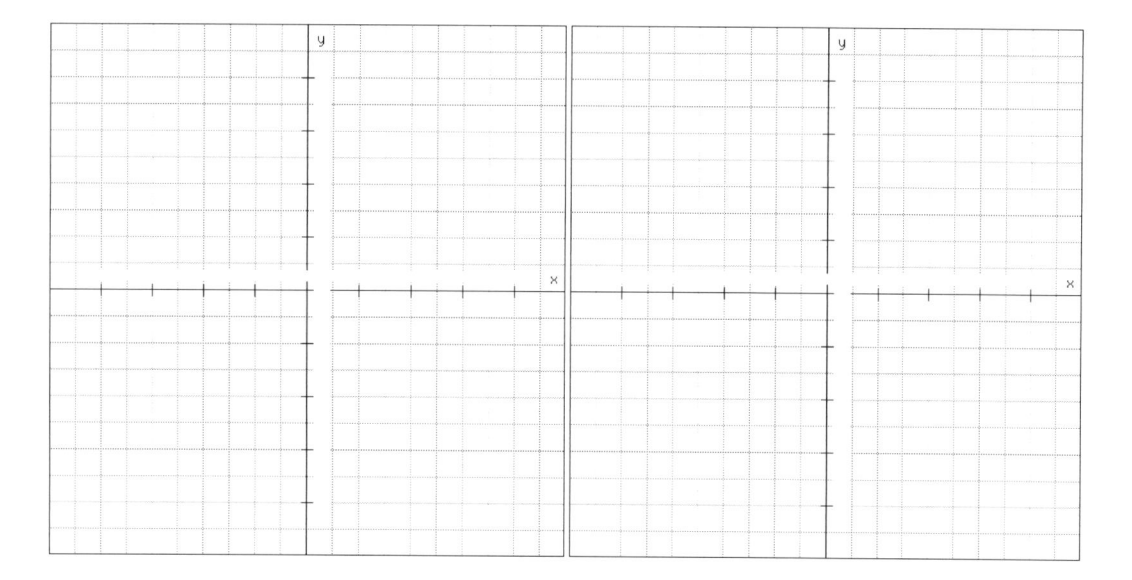

4. Write 2 examples of relations that <u>are not</u> functions:

5. Which one of the following graphs cannot represent function:

6. Draw an example of a curve that is not a function:

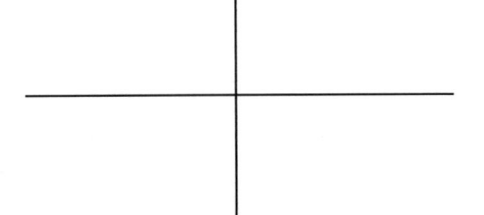

7. Draw an example of a curve that is a function:

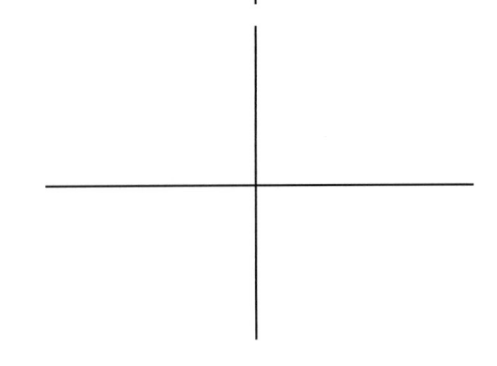

8. The domain of a function is the: _____

9. The Range of a function is the: _____

112

10. Given the Height – age curve for a human.

   a. Sketch an approximate graph:

   Height (cm)

   Age (years)

   b. In your sketch Height(0) = _____, it is the height of _____

   c. In your sketch Height(t) = 100cm. Then t is: _____

   d. State its domain: _____

   e. State its range: _____

11. Out of the following relations circle the ones that are functions:

   a. Person's name → Person's age
   b. City → Number of habitants
   c. City → Names of habitants
   d. Family → Home Address
   e. Satellite's name → Position of satellite
   f. Time → Position of object
   g. One → One
   h. One → Many
   i. Many → One

12. Given the following function that describes the temperature in C° as a function of time (t = 0 corresponds to midnight):

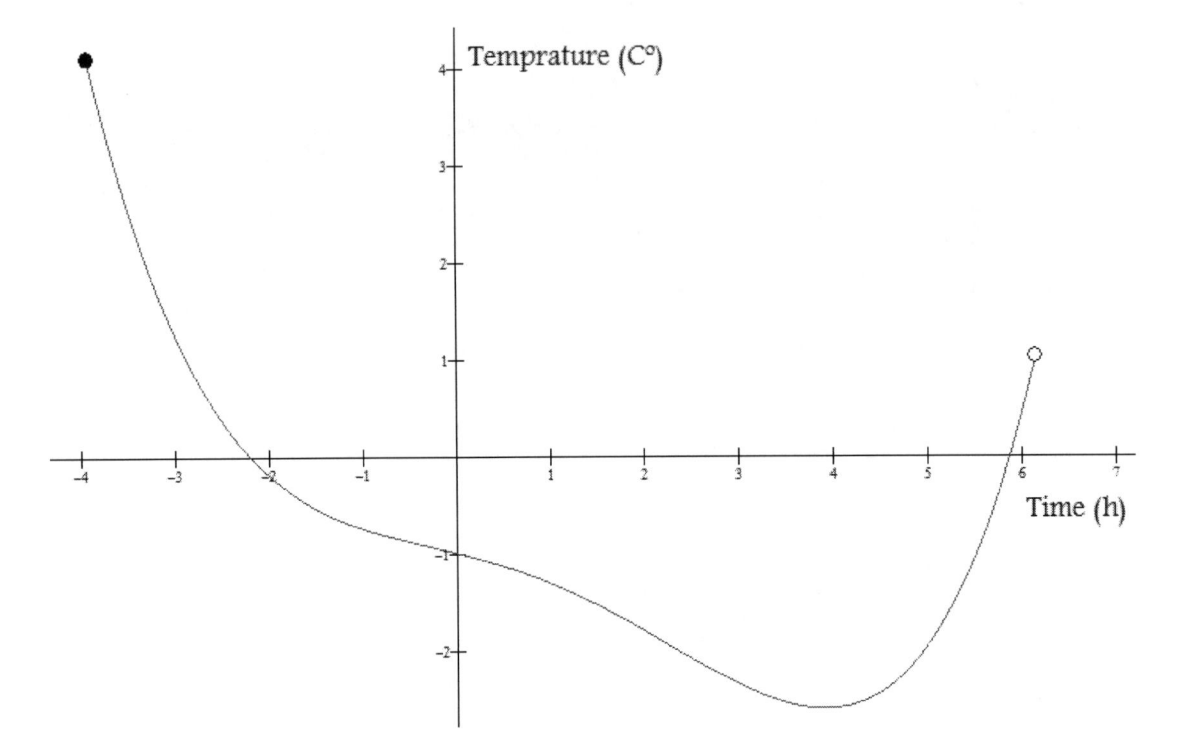

a. f(0) = _____

b. f(2) = _____ = f(__)

c. f(7) = _____

d. f(x) = 3, x = _____

e. f(x) = 0, x = _____

f. f(x) = –2, x = _____

g. State its domain: _____

h. State its range: _____

i. Is this function one to one? One to many? Explain.

114

13. Given the function the describes the change in the benefit (%) given by a certain stock:

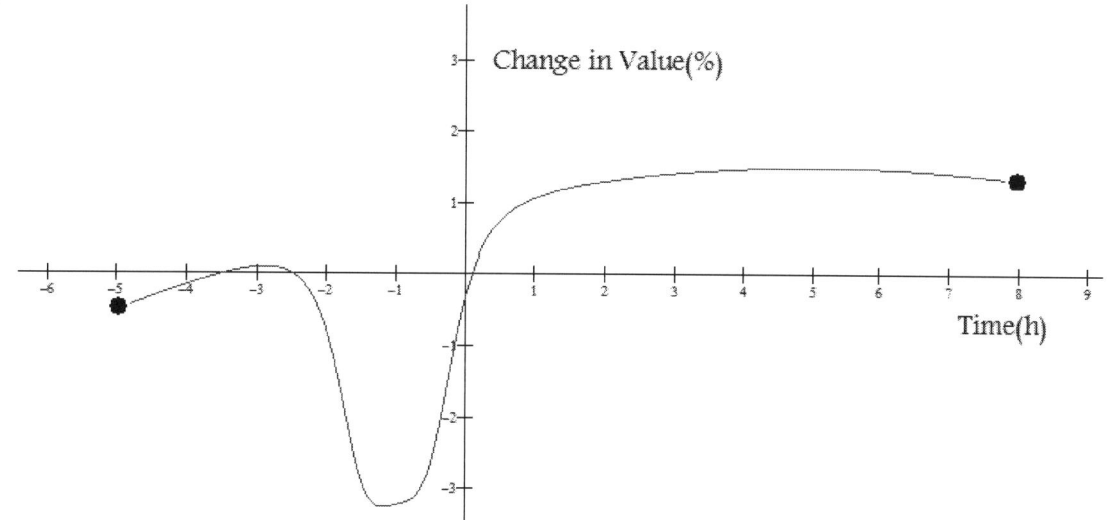

   a. f(x) = 0, x = _____

   b. f(0) = _____ = f(__)

   c. f(–5) = _____

   d. f(1) = _____

   e. f(–2) = _____ = f(__)

   f. f(3) = _____

   g. f(x) = –2, x = _____

   h. Is f(–2) < 0 ?

   i. Is f(–2) < f(–1) ?

   j. State its domain: _____

   k. State its range: _____

   l. Where is the function increasing? _____

   m. Where is the function decreasing? _____

   n. Where is the function stationary? _____

   o. Is this function one to one? One to many? Explain.

115

14. Given the following function:

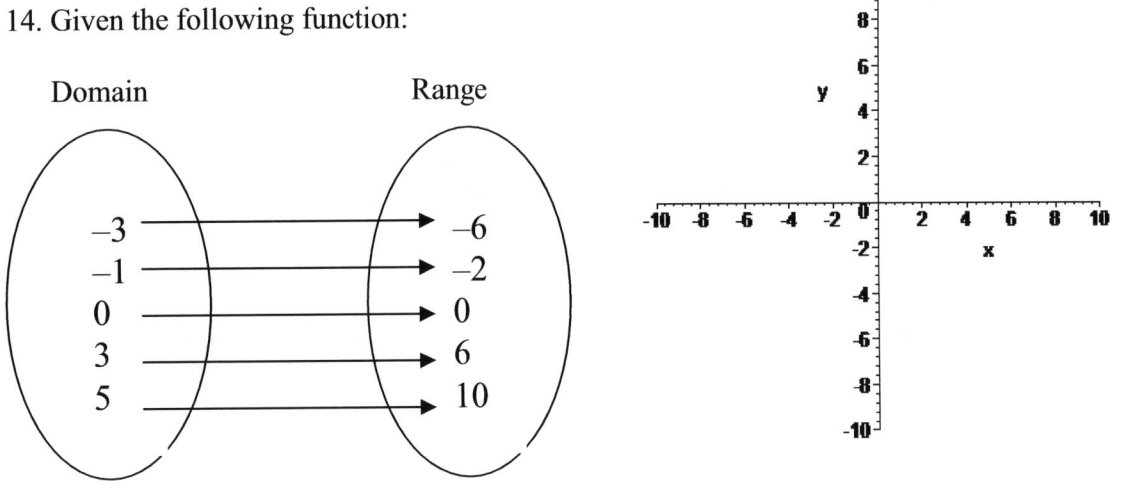

Domain: −3, −1, 0, 3, 5 → Range: −6, −2, 0, 6, 10

a. What are the allowed values for the independent variable (The domain)?

b. What are the allowed values for the dependent variable (The range)?

c. Sketch the function on the graph.

d. Can you write a mathematical expression to express this function?

15. Given the following function:

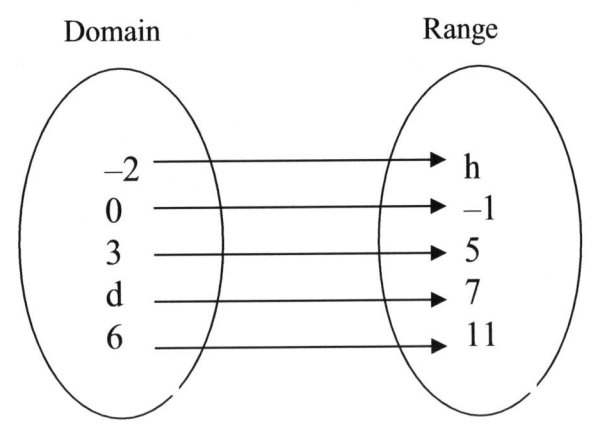

Domain: −2, 0, 3, d, 6 → Range: h, −1, 5, 7, 11

a. Can you write a mathematical expression to express this function?

b. Find h. Find d.

16. Use the graph of the gasoline consumption of a truck to answer:

   a. $f(0) =$ ____
   b. $f(50) =$ ____
   c. $f(5) =$ ____
   d. For what values of x is $f(x) = 12$
   e. Is $f(60) > f(70)$?
   f. For what values of x is $f(x) > 15$?
   g. At what positive speed is the consumption of gasoline minimum?
   h. Where is the function increasing? _____
   i. Where is the function decreasing? _____
   j. Where is the function stationary? _____

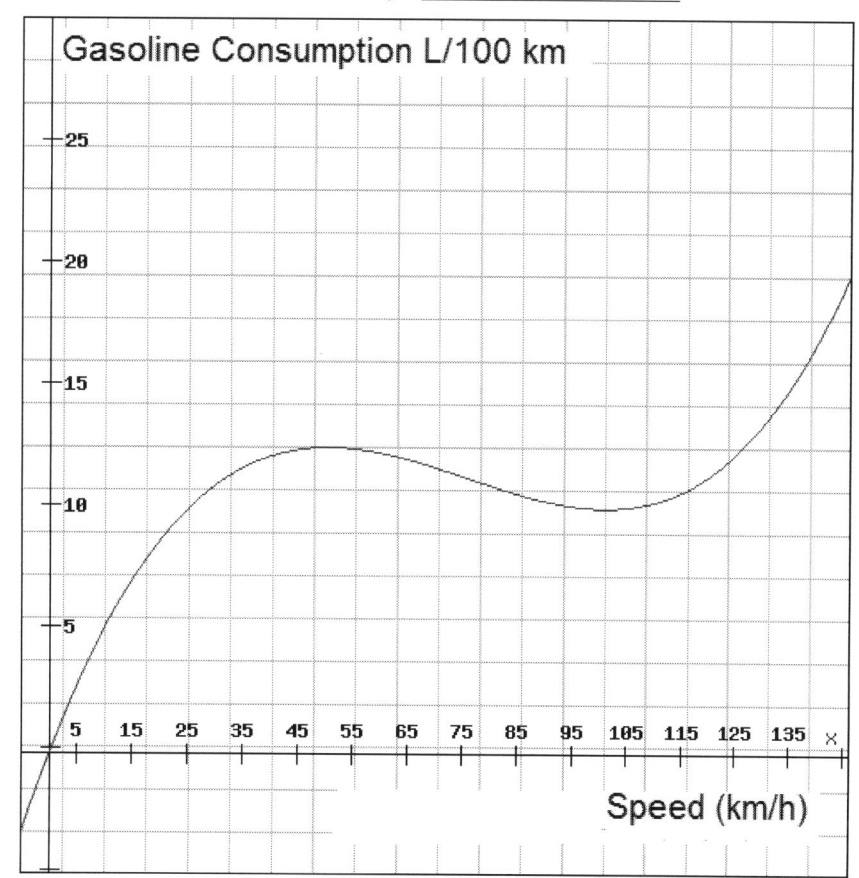

17. Functions can be represented using: _____ or _____.

18. The following graph describes the concentration of a drug injected into the blood as a function of the time (in minutes) since the injection. $t = 0$ corresponds to the time of injection.

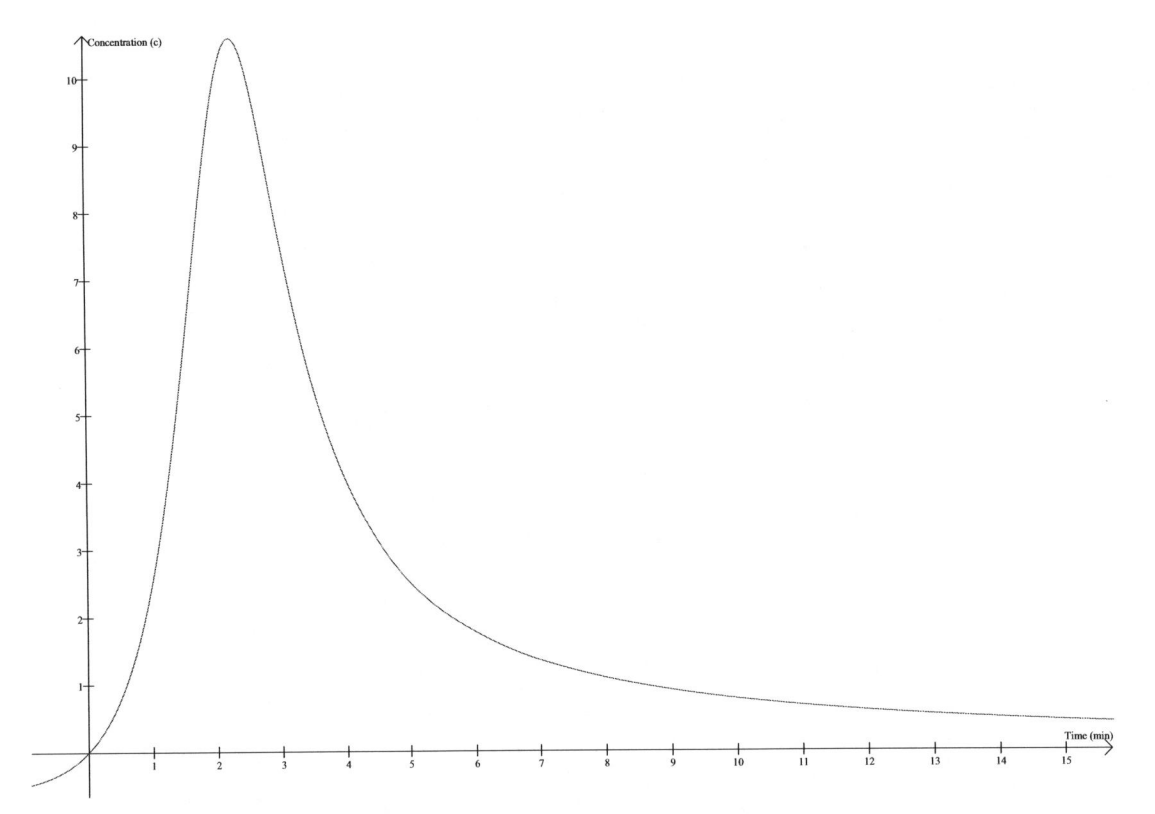

a. What is the concentration of the drug 4 hours after the injection?

b. During what period of time is the concentration increasing?

c. After how long is the concentration maximum?

d. When is the concentration greater than 5c?

e. When is the concentration smaller than 2c?

f. State the domain and range of the function.

19. The graph below shows the temperature in C° on a particular day as a function of time since midnight.

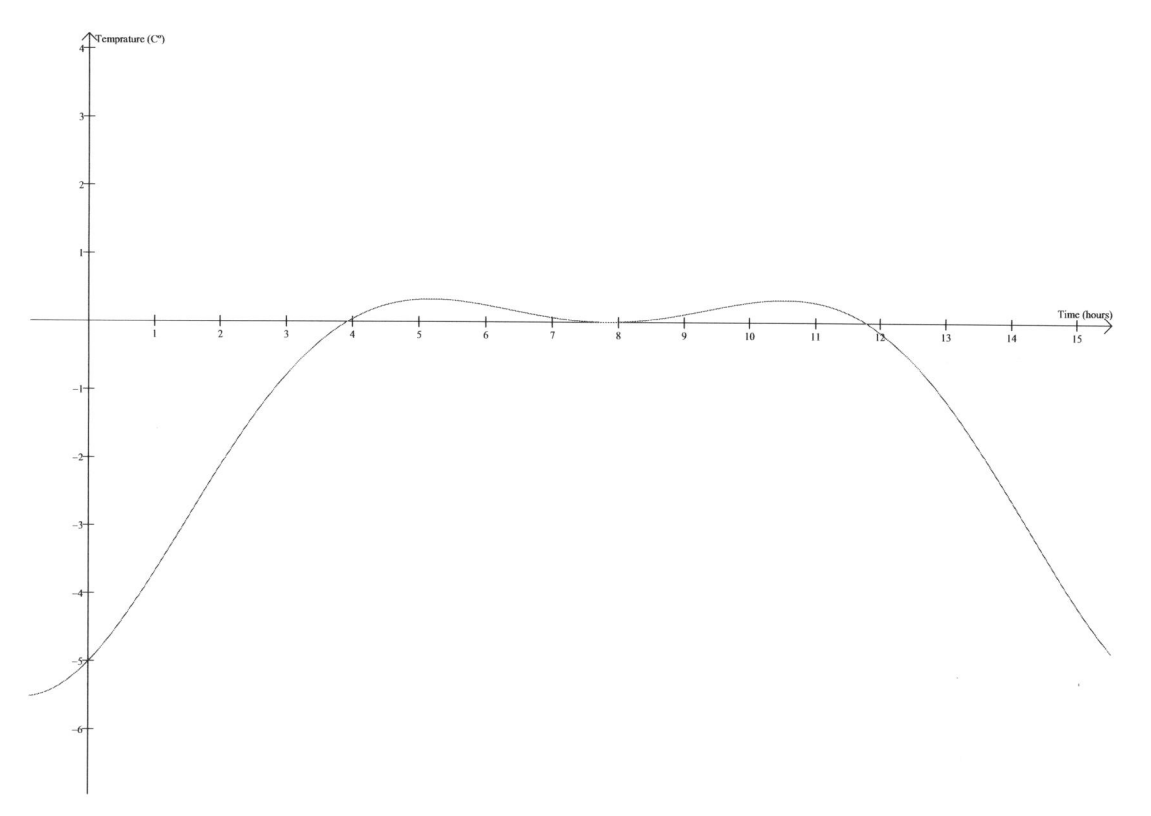

a. What was the temperature at 4:00 a.m.?

b. When was the temperature 0 degrees?

c. When was the temperature below freezing? (less than 0 degrees)

d. When was the temperature increasing?

e. State the domain and range of the function.

2.2. – LINEAR FUNCTIONS

1. Given the function: f(x) = –5

   - Complete the following table:

x	–5	–4	–3	–2	–1	0	1	2	3	4	5
f(x)											

   - Sketch the points of the chart on a graph (use a ruler).

   - State the domain of the function: _____

   - State the y intercept (sketched on the graph: (____, ____)

   - State the x intercept: (____, ____)

   - The function is increasing on the interval: _____

   - The function is decreasing on the interval: _____

   - Sketch the function of the graph used for the points initially drawn

   - State the range of the function: _____

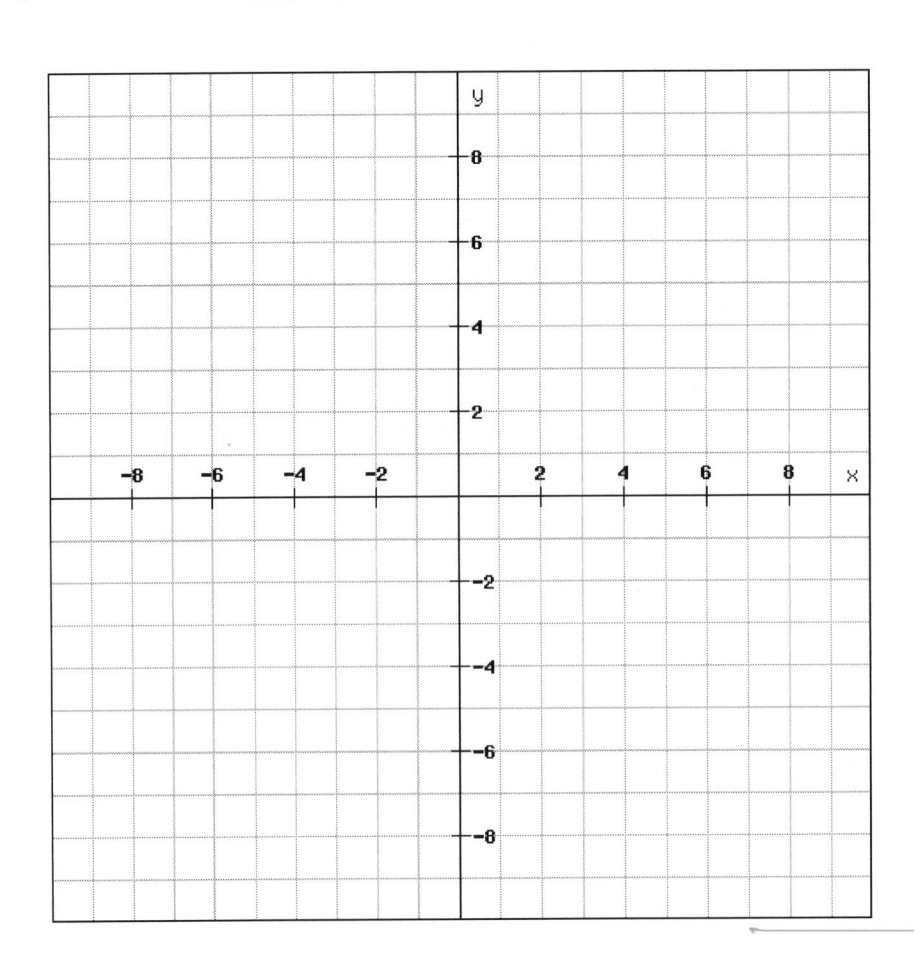

120

2. Given the function: f(x) = x + 3

   - Complete the following table:

x	−5	−4	−3	−2	−1	0	1	2	3	4	5
f(x)											

   - Sketch the points of the chart on a graph (use a ruler).

   - State the domain of the function: _____

   - State the y intercept (sketched on the graph: (____, ____)

   - State the x intercept: (____, ____)

   - The function is increasing on the interval: _____

   - The function is decreasing on the interval: _____

   - Sketch the function of the graph used for the points initially drawn

   - State the range of the function: _____

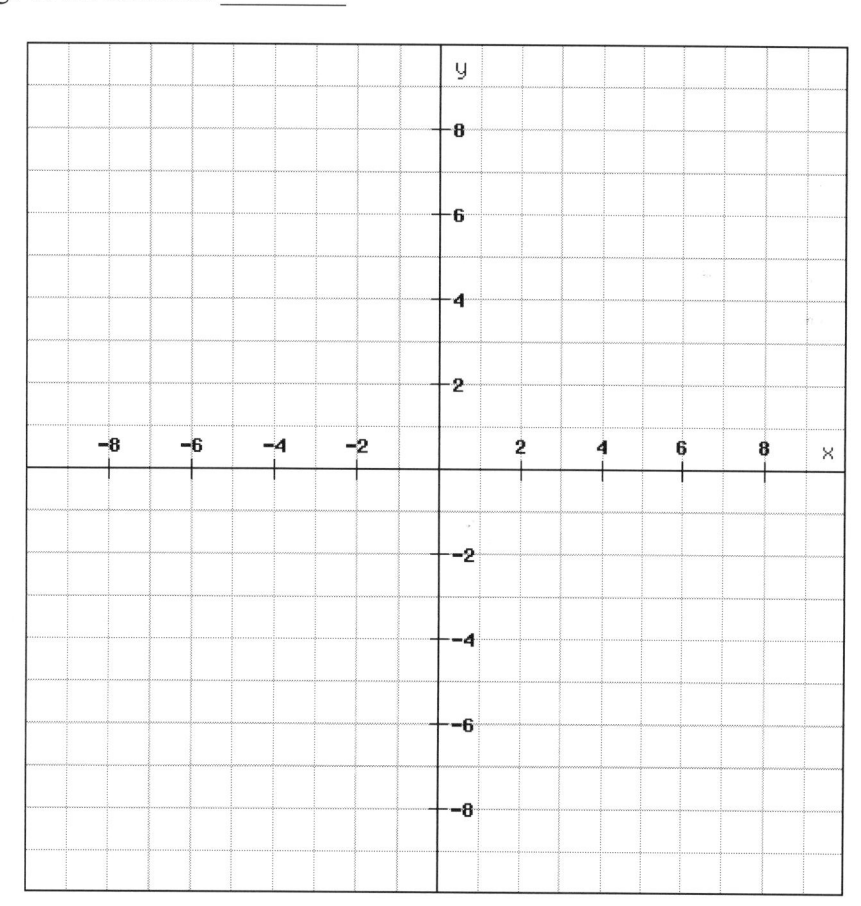

121

3. Given the function: f(x) = –2x – 5

- Complete the following table:

x	–5	–4	–3	–2	–1	0	1	2	3	4	5
f(x)											

- Sketch the points of the chart on a graph (use a ruler).

- State the domain of the function: _____

- State the y intercept (sketched on the graph: (____, ____)

- State the x intercept: (____, ____)

- The function is increasing on the interval: _____

- The function is decreasing on the interval: _____

- Sketch the function of the graph used for the points initially drawn

- State the range of the function: _____

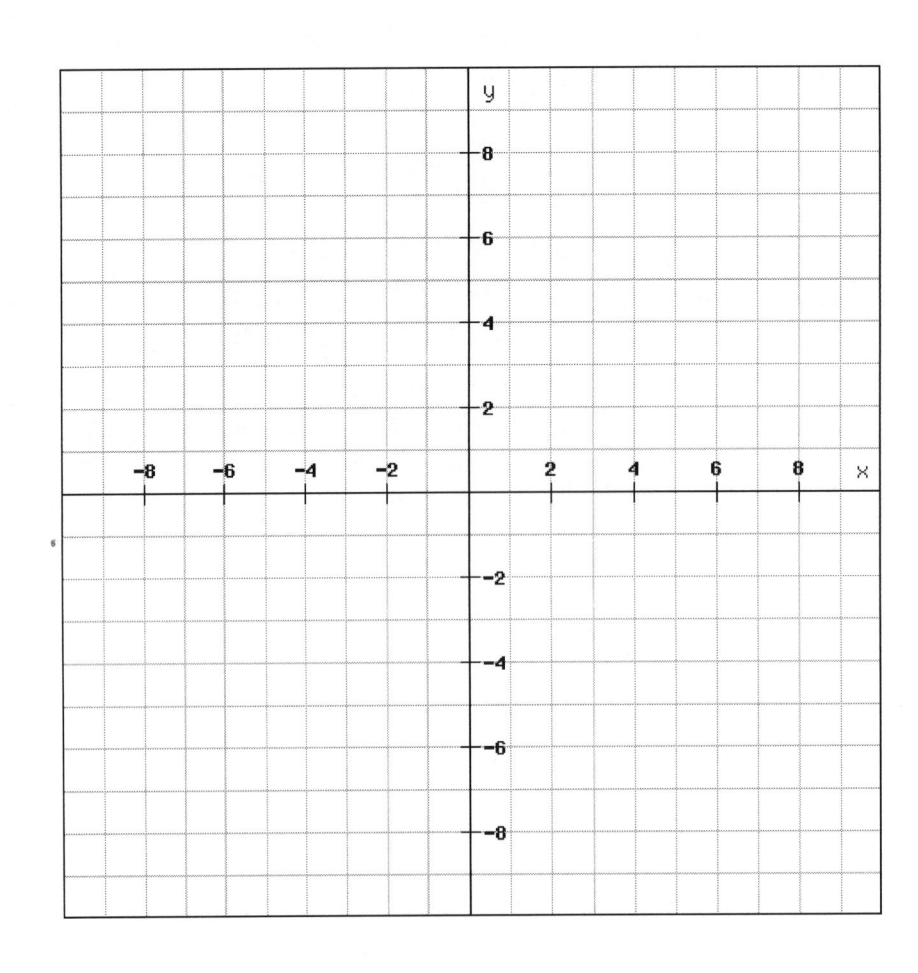

4. Given the function: f(x) = 4x – 3

   - Complete the following table:

x	–5	–4	–3	–2	–1	0	1	2	3	4	5
f(x)											

   - Sketch the points of the chart on a graph (use a ruler).

   - State the domain of the function: _____

   - State the *y* intercept (sketched on the graph: (____, ____)

   - State the *x* intercept: (____, ____)

   - The function is increasing on the interval: _____

   - The function is decreasing on the interval: _____

   - Sketch the function of the graph used for the points initially drawn

   - State the range of the function: _____

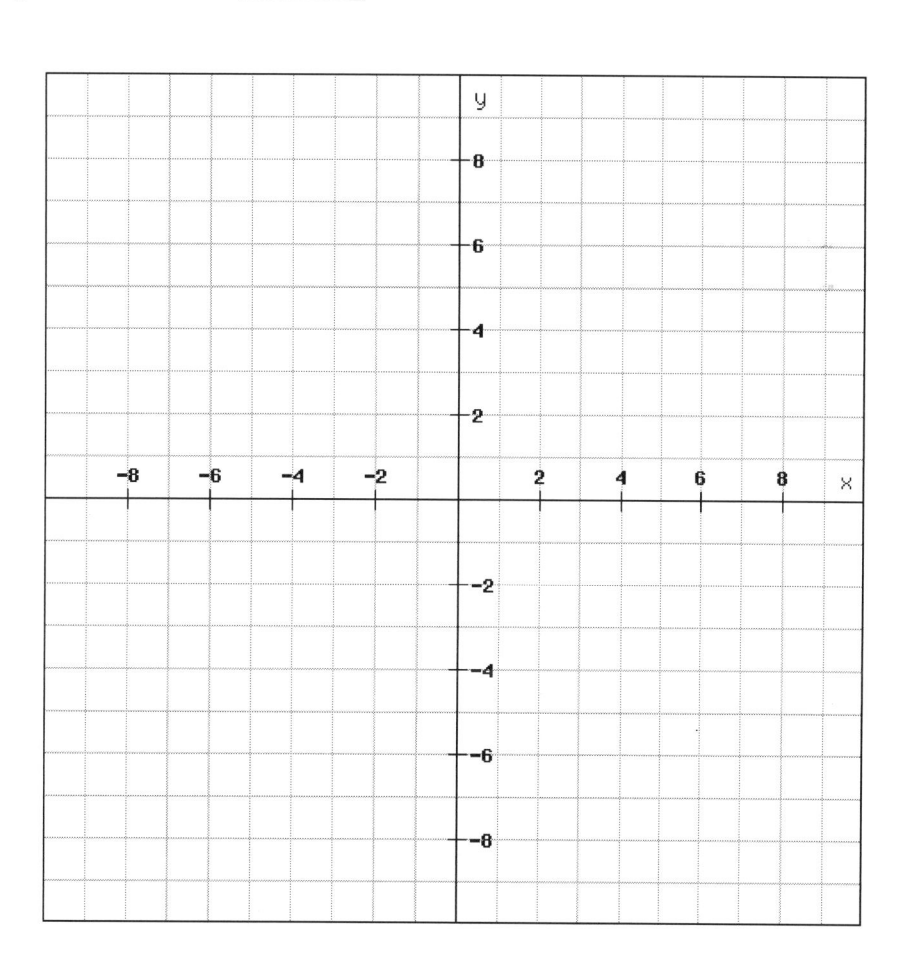

123

5. Given below are the equations for five different lines. Match the function with its graph.

Function	On the graph
f(x) = 20 + 2x	
g(x) = 4x + 20	
s(x) = –30 + 2x	
a(x) = 60 – x	
b(x) = – 2x + 60	

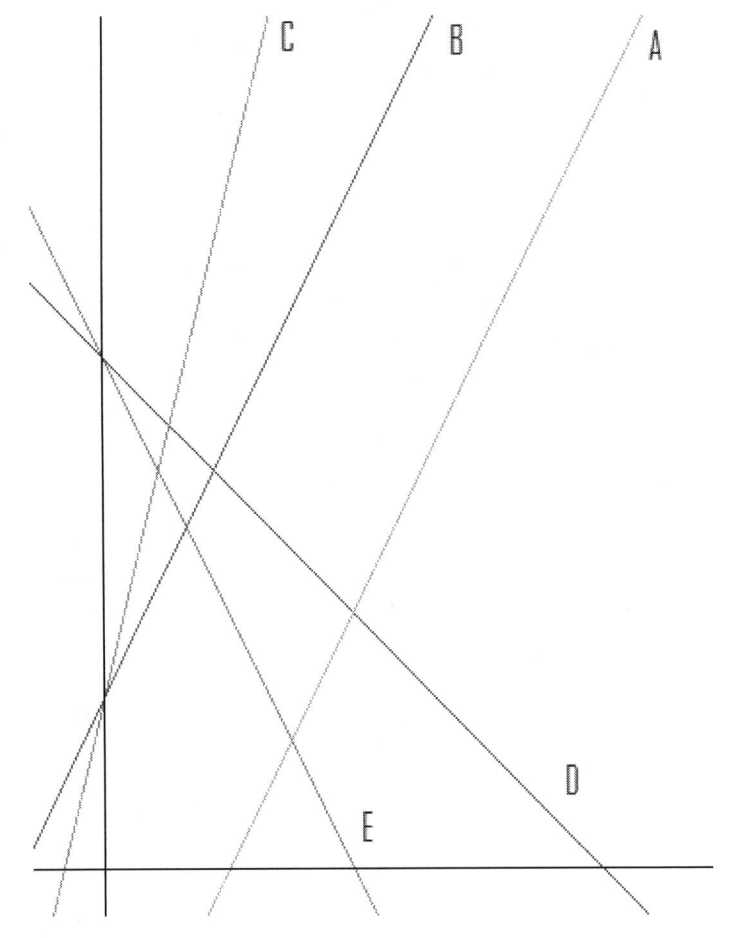

6. The general functions that describes a straight line is _____

7. We know a function is a straight line because _____

8. The y–intercept (also called vertical intercept), tells us where the line crosses the

    _____. The corresponding point is of the form (,).

9. The x–intercept (also called horizontal intercept), tells us where the line crosses the

    _____. The corresponding point is of the form (,).

10. If m > 0, the line _____ left to right. If _____ the line decreases left to right.

11. In case the line is horizontal m is _____ and the line is of the form _____.

12. The larger the value of m is, the _____ the graph of the line is.

13. Given the graph, write, the slope (m), b and the equation of the line:

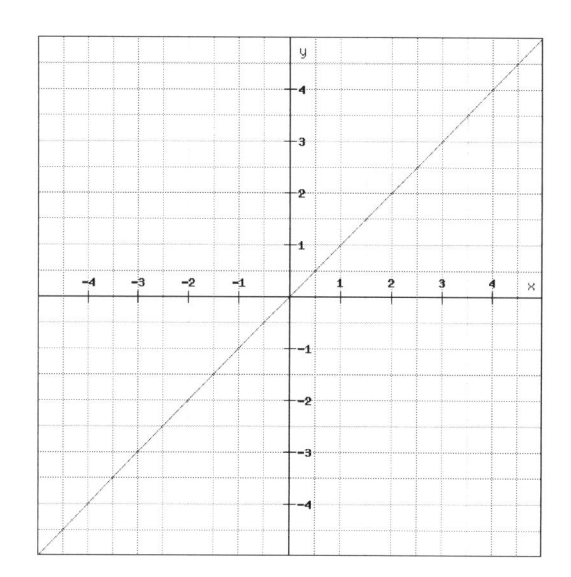

m = _____ b = _____ f(x) = _____

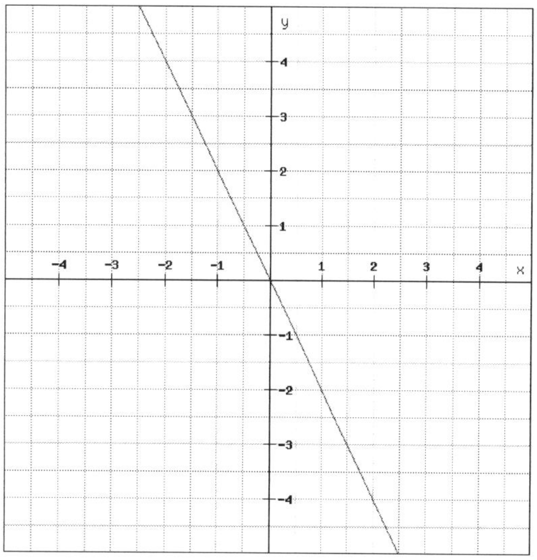

m = _____ b = _____ f(x) = _____

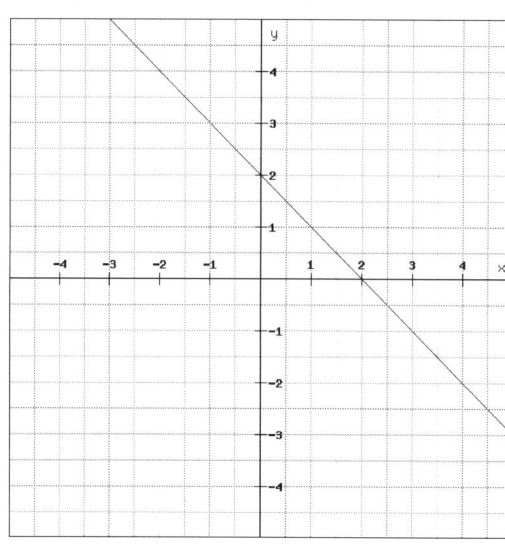

m = _____ b = _____ f(x) = _____

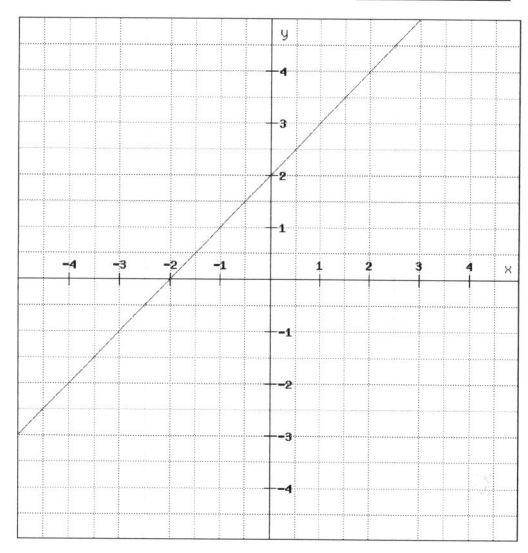

m = _____ b = _____ f(x) = _____

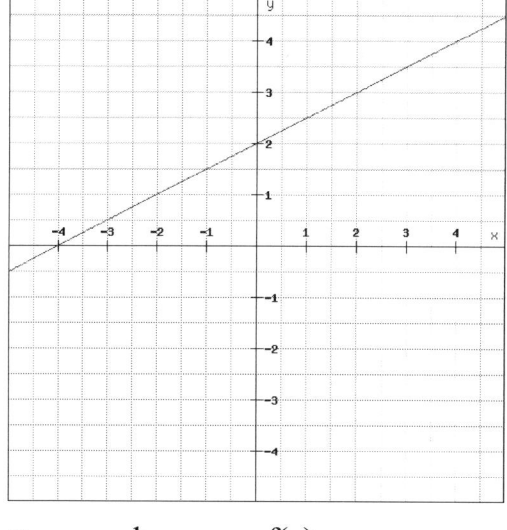

m = _____ b = _____ f(x) = _____

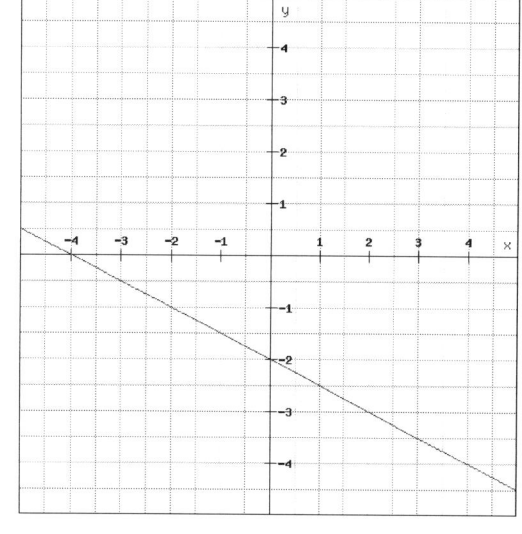

m = _____ b = _____ f(x) = _____

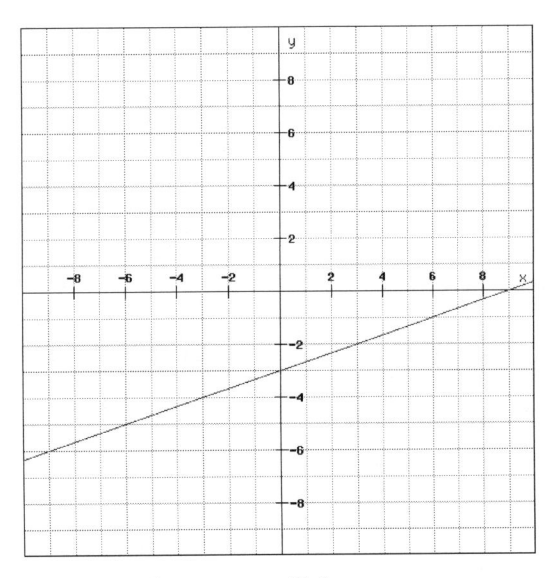

m = _____ b = _____ f(x) = _____

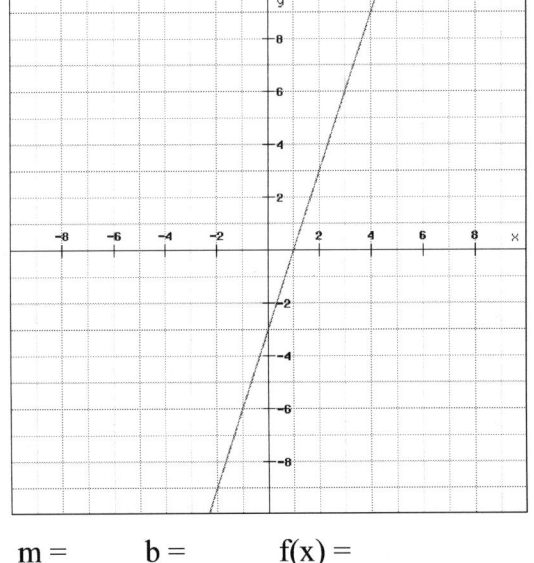

m = _____ b = _____ f(x) = _____

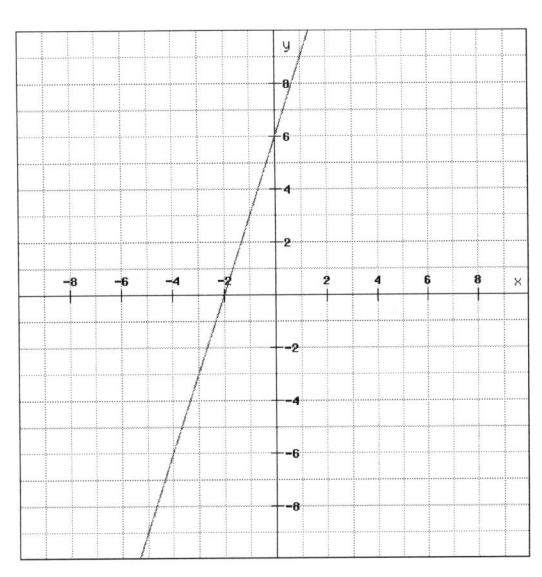

m = _____ b = _____ f(x) = _____

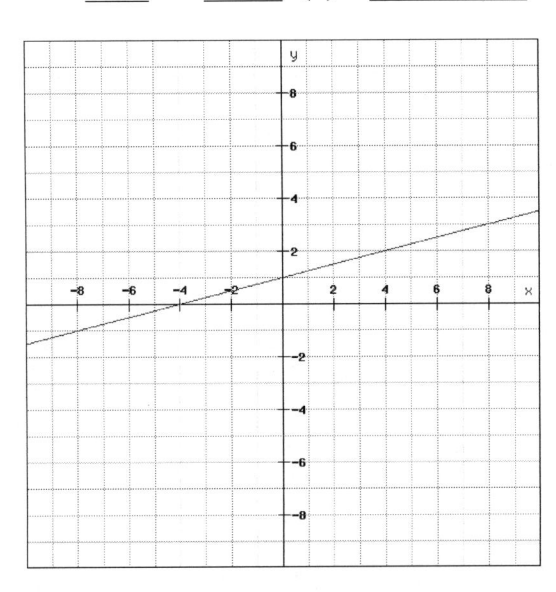

m = _____ b = _____ f(x) = _____

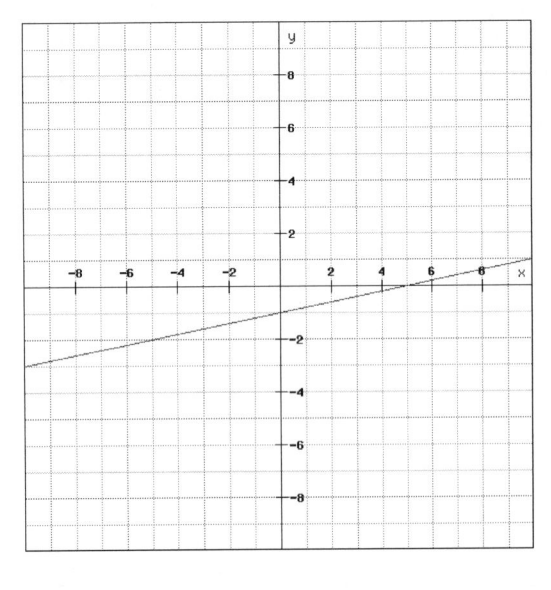

m = _____ b = _____ f(x) = _____

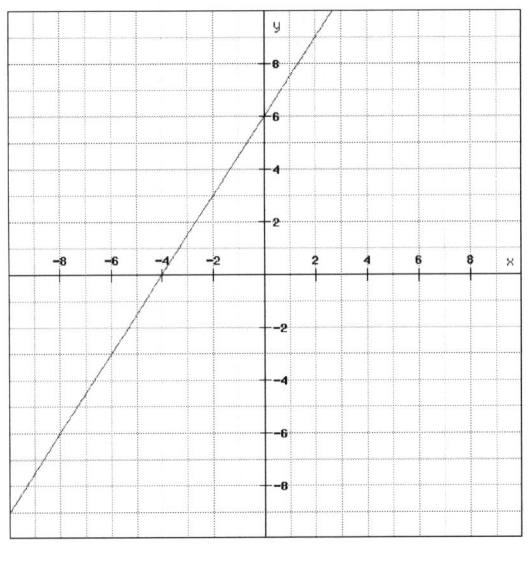

m = _____ b = _____ f(x) = _____

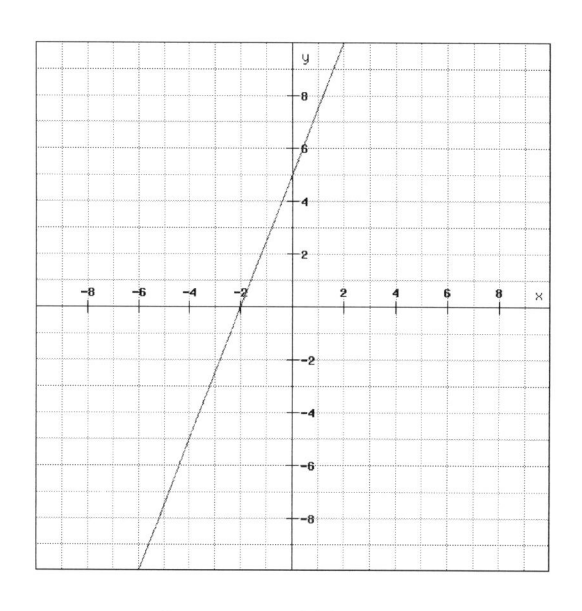

m = _____ b = _____ f(x) 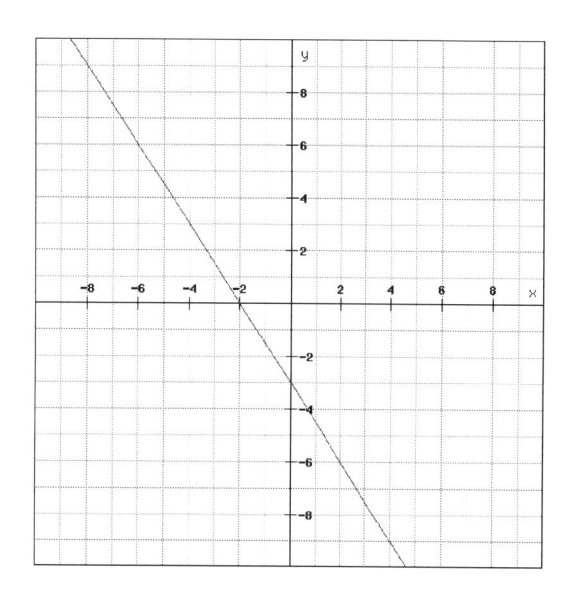 = _____   m = _____ b = _____ f(x) = _____

Analyze the following functions:

1. f(x) = 1

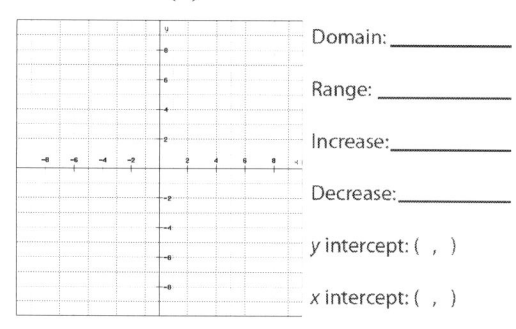

   Domain: _____
   Range: _____
   Increase: _____
   Decrease: _____
   y intercept: (,)
   x intercept: (,)

2. f(x) = 2

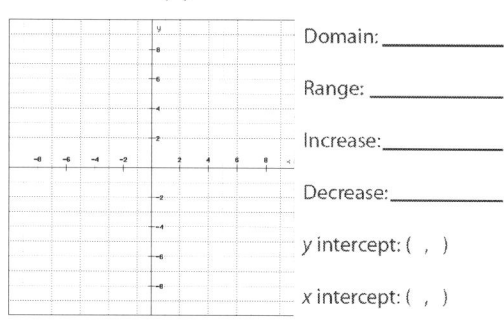

   Domain: _____
   Range: _____
   Increase: _____
   Decrease: _____
   y intercept: (,)
   x intercept: (,)

3. f(x) = –1

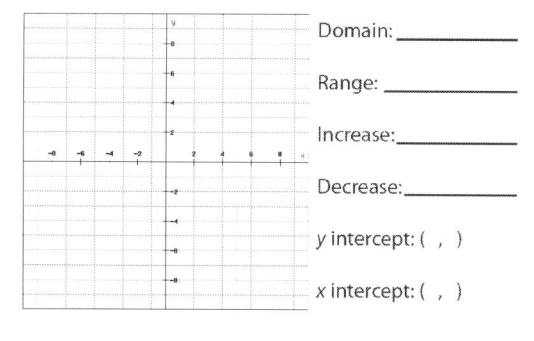

   Domain: _____
   Range: _____
   Increase: _____
   Decrease: _____
   y intercept: (,)
   x intercept: (,)

4. f(x) = 0

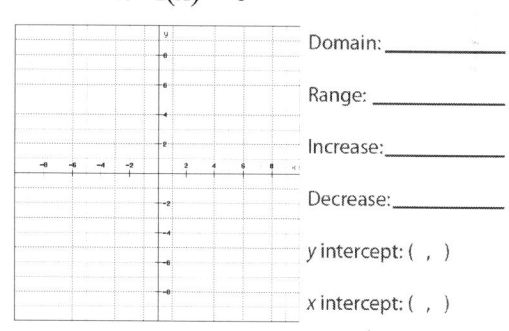

   Domain: _____
   Range: _____
   Increase: _____
   Decrease: _____
   y intercept: (,)
   x intercept: (,)

5. f(x) = x

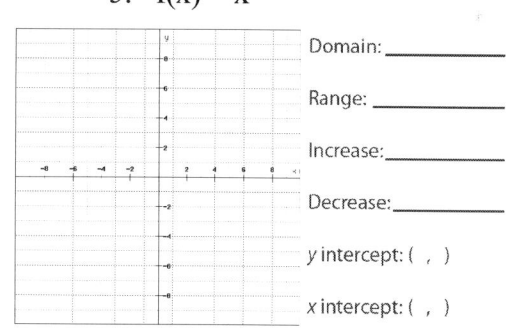

   Domain: _____
   Range: _____
   Increase: _____
   Decrease: _____
   y intercept: (,)
   x intercept: (,)

6. f(x) = x+1

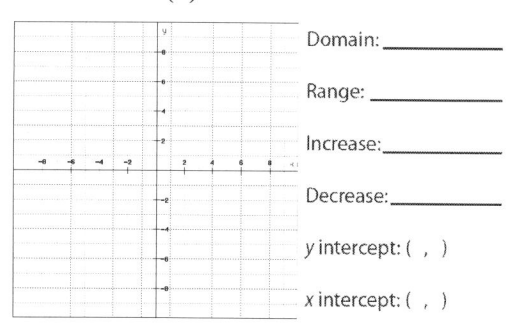

   Domain: _____
   Range: _____
   Increase: _____
   Decrease: _____
   y intercept: (,)
   x intercept: (,)

7. f(x) = –x

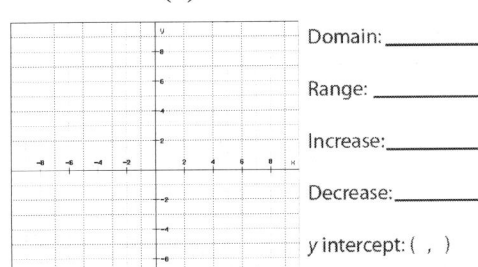

Domain: _____

Range: _____

Increase: _____

Decrease: _____

y intercept: (,)

x intercept: (,)

8. f(x) = –x–2

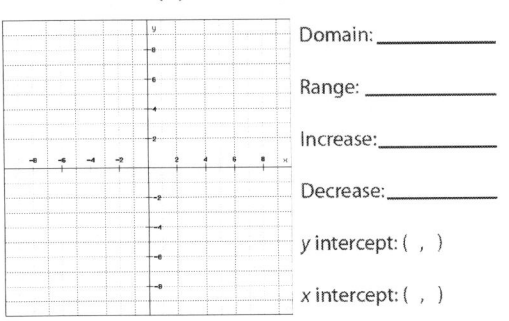

Domain: _____

Range: _____

Increase: _____

Decrease: _____

y intercept: (,)

x intercept: (,)

9. f(x) = 2x

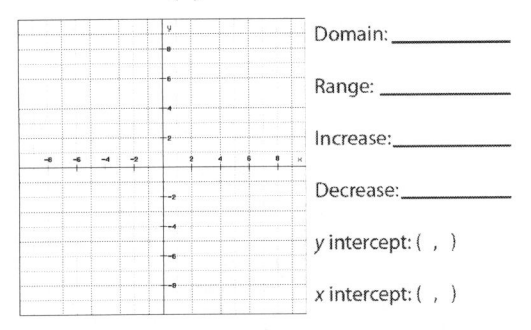

Domain: _____

Range: _____

Increase: _____

Decrease: _____

y intercept: (,)

x intercept: (,)

10. f(x) = 3x – 5

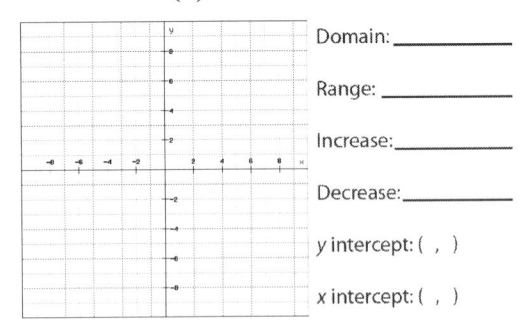

Domain: _____

Range: _____

Increase: _____

Decrease: _____

y intercept: (,)

x intercept: (,)

11. f(x) = 3 – 2x

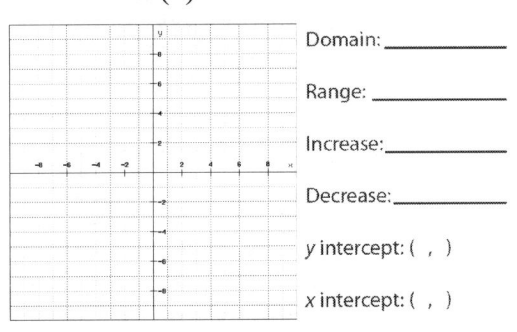

Domain: _____

Range: _____

Increase: _____

Decrease: _____

y intercept: (,)

x intercept: (,)

12. $f(x) = \dfrac{x}{3}$

Domain: _____

Range: _____

Increase: _____

Decrease: _____

y intercept: (,)

x intercept: (,)

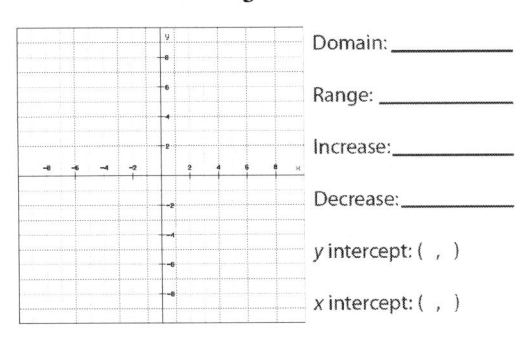

13. f(x) = 2x+1

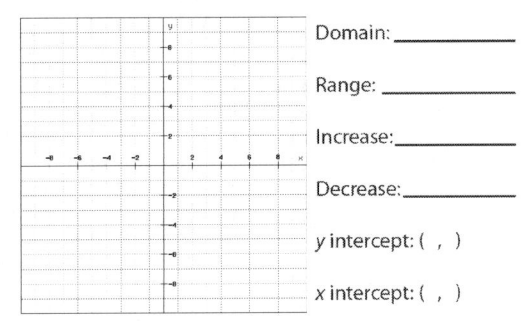

Domain: _____

Range: _____

Increase: _____

Decrease: _____

y intercept: (,)

x intercept: (,)

14. f(x) = 2x–2

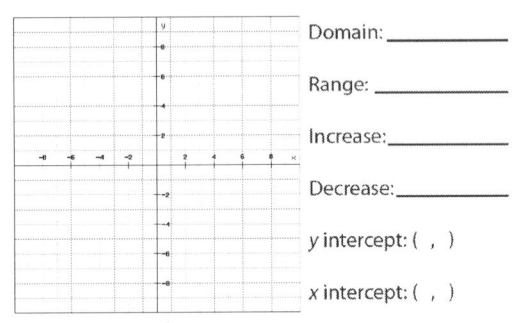

Domain: _____

Range: _____

Increase: _____

Decrease: _____

y intercept: (,)

x intercept: (,)

15. $f(x) = 3x+5$

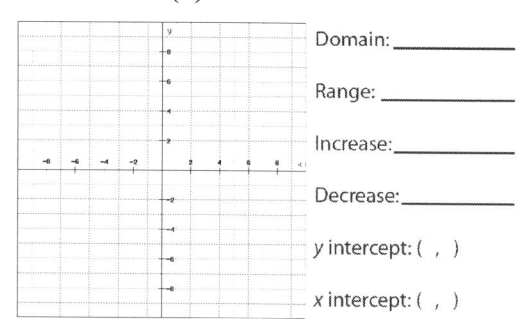

Domain: _____
Range: _____
Increase: _____
Decrease: _____
y intercept: (,)
x intercept: (,)

16. $f(x) = \dfrac{x}{2} - 5$

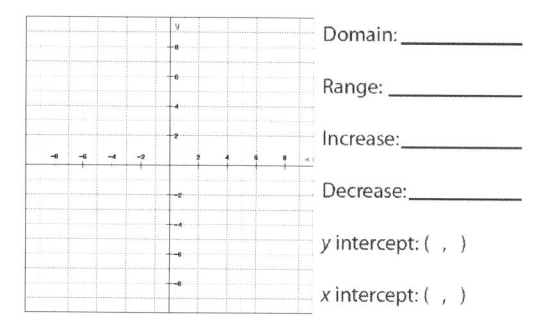

Domain: _____
Range: _____
Increase: _____
Decrease: _____
y intercept: (,)
x intercept: (,)

17. $f(x) = \dfrac{x}{4} + 6$

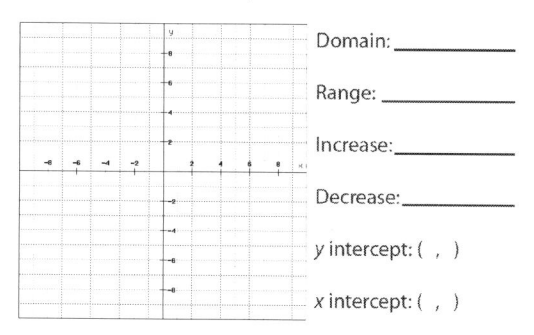

Domain: _____
Range: _____
Increase: _____
Decrease: _____
y intercept: (,)
x intercept: (,)

18. $f(x) = \dfrac{3}{2}x - 5$

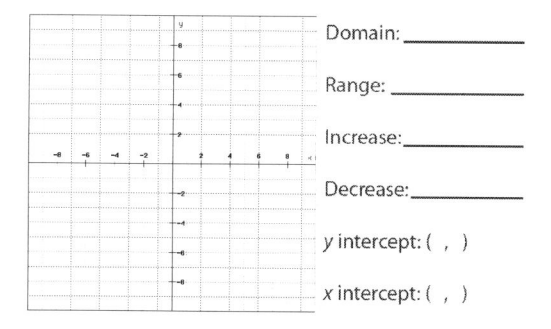

Domain: _____
Range: _____
Increase: _____
Decrease: _____
y intercept: (,)
x intercept: (,)

19. $f(x) = -\dfrac{3}{2}x - \dfrac{3}{2}$

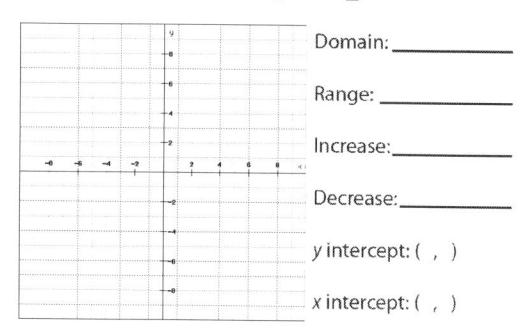

Domain: _____
Range: _____
Increase: _____
Decrease: _____
y intercept: (,)
x intercept: (,)

20. $f(x) = -\dfrac{1}{2}x - \dfrac{3}{2}$

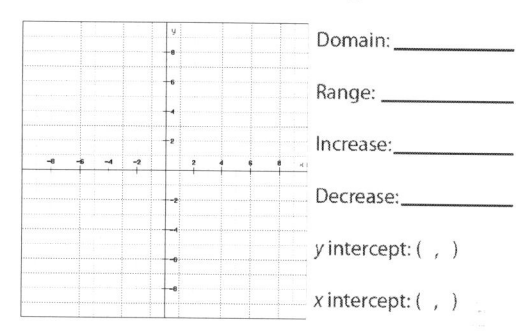

Domain: _____
Range: _____
Increase: _____
Decrease: _____
y intercept: (,)
x intercept: (,)

21. $f(x) = \dfrac{7}{2}x - \dfrac{1}{4}$

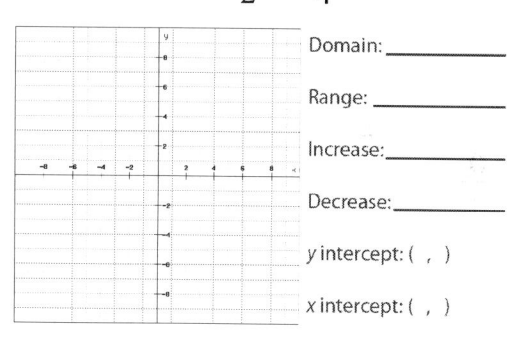

Domain: _____
Range: _____
Increase: _____
Decrease: _____
y intercept: (,)
x intercept: (,)

22. $f(x) = -\dfrac{9}{5}x + \dfrac{8}{3}$

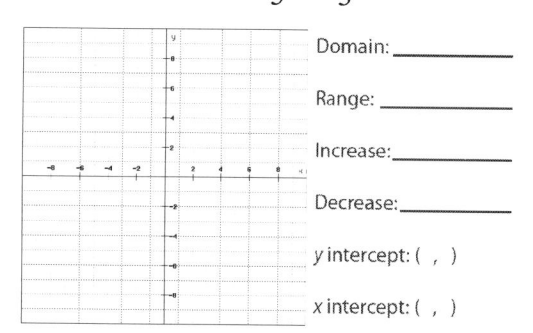

Domain: _____
Range: _____
Increase: _____
Decrease: _____
y intercept: (,)
x intercept: (,)

23. 3x + 2y = 2

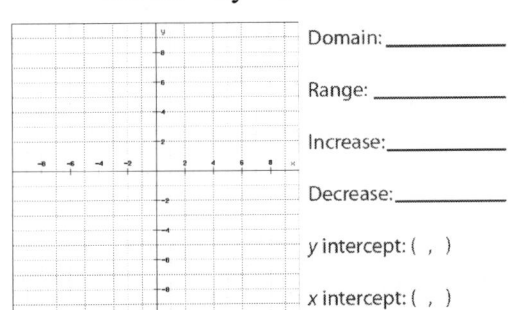

Domain: _____
Range: _____
Increase: _____
Decrease: _____
y intercept: (,)
x intercept: (,)

27. y + 2x − 3 = 1

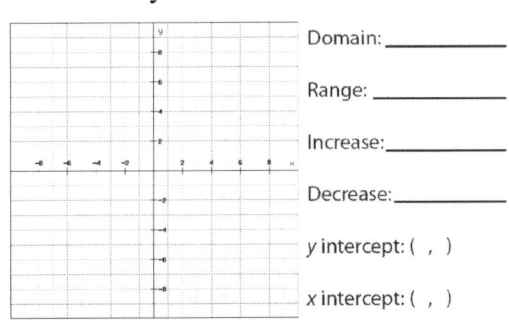

Domain: _____
Range: _____
Increase: _____
Decrease: _____
y intercept: (,)
x intercept: (,)

24. 4x − 2y − 3 = 1

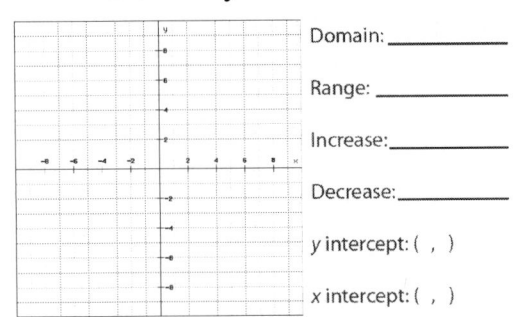

Domain: _____
Range: _____
Increase: _____
Decrease: _____
y intercept: (,)
x intercept: (,)

28. 5y + 5x = 5

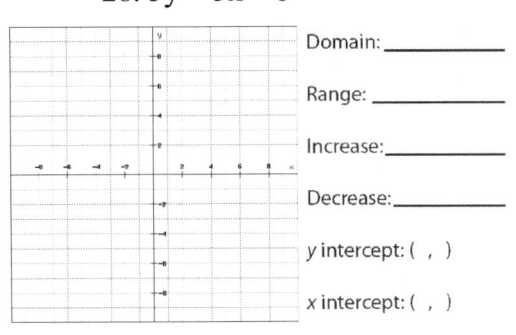

Domain: _____
Range: _____
Increase: _____
Decrease: _____
y intercept: (,)
x intercept: (,)

25. −2y + 3x = −5

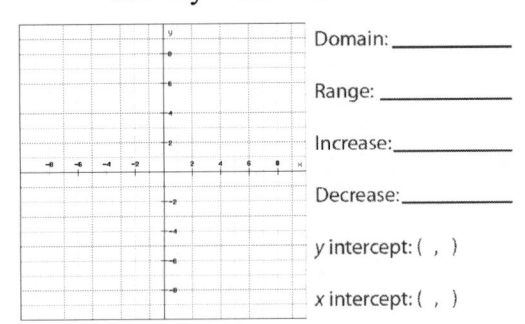

Domain: _____
Range: _____
Increase: _____
Decrease: _____
y intercept: (,)
x intercept: (,)

29. 2x − 2y − 3 = 1

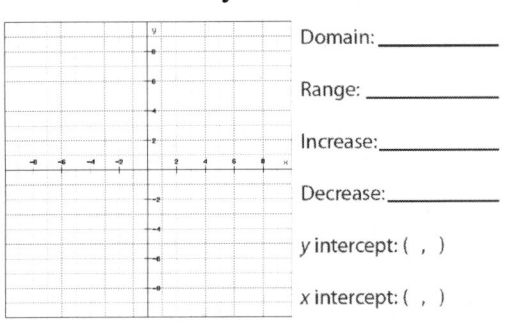

Domain: _____
Range: _____
Increase: _____
Decrease: _____
y intercept: (,)
x intercept: (,)

26. y − x = 2

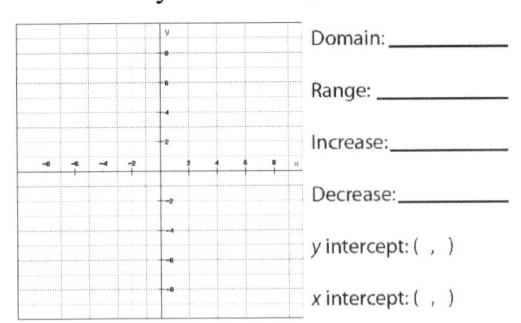

Domain: _____
Range: _____
Increase: _____
Decrease: _____
y intercept: (,)
x intercept: (,)

30. x − 2y − 150 = 0

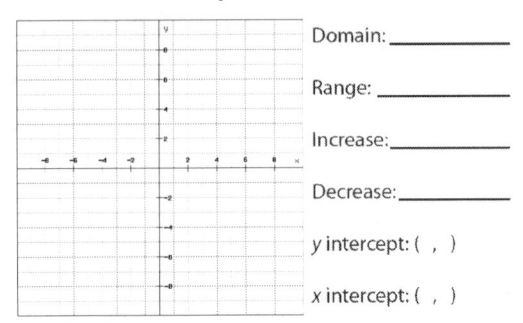

Domain: _____
Range: _____
Increase: _____
Decrease: _____
y intercept: (,)
x intercept: (,)

31. Write the equation of the line that has a slope of 2 and passes through the point (2, 4) in the forms: $y = mx + b$ and $ax + by + c = 0$, $(a, b \in Z)$

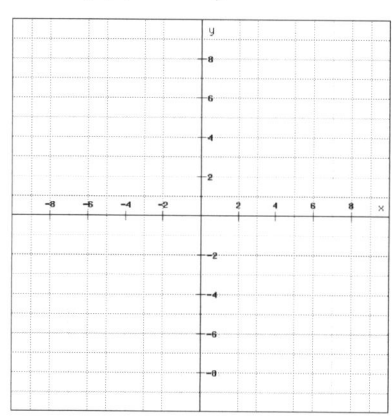

32. Write the equation of the line that has a slope of $-\dfrac{1}{2}$ and passes through the point (−2, −3) in the forms: $y = mx + b$ and $ax + by + c = 0$, $(a, b \in Z)$

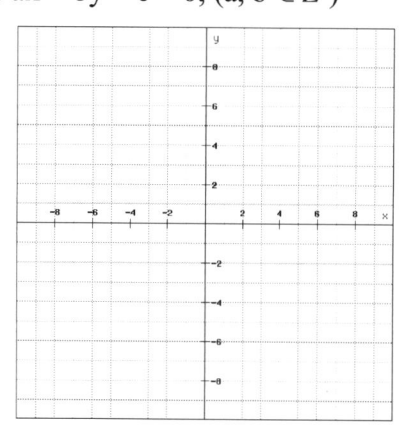

33. Write the equation of the line that has a slope of $-\dfrac{5}{2}$ and passes through the point (−1, 2) in the forms: $y = mx + b$ and $ax + by + c = 0$, $(a, b \in Z)$

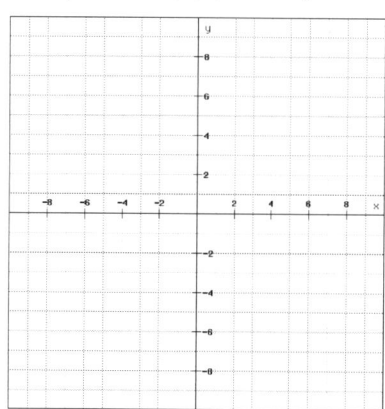

34. Find the equation of the line that passes through the points (1, 1), (2, 4), indicate its y and x intercepts and sketch it. Write its equation in the forms: $y = mx + b$ and $ax + by + c = 0$, $(a, b \in Z)$

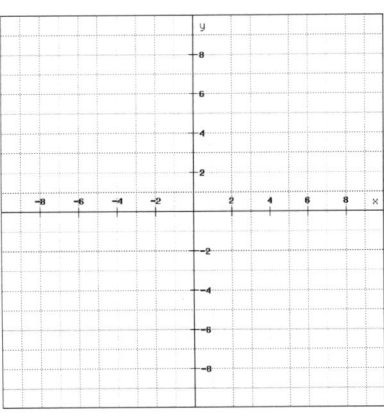

35. Find the equation of the line that passes through the points (−1, −5), (4, 3), indicate its y and x intercepts and sketch it. Write its equation in the forms: $y = mx + b$ and $ax + by + c = 0$, $(a, b \in Z)$

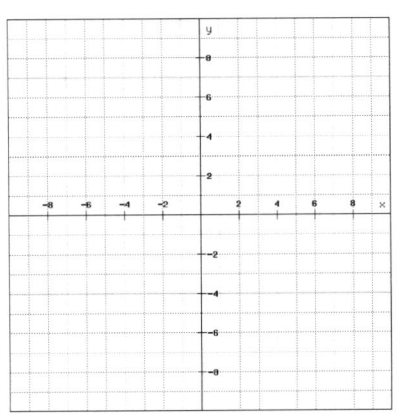

36. Find the equation of the line that passes through the points (−5, 1), (−2, 4), indicate its y and x intercepts, sketch it and write it in both formas $y = mx + b$ and $ax + by + c = 0$, $(a, b \in Z)$

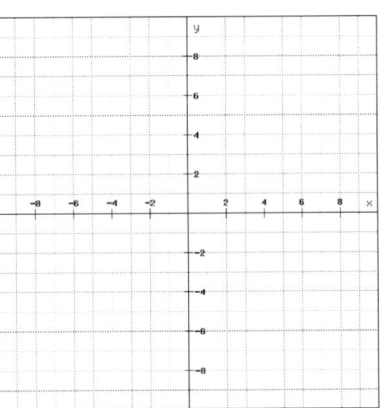

37. Write the equation of the line that is parallel to the line y = 5x – 2 and passes through the point (–2, –1). Write its equation in the forms: y = mx + b and ax + by + c = 0, (a, b ∈ Z)

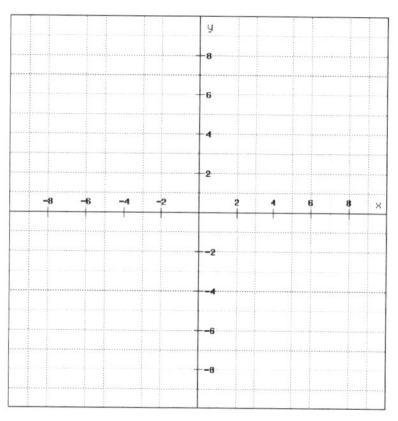

38. Write the equation of the line that is parallel to the line y = –0.5x – 1 and passes through the point (–3, 6). Write its equation in the forms: y = mx + b and ax + by + c = 0, (a, b ∈ Z)

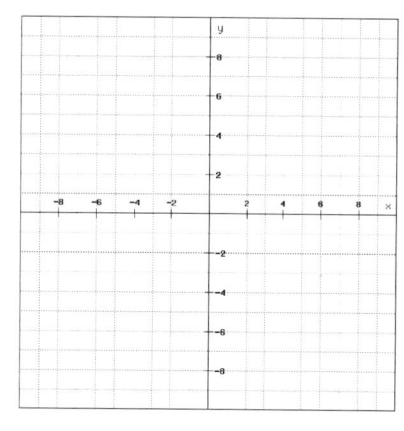

39. Sketch and write the equation of the line with a slope of $-\dfrac{1}{5}$ that passes through the point (0,2).

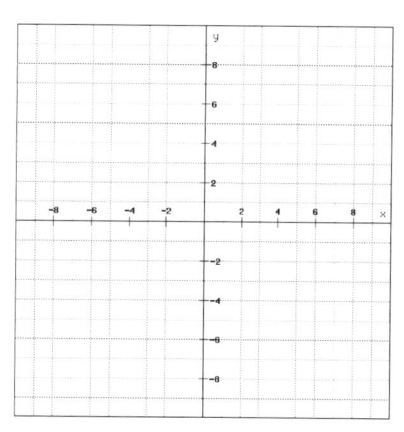

40. Sketch and write the equation of the lines with a slope: $1, 2, -3, -1, -\dfrac{1}{2}, -\dfrac{1}{3}$, that pass through the point (0,0).

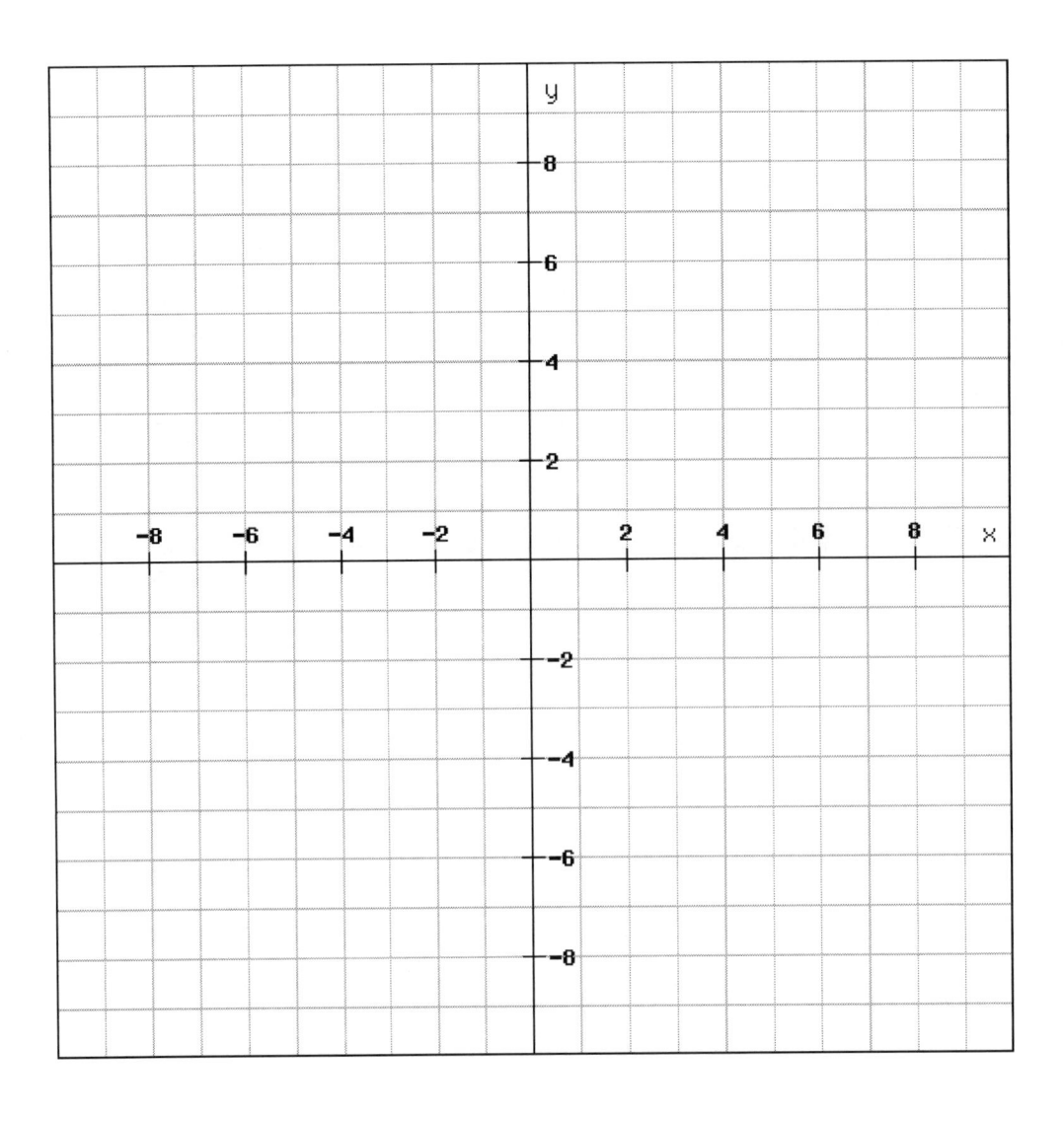

41. Sketch and write the equation of the line with a slope of –3 that passes through the point (0,–3).

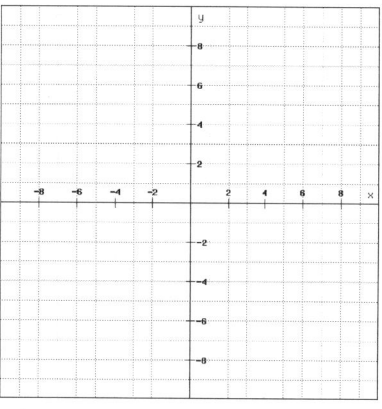

42. Sketch and write the equation of the line with a slope of 2 that passes through the point (2,0)

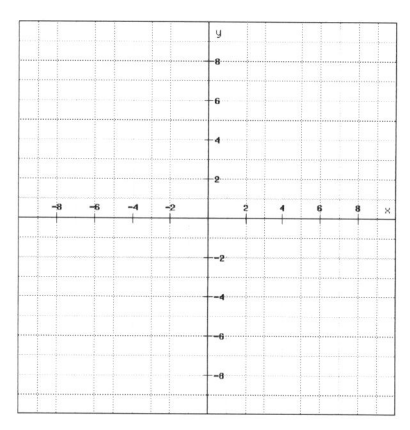

43. Sketch and write the equation of the line with a slope of $-\dfrac{1}{2}$ that passes through the point (–2,0)

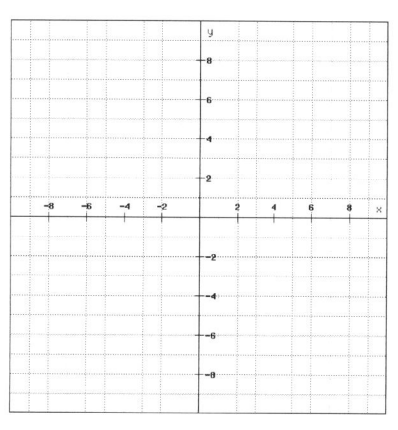

44. Sketch and write the equation of the line with a slope of 2 that passes through the point (−4, 2)

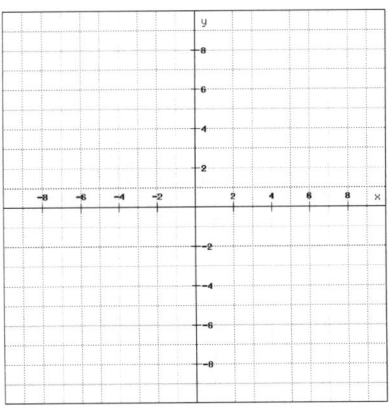

45. Find the intersection between the lines $f(x) = 2x - 3$ and $f(x) = -5x - 2$

46. Find the intersection between the lines $f(x) = -12x - 13$ and $f(x) = 15x + 20$.

DISTANCE AND MIDPOINT BETWEEN 2 POINTS

47. Given the points (1, 2) and (5, 8). Find the distance between them. Find the midpoint. Sketch to illustrate your answer.

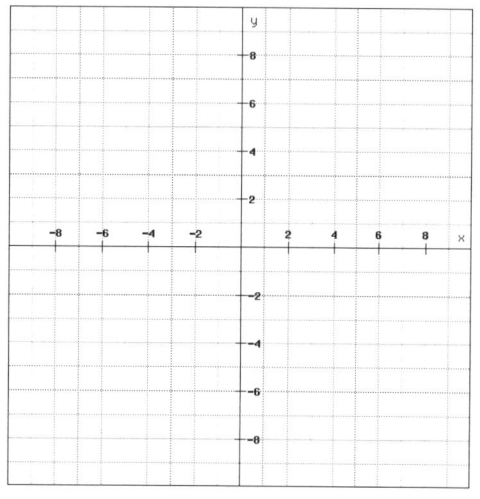

48. Given the points (–3, 2) and (5, –6). Find the distance between them. Find the midpoint. Sketch to illustrate your answer.

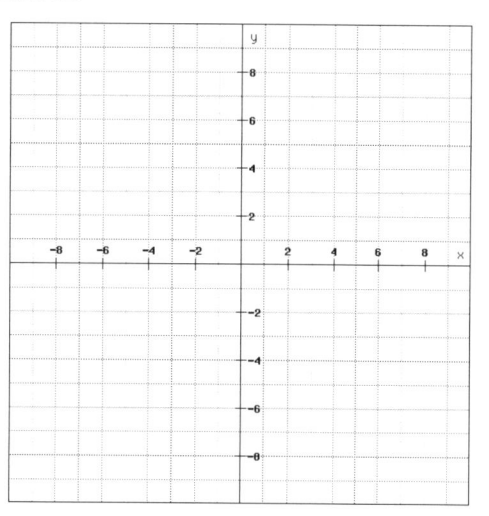

49. Given the points (–1, –6) and (–5, –1). Find the distance between them. Find the midpoint. Sketch to illustrate your answer.

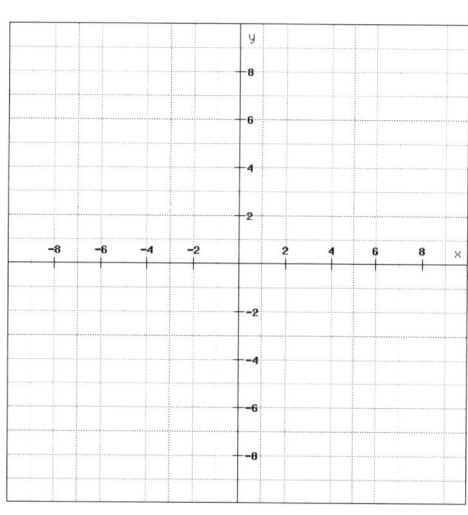

PERPENDICULAR LINES (m m⊥ = −1)

50. Find the equation of a line perpendicular to the line y = 3x − 2 that passes through the point (3, 12). Sketch to illustrate your answer.

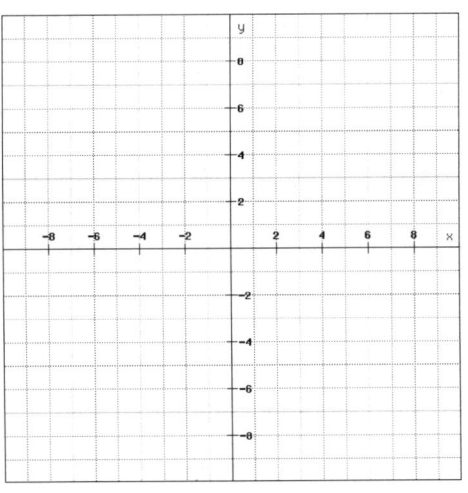

51. Find all the lines perpendicular to the line y = −3x + 4. Fin the ones that passes through the point (−3, 1). Sketch to illustrate your answer.

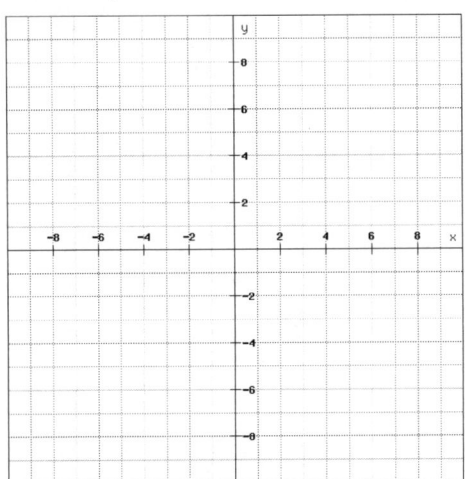

52. Find a line perpendicular to the line $y = -\dfrac{2}{5}x + 1$ that passes through the point (−1, −7). Sketch to illustrate your answer.

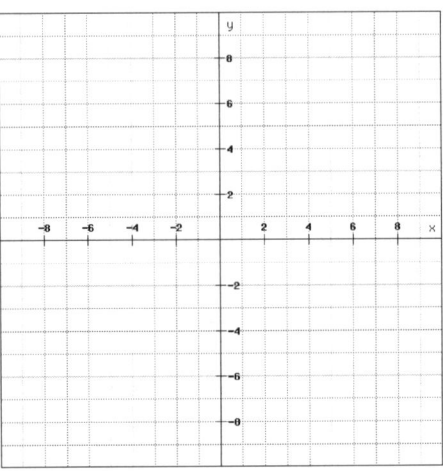

53. Given that the slope of one of the lines is 3 and that the lines are perpendicular, find the **exact** coordinates of the point of intersection of the two lines.

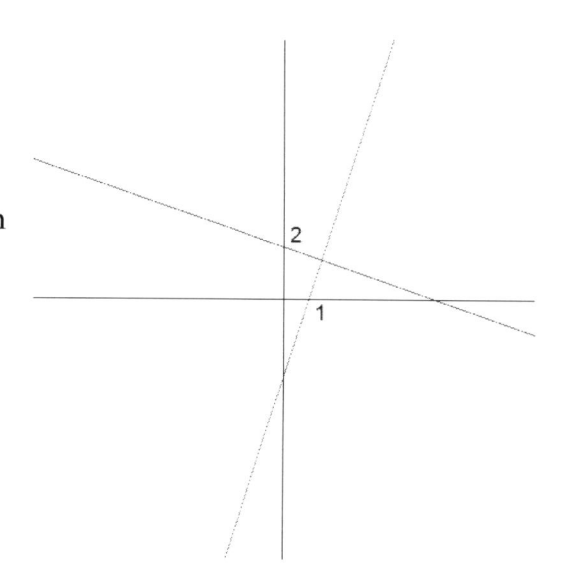

Application

1. The price of a new toy (in US$) is $C(t) = 20 - 0.5t$, t given in days.

   a. Sketch the corresponding graph.

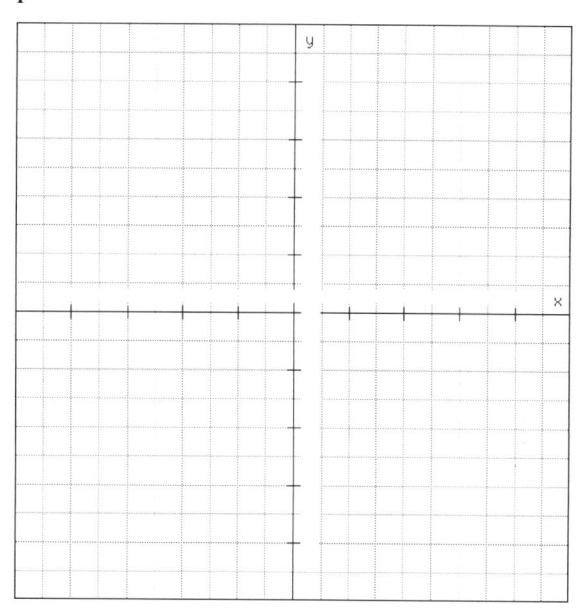

   b. What was the initial price of the toy? _____

   c. Find the price of the toy after 10 days

   d. What is the domain of the function, argument the answer,

   e. What is the range of the function.

   f. What is the meaning of 0.5? Does it have units? What are they?

2. You need to rent a car for one day and to compare the charges of 3 different companies. Company I charges 20$ per day with additional cost of 0.20$ per mile. Company II charges 30$ per day with additional cost of 0.10$ per mile. Company III charges 60$ per day with no additional mileage charge.

   a. Write the cost function for each one of the companies.

   b. Sketch all 3 graphs on the same axes system.

   c. Comment on the circumstances in which renting a car from each one of the companies is best.

2.3. – QUADRATIC FUNCTIONS

Introduction:

1. Given the functions: $f(x) = x^2$, $g(x) = x^2 - 2$. Complete the following table:

x	−5	−4	−3	−2	−1	0	1	2	3	4	5	6
f(x)												
g(x)												

- Sketch the points of the chart on a graph.

- State the domain of the functions: : f(x):_____, g(x):_____

- State the y intercepts: f(x): (____, ____), g(x): (____, ____)

- State the x intercept(s): f(x): (____, ____), g(x): (____, ____),(____, ____)

- Write in all possible forms:

- Find the max/min point(s): f(x): (____, ____), g(x): (____, ____)

- The functions are increasing on the interval: f(x):_____, g(x):_____

- The functions are decreasing on the interval: f(x):_____, g(x):_____

- Sketch the functions of the graph used for the points initially drawn

- State the range of the function: f(x):_____, g(x):_____

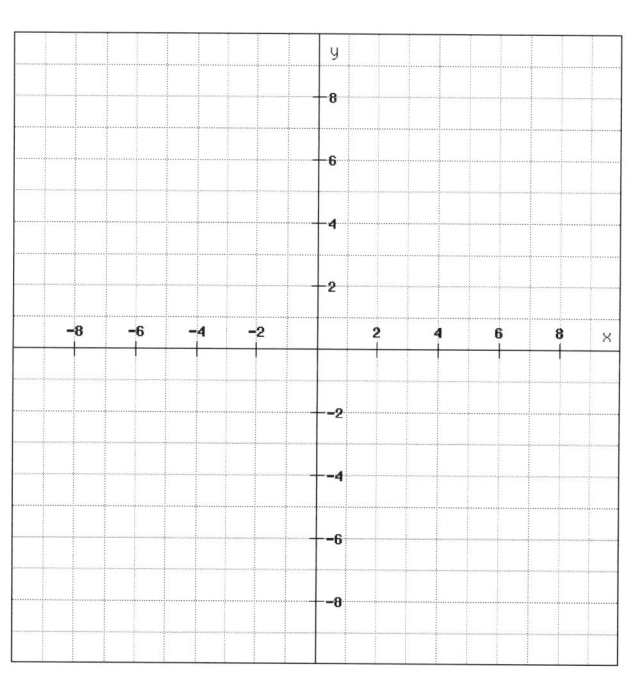

2. Given the functions: $f(x) = (x-2)^2$, $g(x) = (x+3)^2 - 2$. Complete the following chart:

x	−5	−4	−3	−2	−1	0	1	2	3	4	5	6
f(x)												
g(x)												

- Sketch the points of the chart on a graph.

- State the domain of the functions: : f(x):_____, g(x):_____

- State the y intercepts: f(x): (___, ___), g(x): (___, ___)

- State the x intercept(s): f(x): (___, ___), g(x): (___, ___),(___, ___)

- Write in all possible forms:

- Find the max/min point(s): f(x): (___, ___), g(x): (___, ___)

- The functions are increasing on the interval: f(x):_____, g(x):_____

- The functions are decreasing on the interval: f(x):_____, g(x):_____

- Sketch the functions of the graph used for the points initially drawn

- State the range of the function: f(x):_____, g(x):_____

- State its axes of symmetry:

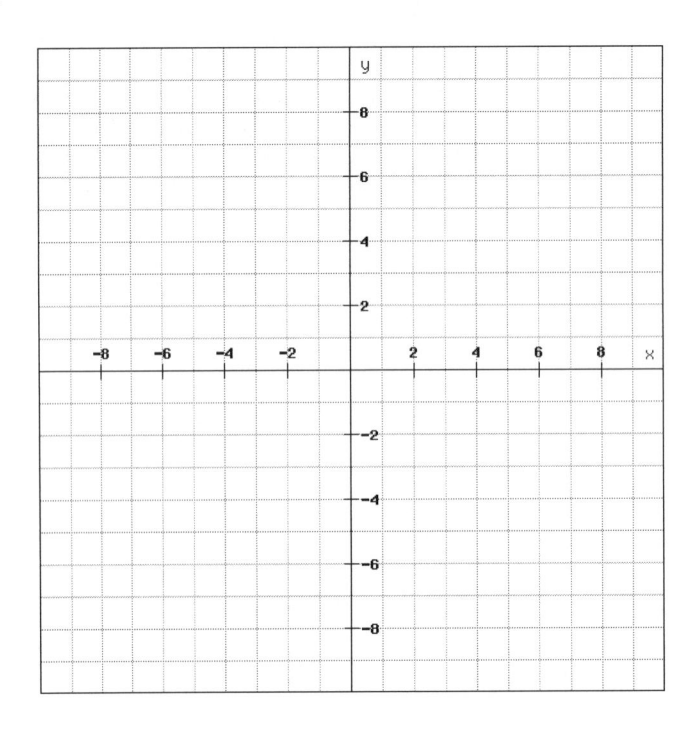

142

3. Given the functions: f(x) = (x + 2)(x − 4), g(x) = 2(x + 2)(x − 4) Complete the following chart:

x	−5	−4	−3	−2	−1	0	1	2	3	4	5	6
f(x)												
g(x)												

- Sketch the points of the chart on a graph.

- State the domain of the functions: : f(x):_____, g(x):_____

- State the y intercepts: f(x): (___, ___), g(x): (___, ___)

- State the x intercept(s): f(x): (___, ___), (___, ___)

   g(x): (___, ___),(___, ___)

- Write in all possible forms:

- Find the max/min point(s): f(x): (___, ___), g(x): (___, ___)

- The functions are increasing on the interval: f(x):_____, g(x):_____

- The functions are decreasing on the interval: f(x):_____, g(x):_____

- Sketch the functions of the graph used for the points initially drawn

- State the range of the function: f(x):_____, g(x):_____

- State its axes of symmetry:

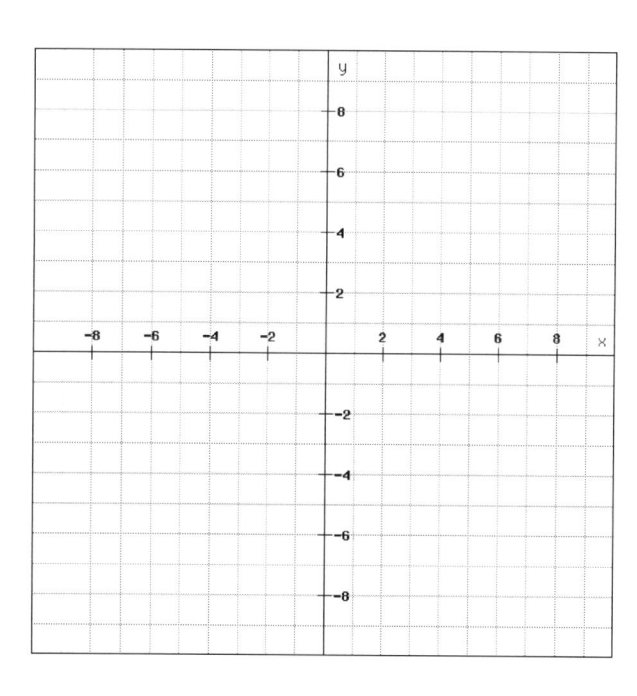

In general, a quadratic function f can be written in several different ways:

a. $f(x) = ax^2 + bx + c$ **standard form**, where a, b and c are constants
b. $f(x) = a(x-r)(x-s)$ **factored form**, where a, r and s are constants
c. $f(x) = a(x-h)^2 + k$ **vertex form**, where a, h and k are constants

Example:

Vertex form: $f(x) = 3(x-2)^2 - 3$
Partial factored form: $f(x) = 3(x-1)(x-3)$
Standard form: $f(x) = 3x^2 + 12x + 9$

Complete the sentences:

1. The graph of a quadratic function is called a _____.

2. In factored form, the numbers r and s represent the _____ of f.

3. In vertex form, the point (h, k) is called the _____ of the parabola. The axis of symmetry of the parabola is the line _____.

4. The graph of the parabola opens upwards if _____ and downwards if _____.

5. In case $f(x) = x^2 + 1$, the function can be written in _____ form(s) only. Why?

6. In case $f(x) = x^2 - 1$, the function can be written in _____ form(s) only. Show your answer:

7. A parabola has its vertex at the point (2, 3) and goes through the point (6, 11). Find the expression of the function.

8. A parabola has its vertex at the point (– 2, 4) and passes through the point (2, – 6). Find the expression of the function.

9. Write the analytical expression that corresponds the following functions in all possible forms, assume $a = 1$ or -1 in all cases:

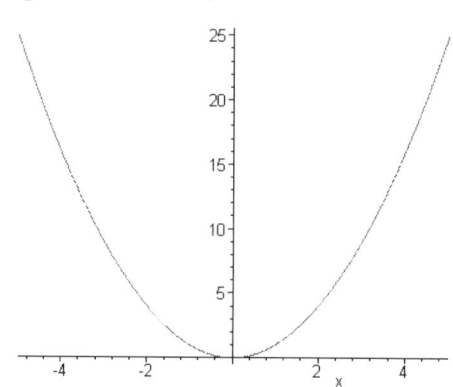

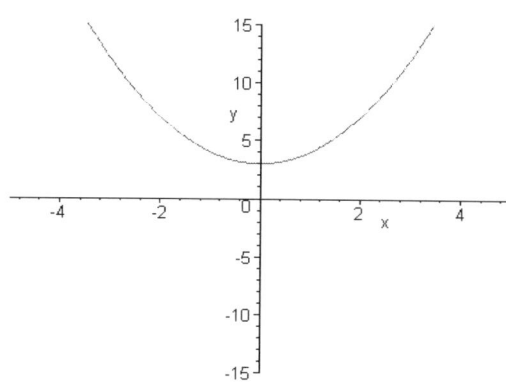

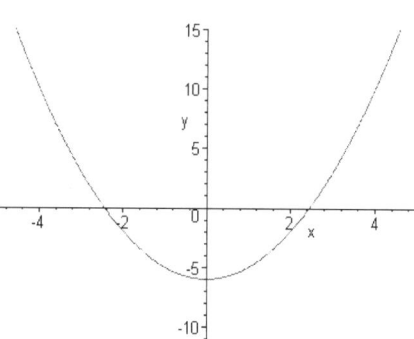

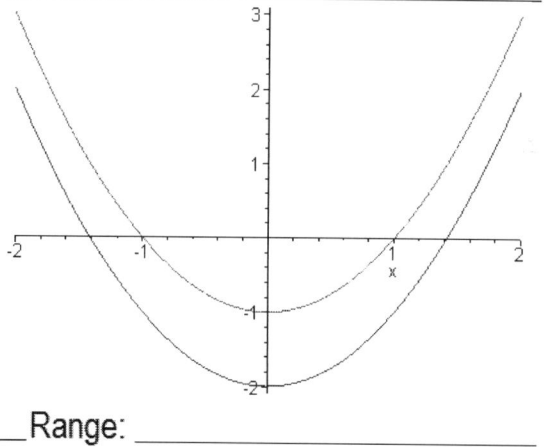

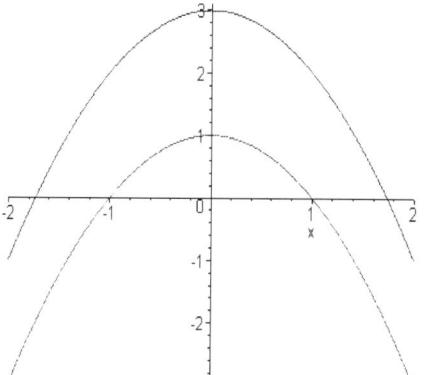

Range: _____ Range: _____
Vertex form: _____ Vertex form: _____
Factorized form: _____ Factorized form: _____
Standard form: _____ Standard form: _____

Range: _____ Range: _____
Vertex form: _____ Vertex form: _____
Factorized form: _____ Factorized form: _____
Standard form: _____ Standard form: _____

Range: _____ Range: _____
Vertex form: _____ Vertex form: _____
Factorized form: _____ Factorized form: _____
Standard form: _____ Standard form: _____

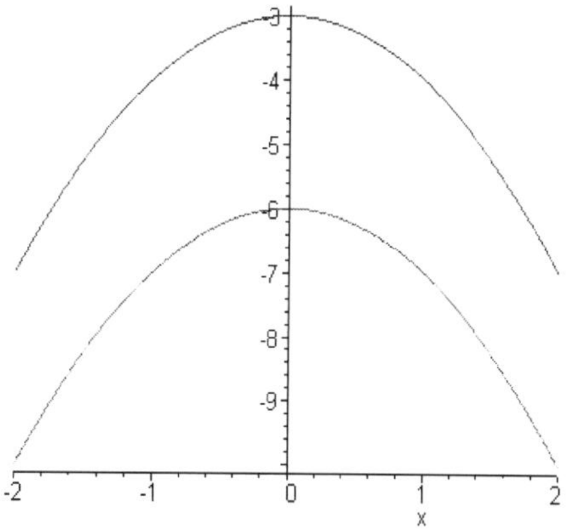

10. Complete the tables:

Function	On the graph
$f(x) = x^2$	
$f(x) = \dfrac{x^2}{2}$	
$f(x) = \dfrac{x^2}{3}$	
$f(x) = 2x^2$	

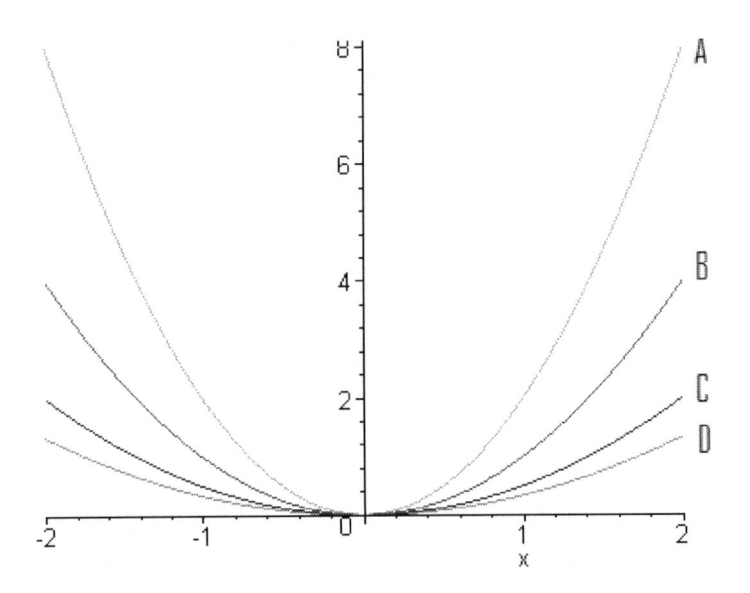

Conclusion:

11. Complete the table:

Function	On the graph
$f(x) = x^2 + 2$	
$f(x) = x^2 - 2$	
$f(x) = x^2 - 3$	
$f(x) = 2x^2 + 2$	

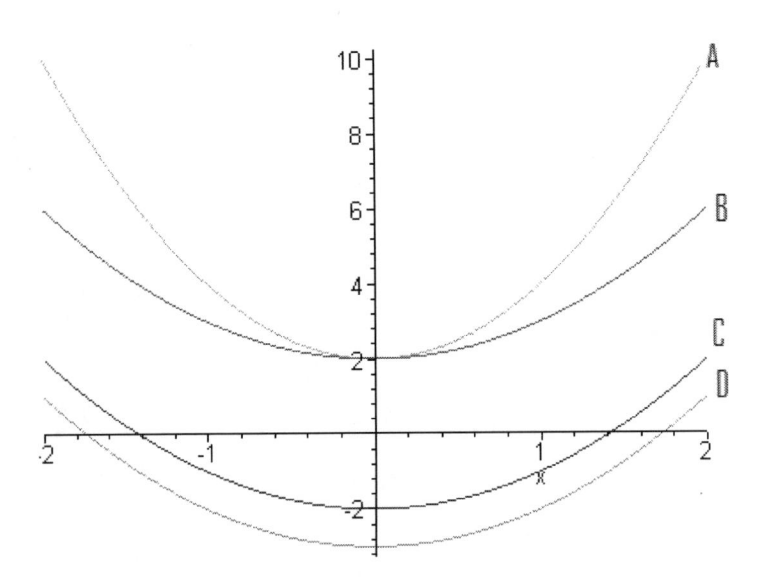

Conclusion:

12. Complete the table:

Function	On the graph
$f(x) = -x^2 + 2$	
$f(x) = x^2 - 4$	
$f(x) = -x^2 + 3$	
$f(x) = 2x^2 + 2$	

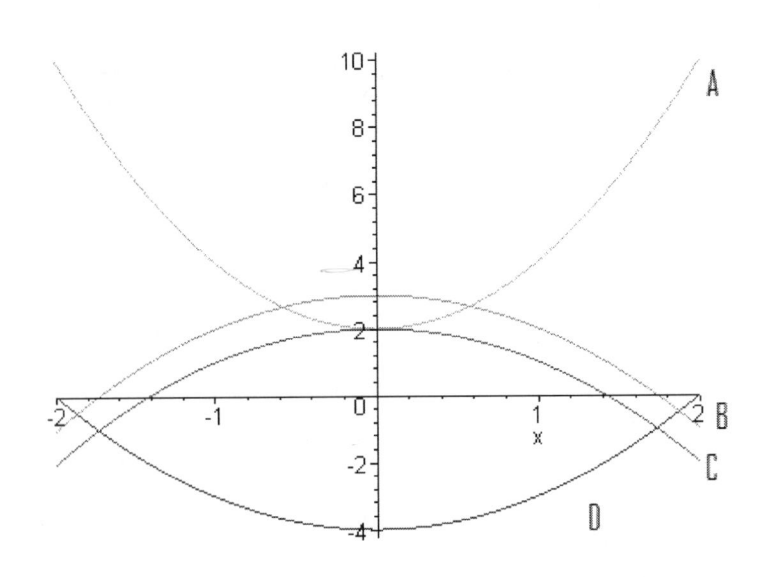

146

13. Write the expression of the function in all possible forms, indicate the range assume $a = 1$ or -1 in all cases:

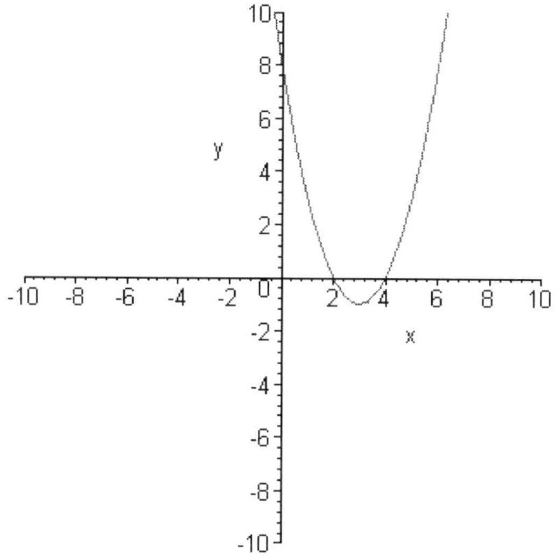

Range: ____________________

Vertex form: ____________________

Factorized form: ____________________

Standard form: ____________________

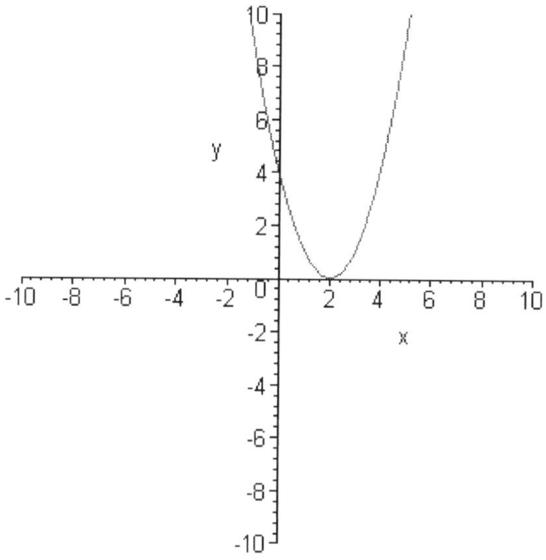

Range: ____________________

Vertex form: ____________________

Factorized form: ____________________

Standard form: ____________________

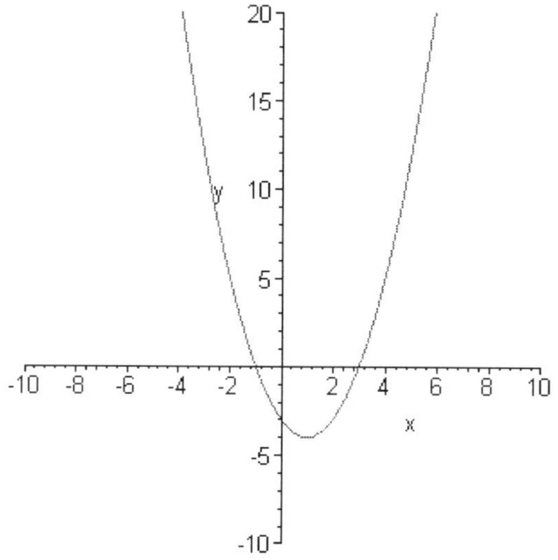

Range: ____________________

Vertex form: ____________________

Factorized form: ____________________

Standard form: ____________________

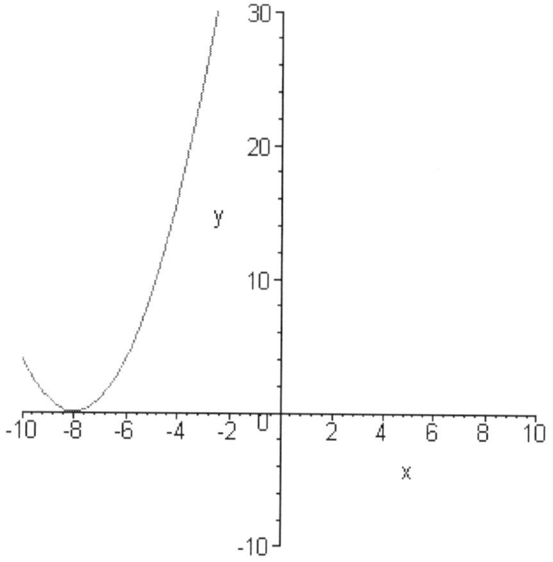

Range: ____________________

Vertex form: ____________________

Factorized form: ____________________

Standard form: ____________________

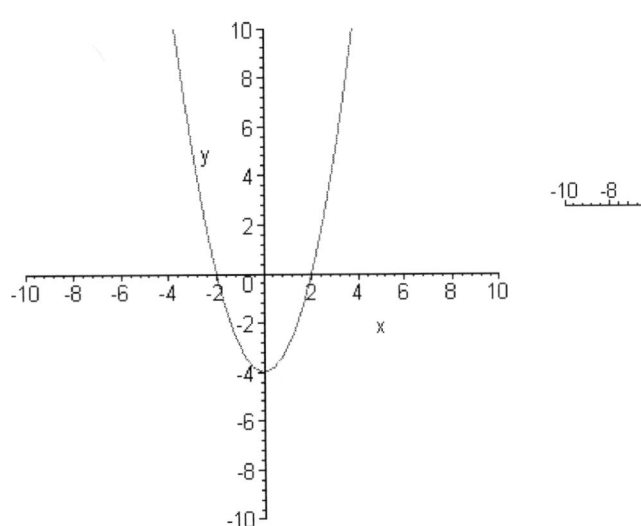

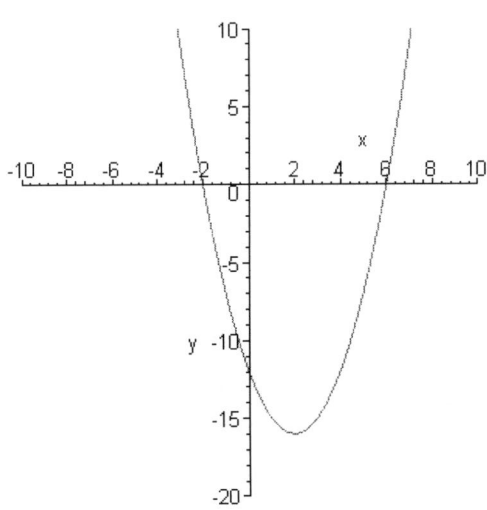

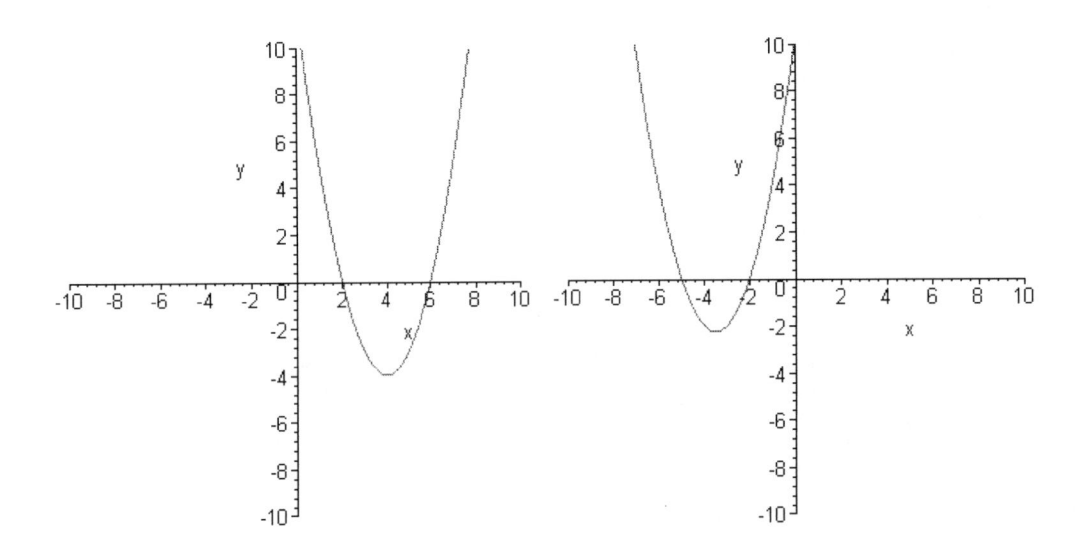

Range: _____   Range: _____
Vertex form: _____   Vertex form: _____
Factorized form: _____   Factorized form: _____
Standard form: _____   Standard form: _____

Range: _____   Range: _____
Vertex form: _____   Vertex form: _____
Factorized form: _____   Factorized form: _____
Standard form: _____   Standard form: _____

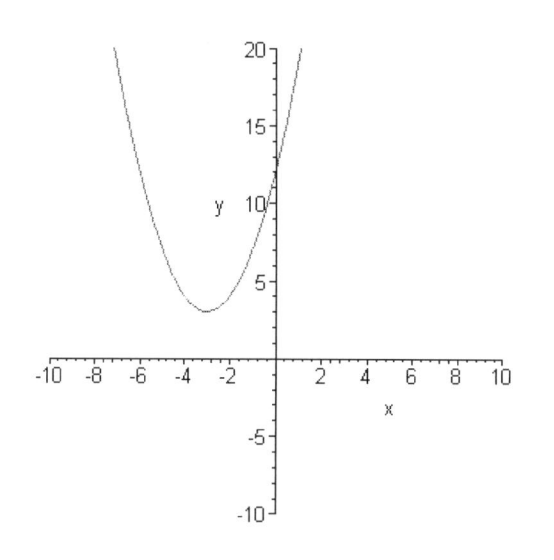

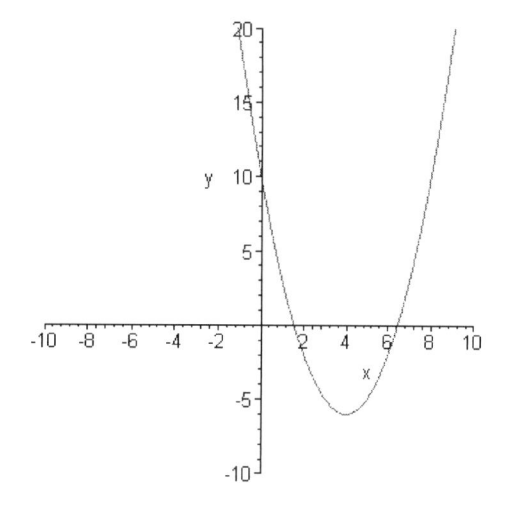

Range: _____   Range: _____
Vertex form: _____   Vertex form: _____
Factorized form: _____   Factorized form: _____
Standard form: _____   Standard form: _____

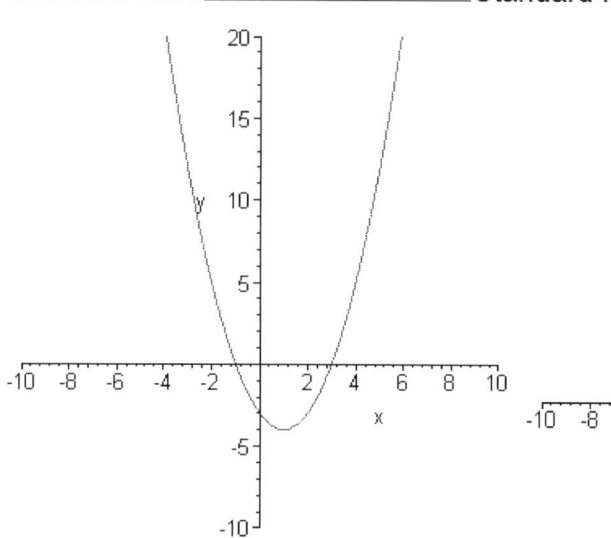

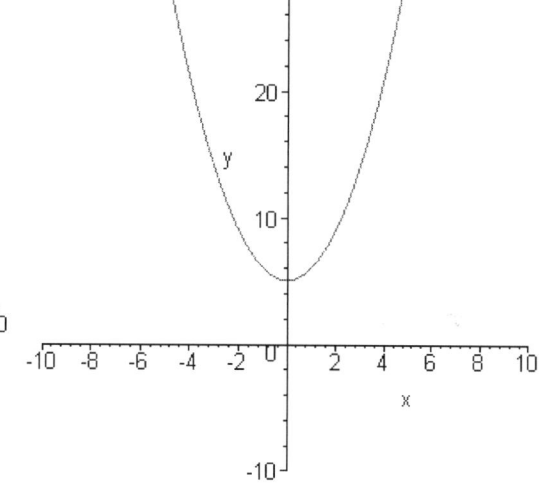

Range: _____   Range: _____
Vertex form: _____   Vertex form: _____
Factorized form: _____   Factorized form: _____
Standard form: _____   Standard form: _____

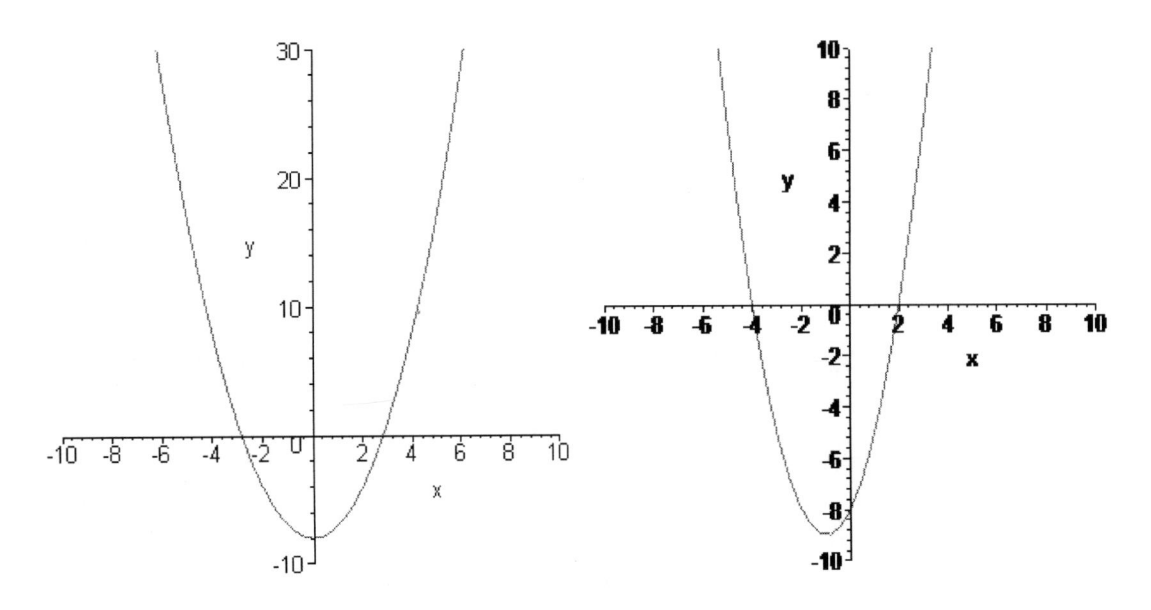

Range: _____ Range: _____
Vertex form: _____ Vertex form: _____
Factorized form: _____ Factorized form: _____
Standard form: _____ Standard form: _____

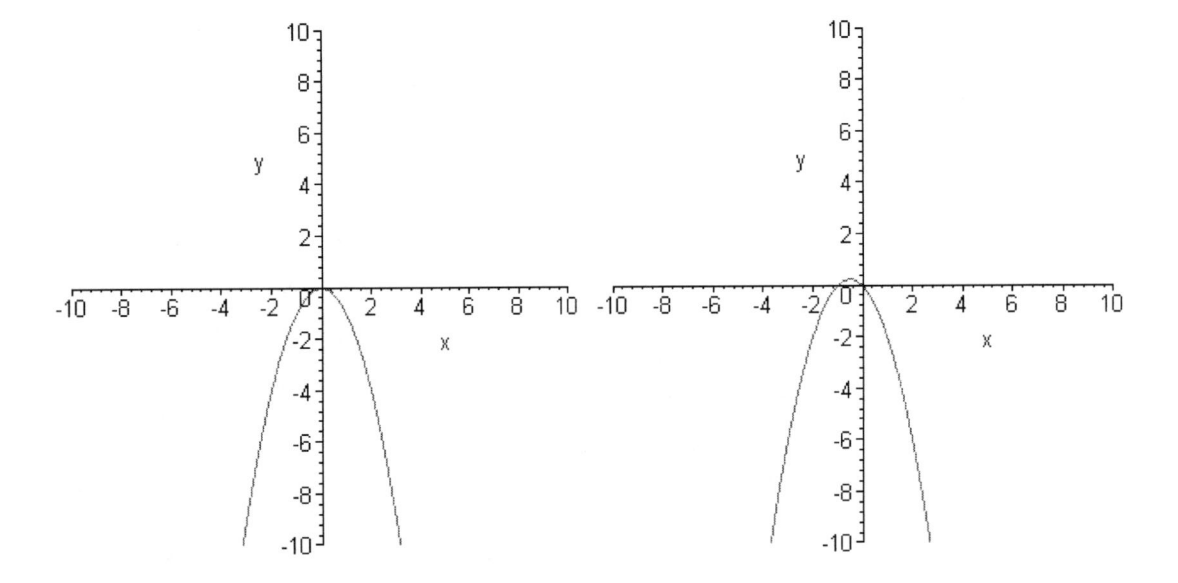

Range: _____ Range: _____
Vertex form: _____ Vertex form: _____
Factorized form: _____ Factorized form: _____
Standard form: _____ Standard form: _____

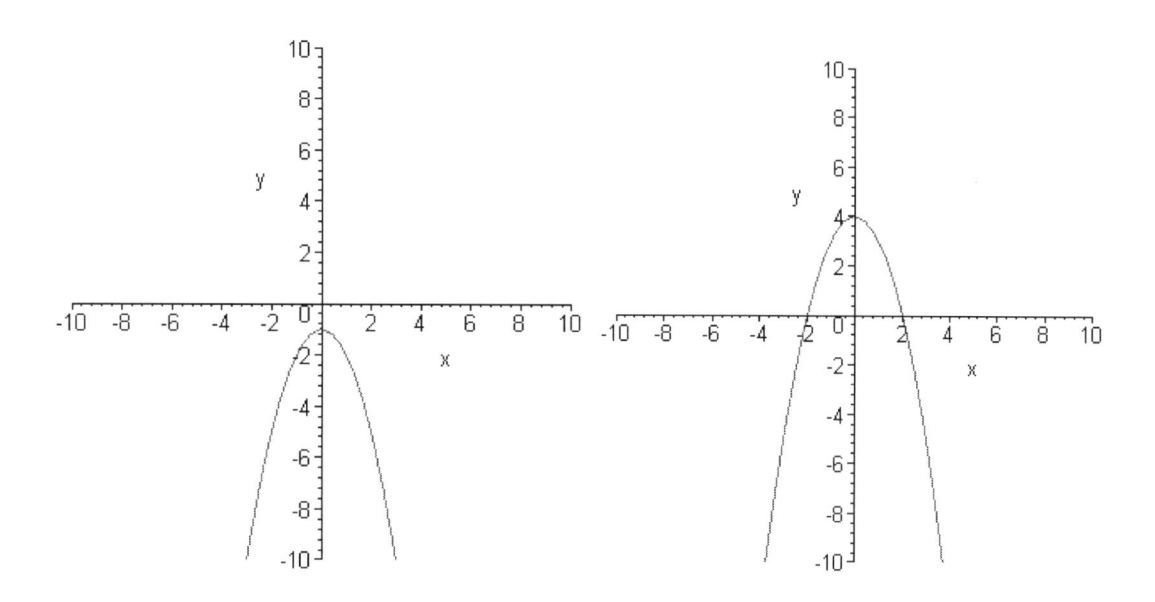

Range: _____   Range: _____
Vertex form: _____   Vertex form: _____
Factorized form: _____   Factorized form: _____
Standard form: _____   Standard form: _____

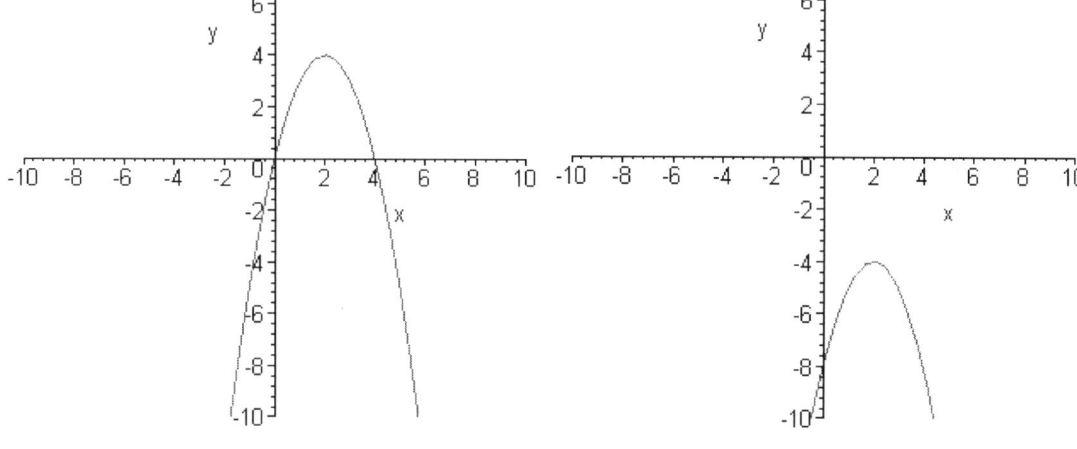

Range: _____   Range: _____
Vertex form: _____   Vertex form: _____
Factorized form: _____   Factorized form: _____
Standard form: _____   Standard form: _____

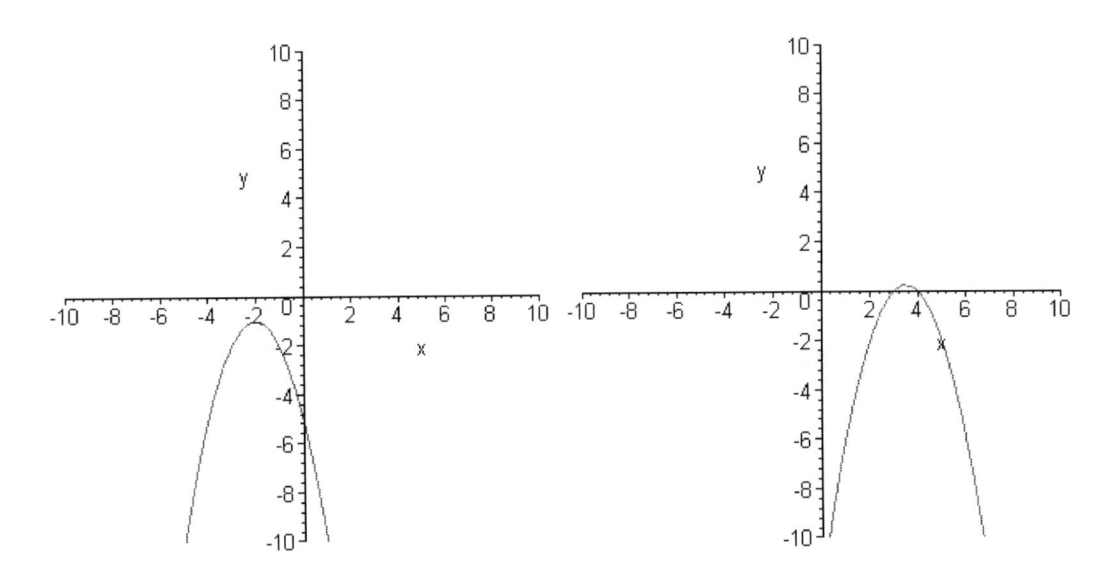

Range: _____ Range: _____
Vertex form: _____ Vertex form: _____
Factorized form: _____ Factorized form: _____
Standard form: _____ Standard form: _____

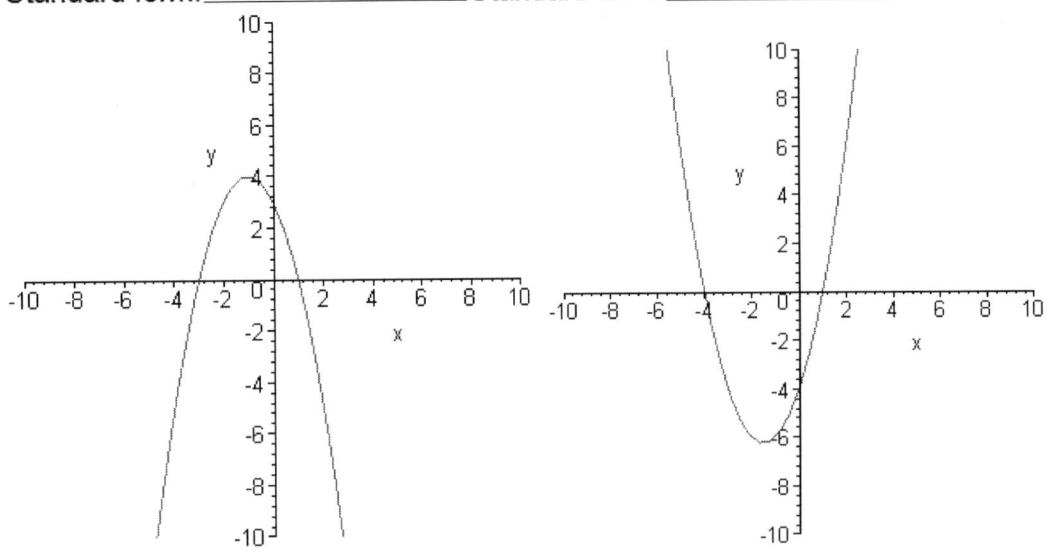

Range: _____ Range: _____
Vertex form: _____ Vertex form: _____
Factorized form: _____ Factorized form: _____
Standard form: _____ Standard form: _____

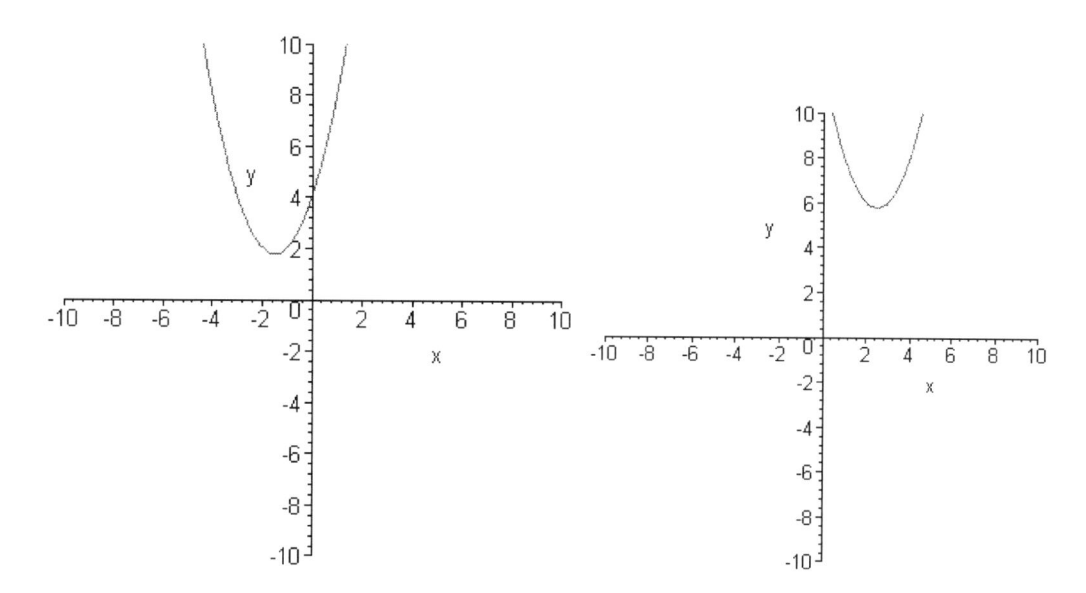

Range: _____ Range: _____
Vertex form: _____ Vertex form: _____
Factorized form: _____ Factorized form: _____
Standard form: _____ Standard form: _____

14. Analyze the following functions:

   1. $f(x) = -3$

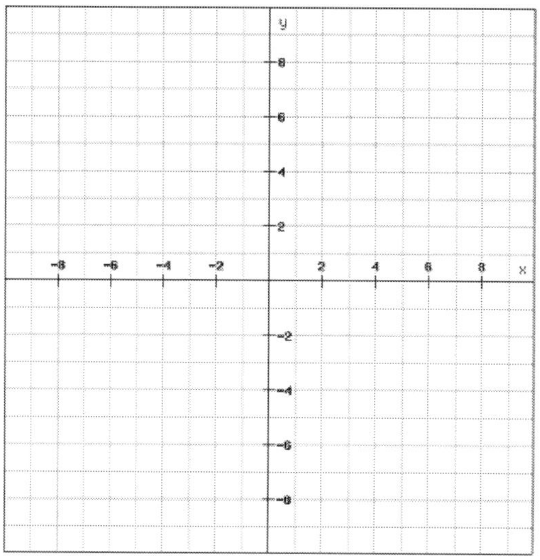

Vertex form: _____

Factorized form: _____

Domain: _____ Range: _____

y intercept: (___, ___)

x intercept(s): (___, ___), (___, ___)

Increases: _____ Decreases: _____

153

2. f(x) = 5x

Vertex form: _____

Factorized form:_____

Domain: _____ Range: _____

y intercept:(__, __) Vertex:(__, __) Max/Min

x intercept(s):(___, ___), (___, ___)

Increases: _____ Decreases: _____

3. f(x) = x² + 8x + 19

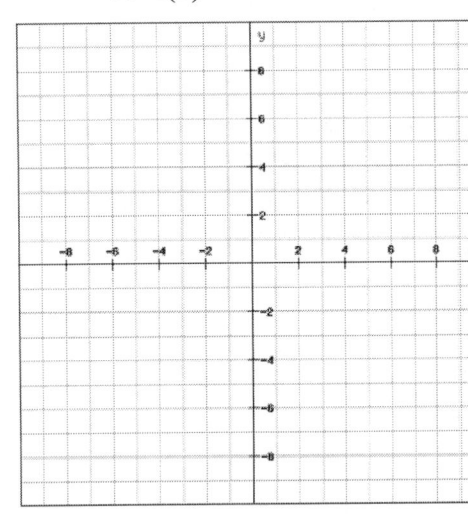

Vertex form: _____

Factorized form:_____

Domain: _____ Range: _____

y intercept:(__, __) Vertex:(__, __) Max/Min

x intercept(s):(___, ___), (___, ___)

Increases: _____ Decreases: _____

4. f(x) = 10x² − 8x − 2

Vertex form: _____

Factorized form:_____

Domain: _____ Range: _____

y intercept:(__, __) Vertex:(__, __) Max/Min

x intercept(s):(___, ___), (___, ___)

Increases: _____ Decreases: _____

5. f(x) = x² + 4x + 1

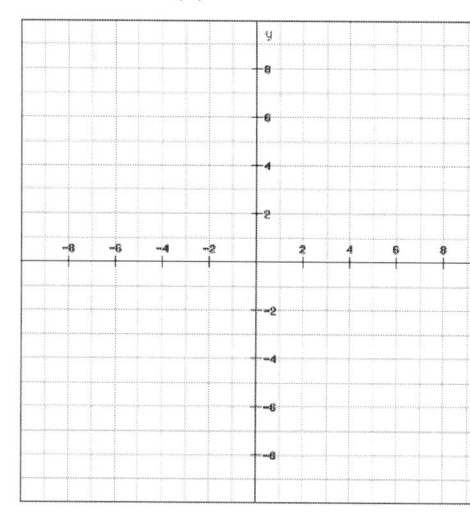

Vertex form: _____

Factorized form: _____

Domain: _____ Range: _____

y intercept: (__, __)   Vertex: (__, __) Max/Min

x intercept(s): (___, ___), (___, ___)

Increases: _____ Decreases: _____

6. f(x) = 4x² − 14x + 6

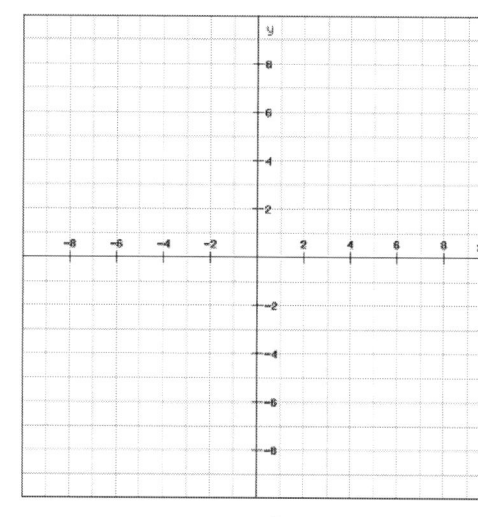

Vertex form: _____

Factorized form: _____

Domain: _____ Range: _____

y intercept: (__, __)   Vertex: (__, __) Max/Min

x intercept(s): (___, ___), (___, ___)

Increases: _____ Decreases: _____

7. f(x) = 2x² − 3x − 5

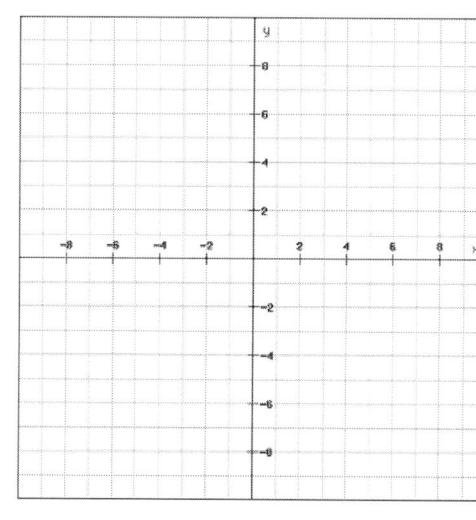

Vertex form: _____

Factorized form: _____

Domain: _____ Range: _____

y intercept: (__, __)   Vertex: (__, __) Max/Min

x intercept(s): (___, ___), (___, ___)

Increases: _____ Decreases: _____

8. $f(x) = x^2 + 3x - 10$

Vertex form: _____

Factorized form: _____

Domain: _____ Range: _____

y intercept: (__, __)   Vertex: (__, __) Max/Min

x intercept(s): (___, ___), (___, ___)

Increases: _____ Decreases: _____

9. $f(x) = x^2 + 7x - 1$

Vertex form: _____

Factorized form: _____

Domain: _____ Range: _____

y intercept: (__, __)   Vertex: (__, __) Max/Min

x intercept(s): (___, ___), (___, ___)

Increases: _____ Decreases: _____

10. $f(x) = x^2 + 2x + 7$

Vertex form: _____

Factorized form: _____

Domain: _____ Range: _____

y intercept: (__, __)   Vertex: (__, __) Max/Min

x intercept(s): (___, ___), (___, ___)

Increases: _____ Decreases: _____

11. $f(x) = x^2 + x - 1$

Vertex form: _____

Factorized form: _____

Domain: _____ Range: _____

y intercept: (__, __)   Vertex: (__, __) Max/Min

x intercept(s): (__, __), (__, __)

Increases: _____ Decreases: _____

12. $f(x) = x^2 + 2x + 1$

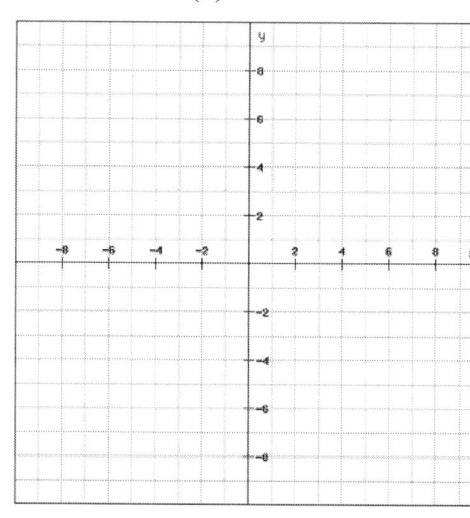

Vertex form: _____

Factorized form: _____

Domain: _____ Range: _____

y intercept: (__, __)   Vertex: (__, __) Max/Min

x intercept(s): (__, __), (__, __)

Increases: _____ Decreases: _____

13. $f(x) = x^2 + 1$

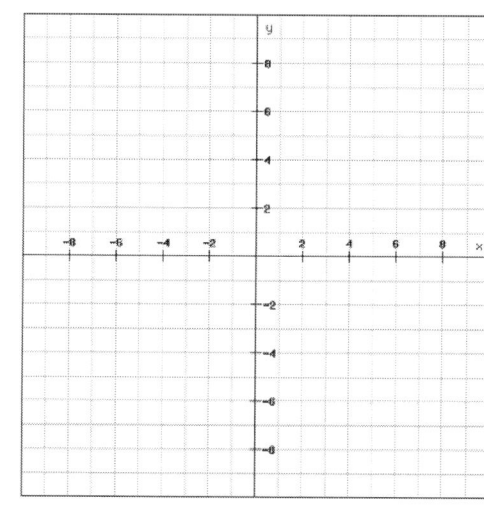

Vertex form: _____

Factorized form: _____

Domain: _____ Range: _____

y intercept: (__, __)   Vertex: (__, __) Max/Min

x intercept(s): (__, __), (__, __)

Increases: _____ Decreases: _____

14. $f(x) = x^2 - 1$

Vertex form: _____

Factorized form: _____

Domain: _____ Range: _____

y intercept:(__, __) Vertex:(__, __) Max/Min

x intercept(s):(___, ___), (___, ___)

Increases: _____ Decreases: _____

15. $f(x) = x^2 + 3x$

Vertex form: _____

Factorized form: _____

Domain: _____ Range: _____

y intercept:(__, __) Vertex:(__, __) Max/Min

x intercept(s):(___, ___), (___, ___)

Increases: _____ Decreases: _____

16. $f(x) = x^2 + 5x$

Vertex form: _____

Factorized form: _____

Domain: _____ Range: _____

y intercept:(__, __) Vertex:(__, __) Max/Min

x intercept(s):(___, ___), (___, ___)

Increases: _____ Decreases: _____

17. $f(x) = x^2 - 3x$

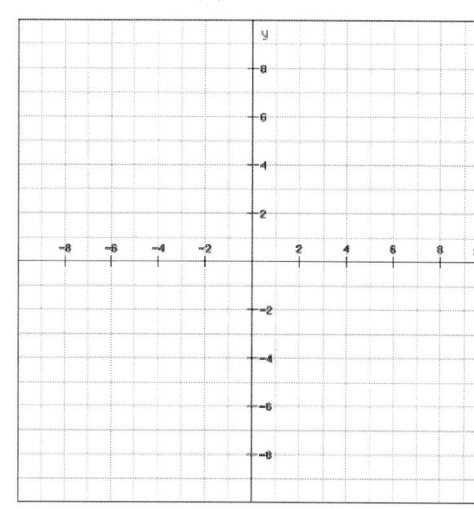

Vertex form: _____

Factorized form: _____

Domain: _____ Range: _____

y intercept:(__, __) Vertex:(__, __) Max/Min

x intercept(s):(__, __), (__, __)

Increases: _____ Decreases: _____

18. $f(x) = x^2 - 7x$

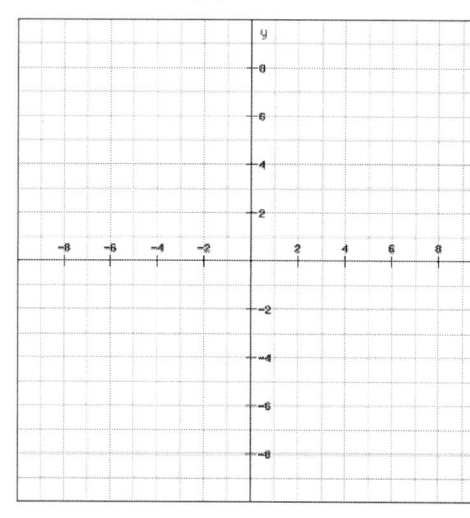

Vertex form: _____

Factorized form: _____

Domain: _____ Range: _____

y intercept:(__, __) Vertex:(__, __) Max/Min

x intercept(s):(__, __), (__, __)

Increases: _____ Decreases: _____

19. $f(x) = x^2 + 4x + 6$

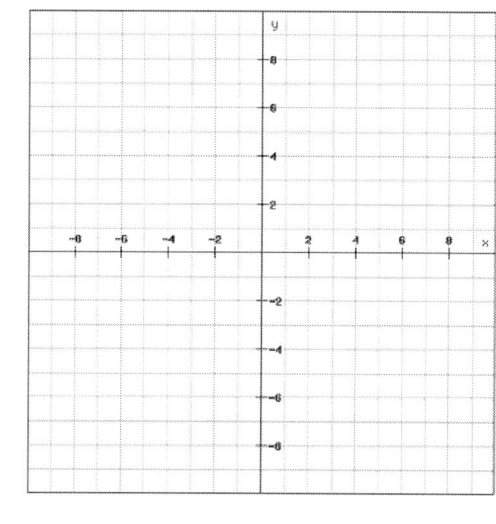

Vertex form: _____

Factorized form: _____

Domain: _____ Range: _____

y intercept:(__, __) Vertex:(__, __) Max/Min

x intercept(s):(__, __), (__, __)

Increases: _____ Decreases: _____

20. f(x) = –2x² – 16x – 29

Vertex form: _____

Factorized form: _____

Domain: _____ Range: _____

y intercept:(__, __)   Vertex:(__, __) Max/Min

x intercept(s):(___, ___), (___, ___)

Increases: _____ Decreases: _____

21. f(x) = x² – 6x + 4

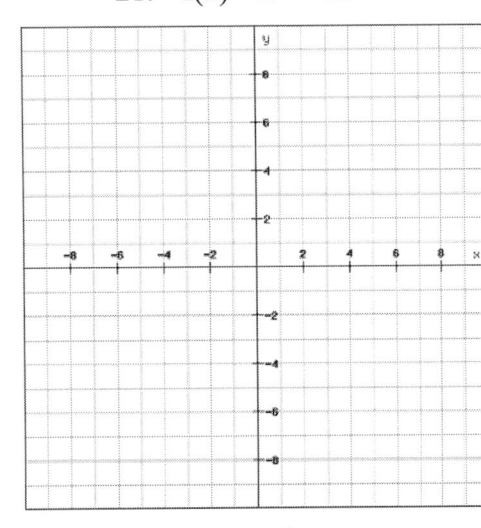

Vertex form: _____

Factorized form: _____

Domain: _____ Range: _____

y intercept:(__, __)   Vertex:(__, __) Max/Min

x intercept(s):(___, ___), (___, ___)

Increases: _____ Decreases: _____

22. f(x) = x² – 7x + 2

Vertex form: _____

Factorized form: _____

Domain: _____ Range: _____

y intercept:(__, __)   Vertex:(__, __) Max/Min

x intercept(s):(___, ___), (___, ___)

Increases: _____ Decreases: _____

23. $f(x) = x^2 + 3x + 10$

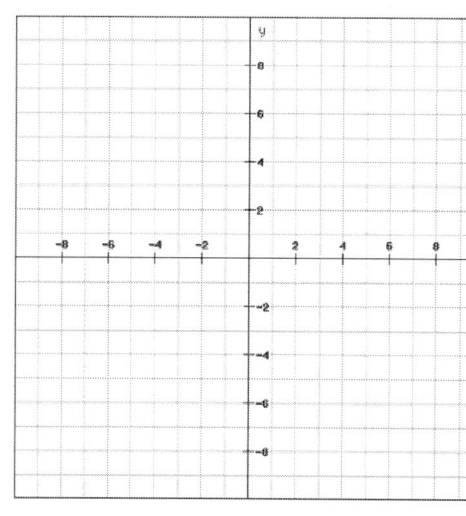

Vertex form: _____

Factorized form: _____

Domain: _____ Range: _____

y intercept:(__, __) Vertex:(__, __) Max/Min

x intercept(s):(__, __), (__, __)

Increases: _____ Decreases: _____

24. $f(x) = x^2 + 5$

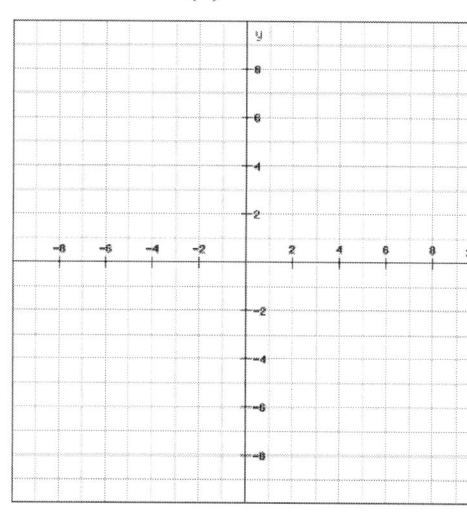

Vertex form: _____

Factorized form: _____

Domain: _____ Range: _____

y intercept:(__, __) Vertex:(__, __) Max/Min

x intercept(s):(__, __), (__, __)

Increases: _____ Decreases: _____

25. $f(x) = x^2 - 3$

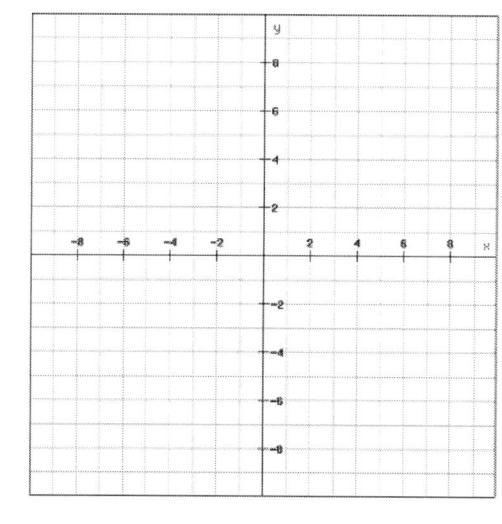

Vertex form: _____

Factorized form: _____

Domain: _____ Range: _____

y intercept:(__, __) Vertex:(__, __) Max/Min

x intercept(s):(__, __), (__, __)

Increases: _____ Decreases: _____

26. $f(x) = x^2 - 7x$

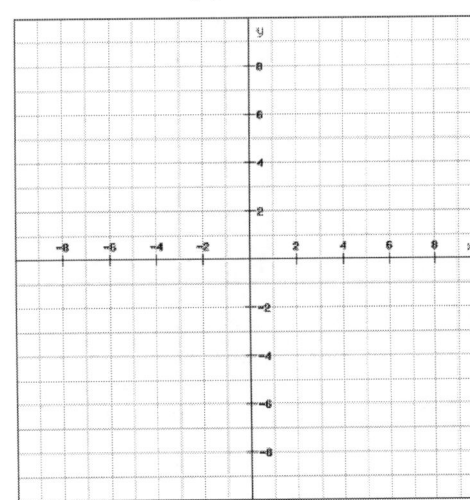

Vertex form: _____

Factorized form: _____

Domain: _____ Range: _____

y intercept:(__, __) Vertex:(__, __) Max/Min

x intercept(s):(__, __), (__, __)

Increases: _____ Decreases: _____

27. $f(x) = x^2 + 3x - 5$

Vertex form: _____

Factorized form: _____

Domain: _____ Range: _____

y intercept:(__, __) Vertex:(__, __) Max/Min

x intercept(s):(__, __), (__, __)

Increases: _____ Decreases: _____

28. $f(x) = 5x^2 - 3$

Vertex form: _____

Factorized form: _____

Domain: _____ Range: _____

y intercept:(__, __) Vertex:(__, __) Max/Min

x intercept(s):(__, __), (__, __)

Increases: _____ Decreases: _____

29. $f(x) = 5x^2 - 10x$

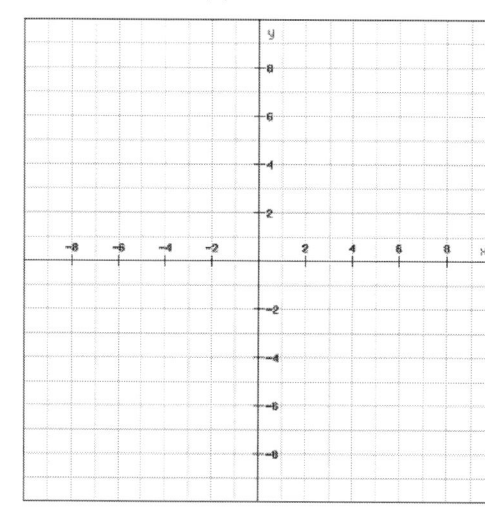

Vertex form: _____

Factorized form: _____

Domain: _____   Range: _____

y intercept: (__, __)   Vertex: (__, __) Max/Min

x intercept(s): (__, __), (__, __)

Increases: _____ Decreases: _____

30. $f(x) = -5x^2$

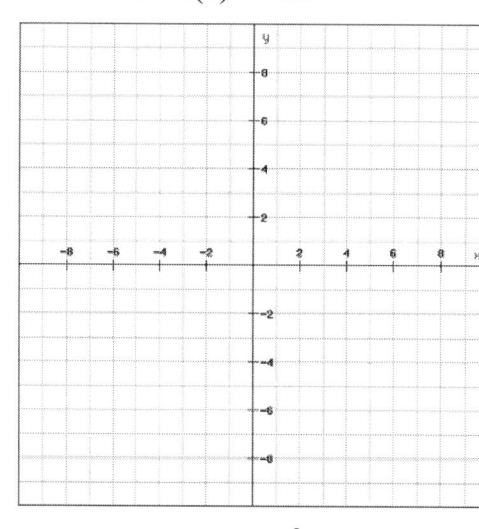

Vertex form: _____

Factorized form: _____

Domain: _____   Range: _____

y intercept: (__, __)   Vertex: (__, __) Max/Min

x intercept(s): (__, __), (__, __)

Increases: _____ Decreases: _____

31. $f(x) = -x^2 + 6x - 8$

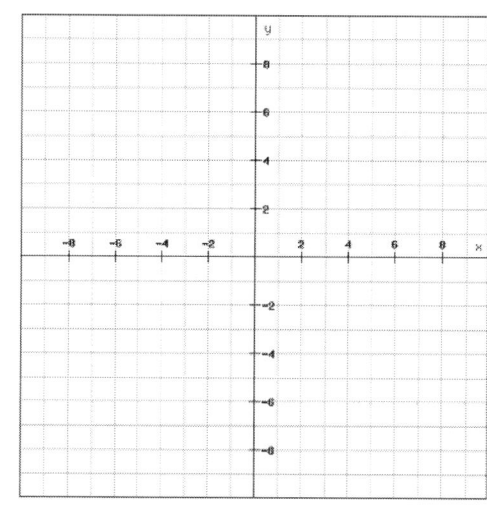

Vertex form: _____

Factorized form: _____

Domain: _____   Range: _____

y intercept: (__, __)   Vertex: (__, __) Max/Min

x intercept(s): (__, __), (__, __)

Increases: _____ Decreases: _____

32. $f(x) = -x^2 - 6x + 2$

Vertex form: _____

Factorized form: _____

Domain: _____ Range: _____

y intercept:(__, __)　Vertex:(__, __) Max/Min

x intercept(s):(___, ___), (___, ___)

Increases: _____ Decreases: _____

33. $f(x) = -x^2 + x - 5$

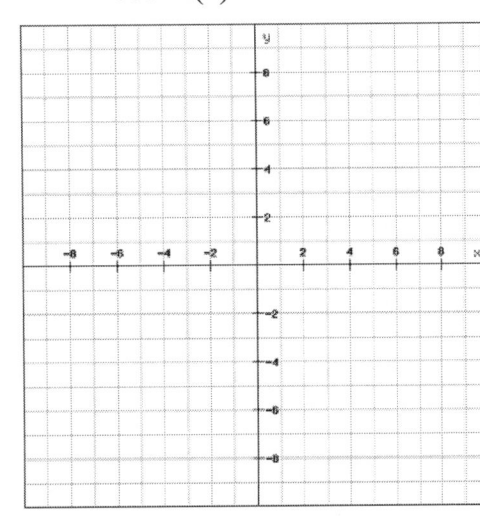

Vertex form: _____

Factorized form: _____

Domain: _____ Range: _____

y intercept:(__, __)　Vertex:(__, __) Max/Min

x intercept(s):(___, ___), (___, ___)

Increases: _____ Decreases: _____

34. $f(x) = -x^2 - 4x - 4$

Vertex form: _____

Factorized form: _____

Domain: _____ Range: _____

y intercept:(__, __)　Vertex:(__, __) Max/Min

x intercept(s):(___, ___), (___, ___)

Increases: _____ Decreases: _____

164

35. $f(x) = -x^2 + 3$

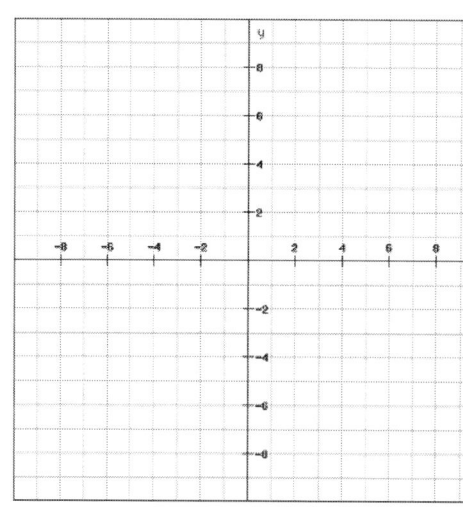

Vertex form: _____

Factorized form: _____

Domain: _____ Range: _____

y intercept:(__, __) Vertex:(__, __) Max/Min

x intercept(s):(___, ___), (___, ___)

Increases: _____ Decreases: _____

36. $f(x) = 3x^2$

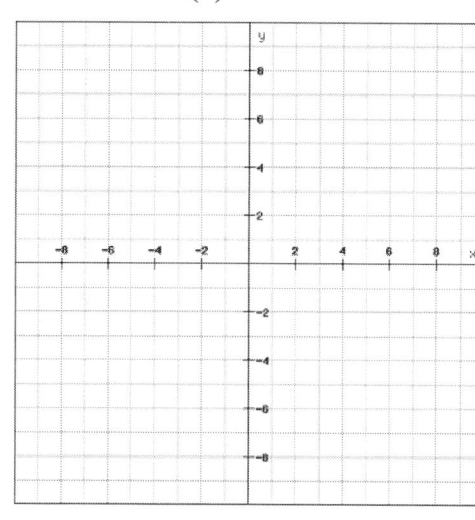

Vertex form: _____

Factorized form: _____

Domain: _____ Range: _____

y intercept:(__, __) Vertex:(__, __) Max/Min

x intercept(s):(___, ___), (___, ___)

Increases: _____ Decreases: _____

37. $f(x) = 2((x + 3)x + 4)$

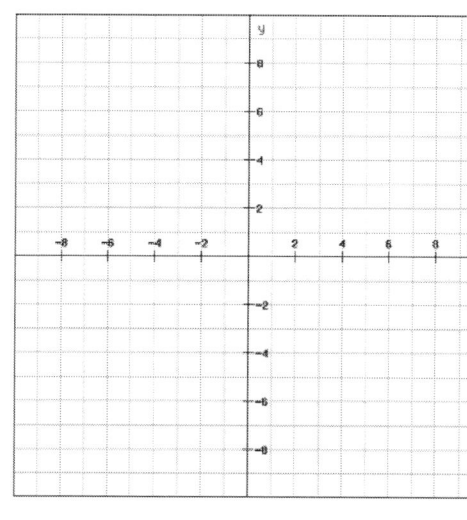

Vertex form: _____

Factorized form: _____

Domain: _____ Range: _____

y intercept:(__, __) Vertex:(__, __) Max/Min

x intercept(s):(___, ___), (___, ___)

Increases: _____ Decreases: _____

38. $f(x) = \dfrac{2x - 4x^2}{2}$

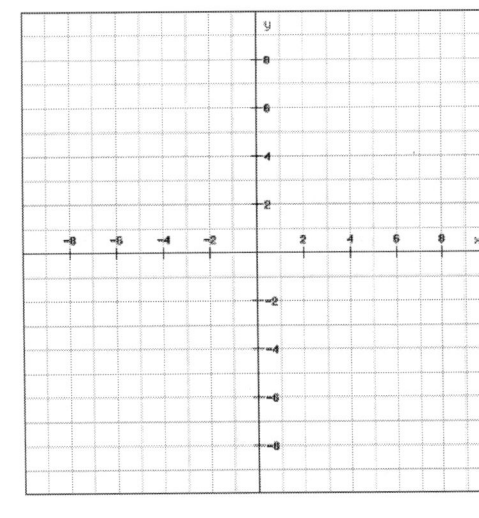

Vertex form: _____

Factorized form: _____

Domain: _____ Range: _____

y intercept:(__, __)   Vertex:(__, __) Max/Min

x intercept(s):(__, __), (__, __)

Increases: _____ Decreases: _____

39. $f(x) = \dfrac{4x^2 + 8x}{4} - 2$

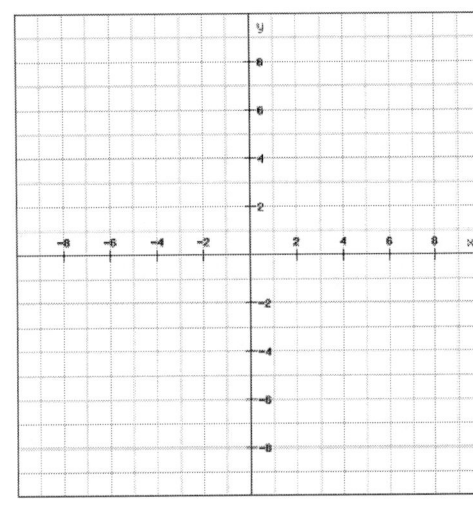

Vertex form: _____

Factorized form: _____

Domain: _____ Range: _____

y intercept:(__, __)   Vertex:(__, __) Max/Min

x intercept(s):(__, __), (__, __)

Increases: _____ Decreases: _____

40. $f(x) = \dfrac{(x-3)(x+4)}{2} - 1$

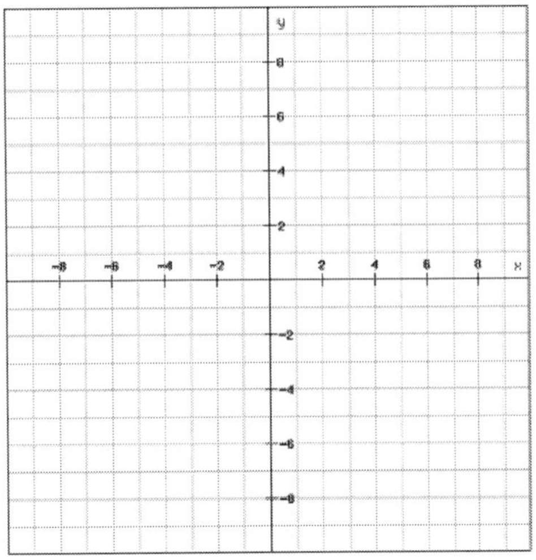

Vertex form: _____

Factorized form: _____

Domain: _____ Range: _____

y intercept:(__, __)   Vertex:(__, __) Max/Min

x intercept(s):(__, __), (__, __)

Increases: _____ Decreases: _____

166

41. What are the coordinates of the vertex of $y = 7(x + 3)^2 + 4$? (___, ___)

42. What are the coordinates of the vertex of $y = -2(x - 4)^2 + 2$? (___, ___)

43. The graph of the relation $x = -5(y + 2)^2 + 6$ is a parabola. Which way does this parabola open? (up, down, left or right).

44. What value of b makes the expression $x^2 + 8x + b$ a perfect square? What is the axis of symmetry in this case?

45. When a quadratic function can be written as a perfect square on the graph it means that _____.

46. what are the zeros of the quadratic relation $y = 10x^2 - 20x$, What is the axis of symmetry in this case?

47. Find the roots (zeros) of the equation $20(6 + 5x)(12 - x) = 0$. What is the axis of symmetry in this case?

48. The quadratic equation is used to find the _____ of the quadratic function. In case this equation has _____ it means the quadratic function is completely _____ or _____ the x axis and the value of $b^2 - 4ac$ _____. In case $b^2 - 4ac$ is _____ the quadratic function will have _____ and lastly if $b^2 - 4ac$ is _____ the quadratic function will have _____.

   If $b^2 - 4ac$ ___ 0 there are _____ Example: _____

   If $b^2 - 4ac$ ___ 0 there are _____ Example: _____

   If $b^2 - 4ac$ ___ 0 there are _____ Example: _____

49. What values of b make the relation $y = 6x^2 + bx + 5$ have no zeros?

50. Under what conditions will the parabola with equation $y = a(x - h)^2 + k$ have two x–intercepts?

51. How many zeros does the quadratic relation $y = -1.7(x + 13.2)^2 - 3.1$ have?

52. A parabola has its vertex in the third quadrant and opens down. A possible value for $b^2 - 4ac$ can be _____

53. Write the equation, in vertex form, of a parabola that has its vertex in the second quadrant, contains two zeros, and is narrower than $y = x^2$

54. Write the equation, in vertex form, of a parabola that has its vertex in the third quadrant, contains two zeros, and is wider than $y = x^2$

55. Give the relation $y = -4(x - 2)^2 + 7$, state its axis of symmetry:

56. Determine the value of the vertex of the relation $y = -(x - 3)(x + 1)$. Is the vertex a maximum or a minimum? Write down the axis of symmetry.

57. The parabola $y = -4(x - 2)^2 + 7$ is reflected about the x–axis. Write the equation of the image parabola.

Inequalities of the 2nd degree – use a graph to solve

1. $x^2 > 0$ $x^2 < 0$

2. $x^2 + 1 > 0$ $x^2 + 1 < 0$

3. $x^2 - 1 > 0$ $x^2 - 1 < 0$

4. $x^2 - 3 \geq 0$ $x^2 - 3 \leq 0$

5. $x^2 - 3x > 0$ $\qquad\qquad\qquad$ $x^2 - 3x < 0$

6. $2x^2 + 4 > 0$ $\qquad\qquad\qquad$ $2x^2 + 4 < 0$

7. $x^2 - 3x + 2 > 0$ $\qquad\qquad\qquad$ $x^2 - 3x + 2 < 0$

8. $x^2 + 2x - 3 > 0$ $\qquad\qquad\qquad$ $x^2 + 2x - 3 < 0$

9. $2x^2 + 8x - 10 > 0$ $\qquad\qquad\qquad$ $2x^2 + 8x - 10 < 0$

10. $x^2 - 2x + 1 > 0$ $\qquad\qquad\qquad$ $2x^2 + 2x \leq 0$

11. $x^2 + 11x + 10 > 0$ $\qquad\qquad\qquad$ $2x^2 + 3x + 1 < 0$

Application:

1. The height of a ball kicked upwards is given by $h(t) = 40t - 16t^2$ meters, where t is measured in seconds.

   a. Sketch the corresponding function, label the axes.

   b. Calculate $h(1)$ and give a practical interpretation to your answer.

   c. Calculate the zeros of $h(t)$ and explain the meaning in the context of the problem.

   d. Solve the equation $h(t) = 10$ and explain the meaning of the solutions in the context of the problem.

   e. Obtain the maximum height of the ball and the instant in which it reaches it.

2. The width of a rectangle is three times is length, its area is 243 m². Find its perimeter.

3. Find 2 consecutive even numbers that when their sum is squared 100 is obtained.

4. The efficiency of an engine as a function of the concentration of a certain chemical component is given by $f(x) = -0.5x^2 + x$, $0 \leq x \leq 2$.

   a. Sketch the function in its domain.

   b. Find the concentration of the chemical for which the efficiency is maximized. What is the efficiency in this case?

5. A hundred meters of fencing is available to enclose a rectangular field along side of a River, What dimensions will produce the maximum area that can be enclosed?

2.4. – TRANSLATIONS AND REFLECTIONS

Vertical translation: f(x) → f(x) + a

1. Given the function $f(x) = x^2$, write the expression for f(x) + 1. Sketch the functions. What kind of translation is that?

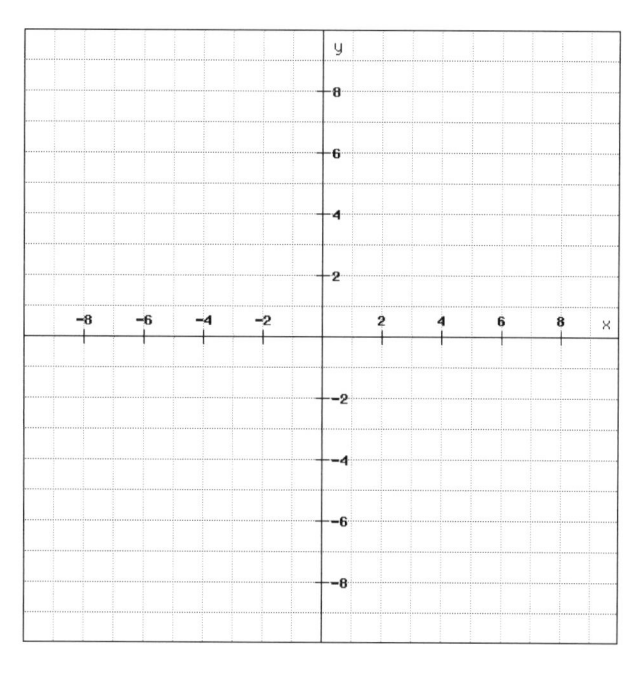

2. Given the function $f(x) = (x+1)^2$, write the expression for f(x) – 3. Sketch the functions. What kind of translation is that?

173

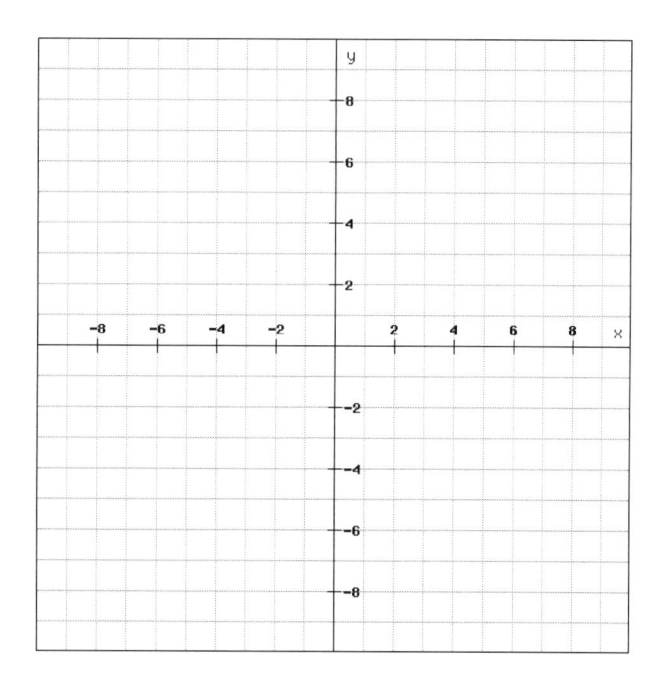

Horizontal Translation (f(x) → f(x + b)):

3. Given the function $f(x) = x^2$, write the expression for $f(x - 3)$. Sketch the function. What kind of translation is that?

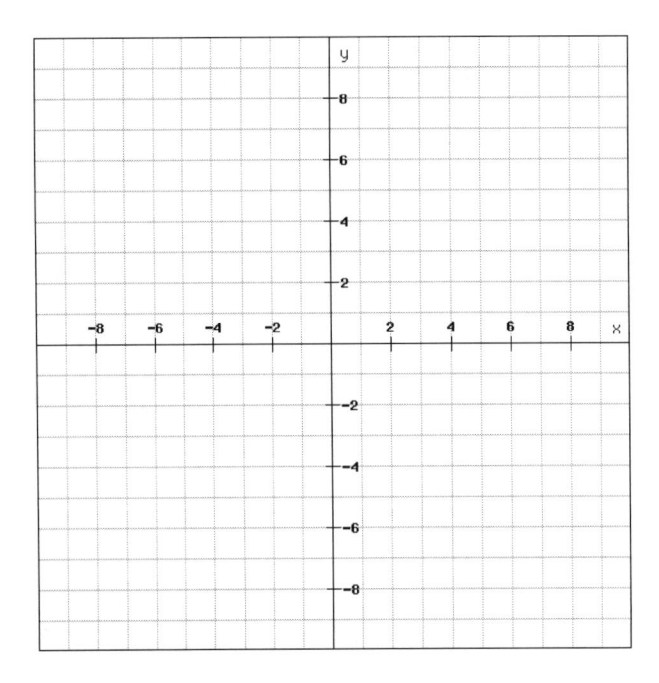

4. Given the function $f(x) = 2 - x^2$, write the expression for $f(x + 1)$. Sketch the function. What kind of translation is that?

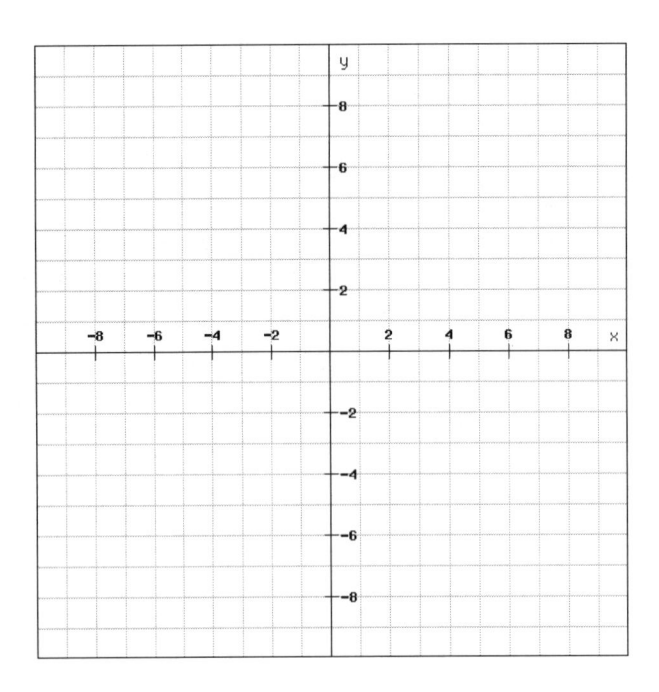

5. Given the function $f(x) = x^2$, write the expression for $f(x + 3)$. Sketch the function. What kind of translation is that?

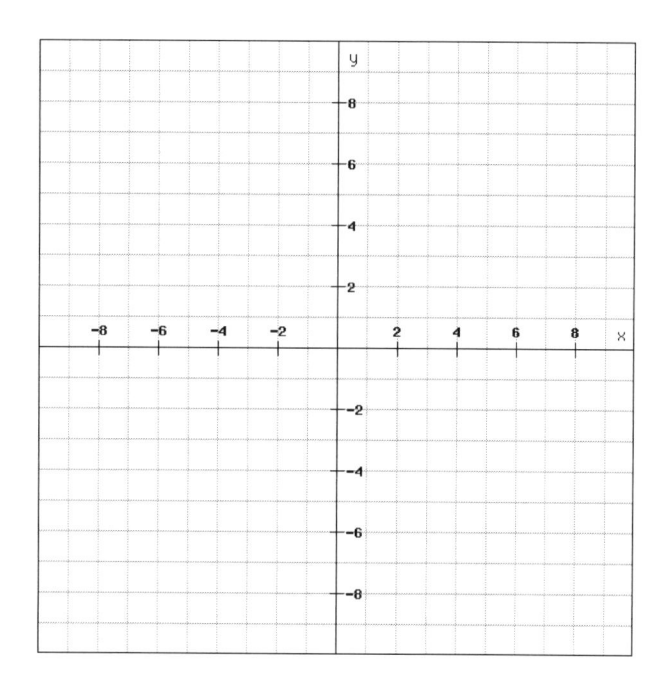

6. Given the function $f(x) = (x+2)^2 - 1$, write the expression for $f(x - 3) + 5$. Sketch the function. What kind of translation is that?

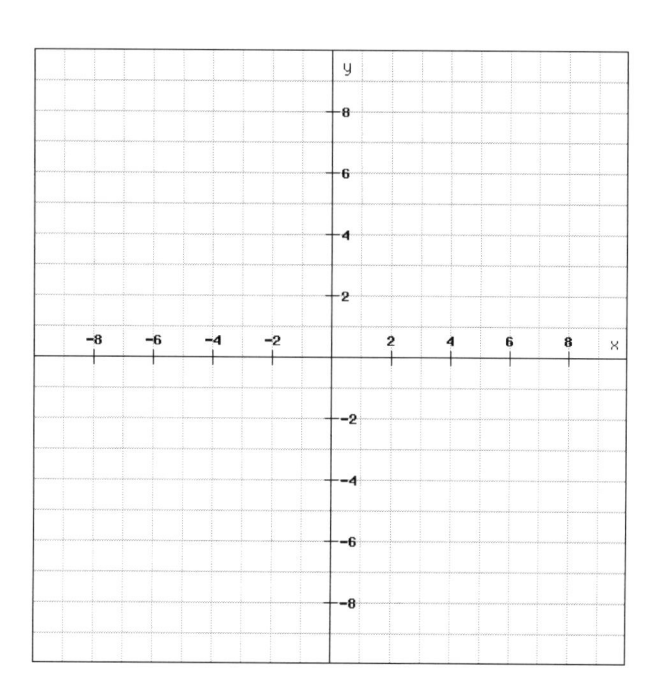

175

Horizontal and Vertical translation: f(x) → f(x + b) + a

7. Given the function $f(x) = x^2$, write the expression for $f(x - 3) + 1$. Sketch the function. What kind of translation is that?

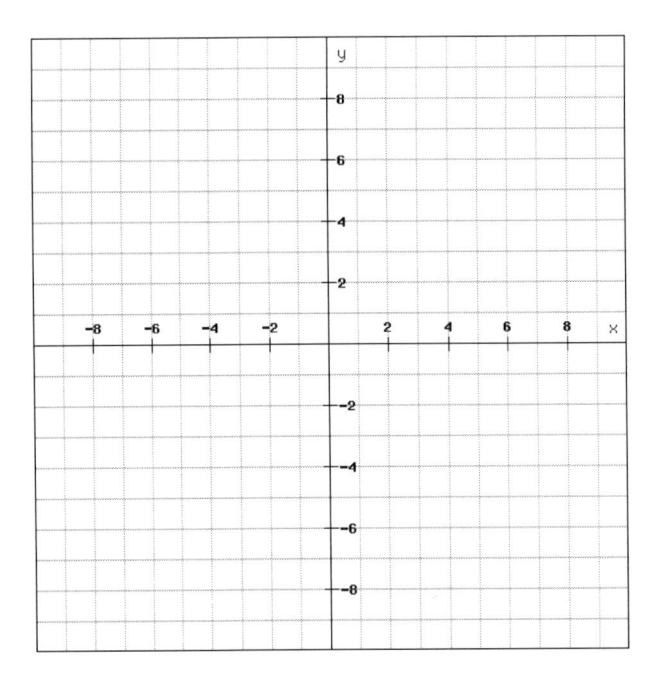

8. Given the function $f(x) = 1 - x^2$, write the expression for $f(x + 2) - 3$. Sketch the function. What kind of translation is that?

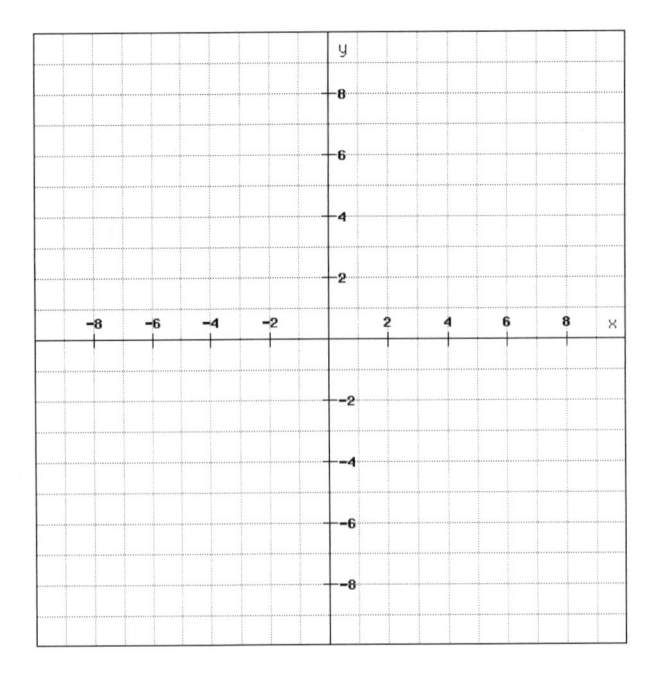

176

Vertical Dilation (change of amplitude): f(x) → pf(x)

9. Given the function $f(x) = x^2$, write the expression for $2f(x)$. Sketch the function. What kind of Dilation is that?

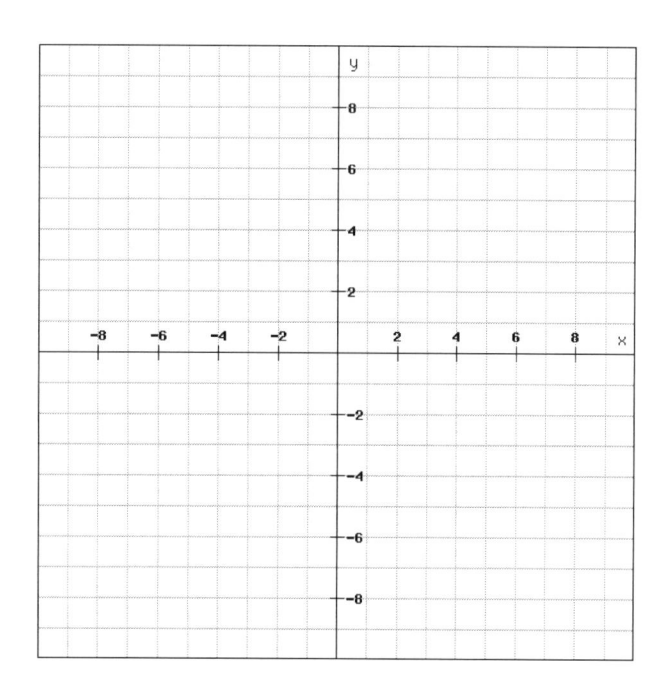

10. Given the function $f(x) = 6 - x^2$, write the expression for $\frac{1}{3}f(x)$. Sketch the function. What kind of Dilation is that?

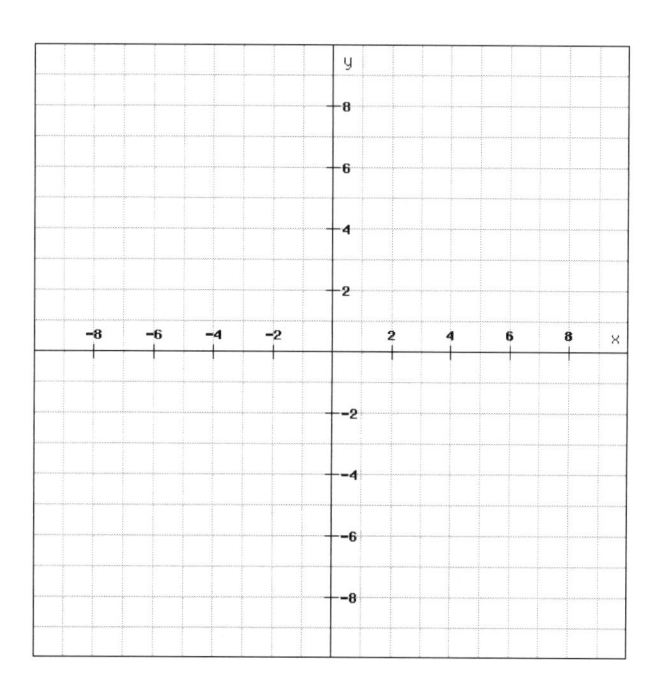

11. Given the function f(x) = x^2, write the expression for 3f(x –3) – 4. Sketch the function. Describe the sequence of transformations applied, pay attention to order.

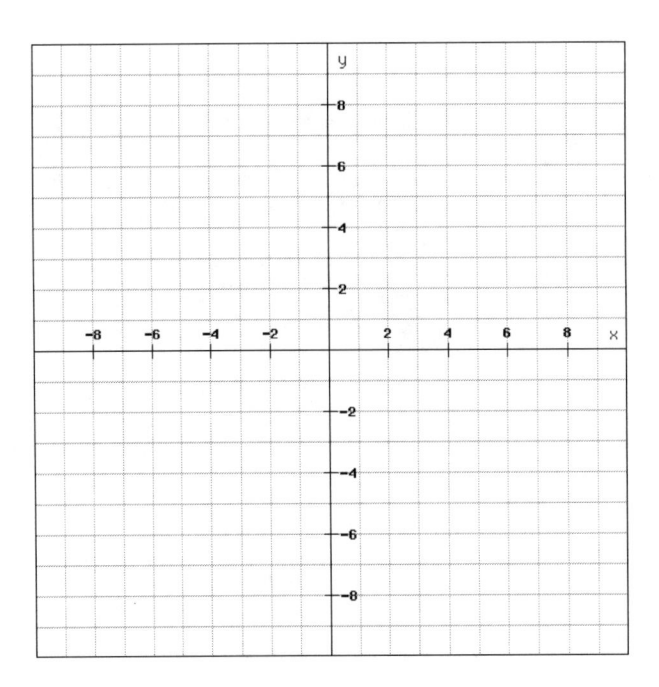

Horizontal Dilation (change of scale): $f(x) \to f(\frac{1}{b}x)$

12. Given the function f(x) = x^2, write the expression for f(2x). Sketch the function. What kind of Dilation is that?

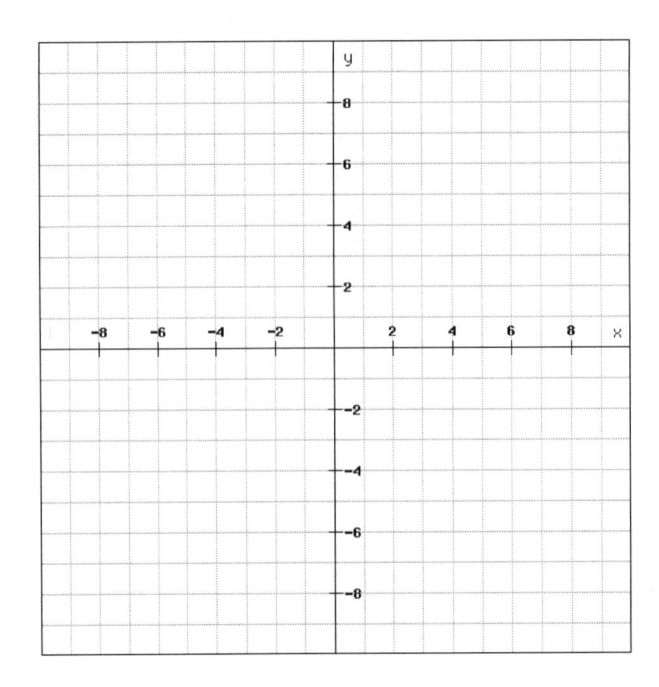

178

13. Given the function $f(x) = (x + 1)^2$, write the expression for $f(\frac{1}{3}x)$. Sketch the function. What kind of Dilation is that?

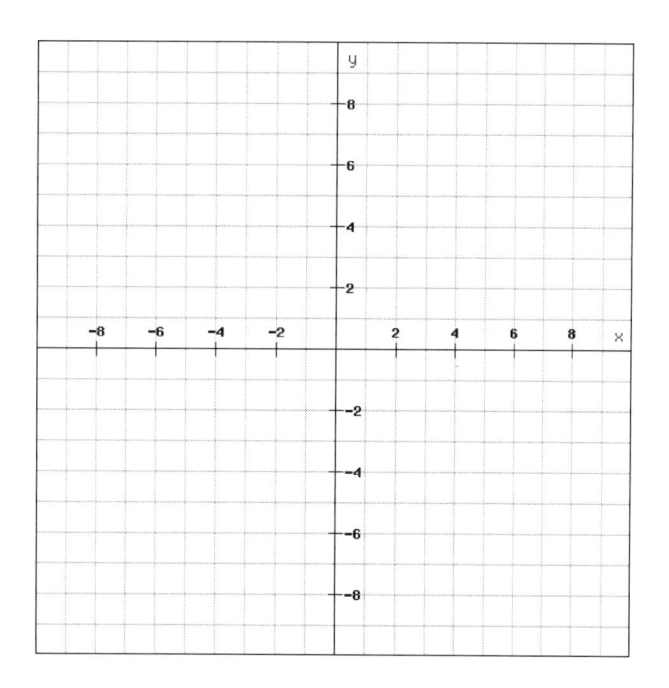

14. Given the function $f(x) = 6 + x^2$, write the expression for $\frac{1}{3}f(2x)$. Sketch the function. What kinds of Dilations/Translations are applied?

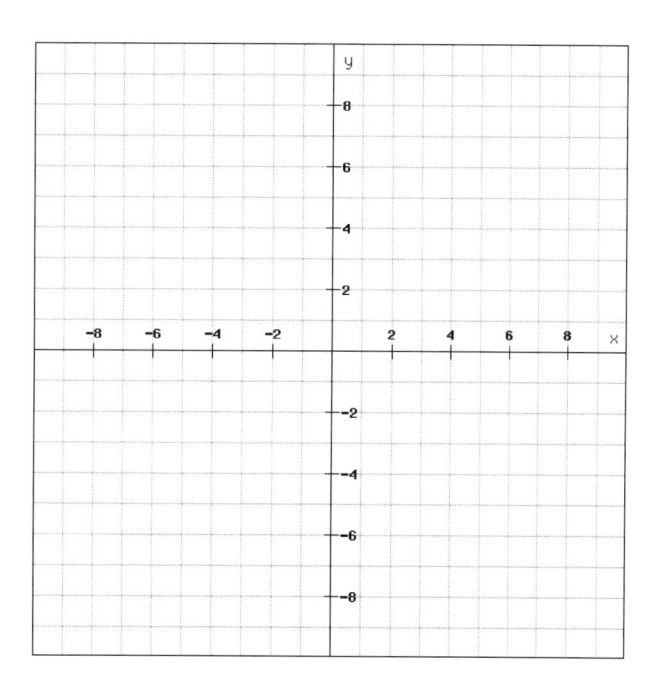

Reflections about x axis: f(x) → –f(x)

15. Given the function $f(x) = (x - 2)^2$, write the expression for $-f(x)$. Sketch the function. What kind of Reflection is that?

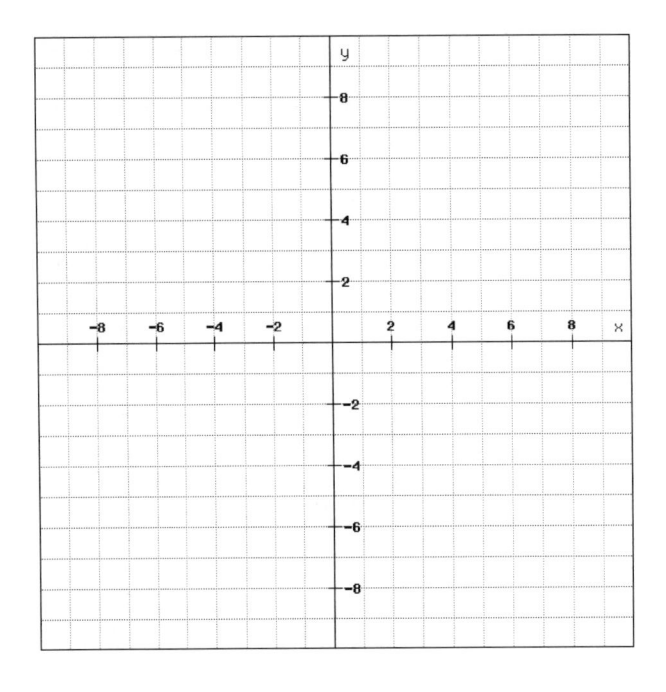

16. Given the function $f(x) = (x - 4)^2$, write the expression for $-f(3x)$. Sketch the function. What kinds of Transformations/Reflections are applied?

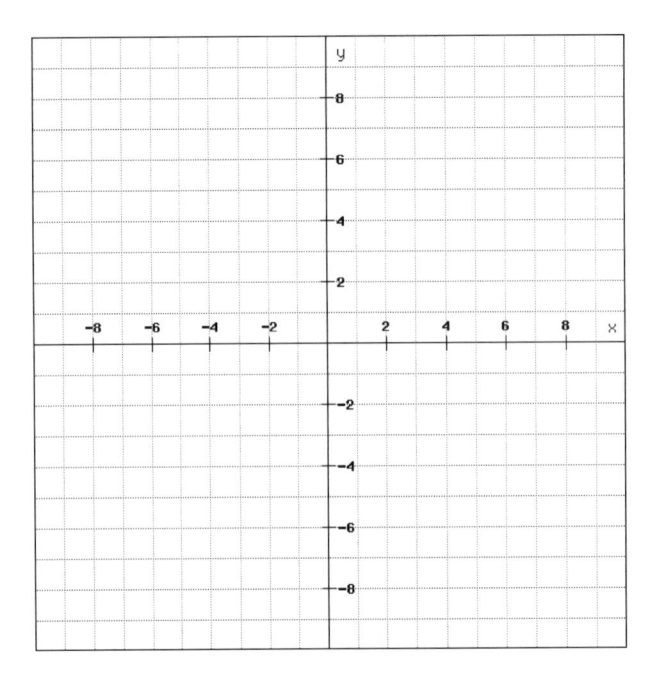

180

Reflections about y axis: f(x) → f(–x)

17. Given the function f(x) = 2x – 4, write the expression for f(–x). Sketch the function. What kind of Reflection is that?

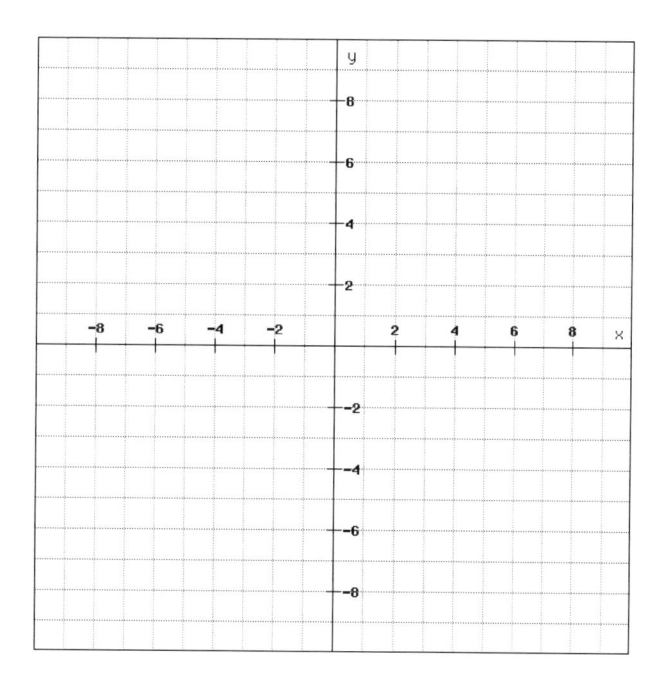

18. Given the function f(x) = (x + 2)² – 7, write the expression for –2f(–x). Sketch the function. What kind of Transformation is that?

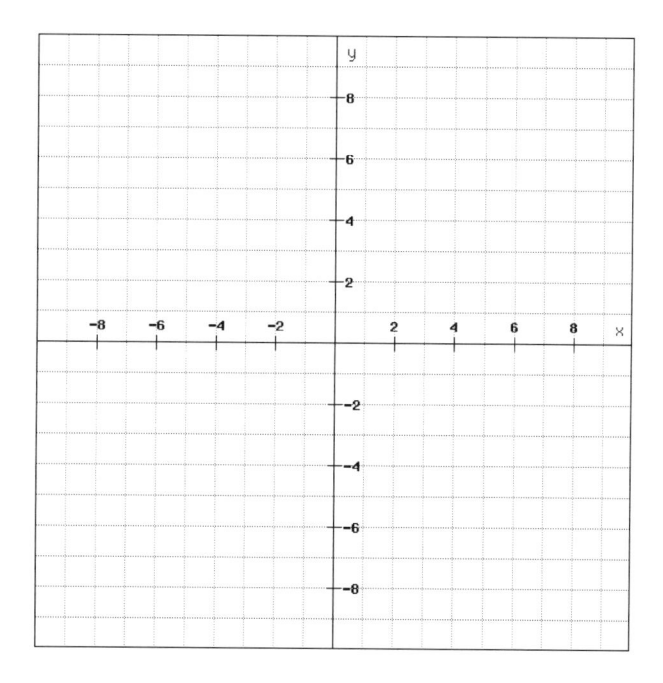

Summarizing:

Vertical Translations: $g(x) = f(x) + k$. The graph is translated k units upward if $k > 0$ and k units downward if $k < 0$.

Horizontal translations: $g(x) = f(x + c)$. The graph is translated c units to the left if $c > 0$ and c units to the right if $c < 0$.

Vertical Dilation (Change of amplitude and/or reflection about the x axis):

$g(x) = Af(x)$.

The amplitude of the graph is increased by a factor of A if $|A| > 1$ and decreased by a factor of A if $|A| < 1$. In addition, if $A < 0$ the graph is inverted (Reflection about x axis)

Horizontal Dilation (Change of scale and/or reflection about the y axis):

$g(x) = f(ax)$.

The graph is "compressed" if $|a| > 1$ and "stretched out" if $|a| < 1$. In addition, if $a < 0$ the graph is reflected about the y–axis.

Exercises:

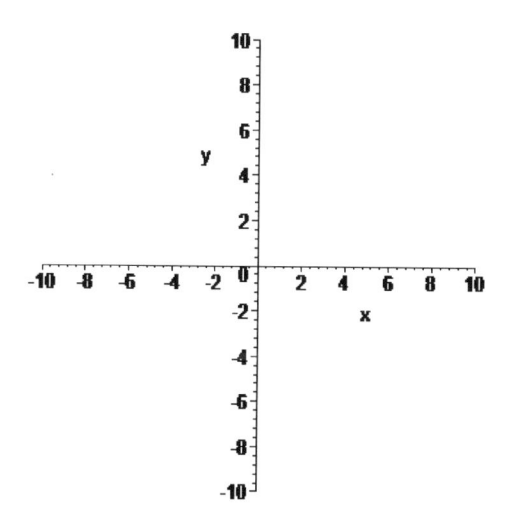

1. Consider the function $f(x) = x^2$

   a. Write the expression of the function

   $g(x) = f(x) + 2 =$ _____

   b. This is a _____ translation.

   c. Sketch both functions on the same graph.

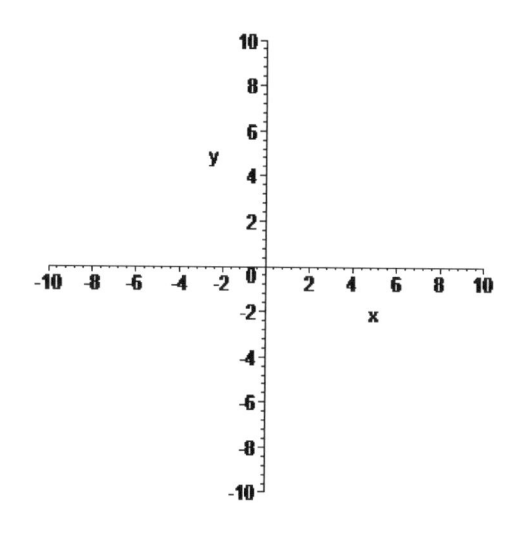

2. Consider the function $f(x) = (x - 2)(x + 3)$

   a. Write the expression of the function

   $g(x) = f(x) - 3 =$ _____

   b. This is a _____ translation.

   c. Sketch both functions on the same graph.

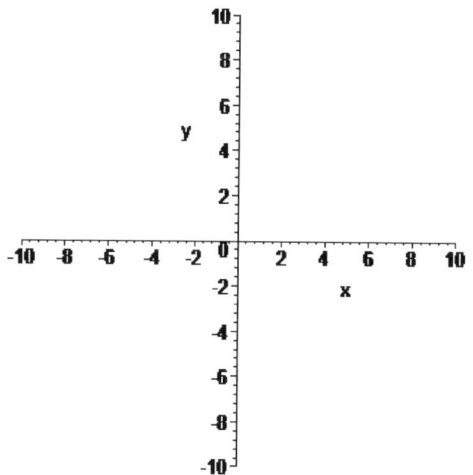

3. Consider the function $f(x) = -2x^2$

   a. Write the expression of the function

   $g(x) = f(x+1) - 5 =$ _____

   b. This is a _____ translation and a

   _____ translation.

   c. Sketch both functions on the same graph.

183

4. Consider the function $f(x) = 2(x-3)^2$

    a. Write the expression of the function

    $g(x) = -f(x) = $ _____

    b. This is a _____ about the

    _____

    c. Sketch both functions on the same graph.

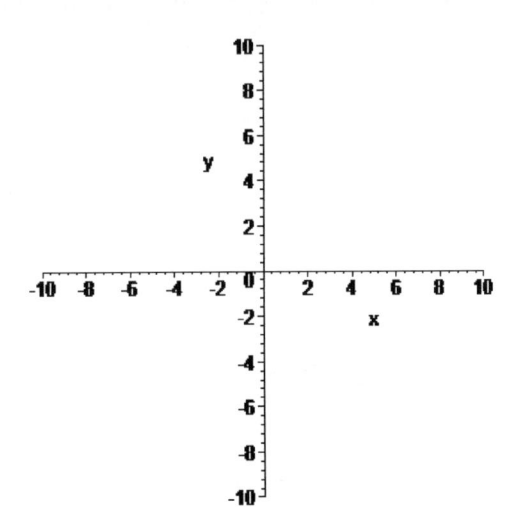

5. Consider the function $f(x) = (x+2)^2 - 1$

    a. Write the expression of the function

    $g(x) = f(-x) = $ _____

    b. This is a _____ about the

    _____

    c. Sketch both functions on the same graph.

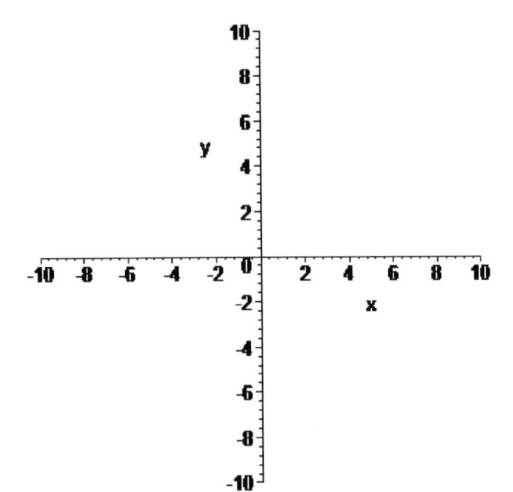

6. Consider the function $f(x) = -(x-2)^2 + 5$

    a. Write the expression of the function

    $g(x) = 3f(x) = $ _____

    b. This is a _____

    with scale factor _____

    c. Sketch both functions on the same graph.

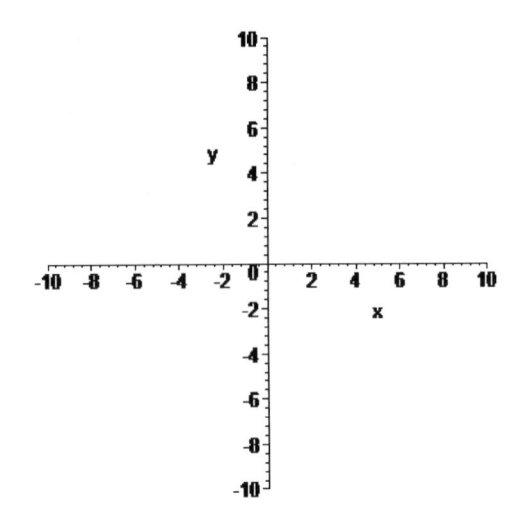

184

7. Consider the function $f(x) = (x - 5)^2 + 2$

   a. Write the expression of the function

   $g(x) = f(\frac{x}{2}) = $ _____

   b. This is a _____

   with scale factor _____

   c. Sketch both functions on the same graph.

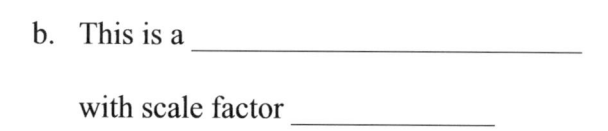

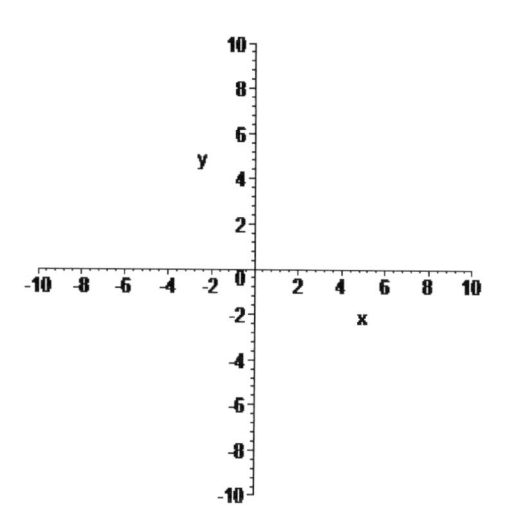

8. Consider the function $f(x) = x^2 - 6$

   a. Write the expression of the function

   $g(x) = -f(3x) = $ _____

   b. This is a _____

   and a _____

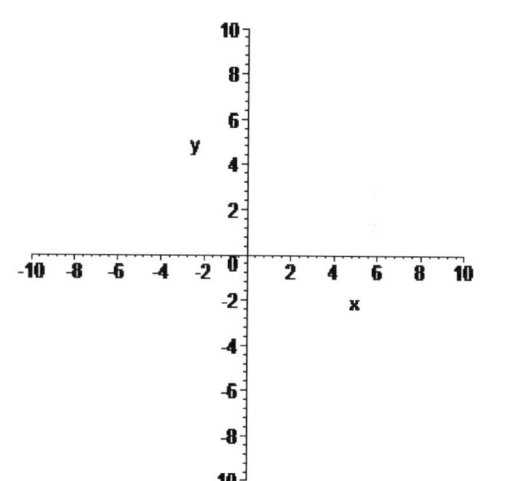

   c. Sketch both functions on the same graph.

9. Write the expression for the function $f(x) = \dfrac{x}{x^2 + 1}$ shifted 2 positions up and 3 left.

10. Write the expression for the function $f(x) = \dfrac{x - 1}{x^3 + 1}$ shifted 5 positions down and 4 right.

185

11. Write the expression for the function $f(x) = \dfrac{x}{x^2+1}$ dilated vertically 3 times.

12. Write the expression for the function $f(x) = \dfrac{x+1}{x^2+1}$ dilated horizontally 3 times, shifted 2 positions to the right and 1 up.

13. The function $f(x) = x^2$ is transformed to $g(x) = (x-2)^2 + 5$. Write the sequence of transformations applied.

14. The function $f(x) = x^2$ is transformed to $g(x) = 2(x+1)^2 + 5$. Write the sequence of transformations applied.

15. The function $f(x) = -x^2$ is transformed to $g(x) = (x-1)^2 - 5$. Write the sequence of transformations applied.

16. The function $f(x) = (x-7)^2$ is transformed to $g(x) = -6(x+3)^2 - 2$. Write the sequence of transformations applied.

17. Given f(x) = x^2, f(–x) = _____. Is it true that f(x) = f(–x) in this case? _____

18. Given f(x) = x^3, f(–x) = _____. Is it true that f(x) = f(–x) in this case? _____

19. Given f(x) = x^3, f(–x) = _____. Is it true that f(x) = –f(–x) in this case? _____

20. Given f(x) = $\dfrac{1-x^2}{x^2+1}$, f(–x) = _____. Is it true that f(x) = f(–x) in this case? _____

21. Given f(x) = $\dfrac{x^3}{x^2+1}$, f(–x) = _____. Is it true that f(x) = –f(–x) in this case? _____

22. Given f(x) = $(x-3)^2$, f(–x) = _____. Is it true that f(x) = f(–x) in this case? _____

___, is it true that f(x) = –f(–x) in this case? _____

23. Functions in which f(x) = f(–x) are called _____. The graphical meaning is that _____

24. Functions in which f(x) = –f(–x) are called _____. The graphical meaning is that _____

2.5. – ABSOLUTE VALUE FUNCTIONS

1. Given the function: $f(x) = |x|$ (absolute value of x) Complete the following table:

x	−5	−4	−3	−2	−1	0	1	2	3	4	5
f(x)											

- Sketch the points of the chart on a graph (use a ruler).

- State the domain of the function: _____

- State the y intercept (sketched on the graph: (____, ____)

- State the x intercept(s): (____, ____), (____, ____)

- Write in all possible forms:

- Find the max/min point(s): (____, ____)

- The function is increasing on the interval: _____

- The function is decreasing on the interval: _____

- Sketch the function of the graph used for the points initially drawn

- State the range of the function: _____

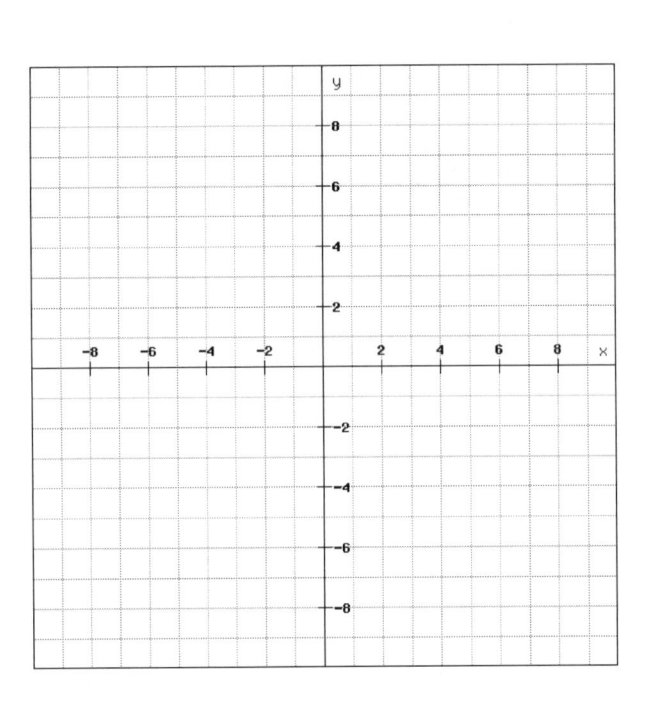

188

2. Given the function: $f(x) = |x + 1|$ Complete the following table:

x	−5	−4	−3	−2	−1	0	1	2	3	4	5
f(x)											

- Sketch the points of the chart on a graph (use a ruler).

- State the domain of the function: _____

- State the y intercept (sketched on the graph: (___, ___)

- State the x intercept(s): (___, ___), (___, ___)

- Write in all possible forms:

- Find the max/min point(s): (___, ___)

- The function is increasing on the interval: _____

- The function is decreasing on the interval: _____

- Sketch the function of the graph used for the points initially drawn

- State the range of the function: _____

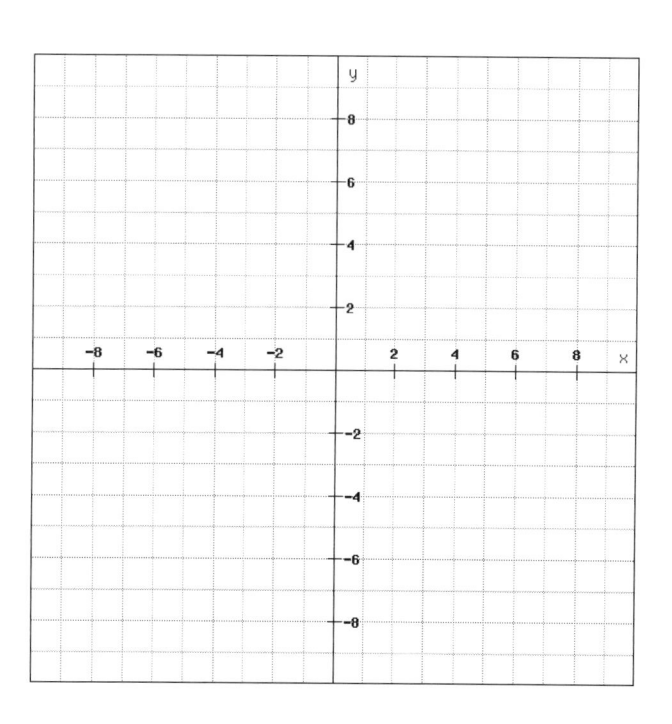

189

3. Given the function: f(x) = |3x − 2| Complete the following table:

x	−5	−4	−3	−2	−1	0	1	2	3	4	5
f(x)											

- Sketch the points of the chart on a graph (use a ruler).

- State the domain of the function: _____

- State the y intercept (sketched on the graph: (____, ____)

- State the x intercept(s): (____, ____), (____, ____)

- Write in all possible forms:

- Find the max/min point(s): (____, ____)

- The function is increasing on the interval: _____

- The function is decreasing on the interval: _____

- Sketch the function of the graph used for the points initially drawn

- State the range of the function: _____

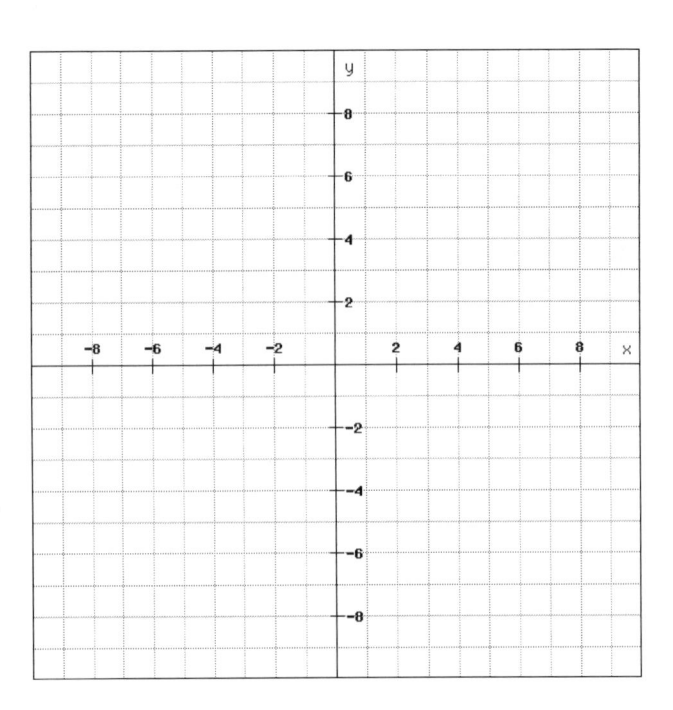

190

4. Given the function: $f(x) = |x - 4| - 3$ Complete the following table:

x	−5	−4	−3	−2	−1	0	1	2	3	4	5
f(x)											

- Sketch the points of the chart on a graph (use a ruler).

- State the domain of the function: _____

- State the y intercept (sketched on the graph: (____, ____)

- State the x intercept(s): (____, ____), (____, ____)

- Write in all possible forms:

- Find the max/min point(s): (____, ____)

- The function is increasing on the interval: _____

- The function is decreasing on the interval: _____

- Sketch the function of the graph used for the points initially drawn

- State the range of the function: _____

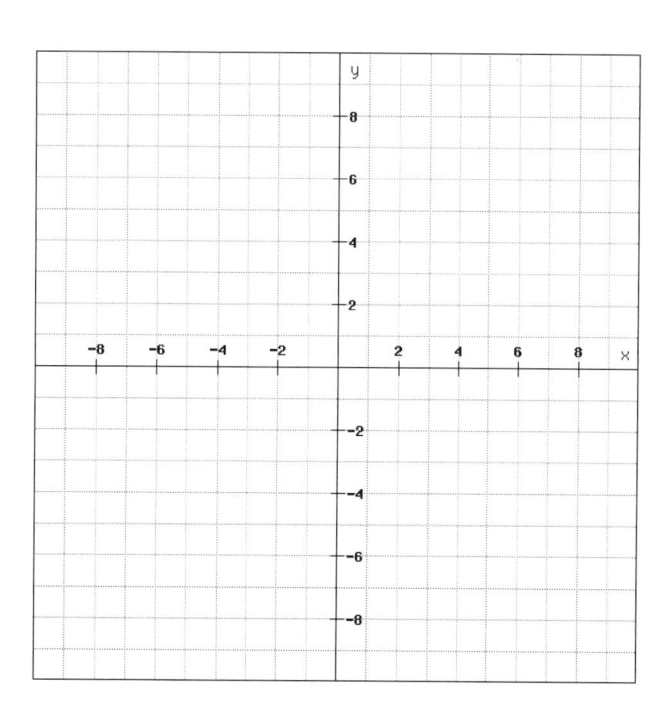

191

5. Given the function: $f(x) = |2x^2 - x|$ Complete the following table:

x	−5	−4	−3	−2	−1	0	1	2	3	4	5
f(x)											

- Sketch the points of the chart on a graph (use a ruler).

- State the domain of the function: _____

- State the y intercept (sketched on the graph: (____, ____)

- State the x intercept(s): (____, ____), (____, ____)

- Write in all possible forms:

- Find the max/min point(s): (____, ____)

- The function is increasing on the interval: _____

- The function is decreasing on the interval: _____

- Sketch the function of the graph used for the points initially drawn

- State the range of the function: _____

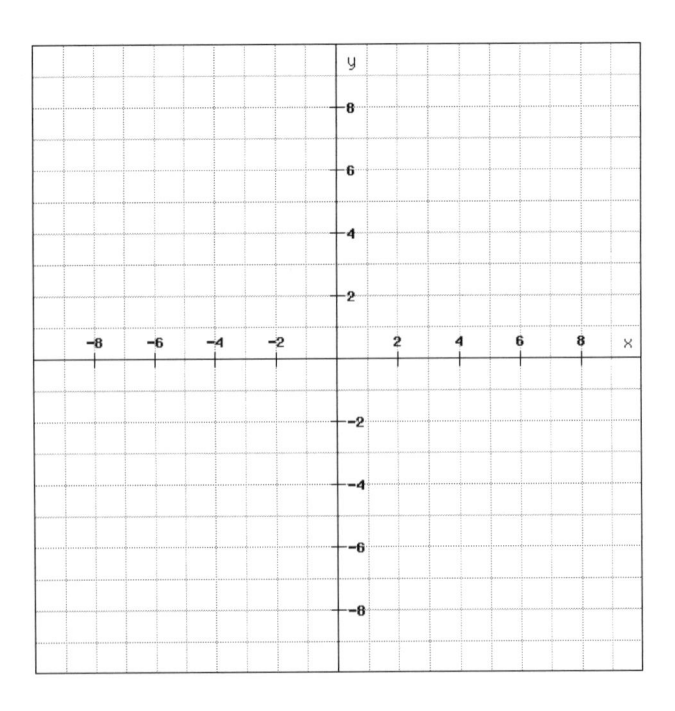

192

6. Given the graph, complete the table below:

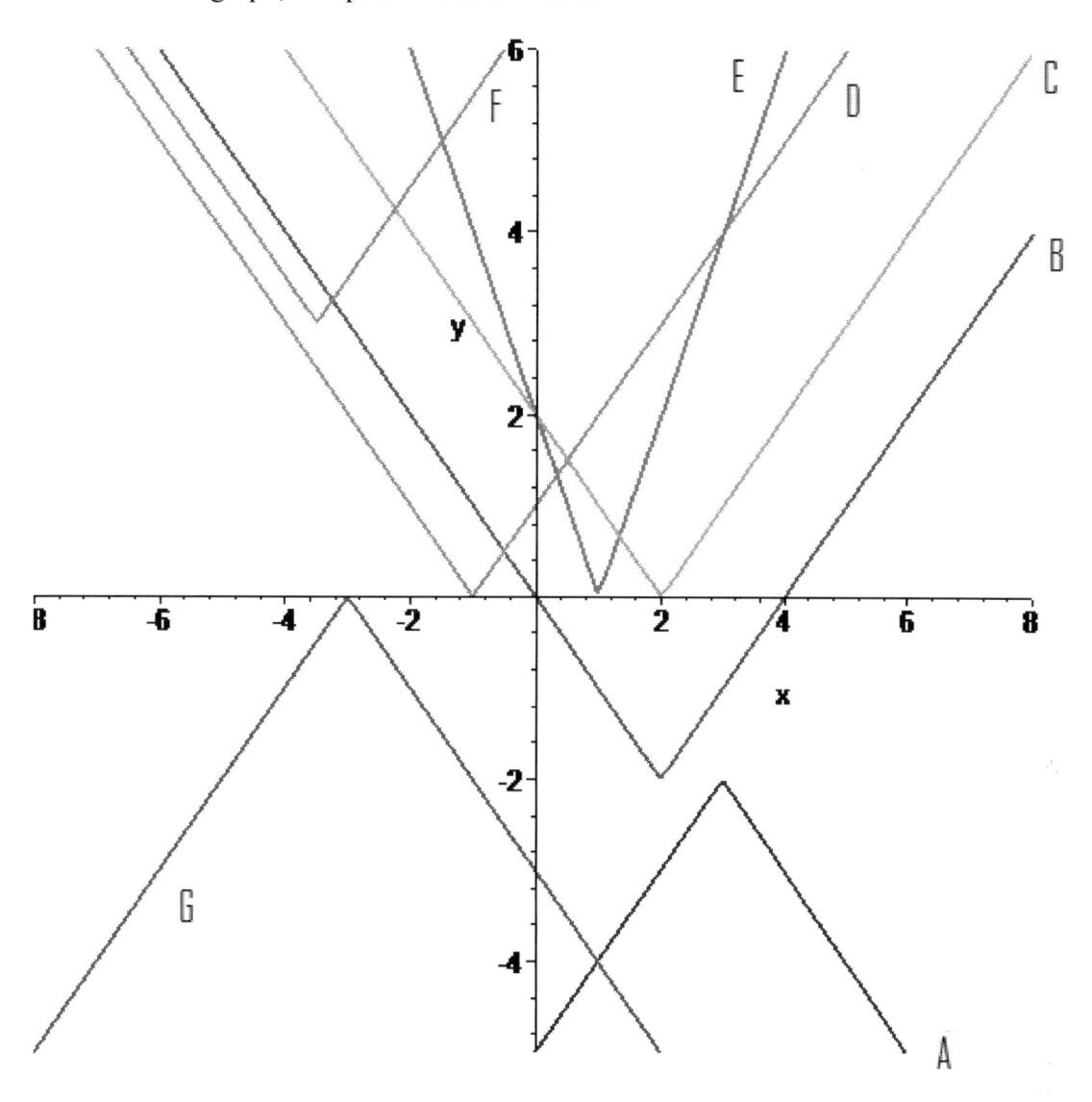

Function	On the graph
$f(x) = |x+1|$	
$f(x) = -|x-3|-2$	
$f(x) = |2x-2|$	
$f(x) = |x-2|-2$	
$f(x) = |x+3.5|+3$	
$-f(x) = |x+3|$	
$f(x) = |x-2|$	

7. Given the function $f(x) = |x|$

   a. Write the same function translated 2 positions up.

   b. Write the same function translated 2 positions left.

   c. Write the same function translated 4 positions up and 3 right.

   d. Sketch all 3 functions

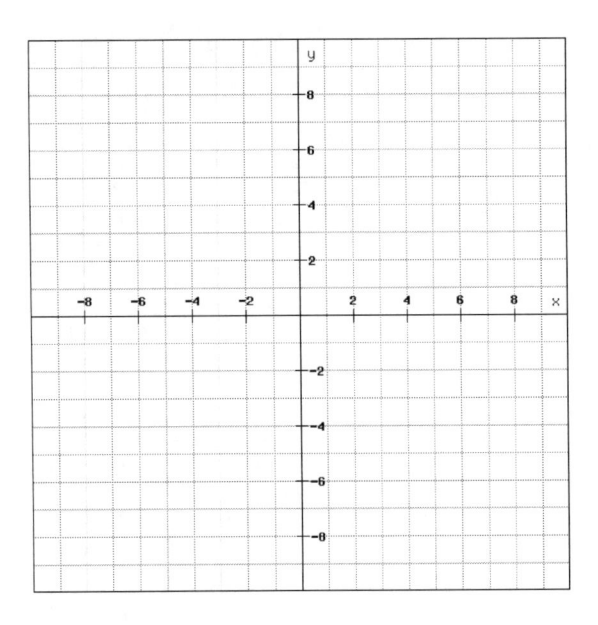

9. Given the function $f(x) = |-3x - 2|$

   a. Write the same function translated 1 positions up.

   b. Write the same function translated 3 positions left.

   c. Write the same function translated 6 positions up and 13 right.

   e. Sketch all 3 functions

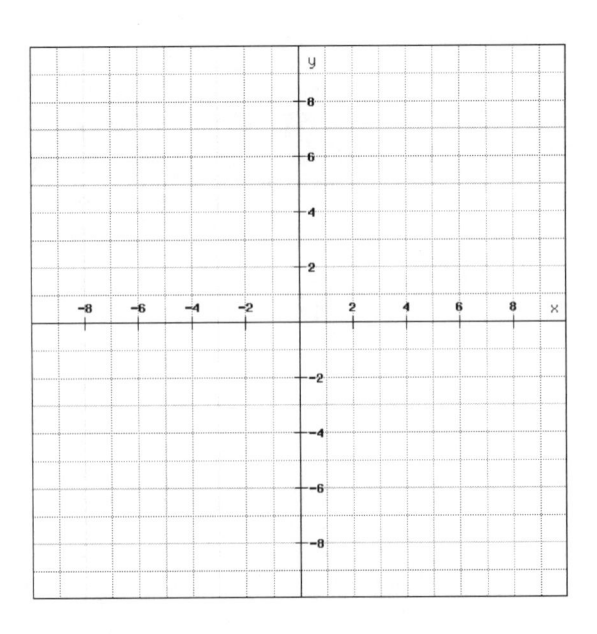

Analyze the following functions:

1. f(x) = |5|

Hybrid form: f(x) = {

Domain: _____ Range: _____

y intercept   Max/Min:(__, __)

x intercept(s):(__, __), (__, __)

Increases: _____ Decreases: _____

2. f(x) = |−3|

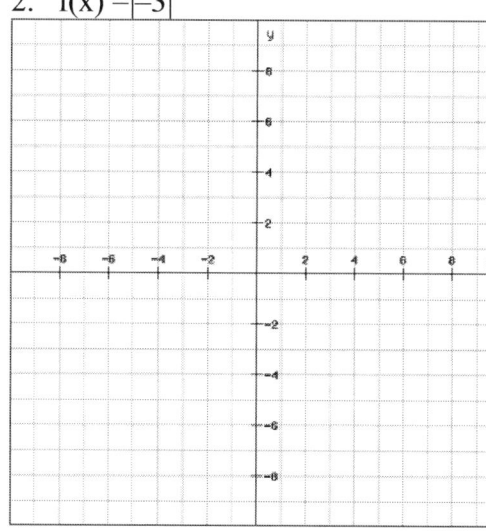

Hybrid form: f(x) = {

Domain: _____ Range: _____

y intercept   Max/Min:(__, __)

x intercept(s):(__, __), (__, __)

Increases: _____ Decreases: _____

3. f(x) = |5x|

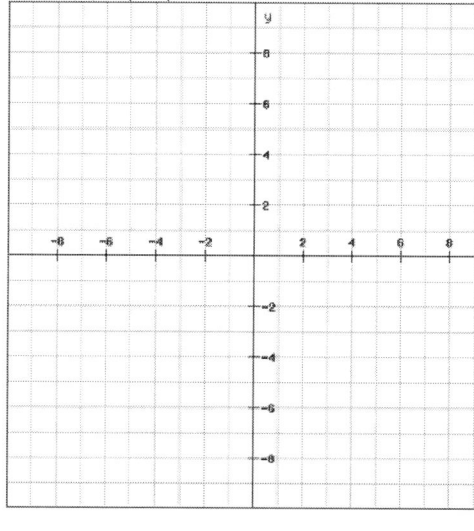

Hybrid form: f(x) = {

Domain: _____ Range: _____

y intercept   Max/Min:(__, __)

x intercept(s):(__, __), (__, __)

Increases: _____ Decreases: _____

4. f(x) = |5x+1|

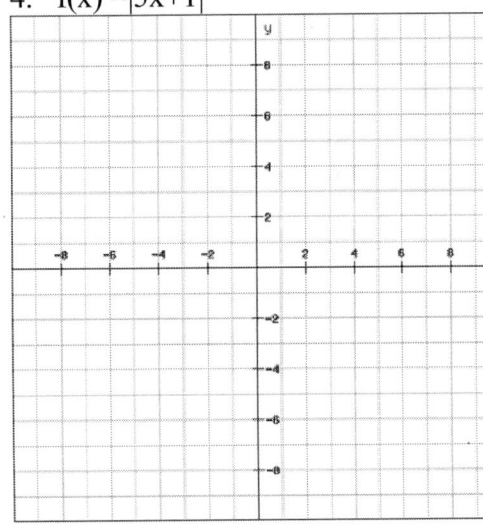

Hybrid form: f(x) = {

Domain: _____ Range: _____

y intercept _____ Max/Min:(__, __)

x intercept(s):(___, ___), (___, ___)

Increases: _____ Decreases: _____

5. f(x) = |−2x| + 1

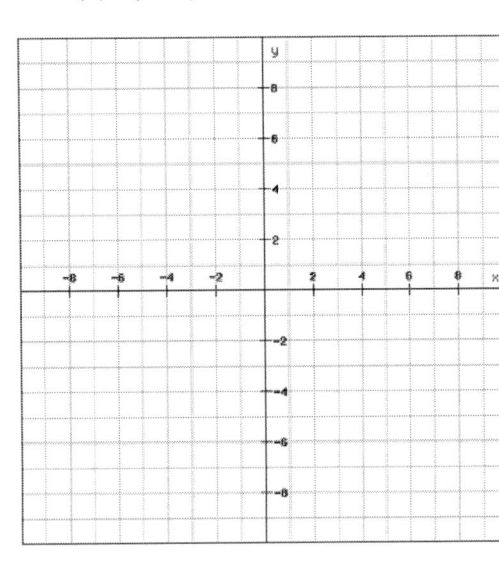

Hybrid form: f(x) = {

Domain: _____ Range: _____

y intercept _____ Max/Min:(__, __)

x intercept(s):(___, ___), (___, ___)

Increases: _____ Decreases: _____

6. f(x) = |−2x − 3|

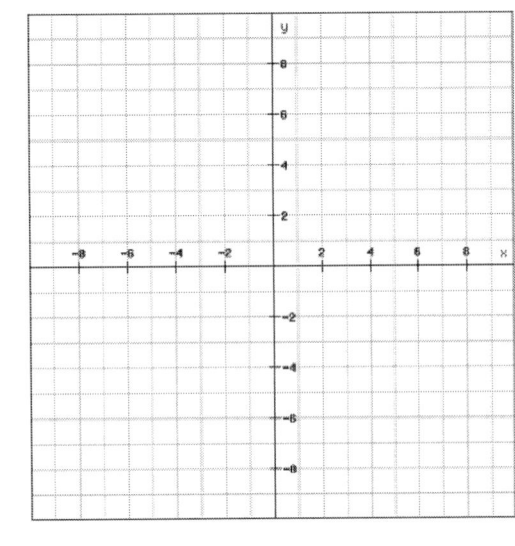

Hybrid form: f(x) = {

Domain: _____ Range: _____

y intercept _____ Max/Min:(__, __)

x intercept(s):(___, ___), (___, ___)

Increases: _____ Decreases: _____

7. $f(x) = |-2x + 3| - 2$

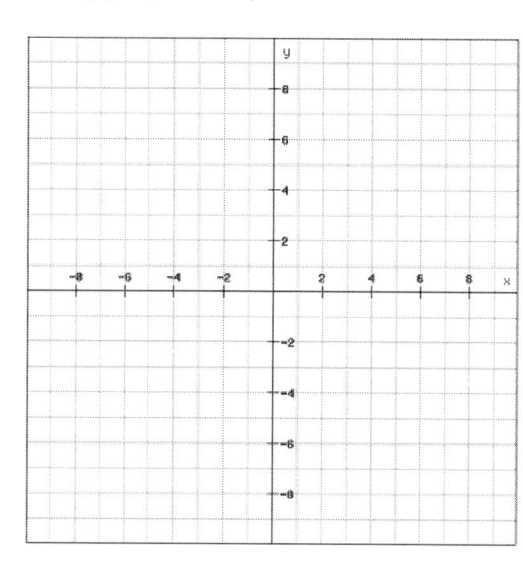

Hybrid form: f(x) = {

Domain: _____   Range: _____

y intercept _____   Max/Min:(__, __)

x intercept(s):(__, __), (__, __)

Increases: _____ Decreases: _____

8. $f(x) = |x|^2 + 2|x|$

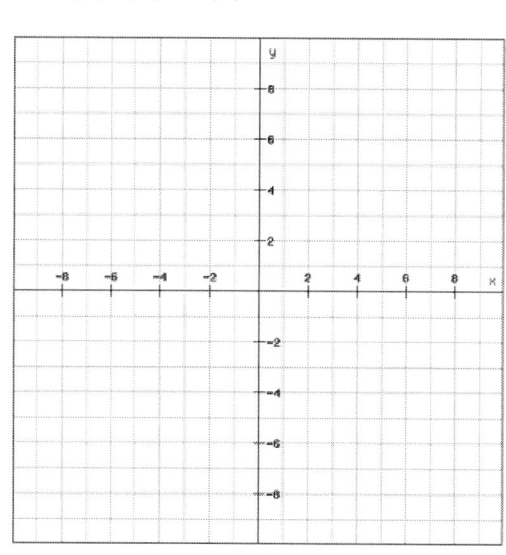

Hybrid form: f(x) = {

Domain: _____   Range: _____

y intercept _____   Max/Min:(__, __)

x intercept(s):(__, __), (__, __)

Increases: _____ Decreases: _____

9. $f(x) = |x|^2 + 7|x| - 1$

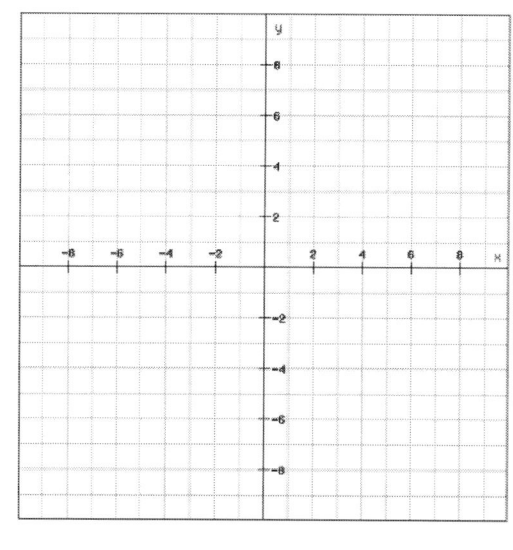

Hybrid form: f(x) = {

Domain: _____   Range: _____

y intercept _____   Max/Min:(__, __)

x intercept(s):(__, __), (__, __)

Increases: _____ Decreases: _____

10. $f(x) = |x^2 + 2x + 7|$

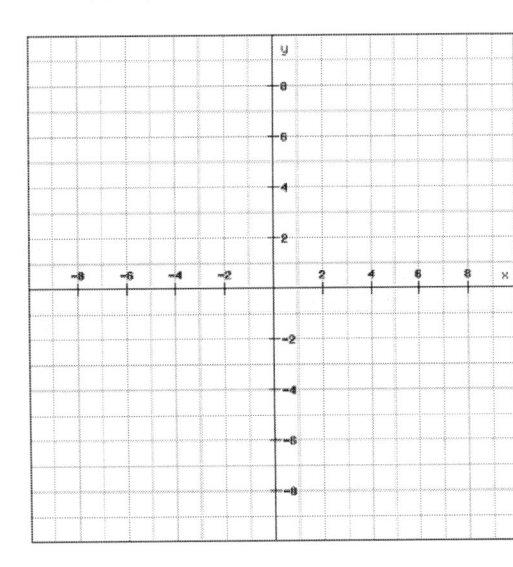

Hybrid form: $f(x) = \begin{cases} & \end{cases}$

Domain: _____ Range: _____

y intercept _____ Max/Min:(__, __)

x intercept(s):(__, __), (__, __)

Increases: _____ Decreases: _____

11. $f(x) = |x^2 + x - 1|$

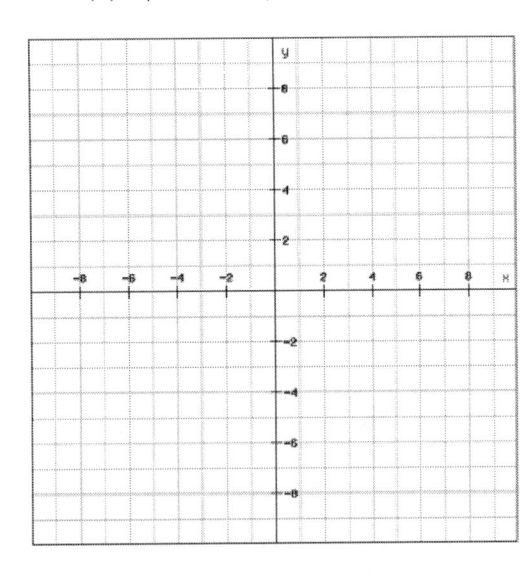

Hybrid form: $f(x) = \begin{cases} & \end{cases}$

Domain: _____ Range: _____

y intercept _____ Max/Min:(__, __)

x intercept(s):(__, __), (__, __)

Increases: _____ Decreases: _____

12. $f(x) = |x|^2 + 2|x| + 1$

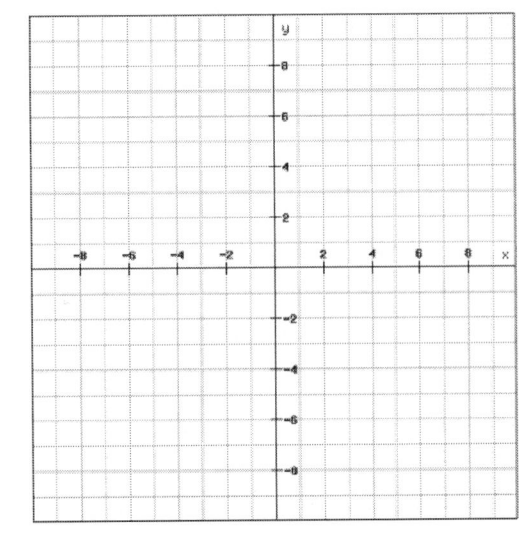

Hybrid form: $f(x) = \begin{cases} & \end{cases}$

Domain: _____ Range: _____

y intercept _____ Max/Min:(__, __)

x intercept(s):(__, __), (__, __)

Increases: _____ Decreases: _____

13. $f(x) = |x^2 + 1| + 2$

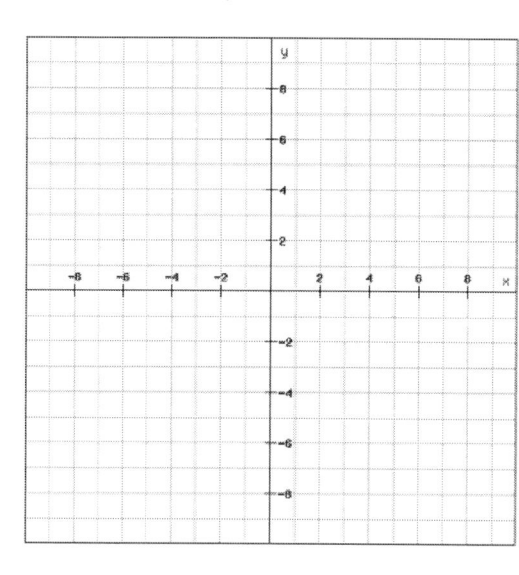

Hybrid form: $f(x) = \begin{cases} \end{cases}$

Domain: _____ Range: _____

y intercept   Max/Min:(__, __)

x intercept(s):(__, __), (__, __)

Increases: _____ Decreases: _____

14. $f(x) = |x|^2 - 1$

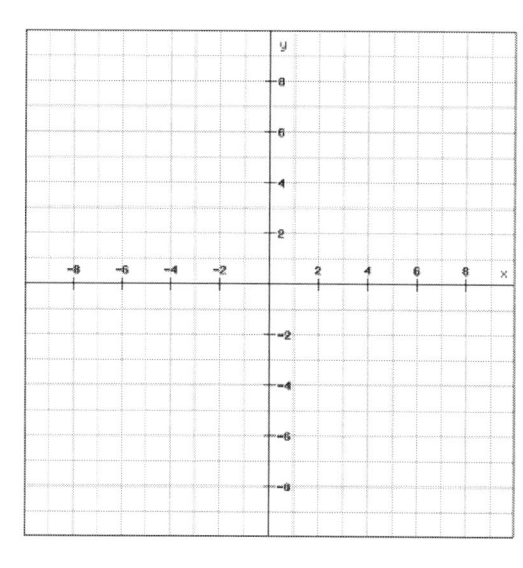

Hybrid form: $f(x) = \begin{cases} \end{cases}$

Domain: _____ Range: _____

y intercept   Max/Min:(__, __)

x intercept(s):(__, __), (__, __)

Increases: _____ Decreases: _____

15. $f(x) = |x^2 - 2|$

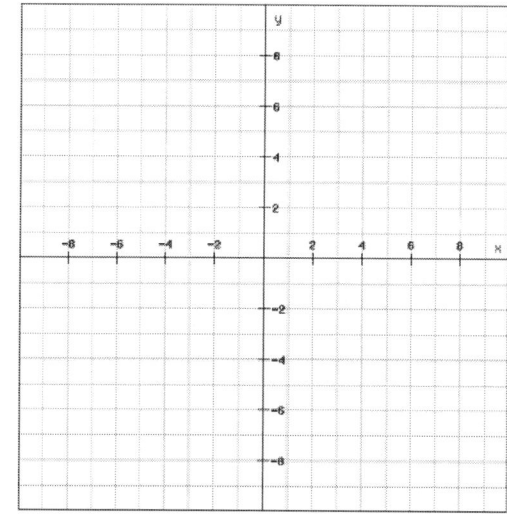

Hybrid form: $f(x) = \begin{cases} \end{cases}$

Domain: _____ Range: _____

y intercept   Max/Min:(__, __)

x intercept(s):(__, __), (__, __)

Increases: _____ Decreases: _____

16. f(x) = |x² − 2x|

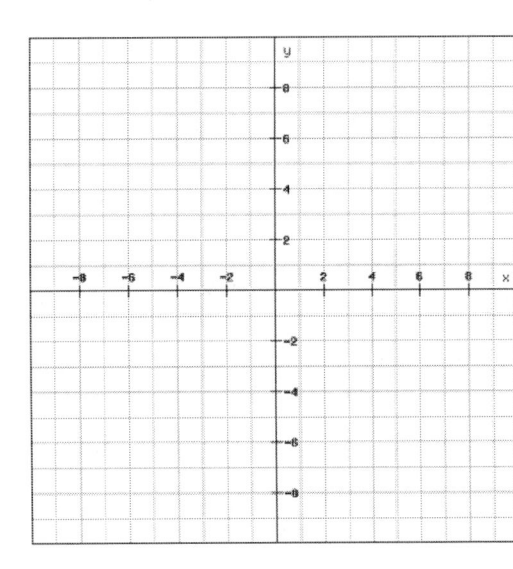

Hybrid form: f(x) = {

Domain: _____ Range: _____

y intercept _____ Max/Min:(__, __)

x intercept(s):(__, __), (__, __)

Increases: _____ Decreases: _____

17. f(x) = |5x² − 10x| − 2

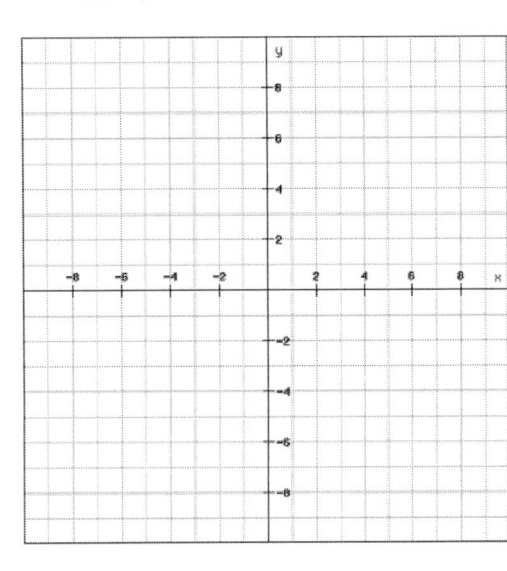

Hybrid form: f(x) = {

Domain: _____ Range: _____

y intercept _____ Max/Min:(__, __)

x intercept(s):(__, __), (__, __)

Increases: _____ Decreases: _____

18. f(x) = |−5x²|

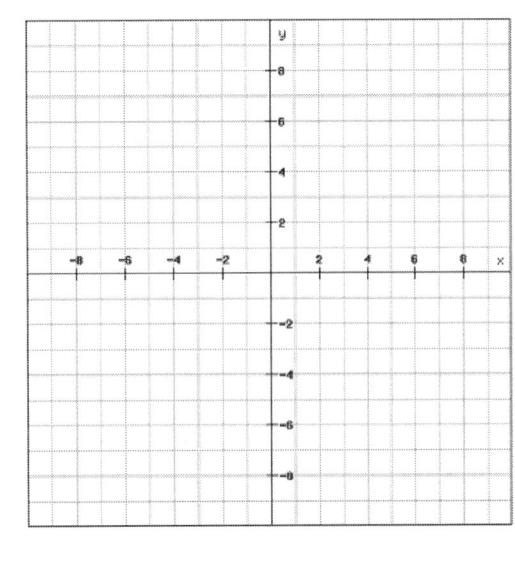

Hybrid form: f(x) = {

Domain: _____ Range: _____

y intercept _____ Max/Min:(__, __)

x intercept(s):(__, __), (__, __)

Increases: _____ Decreases: _____

19. $f(x) = |-x^2 + 6x - 8|$

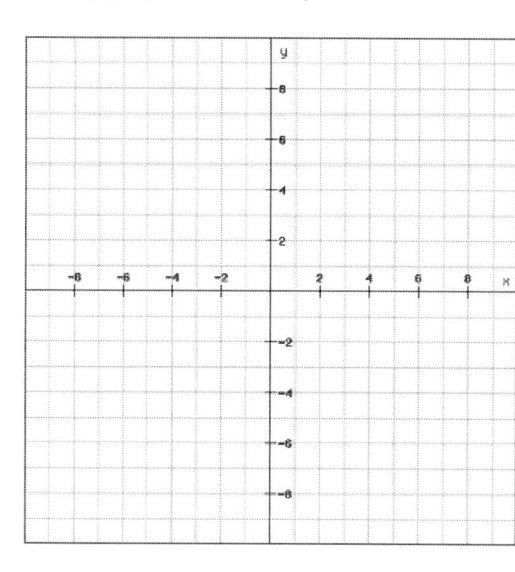

Hybrid form: $f(x) = \begin{cases} & \end{cases}$

Domain: _____ Range: _____

y intercept _____ Max/Min:(___, ___)

x intercept(s):(___, ___), (___, ___)

Increases: _____ Decreases: _____

20. $f(x) = -|x|^2 - 6|x| + 2$

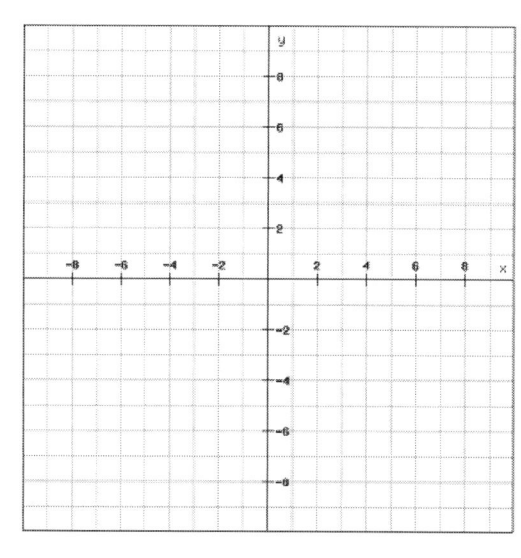

Hybrid form: $f(x) = \begin{cases} & \end{cases}$

Domain: _____ Range: _____

y intercept _____ Max/Min:(___, ___)

x intercept(s):(___, ___), (___, ___)

Increases: _____ Decreases: _____

21. $f(x) = |-x^2 + x - 5|$

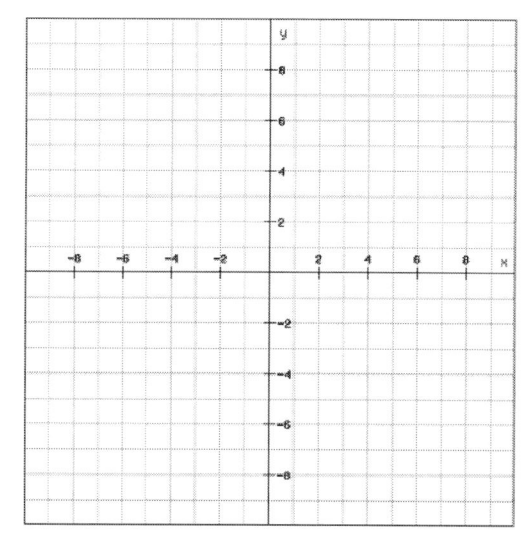

Hybrid form: $f(x) = \begin{cases} & \end{cases}$

Domain: _____ Range: _____

y intercept _____ Max/Min:(___, ___)

x intercept(s):(___, ___), (___, ___)

Increases: _____ Decreases: _____

22. $f(x) = |-x^2 - 4x - 4|$

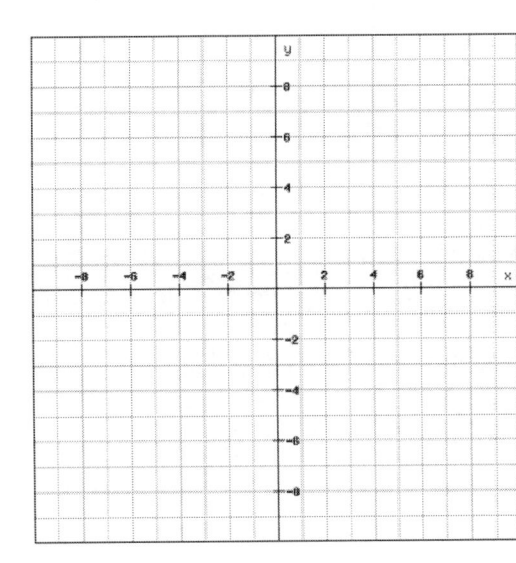

Hybrid form: $f(x) = \begin{cases} & \\ & \end{cases}$

Domain: _____ Range: _____

y intercept   Max/Min:(__, __)

x intercept(s):(__, __), (__, __)

Increases: _____ Decreases: _____

23. $f(x) = |-x^2 + 3|$

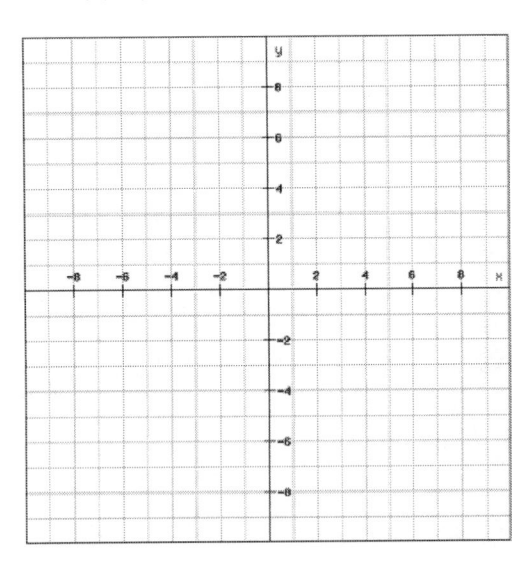

Hybrid form: $f(x) = \begin{cases} & \\ & \end{cases}$

Domain: _____ Range: _____

y intercept   Max/Min:(__, __)

x intercept(s):(__, __), (__, __)

Increases: _____ Decreases: _____

24. $f(x) = |x| - |x|^2$

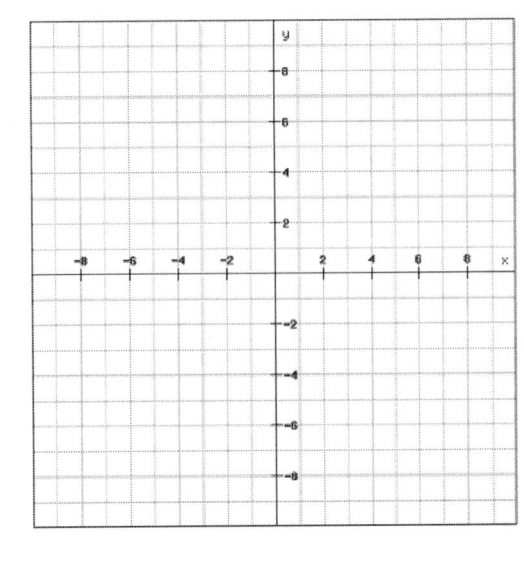

Hybrid form: $f(x) = \begin{cases} & \\ & \end{cases}$

Domain: _____ Range: _____

y intercept   Max/Min:(__, __)

x intercept(s):(__, __), (__, __)

Increases: _____ Decreases: _____

25. f(x) = |x − 6| − 2

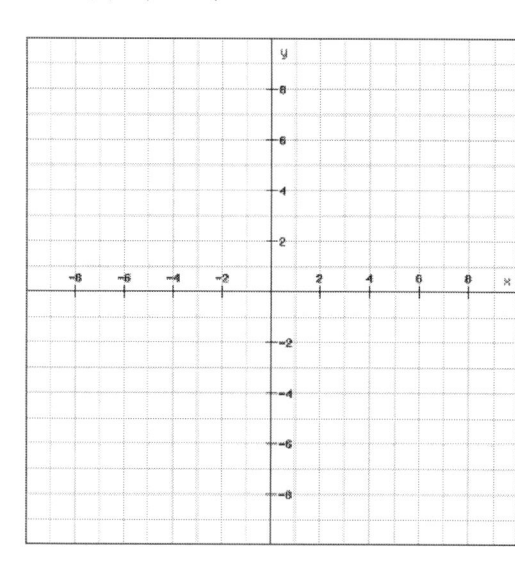

Hybrid form: f(x) = {

Domain: _____   Range: _____

y intercept   Max/Min:(__, __)

x intercept(s):(___, ___), (___, ___)

Increases: _____ Decreases: _____

26. f(x) = − |x − 3| + 5

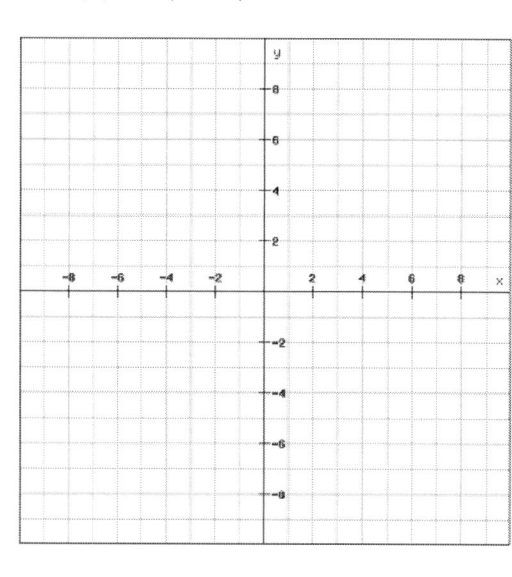

Hybrid form: f(x) = {

Domain: _____   Range: _____

y intercept   Max/Min:(__, __)

x intercept(s):(___, ___), (___, ___)

Increases: _____ Decreases: _____

27. f(x) = |5x² − 3|

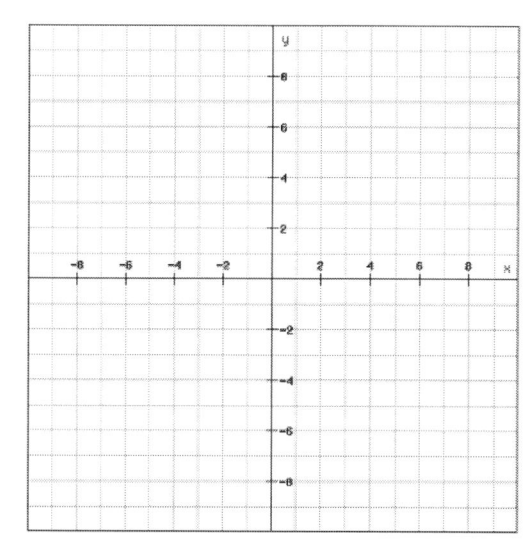

Hybrid form: f(x) = {

Domain: _____   Range: _____

y intercept   Max/Min:(__, __)

x intercept(s):(___, ___), (___, ___)

Increases: _____ Decreases: _____

28. $f(x) = |3x^2| + 1$

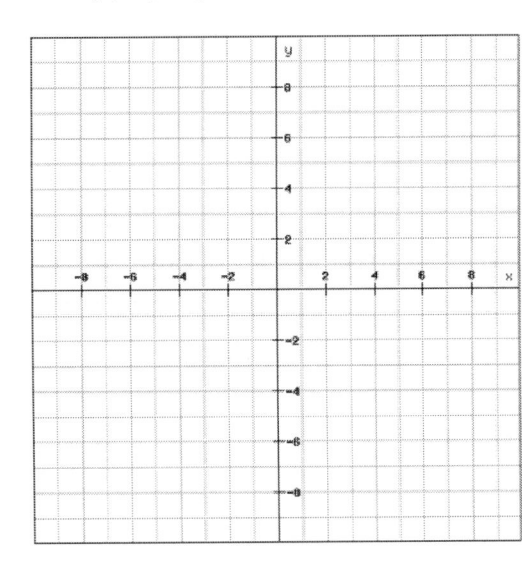

Hybrid form: $f(x) = \begin{cases} & \\ & \end{cases}$

Domain: _____ Range: _____

y intercept   Max/Min:(__, __)

x intercept(s):(__, __), (__, __)

Increases: _____ Decreases: _____

29. $f(x) = |x^2 + 3x + 4|$

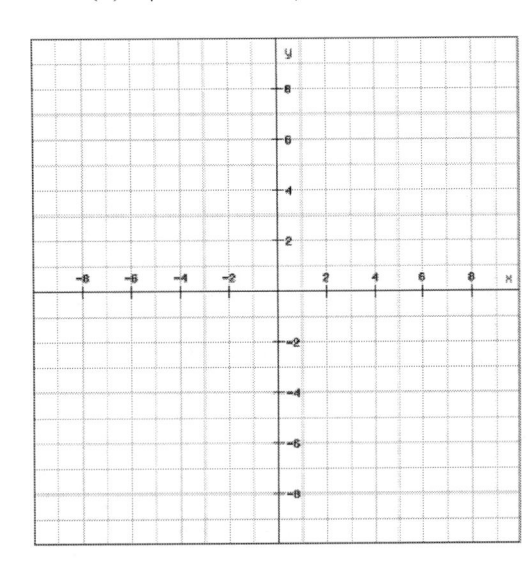

Hybrid form: $f(x) = \begin{cases} & \\ & \end{cases}$

Domain: _____ Range: _____

y intercept   Max/Min:(__, __)

x intercept(s):(__, __), (__, __)

Increases: _____ Decreases: _____

30. $f(x) = -|x - 5|$

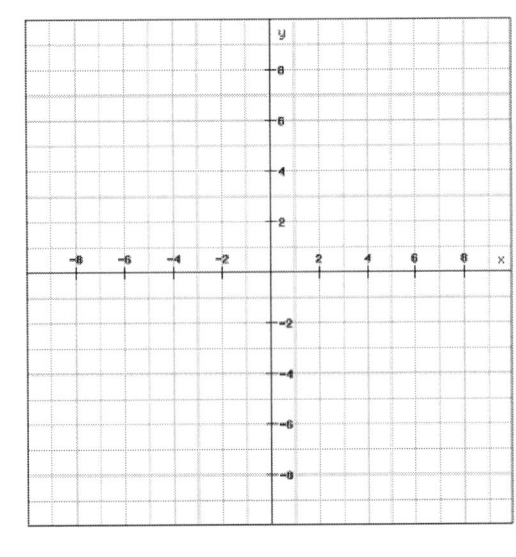

Hybrid form: $f(x) = \begin{cases} & \\ & \end{cases}$

Domain: _____ Range: _____

y intercept   Max/Min:(__, __)

x intercept(s):(__, __), (__, __)

Increases: _____ Decreases: _____

31. f(x) = |−4x + 3| + 3

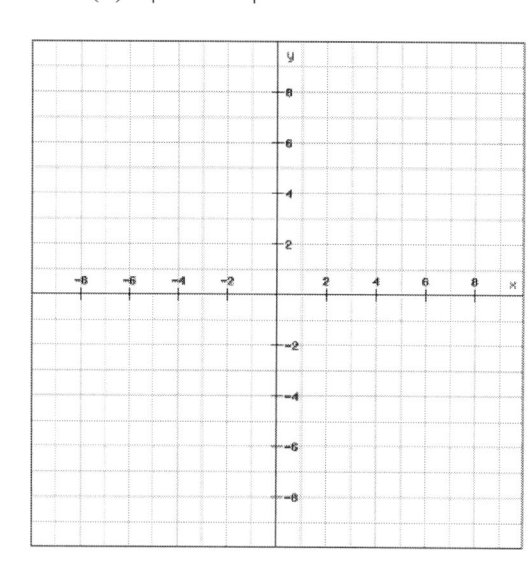

Hybrid form: f(x) = {

Domain: _____ Range: _____

y intercept   Max/Min:(__, __)

x intercept(s):(___, ___), (___, ___)

Increases: _____ Decreases: _____

32. f(x) = |−12x − 13|

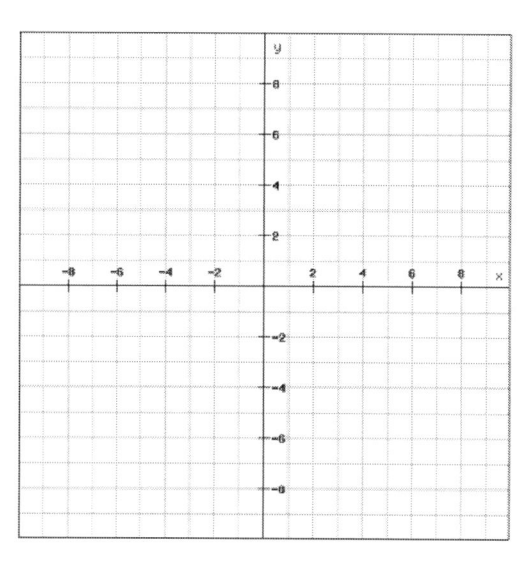

Hybrid form: f(x) = {

Domain: _____ Range: _____

y intercept   Max/Min:(__, __)

x intercept(s):(___, ___), (___, ___)

Increases: _____ Decreases: _____

33. f(x) = |x + 3| + |x + 2|

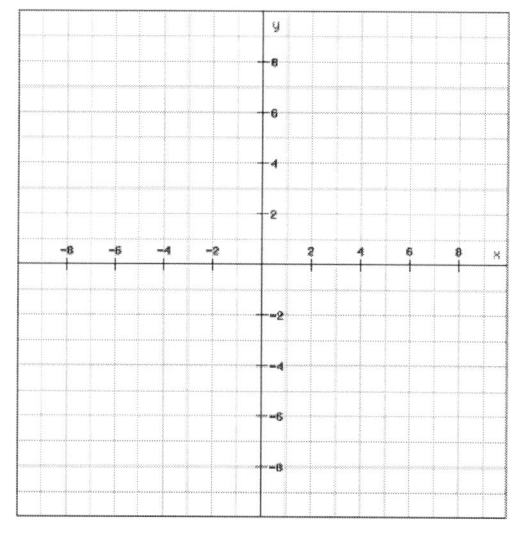

Hybrid form: f(x) = {

Domain: _____ Range: _____

y intercept   Max/Min:(__, __)

x intercept(s):(___, ___), (___, ___)

Increases: _____ Decreases: _____

34. f(x) = |−2x − 2| − |2x − 1|

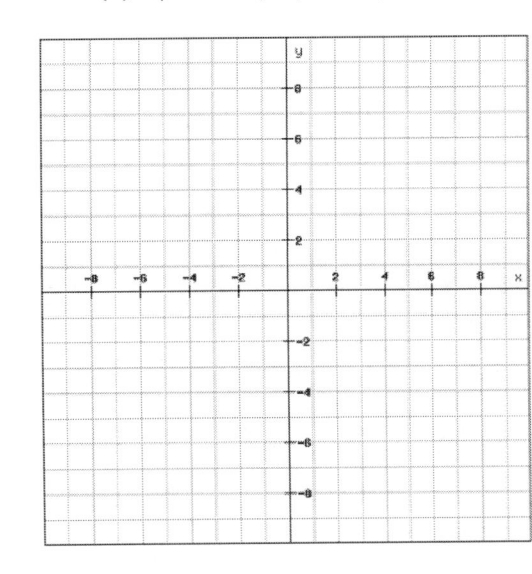

Hybrid form: f(x) = {

Domain: _____   Range: _____

y intercept   Max/Min:(__, __)

x intercept(s):(__, __), (__, __)

Increases: _____ Decreases: _____

35. f(x) = |x + 3| + |2x + 1|

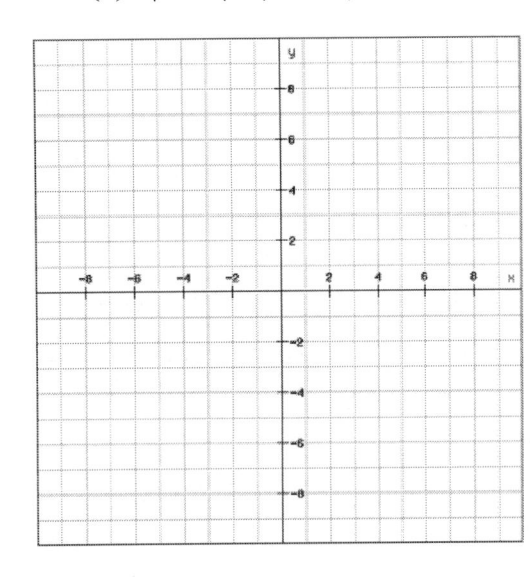

Hybrid form: f(x) = {

Domain: _____   Range: _____

y intercept   Max/Min:(__, __)

x intercept(s):(__, __), (__, __)

Increases: _____ Decreases: _____

36. f(x) = |−2x + 4| − |3x + 2|

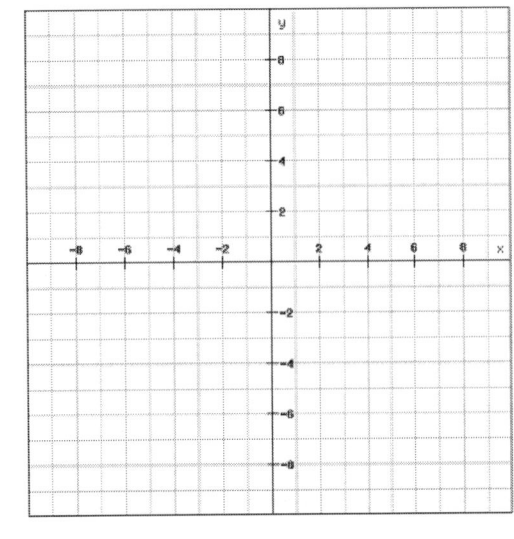

Hybrid form: f(x) = {

Domain: _____   Range: _____

y intercept   Max/Min:(__, __)

x intercept(s):(__, __), (__, __)

Increases: _____ Decreases: _____

37. f(x) = |3x – 4| + |2x – 2|

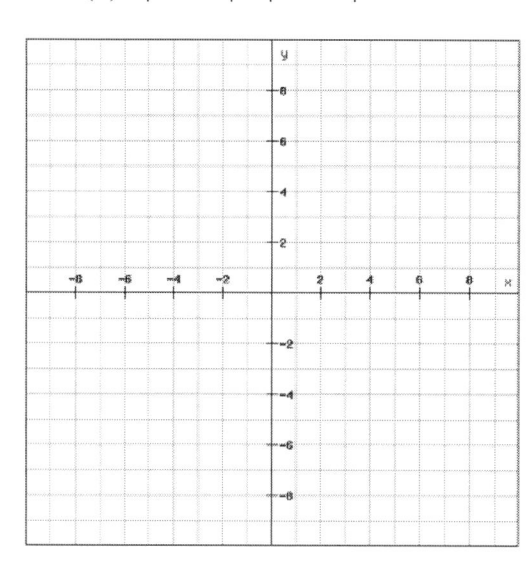

Hybrid form: f(x) = {

Domain: _____   Range: _____

y intercept   Max/Min:(__, __)

x intercept(s):(__, __), (__, __)

Increases: _____ Decreases: _____

38. f(x) = |x + 1||x + 2|

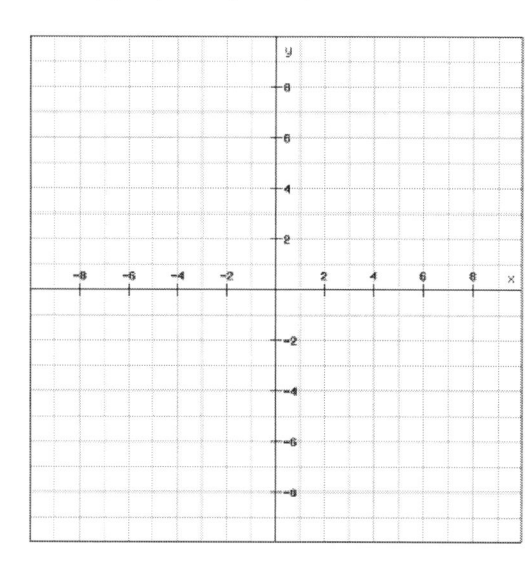

Hybrid form: f(x) = {

Domain: _____   Range: _____

y intercept   Max/Min:(__, __)

x intercept(s):(__, __), (__, __)

Increases: _____ Decreases: _____

39. f(x) = – |x + 1||x + 2|

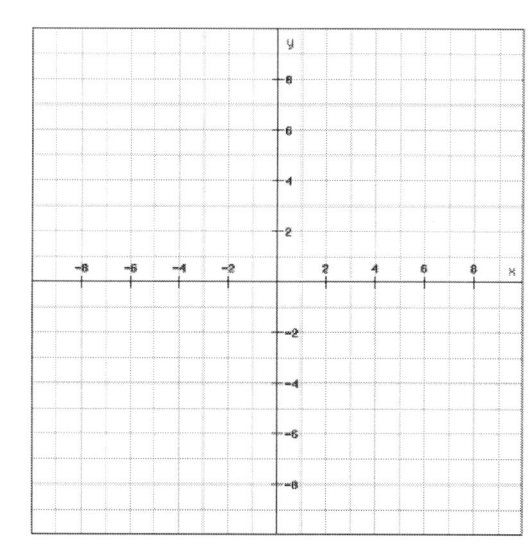

Hybrid form: f(x) = {

Domain: _____   Range: _____

y intercept   Max/Min:(__, __)

x intercept(s):(__, __), (__, __)

Increases: _____ Decreases: _____

2.6. – RATIONAL FUNCTIONS

1. Given the functions: $f(x) = \dfrac{1}{x}$, $g(x) = \dfrac{2}{x}$, Complete the following table:

x	−10	−2	−1	−0.5	−0.1	−0.01	0	0.01	0.1	1	2	10
f(x)												
g(x)												

- Sketch the points of the table on a graph.

- State the domain of the functions: : f(x):_____ , g(x):_____

- State the y intercepts: f(x): (____ , ____), g(x): (____ , ____)

- State the x intercept(s): f(x): (____ , ____), g(x): (____ , ____)

- Write the corresponding limits and the equation of the vertical asymptote:

  f(x): _____   g(x): _____

- Write the corresponding limits and the equation of the horizontal asymptote: ____

  f(x): _____   g(x): _____

- The functions are increasing on the interval: f(x):_____ , g(x):_____

- The functions are decreasing on the interval: f(x):_____ , g(x):_____

- State the range of the functions: f(x):_____ , g(x):_____

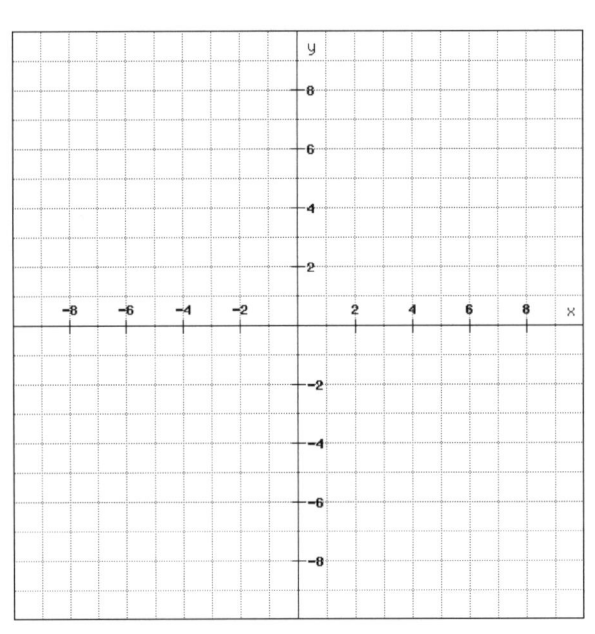

208

2. Given the functions: $f(x) = -3\dfrac{1}{x}$, $g(x) = \dfrac{-2}{x}$, Complete the following table:

x	−10	−2	−1	−0.5	−0.1	−0.01	0	0.01	0.1	1	2	10
f(x)												
g(x)												

- Sketch the points of the table on a graph.

- State the domain of the functions: : f(x):_____, g(x):_____

- State the y intercepts: f(x): (____, ____), g(x): (____, ____)

- State the x intercept(s): f(x): (____, ____), g(x): (____, ____)

- Write the corresponding limits and the equation of the vertical asymptote:

  f(x): _____   g(x): _____

- Write the corresponding limits and the equation of the horizontal asymptote: ____

  f(x): _____   g(x): _____

- The functions are increasing on the interval: f(x):_____, g(x):_____

- The functions are decreasing on the interval: f(x):_____, g(x):_____

- State the range of the functions: f(x):_____, g(x):_____

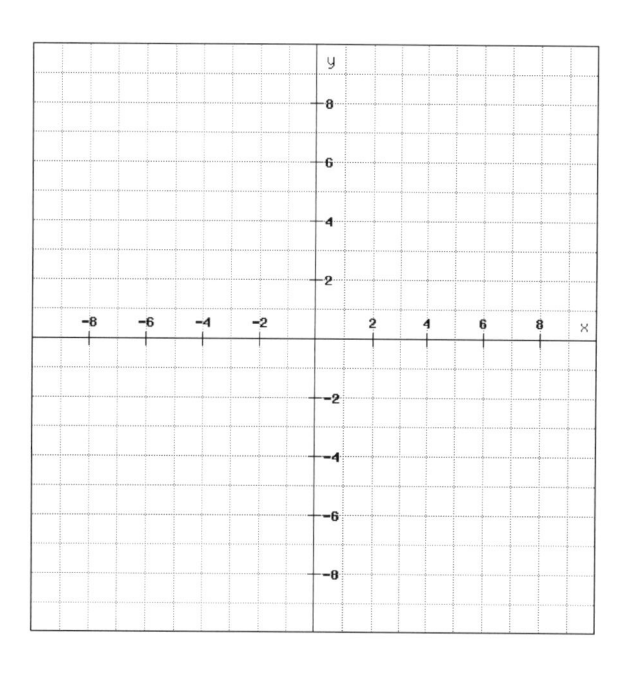

3. Given the functions: $f(x) = \dfrac{1}{x} + 2$, $g(x) = \dfrac{2}{x} - 3$, Complete the following table:

x	−10	−2	−1	−0.5	−0.1	−0.01	0	0.01	0.1	1	2	10
f(x)												
g(x)												

- Sketch the points of the table on a graph.

- State the domain of the functions: : f(x):_____, g(x):_____

- State the y intercepts: f(x): (____, ____), g(x): (____, ____)

- State the x intercept(s): f(x): (____, ____), g(x): (____, ____)

- Write the corresponding limits and the equation of the vertical asymptote:

    f(x): _____   g(x): _____

- Write the corresponding limits and the equation of the horizontal asymptote: ____

    f(x): _____   g(x): _____

- The functions are increasing on the interval: f(x):_____, g(x):_____

- The functions are decreasing on the interval: f(x):_____, g(x):_____

- State the range of the functions: f(x):_____, g(x):_____

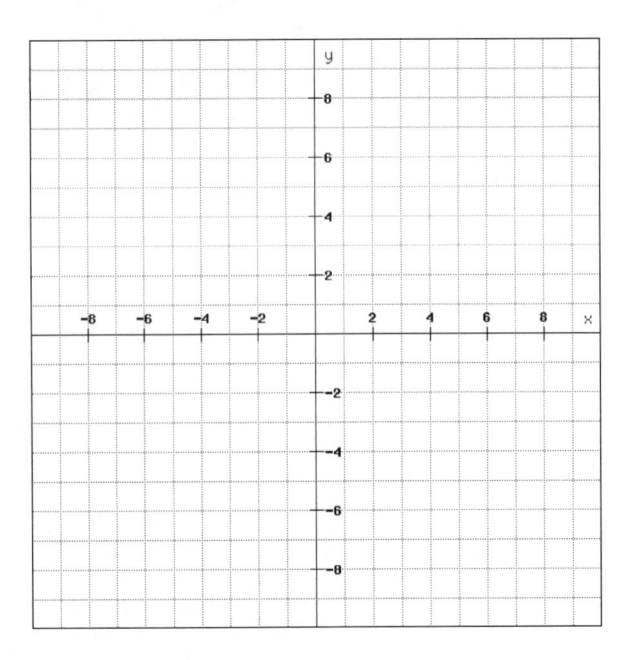

4. Given the functions: $f(x) = \dfrac{1}{x+2}$, $g(x) = \dfrac{-2}{x-4}$, Complete the following table values:

x									
f(x)									
g(x)									

- Sketch the points of the table on a graph.

- State the domain of the functions: : f(x):_____, g(x):_____

- State the y intercepts: f(x): (____, ____), g(x): (____, ____)

- State the x intercept(s): f(x): (____, ____), g(x): (____, ____)

- Write the corresponding limits and the equation of the vertical asymptote:

  f(x): _____   g(x): _____

- Write the corresponding limits and the equation of the horizontal asymptote:

  f(x): _____   g(x): _____

- The functions are increasing on the interval: f(x):_____, g(x):_____

- The functions are decreasing on the interval: f(x):_____, g(x):_____

- State the range of the functions: f(x):_____, g(x):_____

211

5. Given the functions: $f(x) = \dfrac{1}{x-3} + 2$, $g(x) = \dfrac{4}{x-5} - 2$, Complete the following table:

x										
f(x)										
g(x)										

- Sketch the points of the table on a graph.

- State the domain of the functions: : f(x):_____, g(x):_____

- State the y intercepts: f(x): (____, ____), g(x): (____, ____)

- State the x intercept(s): f(x): (____, ____), g(x): (____, ____)

- Write the corresponding limits and the equation of the vertical asymptote:

    f(x): _____   g(x): _____

- Write the corresponding limits and the equation of the horizontal asymptote: ____

    f(x): _____   g(x): _____

- The functions are increasing on the interval: f(x):_____, g(x):_____

- The functions are decreasing on the interval: f(x):_____, g(x):_____

- State the range of the functions: f(x):_____, g(x):_____

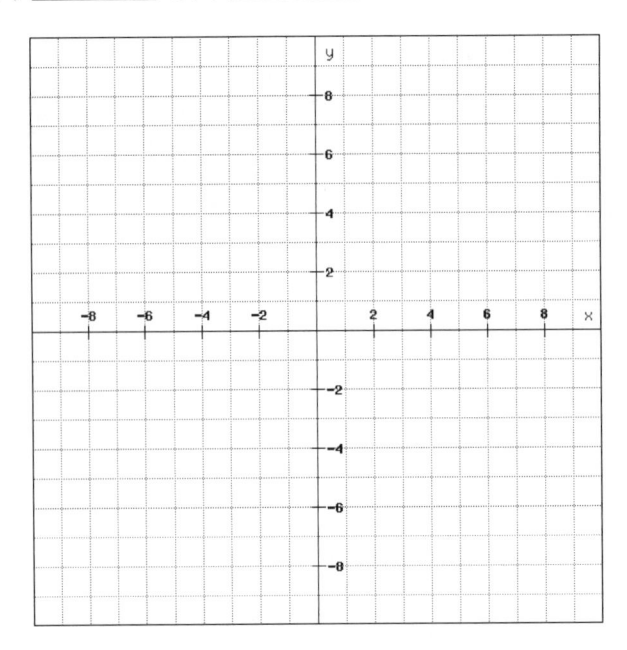

212

6. Given the function $f(x) = \dfrac{1}{x}$ Write the same function translated:

   a. 2 positions up: _____ 2 positions left: _____

   b. 4 positions up and 3 right: _____

7. Given the function $f(x) = \dfrac{3}{x}$

   a. 3 positions down: _____ 5 positions right: _____

   b. 0.5 positions up and $\dfrac{3}{7}$ right: _____

8. Given the function $f(x) = \dfrac{-3}{x} + 1$

   a. 6 positions down: _____ 5 positions left: _____

   b. 12 positions up and 10 right: _____

   c. Write in different forms: _____

9. Given the function $f(x) = \dfrac{7}{2x} + 5$

   a. 1 positions down: _____ 7 positions right: _____

   b. 2 positions up and 1 left: _____

   c. Write in different forms: _____

10. Given the function $f(x) = \dfrac{x+3}{2x+6}$

    a. State its domain: _____

    b. Write in different forms: _____

    c. Sketch the function. Is this a Rational function? Explain

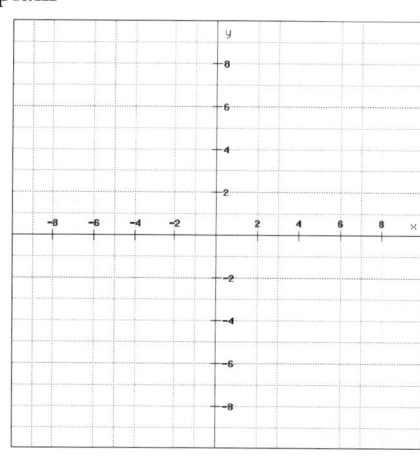

213

Analyze the following functions:

1. $f(x) = \dfrac{1}{2x}$

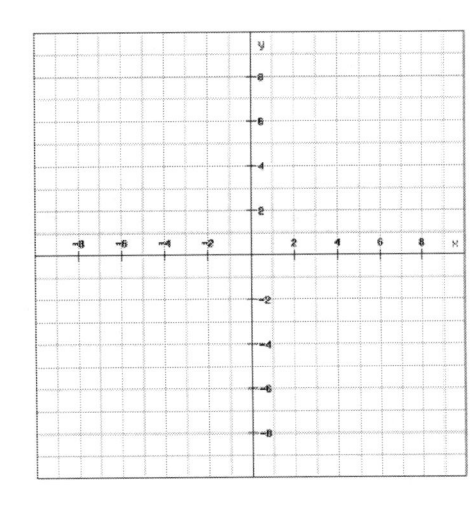

Horizontal asymptote: _____ Domain: _____
Lim   Range: _____
Lim   Increases: _____
Vertical asymptote: _____ Decreases: _____
Lim   y intercept:(___, ___)
Lim   x intercept:(___, ___)

2. $f(x) = -2\dfrac{1}{x}$

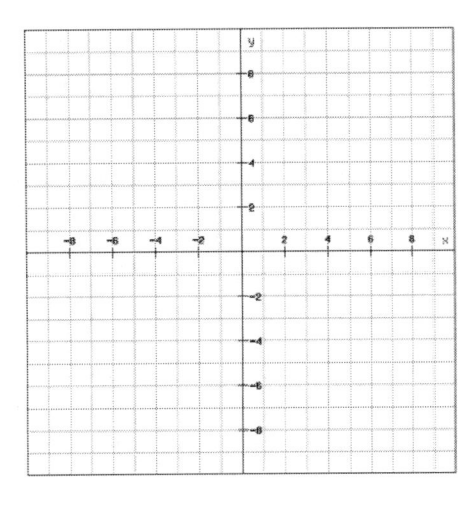

Horizontal asymptote: _____ Domain: _____
Lim   Range: _____
Lim   Increases: _____
Vertical asymptote: _____ Decreases: _____
Lim   y intercept:(___, ___)
Lim   x intercept:(___, ___)

3. $f(x) = \dfrac{1}{2+x}$

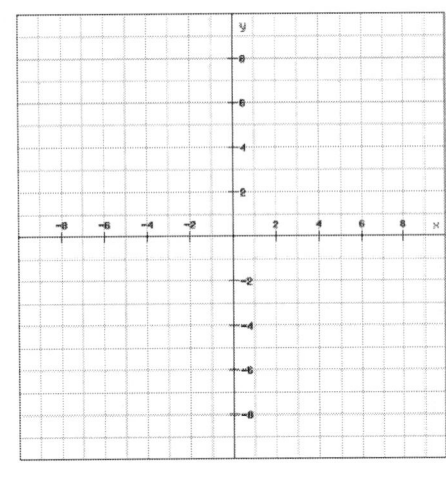

Horizontal asymptote: _____ Domain: _____
Lim   Range: _____
Lim   Increases: _____
Vertical asymptote: _____ Decreases: _____
Lim   y intercept:(___, ___)
Lim   x intercept:(___, ___)

4. $f(x) = \dfrac{1}{1-x}$

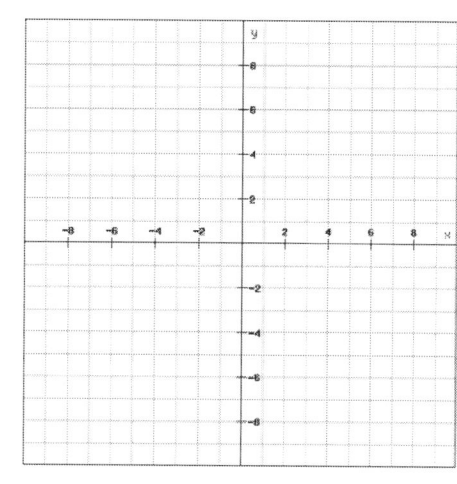

Horizontal asymptote: _____ Domain: _____
Lim
Range: _____
Lim
Increases: _____
Vertical asymptote: _____ Decreases: _____
Lim
y intercept:(___, ___)
Lim
x intercept:(___, ___)

5. $f(x) = -\dfrac{2}{x+1}$

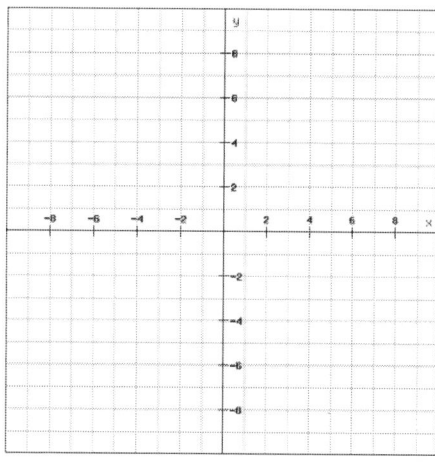

Horizontal asymptote: _____ Domain: _____
Lim
Range: _____
Lim
Increases: _____
Vertical asymptote: _____ Decreases: _____
Lim
y intercept:(___, ___)
Lim
x intercept:(___, ___)

6. $f(x) = \dfrac{5}{2x} + 1$

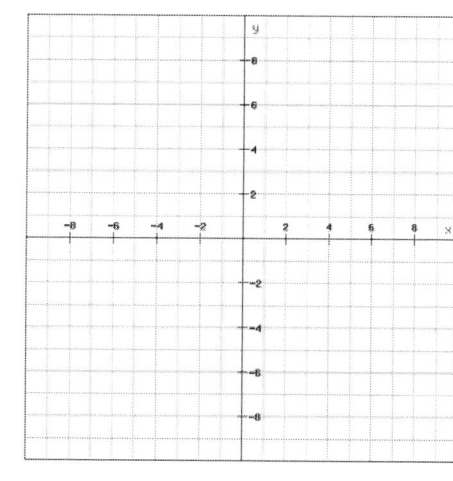

Horizontal asymptote: _____ Domain: _____
Lim
Range: _____
Lim
Increases: _____
Vertical asymptote: _____ Decreases: _____
Lim
y intercept:(___, ___)
Lim
x intercept:(___, ___)

7. $f(x) = -\dfrac{2x}{x+1}$ (use division to write it in the form $f(x) = \dfrac{a}{mx+b} + c$)

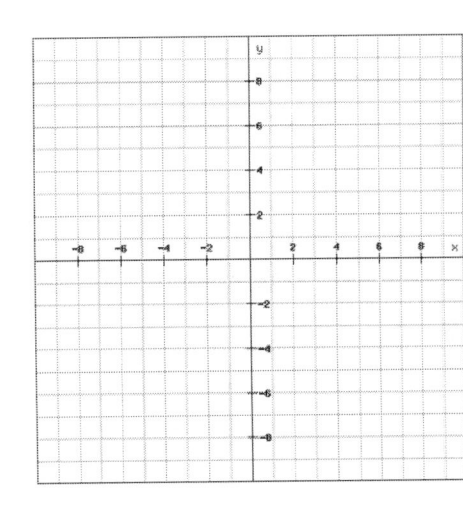

Horizontal asymptote:_____ Domain: _____

Lim

Range: _____

Lim

Increases: _____

Vertical asymptote: _____ Decreases: _____

Lim

y intercept:(___, ___)

Lim

x intercept:(___, ___)

8. $f(x) = \dfrac{2-x}{x+3}$ (use division/otherwise to write it in the form $f(x) = \dfrac{a}{mx+b} + c$)

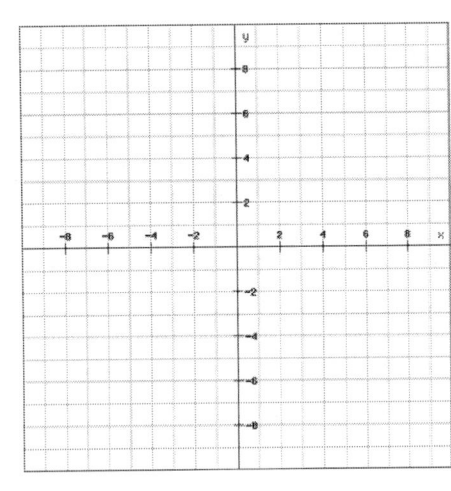

Horizontal asymptote:_____ Domain: _____

Lim

Range: _____

Lim

Increases: _____

Vertical asymptote: _____ Decreases: _____

Lim

y intercept:(___, ___)

Lim

x intercept:(___, ___)

9. $f(x) = \dfrac{2}{7-x} + 4$

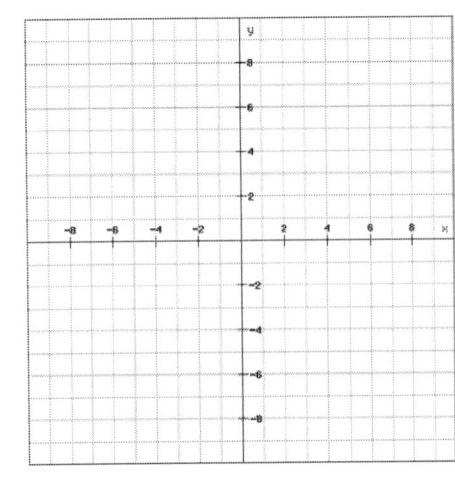

Horizontal asymptote:_____ Domain: _____

Lim

Range: _____

Lim

Increases: _____

Vertical asymptote: _____ Decreases: _____

Lim

y intercept:(___, ___)

Lim

x intercept:(___, ___)

10. $f(x) = \dfrac{3x+3}{2x-1}$ (use division/otherwise to write it in the form $f(x) = \dfrac{a}{mx+b} + c$)

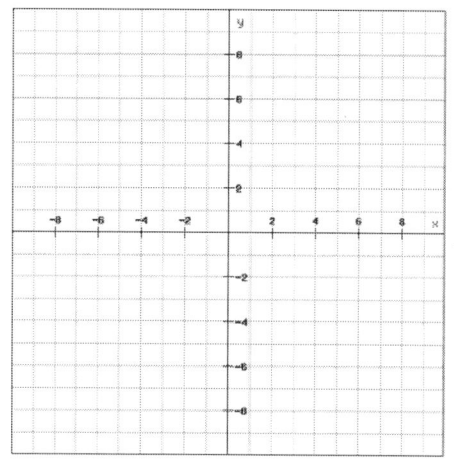

Horizontal asymptote:_____ Domain:_____
Lim
Range:_____
Lim
Increases:_____
Vertical asymptote:_____ Decreases:_____
Lim
y intercept:(___, ___)
Lim
x intercept:(___, ___)

11. $f(x) = -\dfrac{4}{x+4} - 2$

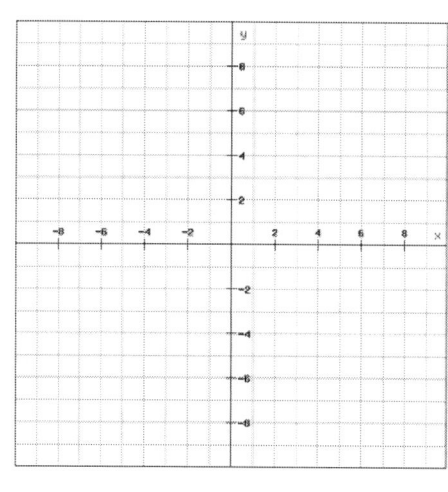

Horizontal asymptote:_____ Domain:_____
Lim
Range:_____
Lim
Increases:_____
Vertical asymptote:_____ Decreases:_____
Lim
y intercept:(___, ___)
Lim
x intercept:(___, ___)

12. $f(x) = \dfrac{x^2 - 2x}{x-2}$

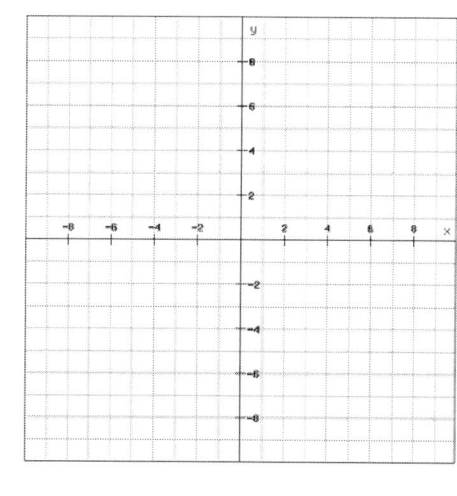

Horizontal asymptote:_____ Domain:_____
Lim
Range:_____
Lim
Increases:_____
Vertical asymptote:_____ Decreases:_____
Lim
y intercept:(___, ___)
Lim
x intercept:(___, ___)

13. $f(x) = \dfrac{8x+3}{4x-2}$ (use division/otherwise to write it in the form $f(x) = \dfrac{a}{mx+b} + c$)

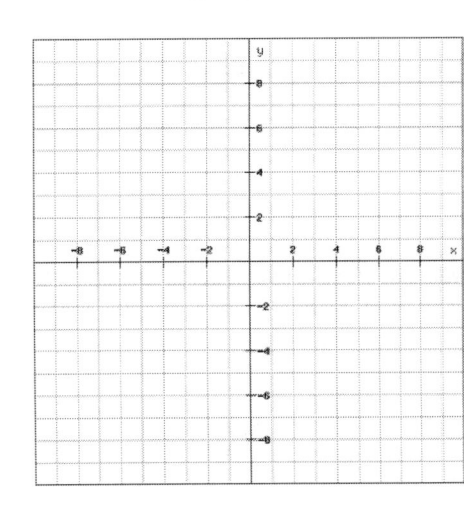

Horizontal asymptote:_____ Domain:_____
Lim
Range:_____
Lim
Increases:_____
Vertical asymptote:_____ Decreases:_____
Lim
y intercept:(___, ___)
Lim
x intercept:(___, ___)

14. $f(x) = \dfrac{x-2}{x-3}$ (use division/otherwise to write it in the form $f(x) = \dfrac{a}{mx+b} + c$)

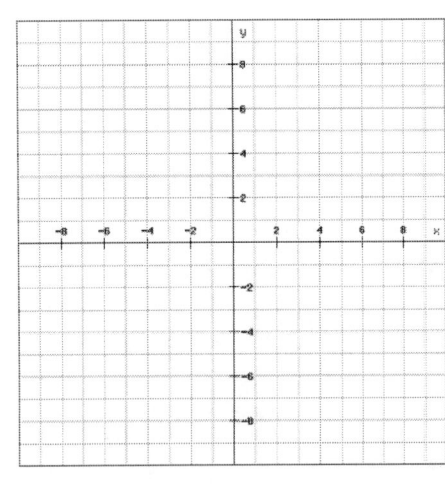

Horizontal asymptote:_____ Domain:_____
Lim
Range:_____
Lim
Increases:_____
Vertical asymptote:_____ Decreases:_____
Lim
y intercept:(___, ___)
Lim
x intercept:(___, ___)

15. $f(x) = \dfrac{3x-5}{4x+3}$ (use division/otherwise to write it in the form $f(x) = \dfrac{a}{mx+b} + c$)

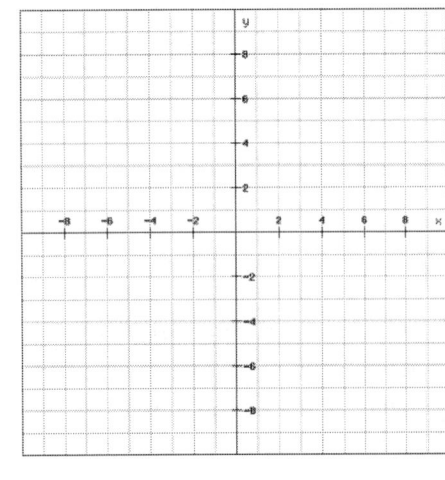

Horizontal asymptote:_____ Domain:_____
Lim
Range:_____
Lim
Increases:_____
Vertical asymptote:_____ Decreases:_____
Lim
y intercept:(___, ___)
Lim
x intercept:(___, ___)

16. $f(x) = \dfrac{6}{4x+3} - 5$

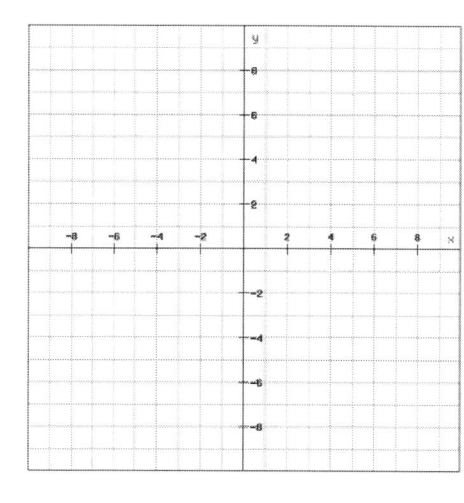

Horizontal asymptote:_____ Domain:_____

Lim

Lim

Range:_____

Increases:_____

Vertical asymptote:_____ Decreases:_____

Lim

y intercept:(___, ___)

Lim

x intercept:(___, ___)

17. $f(x) = \dfrac{3x - x^2}{x - 3}$

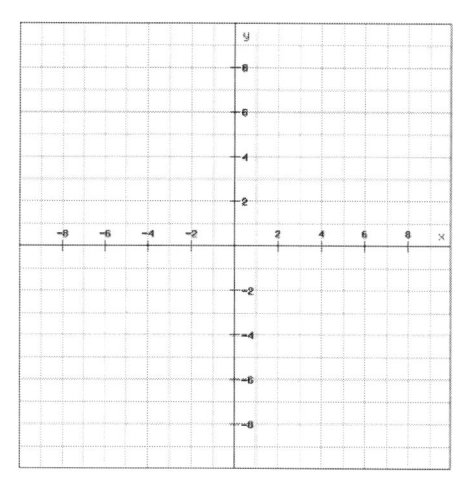

Horizontal asymptote:_____ Domain:_____

Lim

Range:_____

Lim

Increases:_____

Vertical asymptote:_____ Decreases:_____

Lim

y intercept:(___, ___)

Lim

x intercept:(___, ___)

18. $f(x) = \dfrac{3x - 2}{x - 3}$ (use division/otherwise to write it in the form $f(x) = \dfrac{a}{mx+b} + c$)

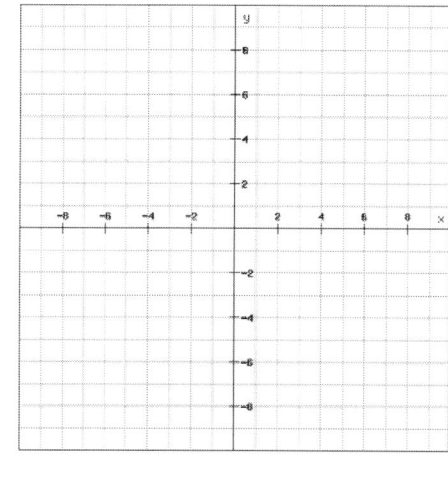

Horizontal asymptote:_____ Domain:_____

Lim

Range:_____

Lim

Increases:_____

Vertical asymptote:_____ Decreases:_____

Lim

y intercept:(___, ___)

Lim

x intercept:(___, ___)

19. $f(x) = \dfrac{4x-1}{-2x-3}$ (use division/otherwise to write it in the form $f(x) = \dfrac{a}{mx+b} + c$)

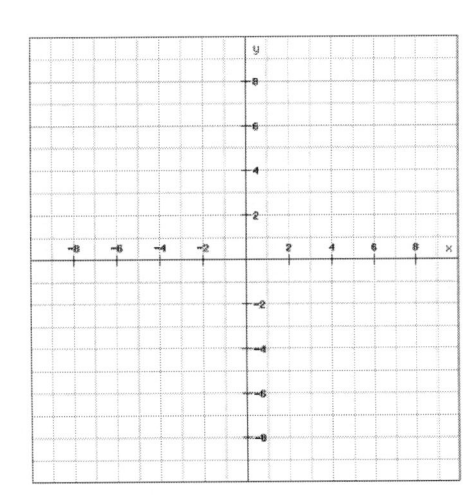

Horizontal asymptote:_____ Domain: _____

Lim

Range: _____

Lim

Increases: _____

Vertical asymptote: _____ Decreases: _____

Lim

y intercept:(___, ___)

Lim

x intercept:(___, ___)

20. $f(x) = \dfrac{4x}{8x-5}$ (use division/otherwise to write it in the form $f(x) = \dfrac{a}{mx+b} + c$)

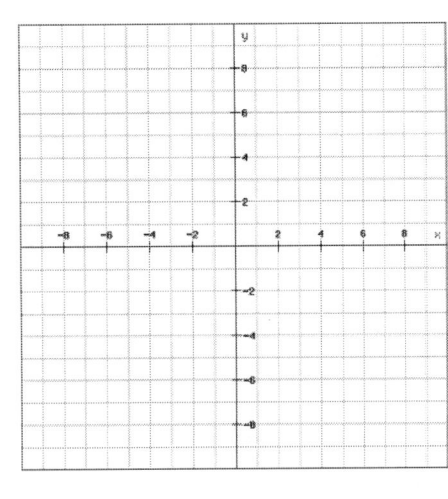

Horizontal asymptote:_____ Domain: _____

Lim

Range: _____

Lim

Increases: _____

Vertical asymptote: _____ Decreases: _____

Lim

y intercept:(___, ___)

Lim

x intercept:(___, ___)

21. $f(x) = \dfrac{x^2 + 4x + 3}{x+1} + 3$

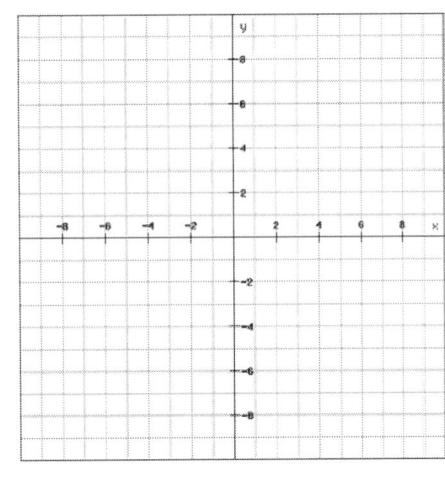

Horizontal asymptote:_____ Domain: _____

Lim

Range: _____

Lim

Increases: _____

Vertical asymptote: _____ Decreases: _____

Lim

y intercept:(___, ___)

Lim

x intercept:(___, ___)

22. $f(x) = \dfrac{4x+3}{5x+3}$ (use division/otherwise to write it in the form $f(x) = \dfrac{a}{mx+b} + c$)

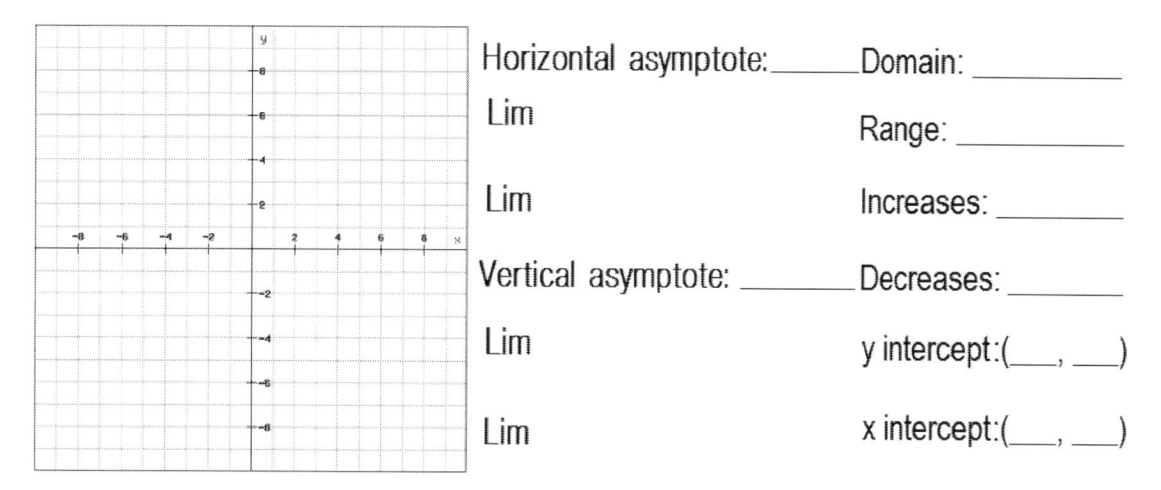

Horizontal asymptote: _____ Domain: _____

Lim

Range: _____

Lim

Increases: _____

Vertical asymptote: _____ Decreases: _____

Lim

y intercept:(___, ___)

Lim

x intercept:(___, ___)

23. On making a certain product there is a fixed cost of 2 Euros and a variable cost per product. The variable cost is 90 Euros for 1 product, 45 Euros for 2 products, 30 Euros for 3 products etc.

   a. What is the total cost of making a product in case 4 products are made?

   b. Write a function for the cost of a product.

   c. Sketch the function obtained on a graph, label the graph.

   d. What is the cost of a product in case a large number of products is made.

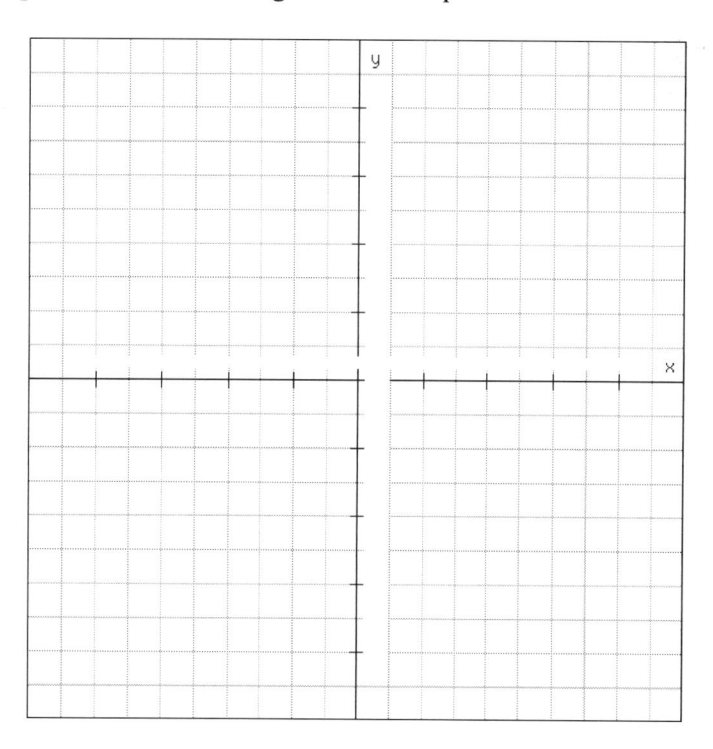

24. The cost per unit C(x) to produce x units of a product is given by $C(x) = \dfrac{300}{x+10}$

   a. What is the cost per unit when 180 units are produced?

   b. If the cost per unit is $1.50, how many units have been produced?

25. In the following formula, S(x) is the minimum number of hours of studying required to attain a test score of x $C(x) = \dfrac{0.32x}{100.5 - x}$

   a. How many hours of study are needed to score 85?

   b. What score can you get if you study 8 hours?

   c. How many hours of study are needed to score 100?

   d. State the domain of the function: _____

   e. Sketch the function in the domain found.

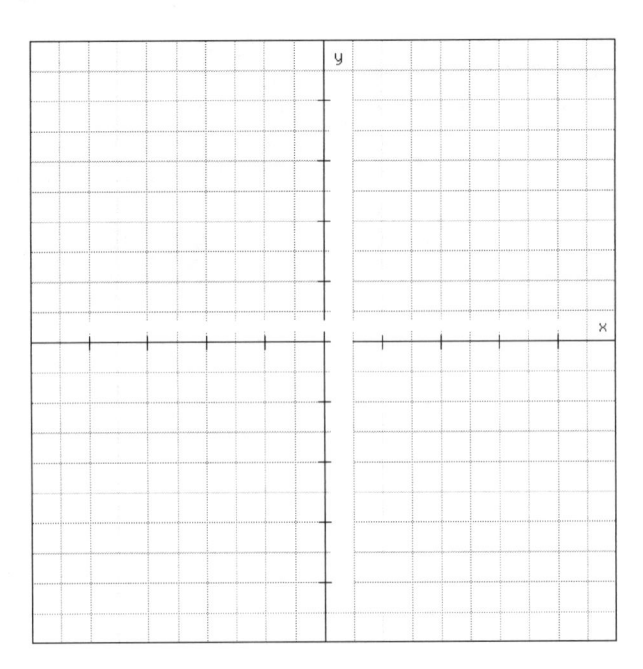

2.7. – EXPONENTIAL FUNCTIONS

1. Given the functions: $f(x) = 2^x$, $g(x) = 3^x$, Complete the following chart:

x	−5	−4	−3	−2	−1	0	1	2	3	4	5	6
f(x)												
g(x)												

- Sketch the points of the table on a graph.

- State the domain of the functions: : f(x):_____, g(x):_____

- State the *y* intercepts: f(x): (___, ___), g(x): (___, ___)

- State the *x* intercept(s): f(x): (___, ___), g(x): (___, ___)

- Write the corresponding limits and the equation of the vertical asymptote:

    f(x): _____   g(x): _____

- Write the corresponding limits and the equation of the horizontal asymptote: ___

    f(x): _____   g(x): _____

- The functions are increasing on the interval: f(x):_____, g(x):_____

- The functions are decreasing on the interval: f(x):_____, g(x):_____

- State the range of the functions: f(x):_____, g(x):_____

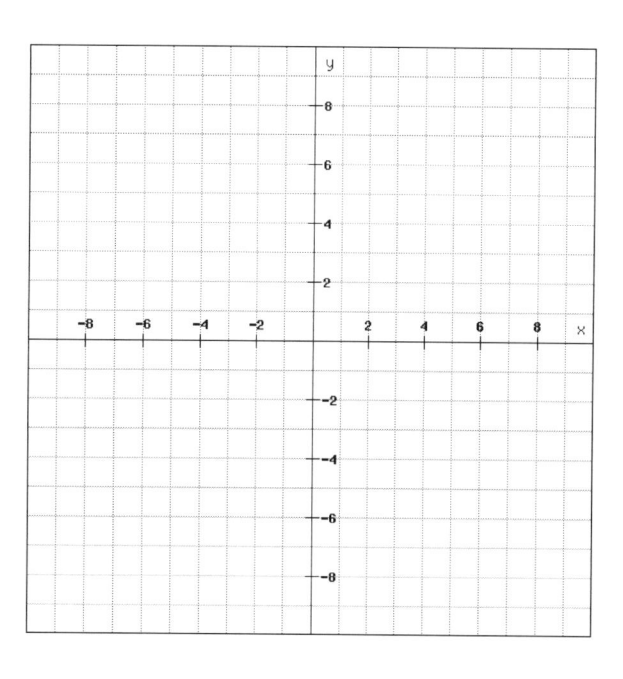

223

2. Given the functions: $f(x) = 2^{-x}$, $g(x) = 3^{-x}$, Complete the following chart:

x	−5	−4	−3	−2	−1	0	1	2	3	4	5	6
f(x)												
g(x)												

- Sketch the points of the table on a graph.

- State the domain of the functions: : f(x):_____, g(x):_____

- State the y intercepts: f(x): (___, ___), g(x): (___, ___)

- State the x intercept(s): f(x): (___, ___), g(x): (___, ___)

- Write the corresponding limits and the equation of the vertical asymptote:

  f(x): _____   g(x): _____

- Write the corresponding limits and the equation of the horizontal asymptote: ____

  f(x): _____   g(x): _____

- The functions are increasing on the interval: f(x):_____, g(x):_____

- The functions are decreasing on the interval: f(x):_____, g(x):_____

- State the range of the functions: f(x):_____, g(x):_____

- Write in mote forms:

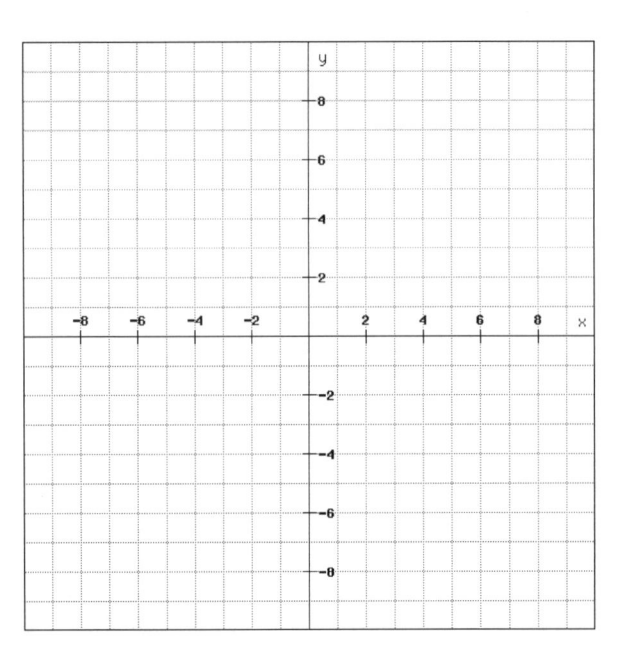

224

3. Given the functions: $f(x) = -2^x$, $g(x) = -3^x$, Complete the following chart:

x	−5	−4	−3	−2	−1	0	1	2	3	4	5	6
f(x)												
g(x)												

- Sketch the points of the table on a graph.

- State the domain of the functions: : f(x):_____, g(x):_____

- State the y intercepts: f(x): (____, ____), g(x): (____, ____)

- State the x intercept(s): f(x): (____, ____), g(x): (____, ____)

- Write the corresponding limits and the equation of the vertical asymptote:

  f(x): _____   g(x): _____

- Write the corresponding limits and the equation of the horizontal asymptote: ____

  f(x): _____   g(x): _____

- The functions are increasing on the interval: f(x):_____, g(x):_____

- The functions are decreasing on the interval: f(x):_____, g(x):_____

- State the range of the functions: f(x):_____, g(x):_____

- Write in mote forms:

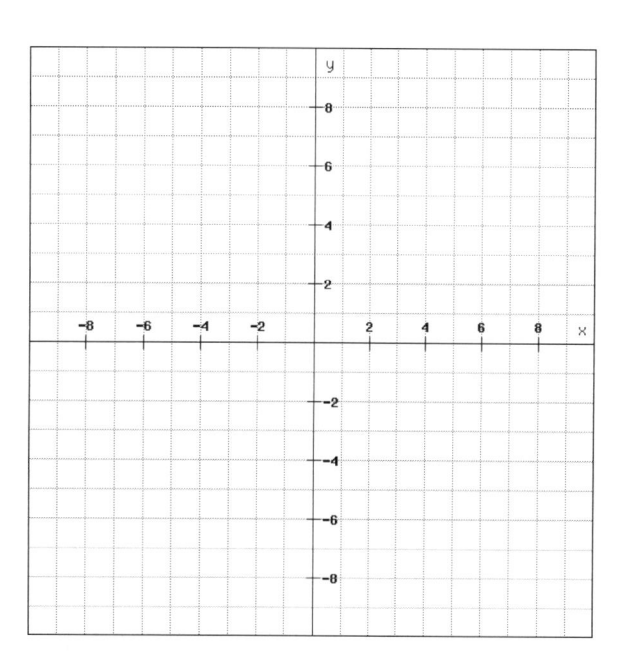

4. Given the functions: $f(x) = -2^{-x}$, $g(x) = -3^{-x}$, Complete the following chart:

x	−5	−4	−3	−2	−1	0	1	2	3	4	5	6
f(x)												
g(x)												

- Sketch the points of the table on a graph.

- State the domain of the functions: : f(x):_____, g(x):_____

- State the y intercepts: f(x): (____, ____), g(x): (____, ____)

- State the x intercept(s): f(x): (____, ____), g(x): (____, ____)

- Write the corresponding limits and the equation of the vertical asymptote:

    f(x): _____   g(x): _____

- Write the corresponding limits and the equation of the horizontal asymptote: ____

    f(x): _____   g(x): _____

- The functions are increasing on the interval: f(x):_____, g(x):_____

- The functions are decreasing on the interval: f(x):_____, g(x):_____

- State the range of the functions: f(x):_____, g(x):_____

- Write in mote forms:

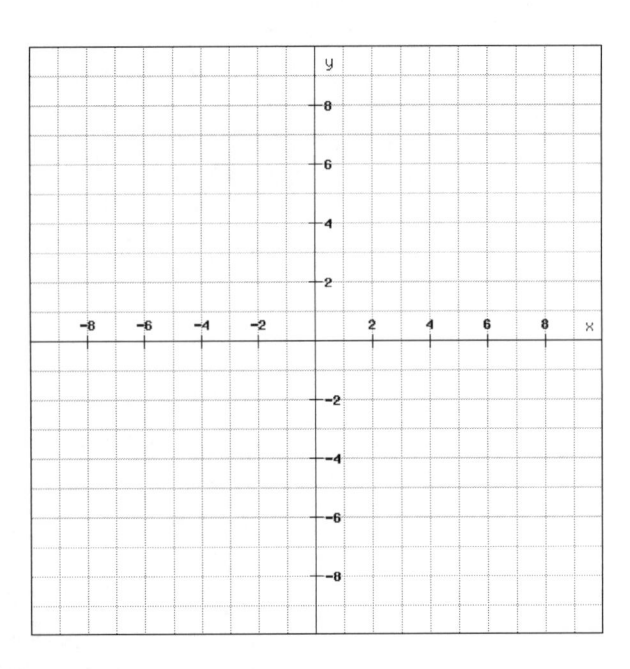

226

5. Given the function: $f(x) = -5 \times 4^{-2x} + 1$, Complete the following chart:

x	−5	−4	−3	−2	−1	0	1	2	3	4	5	6
f(x)												
g(x)												

- Sketch the points of the table on a graph.

- State the domain of the functions: : f(x):_____, g(x):_____

- State the y intercepts: f(x): (____, ____), g(x): (____, ____)

- State the x intercept(s): f(x): (____, ____), g(x): (____, ____)

- Write the corresponding limits and the equation of the vertical asymptote:

    f(x): _____   g(x): _____

- Write the corresponding limits and the equation of the horizontal asymptote: ____

    f(x): _____   g(x): _____

- The functions are increasing on the interval: f(x):_____, g(x):_____

- The functions are decreasing on the interval: f(x):_____, g(x):_____

- State the range of the functions: f(x):_____, g(x):_____

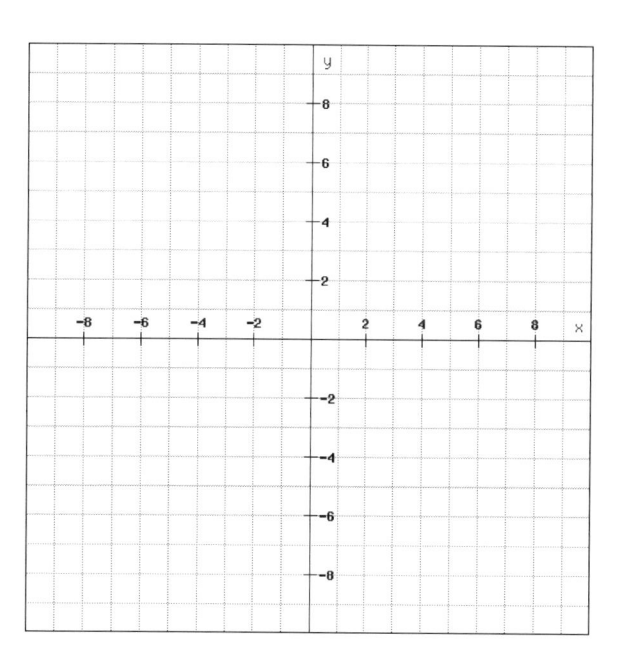

- Write in mote forms:

227

6. Given the graph of the function $f(x) = \left(\dfrac{1}{2}\right)^x = (\_\_)^x = \underline{}$ sketch, on the same set of axes, the graphs of the functions:

$g(x) = \left(\dfrac{1}{2}\right)^{x-2} = (\_\_)^{x-2} = \underline{} = \underline{}$

$d(x) = \left(\dfrac{1}{2}\right)^{x} - 2 = \underline{}$

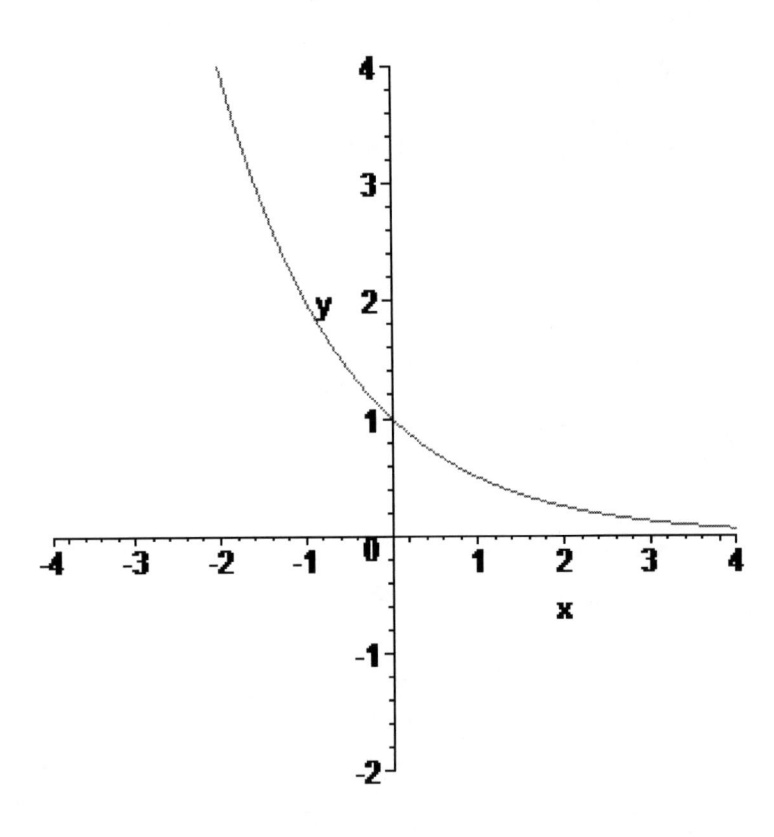

228

7. Given the graph, complete the table below:

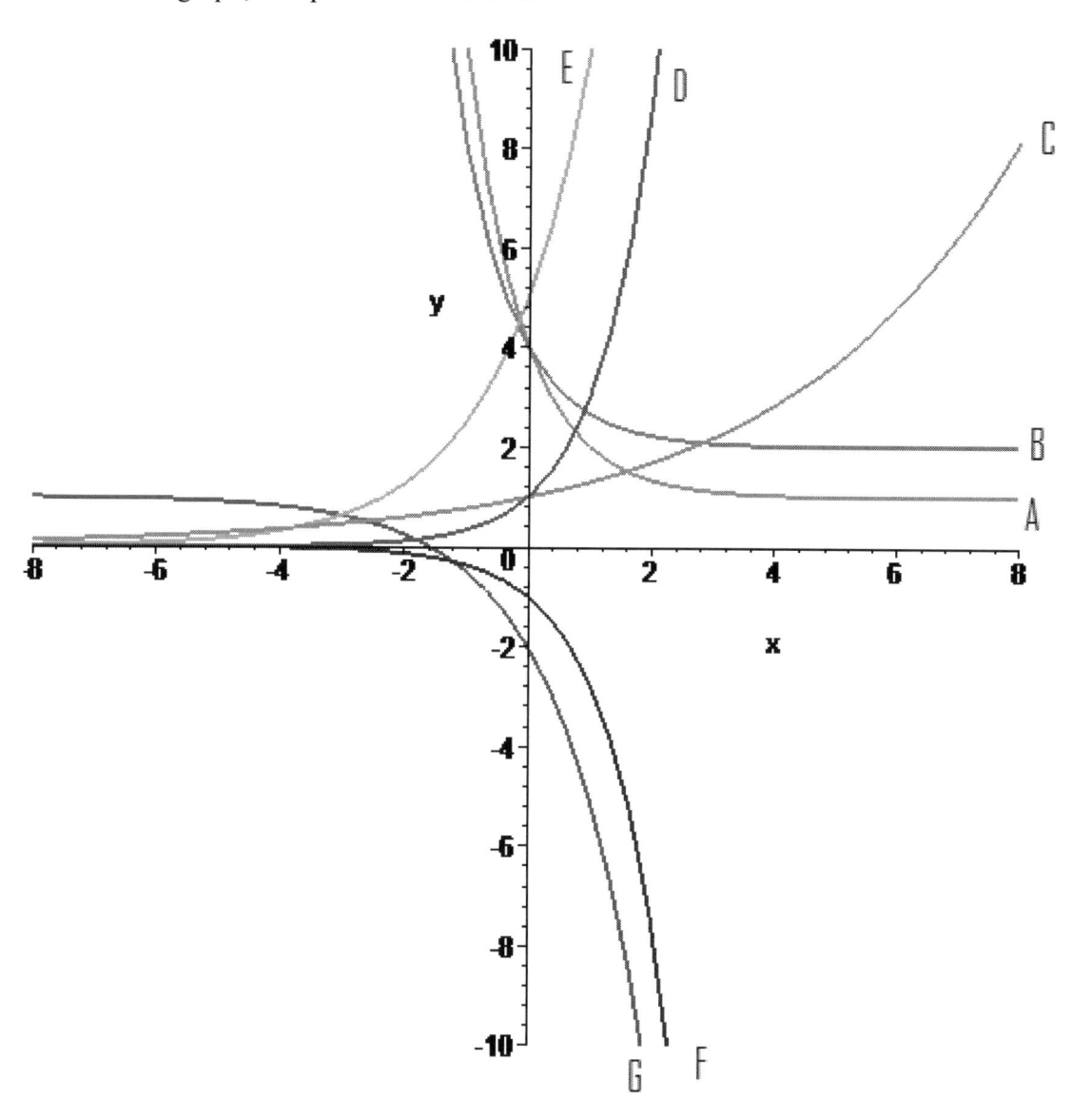

Function	On the graph
$f(x) = 5 \times 2^x$	
$f(x) = 2 + 2 \times 3^{-x}$	
$f(x) = 3 \times 3^{-x} + 1$	
$f(x) = (1.3)^x$	
$f(x) = -e^x$	
$f(x) = 3^x$	
$f(x) = -3 \times 2^x + 1$	

8. Given the function $f(x) = e^x$

   a. Write the same function translated 2 positions up.

   b. Write the same function translated 2 positions left.

   c. Write the same function translated 4 positions up and 3 right.

   d. Sketch all three functions:

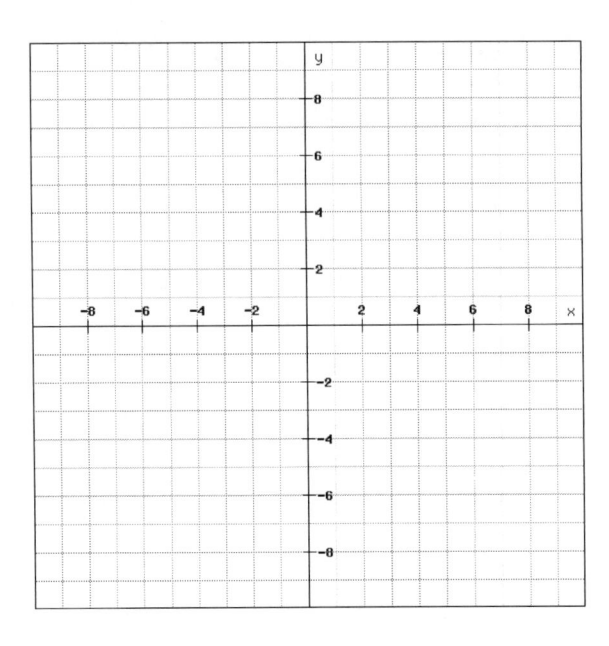

9. Given the function $f(x) = -3 \times 6^{-2x} + 1$

   a. Write the same function translated 2 positions up.

   b. Write the same function translated 2 positions left.

   c. Write the same function translated 4 positions up and 3 right.

   d. Sketch all three functions:

230

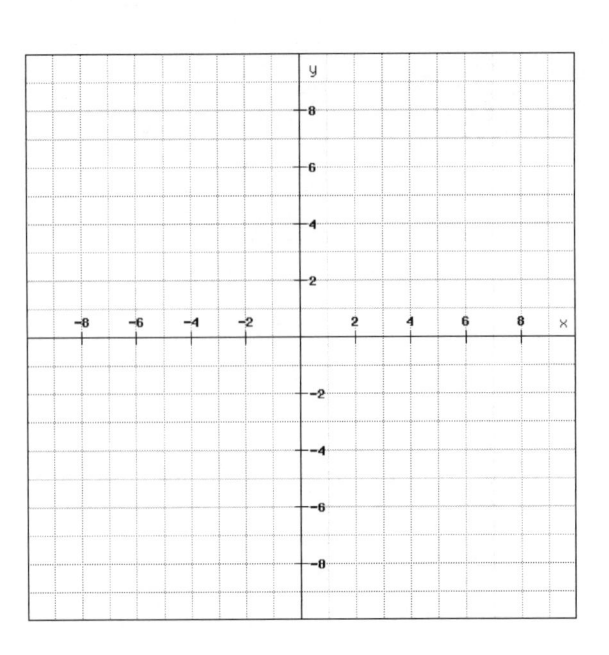

Analyze the functions:

1. $f(x) = 4^x$

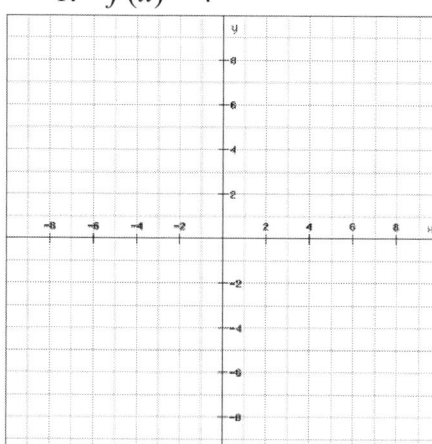

Horizontal asymptote: _____ Domain: _____
Lim   Range: _____
Lim   Increases: _____
Vertical asymptote: _____   Decreases: _____
Lim   y intercept:(___, ___)
Lim   x intercept:(___, ___)

2. $f(x) = -3^x$

Horizontal asymptote: _____ Domain: _____
Lim   Range: _____
Lim   Increases: _____
Vertical asymptote: _____   Decreases: _____
Lim   y intercept:(___, ___)
Lim   x intercept:(___, ___)

3. $f(x) = 2^{-x}$

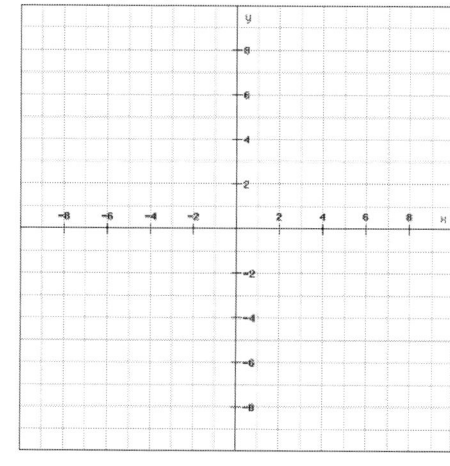

Horizontal asymptote: _____ Domain: _____
Lim   Range: _____
Lim   Increases: _____
Vertical asymptote: _____   Decreases: _____
Lim   y intercept:(___, ___)
Lim   x intercept:(___, ___)

4. $f(x) = -2^{-x}$

Horizontal asymptote: _____ Domain: _____
Lim   Range: _____
Lim   Increases: _____
Vertical asymptote: _____   Decreases: _____
Lim   y intercept: (___, ___)
Lim   x intercept: (___, ___)

5. $f(x) = \left(\dfrac{1}{4}\right)^x$

Horizontal asymptote: _____ Domain: _____
Lim   Range: _____
Lim   Increases: _____
Vertical asymptote: _____   Decreases: _____
Lim   y intercept: (___, ___)
Lim   x intercept: (___, ___)

6. $f(x) = 3\left(\dfrac{2}{7}\right)^x$

Horizontal asymptote: _____ Domain: _____
Lim   Range: _____
Lim   Increases: _____
Vertical asymptote: _____   Decreases: _____
Lim   y intercept: (___, ___)
Lim   x intercept: (___, ___)

7. $f(x) = -2^{x+5}$

Horizontal asymptote:_____ Domain:_____

Lim

Lim

Vertical asymptote:_____ Decreases:_____

Lim

Lim

Range:_____

Increases:_____

y intercept:(___, ___)

x intercept:(___, ___)

8. $f(x) = \left(\dfrac{2}{3}\right)^x$

Horizontal asymptote:_____ Domain:_____

Lim

Lim

Vertical asymptote:_____ Decreases:_____

Lim

Lim

Range:_____

Increases:_____

y intercept:(___, ___)

x intercept:(___, ___)

9. $f(x) = 3 \cdot 7^{x-4}$

Horizontal asymptote:_____ Domain:_____

Lim

Lim

Vertical asymptote:_____ Decreases:_____

Lim

Lim

Range:_____

Increases:_____

y intercept:(___, ___)

x intercept:(___, ___)

10. $f(x) = -7^{x-2} + 2$

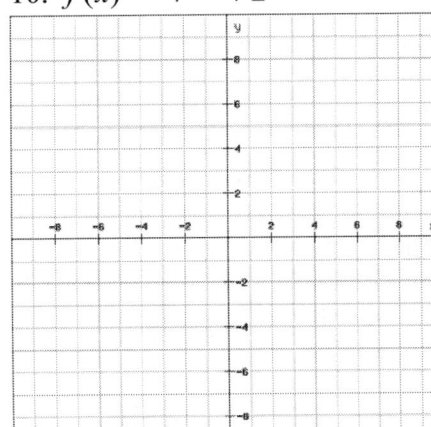

Horizontal asymptote: _____ Domain: _____

Lim

Range: _____

Lim

Increases: _____

Vertical asymptote: _____ Decreases: _____

Lim

y intercept: (___, ___)

Lim

x intercept: (___, ___)

11. $f(x) = 2 \cdot 5^{-x-2} - 5$

Horizontal asymptote: _____ Domain: _____

Lim

Range: _____

Lim

Increases: _____

Vertical asymptote: _____ Decreases: _____

Lim

y intercept: (___, ___)

Lim

x intercept: (___, ___)

12. $f(x) = -3^{-x-3} + 4$

Horizontal asymptote: _____ Domain: _____

Lim

Range: _____

Lim

Increases: _____

Vertical asymptote: _____ Decreases: _____

Lim

y intercept: (___, ___)

Lim

x intercept: (___, ___)

13. $f(x) = -e^x$

Horizontal asymptote:_____ Domain:_____
Lim
        Range:_____
Lim
        Increases:_____
Vertical asymptote:_____ Decreases:_____
Lim
        y intercept:(___, ___)
Lim
        x intercept:(___, ___)

14. $f(x) = e^{x+2}$

Horizontal asymptote:_____ Domain:_____
Lim
        Range:_____
Lim
        Increases:_____
Vertical asymptote:_____ Decreases:_____
Lim
        y intercept:(___, ___)
Lim
        x intercept:(___, ___)

15. $f(x) = -e^x + 4$

Horizontal asymptote:_____ Domain:_____
Lim
        Range:_____
Lim
        Increases:_____
Vertical asymptote:_____ Decreases:_____
Lim
        y intercept:(___, ___)
Lim
        x intercept:(___, ___)

16. $f(x) = 0.1e^{x+1} + 2$

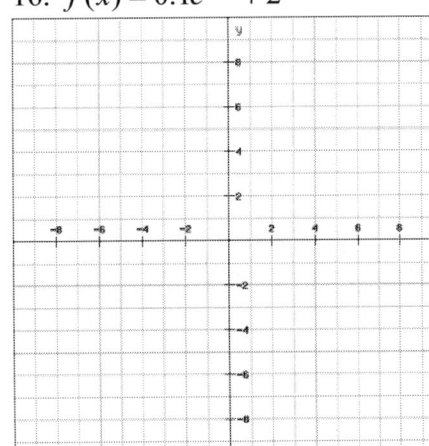

Horizontal asymptote: _____ Domain: _____
Lim   Range: _____
Lim   Increases: _____
Vertical asymptote: _____   Decreases: _____
Lim   y intercept:(___, ___)
Lim   x intercept:(___, ___)

17. $f(x) = 2e^{2x+1} - 4$

Horizontal asymptote: _____ Domain: _____
Lim   Range: _____
Lim   Increases: _____
Vertical asymptote: _____   Decreases: _____
Lim   y intercept:(___, ___)
Lim   x intercept:(___, ___)

18. $f(x) = -2 \cdot 6^{x-2} - 1$

Horizontal asymptote: _____ Domain: _____
Lim   Range: _____
Lim   Increases: _____
Vertical asymptote: _____   Decreases: _____
Lim   y intercept:(___, ___)
Lim   x intercept:(___, ___)

19. $f(x) = 2 \cdot 3^{x-2} - 5$

Horizontal asymptote: _____ Domain: _____
Lim
Range: _____
Lim
Increases: _____
Vertical asymptote: _____ Decreases: _____
Lim
y intercept:(___, ___)
Lim
x intercept:(___, ___)

20. $f(x) = 7 \cdot 5^{x-2} + 2$

Horizontal asymptote: _____ Domain: _____
Lim
Range: _____
Lim
Increases: _____
Vertical asymptote: _____ Decreases: _____
Lim
y intercept:(___, ___)
Lim
x intercept:(___, ___)

21. $f(x) = -2 \cdot 3^{-2x+1} + 4$

Horizontal asymptote: _____ Domain: _____
Lim
Range: _____
Lim
Increases: _____
Vertical asymptote: _____ Decreases: _____
Lim
y intercept:(___, ___)
Lim
x intercept:(___, ___)

Application:

1. The population of a rapidly–growing country starts at 4 million and increases by 10% each year.
   a. Complete the table below:

t(years)	P, population (in millions)	ΔP, increase in population (in millions)
0		
1		
2		
3		
4		

   b. Do you identify a pattern? Can you write a general expression of the population (P) as a function of the time (t)?

   c. Sketch its graph:

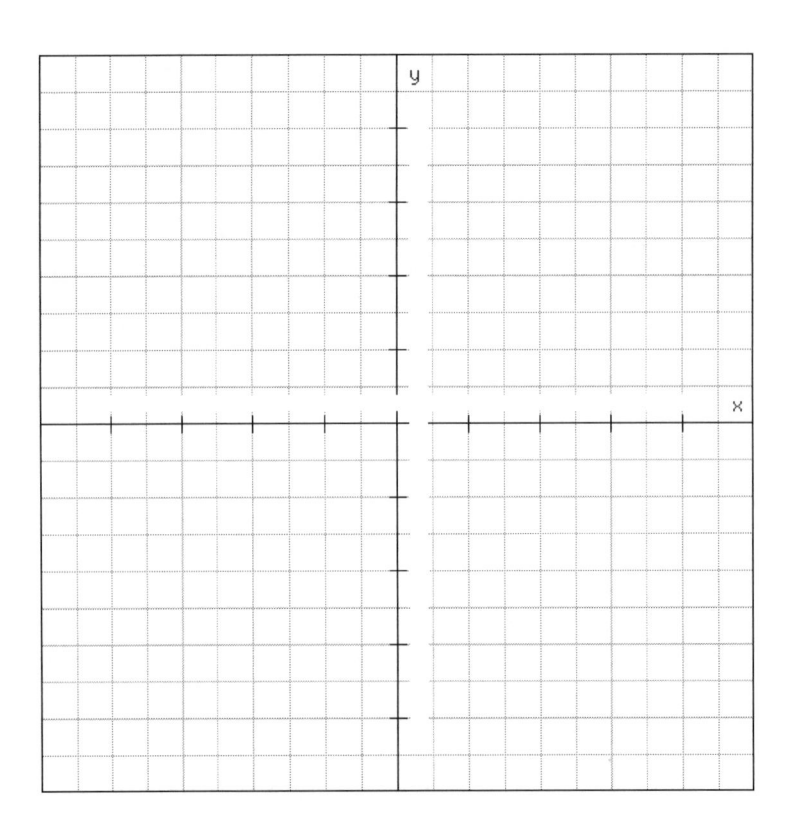

2. Suppose we start with 200 grams of radioactive substance that decays by 20% per year.

   a. First, complete the table below.

t (years)	0	1	2	3	4
Q (grams)					

   b. Find the expression of the function A(t), A the amount of substance and t the time in years.

   c. Sketch its graph.

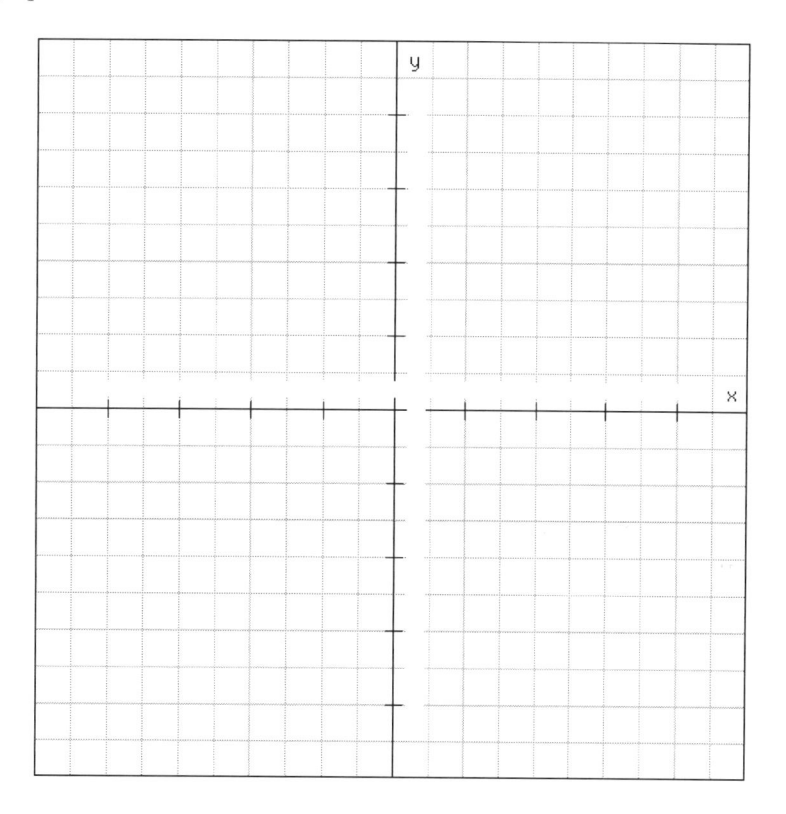

3. Suppose you invest 10000$ in the year 2000 and the investment earns 5.5% annually.

   a. a. Find the expression of the function A(t), A the amount of money and t the time in years.

   b. What will be the investment worth in 2010, 2020, 2030?

239

2.8. – LOGARITHMIC FUNCTIONS

1. Given the functions: $f(x) = \log_2(x)$, $g(x) = \log_3(x)$, Complete the following table:

x	−5	−1	−0.1	0	0.0001	0.001	0.1	1	2	16	81	1024
f(x)												
g(x)												

- Sketch the points of the table on a graph.

- State the domain of the functions: : f(x):_____, g(x):_____

- State the y intercepts: f(x): (___, ___), g(x): (___, ___)

- State the x intercept(s): f(x): (___, ___), g(x): (___, ___)

- Write the corresponding limits and the equation of the vertical asymptote:

    f(x): _____   g(x): _____

- Write the corresponding limits and the equation of the horizontal asymptote: ___

    f(x): _____   g(x): _____

- The functions are increasing on the interval: f(x):_____, g(x):_____

- The functions are decreasing on the interval: f(x):_____, g(x):_____

- State the range of the functions: f(x):_____, g(x):_____

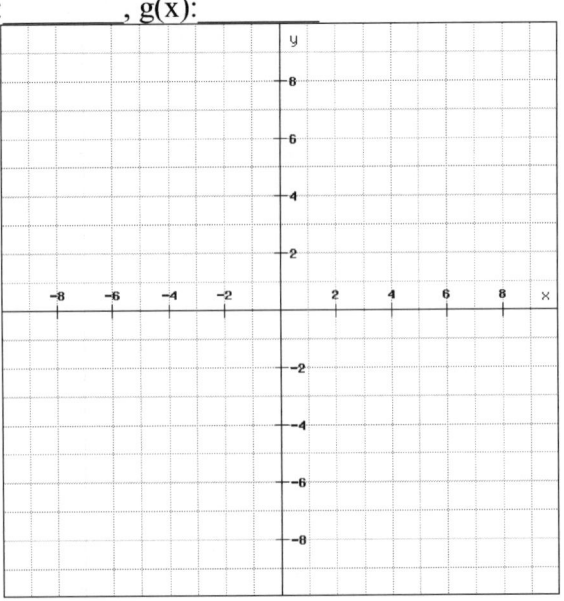

2. Given the functions: $f(x) = \log_1(x)$, $g(x) = \log_{-2}(x)$, Complete the following table:

x	−5	−1	−0.1	0	0.0001	0.001	0.1	1	2	16	81	1024
f(x)												
g(x)												

Conclusion:

3. Given the functions: $f(x) = \log_e(x)$, $g(x) = \log(x)$, Complete the following table:

x	−5	−1	−0.1	0	0.0001	0.001	0.1	1	2	16	81	1024
f(x)												
g(x)												

- Sketch the points of the table on a graph.

- State the domain of the functions: : f(x):_____, g(x):_____

- State the y intercepts: f(x): (___, ___), g(x): (___, ___)

- State the x intercept(s): f(x): (___, ___), g(x): (___, ___)

- Write the corresponding limits and the equation of the vertical asymptote:

    f(x): _____   g(x): _____

- Write the corresponding limits and the equation of the horizontal asymptote: ___

    f(x): _____   g(x): _____

- The functions are increasing on the interval: f(x):_____, g(x):_____

- The functions are decreasing on the interval: f(x):_____, g(x):_____

- State the range of the functions: f(x):_____, g(x):_____

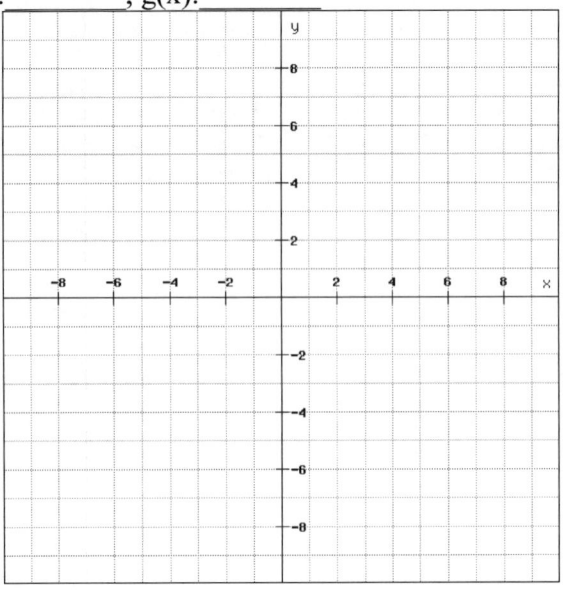

4. Given the functions: $f(x) = \log_4(x) + 4$, $g(x) = \log_3(x) - 3$, Complete the following table:

x	−5	−1	−0.1	0	0.0001	0.001	0.1	1	2	16	81	1024
f(x)												
g(x)												

- Sketch the points of the table on a graph.

- State the domain of the functions: : f(x):_____, g(x):_____

- State the y intercepts: f(x): (____, ____), g(x): (____, ____)

- State the x intercept(s): f(x): (____, ____), g(x): (____, ____)

- Write the corresponding limits and the equation of the vertical asymptote:

  f(x): _____   g(x): _____

- Write the corresponding limits and the equation of the horizontal asymptote: ___

  f(x): _____   g(x): _____

- The functions are increasing on the interval: f(x):_____, g(x):_____

- The functions are decreasing on the interval: f(x):_____, g(x):_____

- State the range of the functions: f(x):_____, g(x):_____

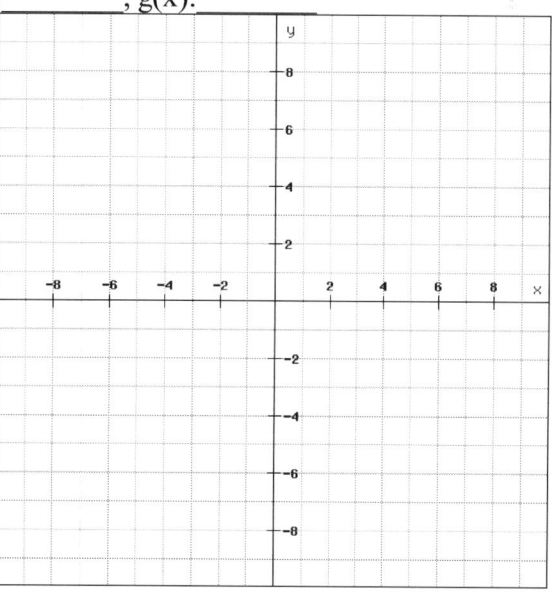

5. Given the functions: $f(x) = \log_2(x - 2)$, $g(x) = \log_3(x + 4)$, Complete the following table:

x	−5	−1	−0.1	0	0.0001	0.001	0.1	1	2	16	81	1024
f(x)												
g(x)												

- Sketch the points of the table on a graph.

- State the domain of the functions: : f(x):_____, g(x):_____

- State the y intercepts: f(x): (____, ____), g(x): (____, ____)

- State the x intercept(s): f(x): (____, ____), g(x): (____, ____)

- Write the corresponding limits and the equation of the vertical asymptote:

    f(x): _____   g(x): _____

- Write the corresponding limits and the equation of the horizontal asymptote: ___

    f(x): _____   g(x): _____

- The functions are increasing on the interval: f(x):_____, g(x):_____

- The functions are decreasing on the interval: f(x):_____, g(x):_____

- State the range of the functions: f(x):_____, g(x):_____

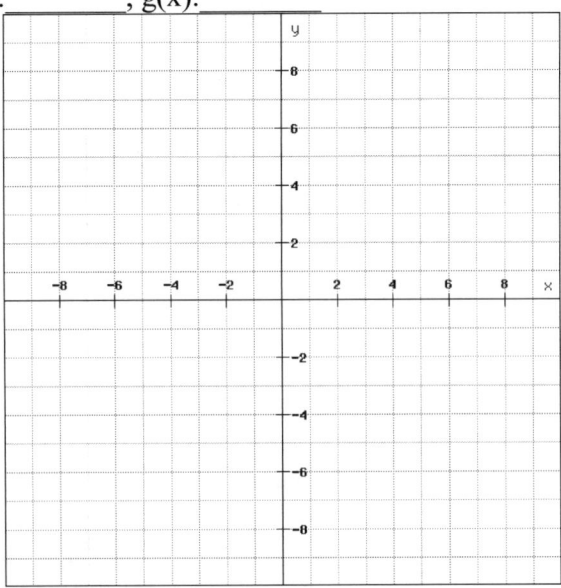

6. Given the functions: $f(x) = \log_2(2x - 5) + 1$, $g(x) = \log_3(3x + 2) - 5$, Ccomplete table:

- Sketch the points of the table on a graph.

- State the domain of the functions: : f(x):_____ , g(x):_____

- State the y intercepts: f(x): (____ , ____), g(x): (____ , ____)

- State the x intercept(s): f(x): (____ , ____), g(x): (____ , ____)

- Write the corresponding limits and the equation of the vertical asymptote:

  f(x): _____   g(x): _____

- Write the corresponding limits and the equation of the horizontal asymptote: ___

  f(x): _____   g(x): _____

- The functions are increasing on the interval: f(x):_____ , g(x):_____

- The functions are decreasing on the interval: f(x):_____ , g(x):_____

- State the range of the functions: f(x):_____ , g(x):_____

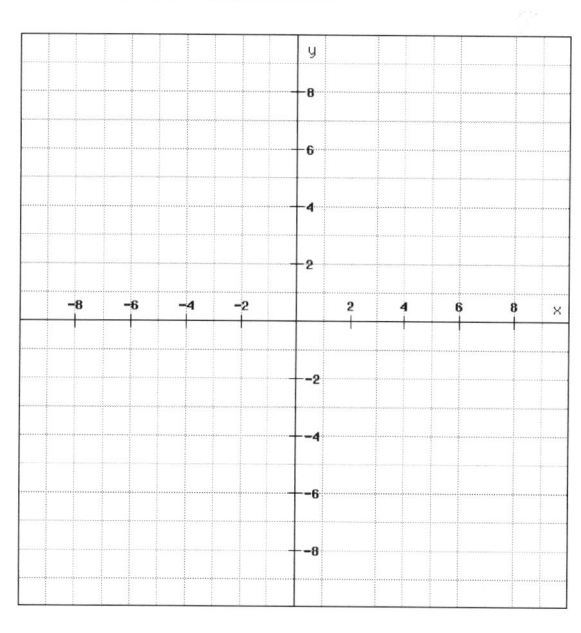

7. Given the graph, complete the table below:

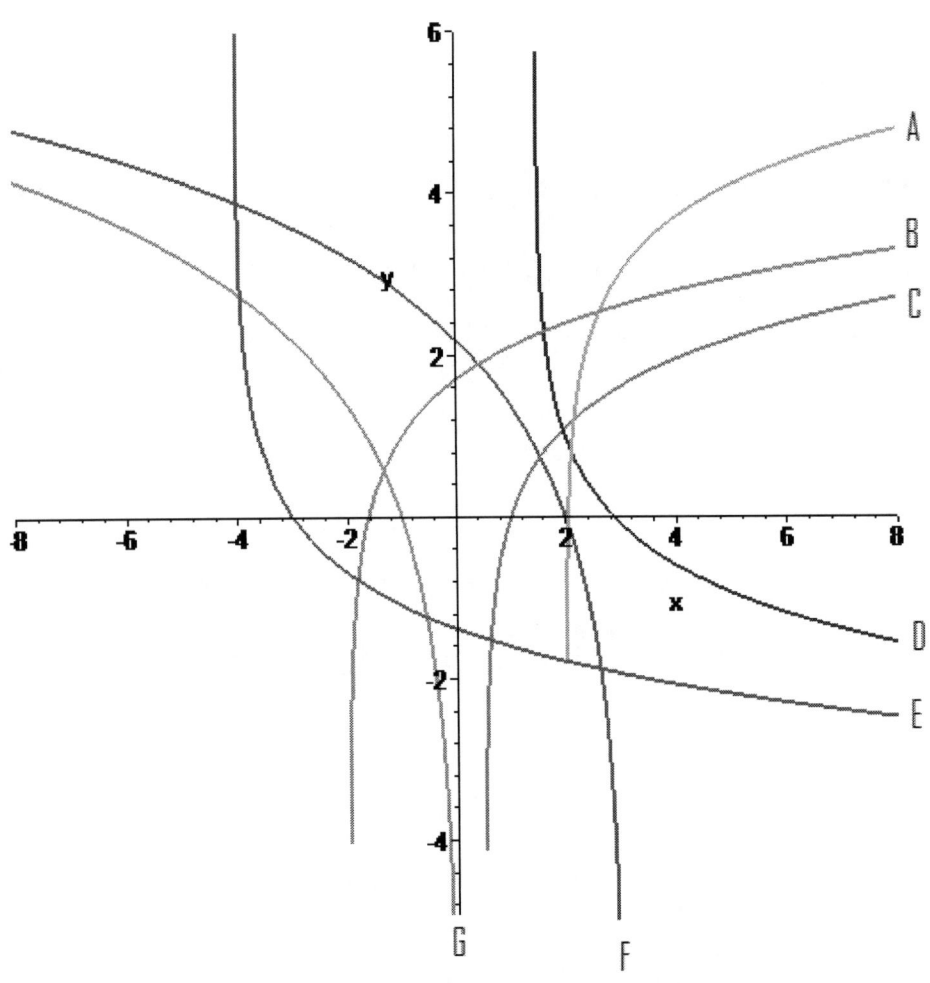

Function	On the graph
$f(x) = 2\ln(-x)$	G
$f(x) = \ln(x+2)+1$	B
$f(x) = 2\ln(3-x)$	F
$f(x) = \ln(2x-1)$	C
$f(x) = -\ln(x+4)$	D
$f(x) = -\ln(2x-3)$	E
$f(x) = \ln(x-2)+3$	A

8. Given the function f(x) = Ln(x)

   a. Write the same function translated 2 positions up.

   b. Write the same function translated 2 positions left.

   c. Write the same function translated 4 positions up and 3 right.

   d. Sketch all 3 functions

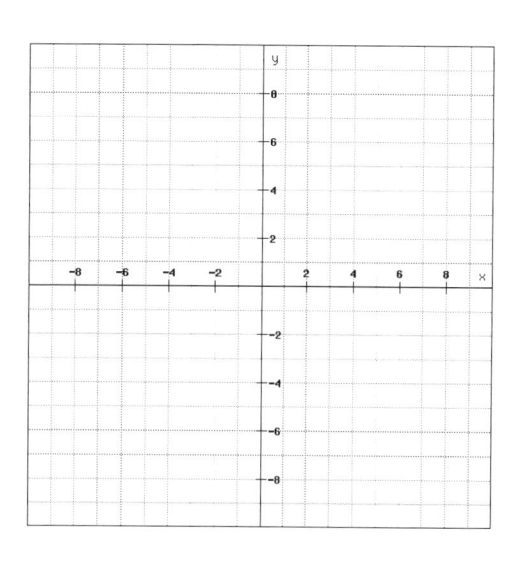

9. Given the function $f(x) = -\log_3(-2x)$

   a. Write the same function translated 2 positions up.

   b. Write the same function translated 2 positions left.

   c. Write the same function translated 4 positions up and 3 right.

   d. Sketch all 3 functions

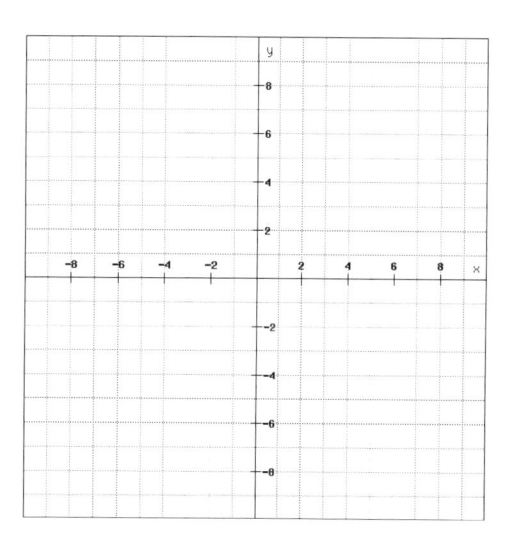

Analyze the following functions:

1. f(x) = log(x) – 2

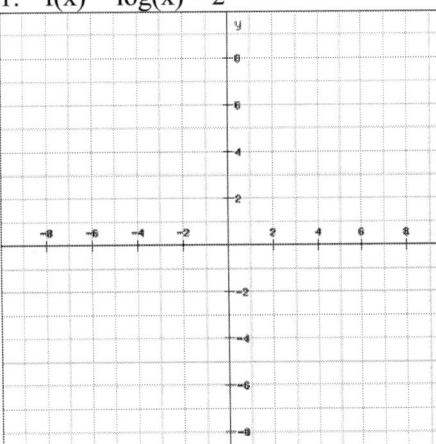

   Horizontal asymptote: _____ Domain: _____
   Lim   Range: _____
   Lim   Increases: _____
   Vertical asymptote: _____ Decreases: _____
   Lim   y intercept:(___, ___)
   Lim   x intercept:(___, ___)

2. f(x) = log(x–1)

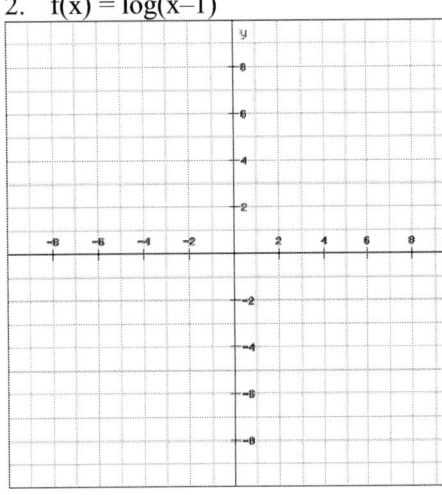

   Horizontal asymptote: _____ Domain: _____
   Lim   Range: _____
   Lim   Increases: _____
   Vertical asymptote: _____ Decreases: _____
   Lim   y intercept:(___, ___)
   Lim   x intercept:(___, ___)

3. f(x) = log(x^2)

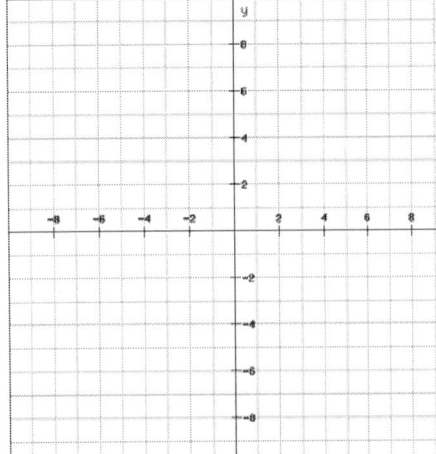

   Horizontal asymptote: _____ Domain: _____
   Lim   Range: _____
   Lim   Increases: _____
   Vertical asymptote: _____ Decreases: _____
   Lim   y intercept:(___, ___)
   Lim   x intercept:(___, ___)

4. f(x) = –log(5 – x)

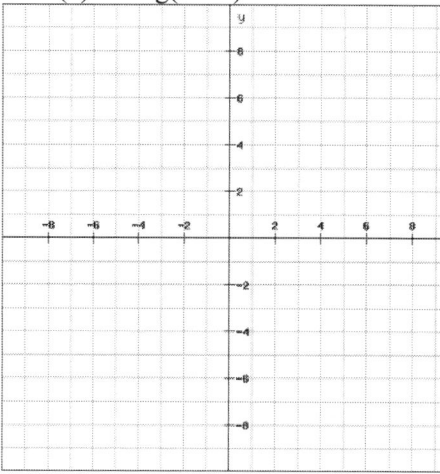

Horizontal asymptote:_____ Domain: _____
Lim   Range: _____
Lim   Increases: _____
Vertical asymptote: _____   Decreases: _____
Lim   y intercept:(___, ___)
Lim   x intercept:(___, ___)

5. f(x) = log(x – 3) + 5

Horizontal asymptote:_____ Domain: _____
Lim   Range: _____
Lim   Increases: _____
Vertical asymptote: _____   Decreases: _____
Lim   y intercept:(___, ___)
Lim   x intercept:(___, ___)

6. f(x) = log(–x + 3) – 2

Horizontal asymptote:_____ Domain: _____
Lim   Range: _____
Lim   Increases: _____
Vertical asymptote: _____   Decreases: _____
Lim   y intercept:(___, ___)
Lim   x intercept:(___, ___)

7. f(x) = –log(x) – 5

Horizontal asymptote: _____   Domain: _____

Lim

Range: _____

Lim

Increases: _____

Vertical asymptote: _____   Decreases: _____

Lim

y intercept:(___, ___)

Lim

x intercept:(___, ___)

8. f(x) = log(2x)

Horizontal asymptote: _____   Domain: _____

Lim

Range: _____

Lim

Increases: _____

Vertical asymptote: _____   Decreases: _____

Lim

y intercept:(___, ___)

Lim

x intercept:(___, ___)

9. f(x) = –log(–2x + 3)

Horizontal asymptote: _____   Domain: _____

Lim

Range: _____

Lim

Increases: _____

Vertical asymptote: _____   Decreases: _____

Lim

y intercept:(___, ___)

Lim

x intercept:(___, ___)

10. f(x) = log(2x – 3) – 1

Horizontal asymptote: _____ Domain: _____
Lim   Range: _____
Lim   Increases: _____
Vertical asymptote: _____ Decreases: _____
Lim   y intercept: (___, ___)
Lim   x intercept: (___, ___)

11. f(x) = log(3x – 5) – 6

Horizontal asymptote: _____ Domain: _____
Lim   Range: _____
Lim   Increases: _____
Vertical asymptote: _____ Decreases: _____
Lim   y intercept: (___, ___)
Lim   x intercept: (___, ___)

12. f(x) = –log(x^2) + 5

Horizontal asymptote: _____ Domain: _____
Lim   Range: _____
Lim   Increases: _____
Vertical asymptote: _____ Decreases: _____
Lim   y intercept: (___, ___)
Lim   x intercept: (___, ___)

13. $f(x) = \log(x^2) - 3$

Horizontal asymptote: _____ Domain: _____

Lim

Range: _____

Lim

Increases: _____

Vertical asymptote: _____ Decreases: _____

Lim

y intercept: (___, ___)

Lim

x intercept: (___, ___)

14. $f(x) = -\log(|x|) - 3$

Horizontal asymptote: _____ Domain: _____

Lim

Range: _____

Lim

Increases: _____

Vertical asymptote: _____ Decreases: _____

Lim

y intercept: (___, ___)

Lim

x intercept: (___, ___)

15. $f(x) = \log(|x - 2|)$

Horizontal asymptote: _____ Domain: _____

Lim

Range: _____

Lim

Increases: _____

Vertical asymptote: _____ Decreases: _____

Lim

y intercept: (___, ___)

Lim

x intercept: (___, ___)

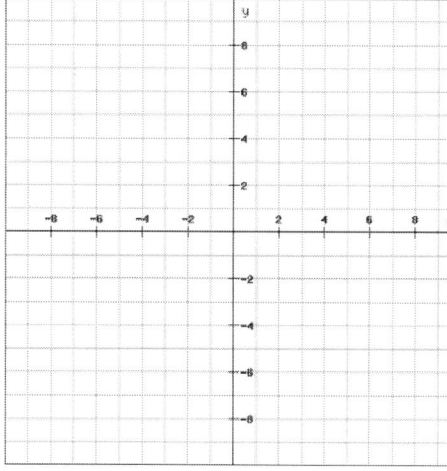

16. f(x) = log(|x + 2|) − 5

Horizontal asymptote: _____
Lim
Lim
Vertical asymptote: _____
Lim
Lim

Domain: _____
Range: _____
Increases: _____
Decreases: _____
y intercept:(___, ___)
x intercept:(___, ___)

17. f(x) = −log(|x + 6|) − 3

Horizontal asymptote: _____
Lim
Lim
Vertical asymptote: _____
Lim
Lim

Domain: _____
Range: _____
Increases: _____
Decreases: _____
y intercept:(___, ___)
x intercept:(___, ___)

18. f(x) = ln(x) − 3

Horizontal asymptote: _____
Lim
Lim
Vertical asymptote: _____
Lim
Lim

Domain: _____
Range: _____
Increases: _____
Decreases: _____
y intercept:(___, ___)
x intercept:(___, ___)

19. f(x) = log(x) − 3

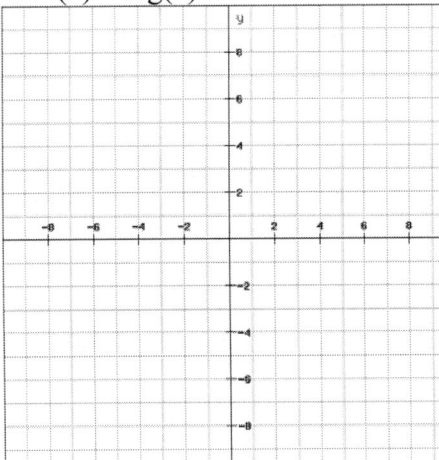

Horizontal asymptote:_____ Domain: _____
Lim   Range: _____
Lim   Increases: _____
Vertical asymptote: _____   Decreases: _____
Lim   y intercept:(___, ___)
Lim   x intercept:(___, ___)

20. f(x) = ln(x) − 2

Horizontal asymptote:_____ Domain: _____
Lim   Range: _____
Lim   Increases: _____
Vertical asymptote: _____   Decreases: _____
Lim   y intercept:(___, ___)
Lim   x intercept:(___, ___)

21. f(x) = ln(−x−1)

Horizontal asymptote:_____ Domain: _____
Lim   Range: _____
Lim   Increases: _____
Vertical asymptote: _____   Decreases: _____
Lim   y intercept:(___, ___)
Lim   x intercept:(___, ___)

22. f(x) = ln(–x²)

Horizontal asymptote:_____ Domain:_____
Lim   Range:_____
Lim   Increases:_____
Vertical asymptote:_____ Decreases:_____
Lim   y intercept:(___, ___)
Lim   x intercept:(___, ___)

23. f(x) = –ln(x+5)

Horizontal asymptote:_____ Domain:_____
Lim   Range:_____
Lim   Increases:_____
Vertical asymptote:_____ Decreases:_____
Lim   y intercept:(___, ___)
Lim   x intercept:(___, ___)

24. f(x) = log₃(4 – 2x) + 1

Horizontal asymptote:_____ Domain:_____
Lim   Range:_____
Lim   Increases:_____
Vertical asymptote:_____ Decreases:_____
Lim   y intercept:(___, ___)
Lim   x intercept:(___, ___)

25. f(x) = ln(2 − 2x) − 3

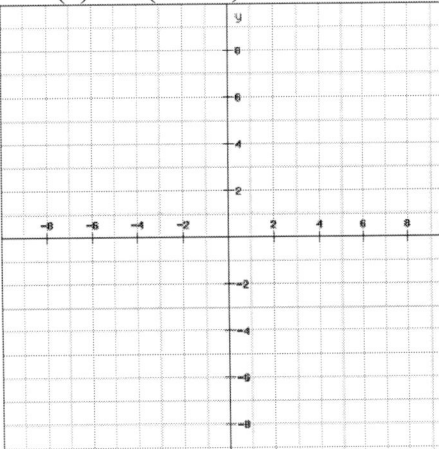

Horizontal asymptote: _____ Domain: _____
Lim   Range: _____
Lim   Increases: _____
Vertical asymptote: _____ Decreases: _____
Lim   y intercept:(___, ___)
Lim   x intercept:(___, ___)

26. f(x) = −ln(x) − 5

Horizontal asymptote: _____ Domain: _____
Lim   Range: _____
Lim   Increases: _____
Vertical asymptote: _____ Decreases: _____
Lim   y intercept:(___, ___)
Lim   x intercept:(___, ___)

27. f(x) = log$_4$(2x)

Horizontal asymptote: _____ Domain: _____
Lim   Range: _____
Lim   Increases: _____
Vertical asymptote: _____ Decreases: _____
Lim   y intercept:(___, ___)
Lim   x intercept:(___, ___)

28. $f(x) = -\log_6(-2x) + 1$

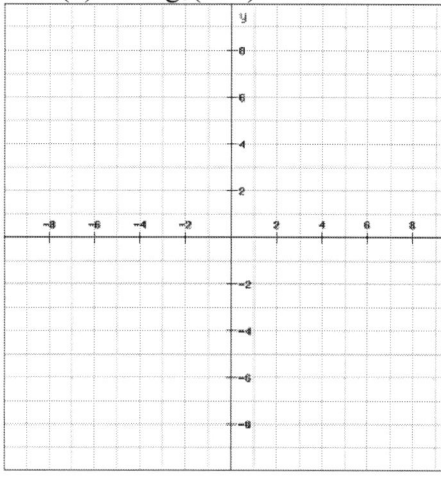

Horizontal asymptote:_____ Domain:_____
Lim Range:_____
Lim Increases:_____
Vertical asymptote:_____ Decreases:_____
Lim y intercept:(___, ___)
Lim x intercept:(___, ___)

29. $f(x) = \ln(-2x - 3) - 1$

Horizontal asymptote:_____ Domain:_____
Lim Range:_____
Lim Increases:_____
Vertical asymptote:_____ Decreases:_____
Lim y intercept:(___, ___)
Lim x intercept:(___, ___)

30. $f(x) = -\log(10x - 5) - 1$

Horizontal asymptote:_____ Domain:_____
Lim Range:_____
Lim Increases:_____
Vertical asymptote:_____ Decreases:_____
Lim y intercept:(___, ___)
Lim x intercept:(___, ___)

31. $f(x) = \ln(x^2) + 1$

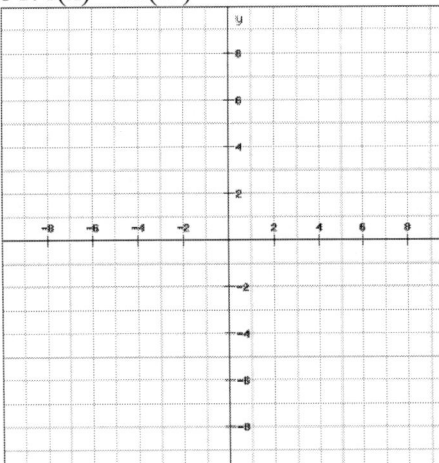

Horizontal asymptote: _____ Domain: _____
Lim   Range: _____
Lim   Increases: _____
Vertical asymptote: _____ Decreases: _____
Lim   y intercept: (___, ___)
Lim   x intercept: (___, ___)

32. $f(x) = -\ln(|x|) + 1$

Horizontal asymptote: _____ Domain: _____
Lim   Range: _____
Lim   Increases: _____
Vertical asymptote: _____ Decreases: _____
Lim   y intercept: (___, ___)
Lim   x intercept: (___, ___)

33. $f(x) = \ln(|x - 2|)$

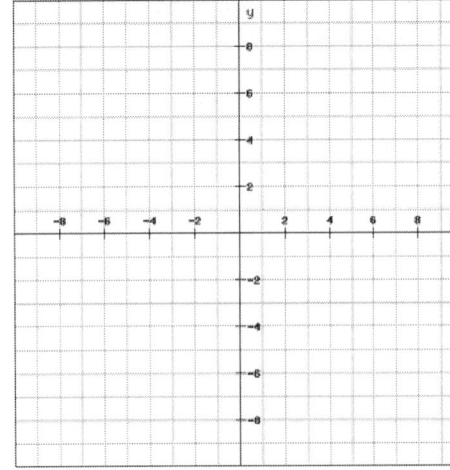

Horizontal asymptote: _____ Domain: _____
Lim   Range: _____
Lim   Increases: _____
Vertical asymptote: _____ Decreases: _____
Lim   y intercept: (___, ___)
Lim   x intercept: (___, ___)

34. The population of a city increases by 5% every year. Find the number of years it will take it to double.

35. The population of a town increases by k% every year; find the time it will take it to triple in terms of k.

36. The population of a city increases by k% every month; find k in case the population grew by 50% after 3 years.

37. The PH level in a substance is given by: $PH = -\log(H^+)$, where H^+ is the concentration of hydrogen ions (only proton) in moles/litter.

   a. Given that the PH level of different substances complete the following table:

Substance	PH Level	Concentration of Hydrogen ions
Battery Acid	0	
Lemon Juice	2	
Milk	6	
Pure Water	7	
Human Blood	7.4	
Great salt lake	10	
Liquid drain cleaner	14	

   b. People who have cancer have about a 100 times more acid blood than normal blood, find their level of PH.

38. Richter scale for measuring an earthquake strength can be approximated by: $R = \log(x)$, where x depends on the strength of the earthquake and the distance from its centre.

   a. Given that in a certain location A the Richter scale measure was 5 and in location B the Richter scale measure was 6. Find how much stronger was the earthquake in location B?

   b. Given that in a certain location A the Richter scale measure was 5 and in location B the earthquake was 3 times as strong, what was the Richter scale measure in location B?

39. The Weber – Fechner law can be approximated by: $S = k\log_{10} I$, where I is the intensity of light and S is the sensation of brightness.

   a. This law means that:
   Big changes in the Intensity will cause _____ changes in the sensation.

   b. Find the change needed in the intensity that will double the sensation of brightness.

40. Decibels (DB) are used for measuring the volume of sound. They are given by: $I = 10\log(P/P_0)$ where P_0 is the minimum intensity of sound detected by the human ear.
   a. What is the threshold in DB of the human ear?

   b. In normal conversation 60 DB will be measured. Express P in terms of P_0. How many times louder is this than the threshold?

   c. In a rock concert 120 DB will be measured. Express P in terms of P_0. How many times louder is this than a normal conversation?

   d. Find the number of DB of a sound twice is strong as the threshold.

260

2.9. – RADICAL FUCNTIONS

1. Given the functions: $f(x) = \sqrt{x}$, $g(x) = -\sqrt{x}$, Complete the following table:

x	−2	−1	0	1	2	3	4	5	6	7	8	9
f(x)												
g(x)												

- Sketch the points of the table on a graph.

- State the domain of the functions: : f(x):_____, g(x):_____

- State the y intercepts: f(x): (____, ____), g(x): (____, ____)

- State the x intercept(s): f(x): (____, ____), g(x): (____, ____)

- Write the corresponding limits and the equation of the vertical asymptote:

    f(x): _____   g(x): _____

- Write the corresponding limits and the equation of the horizontal asymptote: ____

    f(x): _____   g(x): _____

- The functions are increasing on the interval: f(x):_____, g(x):_____

- The functions are decreasing on the interval: f(x):_____, g(x):_____

- State the range of the functions: f(x):_____, g(x):_____

- Write in mote forms:

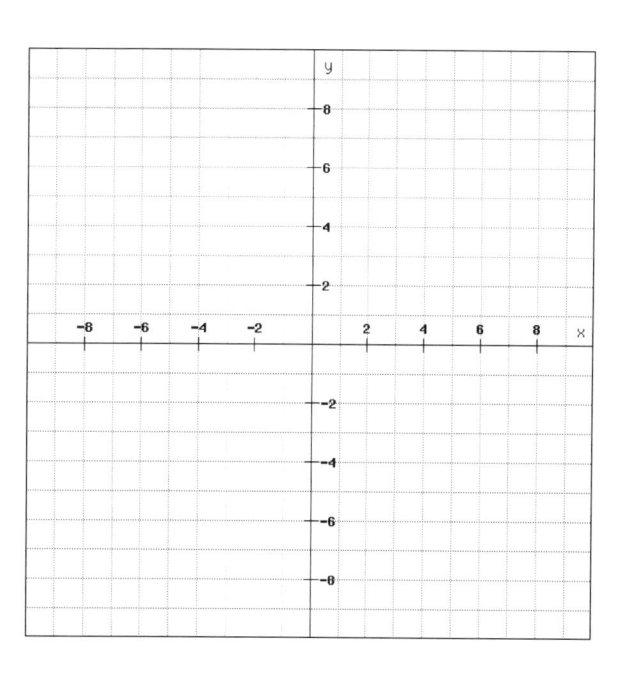

261

2. Given the functions: $f(x) = \sqrt{-x+1}$, $g(x) = -\sqrt{x-3}$, Complete the table:

x	−2	−1	0	1	2	3	4	5	6	7	8	9
f(x)												
g(x)												

- Sketch the points of the table on a graph.

- State the domain of the functions: : f(x):_____, g(x):_____

- State the y intercepts: f(x): (____, ____), g(x): (____, ____)

- State the x intercept(s): f(x): (____, ____), g(x): (____, ____)

- Write the corresponding limits and the equation of the vertical asymptote:

  f(x): _____   g(x): _____

- Write the corresponding limits and the equation of the horizontal asymptote: ____

  f(x): _____   g(x): _____

- The functions are increasing on the interval: f(x):_____, g(x):_____

- The functions are decreasing on the interval: f(x):_____, g(x):_____

- State the range of the functions: f(x):_____, g(x):_____

- Write in mote forms:

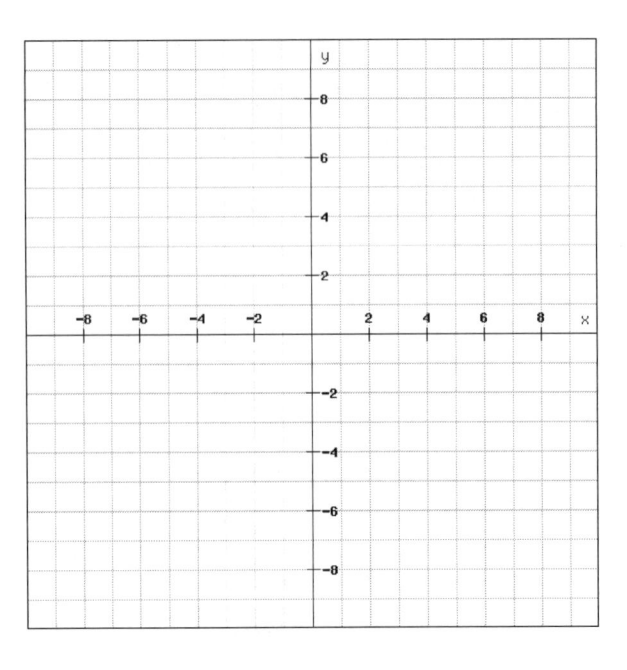

262

3. Given the functions: $f(x) = \sqrt{x+1} + 3$, $g(x) = -\sqrt{x-3} - 6$. Complete the table:

x	−2	−1	0	1	2	3	4	5	6	7	8	9
f(x)												
g(x)												

- Sketch the points of the table on a graph.

- State the domain of the functions: : f(x):_____, g(x):_____

- State the y intercepts: f(x): (___, ___), g(x): (___, ___)

- State the x intercept(s): f(x): (___, ___), g(x): (___, ___)

- Write the corresponding limits and the equation of the vertical asymptote:

    f(x): _____   g(x): _____

- Write the corresponding limits and the equation of the horizontal asymptote: ___

    f(x): _____   g(x): _____

- The functions are increasing on the interval: f(x):_____, g(x):_____

- The functions are decreasing on the interval: f(x):_____, g(x):_____

- State the range of the functions: f(x):_____, g(x):_____

- Write in mote forms:

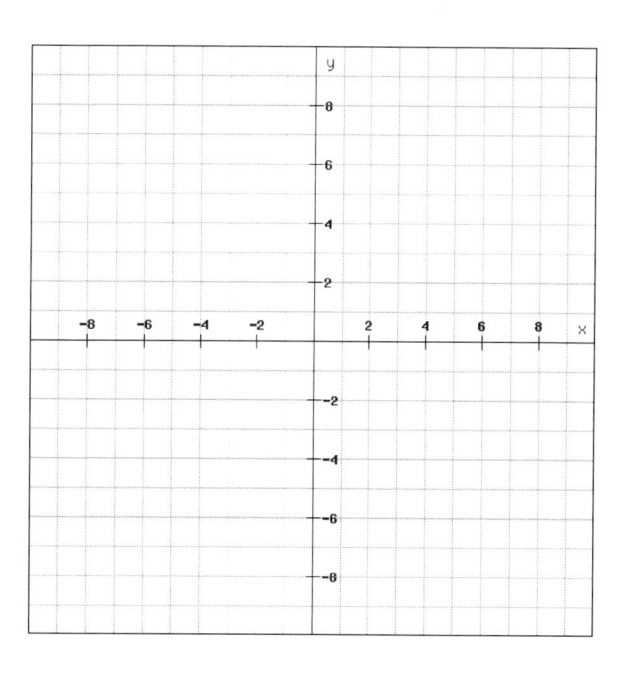

4. Given the graph, complete the table below:

Function	On the graph
$f(x) = 3\sqrt{x-2} - 3$	
$f(x) = \sqrt{3x+2}$	
$f(x) = \sqrt{-2x+1}$	
$f(x) = \sqrt{x+1}$	
$f(x) = \sqrt{-x-2}$	
$f(x) = 2 - \sqrt{x-2}$	
$f(x) = -2\sqrt{x-1}$	
$f(x) = -1 - \sqrt{-x+4}$	
$f(x) = -\sqrt{2x-5} - 1$	

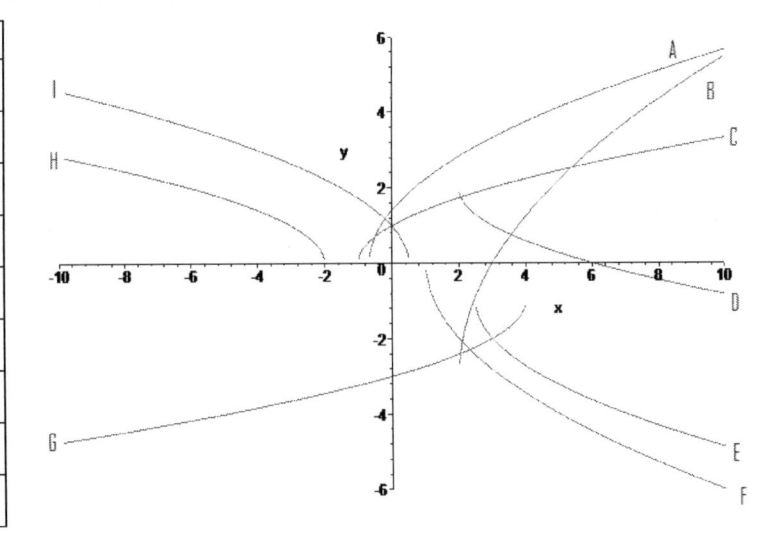

5. Given the function $f(x) = \sqrt{x}$

   a. Write the same function translated 2 positions up.

   b. Write the same function translated 2 positions left.

   c. Write the same function translated 4 positions up and 3 right.

   d. Sketch the 3 functions:

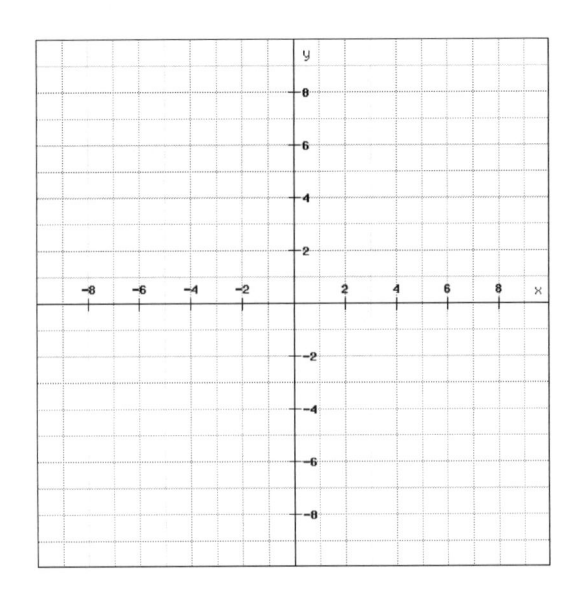

6. Given the function $f(x) = 4\sqrt{-2x+1}$

   a. Write the same function translated 2 positions up.

   b. Write the same function translated 2 positions left.

   c. Write the same function translated 4 positions up and 3 right.

   e. Sketch the 3 functions:

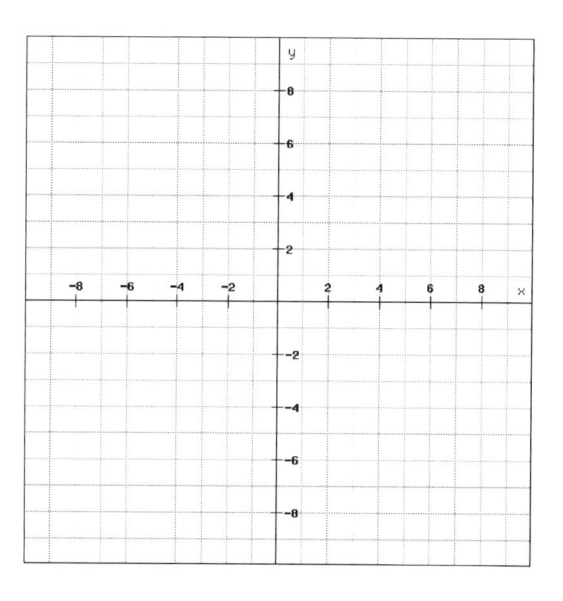

Analyze the following functions:

1. $f(x) = \sqrt{x+3}$

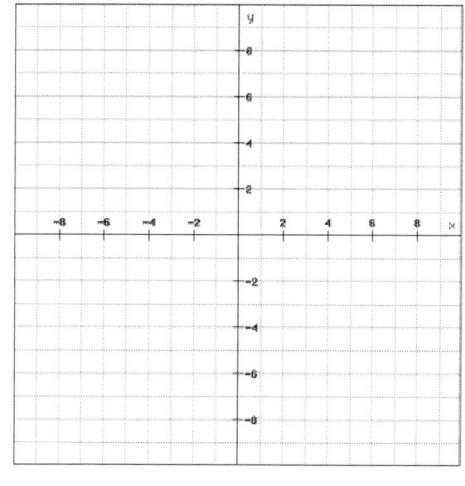

Domain: _____   x intercept:(___, ___)

Range: _____

Increases: _____

Decreases: _____   y intercept:(___, ___)

Max/Min:(___, ___)

265

2. $f(x) = 3\sqrt{x-2}$

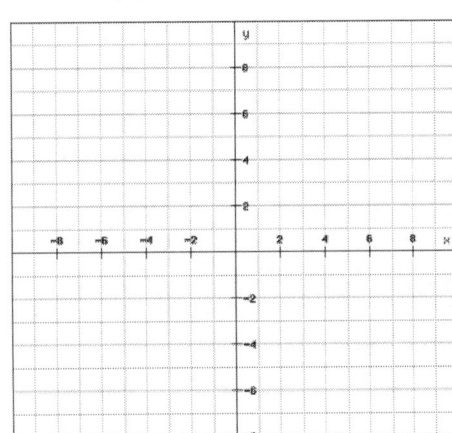

Domain: _____   x intercept:(___, ___)

Range: _____

Increases: _____

Decreases: _____   y intercept:(___, ___)

Max/Min:(___, ___)

3. $f(x) = \sqrt{5x+6}$

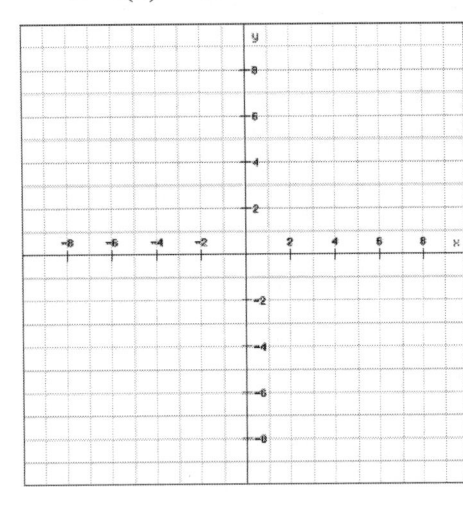

Domain: _____   x intercept:(___, ___)

Range: _____

Increases: _____

Decreases: _____   y intercept:(___, ___)

Max/Min:(___, ___)

4. $f(x) = 2\sqrt{-4x-2}$

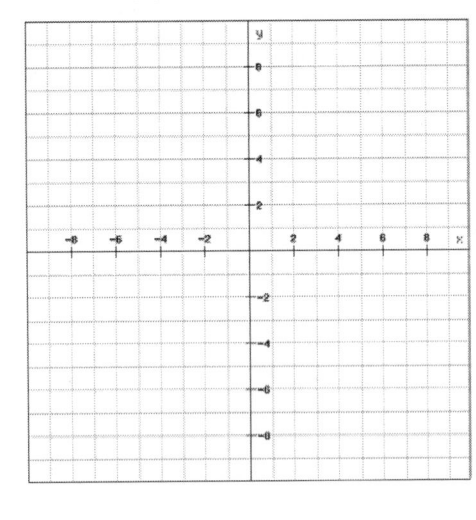

Domain: _____   x intercept:(___, ___)

Range: _____

Increases: _____

Decreases: _____   y intercept:(___, ___)

Max/Min:(___, ___)

5. $f(x) = -\sqrt{x-3}$

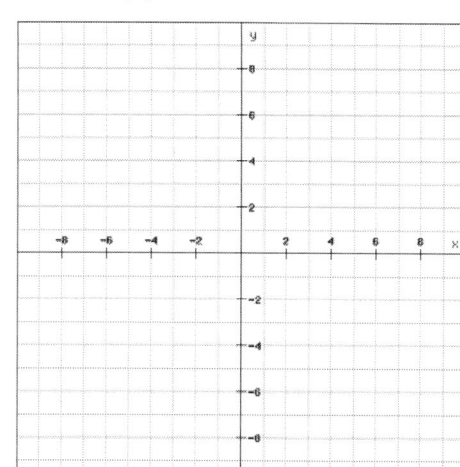

Domain: _____   x intercept:(___, ___)

Range: _____

Increases: _____

Decreases: _____   y intercept:(___, ___)

Max/Min:(___, ___)

6. $f(x) = \sqrt{2x-5}$

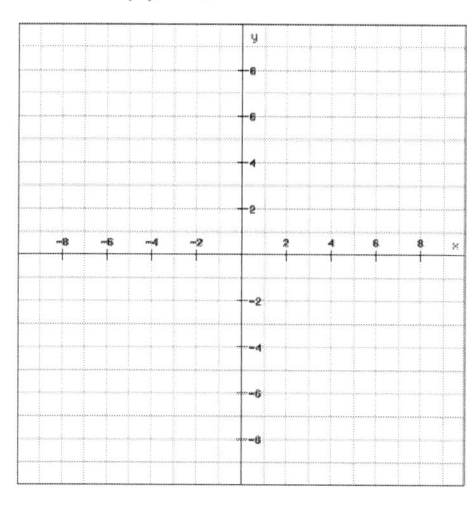

Domain: _____   x intercept:(___, ___)

Range: _____

Increases: _____

Decreases: _____   y intercept:(___, ___)

Max/Min:(___, ___)

7. $f(x) = 2\sqrt{-3x-2}$

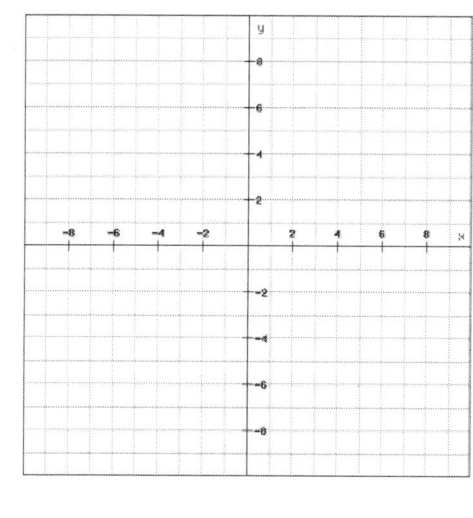

Domain: _____   x intercept:(___, ___)

Range: _____

Increases: _____

Decreases: _____   y intercept:(___, ___)

Max/Min:(___, ___)

8. $f(x) = \sqrt{x-5} + 6$

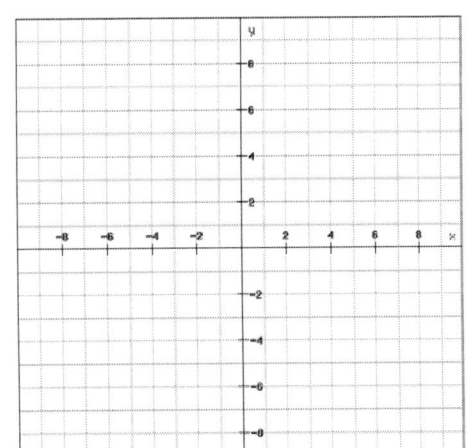

Domain: _____   x intercept: (___, ___)

Range: _____

Increases: _____

Decreases: _____   y intercept: (___, ___)

Max/Min: (___, ___)

9. $f(x) = \sqrt{-x+3} - 8$

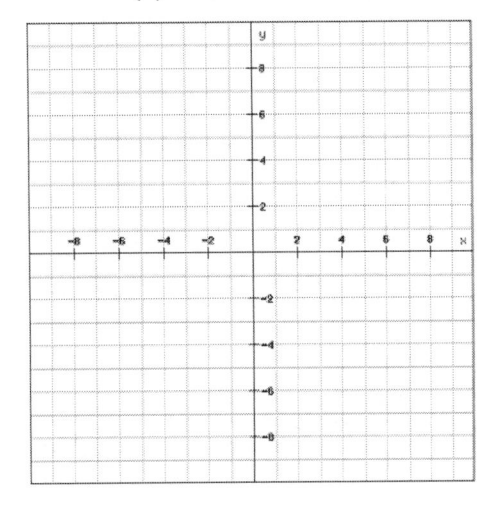

Domain: _____   x intercept: (___, ___)

Range: _____

Increases: _____

Decreases: _____   y intercept: (___, ___)

Max/Min: (___, ___)

10. $f(x) = \sqrt{4x+3} + 4$

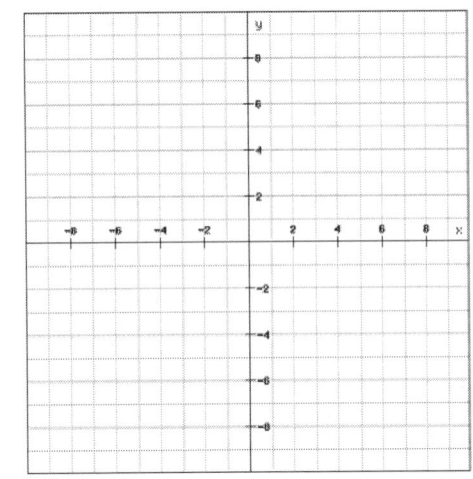

Domain: _____   x intercept: (___, ___)

Range: _____

Increases: _____

Decreases: _____   y intercept: (___, ___)

Max/Min: (___, ___)

11. $f(x) = \sqrt{x-6} - 2$

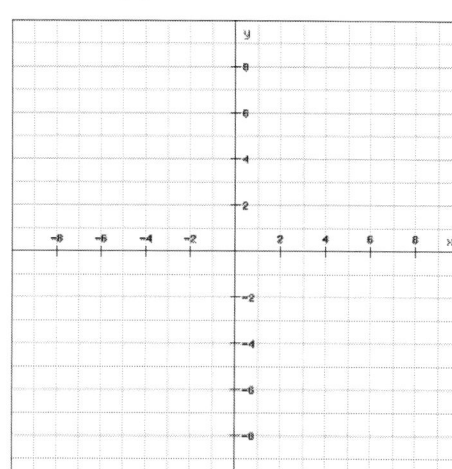

Domain: _____ x intercept:(___, ___)

Range: _____

Increases: _____

Decreases: _____ y intercept:(___, ___)

Max/Min:(___, ___)

12. $f(x) = 5\sqrt{x} - 5$

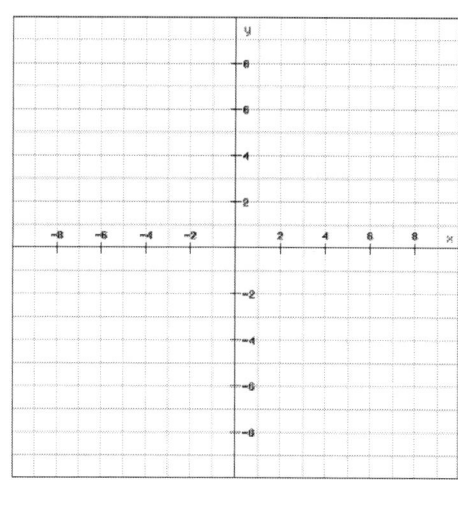

Domain: _____ x intercept:(___, ___)

Range: _____

Increases: _____

Decreases: _____ y intercept:(___, ___)

Max/Min:(___, ___)

13. $f(x) = -\sqrt{-x-3} - 1$

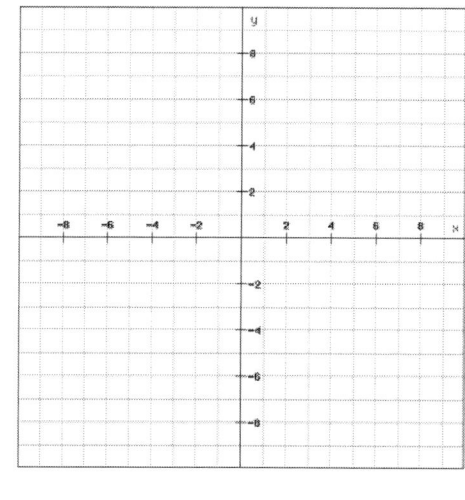

Domain: _____ x intercept:(___, ___)

Range: _____

Increases: _____

Decreases: _____ y intercept:(___, ___)

Max/Min:(___, ___)

14. $f(x) = -2\sqrt{x} + 9$

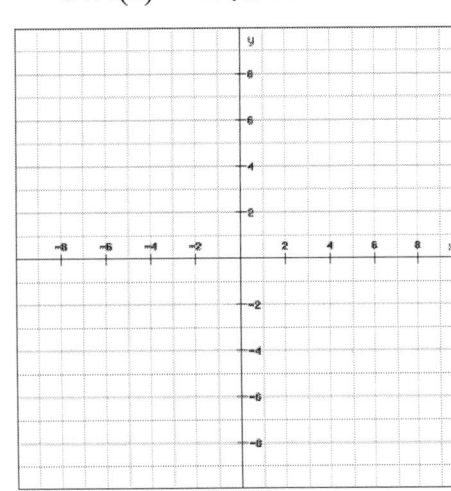

Domain: _____   x intercept:(___, ___)

Range: _____

Increases: _____

Decreases: _____   y intercept:(___, ___)

Max/Min:(___, ___)

15. $f(x) = \left|\sqrt{x+3}\right|$

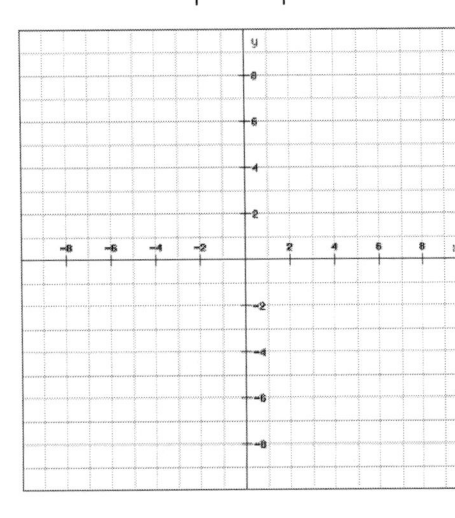

Domain: _____   x intercept:(___, ___)

Range: _____

Increases: _____

Decreases: _____   y intercept:(___, ___)

Max/Min:(___, ___)

16. $f(x) = \left|-\sqrt{x-2}\right|$

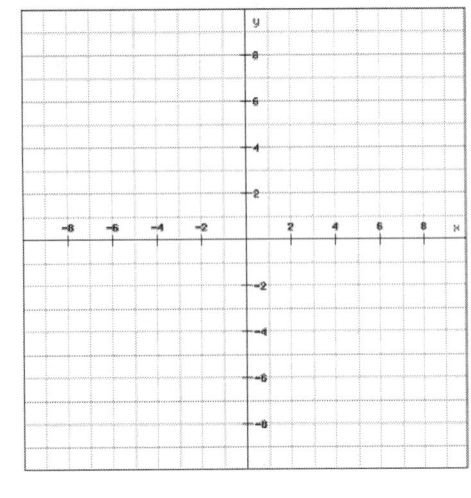

Domain: _____   x intercept:(___, ___)

Range: _____

Increases: _____

Decreases: _____   y intercept:(___, ___)

Max/Min:(___, ___)

17. $f(x) = \left|\sqrt{x+3} - 2\right|$

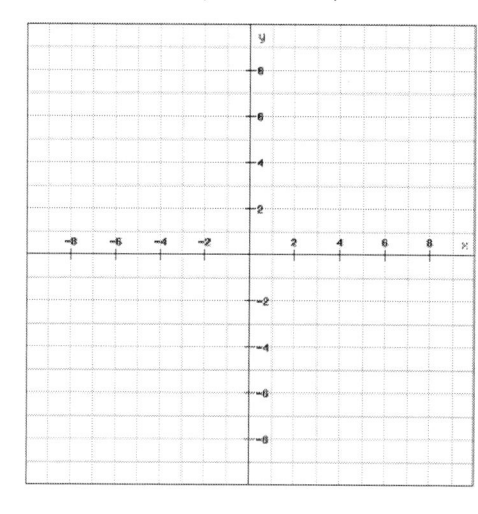

Domain: _____   x intercept:(___, ___)

Range: _____

Increases: _____

Decreases: _____   y intercept:(___, ___)

Max/Min:(___, ___)

18. $f(x) = \sqrt{|x|+3} - 2$

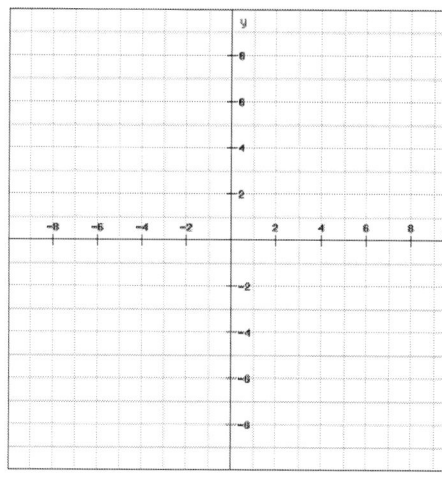

Domain: _____   x intercept:(___, ___)

Range: _____

Increases: _____

Decreases: _____   y intercept:(___, ___)

Max/Min:(___, ___)

19. $f(x) = \sqrt{|x|-1} - 2$

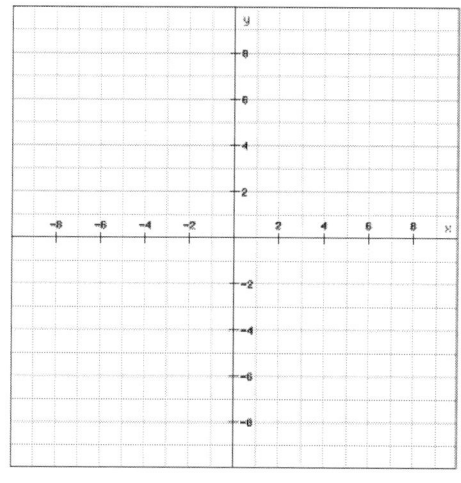

Domain: _____   x intercept:(___, ___)

Range: _____

Increases: _____

Decreases: _____   y intercept:(___, ___)

Max/Min:(___, ___)

2.10. – HYBRID (OR PIECEWISE) FUNCTIONS

1. Analyze a function means that we should discuss the following:

   a. Domain
   b. Range
   c. Interceptions (x and y)
   d. Asymptotes
   e. Critical Points (max, min)
   f. Write in all forms
   g. Decrease and increase intervals
   h. Sketch
   i. Continuity

Analyze the following functions:

2. $f(x) = \begin{cases} -x & x < 0 \\ x & 0 \leq x \end{cases}$

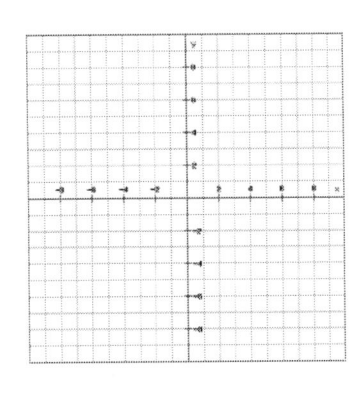

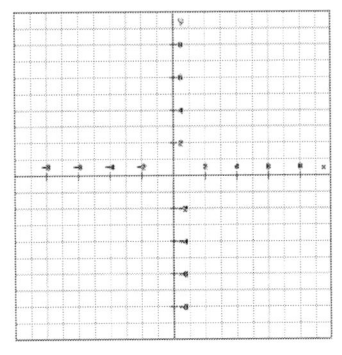

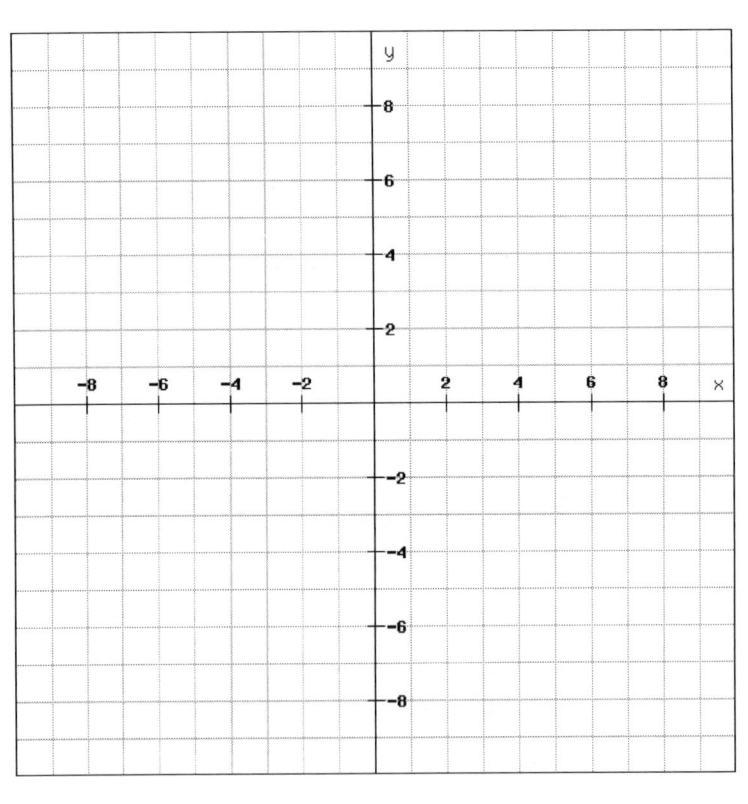

272

3. $f(x) = \begin{cases} -x & x < 2 \\ x & 2 \leq x \end{cases}$

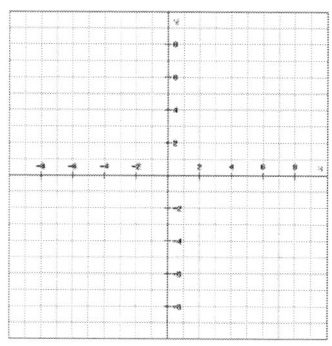

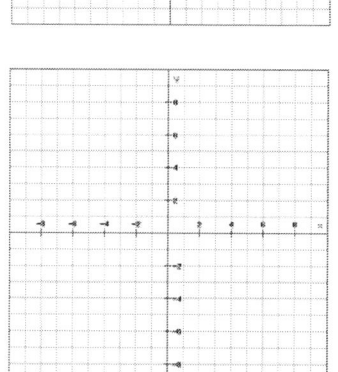

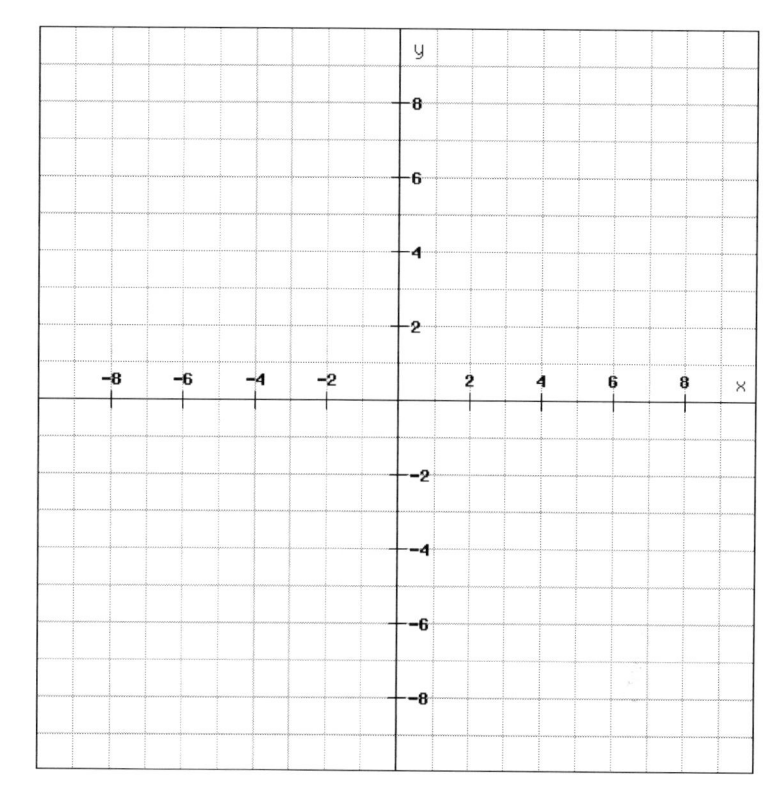

4. $f(x) = \begin{cases} 3 & x < -3 \\ x^2 & -3 \leq x \end{cases}$

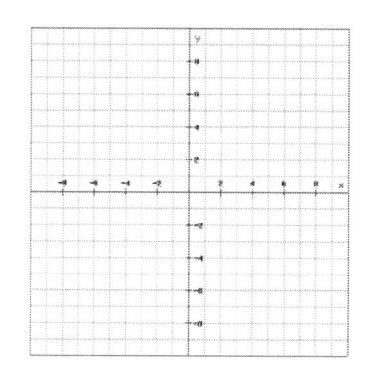

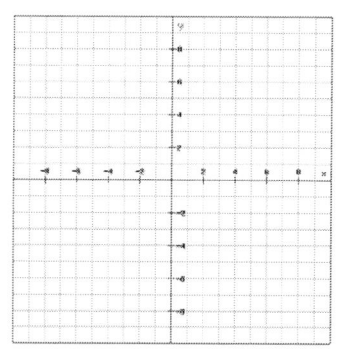

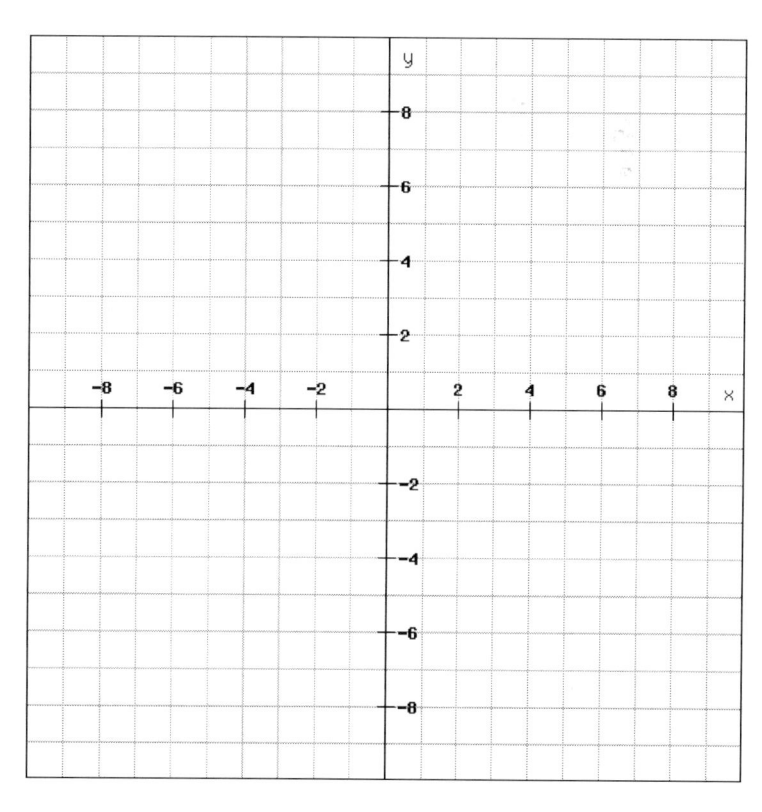

5. $f(x) = \begin{cases} 3x & x \leq 2 \\ -x^2 - 2 & 2 < x \end{cases}$

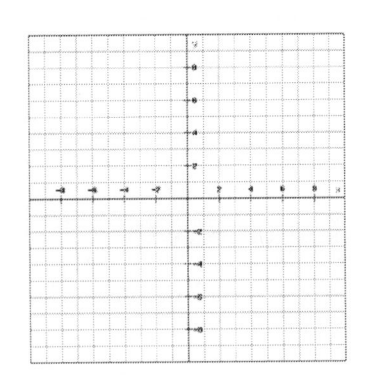

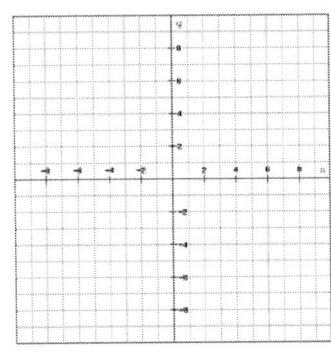

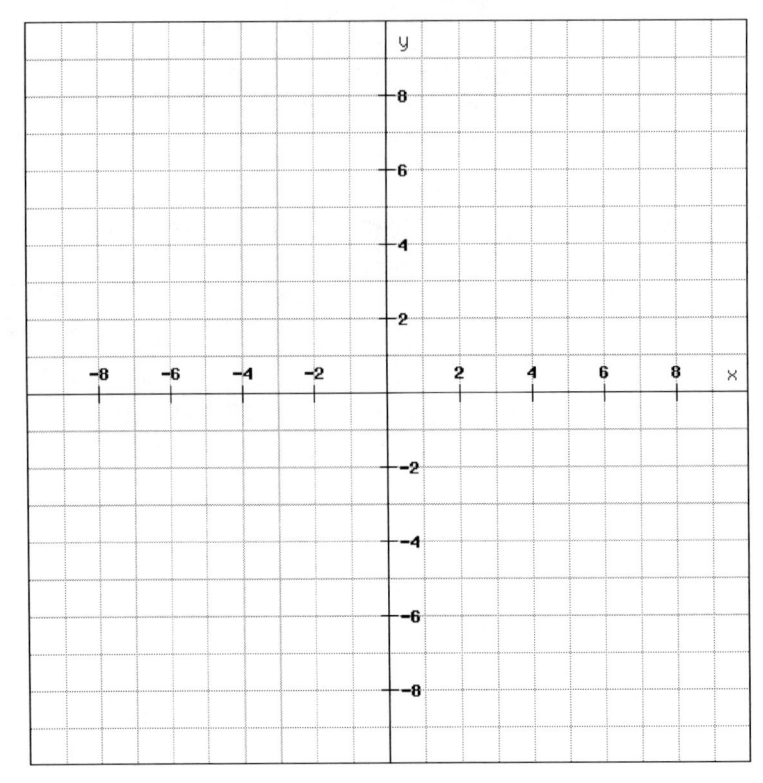

6. $f(x) = \begin{cases} e^x & x \leq 2 \\ -(x-2)^2 & 2 < x \end{cases}$

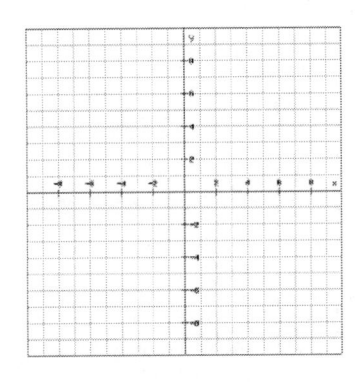

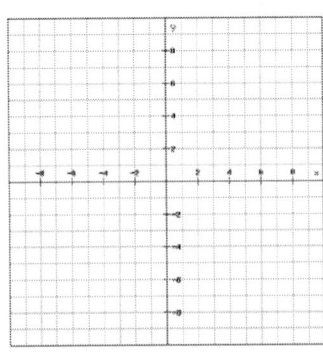

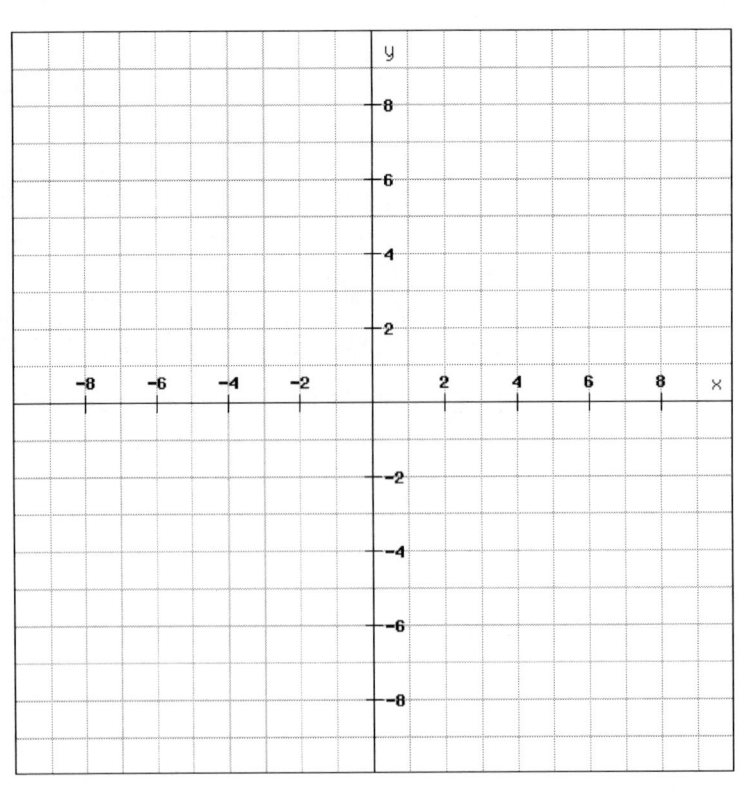

7. $f(x) = \begin{cases} -2^x & x \leq -3 \\ (x+1)^2 - 2 & -3 < x \end{cases}$

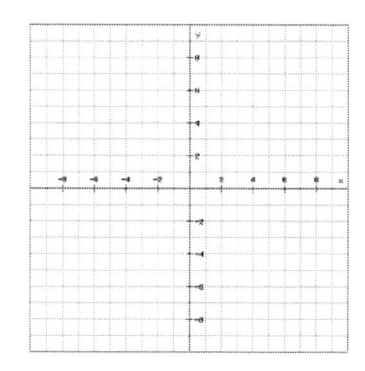

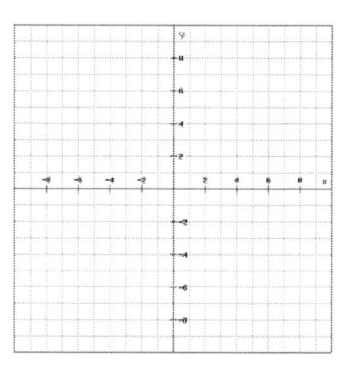

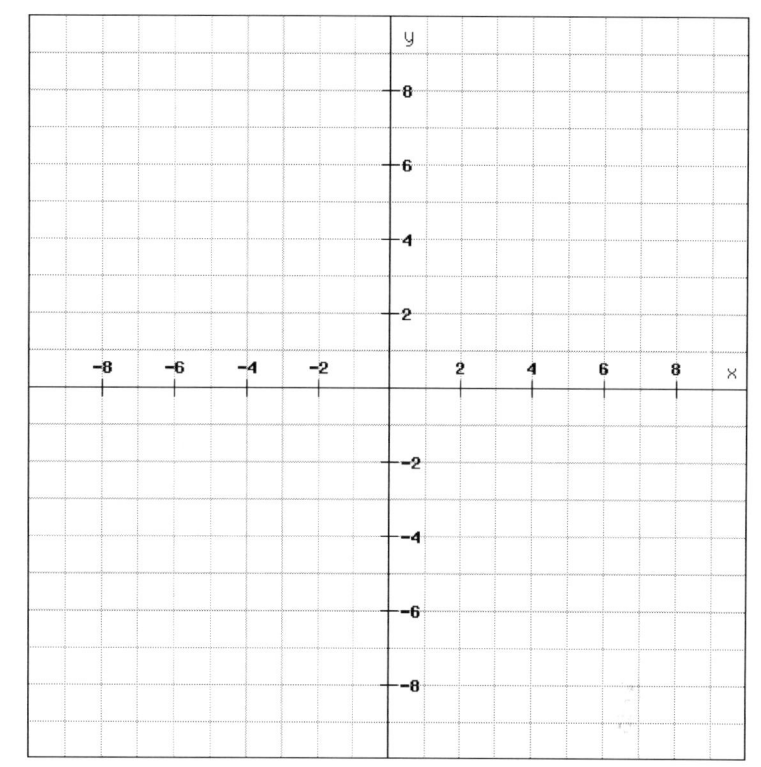

8. $f(x) = \begin{cases} x & x < 2 \\ x^2 - 1 & 2 \leq x \end{cases}$

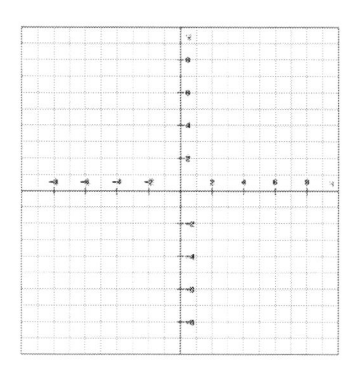

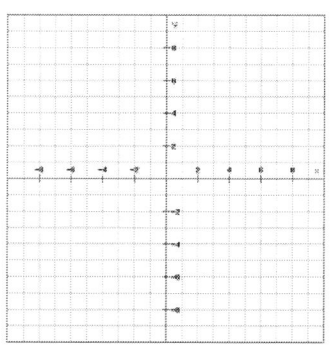

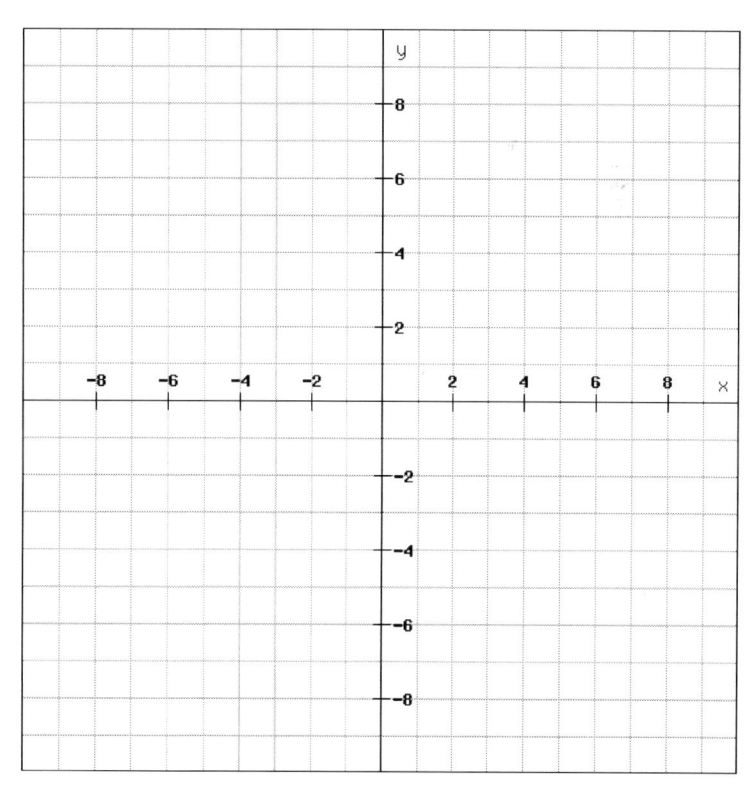

275

9. $f(x) = \begin{cases} -x^2 + 3 & x < -2 \\ x^2 - 1 & -2 \leq x \end{cases}$

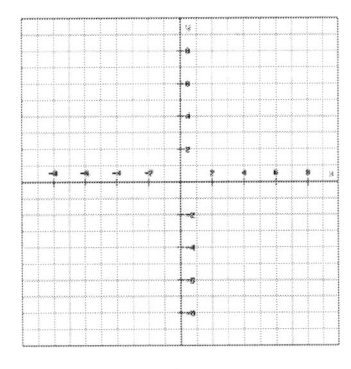

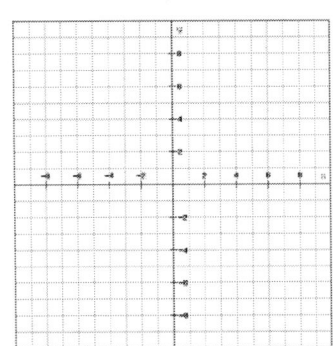

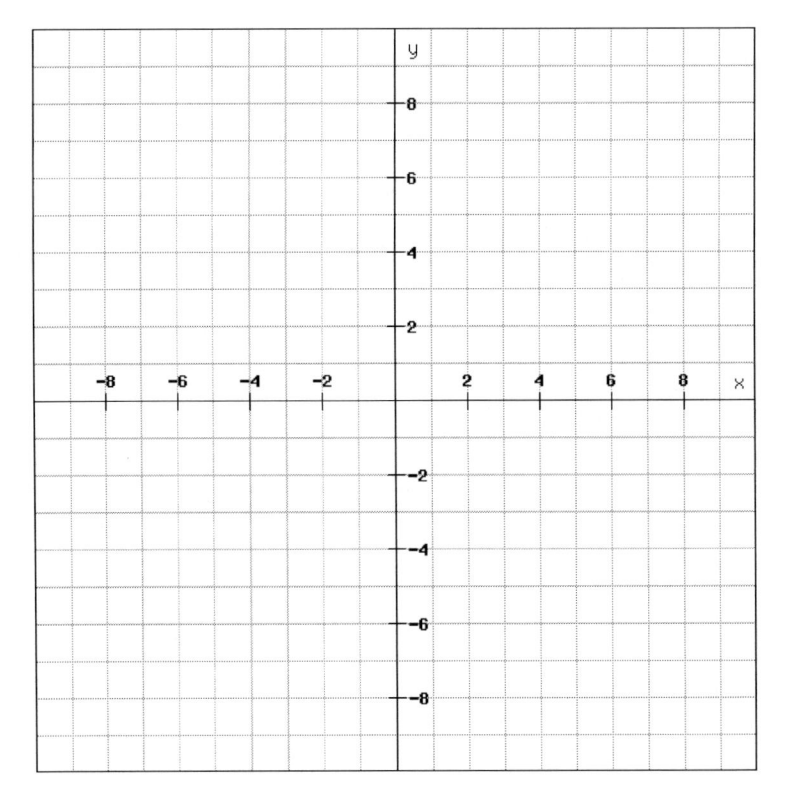

10. $f(x) = \begin{cases} -2x^2 + 47 & x < -5 \\ x + 2 & -5 \leq x \end{cases}$

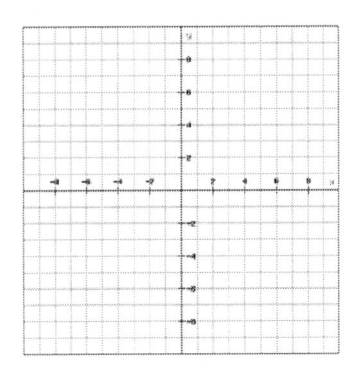

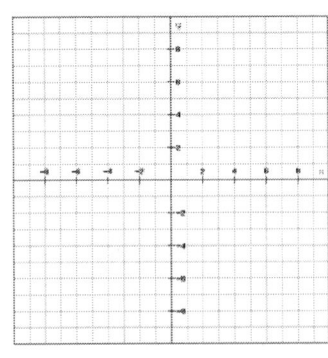

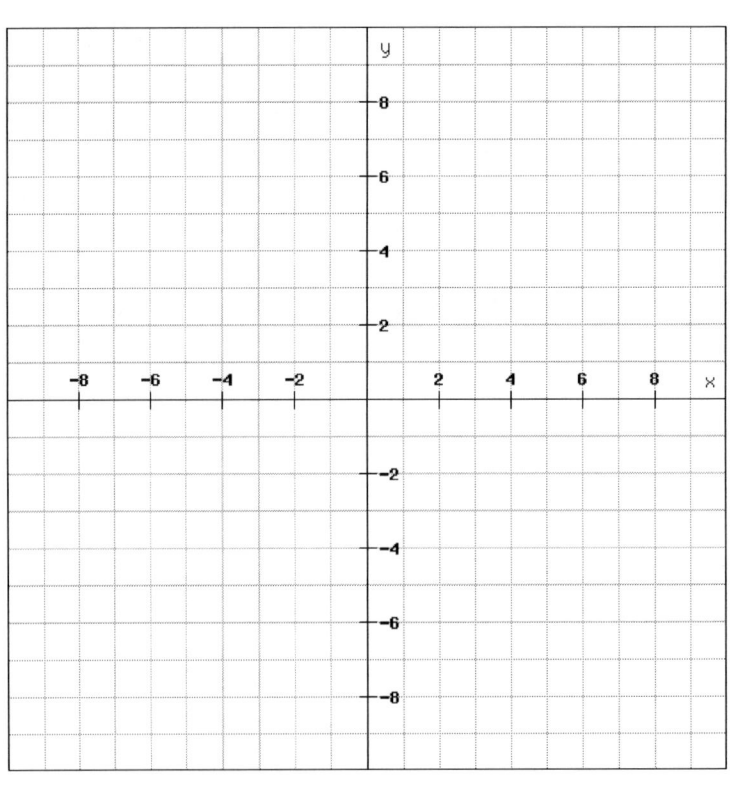

11. $f(x) = \begin{cases} x & x < 3 \\ \ln(x) & 3 < x \end{cases}$

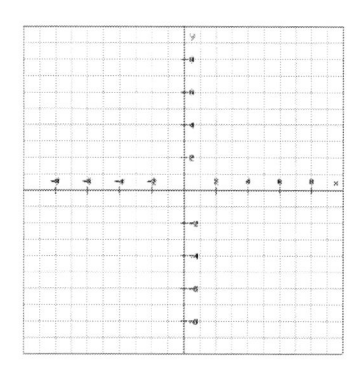

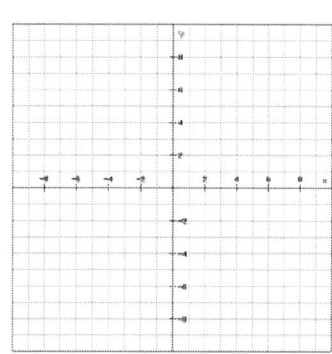

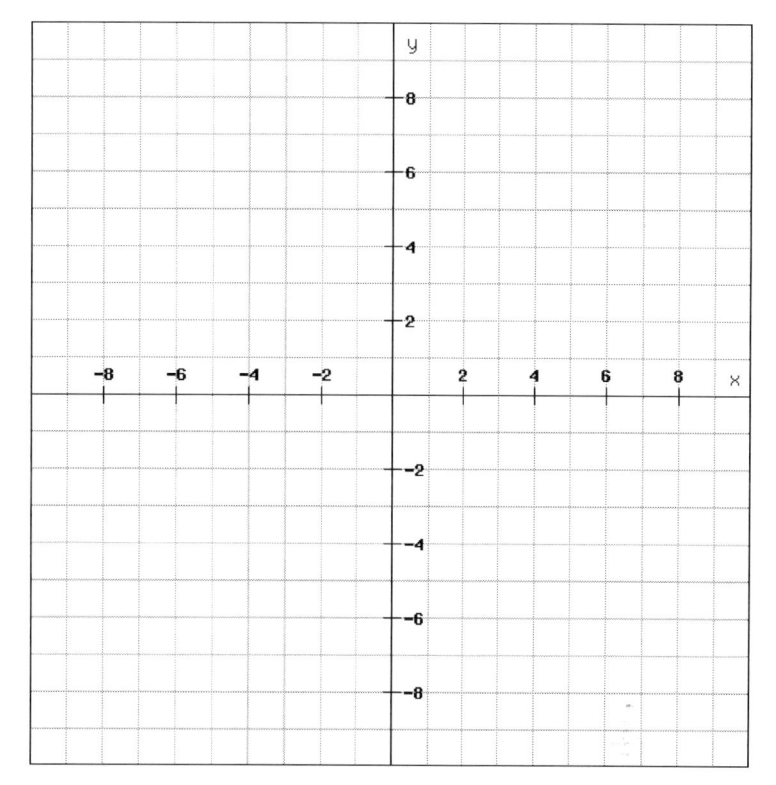

12. $f(x) = \begin{cases} x - \dfrac{8}{3} & x < 3 \\ \dfrac{1}{x} & 3 \leq x \end{cases}$

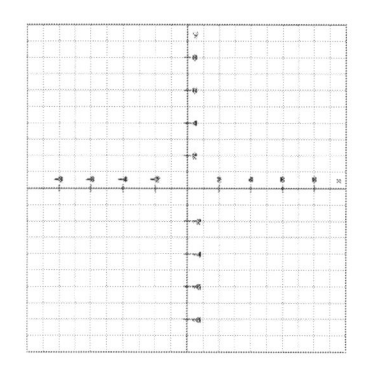

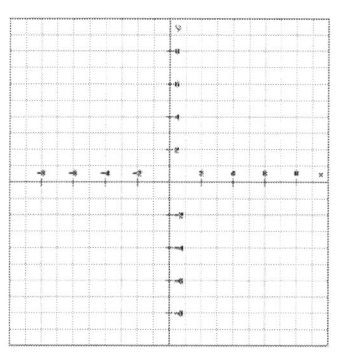

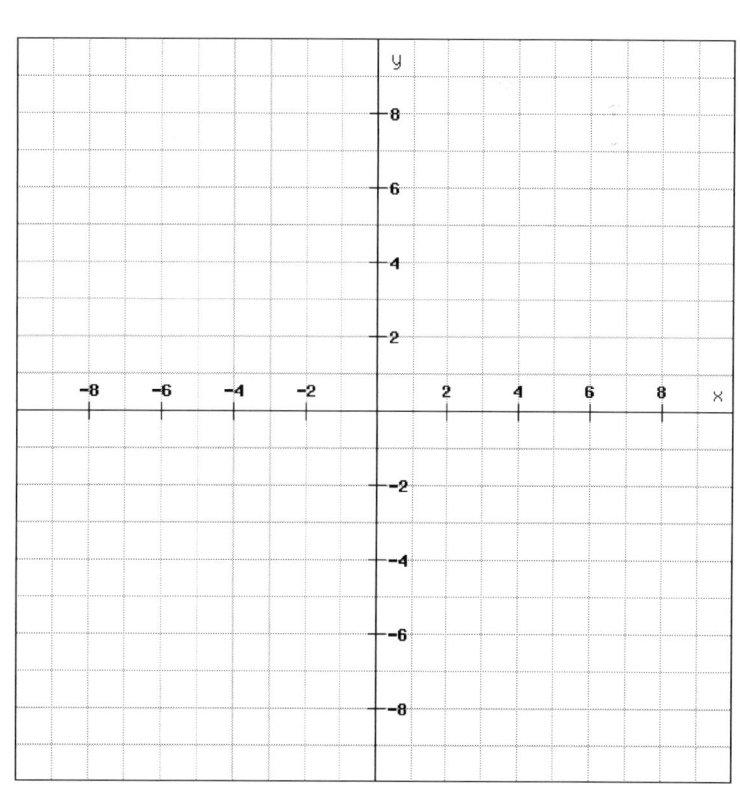

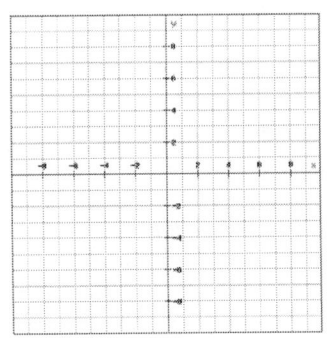

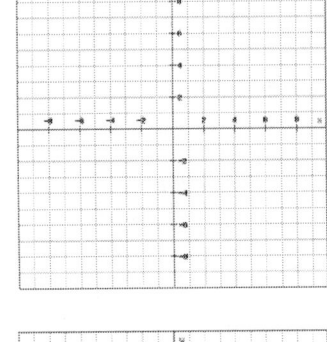

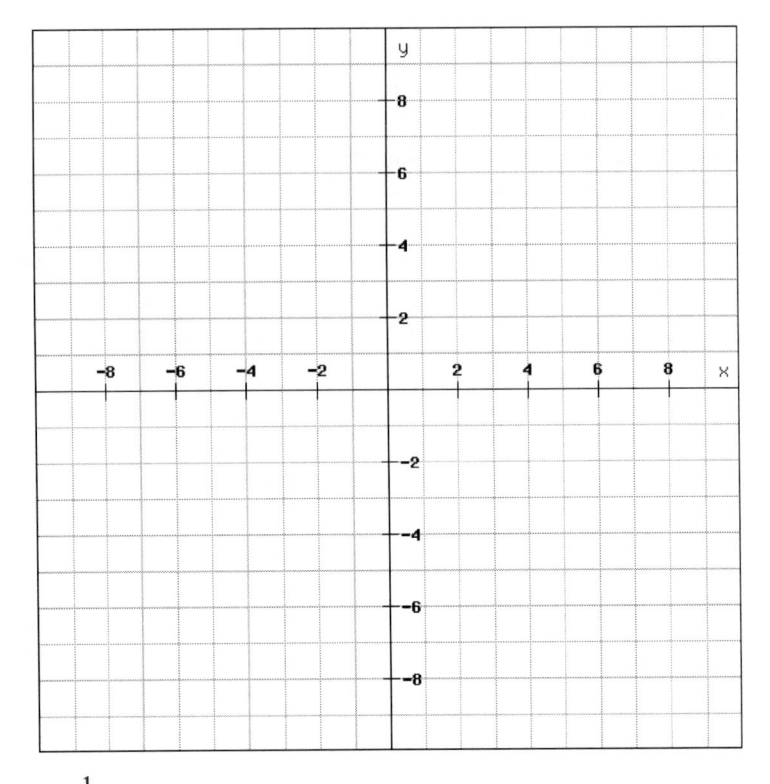

13. $f(x) = \begin{cases} \dfrac{1}{x+1} & x \leq 2 \\ \dfrac{1}{x} & 2 < x \end{cases}$

14. $f(x) = \begin{cases} \dfrac{1}{x+1} & x < \dfrac{-1}{2} \\ \dfrac{1}{x} & \dfrac{-1}{2} < x \end{cases}$

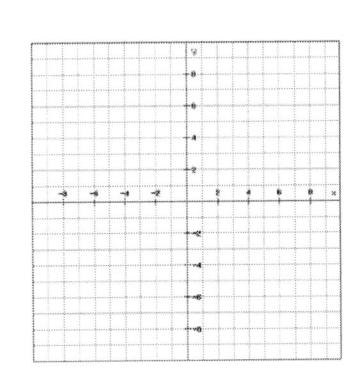

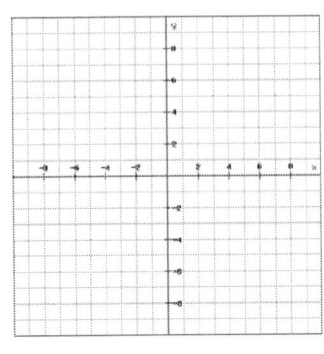

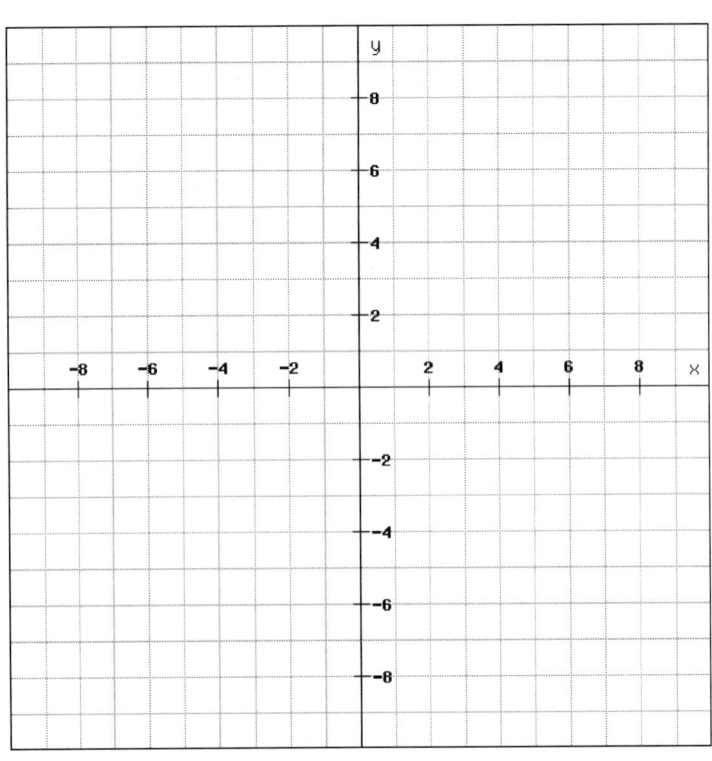

278

15. $f(x) = \begin{cases} \dfrac{1}{x-2} + 2 & x < 3 \\ \ln(x) & 3 \leq x \end{cases}$

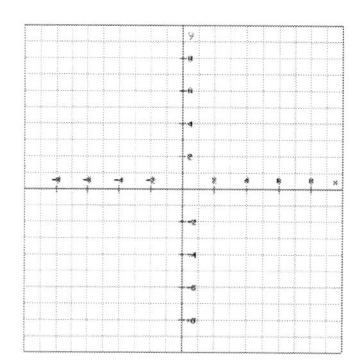

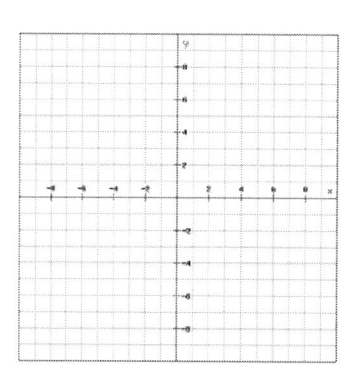

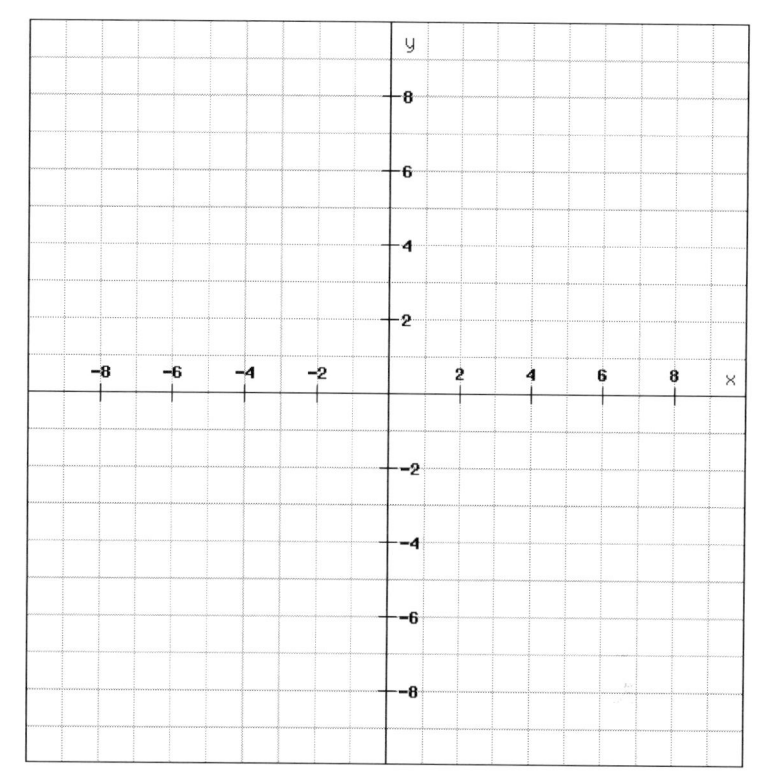

16. $f(x) = \begin{cases} e^x + 2 & x < -2 \\ \dfrac{1}{x} - 2 & -2 \leq x \end{cases}$

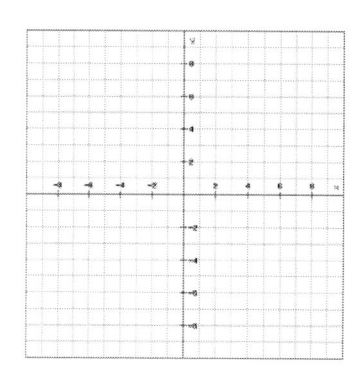

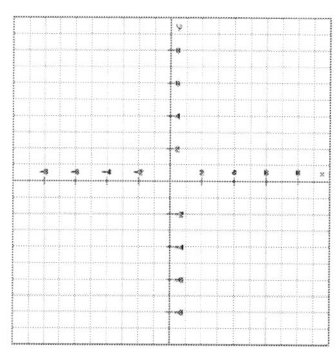

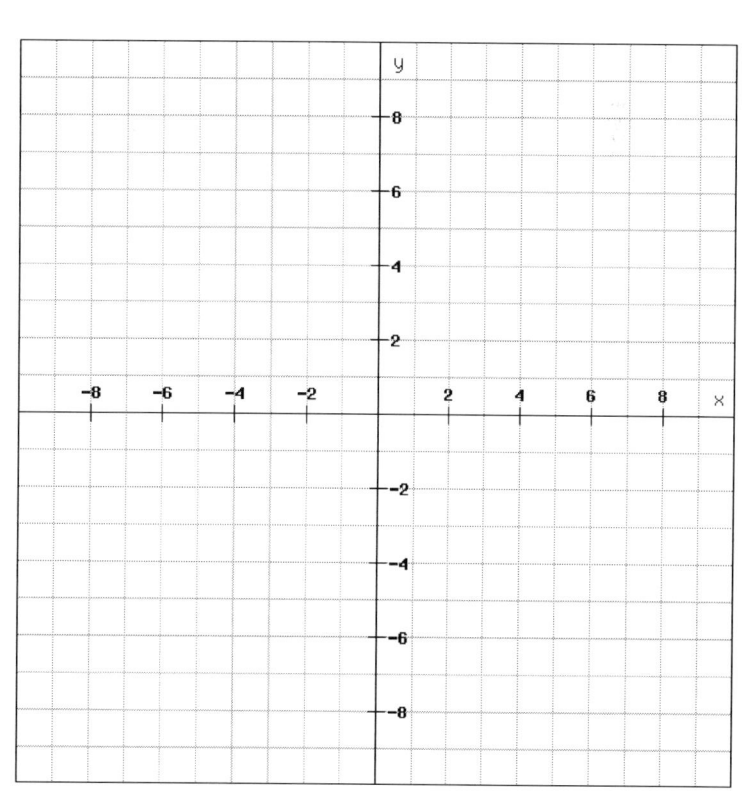

279

17. $f(x) = \begin{cases} e^{(-x)} - 2 & x < 1 \\ \dfrac{1}{x-2} + 1 & 1 \leq x \end{cases}$

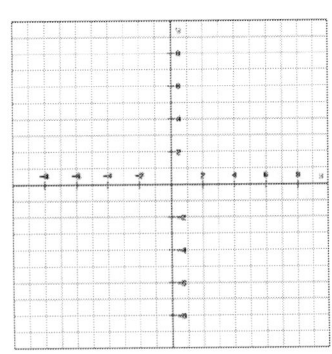

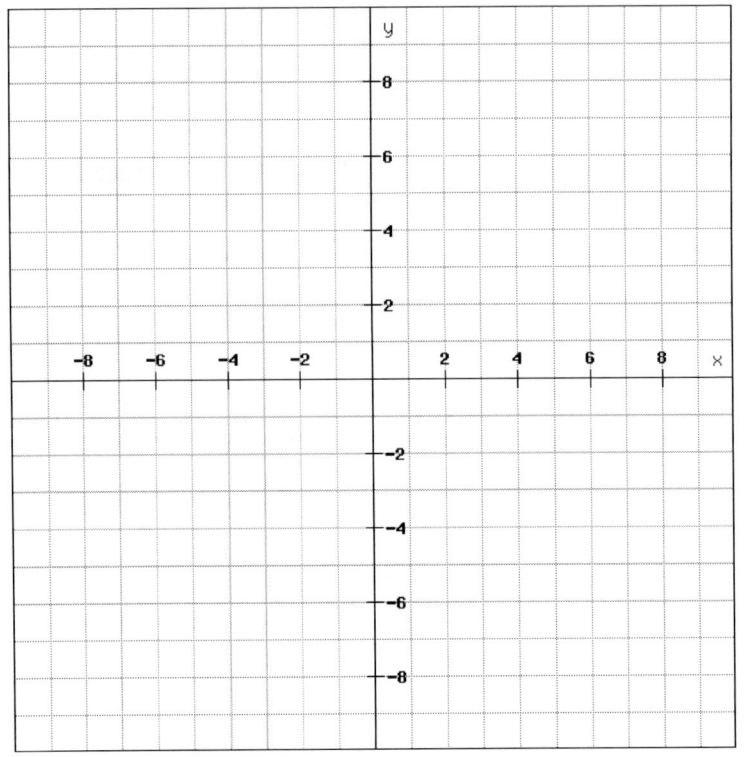

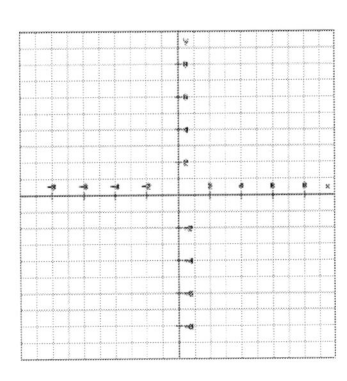

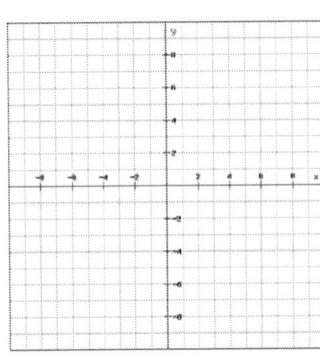

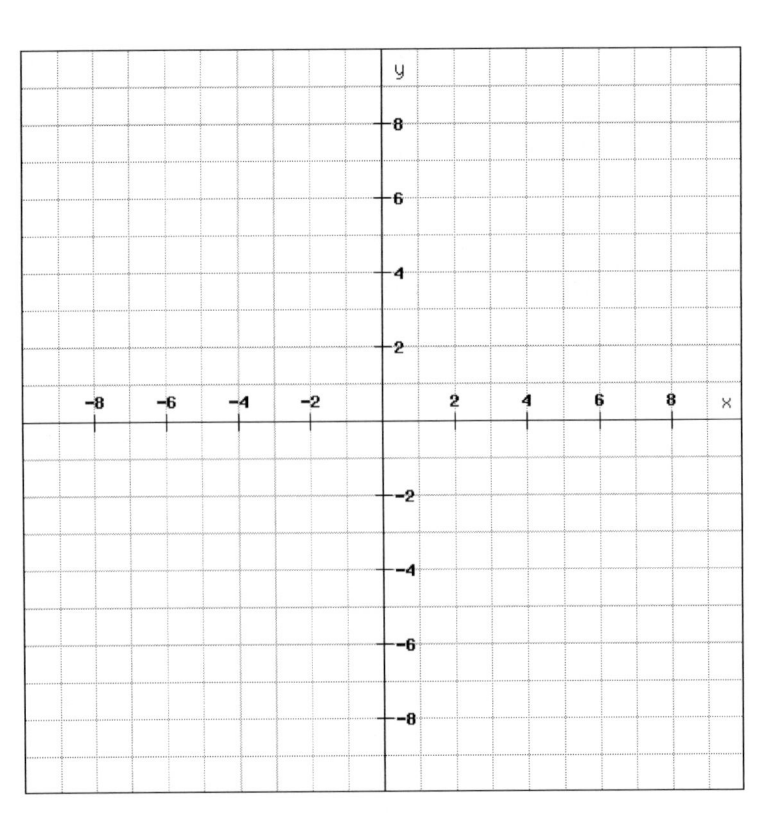

18. $f(x) = \begin{cases} -x^2 - 2 & x < 1 \\ \dfrac{1}{-3+x} & 1 \leq x \end{cases}$

19. $f(x) = \begin{cases} x^2 + 3 & x < 2 \\ \ln(-3 + x) & 2 \leq x \end{cases}$

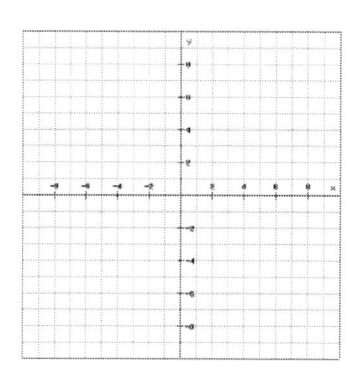

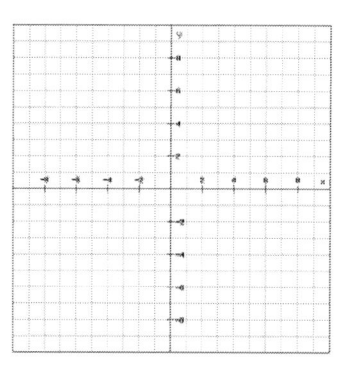

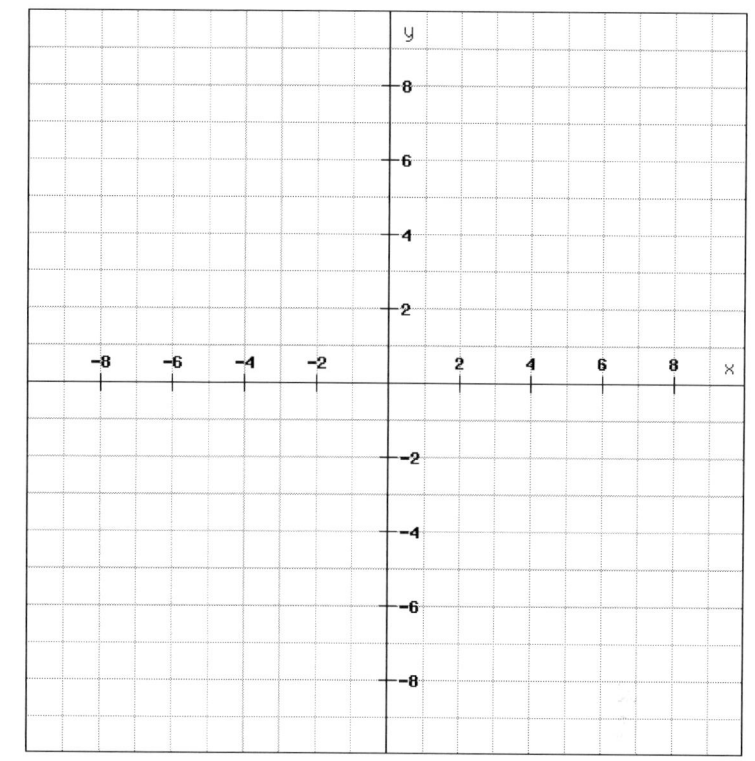

20. $f(x) = \begin{cases} x^2 + 3 & x < 2 \\ \ln(3 + x) & 2 \leq x \end{cases}$

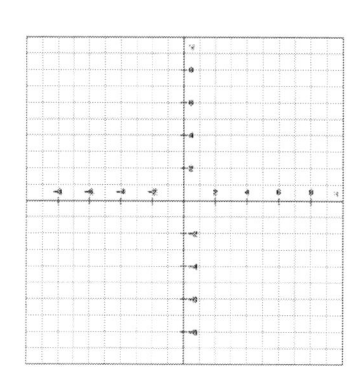

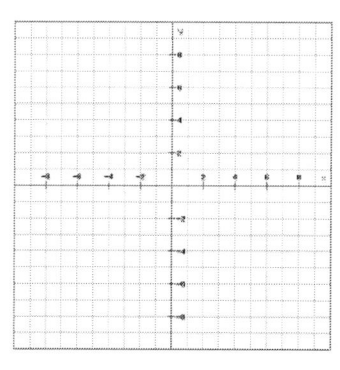

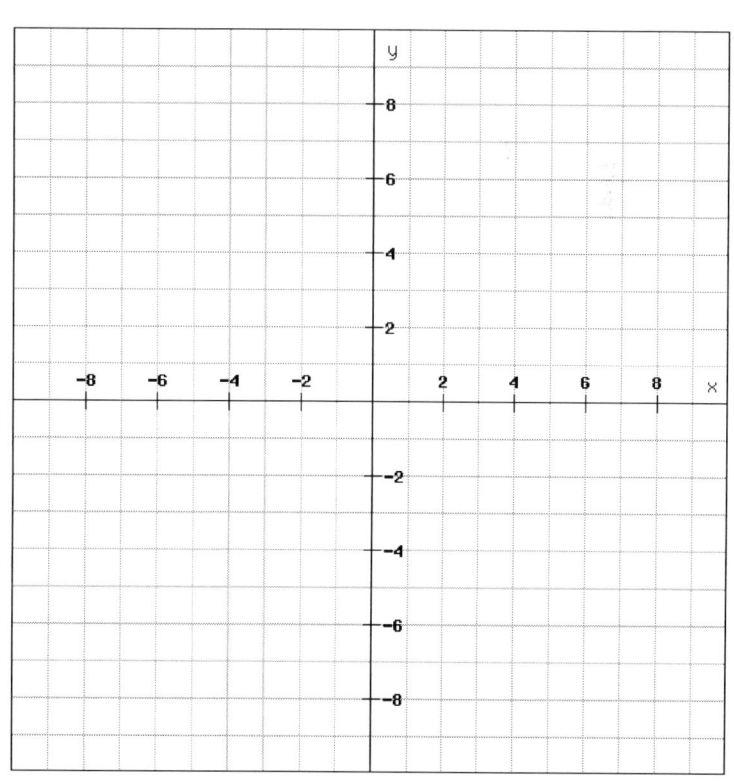

281

21. $f(x) = \begin{cases} 3x - 2 & x < 0 \\ \ln(3 + x) - 1 & 0 \leq x \end{cases}$

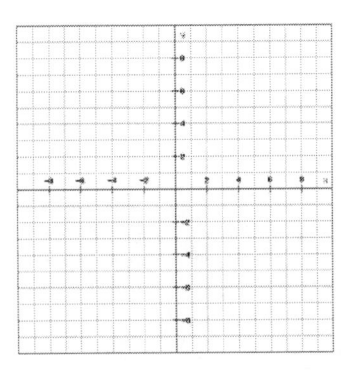

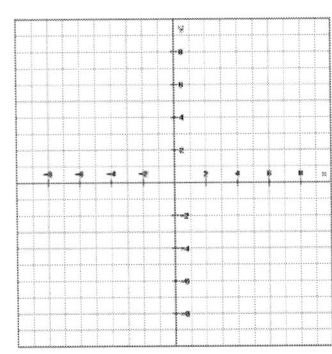

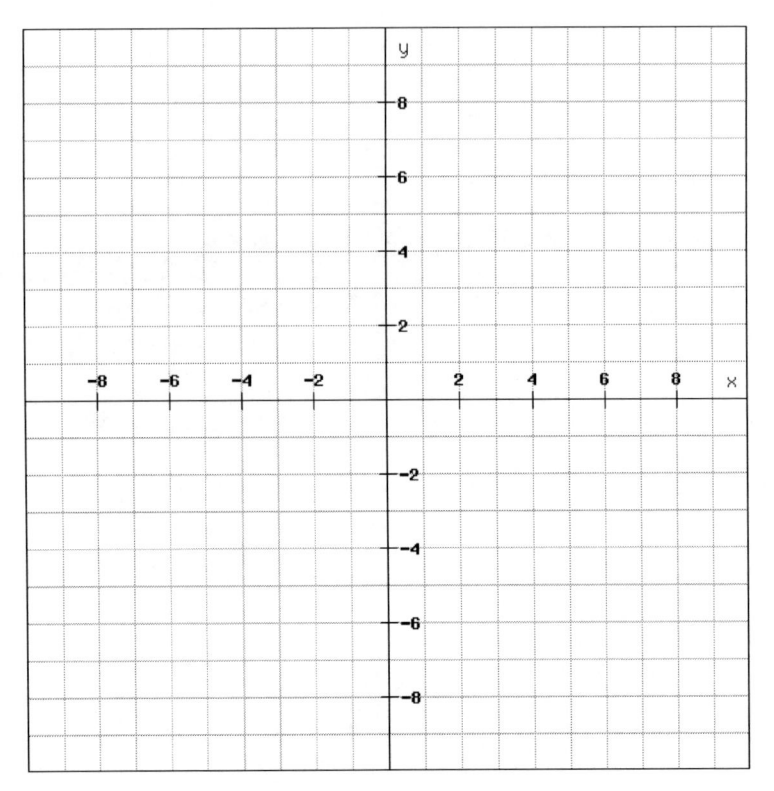

Find the value(s) of *a* for which the following functions will be continuous and then analyze the function:

22. $f(x) = \begin{cases} ax + 7 & x < -3 \\ x + 1 & -3 \leq x \end{cases}$

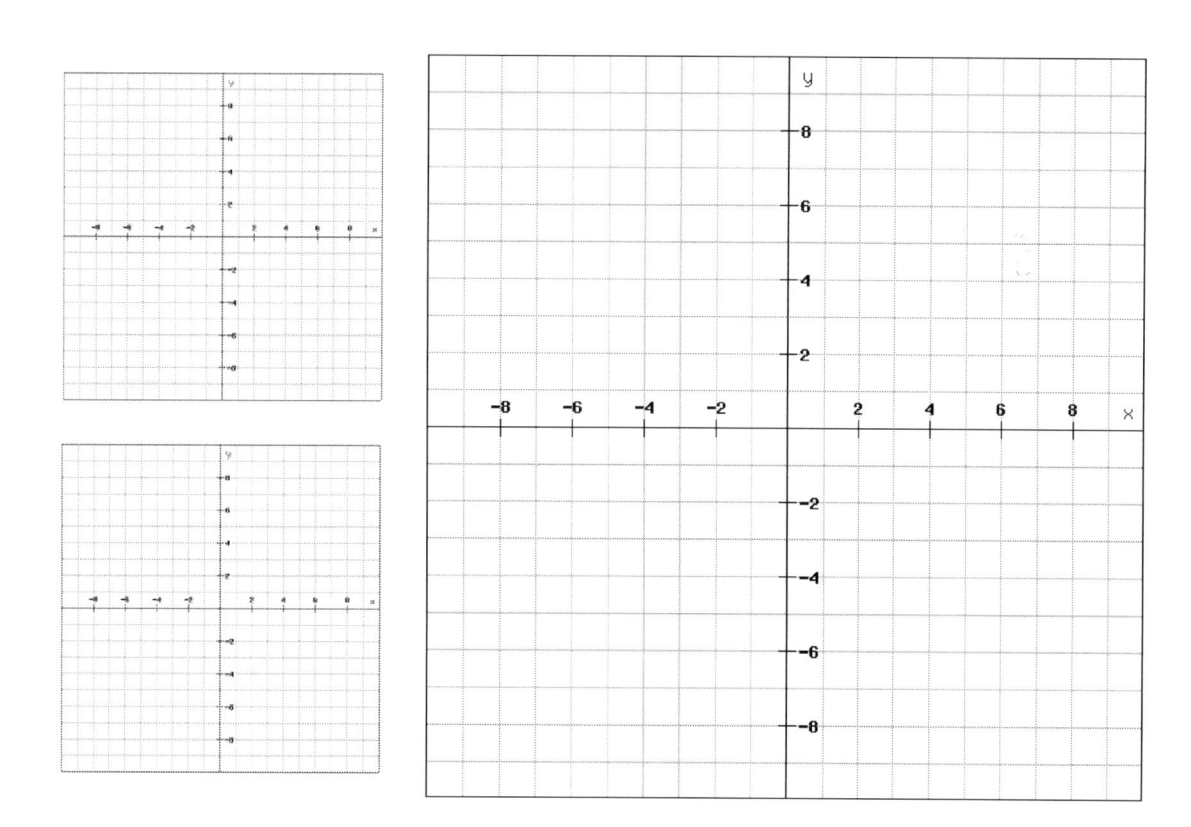

23. $f(x) = \begin{cases} ax^2 + 7 & x < -1 \\ 2x - 6 & -1 \leq x \end{cases}$

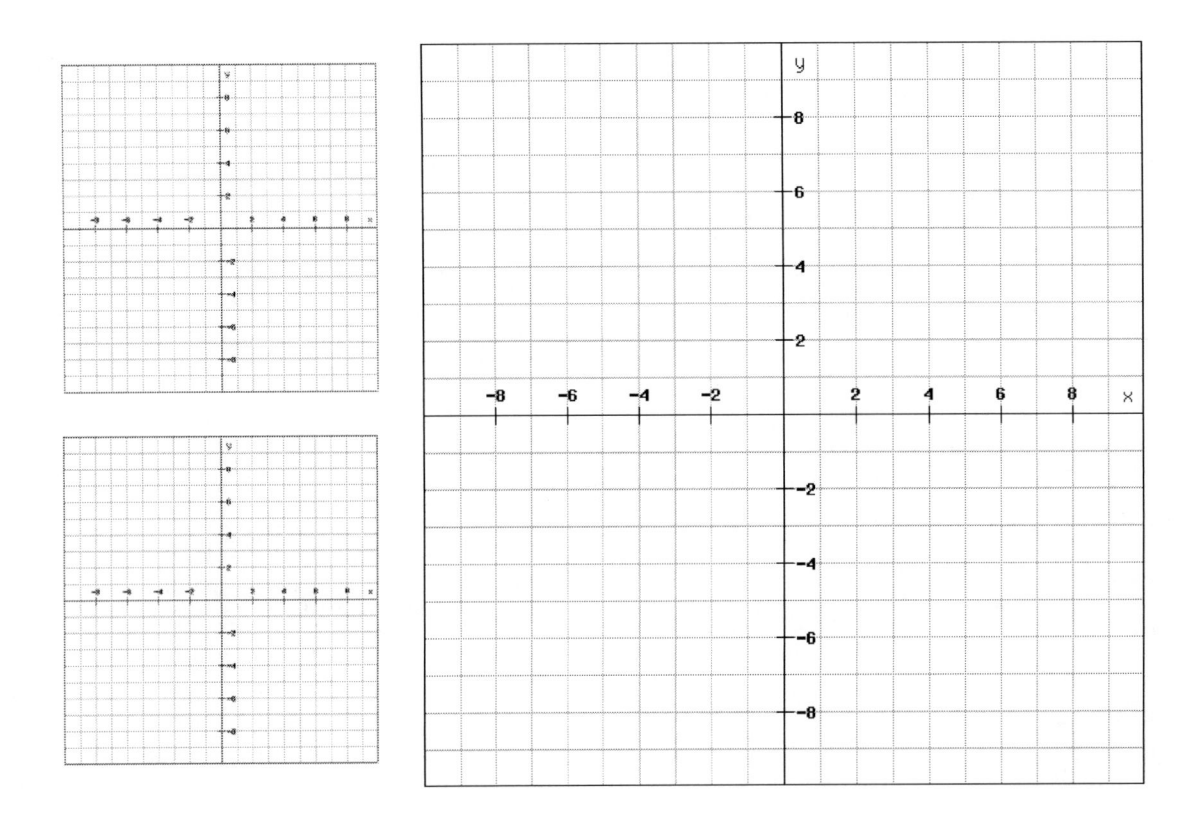

24. $f(x) = \begin{cases} x^2 + a & x < -1 \\ 2x - 6 & -1 \leq x \end{cases}$

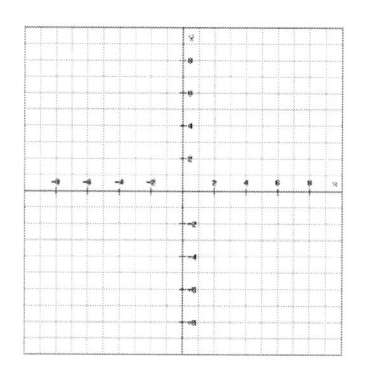

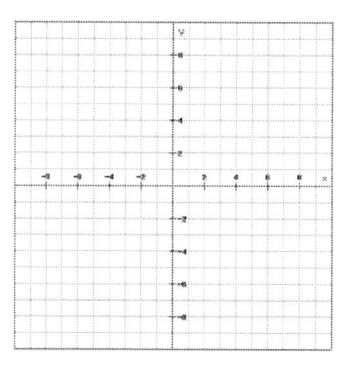

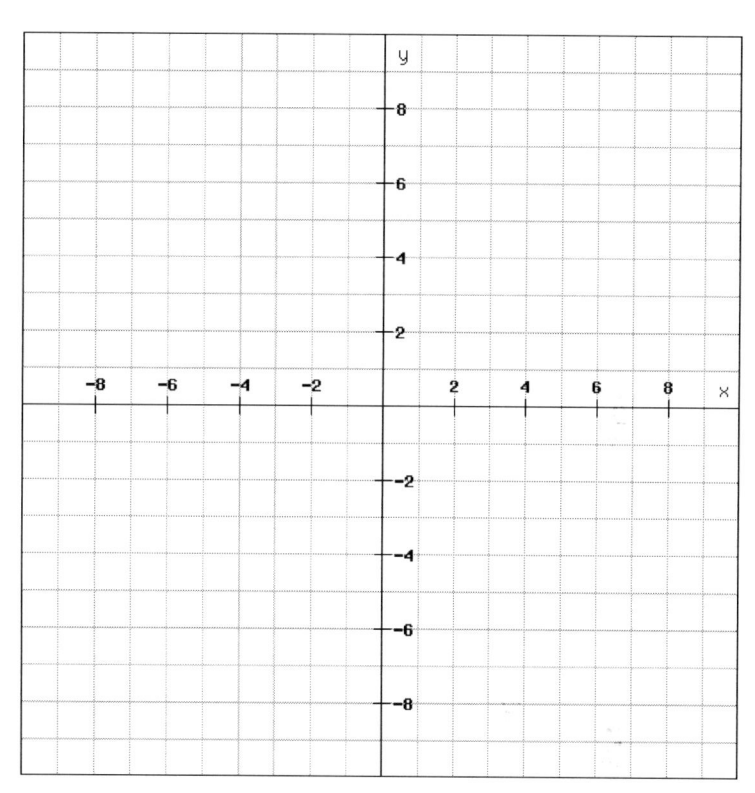

25. $f(x) = \begin{cases} -x^2 + 2 & x < 3 \\ 2x^2 - a & -3 \leq x \end{cases}$

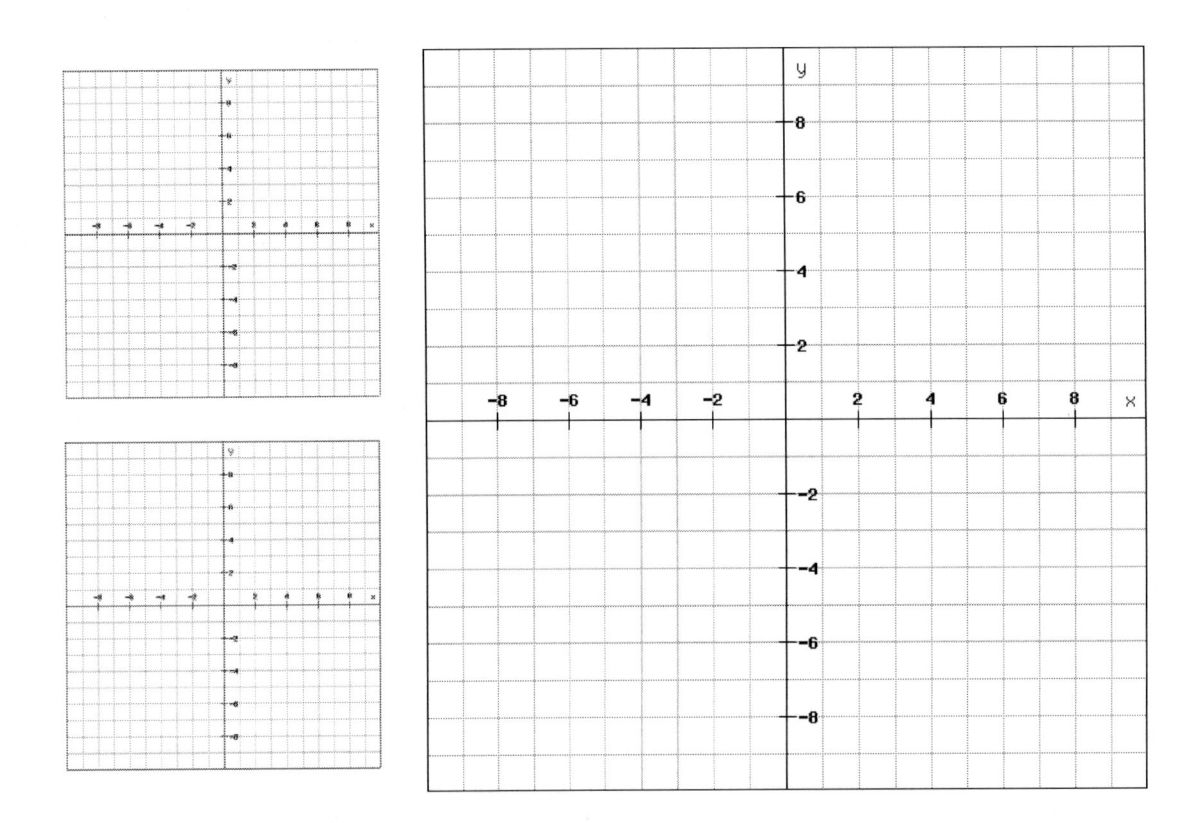

Analyze the following functions:

26. $f(x) = \begin{cases} \sqrt{x} - 1 & x < 2 \\ \dfrac{2}{x} + 1 & 2 \leq x \end{cases}$

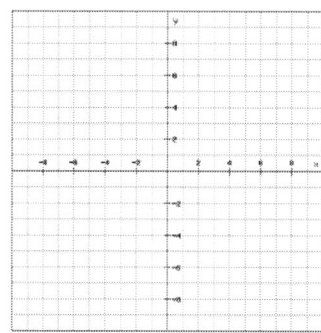

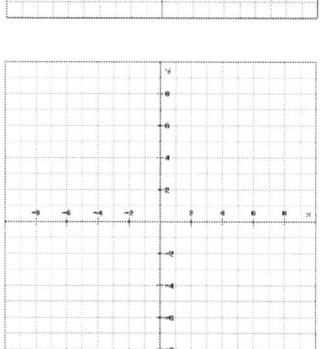

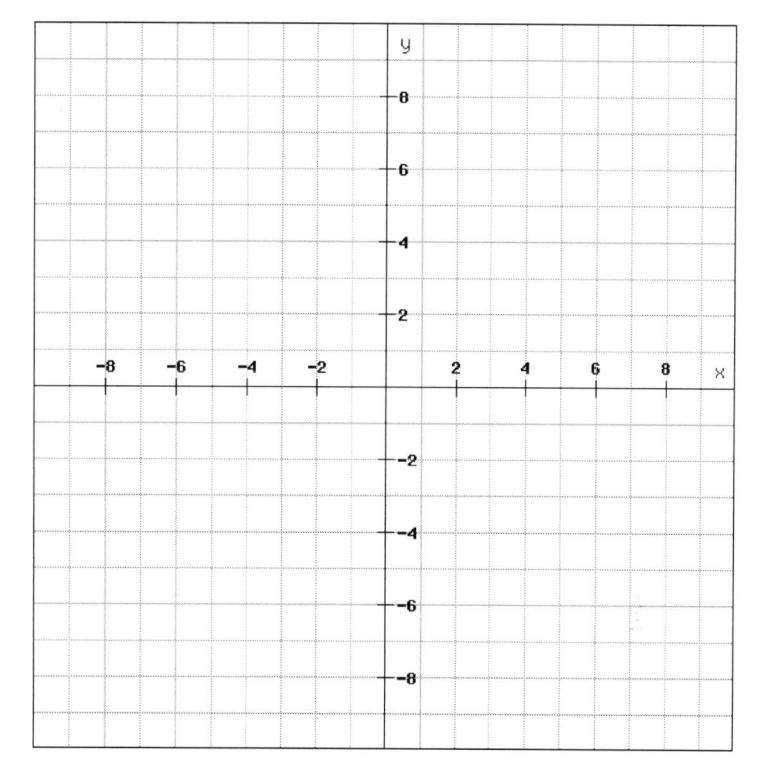

27. $f(x) = \begin{cases} \sqrt{x+2} - 2 & x < 7 \\ \dfrac{16}{x+1} - 1 & 7 \leq x \end{cases}$

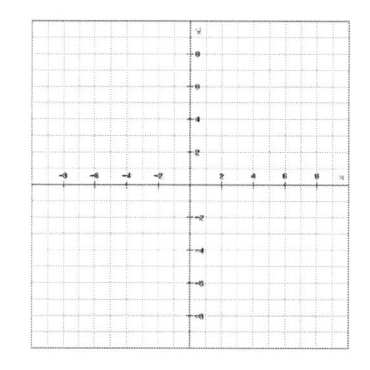

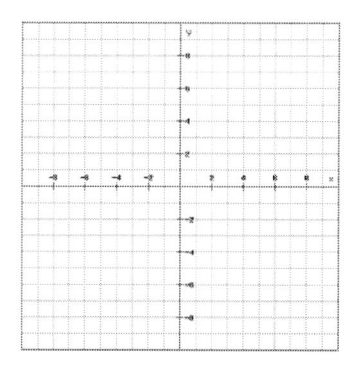

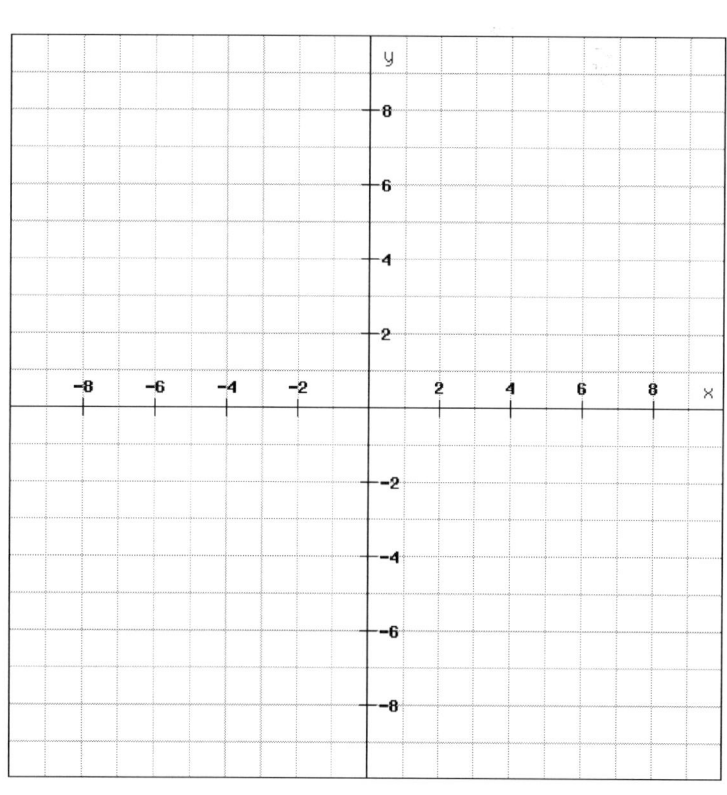

28. The sketch below shows the graph of a function y = f(x) between x = 0 and x = 6. The function f(x) is defined as follows Where a, b, c, d, g, h and k are constants.

$$f(x) = \begin{cases} ax + b & 0 < x \text{ and } x < 2 \\ c & 2 < x \text{ and } x < 4 \\ dx + g & 4 < x \text{ and } x < 6 \\ \sqrt{x + h} + k & 6 < x \text{ and } x < 8 \end{cases}$$

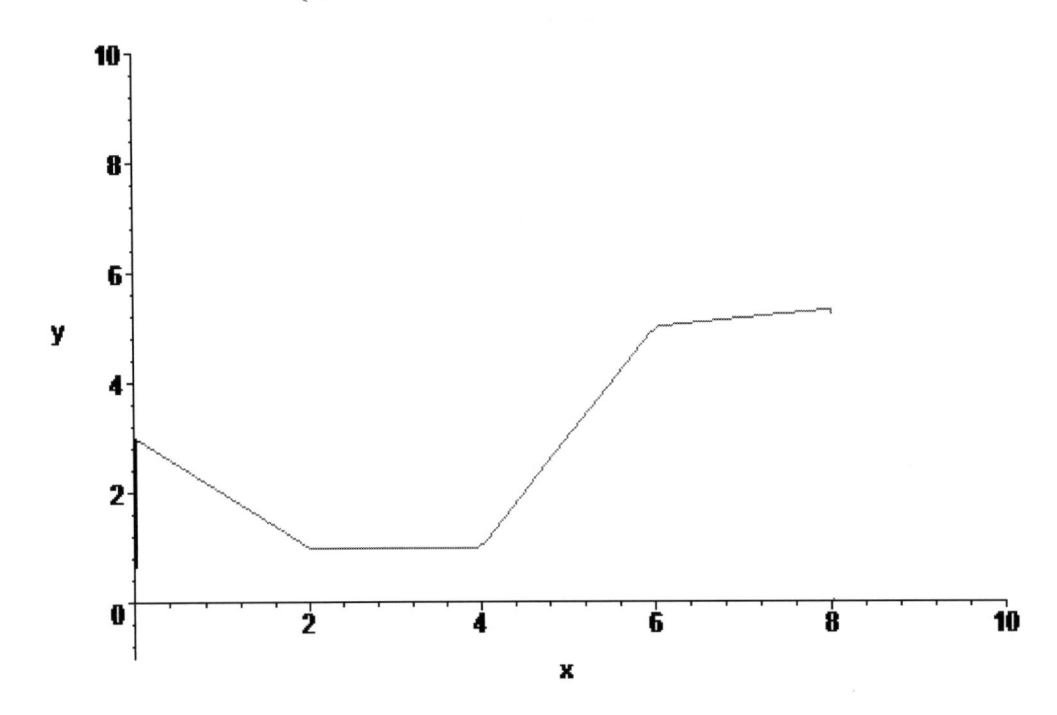

a. Write down the value of c.

b. Find the values of a and b

c. Find the values of d and g

d. Find the values of h and k

288

29. $f(x) = \begin{cases} -1 & x \leq 5 \\ 1 & 5 < x \text{ and } x < 6 \\ 2 & 6 \leq x \end{cases}$

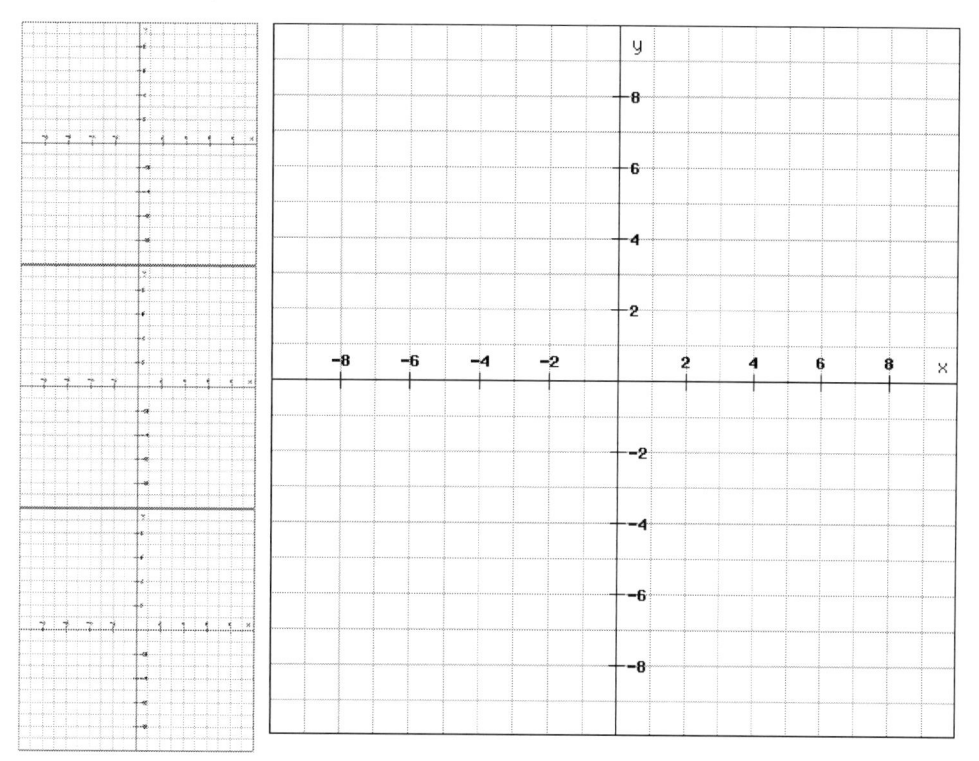

30. $f(x) = \begin{cases} 2x + 7 & x < -6 \\ x + 1 & -6 \leq x \text{ and } x < 2 \\ x^2 & 2 \leq x \end{cases}$

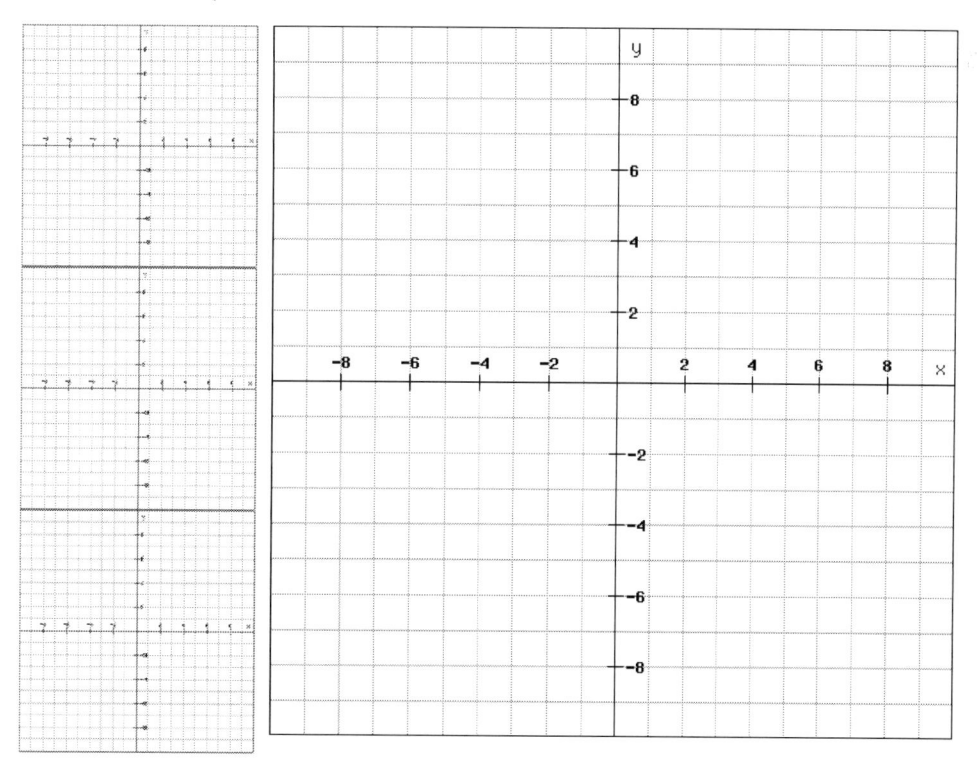

31. $f(x) = \begin{cases} -(3+x)^2 & x \leq -2 \\ x^2 - 5 & -1 < x \text{ and } x < 1 \\ -2x - 5 & 1 \leq x \end{cases}$

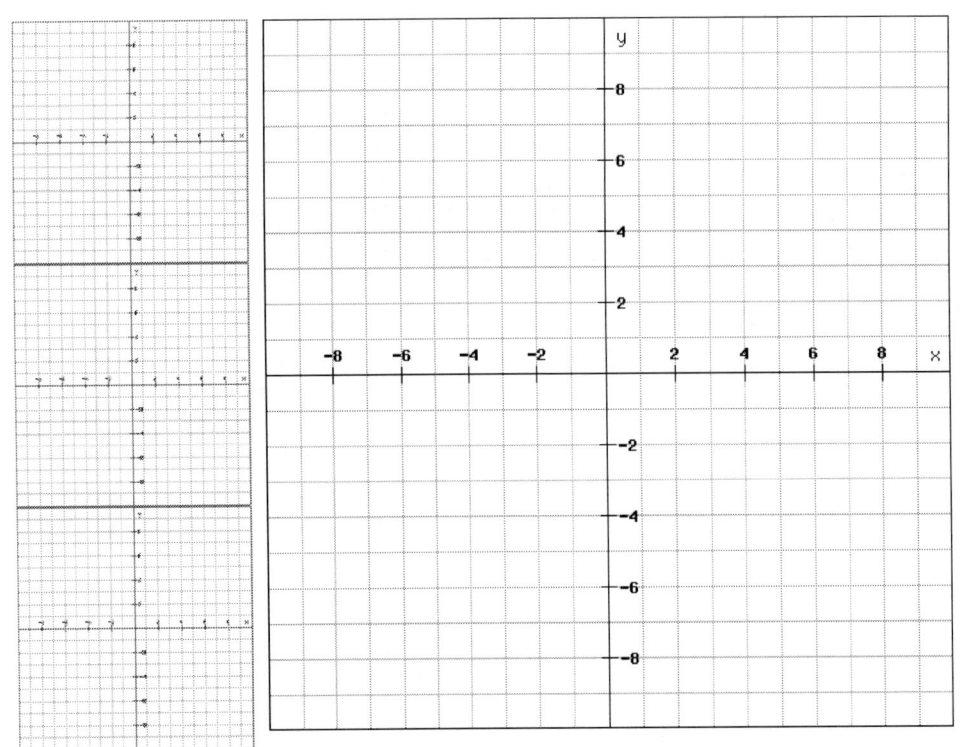

32. $f(x) = \begin{cases} 2x & x \leq -3 \\ (x+2)^2 & -3 < x \text{ and } x \leq 0 \\ \ln(x) & 0 < x \end{cases}$

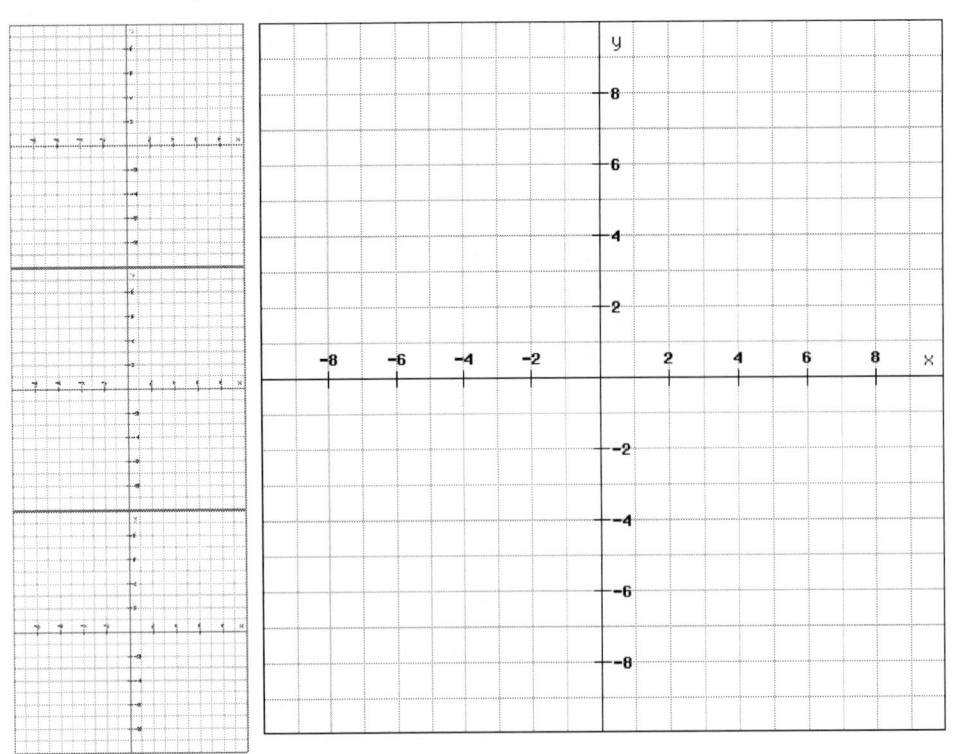

33. $f(x) = \begin{cases} -2x+1 & x \leq 2 \\ e^x & 2 < x \text{ and } x < 4 \\ \dfrac{1}{x} & 4 < x \end{cases}$

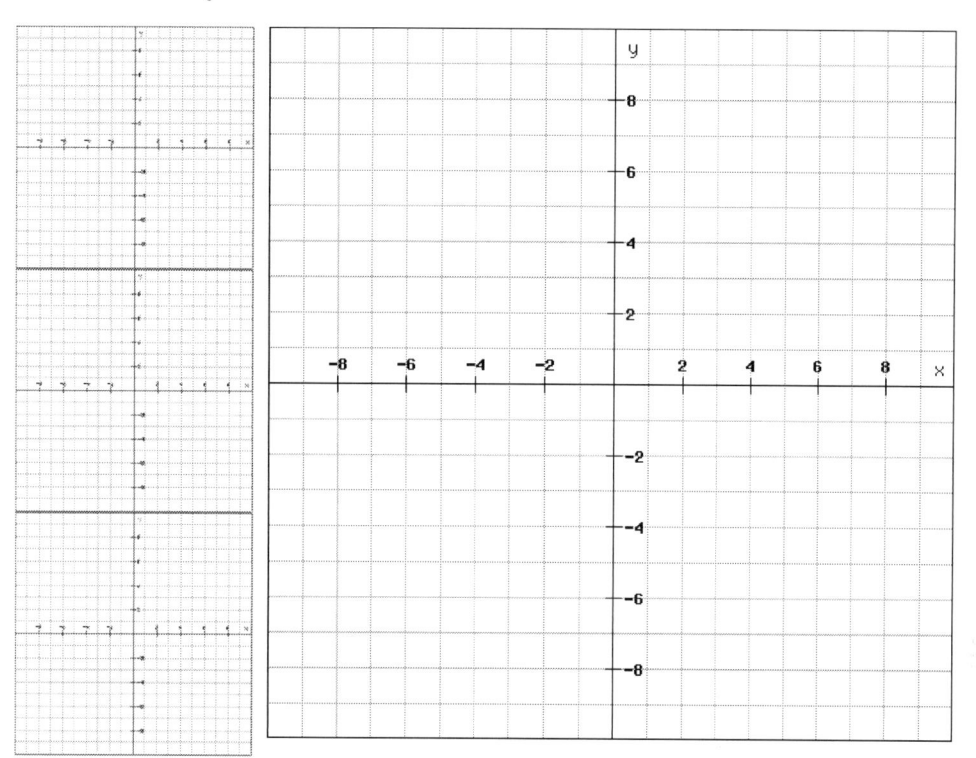

34. $f(x) = \begin{cases} x & x \leq -2 \\ -3x-2 & -2 < x \text{ and } x < 0 \\ \ln(2x+1)-1 & 0 \leq x \end{cases}$

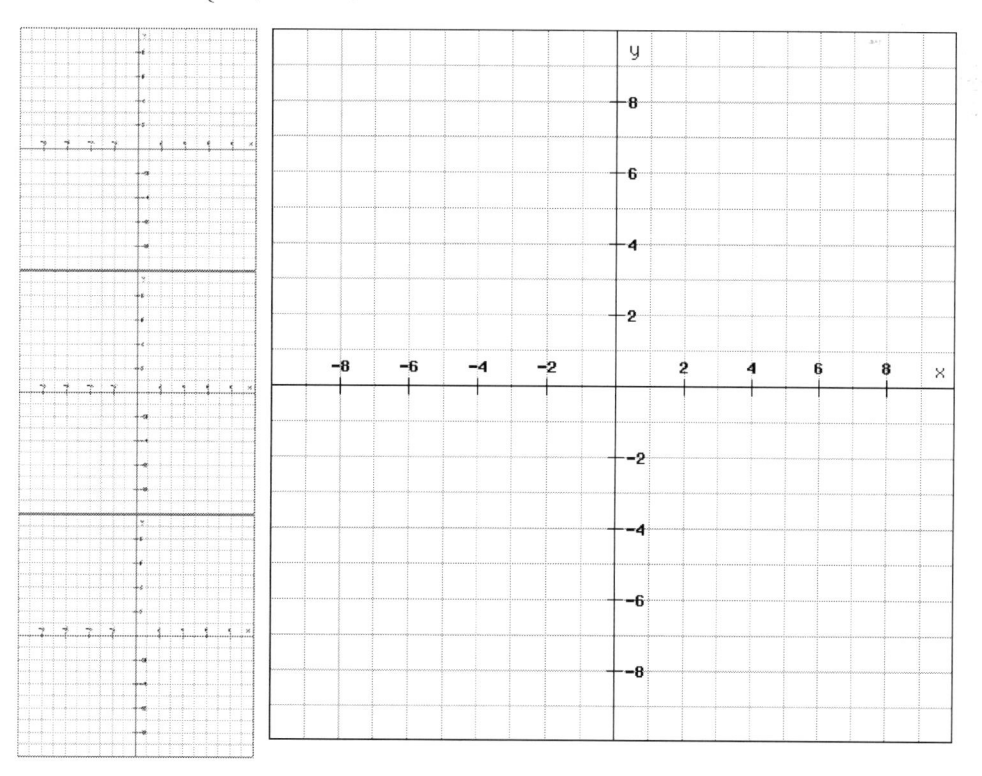

Find the value(s) of *a* for which the following functions will be continuous and then analyze the function:

35. $f(x) = \begin{cases} \sqrt{x+1} & x < 2 \\ \dfrac{a}{x+1} - 1 & 2 \leq x \end{cases}$

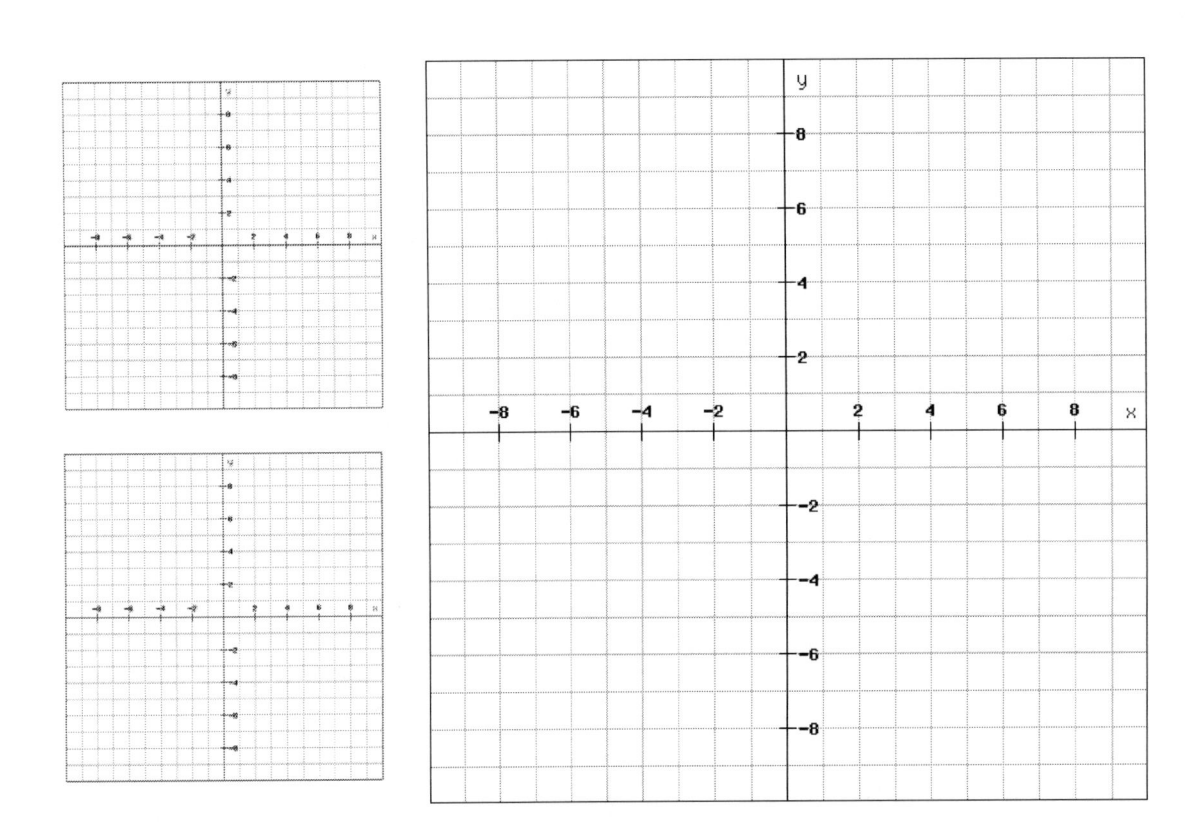

292

36. $f(x) = \begin{cases} \ln(x) + 1 & x < 1 \\ \dfrac{a}{2x+1} - 3 & 1 \le x \end{cases}$

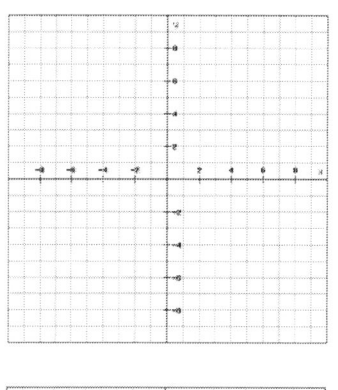

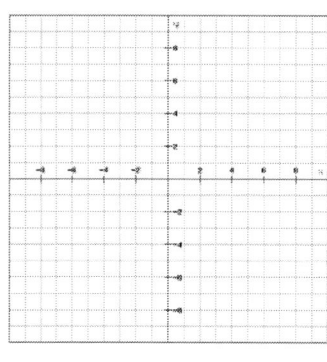

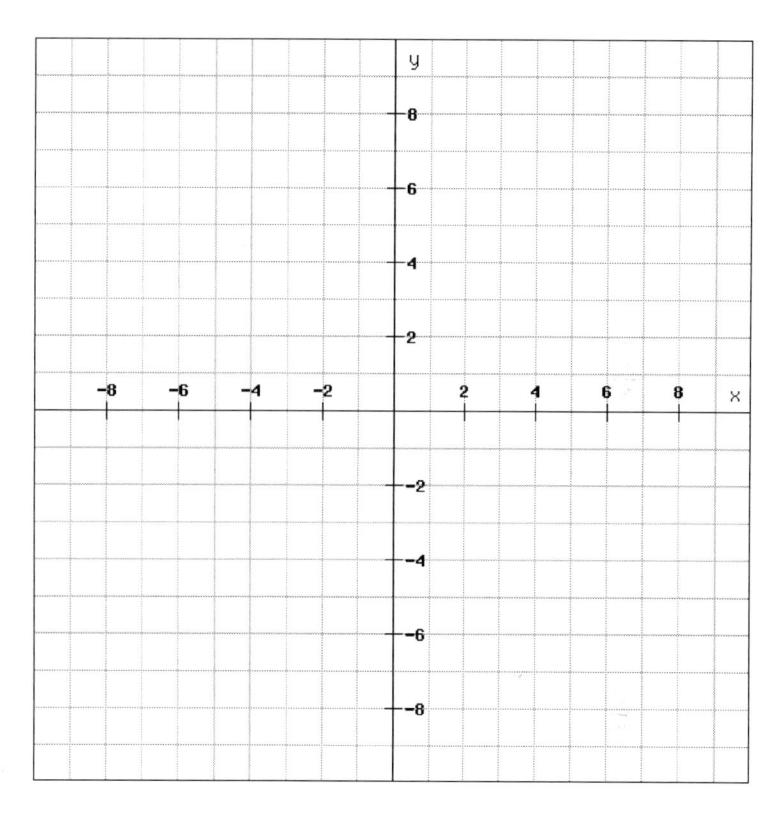

293

37. $f(x) = \begin{cases} x^2 & x < -2 \\ \dfrac{a}{x+3} - 3 & -2 \leq x \end{cases}$

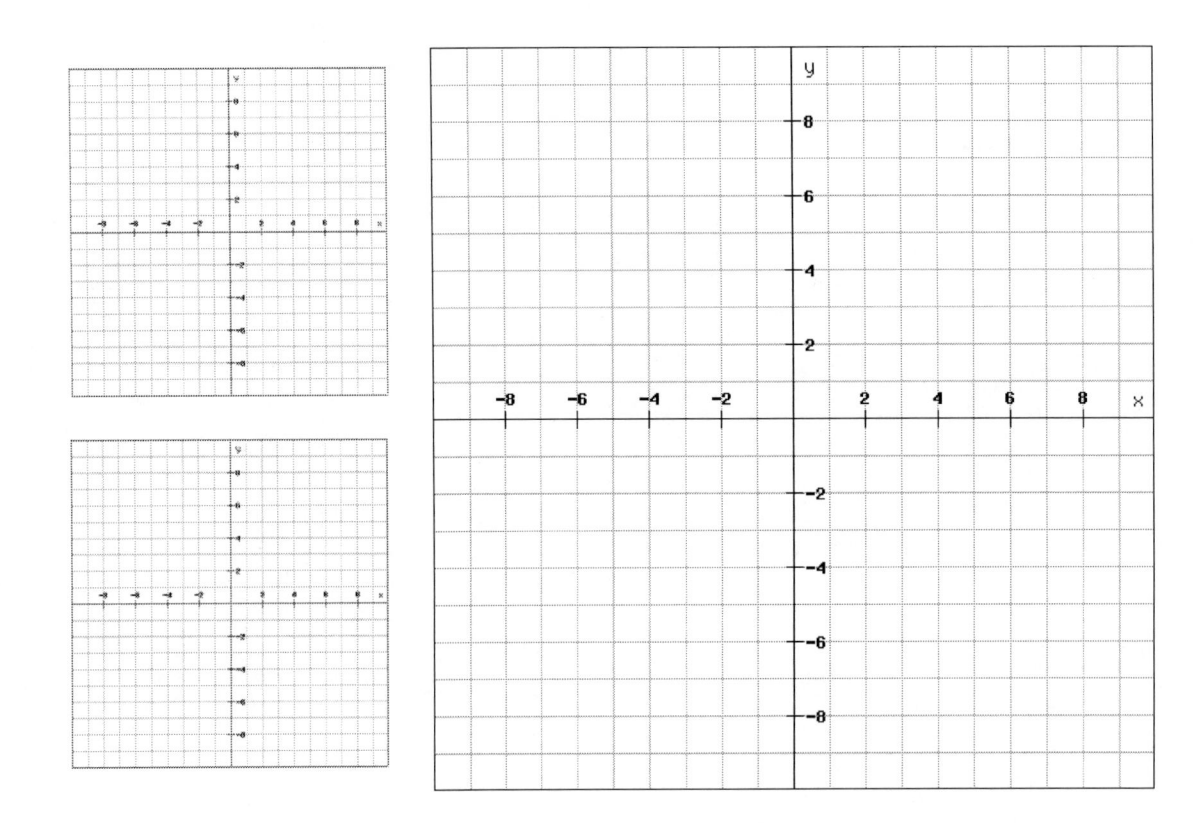

38. $f(x) = \begin{cases} x^2 & x < -2 \\ \sqrt{x+3} - a & -2 \leq x \end{cases}$

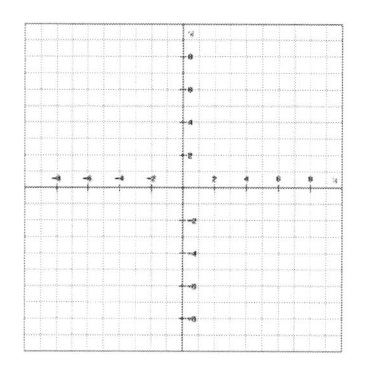

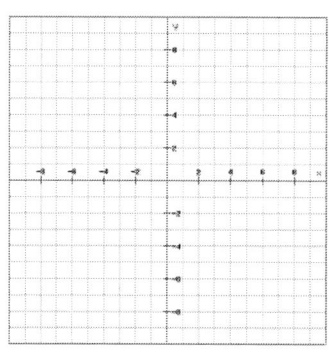

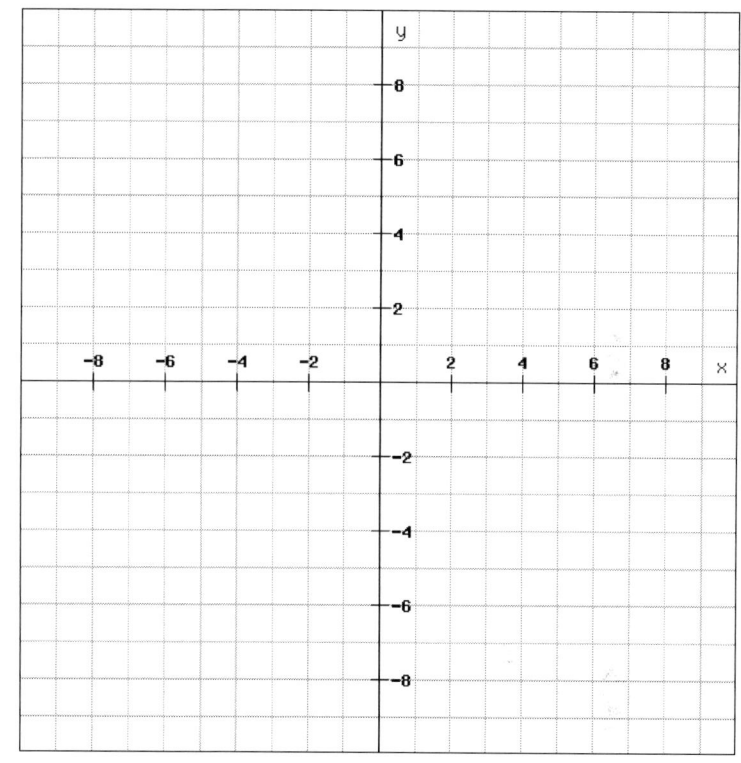

Analyze the following functions:

39. $f(x) = \begin{cases} -x+1 & x < 0 \\ x & 0 \leq x \end{cases}$

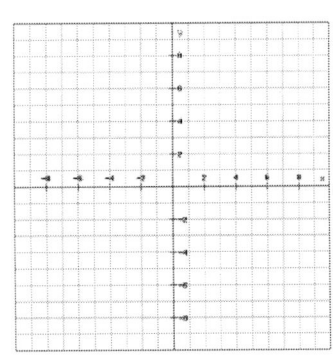

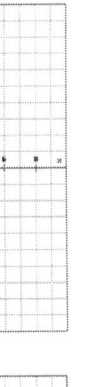

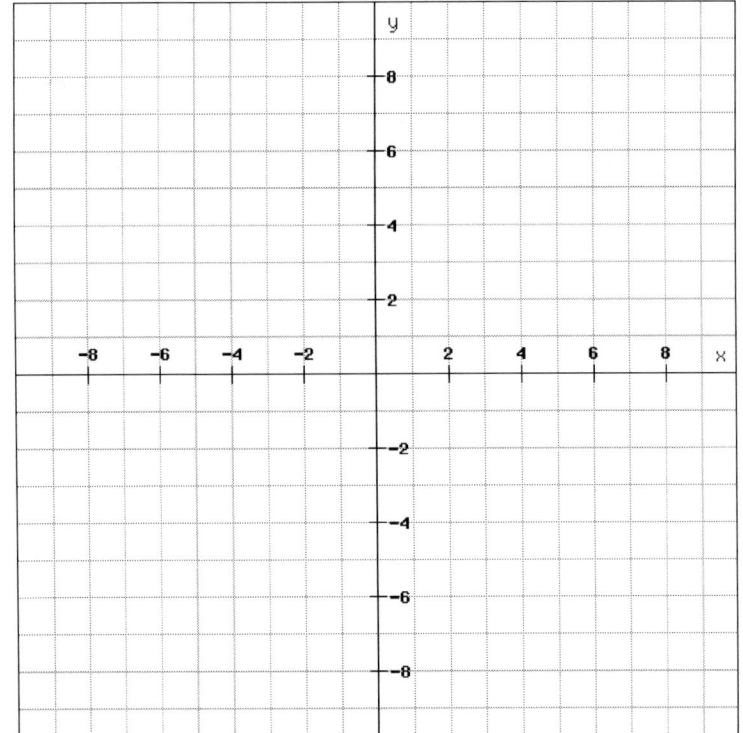

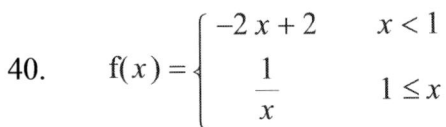

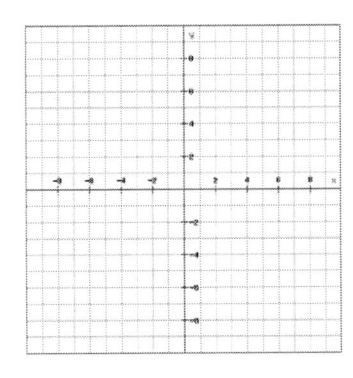

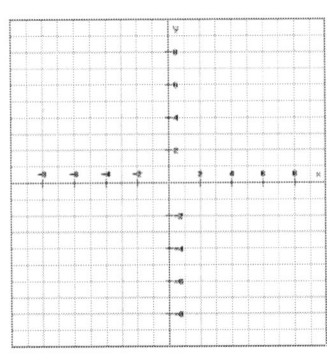

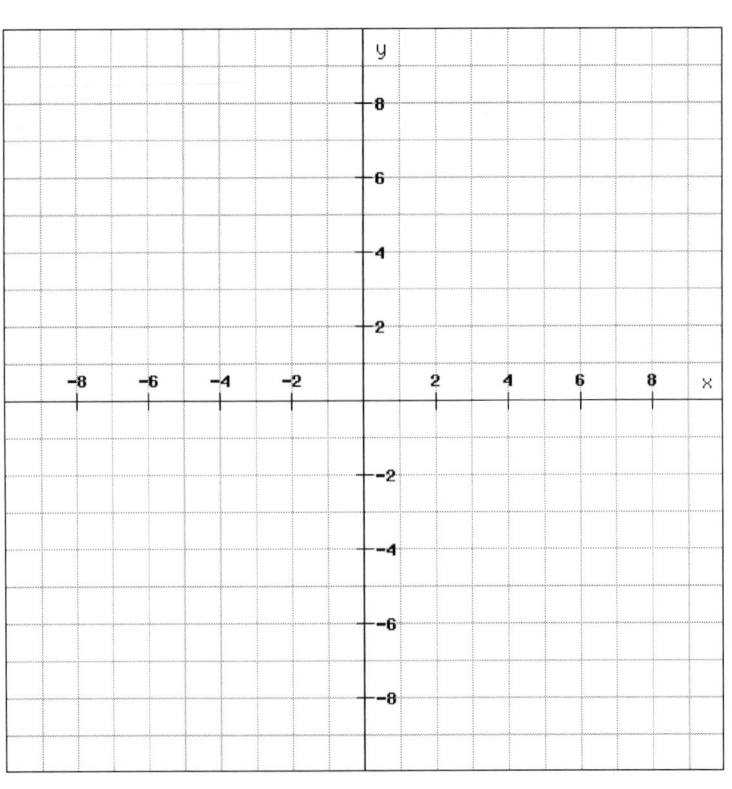

40. $f(x) = \begin{cases} -2x+2 & x < 1 \\ \dfrac{1}{x} & 1 \leq x \end{cases}$

41. $f(x) = \begin{cases} x^2 - 2 & x < -3 \\ \dfrac{1}{x+1} & -3 \leq x \end{cases}$

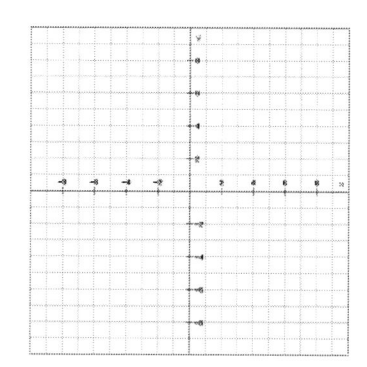

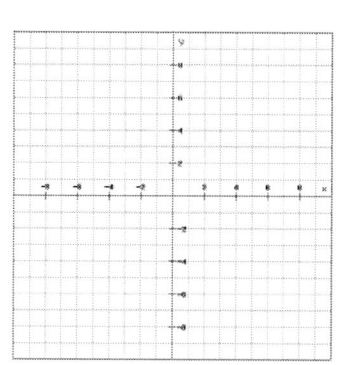

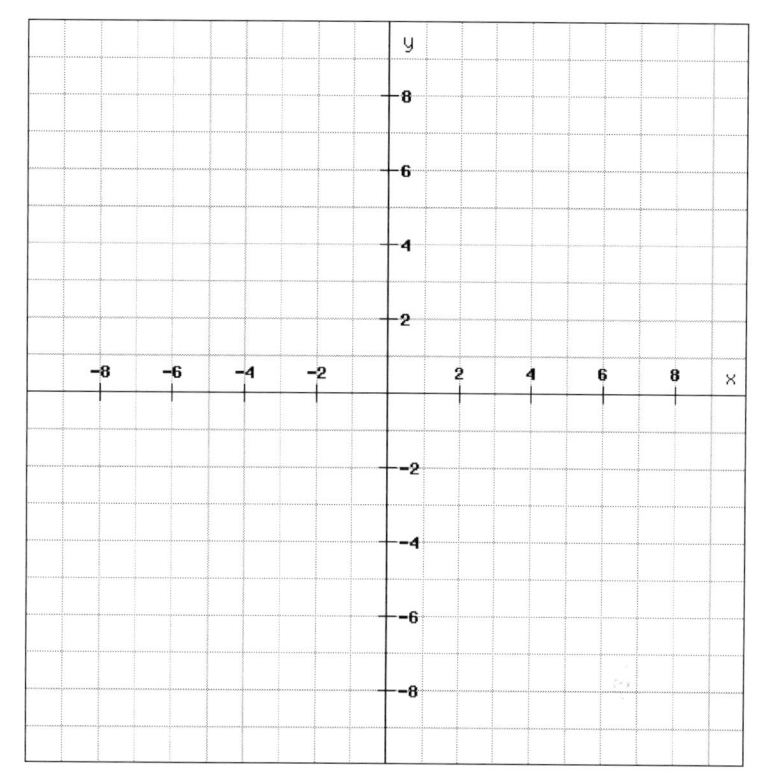

42. $f(x) = \begin{cases} x^2 - 2 & x < 2 \\ \ln(x) & 2 \leq x \end{cases}$

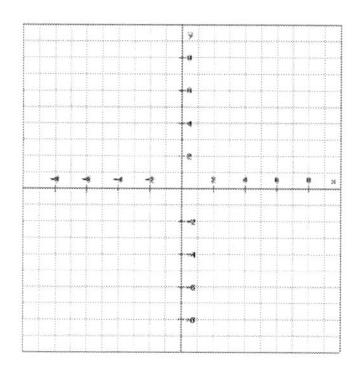

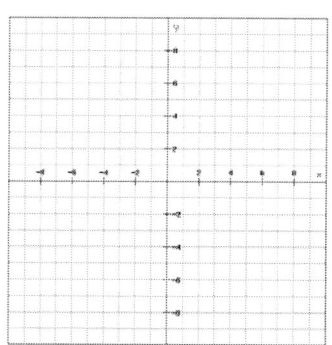

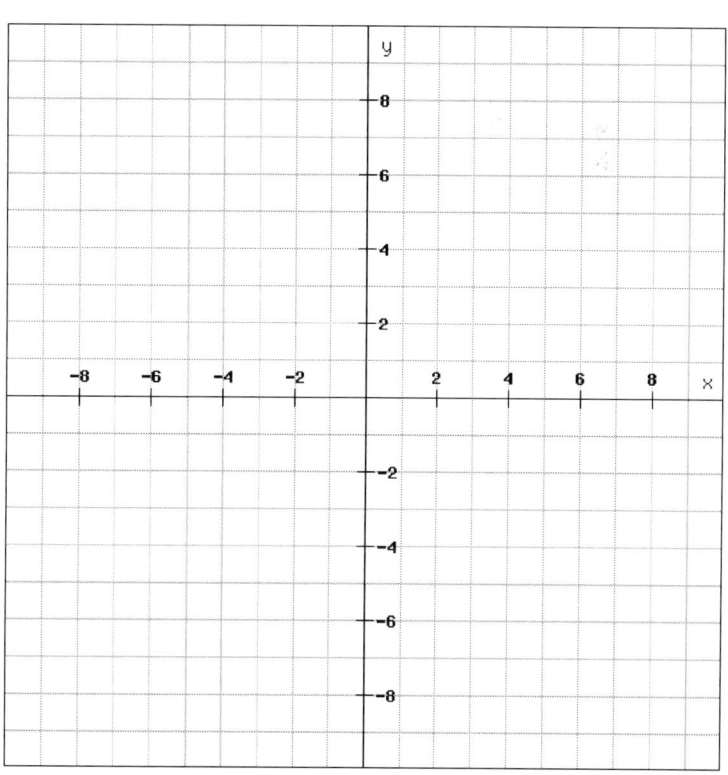

43. Find the value of a that will make f(x) continuous:

$$f(x) = \begin{cases} 2x^2 - 5 & x < 2 \\ a & 2 \leq x \end{cases}$$

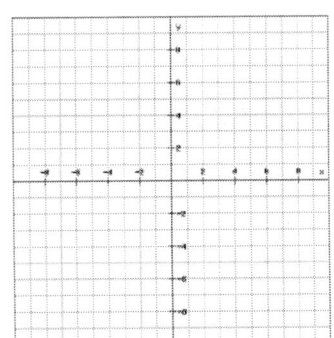

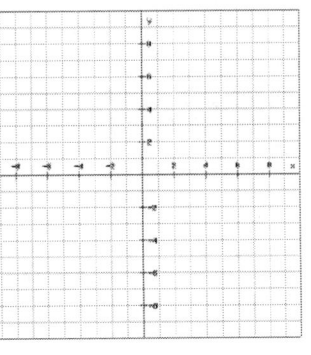

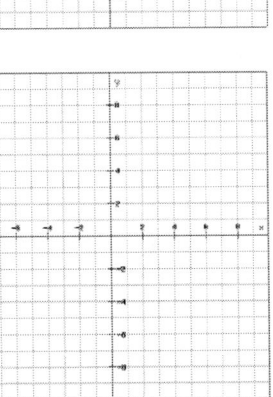

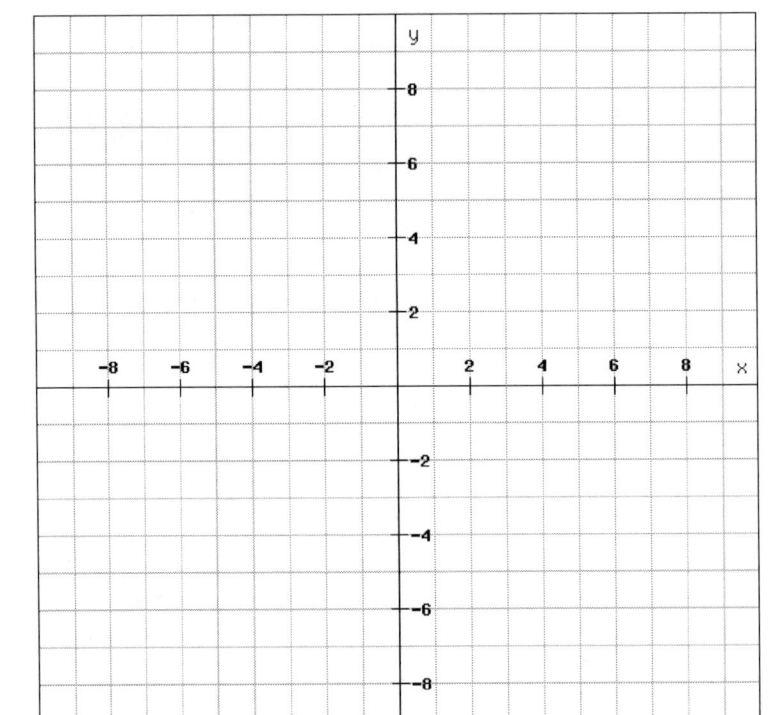

44. $$f(x) = \begin{cases} \ln(x+1) & x < 2 \\ -x^2 & 2 \leq x \end{cases}$$

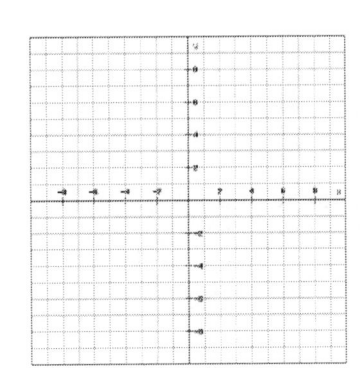

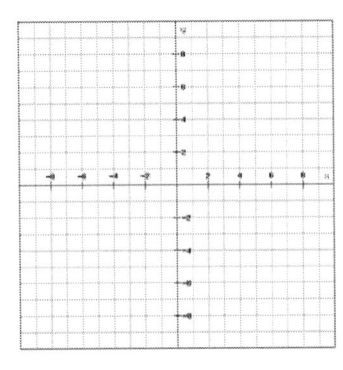

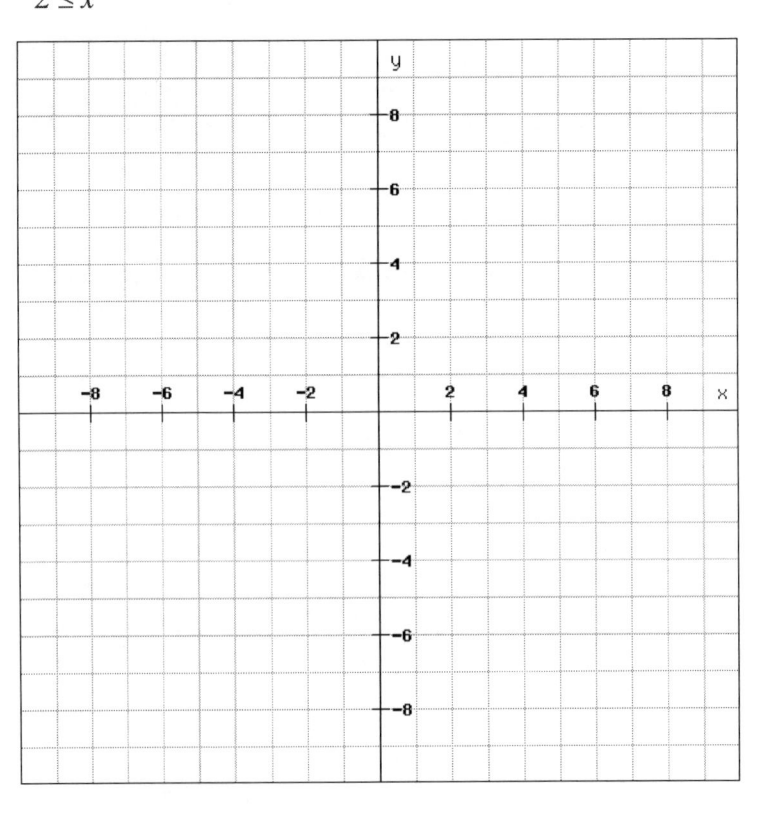

298

45. $f(x) = \begin{cases} \ln(x-1) & x < 2 \\ (x-2)^2 & 2 \leq x \end{cases}$

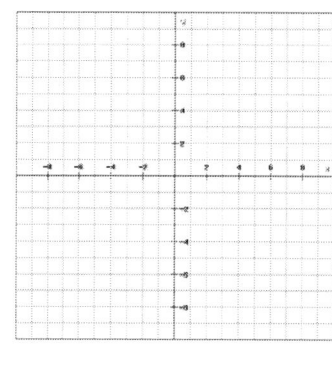

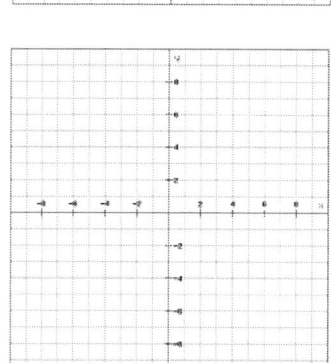

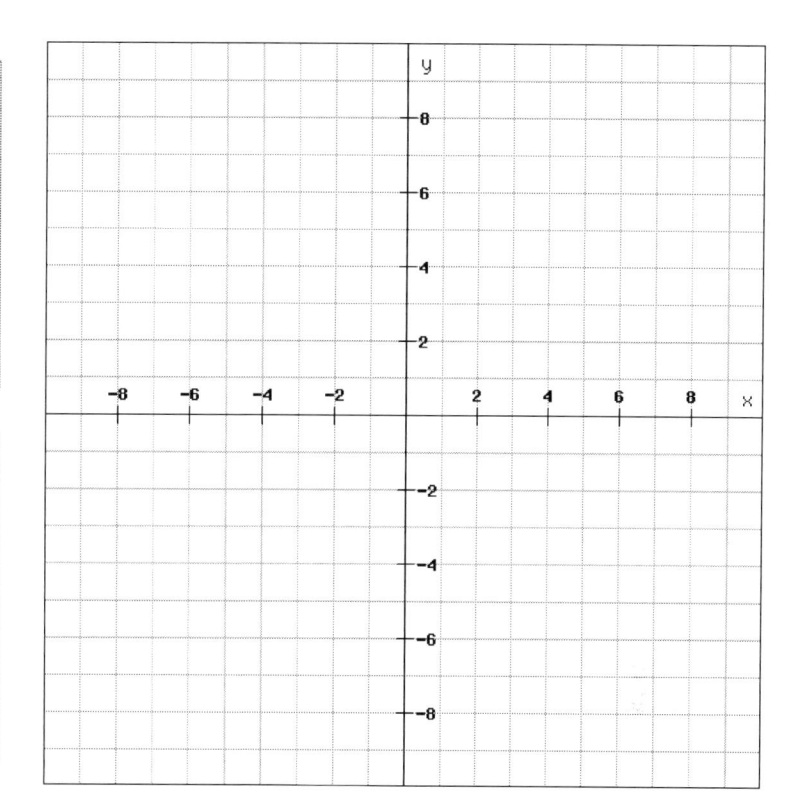

46. Find the value of *a* that will make f(x) continuous:

$f(x) = \begin{cases} x^2 + a & x \leq 1 \\ (x-3)^2 & 1 < x \end{cases}$

47. $f(x) = \begin{cases} 1 & x < 0 \\ x & 0 \leq x \text{ and } x < 2 \\ -(x-3)^2 & 2 \leq x \end{cases}$

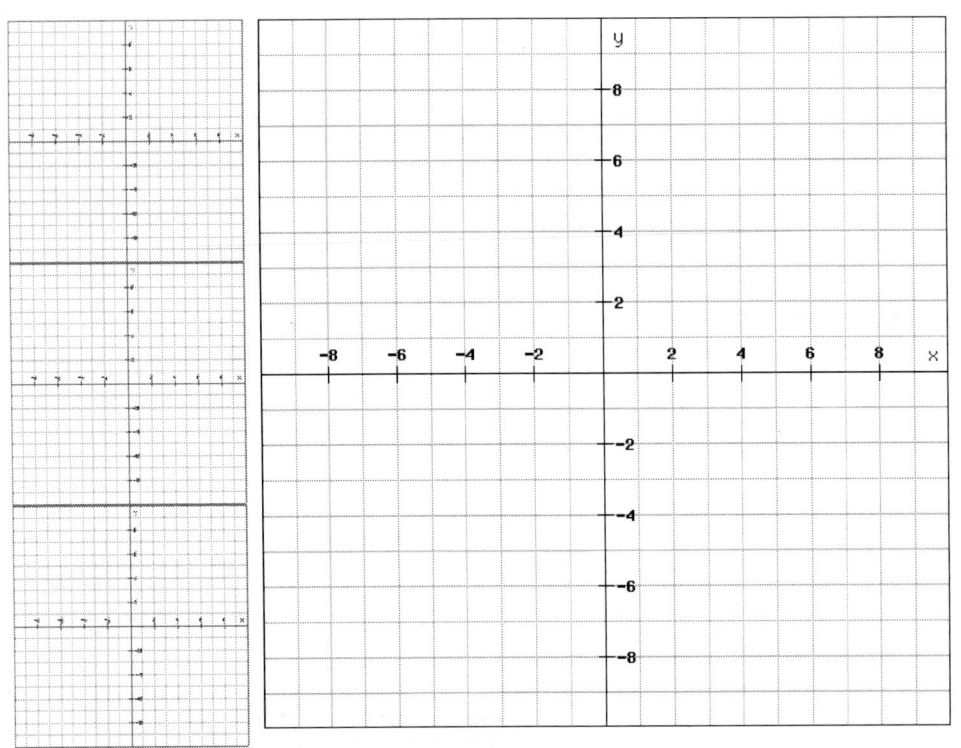

48. $f(x) = \begin{cases} -2x & x < -1 \\ x^2 & -1 \leq x \text{ and } x < 3 \\ (x+1)^2 & 3 \leq x \end{cases}$

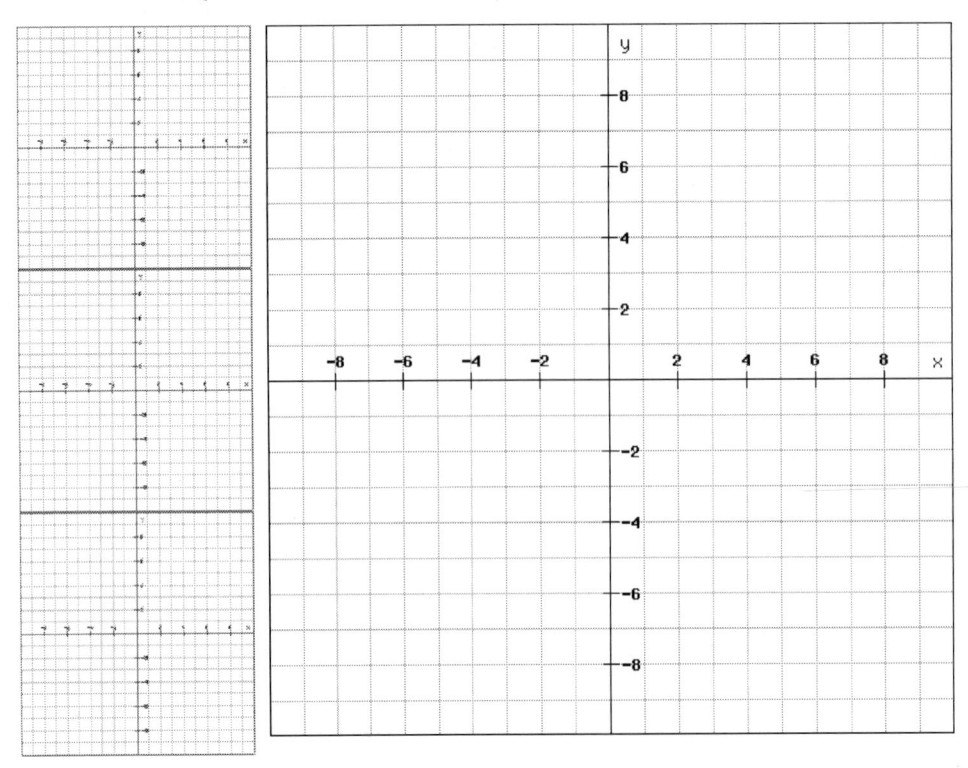

300

49. $f(x) = \begin{cases} x+3 & x < -2 \\ \sqrt{x+4} & -2 \leq x \text{ and } x < 0 \\ -x^2 & 0 \leq x \end{cases}$

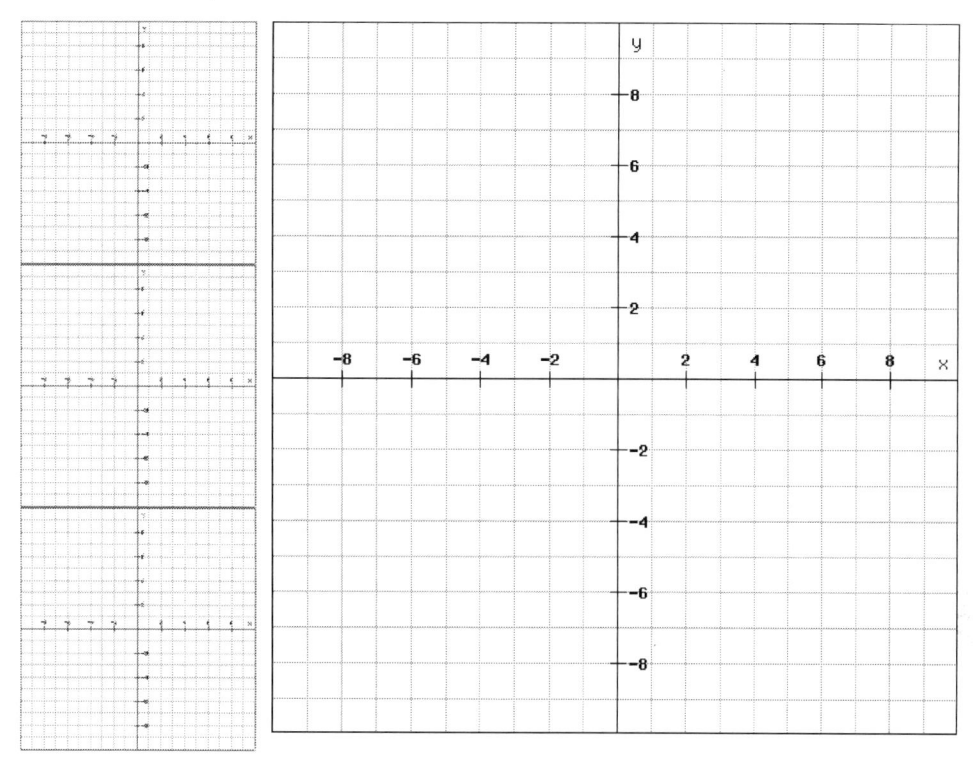

50. $f(x) = \begin{cases} -3x-1 & x < 0 \\ \ln(x-1) & 0 \leq x \text{ and } x < 4 \\ \sqrt{x} & 4 \leq x \end{cases}$

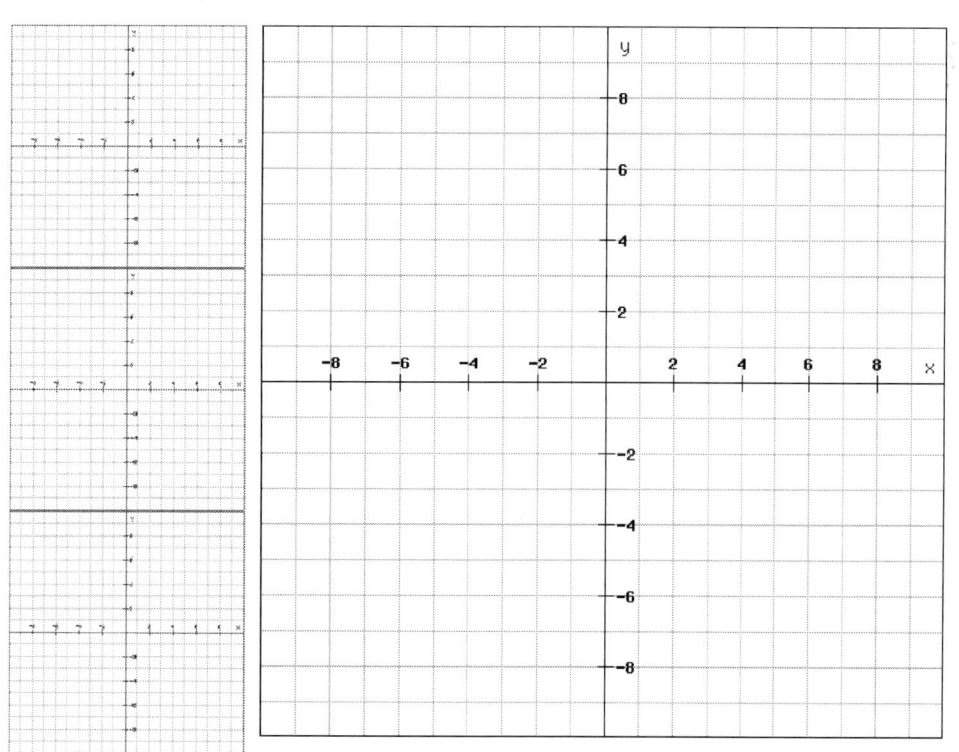

51. $f(x) = \begin{cases} e^x & x < -1 \\ -x^2 & -1 \leq x \text{ and } x < 2 \\ e^{(-x)} & 2 \leq x \end{cases}$

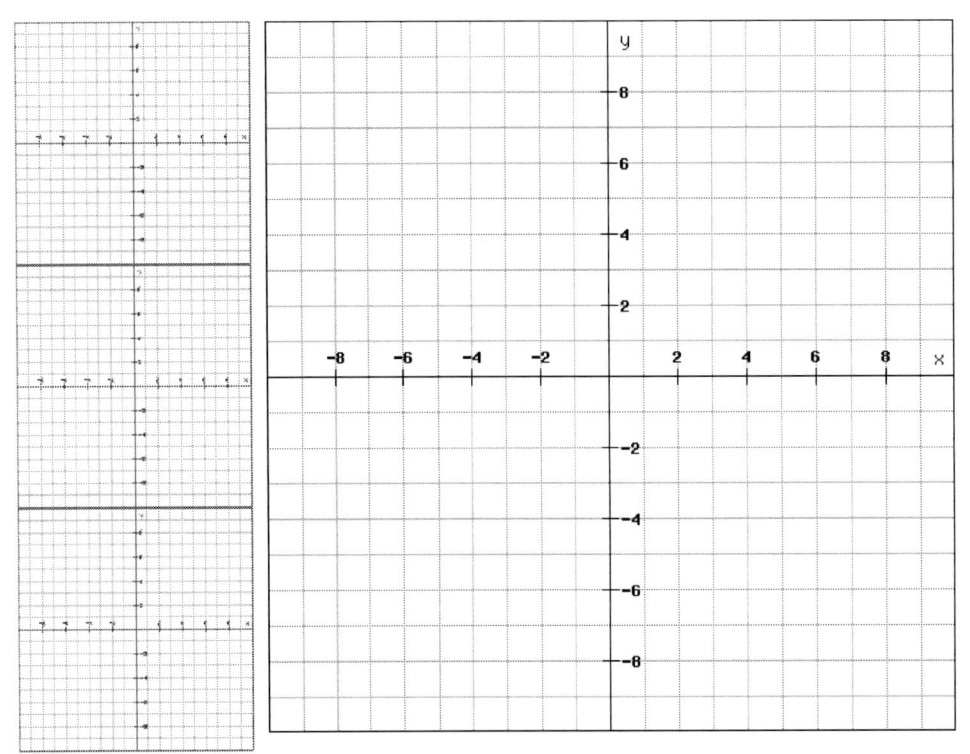

52. $f(x) = \begin{cases} -(x+2)^2 & x < 0 \\ 3^{(-x)} & 0 \leq x \text{ and } x < 3 \\ x - 6 & 3 \leq x \end{cases}$

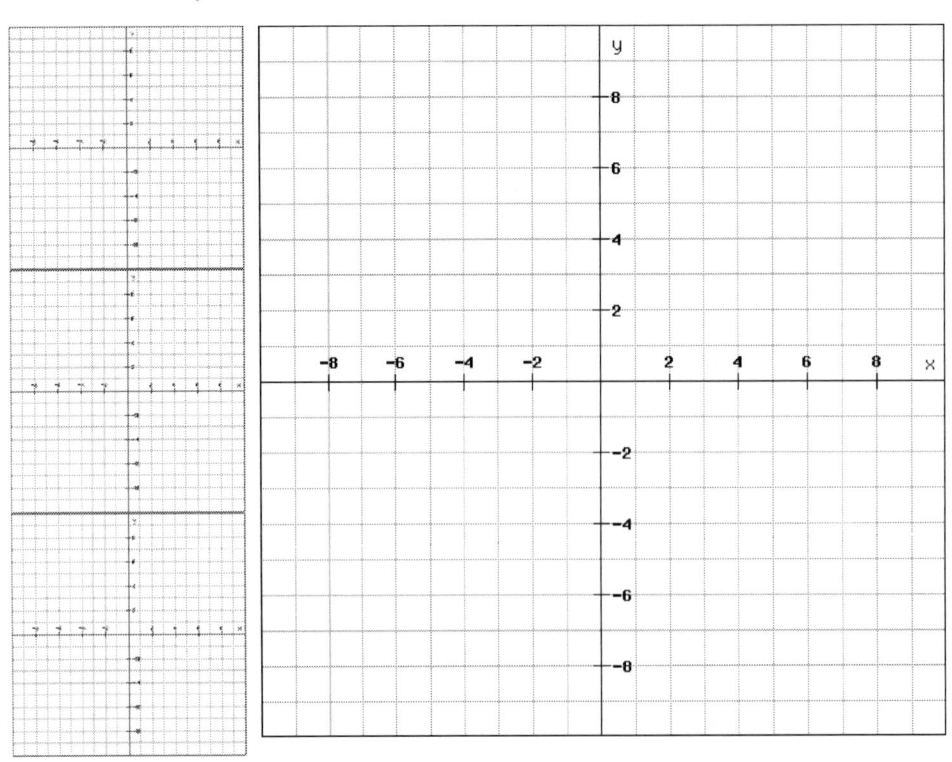

302

53. $f(x) = \begin{cases} x^2 - 1 & x < 0 \\ 2^x & 0 \leq x \text{ and } x < 3 \\ \dfrac{1}{x-6} & 4 \leq x \end{cases}$

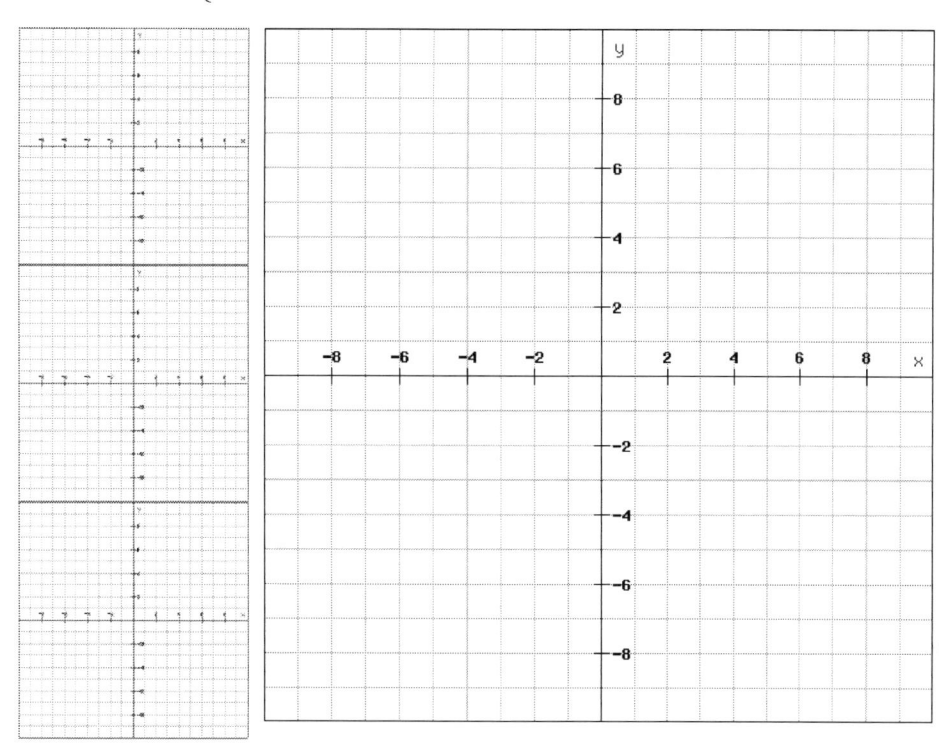

54. $f(x) = \begin{cases} \dfrac{1}{x} & x < -1 \\ e^x & -1 \leq x \text{ and } x < 2 \\ \ln(x) & 2 \leq x \end{cases}$

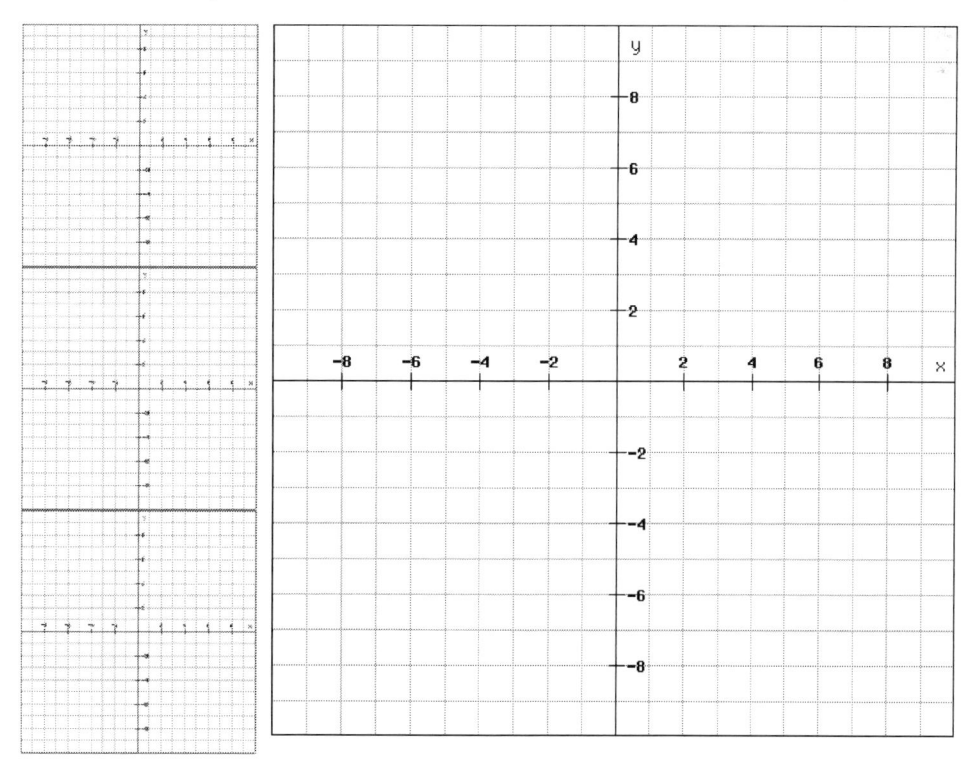

303

55. $f(x) = \begin{cases} \dfrac{1}{x+3} & x < -2 \\ \sqrt{x+2} & -2 \leq x \text{ and } x < 0 \\ \ln(x) & 0 \leq x \end{cases}$

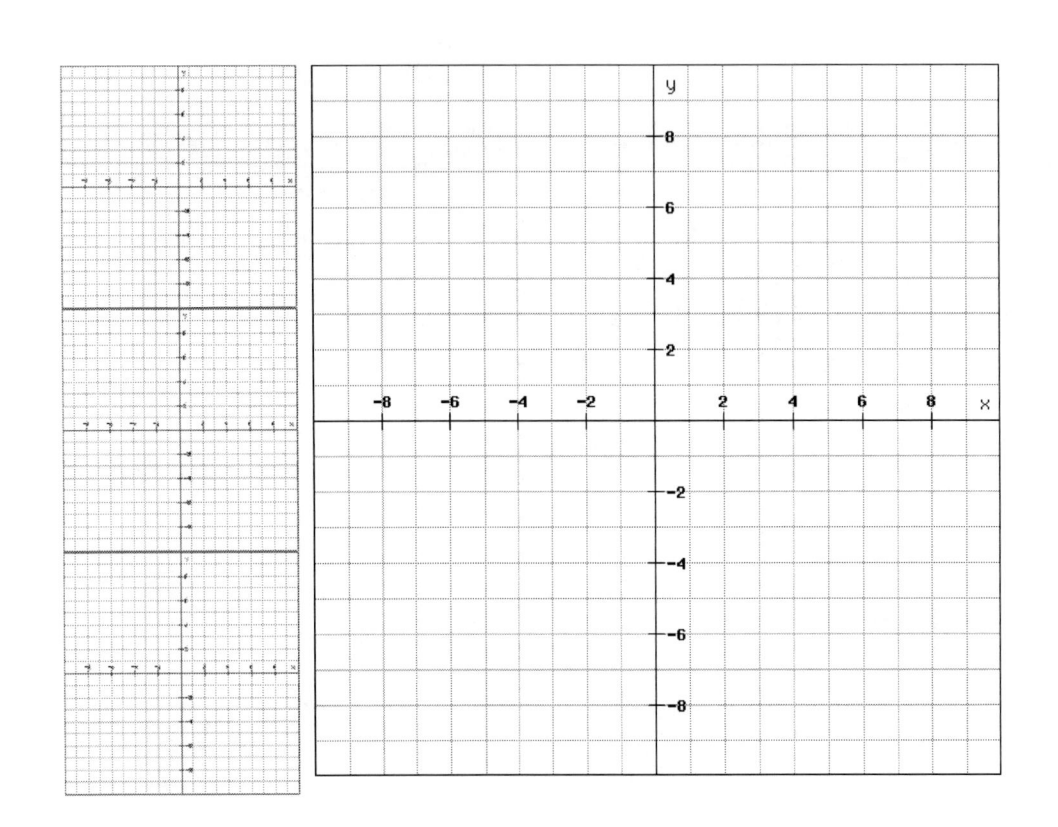

2.11. – COMPOSITE FUCNTIONS

1. Given The functions $f(x) = x + 4$ and $g(x) = 2x^2$, find

    a. $f(g(x)) = $ $g(f(x)) = $

    b. $f(f(x)) = $ $g(g(x)) = $

    c. $f(g(f(x)x)) = $ $g(f(g(x))) = $

2. Given The functions $f(x) = 2x^3 + x$ and $g(x) = \text{Ln}(x + 1)$, find

    a. $f(g(x)) = $ $g(f(x)) = $

    b. $f(f(x)) = $ $g(g(x)) = $

    c. $f(g(f(x)x)) = $ $g(f(g(x))) = $

3. Given The functions $f(x) = \sqrt{x+1}$ and $g(x) = 3^x - 2$, find

    a. $f(g(x)) = $ $g(f(x)) = $

    b. $f(f(x)) = $ $g(g(x)) = $

    c. $f(g(f(x)x)) = $ $g(f(g(x))) = $

4. Given The functions $f(x) = \dfrac{2}{x^2 + 1}$ and $g(x) = \text{Sin}(x + 1)$, find

    a. $f(g(x)) = $ $g(f(x)) = $

    b. $f(f(x)) = $ $g(g(x)) = $

    c. $f(g(f(x)x)) = $ $g(f(g(x))) = $

5. Given The functions $f(x) = \dfrac{1}{x}$ and $g(x) = x^2$, find

    a. $f(g(x)) =$ $g(f(x)) =$

    b. $f(f(x)) =$ $g(g(x)) =$

    c. $f(g(f(x)x)) =$ $g(f(g(x))) =$

6. In general, is $f(g(x)) = g(f(x))$?

7. Given The functions $f(x) = x$ and $g(x) = x^2$, $s(x) = \sin(x^2 + 3)$, $a(x) = \mathrm{Ln}(\dfrac{1}{x})$ find

    a. $f(g(x)) =$ $g(f(x)) =$

    b. $f(s(x)) =$ $s(f(x)) =$

    c. $f(a(x)) =$ $a(f(x)) =$

    d. What is your conclusion?

2.12. – INVERSE FUCNTIONS

1. Given The functions f(x) = x + 4 and g(x) = x – 4, find

    a. f(g(x)) =   g(f(x)) =

2. Given The functions $f(x) = 2x^3$ and $g(x) = \sqrt[3]{\dfrac{x}{2}}$, find

    a. f(g(x)) =   g(f(x)) =

3. What is your conclusion?

4. Given The function $f(x) = \sqrt{x+1}$, find $f^{-1}(x)$

5. Given The function $f(x) = \dfrac{2x-3}{x+5}$, find $f^{-1}(x)$

6. Given The function $f(x) = 2^{3x-5} + 3$, find $f^{-1}(x)$

7. Given The function $f(x) = e^{\sqrt{x-2}} + 5$, find $f^{-1}(x)$

8. Given The function $f(x) = Ln(x^2 + 2) + 3$, find $f^{-1}(x)$

9. Given The function $f(x) = Log_2(2x - 3)$, find $f^{-1}(1)$

10. Given The function $f(x) = (2x - 4)^2$, find $f^{-1}(0)$

11. Given The function f(x) = $x^2 + 2x$, find $f^{-1}(x)$

12. Given the function, sketch the inverse function/curve:

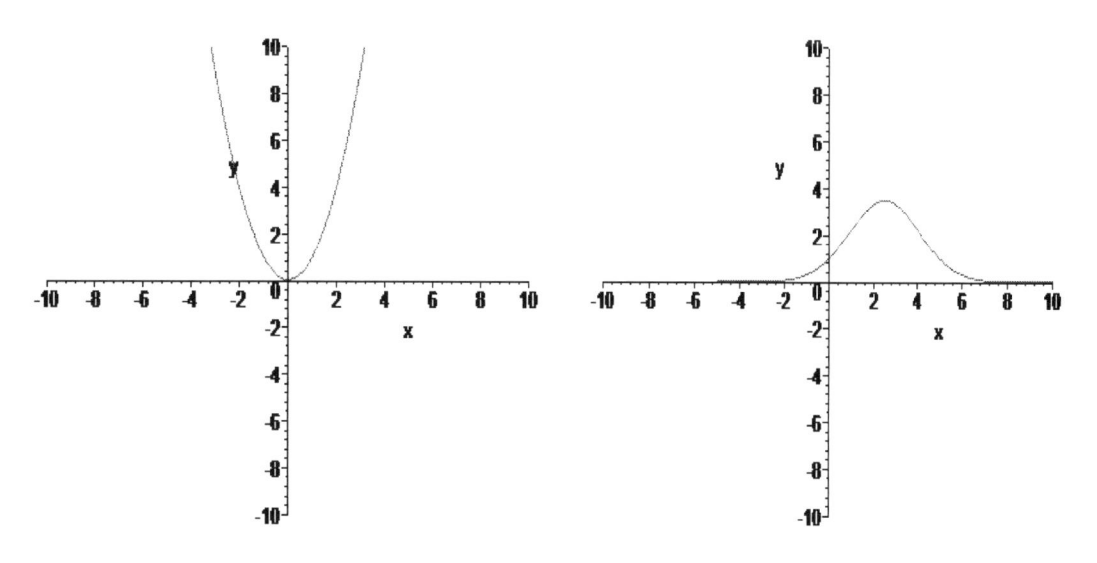

13. Given the function, sketch the inverse function/curve:

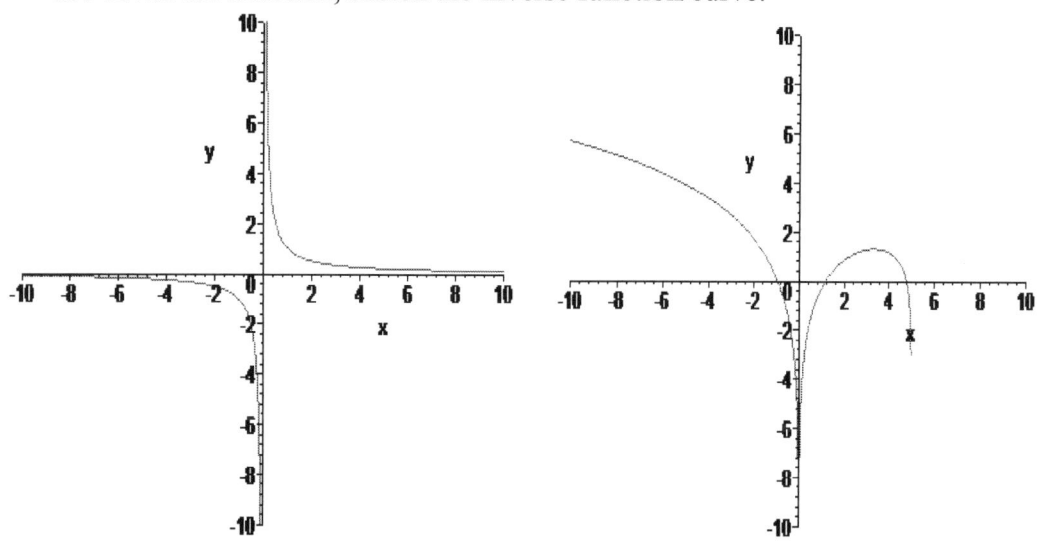

14. Graphically, the inverse function is a _____.

15. (T/F) In case the inverse curve is not a function, the inverse function is not well defined.

CHAPTER 3 – TRIGONOMETRIC FUNCTIONS

3.1. – DEGREES AND RADIANS

Since we were "young" angles were measured in degrees, we were told that the size of a circular angle is 360°. In reality the number 360° is meaningless; it is merely used because of historical reasons. If we go back to the definition of an angle in a circle it is the following:

$$X = -$$

In case that S is the entire circle we obtain:

$$X = \frac{S}{R} = \frac{Length}{of-Circle} = 6.2831... = 2\pi$$

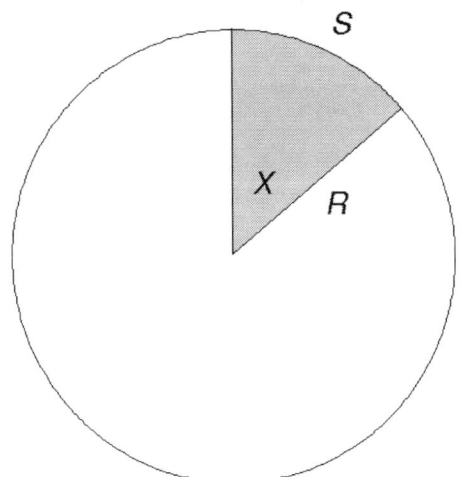

So what we see is that the angle of the entire circle is approximately 6.28 or exactly 2π. That means:

$$2\pi_{rad} = \underline{}°$$

$$1° = \frac{2\pi}{360} rad \approx 0.017_{rad}$$

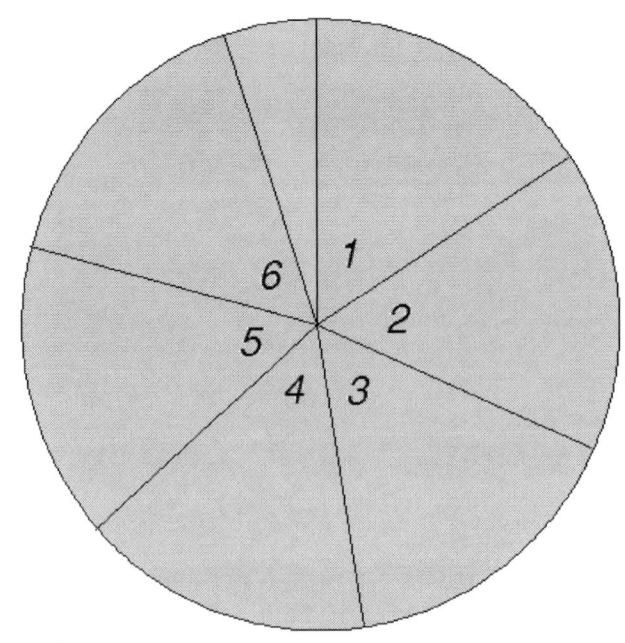

$$1_{rad} = \left(\underline{}\right)° \approx 57.3°$$

In the image we can observe that in a circle 6 radians are equivalent to a bit less than 360°, the exact number is 2π, approximately 6.28 radians.

Exercises:

1. Complete the table:

Degrees	360°	−180°	90°	45°	22.5°
Radians					

2. Complete the table:

Degrees	0°	30°	60°	−120°	150°
Radians					

3. Complete the table:

Degrees	315°	−225°	135°	330°	420°
Radians					

4. Complete the table:

Degrees	54°	18°	−36°	15°	75°
Radians					

5. Complete the table:

Degrees	10°	−9°	12°	3°	7.5°
Radians					

6. Complete the table:

Degrees	5°	1°	−10°	660°	540°
Radians					

7. Complete the table:

Degrees					
Radians	π	$\dfrac{\pi}{10}$	$-\dfrac{5\pi}{3}$	$\dfrac{12\pi}{7}$	$\dfrac{22\pi}{5}$

8. Complete the table:

Degrees					
Radians	1	2.4	3.5	−2	−3.1

9. Given the following circles, find θ or L in each one of the cases (in degrees and radians):

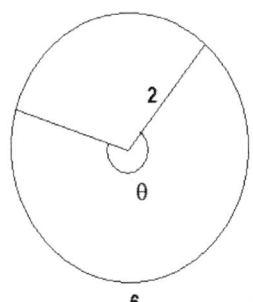

Circle 1 (arc = 2, radius = 6): θ = _____ rad = _____ °

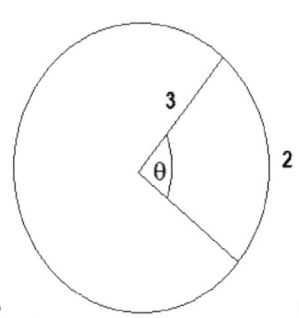

Circle 2 (arc = 3, radius = 2): θ = _____ rad = _____ °

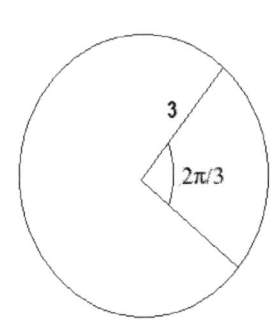

Circle 3 (radius = 3, θ = 2π/3): L = _____

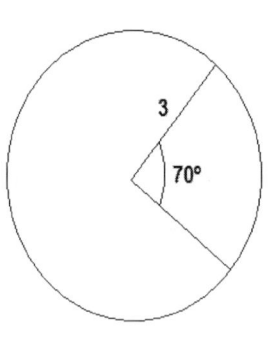

Circle 4 (radius = 3, θ = 70°): L = _____

10. The length of the perimeter of a circle with radius r is _____. The length of the arc that corresponds an angle x° is _____. In case the angle x is measured in radians it would be _____.

312

11. The area of a circle with radius r is _____. The area of the sector that corresponds an angle x° is _____. In case the angle x is measured in radians it would be _____.

12. Given the circle with r = 2cm :

    a. Show the arc corresponding an angle of 45°.
    b. Calculate its length.
    c. Shade Show the corresponding sector area.
    d. Calculate it.

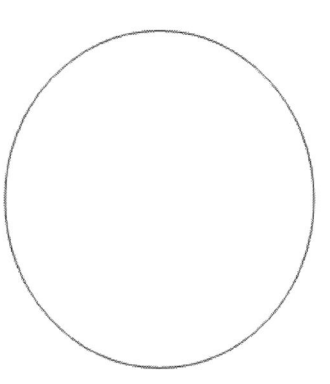

13. Given the circle with r = 3.2m:

    a. Show Shade the arc corresponding an angle of 20°.
    b. Calculate its length.
    c. Shade the corresponding sector area.
    d. Calculate it.

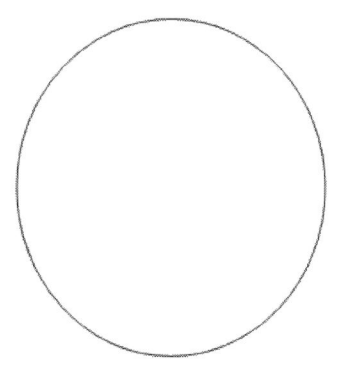

14. Given the circle with r = 3.2m:

    a. Show Shade the arc corresponding an angle of $\frac{\pi}{10} rad$.
    b. Calculate its length.
    c. Shade the corresponding sector area.
    d. Calculate it.

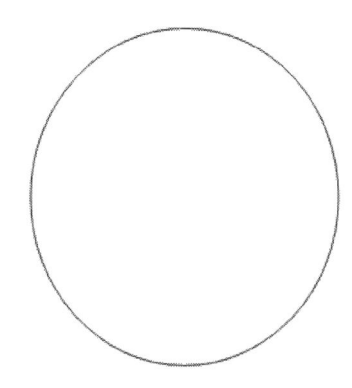

15. Given the circle with r = 3.2m:

    a. Show Shade the arc corresponding an angle of 1 radian.
    b. Calculate its length.
    c. Shade the corresponding sector area.
    d. Calculate it.

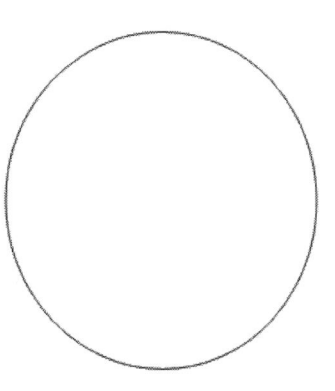

16. Given the following concentric circles with radii 3 cm and 5 cm correspondingly. Calculate the shaded area.

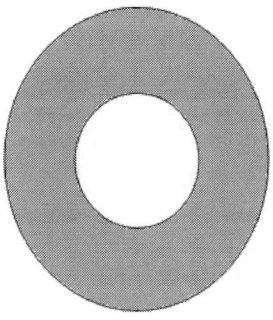

17. Given the following concentric circles with radii 10m and 14m correspondingly. Calculate the shaded area.

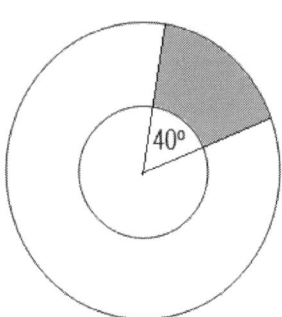

3.2. – TRIGONOMETRIC FUNCTIONS

Definition: The trigonometric functions are defined using the so called "unit circle" which is simply a circle with radius 1:

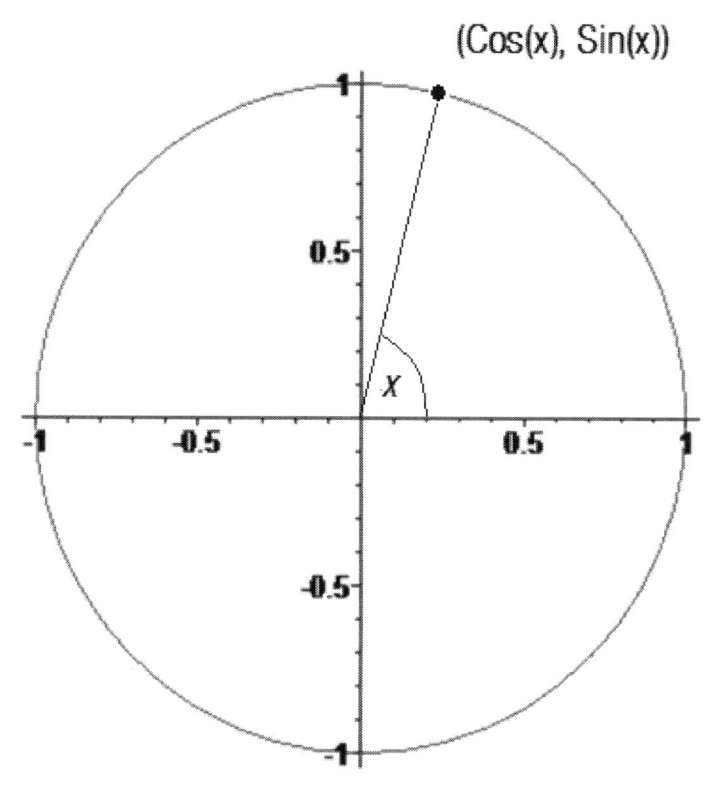

Definition of Sin(x):

1st Quadrant: 3rd Quadrant:

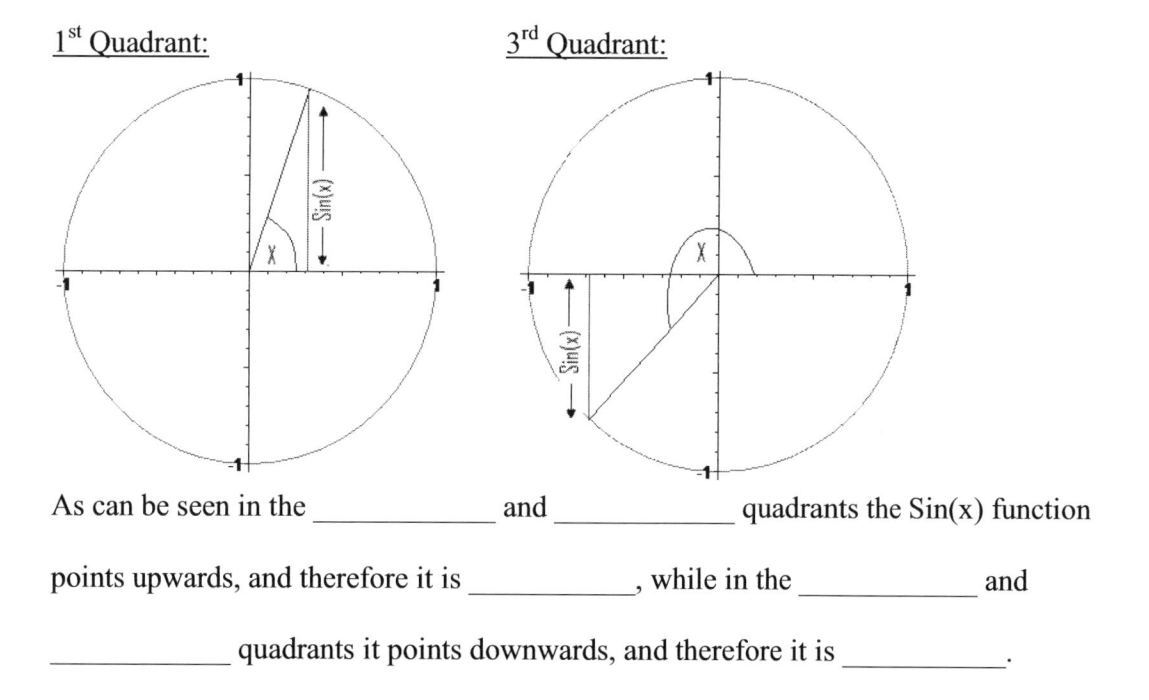

As can be seen in the _____ and _____ quadrants the Sin(x) function points upwards, and therefore it is _____, while in the _____ and _____ quadrants it points downwards, and therefore it is _____.

315

Definition of Cos(x):

2nd Quadrant:

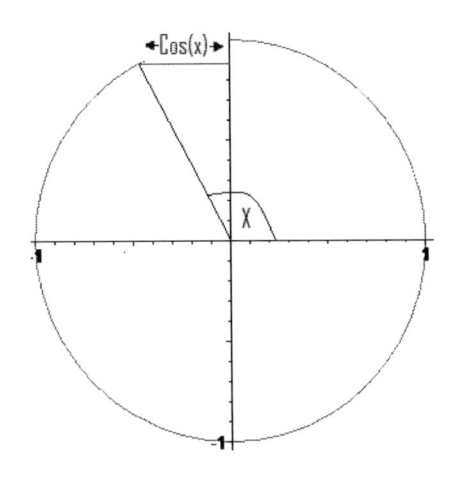

4th Quadrant:

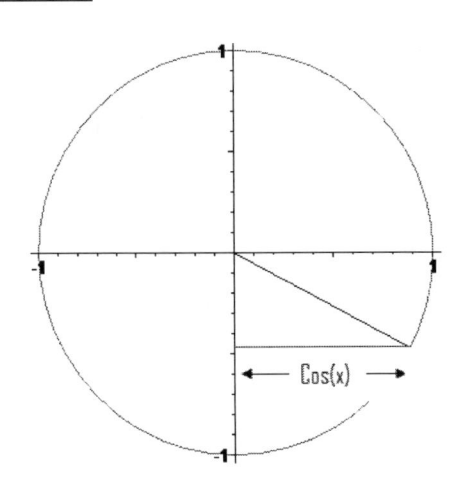

As can be seen in the _____ and _____ quadrants the Sin(x) function points upwards, and therefore it is _____, while in the _____ and _____ quadrants it points downwards, and therefore it is _____.

Exercises:

In each one of the cases sketch the unit circle and the corresponding angle and then find the corresponding value:

1. $Sin(0°)$ =

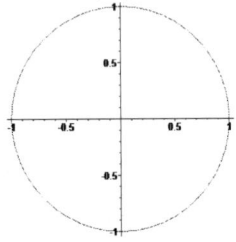

2. $Cos(0_{rad})$ =

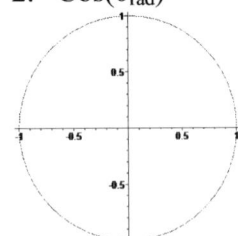

3. $Sin(0_{rad})$ =

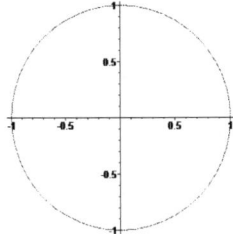

4. $Cos(0°)$ =

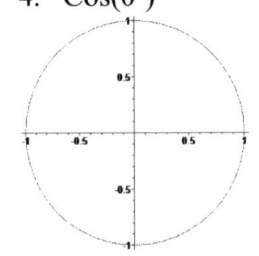

316

5. Sin(90°) =

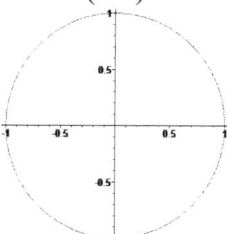

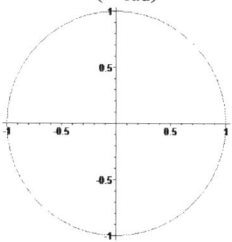

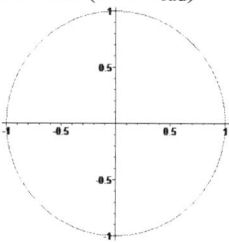

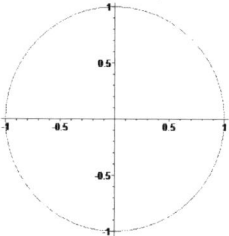

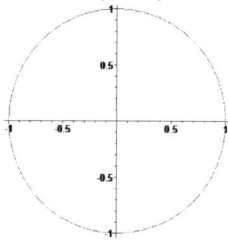

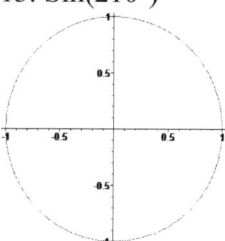

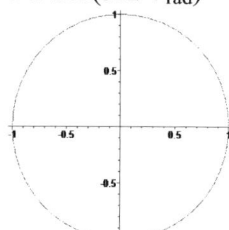

6. Cos(Π_rad) =

7. Sin(3Π/4 _rad) =

8. Cos(225°) =

9. Sin(225°) =

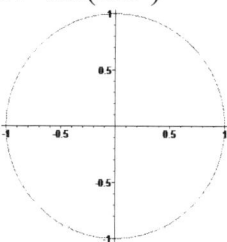

10. Cos(4Π/3 _rad) =

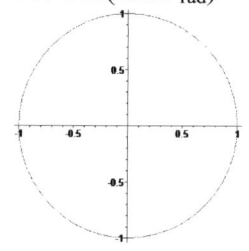

11. Sin(4Π/3 _rad) =

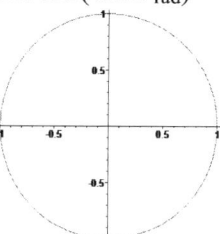

12. Cos(210°) =

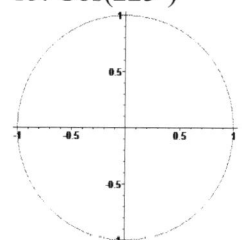

13. Sin(210°) =

14. Sin(3Π/4 _rad) =

15. Cos(225°) =

16. Sin(–225°) =

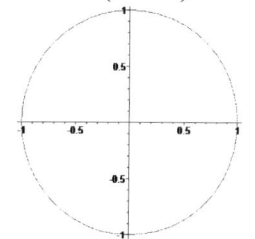

17. Cos(4Π/3 rad) =

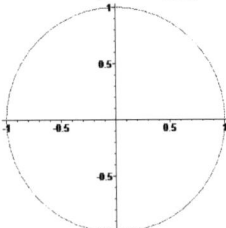

18. Sin(4Π/3 rad) =

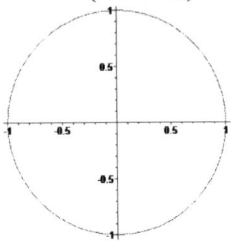

19. Cos(210°) =

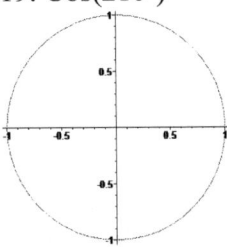

20. Sin(−210°) =

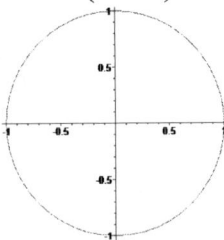

21. Sin(−Π rad) =

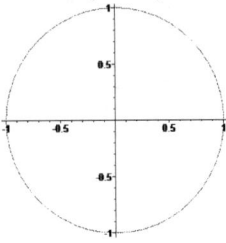

22. Cos(90°) =

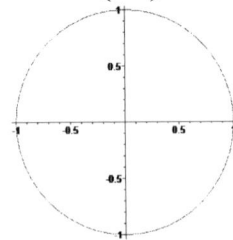

23. Sin(270°) =

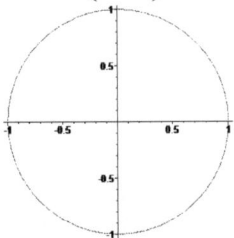

24. Cos(Π/2 rad) =

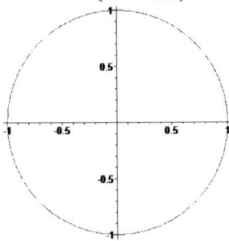

25. Sin(3Π/2 rad) =

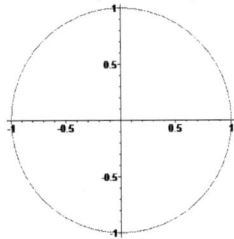

26. Cos(270°) =

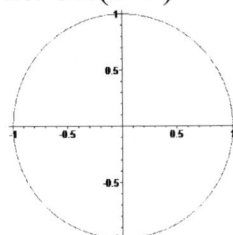

27. Sin(360°) =

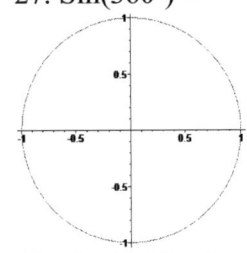

28. Cos(−Π/2 rad) =

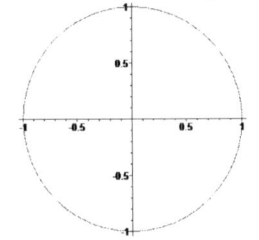

29. Sin(2Π_rad) =

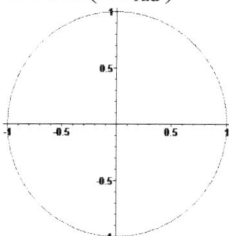

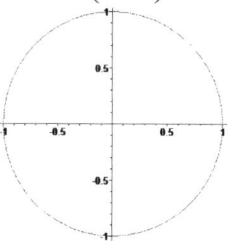

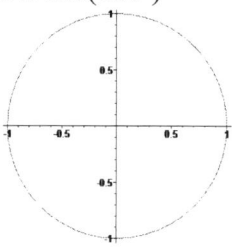

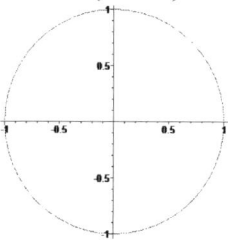

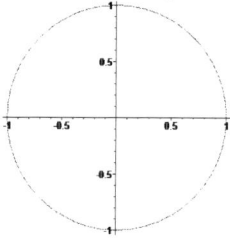

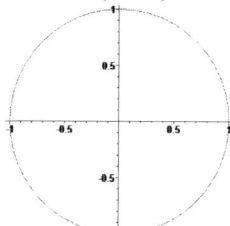

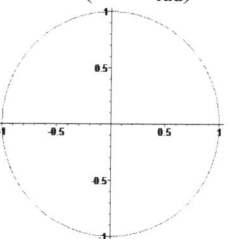

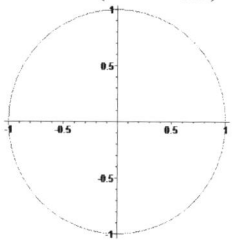

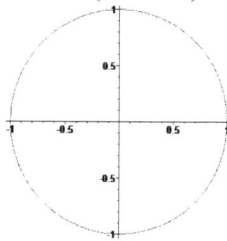

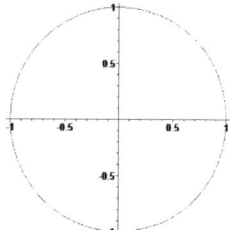

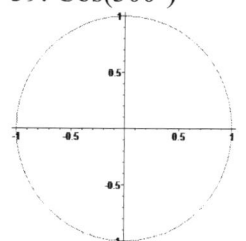

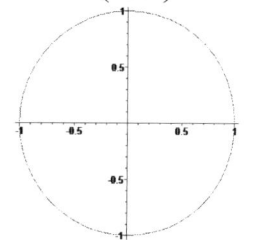

30. Cos(180°) =

31. Sin(180°) =

32. Cos(Π/3_rad) =

33. Sin(Π/4_rad) =

34. Cos(−45°) =

35. Sin(3Π/2 _rad) =

36. Cos(−2Π/3 _rad) =

37. Sin(2Π/3 _rad) =

38. Cos(3Π/4 _rad) =

39. Cos(300°) =

40. Sin(300°) =

41. Cos(2Π rad) =

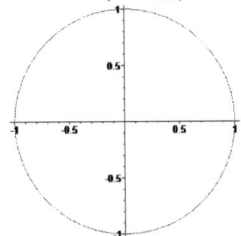

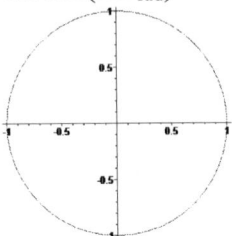

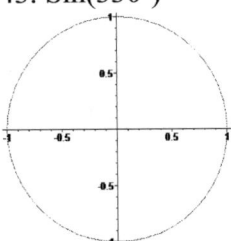

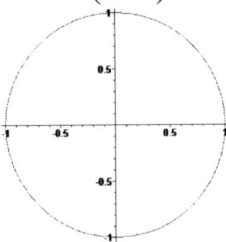

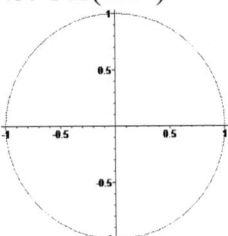

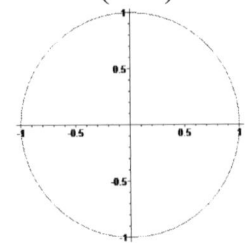

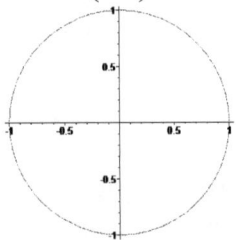

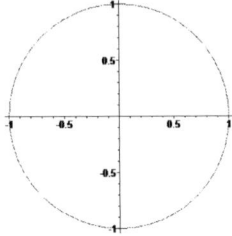

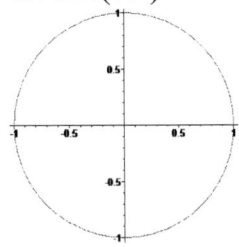

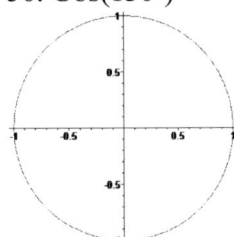

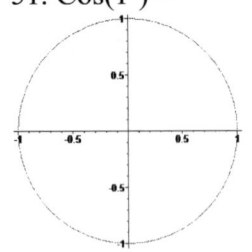

42. Sin(2Π rad) =

43. Sin(330º) =

44. Cos(390º) =

45. Cos(135º) =

46. Sin(135º) =

47. Sin(45º) =

48. Cos(−3Π/2 rad) =

49. Cos(70º) =

50. Cos(130º) =

51. Cos(1º) =

52. Cos(3 rad) =

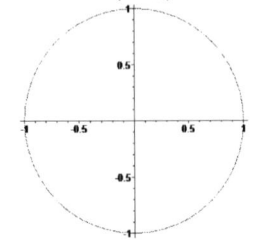

53. Sin(1 rad) =

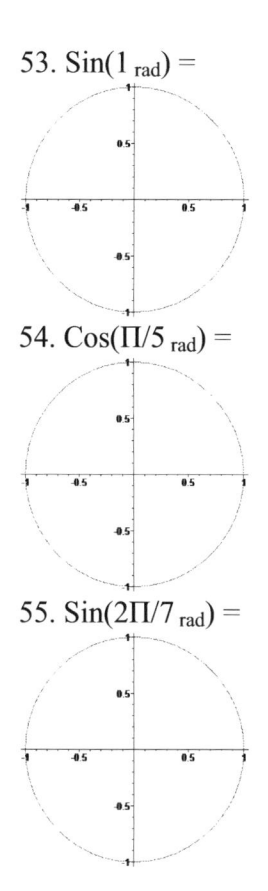

54. Cos(Π/5 rad) =

55. Sin(2Π/7 rad) =

For each one of the following, fill in the blank with an angle between 0° and 360° different than the first one.

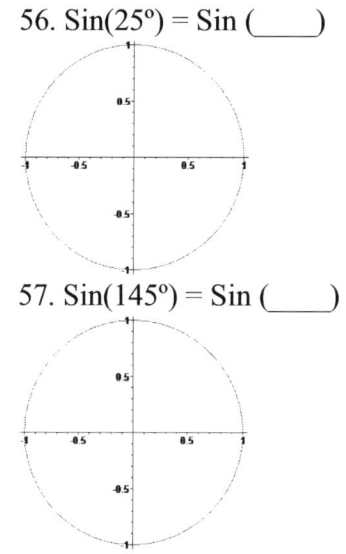

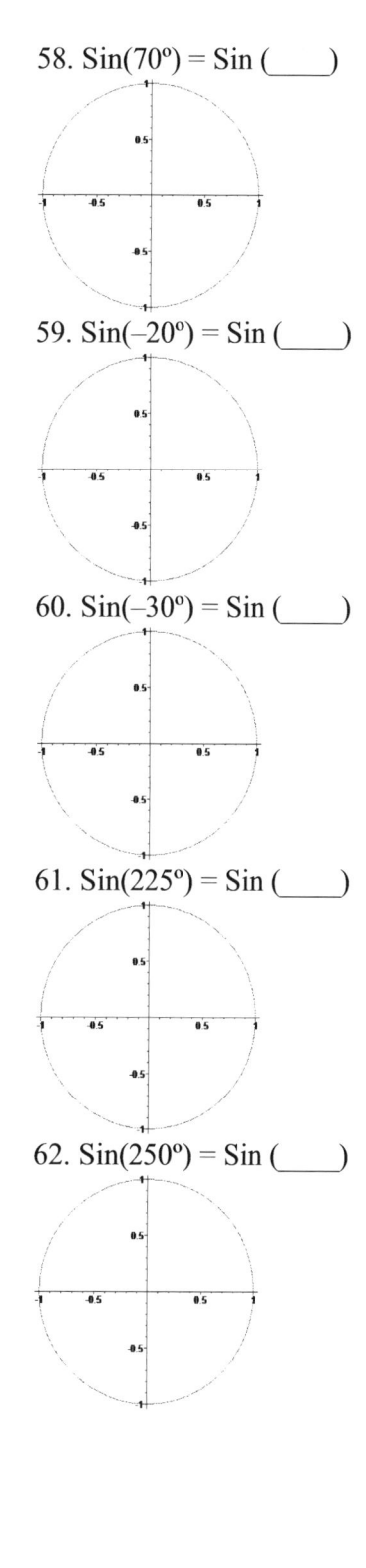

56. Sin(25°) = Sin (____)

57. Sin(145°) = Sin (____)

58. Sin(70°) = Sin (____)

59. Sin(−20°) = Sin (____)

60. Sin(−30°) = Sin (____)

61. Sin(225°) = Sin (____)

62. Sin(250°) = Sin (____)

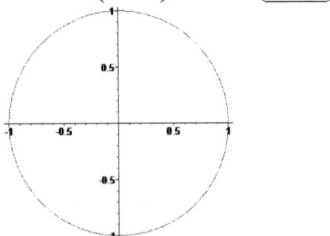

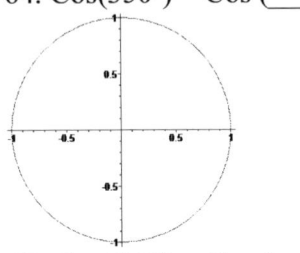

63. Cos(250°) = Cos (____)

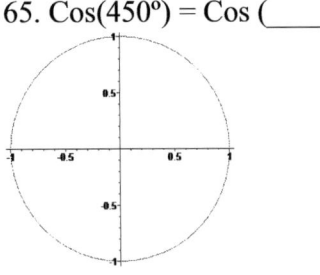

66. Cos(–250°) = Cos (____)

64. Cos(350°) = Cos (____)

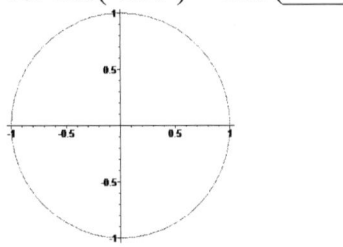

67. Cos(–50°) = Cos (____)

65. Cos(450°) = Cos (____)

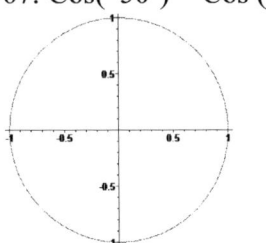

68. Cos(–73°) = Cos (____)

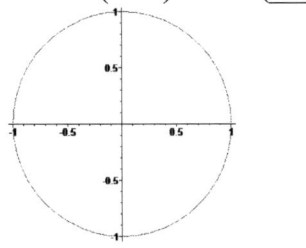

Definitions of Tan (x), Cot(x), Sec(x) Cosec(x)

$Tan(x) = \left(\dfrac{\rule{1cm}{0.4pt}}{\rule{1cm}{0.4pt}}\right), Cos(x) \neq 0$ $\qquad Cot(x) = \left(\dfrac{\rule{1cm}{0.4pt}}{\rule{1cm}{0.4pt}}\right), Sin(x) \neq 0$

$Sec(x) = \left(\dfrac{1}{\rule{1cm}{0.4pt}}\right), Cos(x) \neq 0$ $\qquad Csc(x) = \left(\dfrac{1}{\rule{1cm}{0.4pt}}\right), Sin(x) \neq 0$

In Consequence:

Tan(x) = tg(x) is positive in the _____ and _____ quadrants and

negative in the _____ and _____ quadrants. Cotg(x) = Cot(x) = Cotan(x) is

positive in the _____ and _____ quadrants and negative in the _____ and

_____ quadrants.

322

69. Answer, in terms of a and b:

a. $\sin(\theta) =$ $\cos(\theta) =$

b. $\sin(\theta + 360°) =$

c. $\sin(\theta + 180°) =$

d. $\sin(180° - \theta) =$

e. $\cos(180° - \theta) =$

f. $\sin(360° - \theta) =$

g. $\cos(360° - \theta) =$

h. $\sin(90° - \theta) =$

i. $\cos(90° - \theta) =$

j. $\tan(\theta) =$

k. $\cot(\theta) =$

l. $\sec(\theta) =$

m. $\csc(\theta) =$

n. $\tan(\theta + 180°) =$

o. $\tan(\theta + 90°) =$

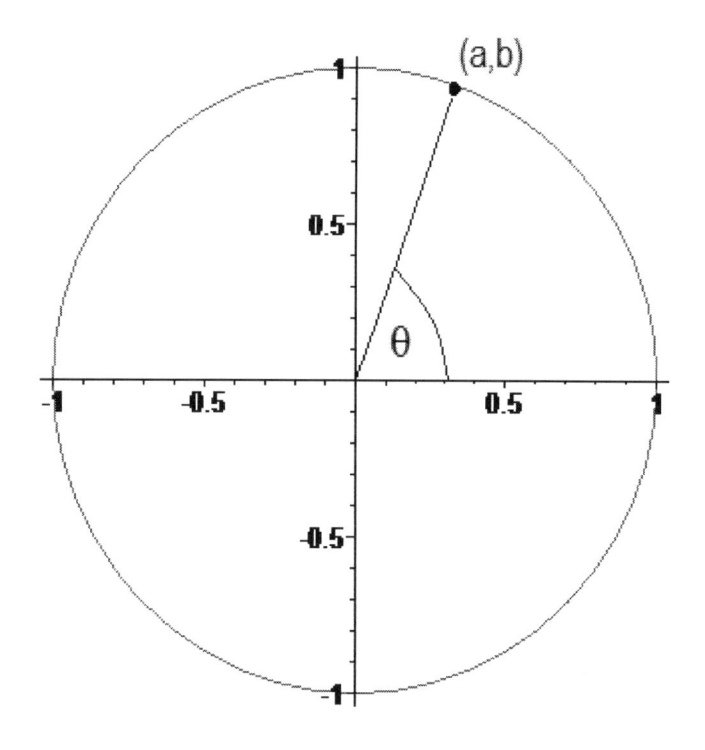

p. $\cos(270° - \theta)$

q. $\sin(270° + \theta)$

Complete the following table:

Angle in degrees	Angle in Radians	Sin(x)	Cos(x)	Tan(x)	Cot(x)	Sec(x)	Csc(x)
0	0						
30°							
45°							
60°							
90°							
120°							
135°							
150°							
180°							
360°							
390°							

Exercises:

1. Given that $\sin(x) = \dfrac{2}{7}$ and $0 < x < \dfrac{\pi}{2}$, find:

   a. $\cos(x) =$

   b. $\tan(x) =$

   c. $\cot(x) =$

   d. $\csc(x) =$

   e. $\sin(2x) =$

   f. $\cos(2x) =$

   g. $\sin(3x) =$

   h. $\cos(3x) =$

   i. $\sin(\pi - x) =$

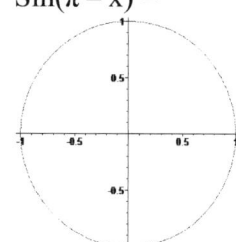

   j. $\cos(\pi - x) =$

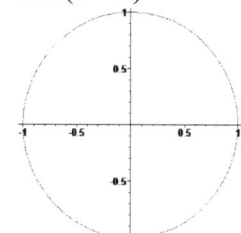

   k. $\sin(2\pi - x) =$

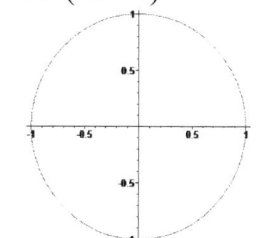

   l. $\cos(2\pi - x) =$

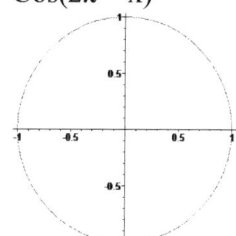

   m. $\sin\left(x + \dfrac{\pi}{2}\right) =$

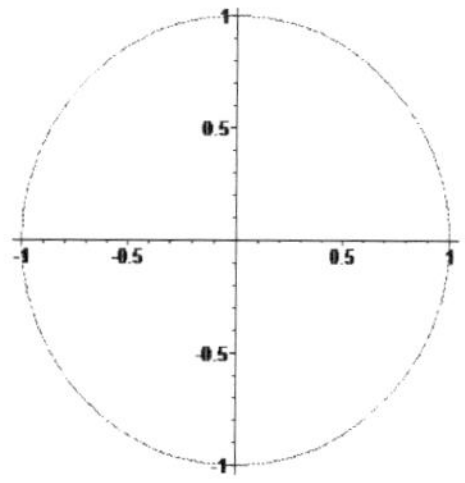

2. Given that $\cos(x) = -\dfrac{1}{6}$ and $\pi < x < \dfrac{3\pi}{2}$, find:

   a. $\sin(x) =$

   b. $\tan(x) =$

   c. $\cot(x) =$

   d. $\csc(x) =$

   e. $\sin(2x) =$

   f. $\cos(2x) =$

   g. $\sin(4x) =$

   h. $\cos(4x) =$

   i. $\sin(\pi - x) =$

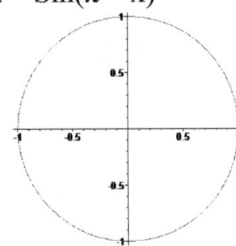

   j. $\cos(\pi - x) =$

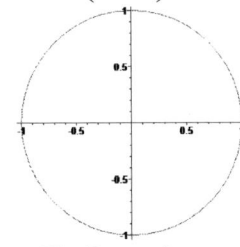

   k. $\sin(2\pi - x) =$

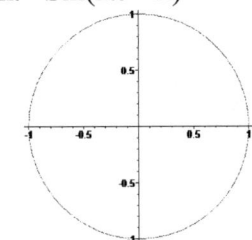

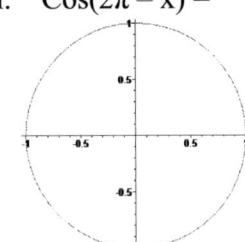

   l. $\cos(2\pi - x) =$

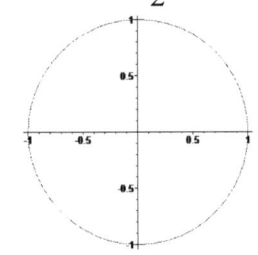

   m. $\cos\left(x + \dfrac{\pi}{2}\right) =$

3. Given that Tan(x) = 3 and $\pi < x < 2\pi$, so x is in the _____ quadrant. find:

   a. Cos(x) =

   b. Tan(x) =

   c. Cot(x) =

   d. Csc(x) =

   e. Tan(2x) =

   f. Sin(3x) =

   g. Cos(3x) =

   h. Sin(π – x) =

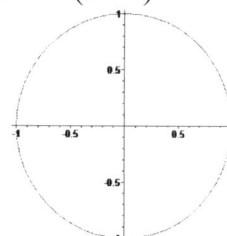

   i. Cos(π – x) =

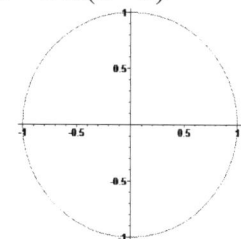

   j. Sin(2π – x) =

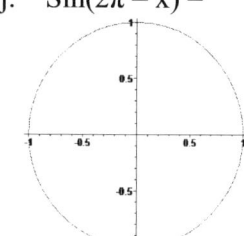

   k. Cos(2π – x) =

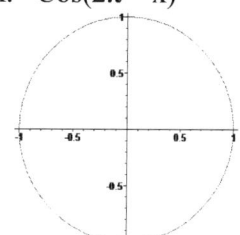

   l. Sin(x + $\dfrac{\pi}{2}$) =

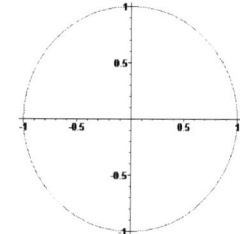

3.3. – TRIGONOMETRIC IDENTITIES

Prove the following identities:

1. $\sin(\theta)\sec(\theta)\cot(\theta) = 1$

2. $\dfrac{\sin(\theta)}{\csc(\theta)} = (\sin(\theta))^2$

3. $\sin(\theta)\tan(\theta) + \cos(\theta) = \sec(\theta)$

4. $\sec(\theta) = \tan(\theta)\csc(\theta)$

5. $(\tan(\theta))^2 + 1 = (\sec(\theta))^2$

6. $\dfrac{\sec(\theta)}{\csc(\theta)} = \tan(\theta)$

7. $(\sec(\theta))^2 - (\tan(\theta))^2 = 1$

8. $\dfrac{\tan(\theta) - \cot(\theta)}{\tan(\theta) + \cot(\theta)} = (\sin(\theta))^2 - (\cos(\theta))^2$

9. $\dfrac{\sin(\theta)\cos(\theta)}{(\cos(\theta))^2 - (\sin(\theta))^2} = \dfrac{\tan(\theta)}{1 - (\tan(\theta))^2}$

10. $\dfrac{1+\tan(\theta)}{1-\tan(\theta)} = \dfrac{1+\cot(\theta)}{\cot(\theta)-1}$

13. $\dfrac{1+\sin(\theta)}{1-\sin(\theta)} - \dfrac{1-\sin(\theta)}{1+\sin(\theta)} = 4\tan(\theta)\sec(\theta)$

11. $\dfrac{1-\sin(\theta)}{1+\sin(\theta)} = (\sec(\theta)-\tan(\theta))^2$

14. $\dfrac{\tan(x)+\tan(y)}{\cot(x)+\cot(y)} = \tan(x)\tan(y)$

12. $\dfrac{1-\cos(\theta)}{1+\cos(\theta)} = (\csc(\theta)-\cot(\theta))^2$

15. $\sin(\theta)\tan(\theta) + \cos(\theta) = \sec(\theta)$

16. $(\sin(x))^2 - (\sin(y))^2 = (\cos(y))^2 - (\cos(x))^2$

17. $(\sin(x))^4 - (\cos(x))^4 = 2(\sin(x))^2 - 1$

18. $\dfrac{1}{1-\sin(\theta)} + \dfrac{1}{1+\sin(\theta)} = 2(\sec(\theta))^2$

19. $3(\sin(x))^2 + 4(\cos(x))^2 = 3 + (\cos(x))^2$

3.4. – TRIGONOMETRIC FUNCTIONS

1. Write next to each one of the functions if it's periodic or not. Determine the period of the periodic ones.

a.

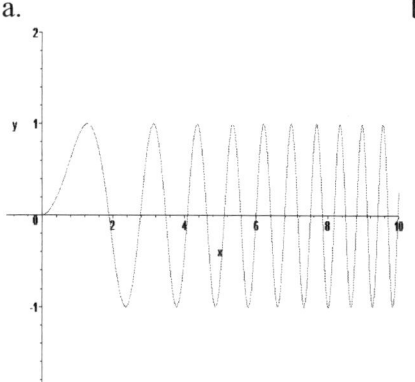

b.

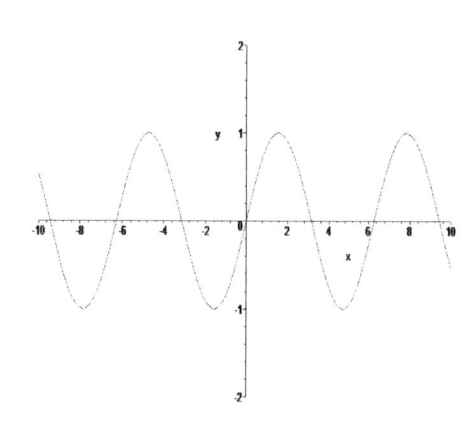

c.

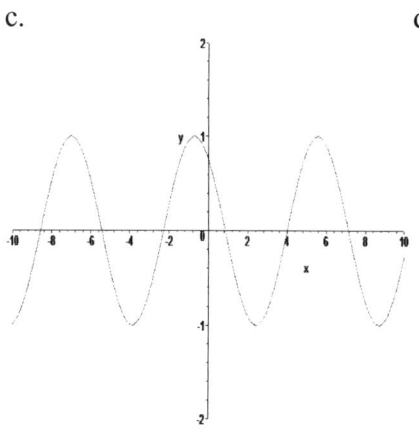

d.

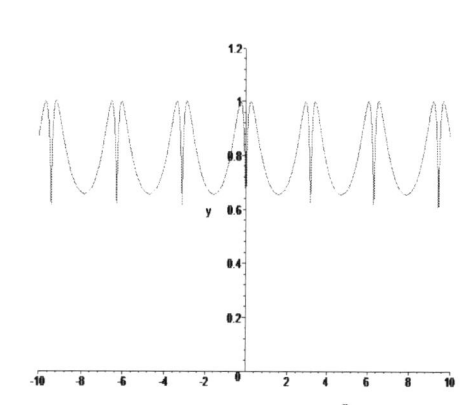

331

2. Given the function f(x) = Sin(x), g(x) = Cos(x), Complete the following table:

x°	0	15	30	45	60	75	90	105	120	135	150	165	180	195	210	225	240	255
Rad																		
f(x)																		
g(x)																		

- Sketch the points of the table on a graph.

- State the domain of the functions: : f(x):_____, g(x):_____

- State the y intercepts: f(x): (____, ____), g(x): (____, ____)

- State the x intercept(s): f(x): (____, ____), g(x): (____, ____)

- Write the corresponding limits and the equation of the vertical asymptote(s): ____

- Write the corresponding limits and the equation of the horizontal asymptote(s): ____

- Find the maximum point(s): f(x):_____, g(x):_____

- Find the minimum point(s): f(x):_____, g(x):_____

- State the range of the function: _____

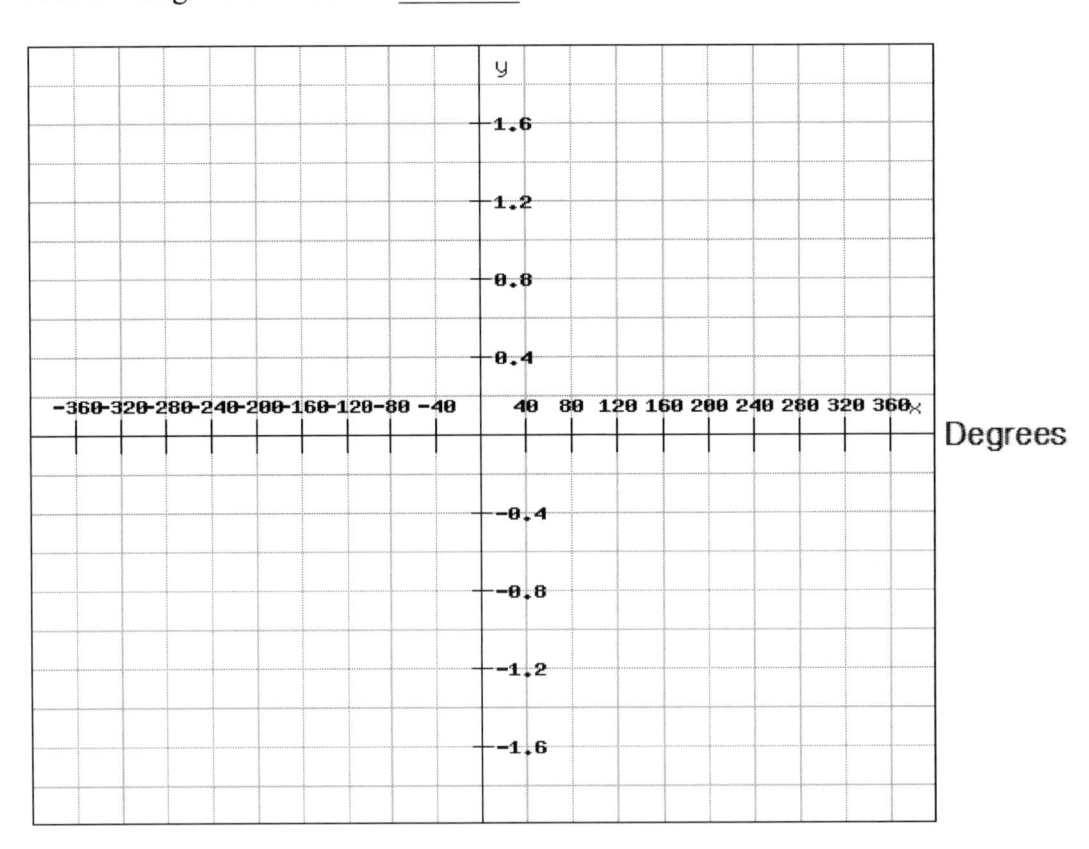

332

3. Given the function f(x) = Sin(x)

   a. Write in all forms the same function translated 2 positions up: _____

   b. Write in all forms the same function translated 3 positions left: _____

   c. Write in all forms the same function translated 3 positions left and 1 up.

   d. Write in all forms the same function translated 4 positions right and 1 up.

   e. Change the function so that the period would be 2.

   f. Change the function so that the period would be 3 and the amplitude 2.

   g. Change the function so that the period would be π and the amplitude 4.

   h. Change the function so that the period would be $\frac{\pi}{3}$ and the amplitude k.

   i. Change the function so that the period would be 6, the amplitude 3, then shift the function 2 positions right and 1 down.

   j. Change the function so that the period would be $\frac{\pi}{3}$, the amplitude 1.3, then shift the function 4 positions left and 2 down.

   k. Change the function so that the period would be $\frac{\pi}{5}$, the amplitude 4, then shift the function π positions left and 5 down.

4. Given the function f(x) = 3Sin(5(x − 2)) + 3

   a. Amplitude = _____

   b. Period = _____

   c. Horizontal Translation = _____

   d. Vertical Translation = _____   Midline: _____

   e. Range: _____

5. Given the function f(x) = −5Cos(3x − 2) − 3.4

   a. Amplitude = _____

   b. Period = _____

   c. Horizontal Translation = _____

   d. Vertical Translation = _____   Midline: _____

   e. Range: _____

6. Given the function $f(x) = 2.4\text{Sin}(\pi x - \frac{\pi}{2}) - 3$

   a. Amplitude = _____

   b. Period = _____

   c. Horizontal Translation = _____

   d. Vertical Translation = _____   Midline: _____

   e. Range: _____

7. Given the function $f(x) = 4 - (2.4)\text{Cos}(2\pi x - \frac{\pi}{3})$

   a. Amplitude = _____

   b. Period = _____

   c. Horizontal Translation = _____

   d. Vertical Translation = _____   Midline: _____

   e. Range: _____

8. Given the function $f(x) = 1 + 4\text{Sin}(\frac{\pi}{3}x - 3)$

   a. Amplitude = _____

   b. Period = _____

   c. Horizontal Translation = _____

   d. Vertical Translation = _____   Midline: _____

   e. Range: _____

9. Given the function $f(x) = -\text{Sin}(\frac{\pi}{5}x - 1) + 1$

   a. Amplitude = _____

   b. Period = _____

   c. Horizontal Translation = _____

   d. Vertical Translation = _____   Midline: _____

   e. Range: _____

10. Given the function $f(x) = 4 - 3\text{Cos}(3x°)$

    a. Amplitude = _____

    b. Period = _____

    c. Horizontal Translation = _____

    d. Vertical Translation = _____   Midline: _____

    e. Range: _____

11. Given the function $f(x) = -\text{Sin}(\frac{x°}{10}) + 1$

    a. Amplitude = _____

    b. Period = _____

    c. Horizontal Translation = _____

    d. Vertical Translation = _____   Midline: _____

    e. Range: _____

12. Given the graph, complete:

   a. Amplitude = _____

   b. Period = _____

   c. Horizontal Translation: _____

   d. Midline: _____

   e. f(x) =

   f. Range: _____

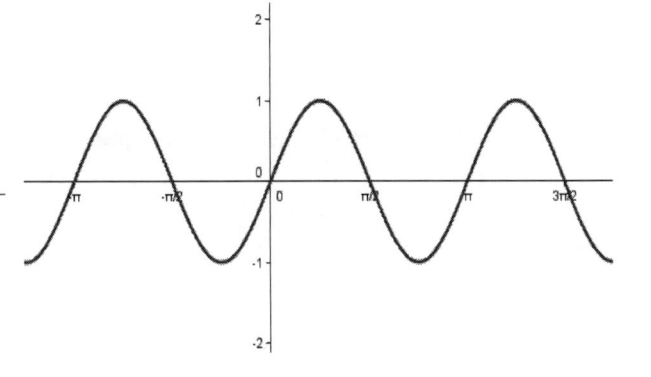

13. Given the graph, complete:

   a. Amplitude = _____

   b. Period = _____

   c. Horizontal Translation: _____

   d. Midline: _____

   e. f(x) =

   f. Range: _____

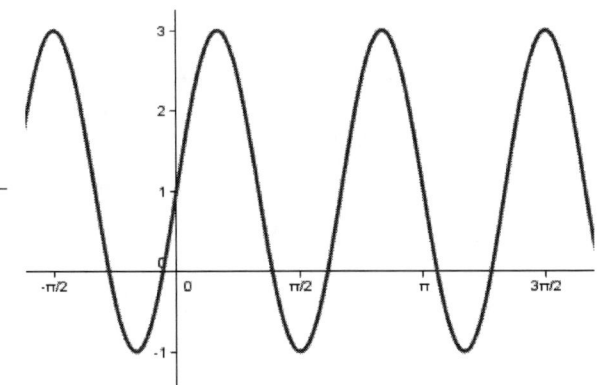

14. Given the graph, complete:

   a. Amplitude = _____

   b. Period = _____

   c. Horizontal Translation: _____

   d. Midline: _____

   e. f(x) =

   f. Range: _____

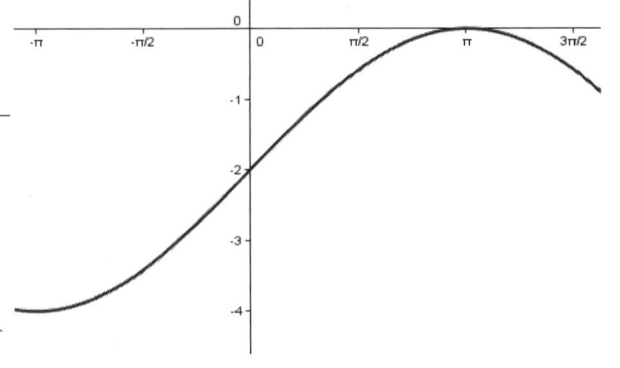

15. Given the graph, complete:

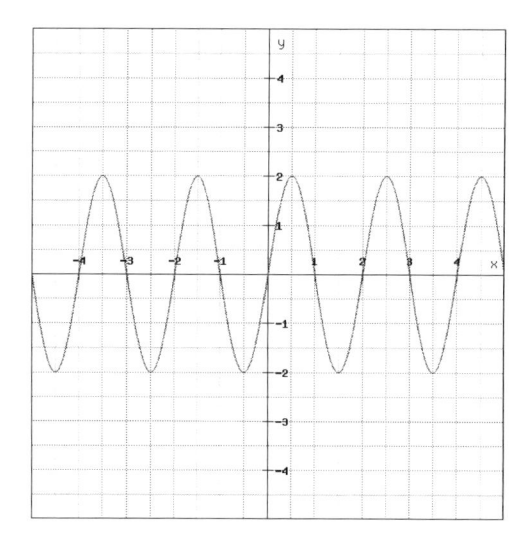

   a. Amplitude = _____

   b. Period = _____

   c. Horizontal Translation: _____

   d. Midline: _____

   e. f(x) =

   f. Range: _____

16. Given the graph, complete:

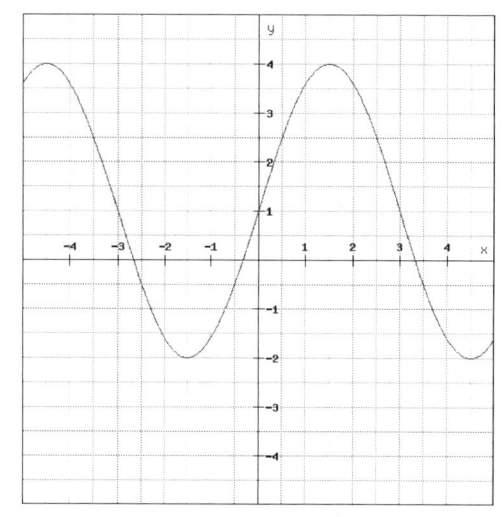

   a. Amplitude = _____

   b. Period = _____

   c. Horizontal Translation: _____

   d. Midline: _____

   e. f(x) =

   f. Range: _____

17. Given the graph, complete:

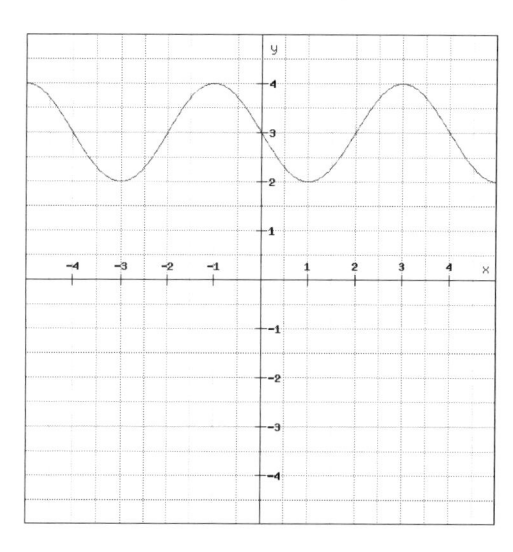

   a. Amplitude = _____

   b. Period = _____

   c. Horizontal Translation: _____

   d. Midline: _____

   e. f(x) =

   f. Range: _____

18. Given the graph, complete:

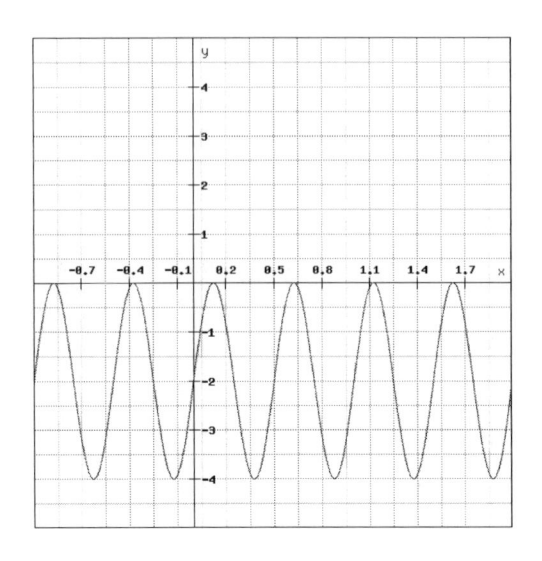

   a. Amplitude = _____

   b. Period = _____

   c. Horizontal Translation: _____

   d. Midline: _____

   e. f(x) =

   f. Range: _____

19. Given the graph, complete:

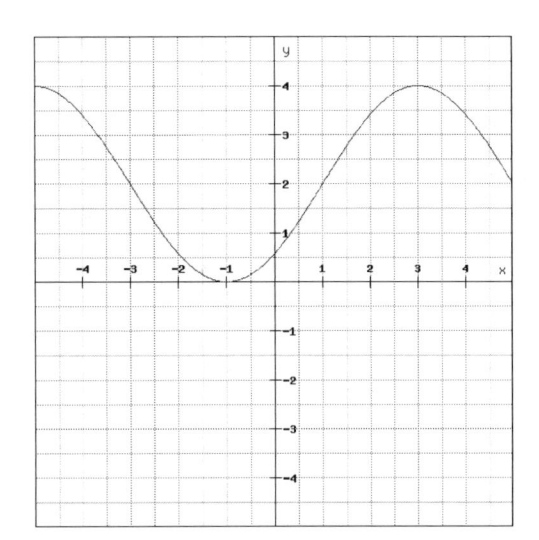

   a. Amplitude = _____

   b. Period = _____

   c. Horizontal Translation = _____

   d. Midline: _____

   e. f(x) =

   f. Range: _____

20. Given the graph, complete:

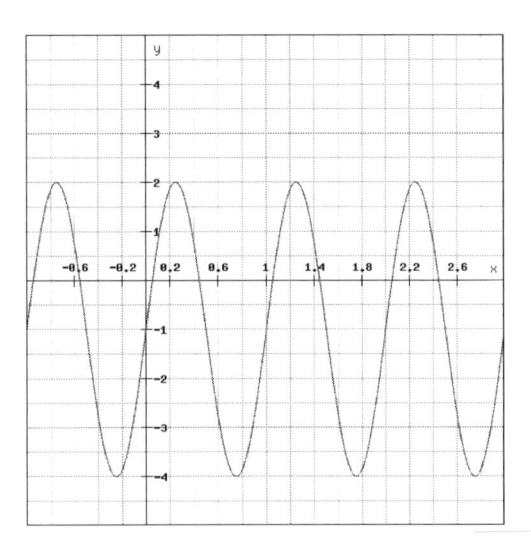

   a. Amplitude = _____

   b. Period = _____

   c. Horizontal Translation = _____

   d. Midline: _____

   e. f(x) =

   f. Range: _____

338

21. Given the graph, complete:

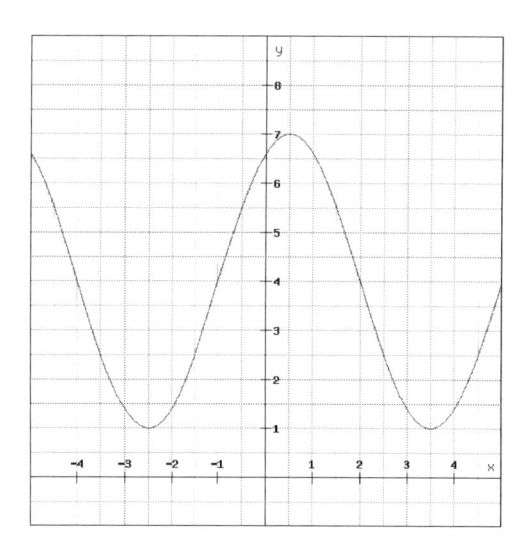

   a. Amplitude = _____

   b. Period = _____

   c. Horizontal Translation: _____

   d. Midline _____

   e. f(x) =

   f. Range: _____

22. Given the graph, complete:

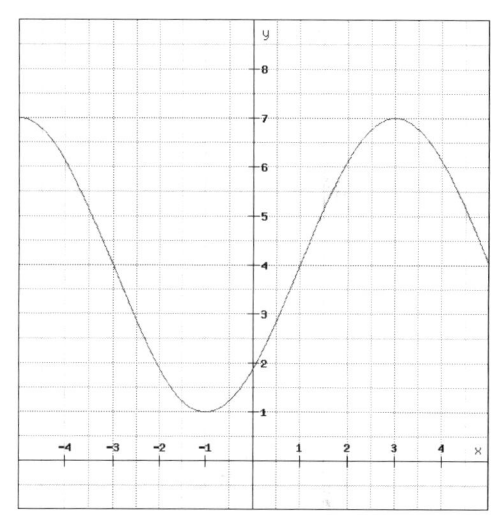

   a. Amplitude = _____

   b. Period = _____

   c. Horizontal Translation: _____

   d. Midline _____

   e. f(x) =

   f. Range: _____

23. Given the graph, complete:

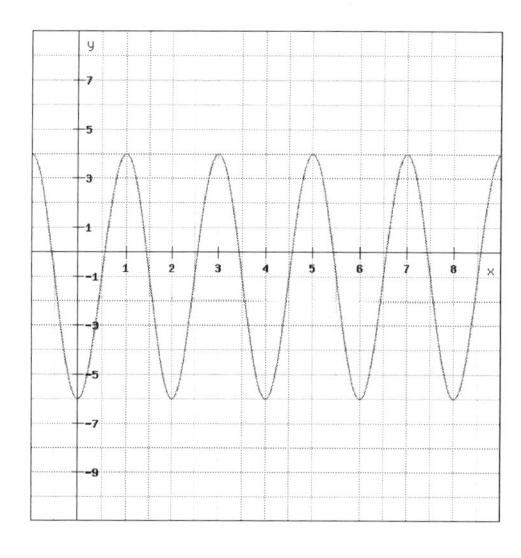

   a. Amplitude = _____

   b. Period = _____

   c. Horizontal Translation: _____

   d. Midline: _____

   e. f(x) =

   f. Range: _____

339

24. Given the function $f(x) = 3 - 2\cos(\pi x - \frac{\pi}{2})$

   a. Amplitude = _____

   b. Period = _____

   c. Horizontal Translation: _____

   d. Vertical Translation: _____

   e. Midline: _____

   f. Range: _____

   g. Sketch the 2 periods of the function, include maximums and minimums.

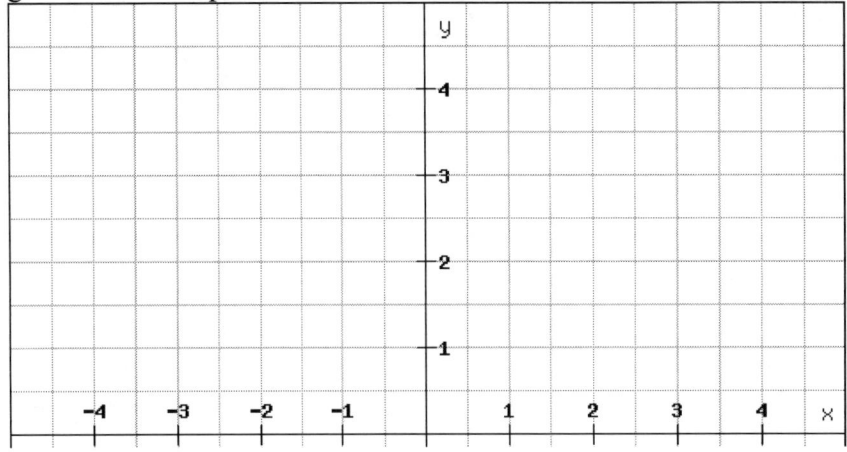

25. Given the function $f(x) = -2\sin(\pi x - \frac{\pi}{2}) + 1$

   a. Amplitude = _____

   b. Period = _____

   c. Horizontal Translation: _____

   d. Vertical Translation: _____

   e. Midline: _____

   f. Range: _____

   g. Sketch the 2 periods of the function, include maximums and minimums.

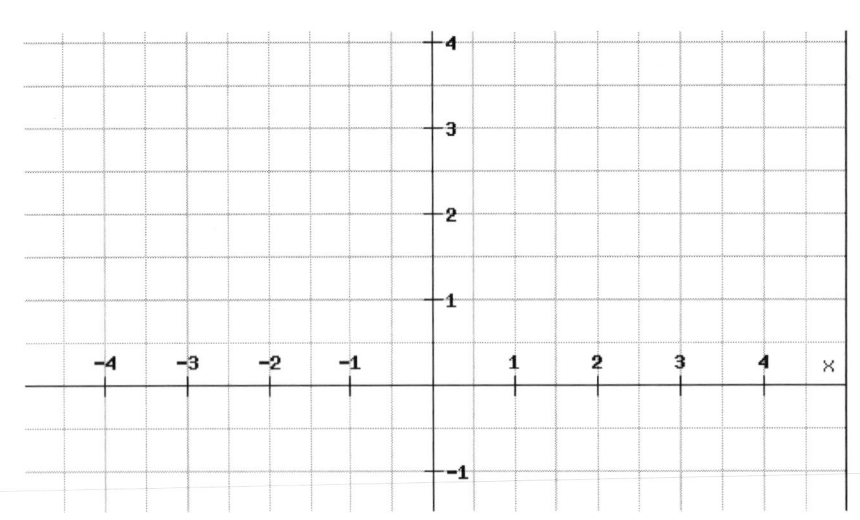

26. Given the function f(x) = Tan(x), Complete the following table:

x°	0	15	30	45	60	75	90	105	120	135	150	165	180	195	210	225	240	255
Rad																		
f(x)																		

- Sketch the points of the table on a graph.

- State the domain of the function: _____

- State the y intercept (sketched on the graph: (____, ____)

- State the x intercept(s): (_____, _____)

- Write the corresponding limits and the equation of the vertical asymptote(s):

- Write the corresponding limits and the equation of the horizontal asymptote:

- Function is increasing on the interval: _____, decreasing on the interval: _____

- Find the max/min point(s): (____, ____)

- State the range of the function: _____

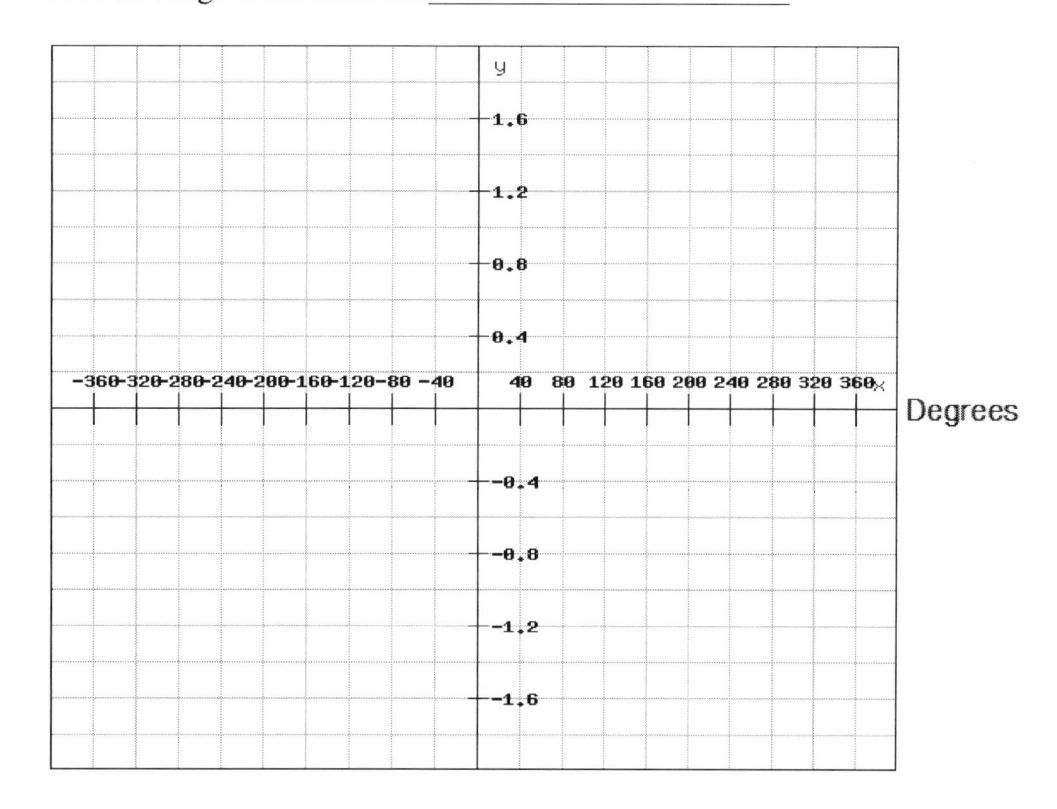

337

27. Given the function f(x) = Tan(x)

   a. Write in all forms the same function translated 2 positions up: _____

   b. Write in all forms the same function translated 3 positions left: _____

   c. Write in all forms the same function translated 3 positions left and 1 up.

   d. Write in all forms the same function translated 4 positions right and 1 up.

   e. Change the function so that the period would be 2.

   f. Change the function so that the period would be 3 and the amplitude 2.

   g. Change the function so that the period would be π.

   h. Change the function so that the period would be $\frac{\pi}{3}$.

   i. Change the function so that the period would be 6, then shift the function 2 positions right and 1 down.

   j. Change the function so that the period would be $\frac{\pi}{3}$, then shift the function 4 positions left and 2 down.

   k. Change the function so that the period would be $\frac{\pi}{5}$, then shift the function π positions left and 5 down.

338

28. Given the graph, complete:

   a. Amplitude = _____

   b. Period = _____

   c. Horizontal Translation: _____

   d. Midline: _____

   e. f(x) =

   f. Range: _____

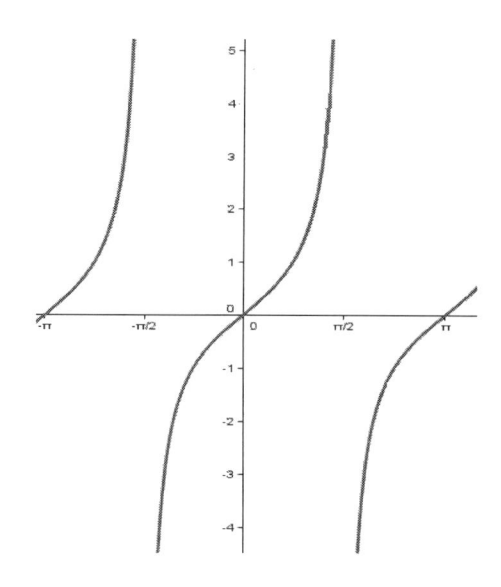

29. Given the graph, complete:

   a. Amplitude = _____

   b. Period = _____

   c. Horizontal Translation: _____

   d. Midline: _____

   e. f(x) =

   f. Range: _____

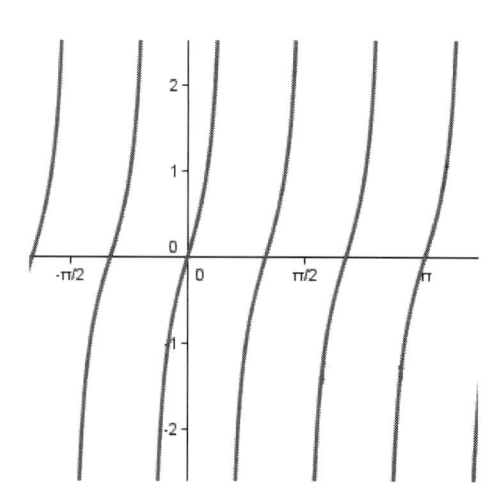

30. Given the graph, complete:

   a. Amplitude = _____

   b. Period = _____

   c. Horizontal Translation: _____

   d. Midline: _____

   e. f(x) =

   f. Range: _____

339

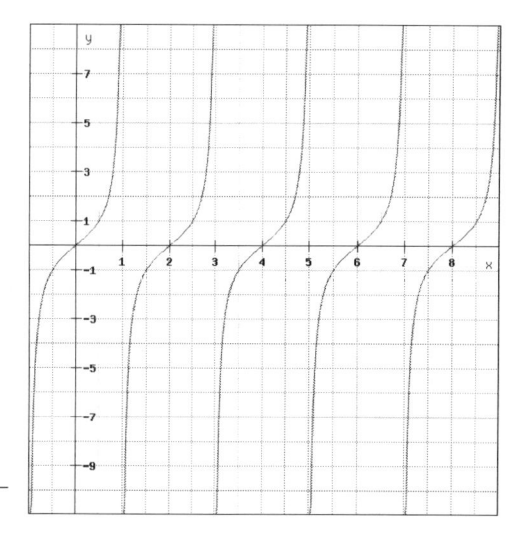

Analyze the following functions (Domain, Amplitude, Period, Range, Interceptions, maximums, minimums, sketch):

1. $f(x) = 2\sin(3x)$
2. $f(x) = \frac{1}{2}\sin(x) + 1$
3. $f(x) = 2\sin(x) + 5$
4. $f(x) = 3\sin(x) - 1$
5. $f(x) = -3\sin(x) - 3$
6. $f(x) = \sin(2x) - 2$
7. $f(x) = -\sin(3x) + 4$
8. $f(x) = -2\sin(\pi x)$
9. $f(x) = \frac{1}{2}\sin(\pi x)$
10. $f(x) = 2\sin(2\pi x)$
11. $f(x) = -\sin(k\pi x)$
12. $f(x) = \sin(\pi x + \pi)$
13. $f(x) = \sin(\frac{\pi}{2}x)$
14. $f(x) = \sin(\frac{\pi}{2}x - \frac{\pi}{2}) - 3$
15. $f(x) = 2\sin(\frac{\pi}{4}x - \frac{\pi}{2})$
16. $f(x) = -2\sin(\frac{\pi}{4}x + \frac{\pi}{2})$
17. $f(x) = \frac{1}{2}\sin(\frac{\pi}{4}x - \pi) + 1$
18. $f(x) = \sin(\pi x - 1)$
19. $f(x) = 2\cos(3x)$
20. $f(x) = \frac{1}{2}\cos(x) + 1$
21. $f(x) = 2\cos(x) + 5$
22. $f(x) = 3\cos(x) - 1$
23. $f(x) = -3\cos(x) - 3$
24. $f(x) = \cos(2x) - 2$
25. $f(x) = -\cos(3x) + 4$
26. $f(x) = -2\cos(\pi x)$
27. $f(x) = \frac{1}{2}\cos(\pi x)$
28. $f(x) = 2\cos(2\pi x)$
29. $f(x) = -\cos(k\pi x)$
30. $f(x) = \cos(\pi x + \pi)$
31. $f(x) = \cos(\frac{\pi}{2}x)$
32. $f(x) = \cos(\frac{\pi}{2}x - \frac{\pi}{2})$
33. $f(x) = 2\cos(\frac{\pi}{4}x - \frac{\pi}{2})$
34. $f(x) = -2\cos(\frac{\pi}{4}x + \frac{\pi}{2})$
35. $f(x) = \frac{1}{2}\cos(\frac{\pi}{4}x - \pi) - 2$
36. $f(x) = \cos(\pi x + 2)$
37.
38. $f(x) = 2\tan(3x)$
39. $f(x) = \frac{1}{2}\tan(x) + 1$
40. $f(x) = 2\tan(x) + 5$
41. $f(x) = 3\tan(x) - 1$
42. $f(x) = -3\tan(x) - 3$
43. $f(x) = \tan(2x) - 2$
44. $f(x) = -\tan(3x) + 4$
45. $f(x) = -2\tan(\pi x)$
46. $f(x) = \frac{1}{2}\tan(\pi x)$
47. $f(x) = 2\tan(2\pi x)$
48. $f(x) = -\tan(k\pi x)$
49. $f(x) = \tan(\pi x + \pi)$
50. $f(x) = \tan(\frac{\pi}{2}x)$
51. $f(x) = \tan(\frac{\pi}{2}x - \frac{\pi}{2})$
52. $f(x) = 2\tan(\frac{\pi}{4}x - \frac{\pi}{2}) + 2$
53. $f(x) = -2\tan(\frac{\pi}{4}x + \frac{\pi}{2})$
54. $f(x) = \frac{1}{2}\tan(\frac{\pi}{4}x - \pi)$
55. $f(x) = \tan(\pi x + 1)$

3.5. – SINE AND COSINE RULE

The sine rule: For any triangle, given the sides a, b and c and their corresponding opposite angles, A, B and C:

$$\frac{Sin(A)}{a} = \frac{Sin(B)}{b} = \frac{Sin(C)}{c}$$

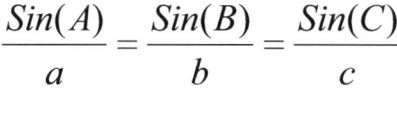

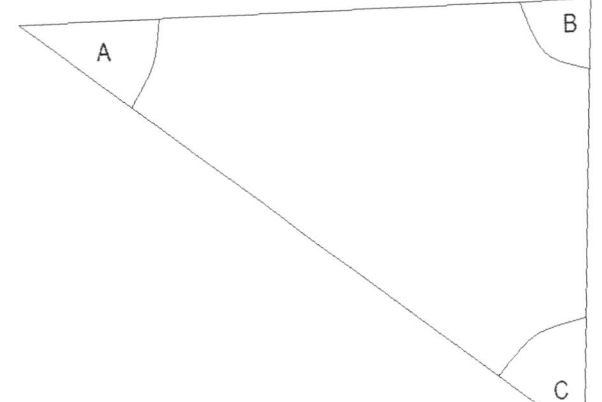

How many equations are written above? ___

    I. _____

    II. _____

    III. _____

The cosine rule: For any triangle, given the sides a, b and c and their corresponding opposite angles, A, B and C:

$$a^2 = b^2 + c^2 - 2bc\cos(A)$$
$$b^2 = a^2 + c^2 - 2ac\cos(B)$$
$$\underline{} = \underline{} + \underline{} - 2\underline{}\cos(\underline{})$$

Given the following triangle:

    a. Find AD in terms of AC and the angle A.

    b. Find the Area of the triangle in terms of CB, AC and the angle A.

    c. Conclusion:

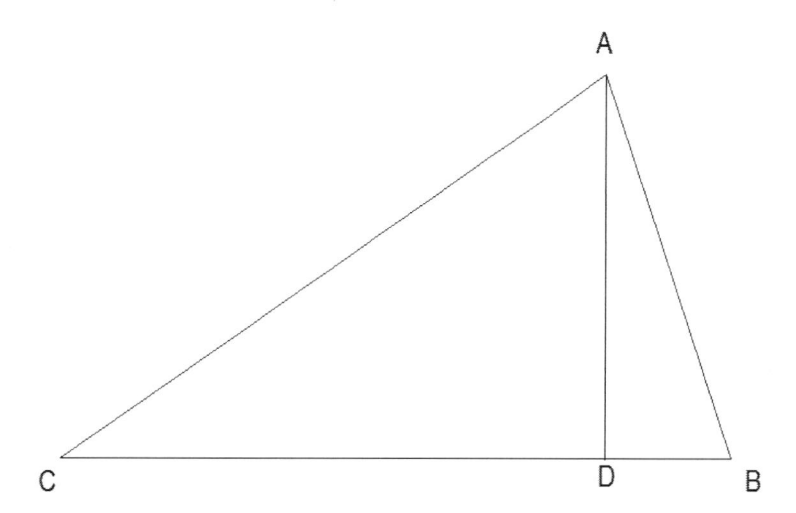

345

Exercises

1. Sketch a right angled triangle with angles: A, B, C and sides a, b, c. Write the Sine and Cosine rule for this triangle.

2. Find all the missing sides, angles and area of the triangles below. If there is more than one set of solutions, try to find them all.

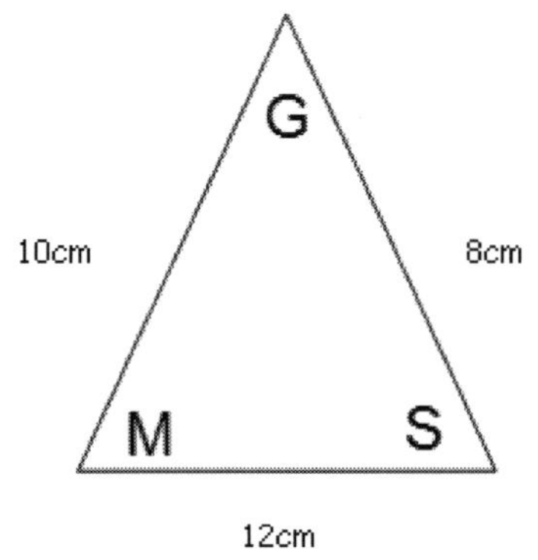
G
10cm
8cm
M
S
12cm

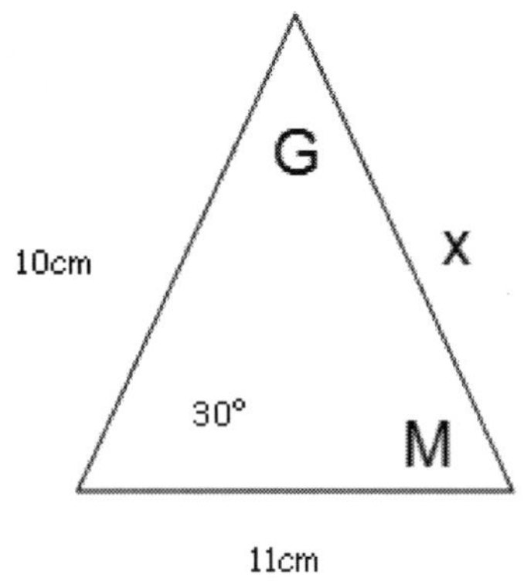
G
10cm
X
30°
M
11cm

Conclusion: The cosine rule must be used in the following cases:

I. ____

II. ____

3. Find all the sides, angles and the area of the following triangles:
   Ambiguous Case (2 possible solutions)

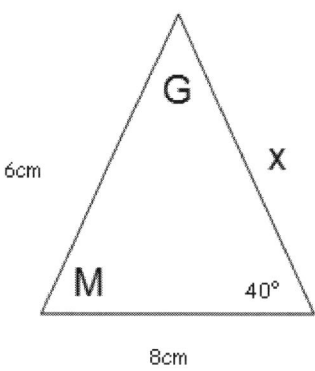

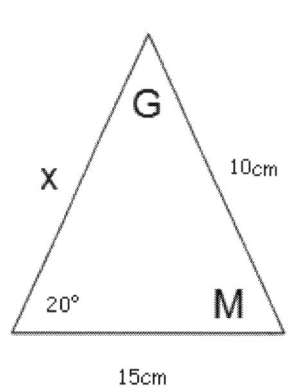

   Triangle with vertices G (top), M (bottom-left), and bottom-right angle = 40°. Side from M to G = 6cm, side from M to bottom-right = 8cm, side opposite M (from G to bottom-right) = x.

   Triangle with vertices G (top), M (bottom-right), and bottom-left angle = 20°. Side from bottom-left to G = x, side from G to M = 10cm, side from bottom-left to M = 15cm.

   Conclusion: _____

4. Find all the sides, angles and the area of the following triangles:

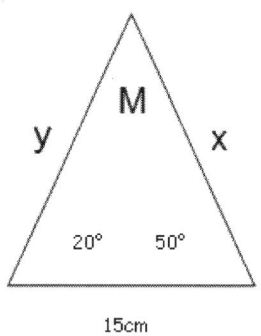

   Triangle with vertex M at top, bottom-left angle = 20°, bottom-right angle = 50°. Side y on the left, side x on the right, base = 15cm.

347

5. Find all the sides, angles and the area of the triangle:

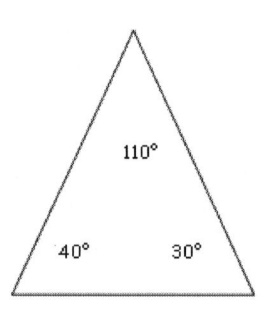

   110°
   40°   30°

6. Find all the sides, angles and the area of the triangle:

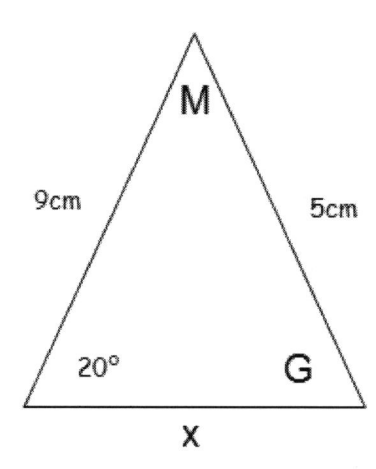

   M
   9cm   5cm
   20°   G
   X

7. Find all the sides, angles and the area of the triangle:

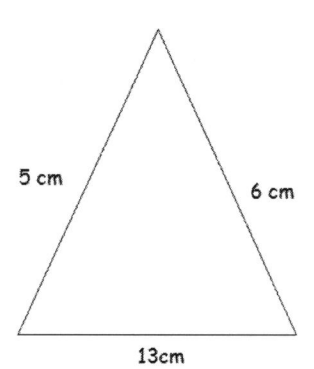

   5 cm   6 cm
   13cm

348

8. Find all the sides, angles and the area of the triangle:

   - Triangle with vertex M at top, vertex G at bottom-left, and bottom-right angle 50°. Side from G to M = 15cm, side from M to bottom-right = 12cm, bottom side labeled x.

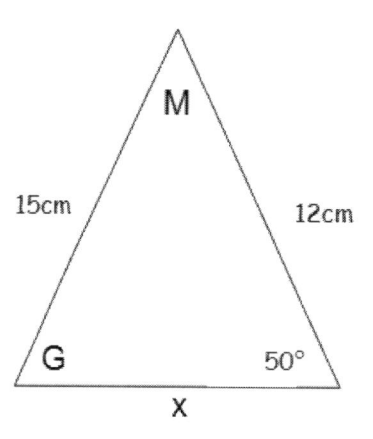

9. Find all the sides, angles and the area of the triangle:

   - Triangle with right side = 8cm, bottom-right angle = 40°, bottom side = 12cm.

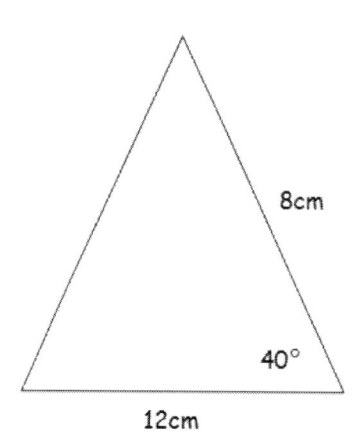

10. Find all the sides, angles and the area of the triangle:

    - Triangle with right side = 6 cm, bottom-right angle = 20°, bottom side = 13cm.

349

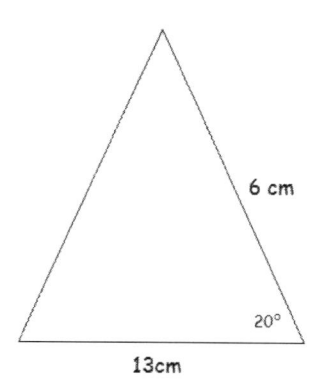

11. Can you identify how many triangles (not to scale) you could draw using the given information? In which example could you find the ambiguous case? Sketch (to scale as possible) both triangles in that case.

a.

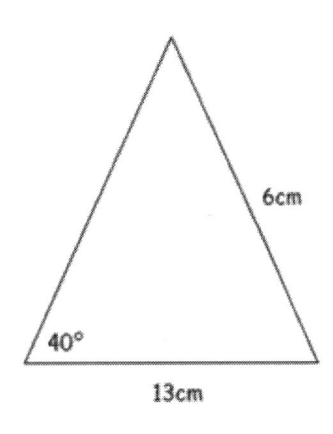

6cm
40°
13cm

b.

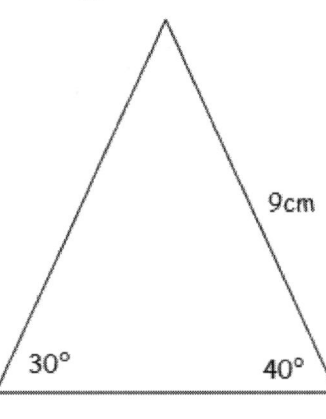

9cm
30°   40°

c.

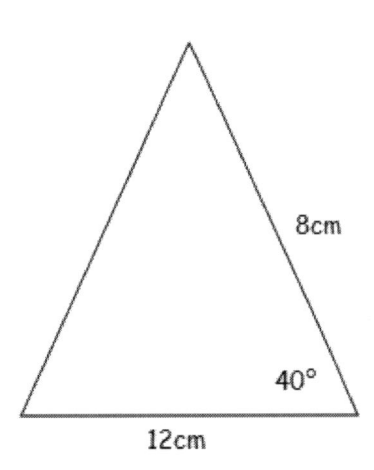

8cm
40°
12cm

d.

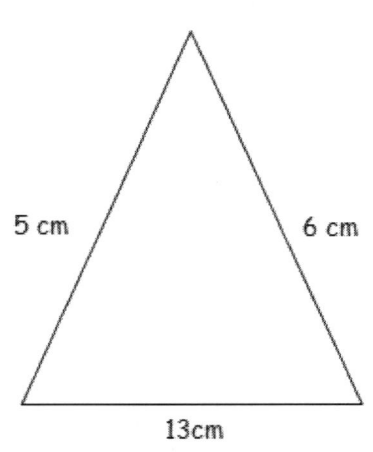

5 cm   6 cm
13cm

e.

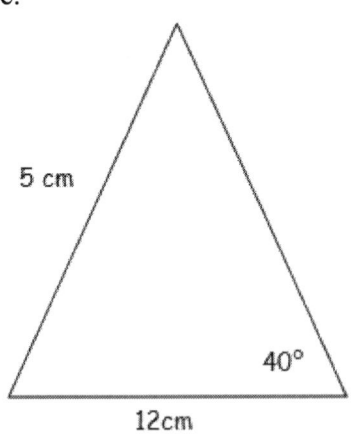

5 cm
40°
12cm

f.

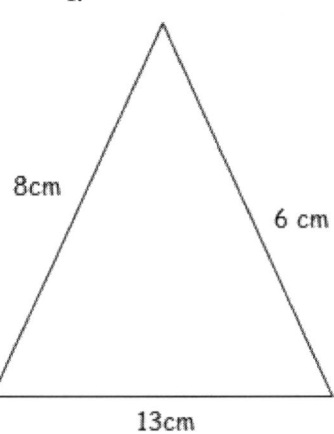

8cm
6 cm
13cm

350

3.6. – TRIGONOMETRIC RATIOS

Following directly from the unit circle are the trigonometric ratios:

$$Sin(x) = \frac{a}{c}$$

$$Cos(x) = \frac{b}{c}$$

$$Tan(x) = \frac{a}{b} = \frac{Sin(x)}{Cos(x)}$$

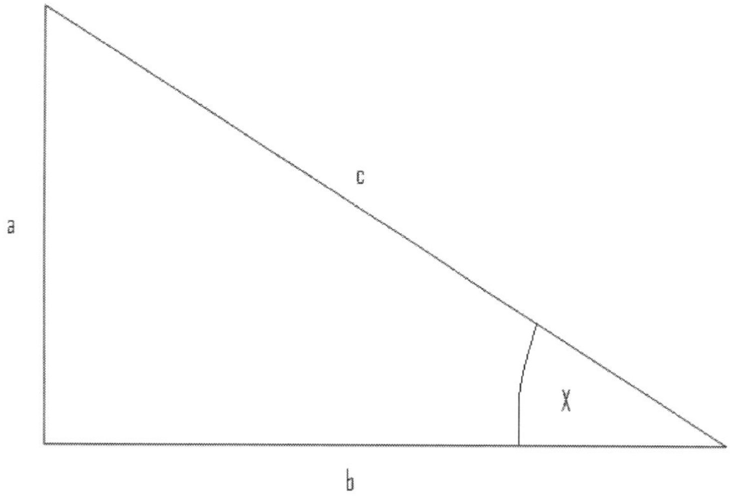

Exercises:

1. Find x and y in the following cases:
    a. 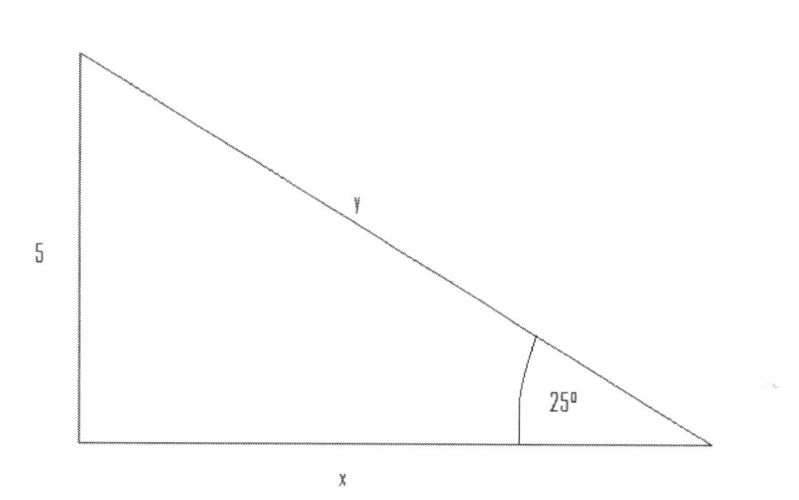

    b.

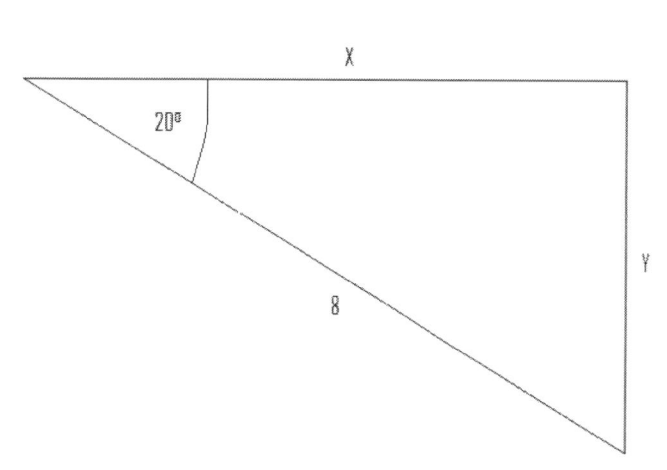

351

2. The Triangle in the diagram (not to scale) is <u>not</u> right angled, find x and y.

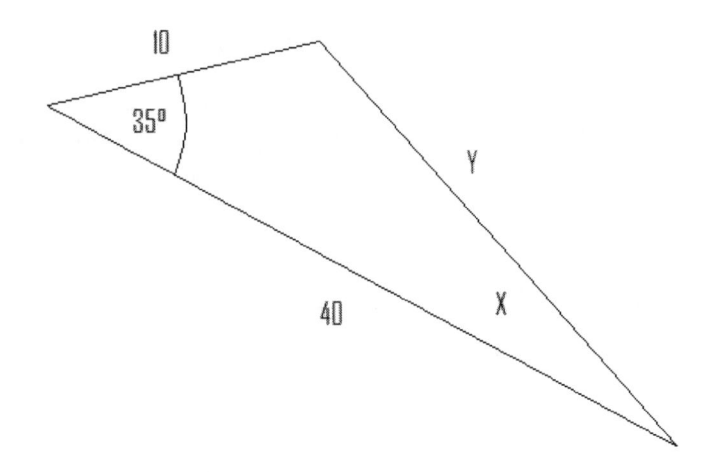

3. The shade formed by building is 100m long. The depression angle of the light as it approaches the ground is 40°.

    a. Sketch a diagram that describes the situation.
    b. Find the height of the building.

4. The height of building is 120m. The depression angle of the light as it approaches the ground is 30°.

    a. Sketch a diagram that describes the situation.
    b. Find the length of the shade on the ground.

5. In its search for food the lion is observing a certain prey located 2 m above the ground. The lion's head forms an angle of 12° as he looks at his prey.

    a. Sketch a diagram that describes the situation.
    b. Find the distance from the lion's mouth to its prey.

6. Measuring the height and distance of objects:

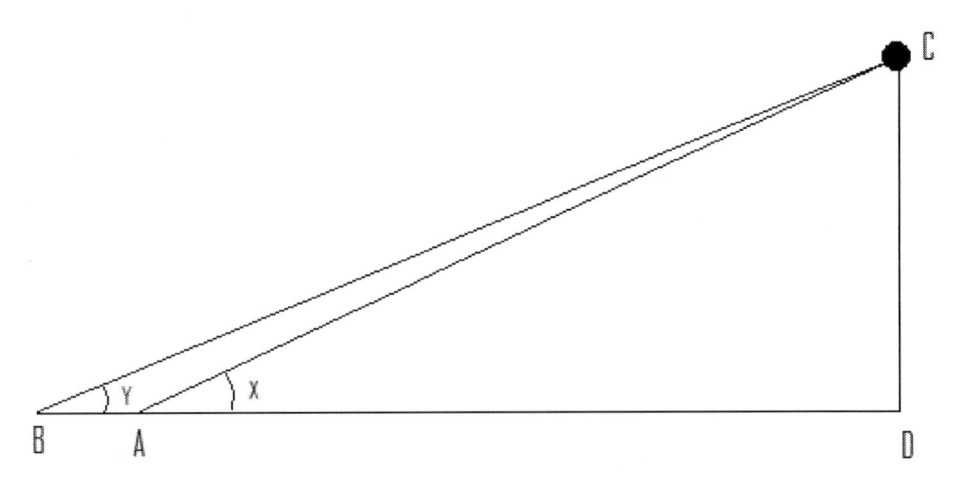

Assuming we start at point A and the object that we want to measure its distance (ground distance AD or Air distance AC) is located at point C. We need to use a device (in real life a **theodolite** is used) the measure the angle x (elevation angle), let's assume that we measured it and got 20°. Later we move a certain distance (backwards or forward) and measure the angle y. Let assume that we moved backwards 4 meters (that is AB = 4m) and the angle y is 18°. Find AD, AC, CD.

3.7. – INVERSE TRIGONOMETRIC FUNCTIONS

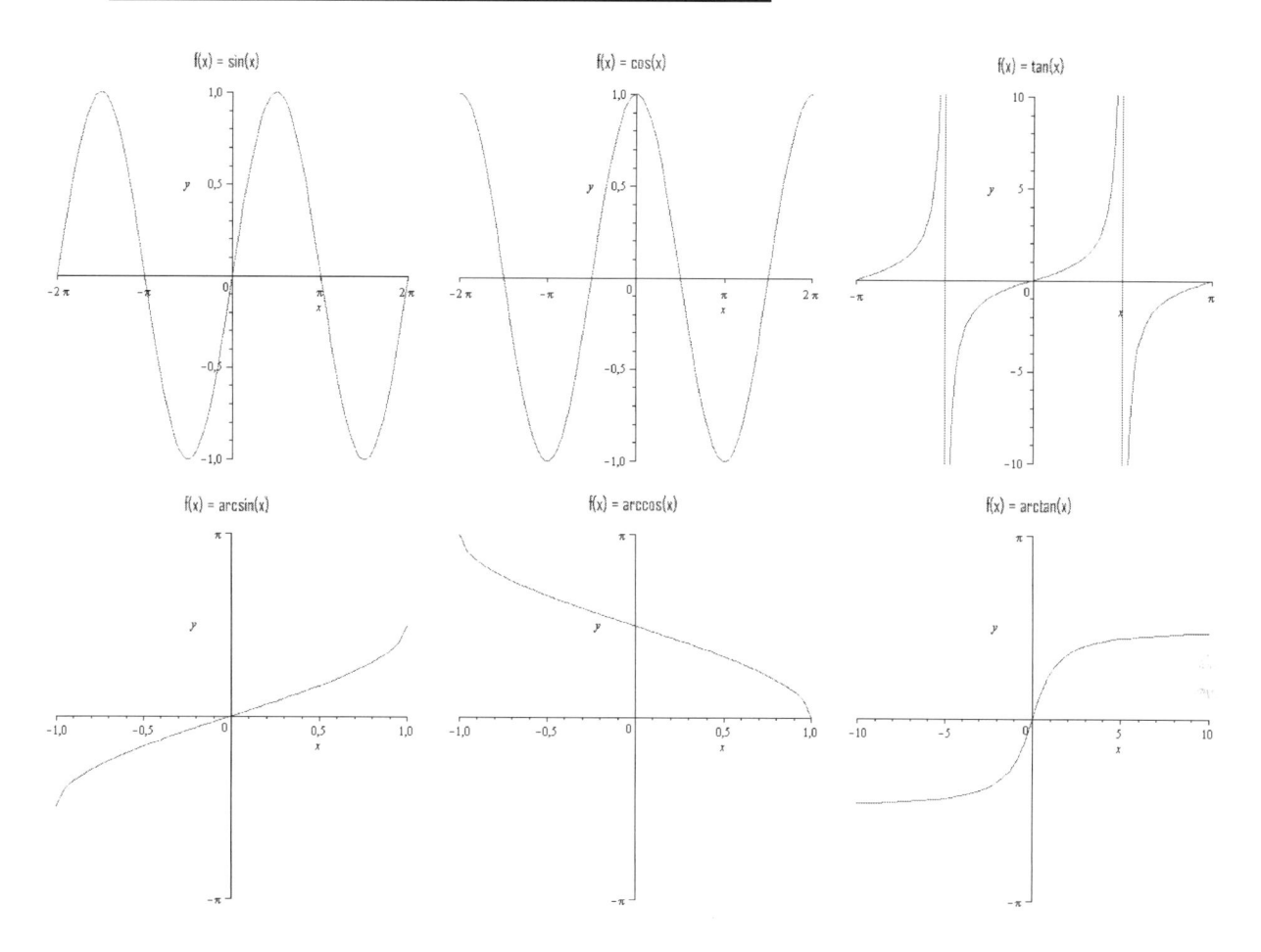

Inverse Trigonometric Function	Domain	Range	In words
$f(x) = \arcsin(x)$	$[-1, 1]$	$[-\frac{\pi}{2}, \frac{\pi}{2}]$	$f(x)$ is the angle (whose sine is x)
$f(x) = \arccos(x)$	$[-1, 1]$	$[0, \pi]$	$f(x)$ is the angle (whose cosine is x)
$f(x) = \arctan(x)$	$[-\infty, \infty]$	$[-\frac{\pi}{2}, \frac{\pi}{2}]$	$f(x)$ is the angle (whose tangent is x)

355

Give your answer(s) in radians and degrees, use GDC only if necessary:

1. Arcsin(0) =

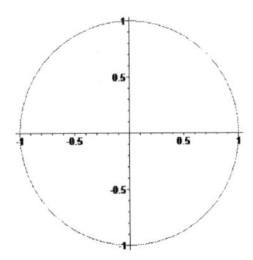

2. Arcos(0) =

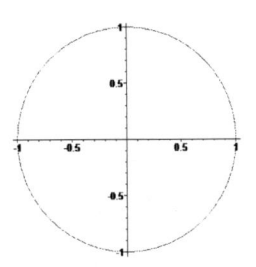

3. Arcsin(1) =

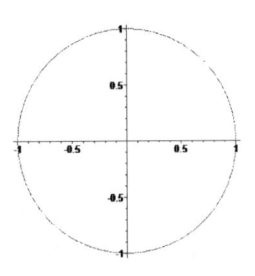

4. Arcos(2) =

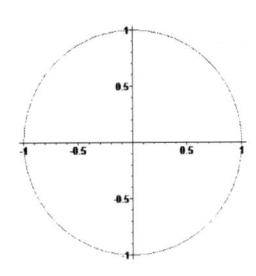

5. Arcsin(0.5) =

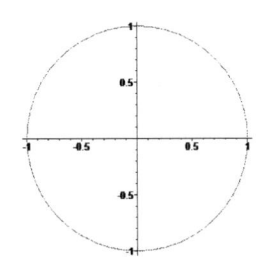

6. Arcos(–0.5) =

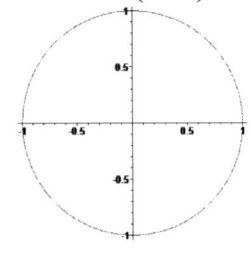

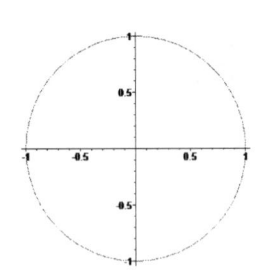

7. $\text{Arcsin}(\frac{\sqrt{3}}{2}) =$

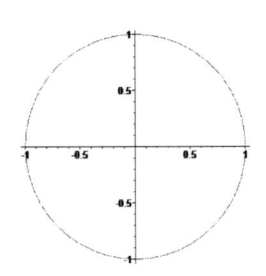

8. $\text{Arcos}(-\frac{\sqrt{3}}{2}) =$

9. Arcsin($\frac{\sqrt{2}}{2}$) =

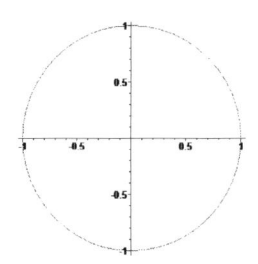

10. Arcos($-\frac{\sqrt{2}}{2}$) =

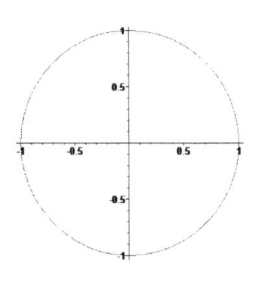

11. Arcsin($\frac{\sqrt{2}}{2}$) =

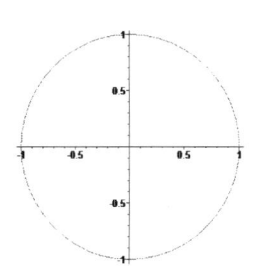

12. Arcsin(–1) =

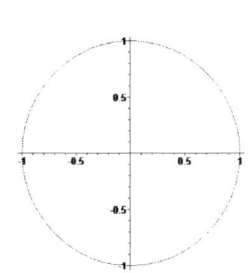

13. Arcos(–1) =

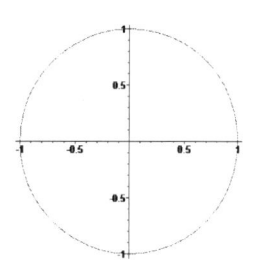

14. Arcsin(0.2) =

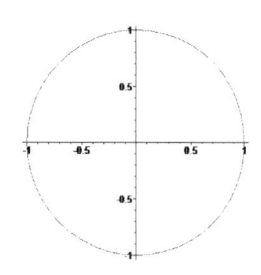

15. Arcos(–0.4) =

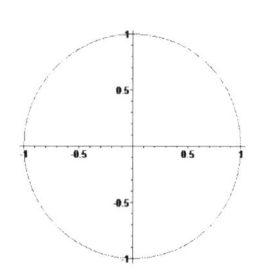

16. Arcsin(1/5) =

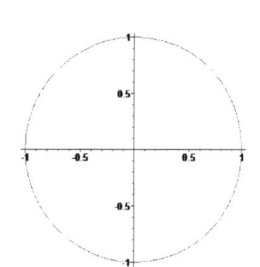

17. Arcos(–5) =

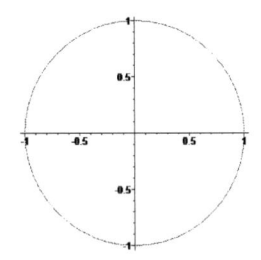

18. Arcsin(0.9) =

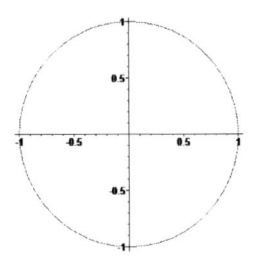

19. Arcsin(–2.4) =

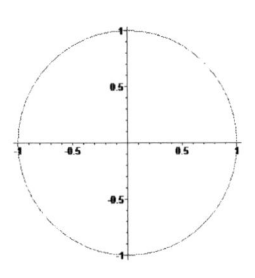

20. Arcos(0.05) =

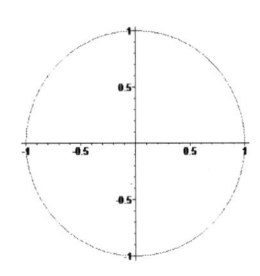

21. Arctan(–5) =

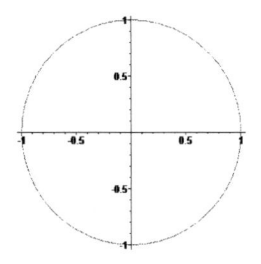

22. Arctan(1) =

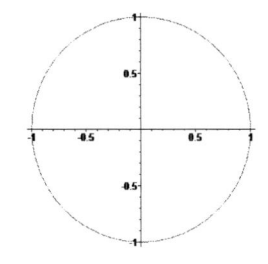

23. Arctan(–2.4) =

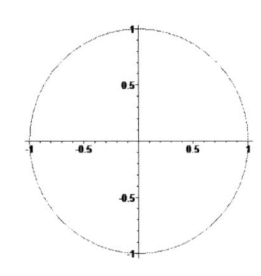

24. Arctan($\frac{1}{\sqrt{3}}$) =

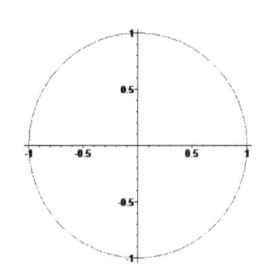

25. Arctan$(-\sqrt{3})$ =

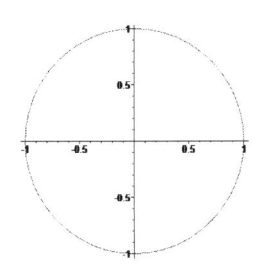

26. Arctan$(\sqrt{3})$ =

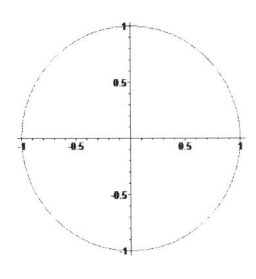

27. Arctan(-1) =

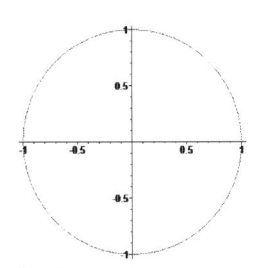

Evaluate:

28. $Arc\sin\left(\dfrac{-1}{2}\right)$

29. $Arc\cos\left(\dfrac{\sqrt{3}}{2}\right)$

30. $Arc\tan(0)$

31. $Arc\cos\left(\sin\left(\dfrac{\sqrt{3}}{2}\right)\right)$

32. $\cos\left(\arcsin\left(\dfrac{2}{5}\right)\right)$

33. $\sin\left(\arcsin\left(\dfrac{\pi}{5}\right)\right)$

34. $\csc\left(\arcsin\left(-\dfrac{2}{7}\right)\right)$

35. $\cos\left(\arctan\left(\dfrac{3}{4}\right)\right)$

36. $\csc\left(\arccos\left(\dfrac{2\sqrt{5}}{5}\right)\right)$

359

3.8. – TRIGONOMETRIC EQUATIONS

Solve the following equations (find all the solutions)

1. $\sin(x) = 1$

   Degrees: $x_1 = $ _____

   Radians: $x_1 = $ _____

2. $\cos(x) = \dfrac{1}{2}$

   Degrees: $x_1 = $ _____

   Radians: $x_1 = $ _____

   Degrees: $x_2 = $ _____

   Radians: $x_2 = $ _____

3. Conclusion, In general trigonometric equations have _____ solutions.

4. $\cos(x) = -2$

5. Solve: $\sin(3x) = \dfrac{1}{2}$, $0 \leq x \leq 2\pi$

6. $\cos(2x - \dfrac{\pi}{4}) = -1$, $0 \leq x \leq 2\pi$

7. $\sin(2x° - 100°) = -\frac{\sqrt{3}}{2}$, $0 \le x \le 360°$

8. $\cos(\frac{\pi}{3}x) = -\frac{1}{2}$, $2\pi \le x \le 4\pi$

9. $\sin(\frac{\pi}{4}x) = 2$, $2\pi \le x \le 4\pi$

10. $\sin(2x) = \frac{1}{3}$, $-2\pi \le x \le 2\pi$

11. $\sin(\frac{3\pi}{7}x) = -\frac{1}{2}$, $0 \le x \le 2\pi$

12. $\sin(\dfrac{\pi}{4}x - \dfrac{\pi}{2}) = -\dfrac{1}{2}$

13. $\cos(\dfrac{\pi}{5}x) = -\dfrac{1}{\sqrt{2}}$

14. $2\cos(\dfrac{1}{5}x) = 1$

15. $4\sin(3x° - 5°) = -\dfrac{2}{5}$

16. $\sin(4x° + 20°) = \dfrac{1}{\sqrt{2}}$

17. $-\text{Tan}(\pi x) = \dfrac{1}{\sqrt{3}}$, $0 \leq x \leq 2\pi$

18. $\text{Tan}(\dfrac{2\pi}{7} x) = \dfrac{1}{\sqrt{3}}$

19. $\text{Tan}(2x°) = 5$, $0 \leq x \leq 360°$

20. $\text{Tan}(2x°) = -1$

21. $\text{Tan}(3x) = \sqrt{3}$

22. $\text{Tan}(2x - \frac{\pi}{3}) = 1$

23. $\sin(x)\cos(x) + 2\cos(x) = 0$

24. $(\cos(x))^2 + \cos(x) = 0$

25. $\tan(x)\sin(2x) + \sin(x)\cos(x) = 0$

26. $(\cos(x))^2 + \cos(x) - 2 = 0$

27. $2(\sin(x))^2 + \sin(x) - 1 = 0$

28. $2(\sin(x))^2 - 7\sin(x) + 6 = 0$

29. $2(\tan(x))^2 - 6\tan(x) + 4 = 0$

3.9. – 3D GEOMETRY

1. Sketch each one of the solids and fill the blanks.

    a. Cuboid   Volume = _____   Surface Area = _____

    b. Right pyramid   Volume = _____   Surface Area = _____

    c. Right prism   Volume = _____   Surface Area = _____

    d. Right cone   Volume = _____   Surface Area = _____

    e. Cylinder   Volume = _____   Surface Area = _____

    f. Sphere   Volume = _____   Surface Area = _____

    g. Hemisphere   Volume = _____   Surface Area = _____

2. In the design process of a certain lamp the following diagram is obtained.

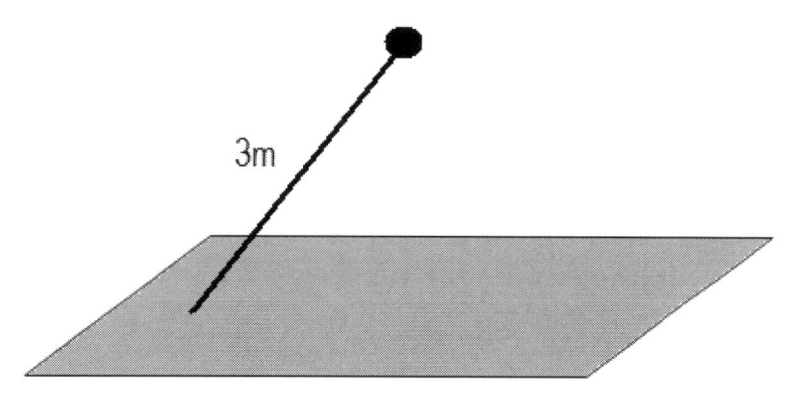

3m

Assuming the sun is directly above the lamp and length of the shadow on the ground is 2.5 meters.

a. Find the angle between the lamp and the ground.
b. Find the height of the lamp above the ground.

3. Given the following diagram (not to scale): ABCD is a rectangle AB = 20 cm, BC = 12 cm, EA = BF = 14 cm. EM = 5 cm.

   a. Find the angle between NB and the base ABCD.
   b. Find the length of the segment MC.
   c. Find the area of MNBC
   d. Find the volume of the cuboid.
   e. Find the surface area of the cuboid.

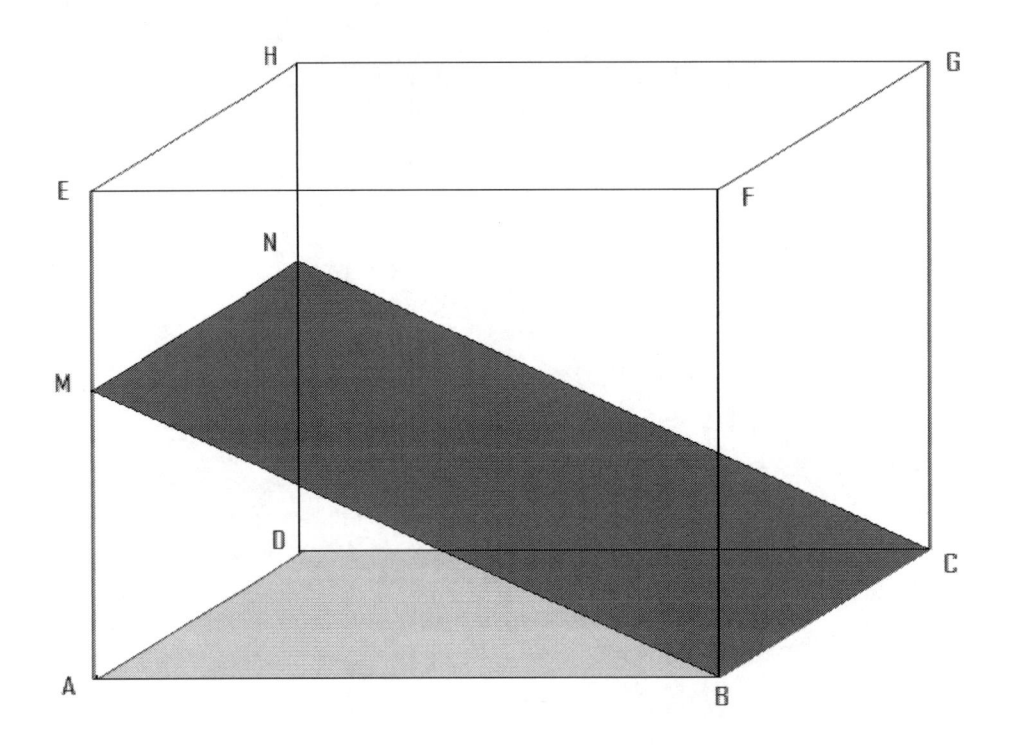

2. Given the following diagram (not to scale): ABCD is a square AB = 10 cm. CG = BF = 12 cm. M is the midpoint of DB.

   a. Find the length DB.
   b. Find the angle between DG and the base ABCD.
   c. Find the angle between GM and the base ABCD.
   d. Find the area of BDG.

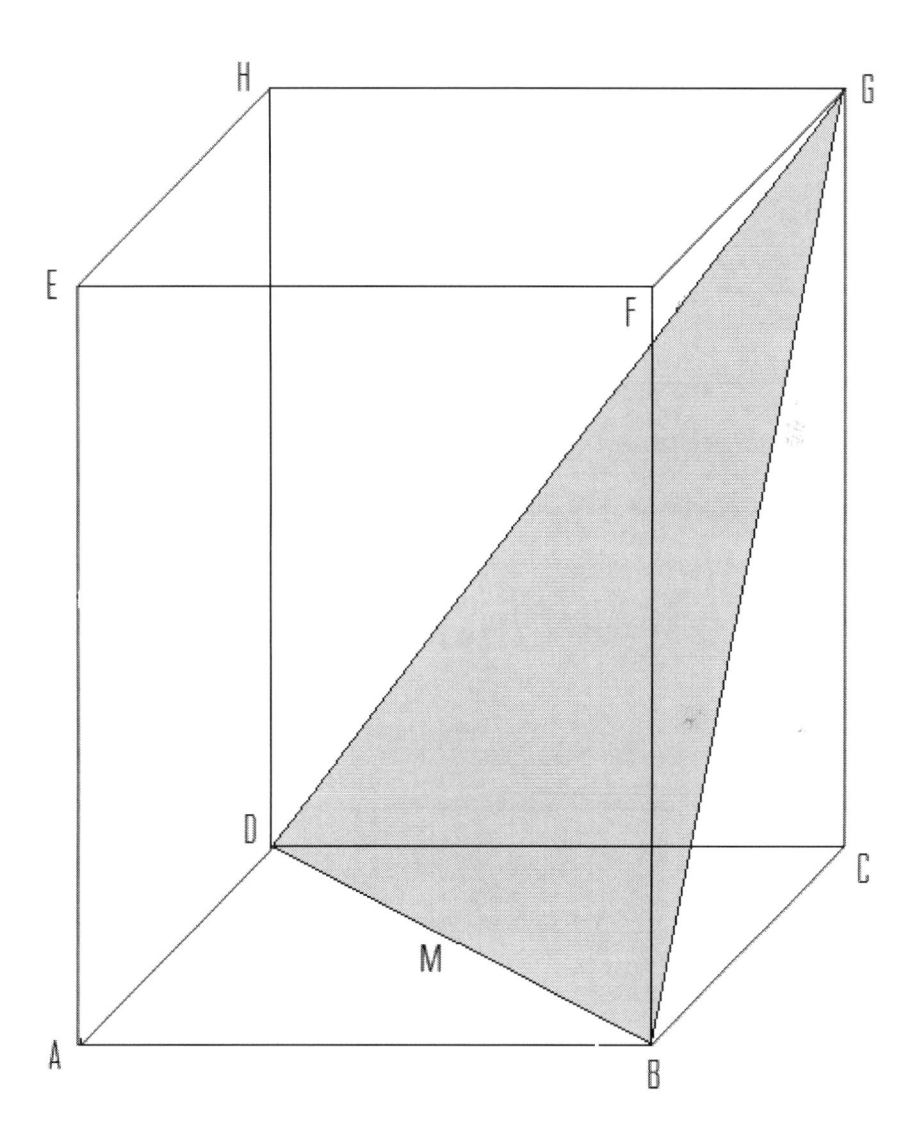

3. In the design process of a modern building a sphere of 5m radius is put on top a cylinder with a radius twice as big. The height of the building is 30m.

   a. Find the volume of the sphere.
   b. Find the height of the cylinder.
   c. Find the volume of the building.
   d. Find the surface area of the building that that is exposed to fresh air.

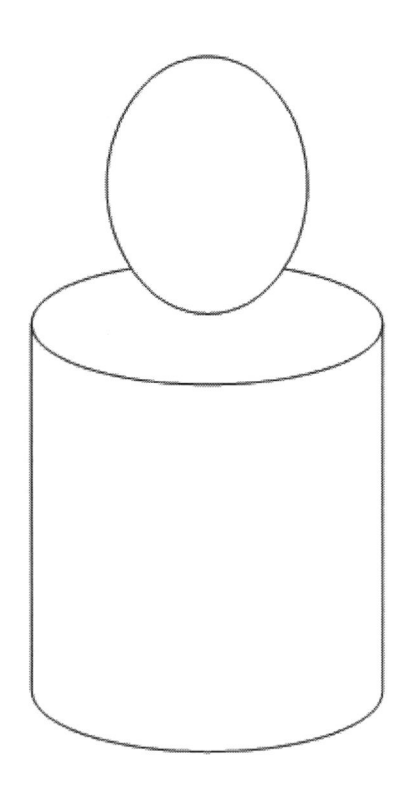

4. Given the following right prism. AB = 12cm, AE = 15cm.

   Find:

   a. The length of AD.
   b. The length of ED.
   c. The length of AF.
   d. The angle FAB.
   e. The surface area of the prism.

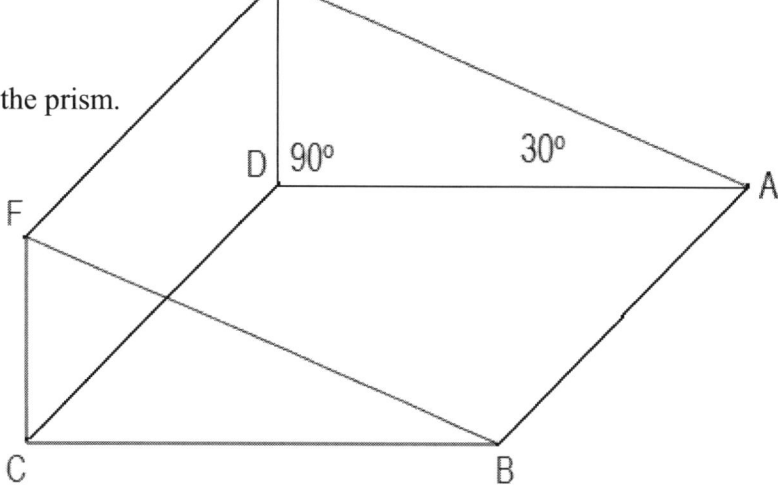

5. An old tower is made of a cone put on top of a cylinder. The radius of both is 5m. The height of the cylinder is 10m. The height of the cone is 60% of the cylinder's height.

   a. Find the height of the tower.
   b. Find the volume of the tower.

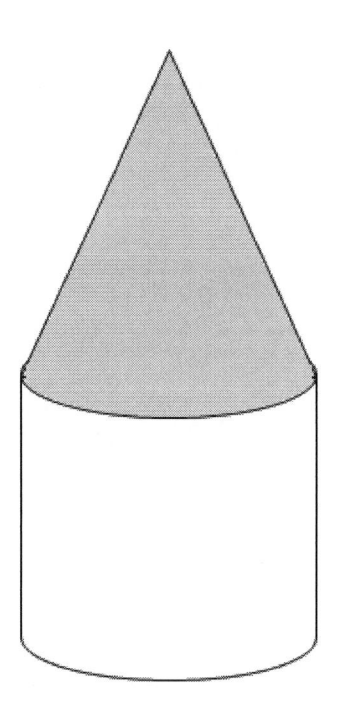

6. Given the following diagram (not to scale): ABCD is a rectangle AB = 9 cm. BC = 7 cm. EF = 10 cm is the height of the right pyramid.

   Find:

   a. The length AE.
   b. The length AF.
   c. The angle between AF and the base ABCD.
   d. The length MF.
   e. The angle between MF and the base ABCD.
   f. The area of FBC.
   g. Find the volume of the pyramid.
   h. Find the surface area of the pyramid.

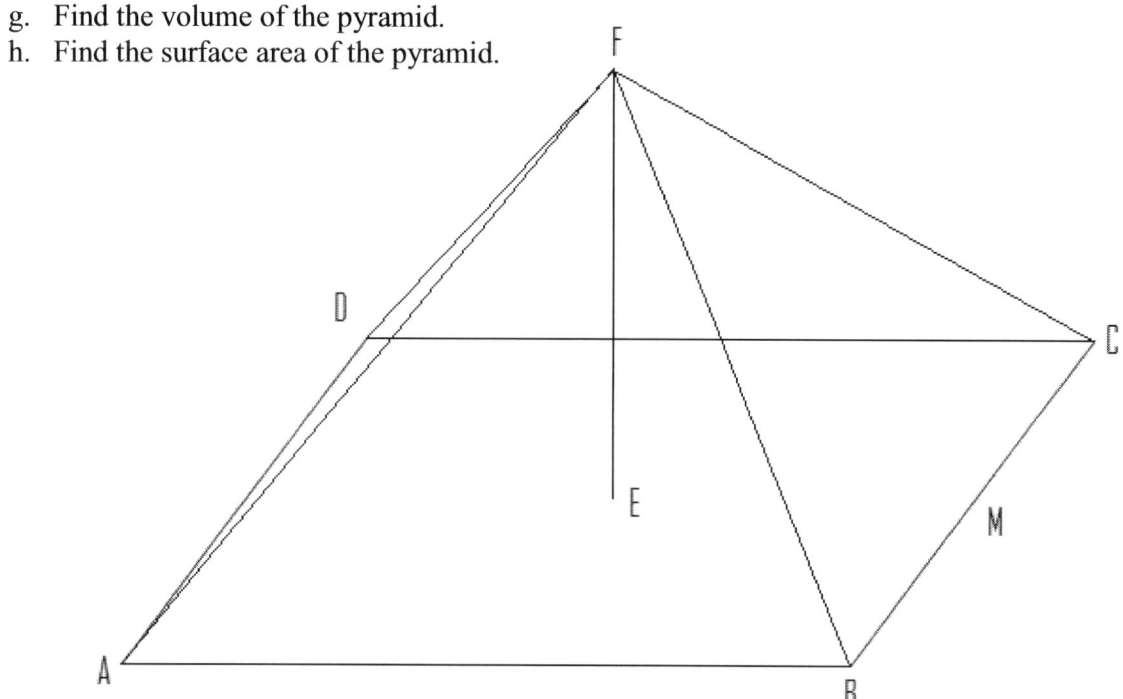

ANSWER KEY
CHAPTER 1 – ALGEBRA

1.1. – TYPES OF NUMBERS

Natural Numbers (N): $N = \{1, 2, 3, 4...\}$

Integers (Z): $Z = \{...-4, -3, -2, -1, 0, 1, 2, 3, 4...\}$

Rational Numbers (Q): $Q = \{\frac{a}{b}, a, b \in Z\}$

Numbers that **can** be written as <u>fractions</u> being both the numerator and the denominator <u>integers</u>.

Examples: $\frac{1}{1}, \frac{2}{3}, \frac{-7}{3}, \frac{4}{-1}, \frac{0}{2}, 0.55, 0.121212...$

Irrational Numbers (Q'): $Q' \neq \{\frac{a}{b}, a, b \in Z\}$ Numbers that <u>cannot</u> be written as fractions, being both the <u>numerator</u> and the <u>denominator</u> integers.

Examples: $\pi, \sqrt{2}, e ...$

Real Numbers (R): $R = Q + Q'$ (Rationals and Irrationals)

Exercises:

1. Natural numbers are contained in the <u>Integer</u> numbers.
2. Integer numbers are contained in the <u>Rational</u> numbers
3. Rational numbers are contained in the <u>Real</u> numbers.
4. Irrational numbers are located <u>in the outermost ring</u>.
5. Shade the area in which the irrational numbers are located:

6. True or False:
   a. All Natural numbers are Integers: <u>True</u>
   b. All Real numbers are Natural: <u>False</u>
   c. All Rational numbers are Real: <u>True</u>
   d. All Real numbers are Rational: <u>False</u>
   e. All Integer numbers are Rational: <u>True</u>
   f. All Real numbers are Irrational: <u>False</u>
   g. Some Irrational numbers are Real and some are not: <u>False</u>
   h. Some Irrational numbers are Integers: <u>False</u>
   i. Some integers are negative: <u>True</u>
   j. Some Irrationals are negative: <u>True</u>
   k. Some Natural numbers are negative: <u>False</u>

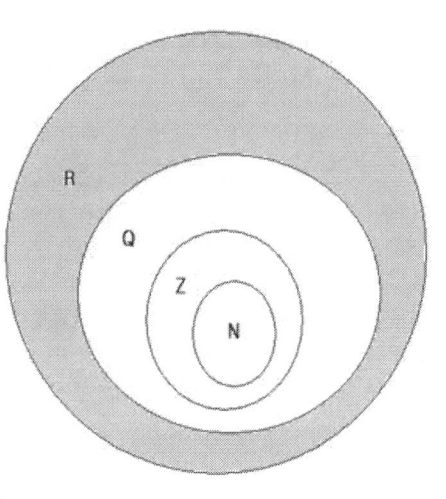

7. Fill the chart with yes or no (follow the example):

Number	Natural	Integer	Rational	Real
-2	no	yes	yes	yes
π	no	no	no	yes
$-3.121212....$	no	no	yes	yes
-15.16	no	no	yes	yes
$\sqrt{3}$	no	no	no	yes
$-2\frac{2}{5}$	no	no	yes	yes
$\sqrt[3]{8}$	yes	yes	yes	yes

8. Fill the numbers column with appropriate numbers and yes or no. Follow the example.

Number	Natural	Integer	Rational	Real
-1	no	yes	yes	yes
0.1	no	no	yes	yes
Does not exist	yes	yes	yes	no
$\sqrt{2}$	no	no	no	yes
$\frac{1}{2}$	no	no	yes	yes
0	no	yes	yes	yes
$0.333...$	no	no	yes	yes
Does not exist		yes	no	

375

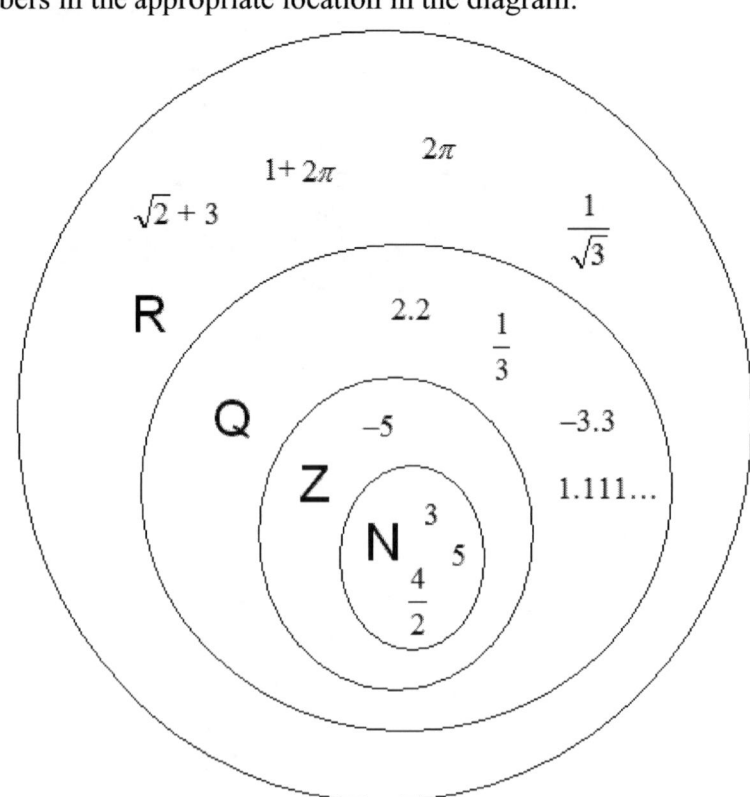

4. Convert the following numbers into the form: $\frac{n}{m}$

1. $0.333... = \frac{1}{3}$
2. $1.111... = \frac{10}{9}$
3. $5.3 = \frac{53}{10}$
4. $5.2828... = \frac{523}{99}$
5. $-2.3535... = \frac{233}{99}$
6. $42.67 = \frac{4267}{100}$
7. $12.355355... = \frac{12343}{999}$
8. $-31.44 = \frac{-3144}{100}$
9. $0.125125... = \frac{125}{99}$
10. $3.22332233... = \frac{32230}{2930}$
11. $1115.36 = \frac{111536}{100}$
12. $122.53 = \frac{12253}{100}$
13. $1.123123... = \frac{1122}{999}$
14. $1.22565656... = \frac{12134}{9900}$
15. $1.5696969... = \frac{1554}{990}$
16. $5.540404040... = \frac{5485}{990}$

5. Given the following diagram:
Write the following numbers in the appropriate location in the diagram:

a. 2.2
b. −5
c. 3
d. $\frac{1}{3}$
e. 5
f. −3.3
g. 1.111...
h. $\frac{1}{\sqrt{3}}$
i. 2π
j. $1+2\pi$
k. $\sqrt{2}+3$
l. $\frac{4}{2}$

6. Circle the right option. The number –2 is:

    a. Integer and Natural.
    b. Positive
    c. Integer and Rational
    d. Natural and Real
    e. Natural and Rational
    f. None of the above

7. Circle the right option. The number 3.41414141..... is:

    a. Integer and Natural.
    b. Natural
    c. Integer and Real
    d. Rational and Integer
    e. Rational
    f. None of the above

8. Circle the right option. The number 3.41 is:

    a. Integer and Natural.
    b. Integer
    c. Rational and Real
    d. Integer and Real
    e. Rational and negative
    f. None of the above

9. Circle the right option. The number $\sqrt{31}$ is:

    a. Integer and Natural.
    b. Integer
    c. Decimal
    d. Integer and Real
    e. Rational
    f. Irrational

10. Circle the right option. The number 5 is:

    a. Natural.
    b. Integer
    c. Real
    d. Integer and Natural
    e. Rational and Natural
    f. All of the above

1.2. – INTERVAL NOTATION

$x \ni (a, b]$ or $\{x| a < x \leq b\}$ means x is between a and b, not including a and including b.

Exercises:

1. Represent the following Intervals on the real line:

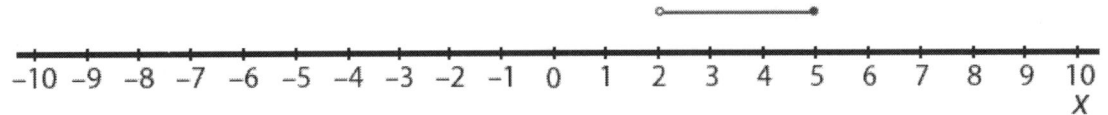

   a. $x \ni (2, 5]$

   b. $x \ni (3, 6)$

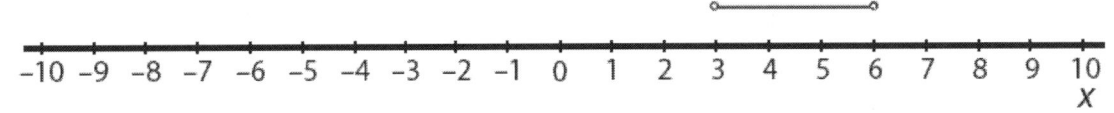

   c. $x \ni [-5, 9]$

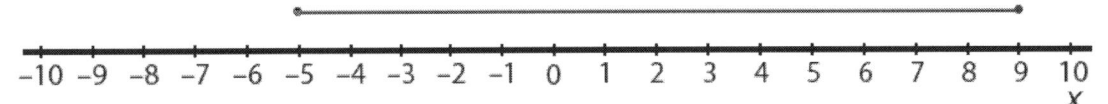

   d. $x \ni [-8, -1)$

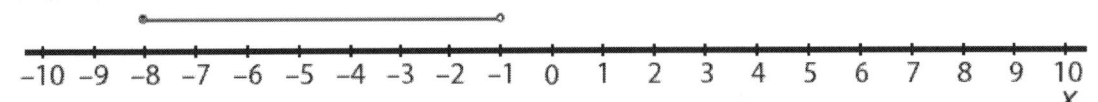

   e. $x \ni [-\infty, -1)$

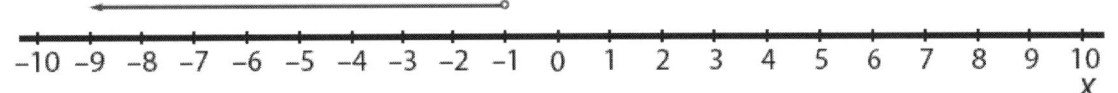

   f. $x \ni [-\infty, 6]$

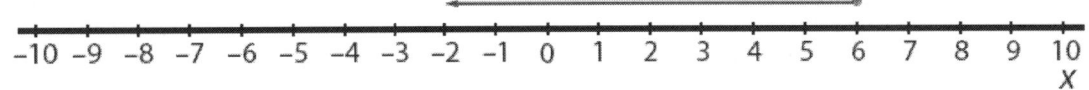

   g. $x \ni (6, \infty]$

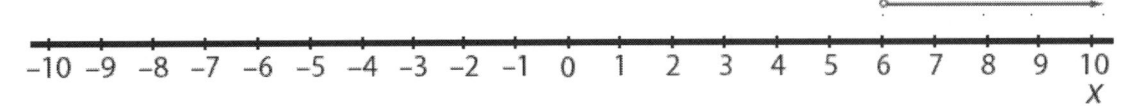

   h. $\{x| 7 < x < 9\}$

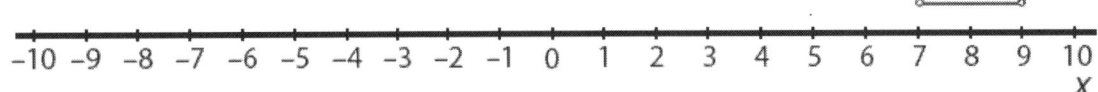

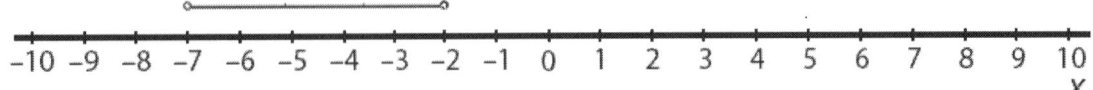

   i. $\{x| -7 < x < -2\}$

   j. $\{x| 1 < x < 2\}$

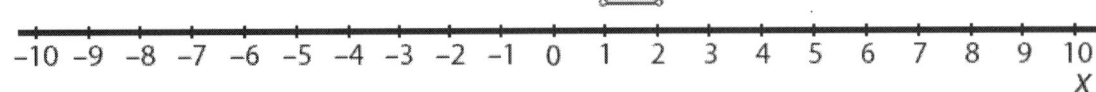

378

k. $\{x|\infty < x < 2\}$ Not Possible

l. $\{x| 1 < x < \infty \}$

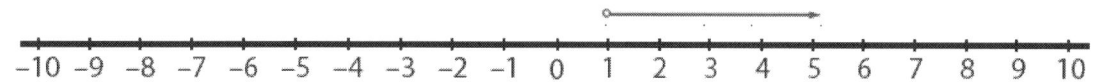

```
-10 -9 -8 -7 -6 -5 -4 -3 -2 -1  0  1  2  3  4  5  6  7  8  9  10
```

2. Write each one of the Intervals using all types of notations:

   a. $x \ni (4, 5) = 4 \leq x \leq 5$

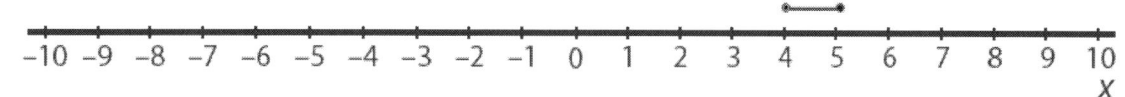

   b. $x \ni (-\infty, 5) = x < 5$

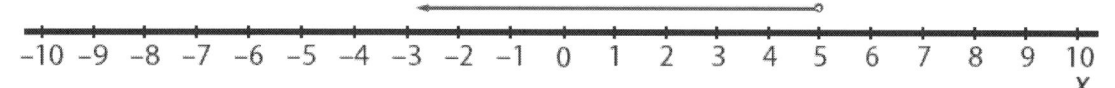

   c. $x \ni (4, 5) = 4 < x < 5$

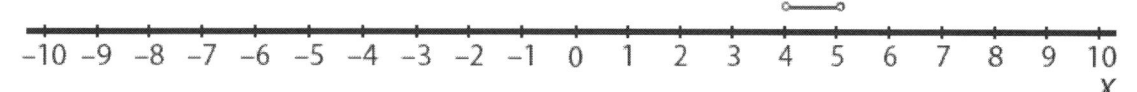

   d. $x \ni (3, \infty] = 3 < x$

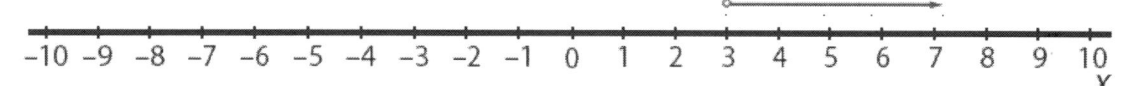

   e. $x \ni]-5, 9] = -5 < x \leq 9$

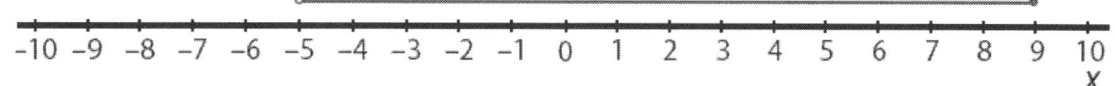

   f. $x \ni [-8, -1[= -8 \leq x < -1$

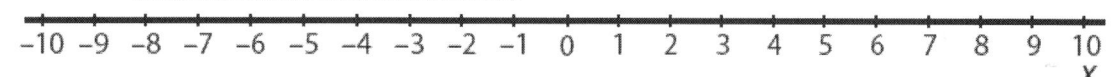

   g. $\{x| 7 < x < 9\} = x \ni (7, 9)$

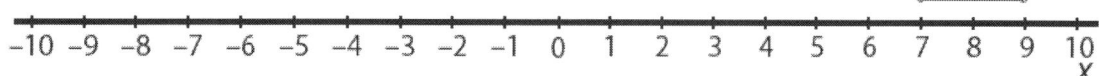

   h. $\{x| -7 < x < -2\} = x \ni (-7, -2)$

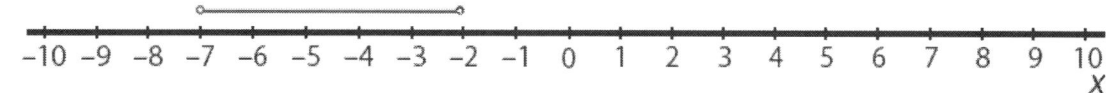

3.
   a. Solve the inequality $3x - 7 \leq 2$ $x \leq 3$

   b. Solve the inequality $-x < -2$. $x > 2$

   c. Represent both solutions on the real line:

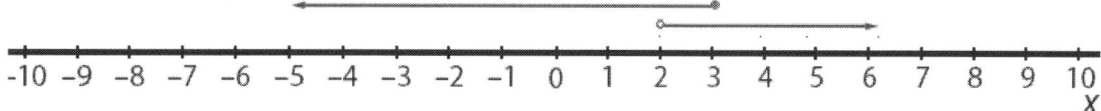

   d. State their intersection: $\{x| 2 < x \leq 3\} = x \ni (2, 3]$

379

4.

    a. Solve the inequality $5x - 2 \leq 2$ $x \leq \dfrac{4}{5}$

    b. Solve the inequality $-2x + 1 > -2$ $x < \dfrac{3}{2}$

    c. Represent both solutions on the real line:

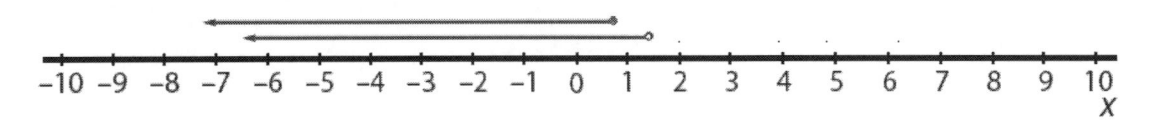

```
  ←――――――――――――――●
         ←―――――――――――○
+――+――+――+――+――+――+――+――+――+――+――+――+――+――+――+――+――+――+――+――+――→
-10 -9 -8 -7 -6 -5 -4 -3 -2 -1  0  1  2  3  4  5  6  7  8  9  10
                                                                X
```

    d. State their intersection: $\{x \mid -\infty < x \leq \dfrac{4}{5}\} = x \ni (-\infty, \dfrac{4}{5}]$

5.

    d. Solve the inequality $5x - 2 \leq -12$ $x \leq -2$

    a. Solve the inequality $-2x - 3 \leq -2$. $x \geq -\dfrac{1}{2}$

    b. Represent both solutions on the real line:

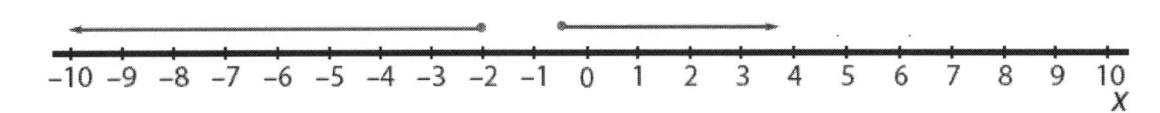

```
  ←―――――――――――――――――――●        ○―――――――――――――→
+――+――+――+――+――+――+――+――+――+――+――+――+――+――+――+――+――+――+――+――+――→
-10 -9 -8 -7 -6 -5 -4 -3 -2 -1  0  1  2  3  4  5  6  7  8  9  10
                                                                X
```

    c. State their intersection: No intersection

380

1.3. – RATIONALIZATION

1. Rationalize the denominator:

   a. $\left(\dfrac{2}{\sqrt{5}}\right)\cdot\left(\dfrac{\sqrt{5}}{\sqrt{5}}\right)=\dfrac{2\sqrt{5}}{5}$

   b. $\left(\dfrac{3}{\sqrt{5}+1}\right)\cdot\left(\dfrac{\sqrt{5}-1}{\sqrt{5}-1}\right)=\dfrac{3(\sqrt{5}-1)}{4}$

   c. $\left(\dfrac{-7}{\sqrt{5}-2}\right)\cdot\left(\dfrac{\sqrt{5}+2}{\sqrt{5}+2}\right)=\dfrac{7(\sqrt{5}+2)}{1}=7(\sqrt{5}+2)$

   d. $\dfrac{\sqrt{2}+3}{-5}$, Denominator already rational

   e. $\left(\dfrac{\sqrt{2}+3}{\sqrt{6}-5}\right)\cdot\left(\dfrac{\sqrt{6}+5}{\sqrt{6}+5}\right)=\dfrac{(\sqrt{2}+3)(\sqrt{6}+5)}{-19}$

   f. $\left(\dfrac{\sqrt{2}}{\sqrt{6}+\sqrt{3}}\right)\cdot\left(\dfrac{\sqrt{6}-\sqrt{3}}{\sqrt{6}-\sqrt{3}}\right)=\dfrac{\sqrt{2}(\sqrt{6}-\sqrt{3})}{3}$

   g. $\left(\dfrac{\sqrt{2}-1}{2\sqrt{5}-\sqrt{3}}\right)\cdot\left(\dfrac{2\sqrt{5}+\sqrt{3}}{2\sqrt{5}+\sqrt{3}}\right)=\dfrac{(\sqrt{2}-1)(2\sqrt{5}+\sqrt{3})}{17}$

   h. $\left(\dfrac{-1}{2\sqrt{a}+b}\right)\cdot\left(\dfrac{2\sqrt{a}-b}{2\sqrt{a}-b}\right)=\left(\dfrac{-2\sqrt{a}+b}{4a-b^2}\right)$

2. Rationalize the numerator:

   a. $\dfrac{\sqrt{4}}{\sqrt{5}}=\dfrac{2}{\sqrt{5}}$

   b. $\left(\dfrac{3-\sqrt{2}}{\sqrt{5}+1}\right)\cdot\left(\dfrac{3+\sqrt{2}}{3+\sqrt{2}}\right)=\dfrac{7}{(\sqrt{5}+1)(3+\sqrt{2})}$

   c. $\left(\dfrac{-7}{\sqrt{5}-2}\right)$, Numerator already rational

   d. $\left(\dfrac{\sqrt{2}+3}{\sqrt{6}-5}\right)\left(\dfrac{\sqrt{2}-3}{\sqrt{2}-3}\right)=\dfrac{-7}{(\sqrt{6}-5)(\sqrt{2}-3)}$

   e. $\left(\dfrac{\sqrt{2}}{\sqrt{x}+\sqrt{3}}\right)\cdot\left(\dfrac{\sqrt{2}}{\sqrt{2}}\right)=\dfrac{2}{\sqrt{2}(\sqrt{x}+\sqrt{3})}$

   f. $\left(\dfrac{\sqrt{b}-a}{2\sqrt{a}-\sqrt{3}}\right)\cdot\left(\dfrac{\sqrt{b}+a}{\sqrt{b}+a}\right)=\dfrac{b-a^2}{(2\sqrt{a}-\sqrt{3})(\sqrt{b}+a)}$

   g. $\left(\dfrac{-3\sqrt{7}+8}{2\sqrt{5}+7}\right)\cdot\left(\dfrac{-3\sqrt{7}-8}{-3\sqrt{7}-8}\right)=\dfrac{-1}{(2\sqrt{5}+7)(-3\sqrt{7}-8)}$

1.4. – EXPONENTS & LOGARITHMS

Product:

$a^0 = 1$
$a^1 = a$
$a^2 = a \times a$
$a^3 = a \times a \times a$
...
$a^3 a^2 = a \cdot a \cdot a \cdot a \cdot a = a^5$

$$a^m a^n = a^{m+n}$$

Division:

$\dfrac{a^5}{a^3} = \dfrac{a \cdot a \cdot a \cdot a \cdot a}{a \cdot a \cdot a} = \dfrac{a \cdot a}{1} = a^2$

$\dfrac{a^2}{a^5} = \dfrac{a \cdot a}{a \cdot a \cdot a \cdot a \cdot a} = \dfrac{1}{a \cdot a \cdot a} = \dfrac{1}{a^3} = a^{-3}$

$$\dfrac{a^m}{a^n} = a^{m-n}$$

Power:

$(a^2)^3 = (a^2)(a^2)(a^2) = a^6$

$\left(\dfrac{a^2}{b}\right)^3 = \left(\dfrac{a^2}{b}\right)\left(\dfrac{a^2}{b}\right)\left(\dfrac{a^2}{b}\right) = \left(\dfrac{a^6}{b^3}\right)$

$$(a^m)^n = a^{mn}$$

$$\left(\dfrac{a^m}{b^k}\right)^n = \left(\dfrac{a^{mn}}{b^{kn}}\right)$$

Radicals:

$(a^3)^{\frac{1}{2}} = a^{\frac{3}{2}} = \sqrt[2]{a^3} = \sqrt{a^3}$

$(a^4)^{\frac{1}{7}} = a^{\frac{4}{7}} = \sqrt[7]{a^4}$

$$(a^m)^{\frac{1}{n}} = a^{\frac{m}{n}} = \sqrt[n]{a^m}$$

Exercises

Write in all possible forms and evaluate without using a calculator (follow example):

1. $4^{-1} = \dfrac{1}{4} = 0.25$

2. $10^0 = \underline{1}$

3. $10^1 = \underline{10}$

4. $10^3 = \underline{1000}$

5. $10^{-1} = \underline{\dfrac{1}{10} = 0.1}$

6. $10^{-2} = \underline{\dfrac{1}{100} = 0.01}$

7. $10^{-3} = \underline{\dfrac{1}{1000} = 0.001}$

8. $10^{-4}\ \underline{\dfrac{1}{10000} = 0.0001}$

9. $2^0 = 1$

10. $2^1 = 2$

11. $2^{-1} = \underline{\dfrac{1}{2} = 0.5}$

12. $2^{-2} = \underline{\dfrac{1}{2^2} = \dfrac{1}{4} = 0.25}$

13. $2^{-3} = \underline{\dfrac{1}{2^3} = \dfrac{1}{8} = 0.125}$

14. $2^{-4} = \underline{\dfrac{1}{2^4} = \dfrac{1}{16} = 0.0625}$

15. $(-1)^0 = \underline{1}$

16. $-1^0 = -1$

17. $(-1)^1 = -1$

18. $-1^1 = -1$

19. $(-1)^{-1} = \underline{\dfrac{1}{-1} = -1}$

20. $-1^2 = -1$

21. $(-1)^2 = 1$

22. $-1^2 = -1$

23. $(-1)^{-2} = \underline{\dfrac{1}{(-1)^2} = \dfrac{1}{1} = 1}$

24. $-1^{-2} = \underline{-\dfrac{1}{1^2} = -\dfrac{1}{1} = -1}$

25. $(-3)^0 = 1$

26. $(-3)^1 = -3$

27. $-3^1 = -3$

28. $(-3)^2 = 9$

29. $-3^2 = -9$

30. $(-3)^{-1} = \underline{\dfrac{1}{(-3)^1} = \dfrac{1}{-3} = -\dfrac{1}{3}}$

31. $-3^{-1} = \underline{-\dfrac{1}{3^1} = -\dfrac{1}{3}}$

32. $(-3)^{-2} = \underline{\dfrac{1}{(-3)^2} = \dfrac{1}{9}}$

33. $-3^{-2} = \underline{-\dfrac{1}{3^2} = -\dfrac{1}{9}}$

34. $9^{\frac{1}{2}} = \underline{\sqrt{9} = \pm 3}$

35. $16^{\frac{3}{4}} = \underline{(2^4)^{\frac{3}{4}} = 2^3 = 8}$

36. $(3^{-1})^2 = \underline{3^{-2} = \dfrac{1}{3^2} = \dfrac{1}{9}}$

37. $(-8^{-3})^{\frac{2}{3}}$

$\underline{(-1)^{\frac{2}{3}}(2^{-9})^{\frac{2}{3}} = \sqrt[3]{1}\left(\dfrac{1}{2^6}\right) = \dfrac{1}{64}}$

38. $\left(\dfrac{1}{2}\right)^0 = 1$

39. $\left(\dfrac{1}{2}\right)^1 = \dfrac{1}{2}$

40. $\left(\dfrac{1}{2}\right)^{-1} = \dfrac{1}{\left(\dfrac{1}{2}\right)} = 2$

41. $\left(\dfrac{1}{2}\right)^2 = \dfrac{1}{4}$

42. $\left(\dfrac{1}{2}\right)^{-2} = \dfrac{1}{\left(\dfrac{1}{2}\right)^2} = 4$

43. $\left(\dfrac{3}{5}\right)^0 = 1$

44. $\left(\dfrac{3}{4}\right)^1 = \dfrac{3}{4}$

45. $\left(\dfrac{2}{5}\right)^{-1} = \dfrac{1}{\left(\dfrac{2}{5}\right)} = \dfrac{5}{2}$

46. $\left(\dfrac{5}{11}\right)^2 = \dfrac{25}{121}$

47. $\left(\dfrac{-11}{2}\right)^{-2} = \dfrac{4}{121}$

48. $\left(\dfrac{3}{-2}\right)^1 = -\dfrac{3}{2}$

49. $\left(\dfrac{-12}{\sqrt{2}}\right)^{-1} = -\dfrac{\sqrt{2}}{12}$

50. $\left(\dfrac{5\sqrt{2}}{11}\right)^2 = \dfrac{50}{121}$

51. $\left(\dfrac{-2\sqrt{5}}{2}\right)^{-2} = \dfrac{1}{5}$

52. $\left(\dfrac{3+5\sqrt{2}}{-2}\right)^2 = \dfrac{59+30\sqrt{2}}{4}$

53. $\left(\dfrac{-12}{2-\sqrt{2}}\right)^{-2} = \dfrac{6-4\sqrt{2}}{144}$

54. $\left(\dfrac{5+\sqrt{2}}{11}\right)^2 = \dfrac{27+10\sqrt{2}}{121}$

55. $\left(\dfrac{-2-\sqrt{5}}{2+\sqrt{2}}\right)^{-2} = \dfrac{9+4\sqrt{5}}{6+4\sqrt{2}}$

56. $\left(\dfrac{-27}{8}\right)^{\frac{2}{3}} = \dfrac{9}{4}$

57. $\left(\dfrac{16}{9}\right)^{\frac{3}{4}} = \left(\dfrac{2^4}{3^2}\right)^{\frac{3}{4}} = \dfrac{2^3}{3^{\frac{3}{2}}} = \dfrac{8}{\sqrt{27}}$

58. $5^{27} 5^{-29} = 5^{-2} = \dfrac{1}{25}$

59. $4^{27} 2^{-49} = 2^5 = 32$

60. $9^{12} 3^{-20} = 3^4 = 81$

61. $(-125)^{\frac{2}{3}} = (-1)^{\frac{2}{3}} (5^3)^{\frac{2}{3}} = \sqrt[3]{1} \cdot 5^2 = 25$

62. $\dfrac{5^{10}}{5^2} = 5^8$

63. $\dfrac{3^{10}}{9^2} 3^{-2} = 3^{10-2-4} = 3^4 = 81$

64. $\left(\dfrac{2}{5}\right)^3 \times \left(\dfrac{5}{3}\right)^3 = \dfrac{2^3 5^3}{5^3 3^3} = \dfrac{8}{27}$

65. $\left(\dfrac{4}{7}\right)^2 \div \left(\dfrac{9}{7}\right)^2 = \dfrac{2^4 7^2}{7^2 3^4} = \dfrac{16}{81}$

66. $\left(\dfrac{2}{5}\right)^3 \cdot \left(\dfrac{3}{5}\right)^{-4} = \dfrac{2^3 3^{-4}}{5^3 5^{-4}} = \dfrac{40}{81}$

67. $\left(\dfrac{3}{4}\right)^5 \div \left(\dfrac{9}{64}\right)^2 = \dfrac{3^5 \cdot 2^{12}}{2^{10} 3^4} = 3 \cdot 2^2 = 12$

68. $\left(\dfrac{7}{5}\right)^7 \div \left(\dfrac{49}{125}\right)^3 = \dfrac{7^7 \cdot 5^9}{5^7 7^6} = 175$

384

69. $\left(\dfrac{2^{-3}}{3^{-2}}\right)^3 \cdot \left(\dfrac{4}{27}\right)^2 = \dfrac{2^{-9} \cdot 2^4}{3^{-6} 3^6} =$

$2^{-5} = \dfrac{1}{32}$

70. $\left(\dfrac{4^2}{5^{-1}}\right)^3 \cdot \left(\dfrac{25^{-1}}{64}\right)^2 = \dfrac{2^{12} 5^{-4}}{5^{-3} 2^{12}} =$

$5^{-1} = \dfrac{1}{5}$

71. $\left(\dfrac{3^{-5}}{4^2}\right)^2 \div \left(\dfrac{9^{-2}}{2^3}\right)^3 = \dfrac{3^{-10} 2^9}{2^8 3^{-12}}$

$= 2 \cdot 3^2 = 18$

72. $\left(\dfrac{5^4}{7^{-3}}\right)^2 \div \left(\dfrac{25^{-1}}{49}\right)^{-3} = \dfrac{5^8 5^{-6}}{7^{-6} 7^6}$

$= 5^2 = 25$

73. $\dfrac{3^{-2}}{9^{\frac{2}{3}}} 27^{\frac{5}{4}} = 3^{-2 + \frac{15}{4} - \frac{4}{3}} = 3^{\frac{5}{12}}$

74. $\dfrac{4^{-4} \sqrt{2}}{8^{-\frac{2}{3}}} 16^{\frac{3}{4}} = 2^{-8 + \frac{1}{2} + 3 + 2} = 2^{-\frac{5}{2}} = \dfrac{1}{\sqrt{32}}$

75. $\sqrt{5} \dfrac{25^2 5^{-1}}{25^{\frac{4}{3}}} 5^{\frac{1}{4}} \sqrt[3]{5} = 5^{\frac{1}{2} + 4 - 1 + \frac{1}{4} + \frac{1}{3} - \frac{8}{3}} = 5^{\frac{17}{12}}$

76. $\dfrac{4^{-2} 2^{-4}}{16^2 (\sqrt[6]{16^4})} 8^{\frac{1}{4}} 2^{-1} = 2^{-4 - 4 + \frac{3}{4} - 1 - 8 - \frac{8}{3}} = 2^{-\frac{227}{12}}$

77. $x\sqrt{x}\sqrt{3} = \sqrt{3}x^{\frac{3}{2}} = \sqrt{3x^3}$

78. $x\sqrt{x} \cdot \sqrt{2x} = x^{\frac{3}{2}} \cdot \sqrt{2} \cdot x^{\frac{1}{2}}$

79. $\dfrac{1}{x\sqrt{x}} = x^{-\frac{3}{2}}$

80. $\dfrac{x\sqrt[3]{x}}{\sqrt{x}} = x^{1 + \frac{1}{3} - \frac{1}{2}} = x^{\frac{7}{6}} = \sqrt[6]{x^7}$

81. $s^n s^{2n} s^2 = s^{3n+2}$

82. $a^{2k} b a^3 b^{2k} a = a^{2k+4} b^{2k+1}$

83. $\dfrac{3^n}{9^n} 27^n = 3^{n+3n-2n} = 3^{2n}$

84. $\dfrac{2^n}{8^{n+1}} 16^{n-2} = 2^{n + 4(n-2) - 3(n+1)} = 2^{2n-11}$

85. $\dfrac{5^{-n}}{125^{2n-2}} 5^{-n+2} = 5^{-n-n+2-3(2n-2)} = 5^{-8n+8}$

86. $\dfrac{x^{-n}}{x^{2n-2}} x^{-n+5} = x^{-4n+7}$

87. $\dfrac{2x^{-n+1}}{2^2 x^{3n+2}} x^{n+5} = 2^{-1} x^{-3n+4}$

88. $\dfrac{2yx^{-2n+3}}{2^5 y^{-1} x^{-4n+2}} x^{-2n+1} = 2^{-4} x^2 y^2$

89. $\dfrac{4^2 y^2 x^{-3} z}{2^2 xz^2 y^{-1} x} x^{-2} z^2 = 2^2 x^{-7} y^3 z$

90. $\dfrac{4^2 y^2 (x^{-2} z^2)^{-2}}{(2^2 x)^3 z^2 y^{-1} x} x^{-2} z^2 = 2^{-2} x^{-1} y^3 z^{-4}$

91. $\dfrac{4^{-2} y^3 (x^{-2} z^3)^{-1}}{(2^{-3} x)^{-3} z^{-2} y^{-1} x} xz^2 = 2^{-13} x^5 y^4 z$

92. $\left(\dfrac{a}{b^2}\right)^2 \div \left(\dfrac{a^{-1}}{b^3}\right)^{-3} \cdot \left(\dfrac{1}{b}\right)^3 = a^{-1} b^2$

93. $\left(\dfrac{ab}{b^2}\right)^{-2} \div \left(\dfrac{(2ba)^{-1}}{b^3}\right)^{-3} \cdot \left(\dfrac{2}{b}\right)^3 = a^{-5} b^{-13}$

94. $\dfrac{a^{-2} b^n (a^{-2n} b^3)^{-1}}{(b^{-3n} a)^3 a^{-2n} b^{-1}} = a^{-5+4n} b^{10n-2}$

95. $\dfrac{a^{-2} b^n (a^{-2n} b^2)^n}{(b^{-3n} a)^n a^{-2n} b^n} =$

$= a^{-2-2n^2-n+2n} b^{n+2n+3n^2-n} = a^{-2n^2+n-2} b^{3n^2+2n}$

96. $\dfrac{3^n a^{-2} b^n (a^{-2n} b^3)^{n+1}}{(9^n b^{-2n} a)^n a^{-2n} b^{n+2}} =$

$3^{n-2n^2} a^{-2n^2-n-2} b^{2n^2+3n+1}$

97. $\dfrac{3^n + 3^{n+1}}{3^{n-1}} = \dfrac{3^n(1+3)}{\left(3^n \cdot \dfrac{1}{3}\right)} = 12$

98. $\dfrac{4^n + 4^{n-1}}{2^{n-2}} = \dfrac{2^{2n}(1+\frac{1}{4})}{\left(2^n \cdot \frac{1}{4}\right)} = 5 \cdot 2^n$

99. $\dfrac{7^{2n} + 7^{2n-1}}{7^{2n-2}} = \dfrac{7^{2n}(1+\frac{1}{7})}{\left(7^{2n} \cdot \frac{1}{49}\right)} = 56$

100. $\dfrac{7^{3n-1} - 7^{3n}}{7^{2n-2}} =$

$\dfrac{7^{3n}(\frac{1}{7}-1)}{\left(7^{2n} \cdot \frac{1}{49}\right)} = -42 \cdot 7^n = -6 \cdot 7^{n+1}$

101. $2^{-1} + 2 = \dfrac{1}{2} + 2 = \dfrac{5}{2}$

102. $3^{-1} - 3^{-2} = \dfrac{1}{3} - \dfrac{1}{9} = -\dfrac{2}{9}$

103. $5^{-1} - 5^{-2} = \dfrac{1}{5} - \dfrac{1}{25} = \dfrac{4}{25}$

104. $3^{-3} + 2^{-2} = \dfrac{1}{27} + \dfrac{1}{4} = \dfrac{31}{108}$

105. $3^{-2} + 4^{-2} = \dfrac{1}{9} + \dfrac{1}{4} = \dfrac{13}{36}$

106. $7^{-2} + 2^{-2} = \dfrac{1}{49} + \dfrac{1}{4} = \dfrac{53}{196}$

107. $8^{-2} - 3^{-2} = \dfrac{1}{64} - \dfrac{1}{9} = -\dfrac{55}{576}$

108. $7^{-2} - 2^{-3} = \dfrac{1}{49} - \dfrac{1}{8} = -\dfrac{41}{392}$

109. $a^{-1} + a^{-1} = \dfrac{1}{a} + \dfrac{1}{a} = \dfrac{2}{a}$

110. $ba^{-1} + a^{-1} = \dfrac{b}{a} + \dfrac{1}{a} = \dfrac{b+1}{a}$

111. $a^{-1} - ba^{-1} = \dfrac{1}{a} - \dfrac{b}{a} = \dfrac{1-b}{a}$

112. $(ba)^{-1} + a^{-1} = \dfrac{1}{ab} + \dfrac{1}{a} = \dfrac{1+b}{ab}$

113. $ba^{-1} + (ba)^{-1} = \dfrac{b}{a} + \dfrac{1}{ab} = \dfrac{b^2+1}{ab}$

LOGARITHMS

1.

Exponential Form	Logarithmic Form
$5^3 = 125$	$\log_5 125 = 3$
$6^2 = 36$	$\log_6 36 = 2$
$x^2 = 64; x = 8$	$\log_x 64 = 2$
$x^3 = 27; x = 3$	$\log_x 27 = 3$
$3^2 = x+1; x = 8$	$\log_3(x+1) = 2$
$e^x = 9; x = \ln(9)$	$\log_e 9 = x$
$e^2 = x$	$\ln x = \log_e x = 2$
$e^{2x-1} = 17; x = \dfrac{\ln 17 + 1}{2}$	$\ln 17 = \log_e 17 = 2x - 1$
$e^2 = 3x+2; x = \dfrac{e^2 - 2}{3}$	$\ln(3x+2) = \log_e(3x+2) = 2$
$4^x = 9$	$\log_4 9 = x$
$6^2 = x$	$\log_6 x = 2$

$2^x = e$	$\log_2 e = x$
$e^4 = x^2; x = e^2$	$\ln(x^2) = \log_e(x^2) = 4$
$10^x = 0.001; x = -3$	$\log 0.001 = x$
$10^x = 200$	$\log 200 = x$
$3^{-2} = \dfrac{1}{9}$	$\log_3 \dfrac{1}{9} = -2$
$2^x = \dfrac{1}{2}; x = -1$	$\log_2 0.5 = x$

Logarithms were "invented" in order to solve equations in which: <u>the variable is the exponent</u>

Evaluate

1. $Log_2(32) = 5$
2. $Log_5(25) = 2$
3. $Log_5(125) = 3$
4. $Log_5(625) = 4$
5. $Log_3(3) = 1$
6. $Log_5(0) = undefined$
7. $Log_5(1) = 0$
8. $Log_a(1) = 0$
9. $Log_2(-3) = undefined$
10. $Log_2(\dfrac{1}{8}) = -3$
11. $Log_7(\dfrac{1}{49}) = -2$
12. $Log_4(32) = \dfrac{5}{2}$
13. $Log_8(32) = \dfrac{5}{3}$
14. $Log_{\frac{1}{2}}(4) = -2$
15. $Log_{\frac{1}{2}}(16) = -4$
16. $Log_{\frac{1}{3}}(81) = -4$

17. $Log_{\frac{1}{2}}(8) = -3$
18. $Log_{\frac{1}{2}}(-8) = undefined$
19. $Log_{\frac{1}{3}}(\dfrac{1}{9}) = 2$
20. $Log_{\frac{1}{5}}(\dfrac{1}{125}) = 3$
21. $Log_1(8) = undefined, 1 \neq b \geq 0$
22. $Log_2(\dfrac{1}{\sqrt{8}}) = -\dfrac{3}{2}$
23. $Log_2(\sqrt[3]{32}) = \dfrac{5}{3}$
24. $Log_3(\sqrt[3]{81}) = \dfrac{4}{3}$
25. $Log_{\sqrt[5]{8}}(\sqrt[5]{8}) = 1$
26. $Log_{\frac{1}{2}}(\sqrt[5]{16}) = -\dfrac{4}{5}$
27. $Log_{17}(\dfrac{17 \sqrt[5]{17}}{17^{\frac{1}{3}}}) = \dfrac{13}{15}$
28. $Log(\sqrt{10}) = \dfrac{1}{2}$

387

29. $Log(\sqrt[3]{10}) = \dfrac{1}{3}$

30. $Log(\sqrt[7]{100}) = \dfrac{2}{7}$

31. $Log(\sqrt[3]{10000}) = \dfrac{4}{3}$

32. $Log(10^{-19}) = -19$

33. $Log(50) - Log(5) = Log(10) = 1$

34. $Log(25) + Log(4) = Log(100) = 2$

35. $Log_3(45) - Log_3(5) = Log_3(9) = 2$

36. $Log_6(18) + Log_6(2) = Log_6(36) = 2$

37. $Log_a(a^x) = x$

38. $Log_a(a^{2x-3}) = 2x - 3$

39. $Log_e(e) = 1$

40. $Ln(e) = 1$

41. $Ln(e^2) = 2$

42. $Ln(e^{\frac{1}{2}}) = \dfrac{1}{2}$

43. $Ln(e^{\frac{2}{5}}) = \dfrac{2}{5}$

44. $Ln(e\sqrt[3]{e^4}) = \dfrac{7}{3}$

45. $\dfrac{Ln(e^{-1})}{Log_{12}(\sqrt{12})} = \dfrac{-1}{\left(\dfrac{1}{2}\right)} = -2$

46. $Ln(1) = 0$

47. $Ln(0) = undefined$

48. $Ln(e^0) = 0$

49. $Ln(e^n) = n$

50. $Ln(\dfrac{1}{\sqrt{e}}) = -\dfrac{1}{2}$

51. $Ln(\dfrac{1}{\sqrt[3]{e^2}}) = -\dfrac{2}{3}$

52. $Log_\pi(\dfrac{1}{\pi^4}) = -4$

53. $Log_\pi(\dfrac{1}{\sqrt{\pi^5}}) = -\dfrac{5}{2}$

54. $Log_a(\dfrac{1}{\sqrt[3]{a^2}}) = -\dfrac{2}{3}$

55. $10^{Log(100)} = 100$

56. $3^{Log_3(9)} = 9$

57. $3^{Log_3(\frac{1}{27})} = \dfrac{1}{27}$

58. $\dfrac{Ln(e^{-1})}{Log_{12}(144)} = \dfrac{-1}{2}$

59. $\dfrac{Ln(3e^5)}{Log_2(64)} = \dfrac{Ln(3e^5)}{8}$

True or False

1. $Log(2x) - Log(3) = Log(2x + 3)$ **F**

2. $Log(x) - Log(9) = 2 \Leftrightarrow \dfrac{x}{9} = 100$ **T**

3. $Log(12) + Log(x) = 1 \Leftrightarrow 12x = 10$ **T**

4. $Log(2) + Log(5) = Log(7)$ **F**

5. $Log(10) - Log(5) = Log(2)$ **T**

6. $Log(20) + Log(2) = Log(22)$ **F**

7. $Log(15) - Log(3) = Log(5)$ **T**

8. $Log(A + B) = Log(A) + Log(B)$ **F**

Simplify

1. $Log_2(2^x 2^{x+y}) = 2x + y$

2. $5^{Log_5(x+y)} = x + y$

3. $Log_7(49^{xy}) = 2xy$

4. $Log_2(xy) - \frac{1}{3}Log_2(x^2) = Log_2(x^{\frac{1}{3}}y)$

5. $Log_2(\frac{8x^2}{y}) - 2Log_2(2x^2y) = Log_2(2x^{-2}y^{-3})$

6. $\frac{1}{2}Log_3(\frac{9xy^2}{y}) - Log_3(27xy) = Log_3(3^{-2}x^{-\frac{1}{2}}y^{-\frac{1}{2}})$

7. $3Log_4((xy)^3) - Log_4(xy) = Log_4((xy)^8)$

8. $Log(2A) + Log(B) - 2Log(AB) = Log(\frac{2}{AB})$

9. $Ln(ab) - Ln((ab)^t) - 2Ln(a) = Ln(a^{-t-1}b^{-t})$

10. If $Log_{10}(8) = x$ and $Log_{10}(3) = y$ express the following in terms of x and y only:

    a. $Log_{10}(24) = x + y$

    b. $Log_{10}(\frac{8}{3}) = x - y$

    c. $Log_{10}(72) = x + 2y$

    d. $Log_{10}(\frac{9}{8}) = 2x - y$

    e. $Log_{10}(720) = 1 + x + 2y$

Change of base

1. $Log_2(5) = \frac{Log_7(5)}{Log_7(2)}$

2. $Log_3(-12) = Undefined$

3. $Log_{22}(51) = \frac{Log_{70}(51)}{Log_{70}(22)}$

4. $Log_{2.3}(1) = \frac{Log_3(1)}{Log_3(2.3)} = 0$

5. $Log_{2.9}(2.9) = \frac{Log_4(2.9)}{Log_4(2.9)} = 1$

6. $Log_3(-5) = undefined$

7. $Log_a(5) = \dfrac{Log_b(5)}{Log_b(a)}$

8. $Log_{12}(5y) = \dfrac{Ln(5y)}{Ln(12)}$

9. $Log_e(2) = \dfrac{Log_7(2)}{Log_7(e)}$

10. $Log(5) = \dfrac{Log_8(5)}{Log_8(10)}$

11. $Ln(15) = \dfrac{Log_3(15)}{Log_3(e)}$

12. $Log_{\sqrt{2}}(5) = \dfrac{Log_{12}(5)}{Log_{12}(\sqrt{2})}$

13. $Log_3(\dfrac{2}{3}) = \dfrac{Log_7(\dfrac{2}{3})}{Log_7(3)}$

14. $Log_5(\dfrac{2}{\sqrt{5}}) = \dfrac{Ln(\dfrac{2}{\sqrt{5}})}{Ln(5)}$

15. Simplify:

  a. $\log_x b \cdot \log_b x = \dfrac{Ln(b)}{Ln(x)} \dfrac{Ln(x)}{Ln(b)} = 1$

  b. $\log_x q \cdot \log_q r \cdot \log_r x = \dfrac{Ln(q)}{Ln(x)} \dfrac{Ln(r)}{Ln(q)} \dfrac{Ln(x)}{Ln(r)} = 1$

Logarithmic Equations

1. $Log_4(x) = 2$
   $x = 16$

2. $Log_{\frac{1}{3}}(x) = 4$
   $x = \sqrt[3]{4}$

3. $Log_{10}(2x+1) = 2$
   $x = \dfrac{99}{2}$

4. $Log_2(64) = x$
   $x = 6$

5. $Ln(x) = 2.7$
   $x = e^{2.7}$

6. $Ln(x+1) = 1.86$
   $x = e^{1.86} - 1$

7. $e^x = 6.27$
   $x = Ln(6.27)$

8. $Log_b(81) = 4$
   $b = 3$

9. $e^{-2x} = 4.12$
   $x = \dfrac{Ln(4.12)}{-2}$

10. $Log_3(x) = Log_3(7) + Log_3(3)$
    $x = 21$

11. $5 \times 9^x = 10$
    $x = \dfrac{Ln(2)}{Ln(9)}$

12. $10e^{4x+1} = 20$
    $x = \dfrac{Ln(2)-1}{4}$

13. $3^t = 2 \cdot 5^{2t}$
    $t = \dfrac{Ln(2)}{Ln(3) - 2Ln(5)}$

14. $3^{t+1} = 4 \cdot 6^{2t-3}$
    $x = \dfrac{Ln(3) + 3Ln(6) - 2Ln(2)}{2Ln(6) - Ln(3)}$

15. $3 \cdot 2^t = 5 \cdot 6^{2t-3}$
    $t = \dfrac{3Ln(3) + Ln(3) - Ln(5)}{2Ln(6) - Ln(2)}$

16. $2 \cdot e^t = 8 \cdot 7^{2t-3}$
    $t = \dfrac{2Ln(2) - 3Ln(7)}{2Ln(7) - 1}$

17. $b^t = c \cdot d^{2t}$
$t = \dfrac{Ln(c)}{Ln(b) - 2Ln(d)}$

18. $a \cdot b^t = c \cdot d^{2t}$
$t = \dfrac{Ln(a) - Ln(c)}{2Ln(d) - Ln(b)}$

19. $e^t + e^t = 2$
$t = 0$

20. $e^{2t} + e^{2t} = 3$
$x = \dfrac{Ln(3) - Ln(2)}{2}$

21. $Ln(x) = 2$
$x = e^2$

22. $Ln(x^2) = 2$
$x = \pm e$

23. $Ln(x^2 - 1) = 2$
$x = \pm\sqrt{e^2 + 1}$

24. $Ln(x+1) - Ln(2x) = -1$
$x = \dfrac{e}{2 - e}$

25. $Ln(x^2 + 1) = 1$
$x = \pm\sqrt{e - 1}$

26. $Log_{10}(x^2 + 2) = 2$
$x = \pm\sqrt{98}$

27. $Ln(x-2) + Ln(x+1) = 0$
$x = \dfrac{\sqrt{13} - 5}{3 - \sqrt{13}}$

28. $Log_2(x) + Log_3(x) = 1$
$x = e^{\frac{Ln(2)Ln(3)}{Ln(6)}}$

29. $Log_2(x) - Log_3(x) = 1$
$x = e^{\frac{Ln(2)Ln(3)}{Ln(3) - Ln(2)}}$

30. $Log_2(x) - 2Log_3(x) = 2$
$x = e^{\frac{2Ln(2)Ln(3)}{Ln(3) - Ln(4)}}$

31. $3Log_2(x) - 2Log_3(x) = 1$
$x = e^{\frac{Ln(2)Ln(3)}{Ln(27) - Ln(4)}}$

32. $Log_2(x) - Log_3(x) = Log_3(x)$
$x = 1$

33. $Log_2(x) - 2Log_x(2) = 0$
$e^{\pm\sqrt{2}Ln(2)}$

34. $Log_2(x) - 2Log_x(2) = 1$
$x = 4, \dfrac{1}{2}$

35. $Log_2(x) - Log_x(3) = 0$
$e^{\pm\sqrt{2}\sqrt{Ln(2)Ln(3)}}$

36. $Log_2(x) - 2Log_x(3) = 0$
$e^{\pm\sqrt{Ln(2)Ln(3)}}$

1.5. – EQUATIONS

1st Degree (Linear Equations)

1. $\dfrac{x}{12} = 5$
   $x = 60$

2. $\dfrac{x}{7} + 2 = 5$
   $x = 21$

3. $\dfrac{2x}{7} + 2 = 5 - 3x$
   $x = \dfrac{21}{23}$

4. $\dfrac{2x}{7} + \dfrac{2}{5} = -2x + 1$
   $x = \dfrac{21}{80}$

5. $\dfrac{2x - 1}{x} = 3$
   $x = -1$

6. $\dfrac{x + 2}{2x} = 5$
   $x = \dfrac{2}{9}$

7. $\dfrac{x - 2}{2x - 1} = 6$
   $x = \dfrac{4}{11}$

8. $\dfrac{2x - 2}{x + 1} = -2$
   $x = 0$

9. $\dfrac{2x}{7} + 1 = \dfrac{-5x}{7}$
   $x = -1$

10. $\dfrac{2x}{7} + 4 = \dfrac{3x}{2}$
    $x = \dfrac{56}{17}$

11. $\dfrac{2}{x} - 3 = \dfrac{3}{2x}$
    $x = \dfrac{1}{6}$

12. $\dfrac{2}{x - 2} - 3 = \dfrac{3}{x - 2}$
    $x = \dfrac{5}{3}$

13. $\dfrac{-2}{x} = \dfrac{3}{x - 2}$
    $x = \dfrac{4}{5}$

14. $\dfrac{4}{x + 1} = \dfrac{4}{x + 2}$
    No Solution

15. $\dfrac{2}{x + 1} = \dfrac{4}{x + 2}$
    $x = 0$

16. $-\dfrac{2}{2x + 1} - 2 = \dfrac{4}{2x + 1}$
    $x = -2$

392

Isolate x

1. $\dfrac{4}{x} = \dfrac{a}{x+6}$
   $x = \dfrac{24}{a-4}$

2. $\dfrac{14}{x+2} = \dfrac{a}{x+2} - a$
   $x = -\dfrac{14+a}{a}$

3. $\dfrac{2}{x+3} - a = \dfrac{a+b}{x+3}$
   $x = \dfrac{2-b-4a}{a}$

4. $\dfrac{5}{2x+1} - 3a = \dfrac{b}{2x+1}$
   $x = \dfrac{5-b-3a}{6a}$

5. $\dfrac{-2x}{a+3} = \dfrac{x+2}{2a-1}$
   $x = -\dfrac{2a+6}{5a+5}$

6. $\dfrac{-5x+1}{2a} = \dfrac{bx}{3a+2}$
   $x = \dfrac{3a+2}{15a+2ab+10}$

7. $\dfrac{a}{x+2} = \dfrac{b}{x+2} - b + 1$
   $x = -\dfrac{a+b+2}{b+1}$

8. $\dfrac{b}{2x-4} - 3 = \dfrac{b}{2x-4} - b + 1$
   No Solution

9. $\dfrac{1}{ax+2} = \dfrac{b}{x+a}$
   $x = \dfrac{a-2b}{ba-1}$

10. $\dfrac{1}{ax+2} = \dfrac{b}{ax+2} - 3$
    $x = \dfrac{b-7}{3a}$

11. $3\dfrac{x}{ax+2} = 3$
    $x = \dfrac{6}{1-3a}$

12. $-3\dfrac{2x}{ax+3} = b$
    $x = -\dfrac{3b}{ab+6}$

13. $\dfrac{2x-3}{2ax+5} = -3b$
    $x = \dfrac{3-15b}{6ab+2}$

14. $\dfrac{x}{ax+2} = \dfrac{2}{a} - 3$
    $x = -\dfrac{4-6a}{3a^2 - a}$

393

2nd degree (Quadratic equations)

a. Solve the following equations using the "complete the square method".
b. Check your answers using the quadratic formula.
c. Write the factorized expression.

1. $x^2 - 4x + 1 = 3$

$(x-2)^2 - 4 + 1 = 3$

$x = \pm\sqrt{6} + 2$

$(x-(\sqrt{6}+2))(x-(-\sqrt{6}+2)) = 0$

2. $x^2 - 4x + 1 = -3$

$(x-2)^2 - 4 + 1 = -3$

$x = 2$

$(x-2)(x-2) = 0$

3. $x^2 - 4x + 1 = -13$

$(x-2)^2 - 4 + 1 = -13$

No Solution

4. $x^2 + 6x + 2 = 2$

$(x+3)^2 - 9 + 2 = 2$

$x = 0, -6$

$(x)(x+6) = 0$

5. $x^2 + 6x + 2 = -10$

$(x+3)^2 - 9 + 2 = -10$

No Solution

6. $x^2 - 3x - 5 = 3$

$\left(x - \dfrac{3}{2}\right)^2 - \dfrac{9}{4} - 5 = 3$

$x = \dfrac{3}{2} \pm \dfrac{\sqrt{41}}{2}$

$\left(x - \left(\dfrac{3}{2} + \dfrac{\sqrt{41}}{2}\right)\right)\left(x - \left(\dfrac{3}{2} - \dfrac{\sqrt{41}}{2}\right)\right) = 0$

7. $x^2 - 3x - 3 = -3$

$\left(x - \dfrac{3}{2}\right)^2 - \dfrac{9}{4} - 3 = -3$

$x = 0, 3$

$(x)(x-3) = 0$

8. $x^2 - 3x - 4 = -1$

$\left(x - \dfrac{3}{2}\right)^2 - \dfrac{9}{4} - 4 = -1$

$x = \dfrac{3}{2} \pm \dfrac{\sqrt{21}}{2}$

$\left(x - \left(\dfrac{3}{2} + \dfrac{\sqrt{21}}{2}\right)\right)\left(x - \left(\dfrac{3}{2} - \dfrac{\sqrt{21}}{2}\right)\right) = 0$

9. $x^2 - 7x - 5 = 3$

$\left(x - \dfrac{7}{2}\right)^2 - \dfrac{49}{4} - 5 = 3$

$x = 8, -1$

$(x+1)(x-8) = 0$

10. $x^2 + x - 3 = 2$

$\left(x + \dfrac{1}{2}\right)^2 - \dfrac{1}{4} - 3 = 2$

$x = -\dfrac{1}{2} \pm \dfrac{\sqrt{21}}{2}$

$\left(x - \left(-\dfrac{1}{2} + \dfrac{\sqrt{21}}{2}\right)\right)\left(x - \left(-\dfrac{1}{2} - \dfrac{\sqrt{21}}{2}\right)\right) = 0$

11. $x^2 - 2x + 4 = 5$
$(x-1)^2 - 1 + 4 = 5$
$x = 1 \pm \sqrt{2}$
$\left(x - \left(1 + \sqrt{2}\right)\right)\left(x - \left(1 - \sqrt{2}\right)\right) = 0$

12. $x^2 + 3x - 1 = 3$
$\left(x + \dfrac{3}{2}\right)^2 - \dfrac{9}{4} - 1 = 3$
$x = 1, -4$
$(x-1)(x+4) = 0$

13. $x^2 + 7x - 3 = 2$
$\left(x + \dfrac{7}{2}\right)^2 - \dfrac{49}{4} - 3 = 2$
$x = -\dfrac{7}{2} \pm \dfrac{\sqrt{69}}{2}$
$\left(x - \left(-\dfrac{7}{2} + \dfrac{\sqrt{69}}{2}\right)\right)\left(x - \left(-\dfrac{7}{2} - \dfrac{\sqrt{69}}{2}\right)\right) = 0$

14. $x^2 + 12x - 4 = -1$
$(x+6)^2 - 36 - 4 = -1$
$x = -6 \pm \sqrt{39}$
$\left(x - \left(-6 + \sqrt{39}\right)\right)\left(x - \left(-6 - \sqrt{39}\right)\right) = 0$

Rational equations 2nd degree

1. $\dfrac{3}{x^2 - 4} = 2$
$x = \pm \dfrac{\sqrt{22}}{2}$

2. $\dfrac{2}{x^2 - 2x + 1} = 1$
$x = 1 \pm \sqrt{3}$

3. $-\dfrac{2}{x^2 - 2x + 3} = 1$
No Solution

4. $\dfrac{x}{x^2 - 4} = 2$
$x = \dfrac{1}{4} \pm \dfrac{\sqrt{65}}{4}$

5. $\dfrac{x}{x-4} = 5$
$x = 5$

6. $\dfrac{x^2}{x^2 - 4x} = 2$
$x = 8$

7. $\dfrac{x^2 - 1}{x - 5} = 2$
No Solution

8. $\dfrac{x}{x-4} + \dfrac{2}{x-4} = 5$
$x = \dfrac{11}{2}$

9. $\dfrac{x}{x-4} + \dfrac{2}{x+3} = -2$
$x = -\dfrac{1}{2} \pm \dfrac{\sqrt{393}}{6}$

10. $\dfrac{x-1}{2x-2} - \dfrac{2x-1}{x+3} = 3$
$x = -\dfrac{13}{9}$

11. $\dfrac{x}{3x+2} - \dfrac{2x-1}{2x+3} = 7$

$x = -\dfrac{89}{92} \pm \dfrac{\sqrt{561}}{92}$

12. $\dfrac{1}{x} + \dfrac{2}{x^2} = 3$

$x = 1, -\dfrac{2}{3}$

13. $\dfrac{1}{x-1} + \dfrac{2}{x^2-1} = 2$

$x = \dfrac{1}{4} \pm \dfrac{\sqrt{41}}{4}$

14. $\dfrac{1}{x-3} - \dfrac{2}{x^2-9} = 4$

$x = \dfrac{1}{8} \pm \dfrac{\sqrt{593}}{8}$

Radical Equations

1. $\sqrt{8x+2} = 0$

$x = -\dfrac{1}{4}$

2. $\sqrt{5x-2} = 6$

$x = \dfrac{38}{5}$

3. $\sqrt{5x^2-2} = 3$

$x = \pm\sqrt{\dfrac{11}{5}}$

4. $\sqrt{x^2+1} = -2$

$x = \pm\sqrt{3}$, Assuming negative root

5. $\sqrt{x^2-2} + 4 = -2$

$x = \pm\sqrt{38}$, Assuming negative root

6. $\sqrt{2x^2-2} + 4x = -2$

No Solution

7. $\sqrt{2x-2} + 3x + 2 = -2$

No Solution

8. $\sqrt{x+1} + \sqrt{x+3} = 2$

$x = -\dfrac{3}{4}$

9. $\sqrt{x-1} + \sqrt{x+3} = 2$

$x = 1$

10. $\sqrt{x-3} + \sqrt{x+3} = 3$

$x = \dfrac{13}{4}$

11. $\sqrt{5x+1} - \sqrt{3x-3} = 2$

$x = 6 \pm 2\sqrt{6}$

12. $\sqrt{8x+2} - \sqrt{3x-3} = 0$

$x = -1$

13. $\sqrt{x-1} + \sqrt{x+2} = -2$

$x = \dfrac{17}{16}$, Assuming negative root

14. $\dfrac{1}{\sqrt{-3x-1}} = \sqrt{-2+x}$

$x = \dfrac{5}{6} \pm \dfrac{\sqrt{37}}{6}$, Assuming negative root

15. $-4\dfrac{1}{\sqrt{6x-2}} = \sqrt{2-5x}$

No Solution

Higher degree simple equations

1. $x^4 - 2x^2 = 0$ $\qquad x = 0, \pm\sqrt{2}$

2. $(2x - 3)(x^2 - 3)(x + 5)(x^3 + 2) = 0$ $\qquad x = \dfrac{3}{2}, \pm\sqrt{3}, -5, \sqrt[3]{-2}$

3. $(2x - 3)(x - 3) = 1$ $\qquad x = \dfrac{9}{4} \pm \dfrac{\sqrt{17}}{4}$

4. $(6x - 7)(3x^2 - 5)(2x + 7)(2x^5 - 64)(4x^4 + 5) = 0$ $\qquad x = \dfrac{7}{26}, \pm\sqrt{\dfrac{5}{3}}, -\dfrac{7}{2}, 2$

5. $3x^5 - x^2 = 0$ $\qquad x = 0, \sqrt[3]{\dfrac{1}{3}}$ $\qquad$ 12. $ax^5 - x^2 = 0$ $\qquad x = 0, \sqrt[3]{\dfrac{1}{a}}$

6. $x^6 - 32x = 0$ $\qquad x = 0, 2$ $\qquad$ 13. $x^4 - 5x^2 + 3 = -1$ $\qquad x = \pm 1, \pm 2$

7. $x^6 - 2x^5 + x^4 = 0$ $\qquad x = 0, 1$ $\qquad$ 14. $x^4 - 10x^2 + 3 = -6$ $\qquad x = \pm 1, \pm 3$

8. $x^3 - 4x^2 + 3x = 0$ $\qquad x = 0, 1, 3$ $\qquad$ 15. $x^6 + 3x^3 - 10 = 0$ $\qquad x = \sqrt[3]{2}, \sqrt[3]{-5}$

9. $2x^3 - 5x = 0$ $\qquad x = 0, \pm\dfrac{\sqrt{10}}{2}$ $\qquad$ 16. $x^8 = -2x^4 - 1$ $\qquad$ No Solution

17. $x^4 - 13x^2 + 36 = 0$ $\qquad x = \pm 2, \pm 3$

10. $2x^3 - x^2 = 0$ $\qquad x = 0, \dfrac{1}{2}$ $\qquad$ 18. $x^5 - 15x^3 + 54x = 0$ $\qquad x = 0, \pm 3, \pm\sqrt{6}$

19. $x^5 + x^3 - 6x = 0$ $\qquad x = 0, \pm\sqrt{2}$

11. $ax^4 - 3x = 0$ $\qquad x = 0, \sqrt[3]{\dfrac{3}{a}}$ $\qquad$ 20. $x^4 = 6x^2 - 5$ $\qquad x = \pm 1, \pm\sqrt{5}$

Rational exponent equations

1. $x^{\frac{1}{2}} = 2$ $\qquad x = 4$ $\qquad$ 4. $x + x^{\frac{1}{2}} = 0$ $\qquad x = 0, 1$

2. $2x^{\frac{2}{3}} = 3$ $\qquad x = \sqrt{\dfrac{27}{8}}$ $\qquad$ 5. $2x - x^{\frac{2}{5}} = 0$ $\qquad x = 0, \dfrac{\sqrt[3]{2}}{4}$

3. $3x^{-\frac{1}{2}} = 2$ $\qquad x = \sqrt{\dfrac{9}{4}}$ $\qquad$ 6. $x^{\frac{1}{3}} + 1 = 0$ $\qquad x = -1$

7. $3x^{\frac{1}{2}} - x^2 = 0$ $x = 0, 3^{\frac{3}{5}}$ 11. $2x^2 - x^{-\frac{3}{2}} = 0$ $x = 2^{-\frac{3}{8}}$

8. $5x^{\frac{4}{3}} = -1$ No Solution   12. $x^{\frac{1}{2}} - 2x^{\frac{1}{6}} = 0$ $x = 0, 8$

9. $3x^{-\frac{3}{4}} = -2$ No Solution

10. $x - 2x^{\frac{2}{3}} = 0$ $x = 0, 8$

Exponential equations

1. $2^x = 2$ $x = 1$ 14. $5^{x-1} = 5^{x(x-1)}$ $x = 1$

2. $2^{x+2} = 2^2$ $x = 0$ 15. $6^{x^2-8} = 6$ $x = \pm 3$

3. $\left(\frac{1}{32}\right) 2^{3x+4} = 4$ $x = 1$ 16. $5^{x-1} = \frac{1}{125}$ $x = -2$

4. $2^{-4x+1} = 8$ $x = -\frac{1}{2}$ 17. $\left(\frac{1}{36}\right)^{2x-3} = \frac{1}{6}$ $x = \frac{7}{4}$

5. $3^{-5x+3} = 9$ $x = \frac{1}{5}$ 18. $6^{2x-3} = -\frac{3}{4}$

6. $\left(\frac{1}{4}\right)^{x+2} = \frac{1}{16}$ $x = 0$ No Solution

                                                                                                                                                  19. $2^x = 3$ $x \in (1, 2)$

7. $2^{x+2} = \frac{-1}{16}$ No Solution   20. $5^x = 3$ $x \in (0, 1)$

                                                                                                                                                  21. $1^x = 2$ No Solution

8. $2^{-2x+1} = 8^x$ $x = \frac{1}{5}$ 22. $2^x = -2$ No Solution

9. $\left(\frac{1}{3}\right)^{4x^2-1} = 9^{2x}$ $x = -\frac{1}{2} \pm \frac{\sqrt{2}}{2}$ 23. $\frac{1}{5^x - 4} = 1$ $x = 1$

10. $\left(\frac{1}{125}\right) 5^{x-1} = 1$ $x = 4$ 24. $\frac{1}{5^x - 24} = 1$ $x = 2$

11. $3^{2x-5} = \frac{1}{3}$ $x = 2$ 25. $\frac{1}{5^{3x} - 24} = 1$ $x = \frac{2}{3}$

12. $3^{2x^2-5} = \frac{1}{27}$ $x = \pm 1$ 26. $\frac{2}{2^x - 7} = 2$ $x = 3$

13. $\left(\frac{1}{5}\right)^{x-1} = -1$ No Solution   27. $\frac{125}{2^{\frac{x}{3}} - 7} = 5$ $x = 15$

398

28. $6^x + 6^{x+1} = \dfrac{7}{6}$ $x = -1$

29. $5^x + 5^{x+1} + 5^{x-1} = \dfrac{31}{5}$ $x = 0$

30. $7^{x-1} + 7^{x-2} = \dfrac{8}{49}$ $x = 0$

31. $7^{x-1} + 7^{x-2} = \dfrac{8}{7}$ $x = 1$

32. $2^x + 2^{x-1} + 2^{x+2} = 11$ $x = -1$

33. $2^x + 2^{x-1} + 2^{x+2} = 22$ $x = 2$

34. $5^{2x} - 6 \times 5^x = -5$ $x = 0, 1$

35. $3^{2x} - 4 \times 3^x - 2 = -5$ $x = 0, 1$

36. $5^{2x} + 4 \times 5^x - 10 = -5$ $x = 0$

37. $8^{2x} - 9 \times 8^x + 8 = 0$ $x = 0, 1$

38. $2 \times 8^{2x} - 18 \times 8^x + 10 = -6$ $x = 0, 1$

39. $3^{2x+1} - 3^{x+2} + 81 = 0$ No Solution

40. $5^{2x-1} - 6 \times 5^{x-1} = -1$ $x = 0, 1$

41. $3^{2x+2} - 4 \times 3^{x+2} + 27 = 0$ $x = 0, 1$

Systems of equations

1. $5x + 1 = 2y$
   $4y + x - 3 = 0$

   $x = \dfrac{1}{11}, y = \dfrac{8}{11}$

2. $5x + 3y = 2 - 2y$
   $-y + 2x - 5 = 0$

   $x = \dfrac{9}{5}, y = -\dfrac{7}{5}$

3. $5x = 2y$
   $-y + 2x = 0$

   $x = 0, y = 0$

4. $x = 2y - 7$
   $4y - 2x = 0$

   No Solution

5. $-5x + 1 = 2y$
   $-4y + x - 3 = x$

   $x = \dfrac{1}{2}, y = -\dfrac{3}{4}$

6. $5x + 1 = 2y$
   $10y - 25x = 10$

   No Solution

7. $2x + 1 = 2y$
   $-4y + 4x + 2 = 0$

   $x = 0, y = \dfrac{1}{2}$

8. $x = 2y$
   $-y + x^2 - 5 = 0$

   $x = -2, y = -1$

   $x = \dfrac{5}{2}, y = \dfrac{5}{4}$

9. $x = 1 - y$
   $-y + x^2 - 5 = 0$

   $x = 2, y = -1$

   $x = -3, y = 4$

10. $x = 1 - y^2$
    $-y^2 + x^2 - 5 = 0$

    $x = -3, y = 2$

    $x = -3, y = -2$

399

1.6. – EQUATIONS/INEQUALITIES WITH ABSOLUTE VALUE

1. $|x| = 5$ $x = \pm 5$
2. $|x| = -5$ No Solution
3. $|x| = 0$ $x = 0$
4. $|x| = -1$ No Solution
5. $|x| < 3$ $x \in (-3, 3)$
6. $|x| > 2$ $x \in (-\infty, -2) \cup (2, \infty)$
7. $|x| > -5$ $x \in \Re$
8. $|x| < -5$ No Solution
9. $|2x| = 1$ $x = \pm \frac{1}{2}$
10. $|x| \geq 0$ $x \in \Re$
11. $|x| \leq 0$ $x = 0$
12. $|2x| < 1$ $x \in (-\frac{1}{2}, \frac{1}{2})$
13. $|2x + 1| = 5$ $x = 2, -3$
14. $|7x + 21| - 5 = -5$ $x = -3$
15. $2 - |5 - 8x| = 15$ No Solution
16. $|4x + 2| = -5$ No Solution
17. $|8x + 12| = 100$ $x = 11, -14$
18. $|2x + 1| < 2$ $x \in (-\frac{13}{2}, -\frac{9}{2})$
19. $|8 - 2x + 1| > 6$ $x \in (-\infty, \frac{3}{2}) \cup (\frac{15}{2}, \infty)$
20. $|5x - 21| > 0$ $x \in \Re, x \neq \frac{21}{5}$
21. $|5x - 21| \geq 0$ $x \in \Re$
22. $|8x + 11| > -2$ $x \in \Re$
23. $|91x + 61| < -2$ No Solution
24. $|8 - 3x| > 8$ $x \in (-\infty, 0) \cup (\frac{16}{3}, \infty)$
25. $|18 - 6x| > 3$ $x \in (-\infty, \frac{5}{2}) \cup (\frac{7}{2}, \infty)$
26. $|1 - 6x| < 7$ $x \in (-1, \frac{4}{3})$
27. $|8 - 5x| \leq 0$ $x = \frac{8}{5}$ $x \in \Re$

28. $|5x - 21| > 1$ $x \in (-\infty, 4) \cup (\frac{22}{5}, \infty)$
29. $|x + 11| = 5$ $x = -6, -16$
30. $|x + 3| \leq 5$ $x \in [-8, 2]$
31. $|x + 11| = -15$ No Solution
32. $|2x + 11| + 2 < 15$ $x \in (-12, 1)$
33. $|3x + 11| = x$ No Solution
34. $|x + 2| = 5 - x$ $x = \frac{3}{2}$
35. $|3x + 1| < 5x$ $x \in (\frac{1}{3}, \infty)$
36. $|x - 4| = 3x$ $x = 1$
37. $|2x - 6| \leq 5 + 2x$ $x \in [\frac{1}{4}, \infty)$
38. $|2x + 4| < 2 - 3x$ $x \in (-\infty, -\frac{2}{5})$
39. $|2x - 2| > 11 - 2x$ $x \in (-\infty, \frac{13}{4})$
40. $|7x - 16| = 5 + 12x$ $x = \frac{11}{19}$
41. $|2x - 6| = 21$ $x = \frac{27}{2}, -\frac{15}{2}$
42. $|2x - 6| \geq 4$ $x \in (-\infty, 1] \cup [5, \infty)$
43. $|3x - 6| + 1 > -4$ $x \in \Re$
44. $|4x - 6| - 4 < -4x$ No Solution
45. $|\frac{1}{2}x - 4| \leq 1 + x$ $x \in [2, \infty)$
46. $|2x + \frac{1}{2}| > 2 - 3x$ $x \in (\frac{3}{10}, \infty)$
47. $|2x - \frac{1}{2}| = 1 - 2x$ $x \in (\frac{3}{8}, \infty)$
48. $|\frac{3}{2}x - 7| \leq 3 + 2x$ $x \in [\frac{8}{7}, \infty)$
49. $|5x - 2| = 1 - x$ $x = \frac{1}{4}, \frac{1}{2}$

1.7. – POLYNOMIALS

<u>Sum, subtraction, multiplication</u>
1. Given the polynomials: $A = 3x + 5x^3 - 7x^{12} - 1$, $B = -3x^2 + 2x^5 - 2x^3$, $C = x^2 + x^3$
   $D = -x + 5 + 5x^4 - 4x^4 + 2x^2 - 4x^5$. Evaluate:
   a. $A + B + C + D = -7x^{12} - 2x^5 + x^4 + 4x^3 + 2x$

   b. $A - 2B + 3D = -7x^{12} - 16x^5 + 3x^4 + 9x^3 + 12x^2 + 14$

   c. $2AC = -14x^{15} - 14x^{14} + 10x^6 + 10x^5 + 6x^4 + 4x^3 - 2x^2$

   d. $-3CB = -6x^8 - 6x^7 + 6x^6 + 15x^5 + 9x^4$

<u>Division</u>
2. Divide $3x^3 + 1$ by x
   $$\frac{3x^3 + 1}{x} = 3x^2 + \frac{1}{x} (\text{Remainder}: 1)$$

3. Divide $-2x^3 - 5$ by $x + 1$
   $$\frac{-2x^3 - 5}{x+1} = -2x^2 + 2x - 2 + \frac{-3}{x+1} (\text{Remainder}: -3)$$

4. Divide $2x^4 + x$ by x
   $$\frac{2x^4 + x}{x} = 2x^3 + 1 (\text{Remainder}: 0)$$

5. Divide $-2x - 5x^3 + 1$ by x
   $$\frac{-5x^3 - 2x + 1}{x} = -5x^4 - 2 + \frac{1}{x} (\text{Remainder}: 1)$$

6. Divide $4 - x^4$ by $x - 1$
   $$\frac{-x^4 + 4}{x-1} = -x^3 - x^2 - x - 1 + \frac{3}{x-1} (\text{Remainder}: 5)$$

7. Divide $2x^3 + 3x - 5$ by $x - 3$
   $$\frac{2x^3 + 3x - 5}{x-3} = 2x^2 + 6x + 21 + \frac{58}{x-3} (\text{Remainder}: 58)$$

8. Divide $4x^4 + x - 5$ by $2x - 3$
   $$\frac{4x^4 + x - 5}{2x-3} = 2x^3 + 3x^2 + \frac{9}{2}x + \frac{29}{4}x + \frac{\left(\frac{67}{4}\right)}{2x-3} (\text{Remainder}: \frac{67}{4})$$

9. Divide $2x^3 + 4x - 7$ by $x^2 - 1$
   $$\frac{2x^3 + 4x - 7}{x^2 - 1} = 2x + \frac{6x - 7}{x^2 - 1} (\text{Remainder}: 6x - 7)$$

10. Divide $5x^4 + x^3 + 2x^2 - 5$ by $-2x + 1$

$$\frac{5x^4 + x^3 + 2x^2 - 5}{-2x+1} = -\frac{5}{2}x^3 - \frac{7}{4}x^2 - \frac{15}{8}x - \frac{15}{16} + \frac{\left(-\frac{65}{16}\right)}{-2x+1} \text{ (Remainder}: -\frac{65}{16})$$

11. Divide $6x^5 + 2x^4 + 2x - 5$ by $x^3 + x$

$$\frac{6x^5 + 2x^4 + 2x - 5}{x^3 + x} = 6x^2 + 2x - 6 + \frac{-2x^2 + 8x - 5}{x^3 + x} \text{ (Remainder}: -2x^2 + 8x - 5)$$

12. Divide $5x^3 + x^4 + 2x^2 - 5$ by $x^4 + 1$

$$\frac{x^4 + 5x^3 + 2x^2 - 5}{x^4 + 1} = 1 + \frac{5x^3 + 2x^2 - 6}{x^4 + 1} \text{ (Remainder}: 5x^3 + 2x^2 - 6)$$

13. When $x^3 - 2x + k$ is divided by $x - 2$ it leaves a remainder of 5, find k.
    $R = P(2) = 8 - 4 + k = 5; k = 1$

14. When $x^3 - 2x + k$ is divided by $x + 1$ it leaves a remainder of 0, find k.
    $R = P(-1) = -1 + 2 + k = 0; k = -1$

15. When $2x^3 - x^2 + kx - 4$ is divided by $x + 2$ it leaves a remainder of 0, find k.
    $R = P(-2) = -16 - 4 - 2k - 4 = 0; k = -12$

16. When $x^3 - x^2 + kx - 4$ is divided by $x - 1$ it leaves a remainder of 2, find k.
    $R = P(1) = 1 - 1 + k - 4 = 2; k = 4$

In each one of the following cases write the corresponding expression and use the Remainder theorem to find the remainder:

1. $2x^3 + 2x - 15$ is divided by $x - 1$
   $2x^3 + 2x - 15 = Q(x - 1) + R$ Substituting $\underline{x = 1}$ on <u>both</u> sides:
   $R = 2 + 2 - 15 = -11$

2. $-4x^4 + 3x^3 - 5x + 1$ is divided by $x + 2$
   $-4x^4 + 3x^3 - 5x + 1 = = Q(x + 2) + R$
   $R = P(-2) = -64 - 24 + 10 + 1 = -77$

3. $3x^3 + 2x - 4$ is divided by $x + 3$
   $3x^3 + 2x - 4 = Q(x + 3) + R$
   $R = P(-3) = -81 - 6 - 4 = -91$

4. $3x^4 + 6x^3 - 33x^2 - 36x + 108$ is divided by $x - 2$
   $3x^4 + 6x^3 - 33x^2 - 36x + 108 = Q(x - 2) + R$
   $R = P(2) = 48 + 48 - 132 - 72 + 108 = 0$

5. $-2x^4 + x^3 + x^2 - 4x - 5$ is divided by $x - 2$
   $-2x^4 + x^3 + x^2 - 4x - 5 = Q(x - 2) + R$
   $R = P(2) = -32 + 8 + 4 - 8 - 5 = -33$

6. $9x^3 + 2x - 4$ is divided by $2x - 3$
   $9x^3 + 2x - 4 = Q(2x - 3) + R$
   $R = P(\frac{3}{2}) = \frac{243}{8} + 3 - 4 = \frac{235}{8}$

7. $x^{44} + x - 5$ is divided by $x - 1$
   $x^{44} + x - 5 = Q(x - 1) + R$
   $R = P(1) = 1 + 1 - 5 = -3$

8. $7x^4 + 14x^3 + 14x^2 + 14x + 7$ is divided by $x + 1$
   $7x^4 + 14x^3 + 14x^2 + 14x + 7 = Q(x + 1) + R$
   $R = P(-1) = 7 - 14 + 14 - 14 + 7 = 0$

9. $4x^{4455} + x^3 - x - 5$ is divided by $x + 1$
   $4x^{4455} + x^3 - x - 5 = Q(x + 1) + R$
   $R = P(-1) = -4 - 1 + 1 - 5 = -9$

10. $2x^3 + 3x^2 - 4x - 3$ is divided by $3x - 4$
    $2x^3 + 3x^2 - 4x - 3 = Q(3x - 4) + R$
    $R = P(\frac{4}{3}) = \frac{47}{27}$

11. In which one of the questions 1 to 10 the divisor is Also a factor of the polynomial? <u>In Questions 4 and 8, the remainder is 0 so $(x - 2)$ and $(x + 1)$ are factors of the polynomial</u>

Factor the following polynomials and solve the equations (real solutions only):

12. $2x^3 + 2x^2 - 2x - 2 = 0$ $2(x-1)(x+1)^2 = 0; x = 1, -1$

13. $2x^3 + 4x^2 + 2x + 4 = 0$ $2(x+2)(x^2+1) = 0; x = -2$

14. $6x + 6 + 3x^3 + 3x^2 = 0$ $3(x+1)(x^2+2) = 0; x = -1$

15. $-4x + 12 + 2x^3 - 6x^2 = 0$ $2(x-3)(x-\sqrt{2})(x+\sqrt{2}) = 0; x = 3, \sqrt{2}, -\sqrt{2}$

16. $x^3 - 4x^2 + 4x - 1 = 0$

    $(x-1)\left(x - \left(\frac{3+\sqrt{5}}{2}\right)\right)\left(x - \left(\frac{3-\sqrt{5}}{2}\right)\right) = 0; x = 1, \frac{3-\sqrt{5}}{2}, \frac{3+\sqrt{5}}{2}$

17. $2x^3 - x^2 - 8x + 4 = 0$ $2(x-2)(x-\frac{1}{2})(x+2) = 0; x = 2, \frac{1}{2}, -2$

18. $5x^3 - 8x^2 - 27x + 18 = 0$ $5(x-3)(x-\frac{3}{5})(x+2) = 0; x = 3, \frac{3}{5}, -2$

19. $-11x^2 - x + 6 + 6x^3 = 0$ $6(x-1)(x-\frac{3}{2})(x+\frac{2}{3}) = 0; x = 1, \frac{3}{2}, -\frac{2}{3}$

20. $4x^3 - 39x + 35 = 0$ $4(x-1)(x-\frac{5}{2})(x+\frac{7}{2}) = 0; x = 1, \frac{5}{2}, -\frac{7}{2}$

21. $5x^3 - 8x^2 - 27x + 18 = 0$ $5(x-3)(x-\frac{3}{5})(x+2) = 0; x = 3, \frac{3}{5}, -2$

22. $9x^3 + 18x^2 - 16x - 32 = 0$ $9(x+2)(x-\frac{4}{3})(x+\frac{4}{3}) = 0; x = -2, \frac{4}{3}, -\frac{4}{3}$

23. $x^3 - 13x - 12 = 0$ $2(x-4)(x+3)(x+1) = 0; x = 4, -3, -1$

24. $2x^3 + 9 - 9x^2 - 2x = 0$ $2(x-1)(x+1)(x-\frac{9}{2}) = 0; x = 1, -1, \frac{9}{2}$

25. $3x^3 + 6x^2 - 4x - 8 = 0$
$(x+2)\left(x - \frac{2\sqrt{3}}{3}\right)\left(x + \frac{2\sqrt{3}}{3}\right) = 0; x = -2, \frac{2\sqrt{3}}{3}, -\frac{2\sqrt{3}}{3}$

26. $x^4 - x^3 - 12x^2 - 4x + 16 = 0$ $(x-1)(x-4)(x+2)^2 = 0; x = 1, 4, -2$

27. $x^4 + 3x^3 - 6x - 4 = 0$
$(x+2)(x+1)(x-\sqrt{2})(x+\sqrt{2}) = 0; x = -1, -2, \sqrt{2}, -\sqrt{2}$

28. $6x^4 + 17x^3 + 7x^2 - 8x - 4 = 0$
$(x+2)(x+1)(x-\frac{2}{3})(x+\frac{1}{2}) = 0; x = -1, -2, -\frac{1}{2}, \frac{2}{3}$

29. The values of a and b if $6x^3 + 7x^2 + ax + b$ is divisible by $(2x - 1)$ and $(x + 1)$
$\frac{5}{2} + \frac{a}{2} + b = 0; \quad 1 - a + b = 0; \quad a = -1, b = -1$

30. $x^3 + ax^2 - 2x + b$ has $(x + 1)$ as a factor, and leaves a remainder of 4 when divided by $(x - 3)$. Find a and b.
$1 + a + b = 0; \quad -21 + 9a + b = 4; \quad a = \frac{13}{4}, b = -\frac{17}{4}$

31. Given that $(x - 1)$ and $(x - 2)$ are factors of $6x^4 + ax^3 - 17x^2 + bx - 4 = 0$, find a and b, and any remaining factors.
$-15 + a + b = 0; \quad 24 + 8a + 2b = 0; \quad a = -9, b = 24$, the remaining factors are:
$\left(x - \left(\frac{-9 + \sqrt{129}}{12}\right)\right)\left(x - \left(\frac{-9 - \sqrt{129}}{12}\right)\right)$

Solutions of polynomials

1. In the equation $x^2 + 3x - 10 = 0 = (x + 5)(x - 2)$ Find:

   $x_1 + x_2 = -3$ $\qquad$ $x_1 \cdot x_2 = -10$ $\qquad$ $-\dfrac{b}{a} = -3$ $\qquad$ $\dfrac{c}{a} = -10$

2. In the equation $2x^2 - 5x - 3 = 0 = (2x + 1)(x - 3)$ Find:

   $x_1 + x_2 = \dfrac{5}{2}$ $\qquad$ $x_1 \cdot x_2 = -\dfrac{3}{2}$ $\qquad$ $-\dfrac{b}{a} = \dfrac{5}{2}$ $\qquad$ $\dfrac{c}{a} = -\dfrac{3}{2}$

3. In the equation $6x^2 - 5x - 6 = 0 = (3x + 2)(2x - 3)$ Find:

   $x_1 + x_2 = \dfrac{5}{6}$ $\qquad$ $x_1 \cdot x_2 = -1$ $\qquad$ $-\dfrac{b}{a} = \dfrac{5}{6}$ $\qquad$ $\dfrac{c}{a} = -1$

4. In the equation $x^3 - 5x^2 - 2x + 24 = 0 = (x + 2)(x - 3)(x - 4)$ Find:

   $x_1 + x_2 + x_3 = 5$ $\qquad$ $x_1 \cdot x_2 \cdot x_3 = -24$ $\qquad$ $-\dfrac{b}{a} = 5$ $\qquad$ $-\dfrac{d}{a} = -24$

5. In the equation $12x^3 - 4x^2 - 3x + 1 = 0 = (2x + 1)(2x - 1)(3x - 1)$ Find:

   $x_1 + x_2 + x_3 = \dfrac{1}{3}$ $\qquad$ $x_1 \cdot x_2 \cdot x_3 = -\dfrac{1}{12}$ $\qquad$ $-\dfrac{b}{a} = \dfrac{1}{3}$ $\qquad$ $-\dfrac{d}{a} = -\dfrac{1}{12}$

6. In the equation $x^4 - 2x^3 - 3x^2 + 8x - 4 = 0 = (x - 1)^2(x - 2)(x + 2)$ Find:

   $x_1 + x_2 + x_3 + x_4 = 2$ $\quad$ $x_1 \cdot x_2 \cdot x_3 \cdot x_4 = -4$ $\quad$ $-\dfrac{b}{a} = 2$ $\quad$ $\dfrac{e}{a} = -4$

7. In the equation:
   $2x^5 + 13x^4 + 27x^3 + 17x^2 - 5x - 6 = 0 = (2x - 1)(x + 1)^2(x + 2)(x + 3)$ Find:

   $x_1 + x_2 + x_3 + x_4 + x_5 = -\dfrac{13}{2}$ $\quad$ $x_1 \cdot x_2 \cdot x_3 \cdot x_4 \cdot x_5 = 3$ $\quad$ $-\dfrac{b}{a} = -\dfrac{13}{2}$ $\quad$ $-\dfrac{f}{a} = 3$

8. Conclusion:

   In the polynomials of even degree:

   $x_1 + x_2 + x_3 + ... = -\dfrac{b}{a}$ $\qquad\qquad$ $x_1 \cdot x_2 \cdot x_3 \cdot ... = \dfrac{independent\ term}{a}$

   In the polynomials of odd degree:

   $x_1 + x_2 + x_3 + ... = -\dfrac{b}{a}$ $\qquad\qquad$ $x_1 \cdot x_2 \cdot x_3 \cdot ... = -\dfrac{independent\ term}{a}$

1.8. – BINOMIAL THEOREM

1. $0! = \underline{1}$ $1! = \underline{1}$ $2! = \underline{2}$ $3! = \underline{6}$ $n! = 1\cdot 2\cdot 3...(n-2)(n-1)n$

2. Definition: $^nC_k = \binom{n}{k} = \dfrac{n!}{(n-k)!k!}$

3. Evaluate: $\binom{6}{2} = \dfrac{6!}{4!2!} = 15$ $\binom{9}{6} = \dfrac{9!}{3!6!} = 84$

    $\binom{4}{0} = \dfrac{4!}{4!0!} = 1$ $\binom{7}{1} = \dfrac{7!}{6!1!} = 7$

4. $\dfrac{5!}{2!3!} = \dfrac{5!}{3!2!}$

5. $\dfrac{n!}{(n-k)!k!} = \dfrac{n!}{k!(n-k)}$

6. $(a+b)^2 = a^2 + 2ab + b^2$
7. $(a+b)^3 = a^3 + 3a^2b + 3ab^2 + b^3$
8. $(a-b)^4 = a^4 - 4a^3b + 6a^2b^2 - 4ab^3 + b^4$
9. $(a-b)^5 = a^5 - 5a^4b + 10a^3b^2 - 10a^2b^3 + 5ab^4 - b^5$
10. $(a+b)^6 = a^6 + 6a^5b + 15a^4b^2 + 20a^3b^3 + 15a^2b^4 + 6ab^5 + b^6$
11. Complete the Pascal Triangle:

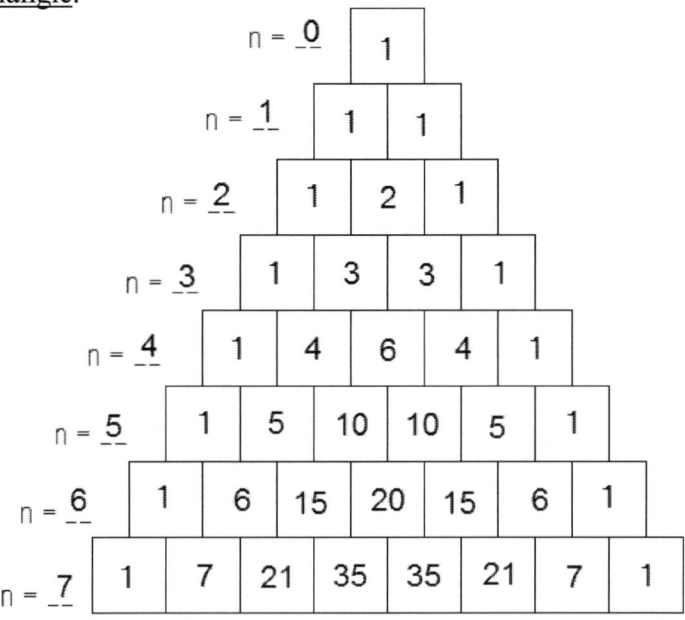

    n = 0: 1
    n = 1: 1 1
    n = 2: 1 2 1
    n = 3: 1 3 3 1
    n = 4: 1 4 6 4 1
    n = 5: 1 5 10 10 5 1
    n = 6: 1 6 15 20 15 6 1
    n = 7: 1 7 21 35 35 21 7 1

12. In conclusion: The coefficients of the binomial $(a+b)^n$ are given by the numbers in the pascal triangle. The same numbers can be obtained by the expression $^nC_k = \binom{n}{k} = \dfrac{n!}{(n-k)!k!}$

13. The binomial theorem can be summarized by…

14. $(2x+3)^5 = (2x)^5 + 5(2x)^4 3 + 10(2x)^3 3^2 + 10(2x)^2 3^3 + 5(2x)3^4 + 3^5 =$
    $= 32x^5 + 240x^4 + 720x^3 + 1080x^2 + 810x + 243$

15. $(2x+3y)^4 = (2x)^4 + 4(2x)^3 3y + 6(2x)^2(3y)^2 + 4(2x)(3y)^3 + (3y)^4 =$
$= 16x^4 + 96x^3 y + 216x^2 y^2 + 216xy^3 + 81y^4$

16. $(a+\frac{1}{a^2})^6 =$

$a^6 + 6a^5 \frac{1}{a^2} + 15a^4 \left(\frac{1}{a^2}\right)^2 + 20a^3 \left(\frac{1}{a^2}\right)^3 + 15a^2 \left(\frac{1}{a^2}\right)^4 + 6a\left(\frac{1}{a^2}\right)^5 + \left(\frac{1}{a^2}\right)^6 =$
$= a^6 + 6a^3 + 15 + 20a^{-3} + 15a^{-6} + 6a^{-9} + a^{-12}$

17. $(\frac{a}{b} - \frac{b}{a})^7$

$\left(\frac{a}{b}\right)^7 - 7\left(\frac{a}{b}\right)^6\left(\frac{b}{a}\right) + 15\left(\frac{a}{b}\right)^5\left(\frac{b}{a}\right)^2 - 21\left(\frac{a}{b}\right)^4\left(\frac{b}{a}\right)^3 + 21\left(\frac{a}{b}\right)^3\left(\frac{b}{a}\right)^4 - 15\left(\frac{a}{b}\right)^2\left(\frac{b}{a}\right)^5 + 7\left(\frac{a}{b}\right)\left(\frac{b}{a}\right)^6 - \left(\frac{b}{a}\right)^7$

$\left(\frac{a}{b}\right)^7 - 7\left(\frac{a}{b}\right)^6 + 15\left(\frac{a}{b}\right)^3 - 21\left(\frac{a}{b}\right) + 21\left(\frac{a}{b}\right)^{-1} - 15\left(\frac{a}{b}\right)^{-3} + 7\left(\frac{a}{b}\right)^{-5} - \left(\frac{a}{b}\right)^{-7}$

18. In each one of the questions 14 to 17 state the number of terms.
    14. <u>6</u>　　　15. <u>5</u>　　　16. <u>7</u>　　　17. <u>8</u>

19. Complete the sentence: a binomial of degree n has <u>n +1</u> terms.

20. The 8th term of the binomial

$(3a^2 + \frac{2}{a})^{13} : t_8 = \binom{13}{7}(3a^2)^6 \left(\frac{2}{a}\right)^7 = 160123392a^5$

21. The 7th term of the binomial

$(3x-5y)^{11} : t_7 = \binom{11}{6}(3x)^5 (5y)^6 = 1754156250 x^5 y^6$

22. The 5th term of the binomial $(3a^2 + y^4)^7 : t_5 = \binom{7}{4}(3a^2)^3 y^4 = 945a^6 y^4$

23. Given the binomial $(\frac{x^2}{2} - \frac{3}{x^3})^{10}$

   a. The first 3 terms: $t_1 = \frac{x^{20}}{2^{10}}, t_2 = \frac{-30x^{15}}{2^9}, t_3 = \frac{405x^{10}}{2^8}$, pattern: x^{20}, x^{15}, x^{10}

   b. The coefficient of x^5: $t_4 = \binom{10}{3} 2^{-7}(-3)^3 = \frac{405}{16}$

   c. The independent term: $t_5 = \binom{10}{4} 2^{-6}(-3)^4 = \frac{8505}{32}$

   d. The middle term: $t_6 = \binom{10}{5} 2^{-5}(-3)^5 x^{-5} = \frac{15309}{8}$, the middle term will exist if n is even (odd number of terms), it will be the (n + 1)/2 term.

407

24. 2 different binomials with first term $16x^{12}$: $(16x^{12}+b)^1$, $(4x^6+b)^2$

25. The constant term in the following cases (identify the pattern first):
    a. $(2x-\dfrac{3}{x^2})^9$; constant term $= -145152$
    b. $(2x+\dfrac{1}{x^2})^4$; No constant term

26. Given the binomial $(\dfrac{x}{2}-\dfrac{1}{x^2})^8$
    a. The first 3 terms and identify the pattern.
    $t_1 = \dfrac{x^8}{256}, t_2 = -\dfrac{x^5}{16}, t_3 = \dfrac{7x^2}{16}$, pattern: $x^8, x^5, x^2, x^{-1}...$
    b. No such term.
    c. No such term.
    d. The middle term. $t_5 = \dfrac{35x^{-4}}{8}$

27. Given $(\dfrac{a}{x}-\dfrac{x^2}{a})^8$ $t_5 = 70a^4 = 70, a = \pm 1$

28. $a = \dfrac{1}{2}$

29. Given the expression $(x-1)^{n+1}-(x-1)^n$.
    a. $(x-1)^n(x-2)$ $a = -2$

    b. The independent term of the expression as a function of n:
    $$\text{Independent Term}(n) = \begin{cases} 2 & n = odd \\ -2 & n = even \end{cases}$$

1.9. – SEQUENCES AND SERIES

Given The following sequences, write the first 3 terms and the term in the 20th position. If possible identify the pattern using text (follow example):

1. $a_n = 3n$ $a_1=3$ $a_2=6$ $a_3=9$ $a_{20}=60$ Pattern: __add 3__

2. $a_n = 3n+1$ $a_1=4$ $a_2=7$ $a_3=10$ $a_{20}=61$ Pattern: __add 3__

3. $a_n = 3n-5$ $a_1=-5$ $a_2=-2$ $a_3=1$ $a_{20}=55$ Pattern: __add 3__

4. $a_n = 2n+1$ $a_1=3$ $a_2=5$ $a_3=7$ $a_{20}=41$ Pattern: __add 2__

5. $a_n = 2n$ $a_1=2$ $a_2=4$ $a_3=6$ $a_{20}=40$ Pattern: __add 2__

6. $a_n = 2n-4$ $a_1=-2$ $a_2=0$ $a_3=2$ $a_{20}=36$ Pattern: __add 2__

7. $a_n = -4n$ $a_1=-4$ $a_2=-8$ $a_3=-12$ $a_{20}=-80$ Pattern: __add –4__

8. $a_n = -4n+10$ $a_1=6$ $a_2=2$ $a_3=-2$ $a_{20}=-70$ Pattern: __add –4__

9. $a_n = -4n-6$ $a_1=-10$ $a_2=-14$ $a_3=-18$ $a_{20}=-86$ Pattern: __add –4__

10. $a_n = \dfrac{n}{3}$ $a_1=\dfrac{1}{3}$ $a_2=\dfrac{2}{3}$ $a_3=1$ $a_{20}=\dfrac{20}{3}$ Pattern: __add $\dfrac{1}{3}$__

11. $a_n = \dfrac{n}{2}$ $a_1=\dfrac{1}{2}$ $a_2=1$ $a_3=\dfrac{3}{2}$ $a_{20}=10$ Pattern: __add $\dfrac{1}{2}$__

12. $a_n = \dfrac{2n}{5}+1$ $a_1=\dfrac{7}{5}$ $a_2=\dfrac{9}{5}$ $a_3=\dfrac{11}{5}$ $a_{20}=9$ Pattern: __add $\dfrac{2}{5}$__

13. $a_n = \dfrac{-3n}{7}+5$ $a_1=\dfrac{32}{7}$ $a_2=\dfrac{29}{7}$ $a_3=\dfrac{26}{7}$ $a_{20}=\dfrac{-25}{7}$ Pattern: __add $-\dfrac{3}{7}$__

14. $a_n = \dfrac{n}{9}-5$ $a_1=\dfrac{-44}{9}$ $a_2=\dfrac{-43}{9}$ $a_3=\dfrac{-42}{9}$ $a_{20}=\dfrac{-25}{9}$ Pattern: __add $\dfrac{1}{9}$__

15. $a_n = \dfrac{n}{10}-1$ $a_1=\dfrac{-9}{10}$ $a_2=\dfrac{-8}{10}$ $a_3=\dfrac{-7}{10}$ $a_{20}=1$ Pattern: __add $\dfrac{1}{10}$__

16. $a_n = \dfrac{3n}{4}+2$ $a_1=\dfrac{11}{4}$ $a_2=\dfrac{14}{4}$ $a_3=\dfrac{17}{4}$ $a_{20}=\dfrac{68}{4}$ Pattern: __add $\dfrac{3}{4}$__

17. $a_n = n^2$ $a_1=1$ $a_2=4$ $a_3=9$ $a_{20}=400$ Pattern: __different__

18. $a_n = n^3$ $a_1=1$ $a_2=8$ $a_3=27$ $a_{20}=8000$ Pattern: __different__

19. $a_n = 2^n$ $a_1=2$ $a_2=4$ $a_3=8$ $a_{20}=2^{20}$ Pattern: __multiply by 2__

20. $a_n = -2^n$ $a_1=-2$ $a_2=-4$ $a_3=-8$ $a_{20}=-2^{20}$ Pattern: __multiply by 2__

21. $a_n = 2^{-n}$ $a_1=\dfrac{1}{2}$ $a_2=\dfrac{1}{4}$ $a_3=\dfrac{1}{8}$ $a_{20}=\dfrac{1}{2^{20}}$ Pattern: __multiply by $\dfrac{1}{2}$__

22. $a_n = -2^{-n}$ $a_1 = -\dfrac{1}{2}$ $a_2 = -\dfrac{1}{4}$ $a_3 = -\dfrac{1}{8}$ $a_{20} = -\dfrac{1}{2^{20}}$ Pattern: __multiply by $\dfrac{1}{2}$__

23. $a_n = (-2)^n$ $a_1 = -2$ $a_2 = 4$ $a_3 = -8$ $a_{20} = 2^{20}$ Pattern: __multiply by -2__

24. $a_n = 2^{n-1}$ $a_1 = 1$ $a_2 = 2$ $a_3 = 4$ $a_{20} = 2^{19}$ Pattern: __multiply by 2__

25. $a_n = 2^{n+2}$ $a_1 = 8$ $a_2 = 16$ $a_3 = 32$ $a_{20} = 2^{22}$ Pattern: __multiply by 2__

26. $a_n = 3 \times 2^n$ $a_1 = 6$ $a_2 = 12$ $a_3 = 24$ $a_{20} = 3 \cdot 2^{20}$ Pattern: __multiply by 2__

27. $a_n = -5 \times 2^{n-1}$ $a_1 = -5$ $a_2 = -10$ $a_3 = -20$ $a_{20} = -5 \cdot 2^{19}$ Pattern: __multiply by 2__

28. $a_n = 5 \times 2^{1-n}$ $a_1 = 5$ $a_2 = \dfrac{5}{2}$ $a_3 = \dfrac{5}{4}$ $a_{20} = \dfrac{5}{2^{19}}$ Pattern: __multiply by $\dfrac{1}{2}$__

29. $a_n = (-3)^{2-n}$ $a_1 = -3$ $a_2 = 1$ $a_3 = -\dfrac{1}{3}$ $a_{20} = \dfrac{1}{3^{18}}$ Pattern: __multiply by $-\dfrac{1}{3}$__

30. $a_n = 2 \times (-3)^n$ $a_1 = -6$ $a_2 = 18$ $a_3 = -54$ $a_{20} = 2 \cdot 3^{20}$ Pattern: __multiply by -3__

31. $a_n = 2 \times (-5)^{n-1}$ $a_1 = 2$ $a_2 = -10$ $a_3 = 50$ $a_{20} = 2 \cdot (-5)^{19}$ Pattern: __multiply by -5__

32. $a_n = (-3)^{n+1}$ $a_1 = 9$ $a_2 = -27$ $a_3 = 81$ $a_{20} = (-3)^{21}$ Pattern: __multiply by -3__

33. $a_n = 1 + 5^{n-2}$ $a_1 = \dfrac{6}{5}$ $a_2 = 2$ $a_3 = 6$ $a_{20} = 1 + 5^{18}$ Pattern: __different__

34. $a_n = 3 \times 2^n$ $a_1 = 6$ $a_2 = 12$ $a_3 = 24$ $a_{20} = 3 \cdot 2^{20}$ Pattern: __multiply by 2__

35. $a_n = -5 \times 2^{n-1}$ $a_1 = -5$ $a_2 = -10$ $a_3 = -20$ $a_{20} = -5 \cdot 2^{19}$ Pattern: __multiply by 2__

36. $a_n = 2 \times 3^n$ $a_1 = 6$ $a_2 = 18$ $a_3 = 54$ $a_{20} = 2 \cdot 3^{20}$ Pattern: __multiply by 3__

37. $a_n = 5^{n-2} + 3$ $a_1 = \dfrac{16}{5}$ $a_2 = 4$ $a_3 = 8$ $a_{20} = 3 + 5^{-18}$ Pattern: __different__

38. $a_n = (-3)^n$ $a_1 = -3$ $a_2 = 9$ $a_3 = -27$ $a_{20} = 3^{20}$ Pattern: __multiply by -3__

39. $a_n = 2 \times (-3)^n$ $a_1 = -6$ $a_2 = 18$ $a_3 = -54$ $a_{20} = 2 \cdot 3^{20}$ Pattern: __multiply by -3__

40. $a_n = 2 \times (-5)^{n-1}$ $a_1 = 2$ $a_2 = -10$ $a_3 = 50$ $a_{20} = 2 \cdot (-5)^{19}$ Pattern: __multiply by -5__

41. $a_n = (-3)^{n+1}$ $a_1 = 9$ $a_2 = -27$ $a_3 = 81$ $a_{20} = -3^{21}$ Pattern: __multiply by -3__

42. $a_n = 1 + 5^{n-2}$ $a_1 = \dfrac{6}{5}$ $a_2 = 2$ $a_3 = 6$ $a_{20} = 1 + 5^{18}$ Pattern: __different__

43. The sequences in which the pattern is add/subtract a number are called
    __Arithmetic__

44. The sequences in which the pattern is multiply/divide (pay attention that dividing by a is the same as multiplying by the inverse) a number are called Geometric

45. $a_n = 2a_{n-1}$ $a_1=1$ $a_2=2$ $a_3=4$ $a_{20}=2^{19}$ Pattern: multiply by 2

46. $a_{n+2} = a_n + a_{n+1}$ $a_1=1$ $a_2=1$ $a_3=2$ $a_{20}=$___ Pattern: Each term is the sum of the previous 2 (Fibonacci)

47. In the last 2 sequences the terms are given in terms of the previous terms

48. (T/**F**) Arithmetic and Geometric sequences are most of the sequences that exist.

49. The terms in a convergent geometric sequence tend to a number, in a none–convergent sequence the terms tend to infinity or negative infinity (or alternate).

50. An example of a convergent geometric sequence: 200, 100, 50, 25…

51. An example of a divergent geometric sequence: 7, 21, 63, 189…

52. An example of a alternating convergent geometric sequence: 80, –40, 20, –10…

53. An example of a none alternating divergent geometric sequence: 2, 10, 50, 250…

54. A convergent geometric sequence is a sequence in which r is between –1 and 1

Given the following sequences:

a. For each one write: arithmetic, geometric convergent, geometric divergent or neither, the next term and their general term (in case they are geometric or arithmetic only).

b. Try to write the general term of the other sequences as well.

55. 1, 2, 3, 4, _5_
$a_n = 1 + (n-1)1$, Arithmetic
$a_n = n$

56. 1, 2, 4, 8, _16_
$a_n = 2^{n-1}$, Geometric

57. 1, 3, 5, 7, ___
$a_n = 1 + (n-1)2$, Arithmetic
$a_n = -1 + 2n$

58. 1, 3, 9, 27, _81_
$a_n = 3^{n-1}$, Geometric

59. 4, 6, 9, 13,5, _20.25_
$a_n = 4\left(\dfrac{3}{2}\right)^{n-1}$, Geometric

60. 4, 1, –2, –5, _–8_
$a_n = 4 + (n-1)(-3)$, Arithmetic
$a_n = 7 - 3n$

61. 5, 0, –4, –7, ___
Neither

62. 10, 1000, 100000, _10000000_
$a_n = 10 \cdot 100^{n-1}$, Geometric

63. 30, 10, $\dfrac{10}{3}$, $\dfrac{10}{9}$, $\dfrac{10}{27}$
$a_n = 30 \cdot \left(\dfrac{1}{3}\right)^{n-1}$, Geometric

64. 2, 10, 50, 250, __1250__
    $a_n = 2 \cdot 5^{n-1}$, Geometric

65. 2, 102, 202, 302, __402__
    $a_n = 2 + (n-1)100$, Arithmetic
    $a_n = -98 + 100n$

66. 1, −1, 1, −1, __1__
    $a_n = (-1)^{n-1}$, Geometric

67. −2, 2, −2, 2, __−2__
    $a_n = -2(-1)^{n-1}$, Geometric

68. 3, −6, 12, −24, __48__
    $a_n = 3(-2)^{n-1}$, Geometric

69. −8, 4, −2, 1, $\underline{\left(-\dfrac{1}{2}\right)}$
    $a_n = -8\left(-\dfrac{1}{2}\right)^{n-1}$, Geometric

70. 5, 1, $\dfrac{1}{5}$, $\dfrac{1}{25}$, $\dfrac{1}{125}$
    $a_n = 5\left(\dfrac{1}{5}\right)^{n-1}$, Geometric

71. 100, 10, 1, $\dfrac{1}{10}$, $\dfrac{1}{100}$
    $a_n = 100\left(\dfrac{1}{10}\right)^{n-1}$, Geometric

72. $\dfrac{3}{4}$, $\dfrac{3}{8}$, $\dfrac{3}{16}$, $\dfrac{3}{32}$
    $a_n = \dfrac{3}{4}\left(\dfrac{1}{2}\right)^{n-1}$, Geometric

73. 12, 11, 10, 9, __8__
    $a_n = 12 + (n-1)(-1)$, Arithmetic
    $a_n = 13 - n$

74. $\dfrac{4}{9}$, $\dfrac{5}{9}$, $\dfrac{6}{9}$, $\dfrac{6}{9}$
    $a_n = \dfrac{4}{9} + (n-1)\left(\dfrac{1}{9}\right)$, Arithmetic
    $a_n = -98 + 100n$

75. 9, 8, 6, 5, 3, 2, ___
    Neither

76. 5, 9, 13, __17__
    $a_n = 5 + (n-1)4$, Arithmetic
    $a_n = 1 + 4n$

77. 1, $\dfrac{3}{2}$, $\dfrac{9}{4}$, $\dfrac{27}{8}$, $\dfrac{81}{16}$
    $a_n = \left(\dfrac{3}{2}\right)^{n-1}$, Geometric

78. 5, $-\dfrac{5}{3}$, $\dfrac{5}{9}$, $-\dfrac{5}{27}$, $\dfrac{5}{81}$
    $a_n = 5\left(-\dfrac{1}{3}\right)^{n-1}$, Geometric

79. −1, −2, −3, __−4__
    $a_n = -1 + (n-1)(-1)$, Arithmetic
    $a_n = -n$

80. −2, 4, −8, __16__
    $a_n = -2(-2)^{n-1}$, Geometric

81. 70, 20, $\dfrac{40}{7}$, $\dfrac{80}{14}$
    $a_n = 70\left(\dfrac{2}{7}\right)^{n-1}$, Geometric

82. 100, 10, 1, $\dfrac{1}{10}$
    $a_n = 100\left(\dfrac{1}{10}\right)^{n-1}$, Geometric

83. $100, -10, 1, \dfrac{-1}{10}, \dfrac{1}{100}$

$a_n = 100\left(-\dfrac{1}{10}\right)^{n-1}$, Geometric

84. $3, 24, 192, \underline{1536}$

$a_n = 3 \cdot 8^{n-1}$, Geometric

85. $90, 9, \dfrac{9}{10}, \dfrac{9}{100}$

$a_n = 90 \cdot \left(\dfrac{1}{10}\right)^{n-1}$, Geometric

86. $\dfrac{3}{2}, \dfrac{4}{3}, \dfrac{5}{4}, \dfrac{6}{5}$

Neither, General term:

$a_n = \dfrac{2+n}{1+n}$ Numerator and denominator are arithmetic.

87. $\dfrac{40}{3}, \dfrac{20}{6}, \dfrac{10}{12}, \dfrac{5}{24}, \dfrac{5}{96}$

$a_n = \dfrac{40}{3}\left(\dfrac{1}{4}\right)^{n-1}$, Geometric

88. $\dfrac{2}{3}, -\dfrac{4}{9}, \dfrac{8}{27}, -\dfrac{16}{81}, \dfrac{32}{243}$

$a_n = \dfrac{2}{3}\left(-\dfrac{2}{3}\right)^{n-1}$, Geometric

89. $-\dfrac{1}{2}, -\dfrac{1}{4}, -\dfrac{1}{8}, -\dfrac{1}{16}, -\dfrac{1}{32}$

$a_n = -\dfrac{1}{2}\left(-\dfrac{1}{2}\right)^{n-1}$, Geometric

90. $\dfrac{1}{7}, -\dfrac{1}{14}, \dfrac{1}{21}, -\dfrac{1}{28}, \dfrac{1}{35}$

Neither, General term:

$a_n = \dfrac{1}{7n}(-1)^{n-1}$

91. $8, 5, 3, 0, \underline{} \ldots$

Neither

92. $3, \dfrac{3}{4}, \dfrac{3}{16}, \dfrac{3}{64}$

$a_n = 3\left(\dfrac{1}{4}\right)^{n-1}$, Geometric

93. $81, -9, 1, -\dfrac{1}{9}, \dfrac{1}{81}$

$a_n = 81\left(-\dfrac{1}{9}\right)^{n-1}$, Geometric

94. $2, -10, 50, -250$

$a_n = 2(-5)^{n-1}$, Geometric

In each one of the following sequences find the term indicated:

95. $1, 4, 7\ldots (a_{31})$ $a_{31} = 1 + 3 \cdot 30 = 91$

96. $-8, -5, -2\ldots (a_{37})$ $a_{37} = -8 + 3 \cdot 36 = 100$

97. $4, -8, 16\ldots (a_{15})$ $a_{15} = 4(-2)^{14}$

98. $32, -8, 2\ldots (a_{11})$ $a_{37} = 32\left(-\dfrac{1}{4}\right)^{10}$

99. $68, -34, 17\ldots (a_9)$ $a_9 = 68\left(-\dfrac{1}{2}\right)^8 = \dfrac{68}{256}$

413

100. 3, 14, 25... (a_9) $a_9 = 3 + 8 \cdot 11 = 91$

101. -4000, 1000, -250,... (a_7) $a_7 = -4000\left(-\dfrac{1}{4}\right)^6 = -\dfrac{125}{128}$

102. The 4th term of a geometric sequence is 3, the 6th term is $\dfrac{27}{4}$.

   a. The ratio of the sequence.
   $a_6 = a_4 r^2; \dfrac{27}{4} = 3r^2 \quad r = \pm\dfrac{3}{2}$

   b. Divergent |r| > 1
   c. a_1
   $a_4 = a_1 r^3; 3 = \pm\left(\dfrac{3}{2}\right)^3 a_1$
   $a_1 = \pm\left(\dfrac{8}{9}\right)$

   d. Find a_{12}
   $a_{12} = \left(\pm\left(\dfrac{8}{9}\right)\right)\left(\pm\left(\dfrac{3}{2}\right)^{11}\right) = \dfrac{3^9}{2^8}$

   e. Sum the first 15 terms.
   $S_{15} = \dfrac{\left(\pm\left(\dfrac{8}{9}\right)\right)\left(\left(\pm\left(\dfrac{3}{2}\right)\right)^{15} - 1\right)}{\pm\left(\dfrac{3}{2}\right) - 1}$

103. The 2nd term of a arithmetic sequence is –2, the 6th term is –4.

   a. Find the difference of the sequence. $a_6 = a_2 + 4d; -4 = -2 + 4d; d = -\dfrac{1}{2}$

   b. a_1 $a_2 = a_1 + d; -2 = a_1 - \dfrac{1}{2}; a_1 = -\dfrac{3}{2}$

   c. a_{12} $a_{12} = a_1 + 11d; a_{12} = -\dfrac{3}{2} - \dfrac{11}{2}; a_{12} = -\dfrac{16}{2} = -8$

   d. Sum of the first 50 terms. $S_{50} = \dfrac{50}{2}\left(\dfrac{-6}{2} - \dfrac{49}{2}\right) = \dfrac{-14700}{4}$

104. The 10th term of a geometric sequence is 5, the 14th term is $\dfrac{80}{81}$

   a. The ratio of the sequence. $a_{14} = a_{10} r^4; \dfrac{80}{81} = 5r^4; r = \pm\dfrac{2}{3}$

   b. a_1 $a_{10} = a_1 r^9; 5 = a_1\left(\pm\dfrac{2}{3}\right)^9; a_1 = 5\left(\pm\dfrac{3}{2}\right)^9$

   c. a_7 $a_{10} = a_7 r^3; 5 = a_7\left(\pm\dfrac{2}{3}\right)^3; a_7 = 5\left(\pm\dfrac{3}{2}\right)^3 = \pm\dfrac{135}{8}$

   d. Sum the first 10 terms. $S_{10} = \dfrac{\left(5\left(\pm\dfrac{3}{2}\right)^9\right)\left(\left(\pm\left(\dfrac{2}{3}\right)\right)^{10} - 1\right)}{\pm\left(\dfrac{2}{3}\right) - 1}$

105. The 7th term of a arithmetic sequence is 120, the 16th term is 201.
   a. The difference of the sequence. $a_{16} = a_7 + 9d; 201 = 120 + 9d; d = 9$
   b. Find a_1 $a_7 = a_1 + 6d$
   $a_1 = 66$

c. Find a_{12} $\quad a_{12} = a_1 + 11d = 66 + 99 = 165$

d. Sum the first 50 terms. $\quad S_{50} = \dfrac{50}{2}(132 + 49 \cdot 9) = 14325$

106. All the terms in a geometric sequence are positive. The first term is 7 and the 3rd term is 28.

$$a_3 = a_1 r^2$$

a. Find the common ratio. $\quad 28 = 7r^2 \quad$ Positive since all terms are positive.
$\quad r = +2$

b. Find the sum of the first 14 terms. $\quad S_{14} = \dfrac{7(2^{14} - 1)}{2 - 1} = 114681$

107. The fifth term of an arithmetic sequence is –20 and the twelfth term is –44.

$$a_{12} = a_5 + 7d$$

a. Find the common difference. $\quad d = -\dfrac{24}{7}$

$$a_5 = a_1 + 4d$$

b. Find the first term of the sequence. $\quad -20 = a_1 - \dfrac{24}{7} \cdot 4$

$$a_1 = -\dfrac{44}{7}$$

c. Calculate eighty–seventh term. $\quad a_{87} = a_1 + 86d = -\dfrac{44}{7} - 86 \cdot \dfrac{24}{7} = -\dfrac{2108}{7}$

d. Sum of the first 150 terms. $\quad S_{150} = \dfrac{150}{2}(-\dfrac{88}{7} - 149 \cdot \dfrac{24}{7}) = -\dfrac{274800}{7}$

108. Sum the following sequences:

a. $3 + 6 + 9 + 12 + \ldots + 69 =$

First find the number of terms using general term $69 = 3 + (n-1)3; n = 23$

Now, sum the 23 terms: $S_{23} = \dfrac{23}{2}(6 + 22 \cdot 3) = 828$

b. $6 + 14 + 22 + 30 + \ldots + 54 =$

First find the number of terms using general term $54 = 6 + (n-1)8; n = 7$

Now, sum the 7 terms: $S_7 = \dfrac{7}{2}(12 + 6 \cdot 8) = 210$

c. $5 + \dfrac{5}{3} + \dfrac{5}{9} + \ldots =$ $\quad S_\infty = \dfrac{a_1(r^\infty - 1)}{r - 1} = \dfrac{5\left(\left(\dfrac{1}{3}\right)^\infty - 1\right)}{\left(\dfrac{1}{3}\right) - 1} = \dfrac{-5}{\left(-\dfrac{2}{3}\right)} = \dfrac{15}{2}$

Attention that $\left(\dfrac{1}{3}\right)^\infty \approx 0$

415

d. $1 + 2 + 3 + 4 + \ldots + 158 =$

First find the number of terms using general term $158 = 1 + (n-1)1; n = 158$

Now, sum the 158 terms: $S_{158} = \dfrac{158}{2}(2 + 157 \cdot 1) = 12561$

e. $9 + 18 + 27 + 36 + \ldots + 900 =$

First find the number of terms using general term $900 = 9 + (n-1)9; n = 100$

Now, sum the 100 terms: $S_{100} = \dfrac{100}{2}(18 + 99 \cdot 9) = 45450$

f. $80 + 20 + 5 + \ldots \; S_\infty = \dfrac{a_1(r^\infty - 1)}{r - 1} = \dfrac{80\left(\left(\frac{1}{4}\right)^\infty - 1\right)}{\left(\frac{1}{4}\right) - 1} = \dfrac{-80}{\left(-\frac{3}{4}\right)} = \dfrac{320}{3}$

Attention that $\left(\dfrac{1}{4}\right)^\infty \approx 0$

109. Consider the arithmetic series $-6 + 1 + 8 + 15 + \ldots$ Find the least number of terms so that the sum of the series is greater than 10000.

$S_n = \dfrac{n}{2}(-12 + (n-1)7) = 10000$ So 55 terms are needed.

$n \approx 54.8$

110. In a theatre there are 20 seats in the first row, 23 in the 2nd, 26 in the 3rd etc. There are 40 rows in the theatre. Find the total number of seats available.

20, 23, 26 … Arithmetic

$S_{40} = \dfrac{40}{2}(40 + 39 \cdot 3) = 3140 \text{ seats}$

111. A ball bounces on the floor. It is released from a height of 160 cm. After the 1st bounce it reaches a height of 120 cm and 90 cm after the 2nd. If the patterns continue find:

   a. The height the ball will reach after the 6th bounce.

   160, 120, 90, … Geometric, $r = \dfrac{120}{160} = \dfrac{90}{120} = \dfrac{3}{4}$

   $a_n = 160 \cdot \left(\dfrac{3}{4}\right)^{n-1}; a_7 = 160 \cdot \left(\dfrac{3}{4}\right)^6 = \dfrac{3645}{128} \approx 28.5 cm$

   Attention that a_7 corresponds to height after the 6th bounce.

   b. The total distance the ball passed after a long period o time.

   $S_\infty = \dfrac{a_1(r^\infty - 1)}{r - 1} = \dfrac{160\left(\left(\frac{3}{4}\right)^\infty - 1\right)}{\left(\frac{3}{4}\right) - 1} = \dfrac{-160}{\left(-\frac{1}{4}\right)} = 640 cm$ $\left(\dfrac{3}{4}\right)^\infty \approx 0$

112. In a certain forest the current population of rabbits is 200 objects. It is known that the population increases by 20% every year.

   a. Find the population of rabbits after a year. $\frac{120}{100} \cdot 200 = 240 \text{ rabbits}$

   b. Find the population of rabbits after 2 years. $\frac{120}{100} \cdot 240 = 288 \text{ rabbits}$

   c. What kind of a sequence is it? State the expression for the population after n years. Geometric. $r = \frac{120}{100} = \frac{6}{5}$ $a_n = 200 \cdot \left(\frac{6}{5}\right)^{n-1}$

   d. Find the total number of rabbits after 10 years (assuming none has died).
   $a_{11} = 200 \cdot \left(\frac{6}{5}\right)^{10} \approx 1240 \text{ rabbits}$

113. In a research it was observed that the number of defective products produced by a machine per year decreases by 10% every year (due to technological improvements). In a certain year the machine made 300 products.

   a. Find the number of defective products produced a year later.
   $\frac{90}{100} \cdot 300 = 270 \text{ defective}$

   b. Find the number of defective products produced 2 years later.
   $\frac{90}{100} \cdot 270 = 243 \text{ defective}$

   c. What kind of a sequence is it? State the expression for the number of errors committed after n years.
   Geometric. $r = \frac{90}{100} = \frac{9}{10}$ $a_n = 300 \cdot \left(\frac{9}{10}\right)^{n-1}$

   d. Find the <u>total number</u> of bad products produced in the first 8 years.
   $S_8 = \frac{300\left(\left(\frac{9}{10}\right)^8 - 1\right)}{\left(\frac{9}{10}\right) - 1} \approx 1710 \text{ defective}$

114. In a certain company the pay scale follows a pattern of an arithmetic sequence (every year). This means:

   a. The salary increases by a certain % every year (True/**False**), explain.
   Since the amount of the increase is fixed, the percentage is not the same one every year. An increase by a percentage corresponds to a geometric sequence.

   b. The salary increases by a certain amount every year (**True**/False), explain
   Since the amount of the increase is fixed, the pattern is identical to an Arithmetic sequence.

417

COMPOUND INTEREST

1. 1200$ are put in account that gives 2% per year. Calculate the amount of money in the account after:
    a. 1 year.   Amount = $1200(1.02) = 1224$ $
    b. 2 years.   Amount = $1200(1.02)^2 = 1248.48$ $

2. To increase an amount A by 5% it should be multiplied by 1.05
3. To increase an amount A by 56% it should be multiplied by 1.56
4. To decrease an amount A by 5% it should be multiplied by 0.95
5. To increase an amount A by 15% it should be multiplied by 1.15
6. To decrease an amount A by 12% it should be multiplied by 0.88
7. To increase an amount A by 230% it should be multiplied by 3.3

8. 1000$ are put in account that takes 5% commission per year. Calculate the amount of money in the account after:
    a. 1 year.   Amount = $1000(0.95) = 950$ $
    b. 2 years.   Amount = $1000(0.95)^2 = 902.5$ $

9. 2000$ are being put in a deposit that pays 5% (per year).

    a. Fill the table:

Number of Years	Interest earned at the end of the year	Amount in deposit ($)
0		2000
1	$\frac{5}{100} \cdot 2000 = 100$	2100
2	$\frac{5}{100} \cdot 2100 = 105$	2205
3	$\frac{5}{100} \cdot 2205 = 110.25$	2315.25
4	$\frac{5}{100} \cdot 2315.25 = 115.7625$	2431.0125
5	$\frac{5}{100} \cdot 2431.0125 = 121.550625$	2552.563125

    b. Observe the numbers in the compound interest column: 2000, 2100, 2205… What kind of a sequence is that? Write its general term.
        Geometric sequence. $a_n = 2000(1.05)^{n-1}$

    c. $a_{21} = 2000(1.05)^{20} \approx 5310$ $ Attention that a_{21} corresponds to "after 20 years" as a_1 corresponds to "after 0 years".

    d. $a_n = 2000(1.05)^{n-1}$ means a_1 corresponds to "after 0 years" while writing
        $a_n = 2000(1.05)^n$ means a_1 corresponds to "after 1 year"

10. A loan of 1200$ is made at 12% per year compounded semiannually, over 5 years the debt will grow to:
    a. $1200(1 + 0.12)^5$
    b. **$1200(1 + 0.06)^{10}$**
    c. $1200(1 + 0.6)^{10}$
    d. $1200(1 + 0.06)^5$
    e. $1200(1 + 0.12)^{10}$

11. A loan of 23200$ is made at 8% per year compounded quarterly, over 6 years the debt will grow to:
    a. $23200(1 + 0.2)^{24}$
    b. $23200(1 + 0.08)^6$
    c. **$23200(1 + 0.02)^{24}$**
    d. $23200(1 + 0.08)^{24}$
    e. $23200(1 + 0.02)^6$

12. A loan of 20$ is made at 12% per year compounded monthly, over 8 years the debt will grow to:
    a. $20(1 + 0.12)^{80}$
    b. $20(1 + 0.01)^8$
    c. $20(1 + 0.012)^{96}$
    d. **$20(1 + 0.01)^{96}$**
    e. $20(1 + 0.06)^{12}$

13. A loan of X$ is made at 12% per year compounded every 4 months, over 5 years the debt will grow to:
    a. $X(1 + 0.12)^4$
    b. $X(1 + 0.4)^5$
    c. $X(1 + 0.4)^{15}$
    d. **$X(1 + 0.04)^{15}$**
    e. $X(1 + 0.012)^{15}$

14. A loan of X$ is made at i% per year compounded every m months, over n years the debt will grow to:

$$Debt = X(1+\frac{mi}{1200})^{\frac{12n}{m}}$$

15. Calculate the total amount owing after two years on a loan of 1500$ if the interest rate is 11% compounded

    a. Annually $Amount = 1500(1+\frac{11}{100})^2 \approx 1848\$$

    b. Semiannually $Amount = 1500(1+\frac{11}{200})^4 \approx 1858\$$

    c. Quarterly $Amount = 1500(1+\frac{11}{400})^8 \approx 1864\$$

    d. Monthly $Amount = 1500(1+\frac{11}{1200})^{24} \approx 1867\$$

16. How much will a client have to repay on a loan of 800$ after 2 years, if the 12% interest is compounded annually.

$$Amount = 800(1+\frac{12}{100})^2 = 1003.52\$$$

17. Find the compound interest **earned** by the deposit. Round to the nearest dollar. $3000 at 12% compounded semiannually for 10 years

$$AmountObtained = 3000(1+\frac{12}{200})^{20} \approx 9620\$$$

$$AmountEarned = 9620 - 3000 = 6620\$$$

18. How many years will it take to a 100$ to double assuming interest rate is 6%. Compounded semiannually.

$$200 = 100(1+\frac{6}{200})^{2n}$$

$$n \approx 11.7$$

So it will take 12 years.

19. How many years will it take to a X$ to triple assuming interest rate is 7%. Compounded quarterly

$$3X = X(1+\frac{7}{400})^{4n}$$

$$n \approx 15.8$$

So it will take 16 years.

20. Find the interest rate given to a certain person in case he made a deposit of 1000$ and obtained 1200$ after 3 years, compounded monthly.

$$1200 = 1000(1+\frac{i}{1200})^{36}$$

$$i \approx 6.09$$

21. Find the interest rate given to a certain person in case he made a deposit of 2500$ and obtained 3000$ after 10 years, compounded yearly.

$$3000 = 2500(1+\frac{i}{100})^{10}$$

$$i \approx 1.84$$

SIGMA NOTATION

1. The sum $\sum_{k=2}^{4} 2^k$ is equal to which of the following?
   a. $2^1 + 2^2 + 2^3 + 2^4$
   b. $2^2 + 2^4$
   c. $2^2 + 3^3 + 4^4$
   d. **$2^2 + 2^3 + 2^4$**

2. The sum $\dfrac{1}{4}\sum_{m=2}^{4} x_m$ is equal to which of the following?

   a. $\dfrac{1}{4}x_2 + \dfrac{1}{4}x_3 + \dfrac{1}{4}x_4$

   b. $\dfrac{1}{4}x_2 + x_3 + x_4$

   c. $\dfrac{1}{2}x_2 + \dfrac{1}{3}x_3 + \dfrac{1}{4}x_4$

   d. $\dfrac{1}{4}(2+3+4)$

3. The sum $\sum_{j=4}^{n} \dfrac{j}{j+1}$ is equal to which of the following?

   a. $\dfrac{1}{2} + \dfrac{3}{4} + \dfrac{5}{6} + \ldots + \dfrac{n}{n+1}$

   b. $\dfrac{1}{2} + \dfrac{2}{3} + \dfrac{3}{4} + \ldots + \dfrac{n}{n+1}$

   c. $\dfrac{4}{5} + \dfrac{5}{6} + \dfrac{6}{7} + \ldots + \dfrac{n}{n+1}$

   d. $\dfrac{4}{5} + \dfrac{5}{6} + \dfrac{6}{7} + \ldots + \dfrac{n+4}{n+5}$

4. Write out fully what is meant by

   a. $\sum_{i=4}^{i=6} 2i - 1 = 7 + 9 + 11$

   b. $\sum_{i=2}^{i=5} \dfrac{i}{i^2+1} = \dfrac{2}{5} + \dfrac{3}{10} + \dfrac{4}{17} + \dfrac{6}{26}$

   c. $\sum_{i=4}^{i=6} (2i-3)^2 = 25 + 49 + 81$

   d. $\sum_{k=3}^{i=7} (2^k + \sqrt{k}) = 8 + \sqrt{3} + 16 + \sqrt{4} + 32 + \sqrt{5} + 64 + \sqrt{6} + 128 + \sqrt{7}$

   e. $\sum_{i=1}^{i=4} (-1)^i \times 3^{2i} = -9 + 81 - 729 + 6561$

5. Write each series using sigma notation:

   a. $4 + 9 + 16 + 25 + 36 + 49 + 64 + 81 = \sum_{i=2}^{i=9} i^2$

   b. $5 + 9 + 13 + 17 + 21 + 25 + 29 + 33\ldots = \sum_{i=1}^{i=\infty} 5 + (i-1)4$

   c. $1 - \dfrac{1}{3} + \dfrac{1}{9} - \dfrac{1}{27} + \dfrac{1}{81} - \dfrac{1}{243} = \sum_{i=1}^{i=6} 1 \cdot \left(-\dfrac{1}{3}\right)^{i-1}$

6. $3 + 6 + 9 + 12 + \ldots$ for 28 terms $= \sum_{i=1}^{i=28} 3+(i-1)3 = \frac{28}{2}(6+27\cdot 3) = 1218$

7. $-3 + 6 - 12 + 24 - 48 + \ldots$ for 35 terms $= \sum_{i=1}^{i=35} -3\cdot(-2)^{i-1} = \frac{-3(2^{35}-1)}{-2-1}$

8. $8.3 + 8.1 + 7.9 + 7.7 + \ldots$ for 100 terms $=$
$\sum_{i=1}^{i=100} 8.3+(i-1)(-0.2) = \frac{100}{2}(16.6+99\cdot(-0.2)) = -160$

9. An infinite geometric series is given by $\sum_{i=1}^{\infty} 2(1-x)^i$

    a. Find the value of x for which the series has a finite sum
    $-1 < (1-x) < 1;\quad 2 > x > 0$

    b. When x = 0.5, find the minimum number of terms needed to give a sum which is greater than 1.9

    $\sum_{i=1}^{n} 2(0.5)^i = \frac{1(0.5^n-1)}{0.5-1} = 1.9$ So 5 terms are needed

    $n \approx 4.32$

422

1.10. – COMPLEX NUMBERS

1. A complex number z is a number of the form $a+bi$ where a, b are <u>real</u> numbers and $i=\sqrt{-1}$ or $i^2=-1$.
2. a is called the <u>real</u> part of z, $a=\text{Re}(z)$, and b is called the <u>imaginary</u> part of z, $b=\text{Im}(z)$
3. z is said to be purely imaginary if and only if $\text{Re}(z)=0$ and $\text{Im}(z)\neq 0$.
4. When $\text{Im}(z)=0$, the complex number z is real.
5. Practice:

   $i^2 = i \cdot i = -1$ $\qquad\qquad i^{65} = i^{64} i = i$

   $i^3 = i^2 \cdot i = -i$ $\qquad\qquad i^{176} = 1$

   $i^4 = i^3 \cdot i = 1$ $\qquad\qquad i^{26} = i^{24} i^2 = -1$

   $i^5 = i^4 \cdot i = i$ $\qquad\qquad i^{99} = i^{96} i^3 = -i$

   $i^6 = i^5 \cdot i = -1$ $\qquad\qquad i^{100} = 1$

   $i^7 = i^6 \cdot i = -i$ $\qquad\qquad i^{133} = i^{132} i = i$

   $i^8 = 1$ $\qquad\qquad\qquad\quad i^{88} = 1$

6. Solve in terms of i:

   a. $x^2+x+1=0 \quad x = -\dfrac{1}{2}+\dfrac{\sqrt{3}}{2}i, -\dfrac{1}{2}-\dfrac{\sqrt{3}}{2}i$

   b. $2x^2+3x+6=0 \quad x = -\dfrac{3}{4}+\dfrac{\sqrt{39}}{4}i, -\dfrac{3}{4}-\dfrac{\sqrt{39}}{4}i$

Operations on Complex Numbers

Let $z_1 = a+bi$ and $z_2 = c+di$. Then

7. $z_1 + z_2 = (a+c)+(b+d)i$
8. $z_1 - z_2 = (a-c)+(b-d)i$
9. $z_1 z_2 = (a+bi)(c+di) = ac-bd+(ad+bc)i$
10. $\dfrac{z_1}{z_2} = \left(\dfrac{a+bi}{c+di}\right)\cdot\left(\dfrac{c-di}{c-di}\right) = \dfrac{ac+bd+(bc-ad)i}{c^2+d^2} = \dfrac{ac+bd}{c^2+d^2}+\dfrac{(bc-ad)}{c^2+d^2}i$
11. $\dfrac{1}{i} = \dfrac{1i}{ii} = -i$
12. $\dfrac{i}{z_2} = \dfrac{i(c-di)}{(c+di)(c-di)} = \dfrac{ic+d}{c^2+d^2} = \dfrac{d}{c^2+d^2}+\dfrac{c}{c^2+d^2}i$
13. Given $z_1 = -4-3i$ and $z_2 = 1-5i$, find

    a. $z_1 + 2z_2 = -2-13i$
    b. $-3z_1 - 2z_2 = 10+19i$
    c. $z_2 - iz_1 = -4-6i$
    d. $z_1 z_2 = (-4-3i)(1-5i) = -19+17i$
    e. $z_1 z_2 z_2 = 66+112i$

    f. $\dfrac{z_1}{z_2} = \dfrac{11}{26}-\dfrac{23}{26}i$

    g. $\dfrac{z_2}{iz_1} = \dfrac{23}{25}-\dfrac{11}{25}i$

423

14. The conjugate number of $z = x + iy$ is $z^* = \underline{x - iy}$ it can also be written as $\bar{z}$
15. Given that $z = x + iy$, answer:

   a. $\frac{1}{2}(z + z^*) = x$

   b. $\frac{1}{2i}(z - z^*) = y$

   c. $zz^* = x^2 + y^2$

   d. z is real if and only if $\bar{z} = z$ (**True**/False)

   e. $\bar{\bar{z}} = z$ (**True**/False)

   f. $z\bar{z} = (x+iy)(x-iy) = x^2 + y^2 = |z|^2$

   Let $z_1 = x + iy$ and $z_2 = a + ib$ be two complex numbers. Answer:

   g. $\overline{z_1 + z_2} = \bar{z_1} + \bar{z_2}$ (**True**/False)
   $x + a - i(y+b) = x - iy + b - ib$

   h. $\overline{z_1 z_2} = \bar{z_1} \cdot \bar{z_2}$ (**True**/False)
   $\overline{(x+iy)(a+ib)} = (x-iy)(a-ib)$
   $xa - yb - i(ya + xb) = xa - yb - i(ya + xb)$

   i. $\overline{\left(\frac{z_1}{z_2}\right)} = \frac{\bar{z_1}}{\bar{z_2}}$ $(z_2 \neq 0)$ (**True**/False)

16. Find the square roots of the complex numbers (using algebra, later we will see how it can be done using DeMoivre's Theorem)

   a. $\sqrt{5-12i} = x + iy$; $5 - 12i = x^2 - y^2 + 2xyi$, equalling imaginary and real parts:
   $5 = x^2 - y^2$ $\quad (-3, 2), (3, -2)$
   $-12 = 2xy$
   So roots of $5 - 12i$ are $z = -3 + 2i, 3 - 2i$

   b. $\sqrt{24+10i} = x + iy$; $24 + 10i = x^2 - y^2 + 2xyi$ equalling imaginary and real parts:
   $24 = x^2 - y^2$ $\quad (5, 1), (-5, -1)$
   $10 = 2xy$
   So roots of $24 + 10i$ are $z = 5 + i, -5 - i$

Geometrical Representation of a Complex Number

1. Complex numbers can be represented graphically on a diagram called **Argand** diagram. The real part is represented as the x coordinate and the imaginary part as the y coordinate.
2. On this plane, a number represented by points on x axis will be **Real**

   For example: Sketch the number 4 on the Argand diagram:

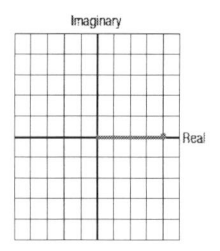

3. Imaginary numbers are represented by points on the **y axis**.

   For example: Sketch the number 2i on the Argand diagram:

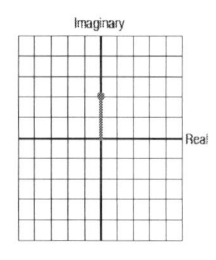

4. The number 0 is represented by the origin **O**.
5. z_1, z_2, z_3 are represented on the Argand diagram. Write down the 3 numbers:

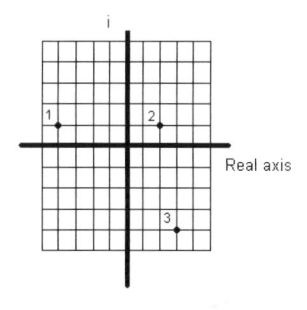

   $z_1 = -4 + i$

   $z_2 = 2 + i$

   $z_3 = 3 - 4i$

Polar Form of a Complex Number

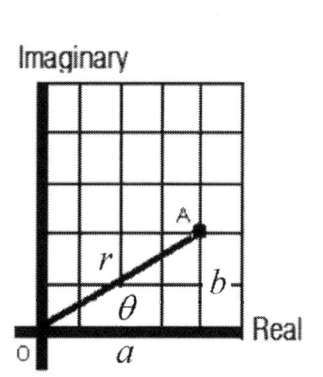

A complex number $z = a + bi$ can be represented by a vector $\overrightarrow{OA}$ as shown in Figure:

1. The length of the vector $\overrightarrow{OA}$, $r = |\overrightarrow{OA}|$, is called the **magnitude** (or **modulus**) of the complex number z, and it is denoted by $|z|$.
2. The angle between the vector $\overrightarrow{OA}$ and the positive real axis is defined to be the **argument** (or amplitude) of z and is denoted by $\arg(z)$ or $\text{amp}(z)$.
3. Show a, b, r and θ on the diagram.
4. In this case $r = \sqrt{20}$ and $\arg(z) = \arctan\left(\dfrac{2}{4}\right) \approx 26.6° \approx 0.464 rad$
5. $A \text{rg}(z)$ has an infinite number of possible values: $\arg(z) = \theta + 2k\pi, k \in Z$.

425

6. In this case possible values of arg(z) are: $26.6° \approx 0.464 rad; 386.6° \approx 3.61 rad$ etc.
7. If arg(z) lies in the interval $-\pi < \theta \leq \pi$, we call this value the ***principal value***.
8. In this case: $z = a + ib =$ **$4 + 2i \approx 2cis(0.464)$**
9. In general $z = a + ib = \sqrt{a^2 + b^2} Cis\left(\arctan\left(\frac{b}{a}\right)\right) = \sqrt{a^2 + b^2} e^{i\left(\arctan\left(\frac{b}{a}\right)\right)}$
10. Sketch the following complex numbers on an Argand diagram and write them in the polar form:

    a. $2 = 2Cis(0) = 2e^{i0}$

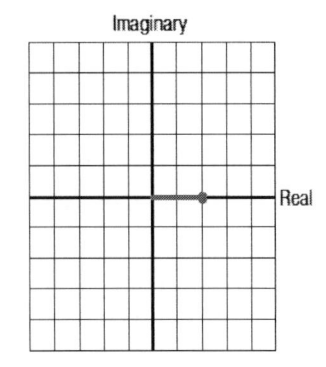

    b. $-5 = 5Cis(\pi) = 5e^{i\pi}$

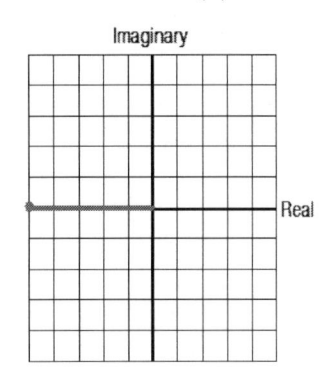

    c. $i = 1Cis(\frac{\pi}{2}) = 1e^{i\frac{\pi}{2}}$

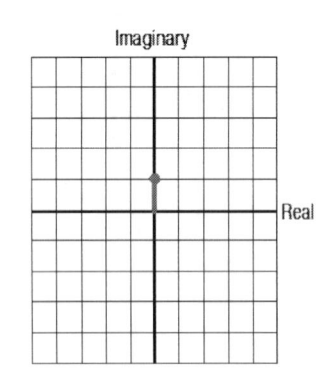

    d. $-3i = 3Cis(\frac{3\pi}{2}) = 3e^{i\frac{3\pi}{2}}$

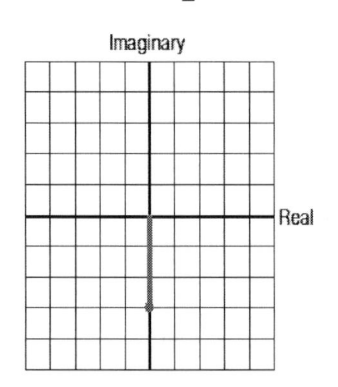

    e. $1 + i = \sqrt{2}Cis(\frac{\pi}{4}) = \sqrt{2}e^{i\frac{\pi}{4}}$

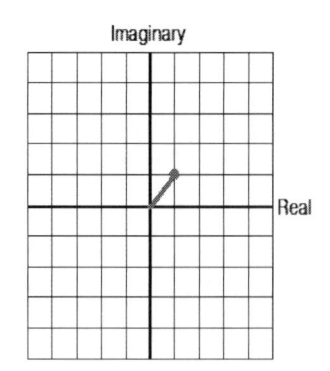

    f. $-5 + 12i \approx 13Cis(1.97) = 13e^{1.97i}$

    (exceeds graph in 2nd quadrant)

g. $3 - 3\sqrt{3}i = 6Cis(-\frac{\pi}{3}) = 6e^{-i\frac{\pi}{3}}$

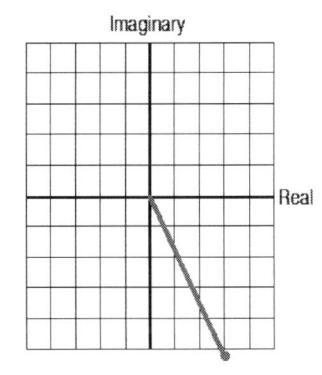

h. $-1 - i = \sqrt{2}Cis(-\frac{3\pi}{4}) = \sqrt{2}e^{-i\frac{3\pi}{4}}$

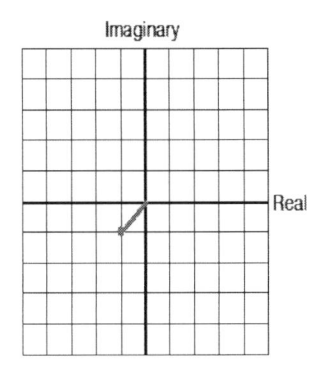

i. $-1 + \sqrt{2}i$

$\approx \sqrt{3}Cis(2.19) = \sqrt{3}e^{i2.19}$

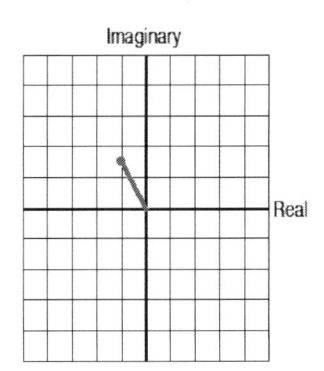

j. $-\sqrt{2}i = \sqrt{2}Cis(\frac{3\pi}{2}) = \sqrt{2}e^{i\frac{3\pi}{2}}$

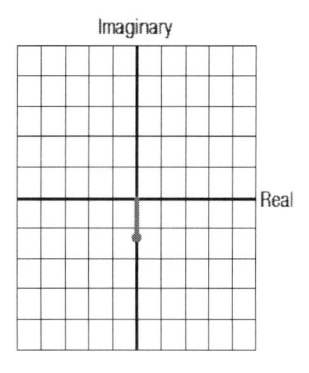

k. $(1 - \sqrt{3}i)^2$

$= -2 - 2\sqrt{3}i = 4Cis(-\frac{2\pi}{3}) = 4e^{-i\frac{2\pi}{3}}$

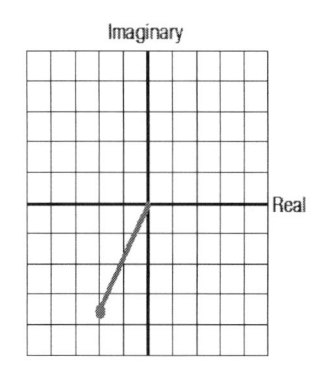

l. $\dfrac{1}{i-2} = \dfrac{1(-i-2)}{(i-2)(-i-2)} = \dfrac{-i-2}{5} = \dfrac{-2}{5} - \dfrac{1}{5}i$

$\approx \dfrac{\sqrt{5}}{5}Cis(-2.68) = \dfrac{\sqrt{5}}{5}e^{-i2.68}$

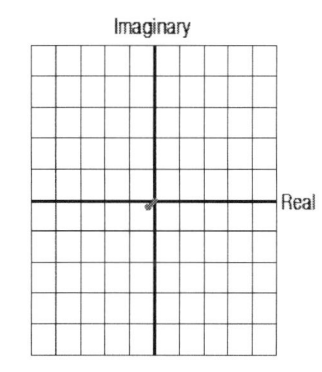

427

Use of Polar Form in Multiplication and Division

Let $z_1 = r_1(\cos\theta_1 + i\sin\theta_1)$, $z_2 = r_2(\cos\theta_2 + i\sin\theta_2)$

15. $|\bar{z}| = |z|$ (**True**/False) Magnitudes are identical:

16. $\arg\bar{z} = -\arg z$ (**True**/False) Angle is negative and same size:

17. Let $z_1 = 1+\sqrt{3}i$ and $z_2 = 3-\sqrt{3}i$. Express z_1 and z_2 in polar form

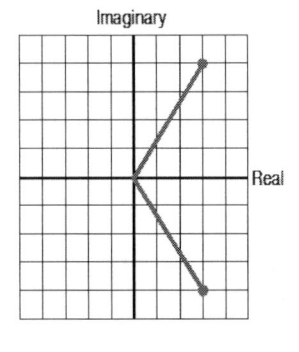

$$z_1 = 2Cis(\frac{\pi}{3}) = 2e^{i\frac{\pi}{3}} \;; z_2 = \sqrt{12}Cis(-\frac{\pi}{6}) = \sqrt{12}e^{-i\frac{\pi}{6}}$$

Find and write in all forms:

a. $z_1 z_2 = 6+2\sqrt{3}i = 4\sqrt{3}Cis(\frac{\pi}{6}) = 4\sqrt{3}e^{\frac{\pi}{6}i}$

b. $z_1(z_2)^2 = 24 = 24Cis(0) = 24e^{0i}$

c. $iz_2 = \sqrt{3}+3i = 2\sqrt{3}Cis(\frac{\pi}{3}) = 2\sqrt{3}e^{\frac{\pi}{3}i}$

d. $\dfrac{z_1}{z_2} = \dfrac{\sqrt{3}}{3}i = \dfrac{\sqrt{3}}{3}Cis(\frac{\pi}{2}) = \dfrac{\sqrt{3}}{3}e^{\frac{\pi}{2}i}$

e. $\dfrac{z_1}{iz_2} = \dfrac{\sqrt{3}}{3} = \dfrac{\sqrt{3}}{3}Cis(0) = \dfrac{\sqrt{3}}{3}e^{0i}$

f. $\left(\dfrac{iz_2}{z_1}\right)^2 = 3 = 3Cis(0) = 3e^{0i}$

DeMoivre's Theorem and nth Roots of a Complex Number

18. Calculate:

a. $(1+i)^{10} = \left(\sqrt{2}Cis(\frac{\pi}{4})\right)^{10} = 32Cis(\frac{5\pi}{2}) = 32i$

b. $(1-\sqrt{3}i)^4 = \left(2Cis(-\frac{\pi}{3})\right)^4 = 16Cis(-\frac{4\pi}{3}) = 16Cis(\frac{2\pi}{3}) = -8+8\sqrt{3}i$

c. $i^{13} = \left(1Cis(\frac{\pi}{2})\right)^{13} = 1Cis(\frac{13\pi}{2}) = 1Cis(\frac{\pi}{2}) = i$

d. $(-2-\sqrt{3}i)^6 \approx \left(\sqrt{7}Cis(-2.43)\right)^6 = 343Cis(-14.6) = 343Cis(-2.00) = -143-180\sqrt{3}i$

e. $\sqrt{(2-\sqrt{3}i)} = (2-2\sqrt{3}i)^{\frac{1}{2}} = \left(4Cis(-\frac{\pi}{3}+2\pi k)\right)^{\frac{1}{2}} = 2Cis(-\frac{\pi}{6}+\pi k) = \sqrt{3}-i, -\sqrt{3}+i$

f. $i^{\frac{1}{3}} = \left(1Cis(\frac{\pi}{2}+2\pi k)\right)^{\frac{1}{3}} = 1Cis(\frac{\pi}{6}+\frac{2\pi k}{3}) = -1, \frac{\sqrt{3}}{2} \pm \frac{1}{2}i$

g. $(1-\sqrt{3}i)^{\frac{3}{2}} = \left(2Cis(-\frac{\pi}{3}+2\pi k)\right)^{\frac{3}{2}} = \sqrt{8}Cis(-\frac{\pi}{2}+3\pi k) = \pm\sqrt{8}i$

19. Solve and sketch the solutions on the Argand diagram:

   a. $z^2 = -1$

   $z = i, -i$

   b. $z^3 = -1$

   $z = (-1)^{\frac{1}{3}} = (1Cis(\pi + 2\pi k))^{\frac{1}{3}} = 1Cis(\frac{\pi + 2\pi k}{3})$

   $k = 0 \quad z = Cis(\frac{\pi}{3}) = \frac{1}{2} + \frac{\sqrt{3}}{2}i$

   $k = 1 \quad z = Cis(\frac{3\pi}{3}) = -1$

   $k = 2 \quad z = Cis(\frac{5\pi}{3}) = \frac{1}{2} - \frac{\sqrt{3}}{2}i$

   For k = 3 etc. Solutions repeat.

   c. $z^4 = -1$

   $z = (-1)^{\frac{1}{4}} = (1Cis(\pi + 2\pi k))^{\frac{1}{4}} = 1Cis(\frac{\pi + 2\pi k}{4})$

   $k = 0 \quad z = Cis(\frac{\pi}{4}) = \frac{1}{\sqrt{2}} + \frac{1}{\sqrt{2}}i$

   $k = 1 \quad z = Cis(\frac{3\pi}{4}) = -\frac{1}{\sqrt{2}} + \frac{1}{\sqrt{2}}i$

   $k = 2 \quad z = Cis(\frac{5\pi}{4}) = -\frac{1}{\sqrt{2}} - \frac{1}{\sqrt{2}}i$

   $k = 3 \quad z = Cis(\frac{7\pi}{4}) = \frac{1}{\sqrt{2}} - \frac{1}{\sqrt{2}}i$

   For k = 4 etc. Solutions repeat.

   d. $z^5 = -1$

   $z = (-1)^{\frac{1}{5}} = (1Cis(\pi + 2\pi k))^{\frac{1}{5}} = 1Cis(\frac{\pi + 2\pi k}{5})$

   $k = 0 \quad z = Cis(\frac{\pi}{5}); k = 1 \quad z = Cis(\frac{3\pi}{5})$

   $k = 2 \quad z = Cis(\frac{5\pi}{5}) = -1$

   $k = 3 \quad z = Cis(\frac{7\pi}{5}); k = 4 \quad z = Cis(\frac{9\pi}{5})$

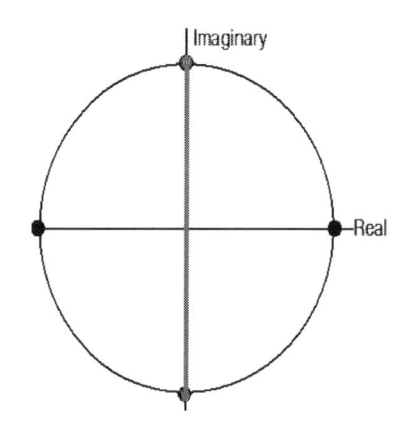

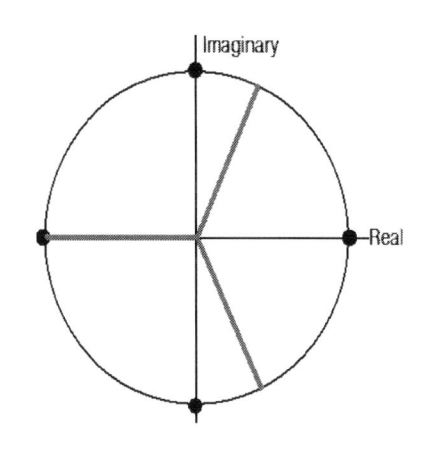

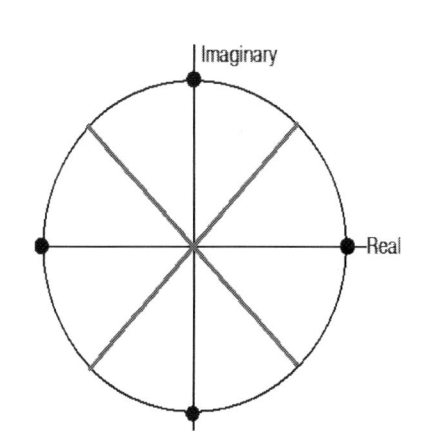

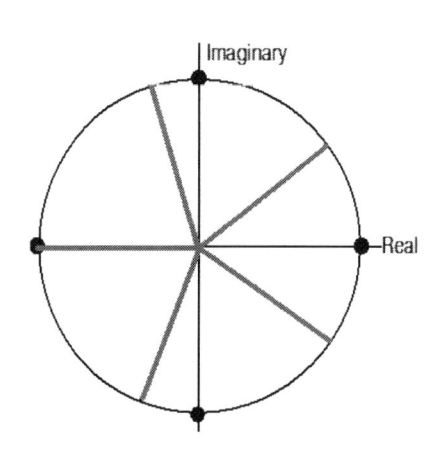

   For k = 5 etc. Solutions repeat.

429

Solve the equations:

e. $z^4 = 16$

$$z = (16)^{\frac{1}{4}} = (16Cis(0+2\pi k))^{\frac{1}{4}} = 2Cis(\frac{0+2\pi k}{4})$$

$k = 0 \quad z = 2Cis(0) = 2$

$k = 1 \quad z = 2Cis(\frac{\pi}{2}) = 2i$

$k = 2 \quad z = 2Cis(\pi) = -2$

$k = 3 \quad z = 2Cis(\frac{3\pi}{2}) = -2i$

f. $z^3 = 8i$

$$z = (8i)^{\frac{1}{3}} = \left(8Cis(\frac{\pi}{2}+2\pi k)\right)^{\frac{1}{3}} = 2Cis(\frac{\pi+4\pi k}{6})$$

$k = 0 \quad z = 2Cis(\frac{\pi}{6}) = \sqrt{3}+i$

$k = 1 \quad z = 2Cis(\frac{5\pi}{6}) = -\sqrt{3}+i$

$k = 2 \quad z = Cis(\frac{3\pi}{2}) = -2i$

g. Find the 4th roots of $1 + \sqrt{3}i$

$$z = (1+\sqrt{3}i)^{\frac{1}{4}} = \left(2Cis(\frac{\pi}{3}+2\pi k)\right)^{\frac{1}{4}} = \sqrt[4]{2}Cis(\frac{\pi+6\pi k}{12})$$

$k = 0 \quad z = \sqrt[4]{2}Cis(\frac{\pi}{12})$

$k = 1 \quad z = \sqrt[4]{2}Cis(\frac{7\pi}{12})$

$k = 2 \quad z = \sqrt[4]{2}Cis(\frac{13\pi}{12})$

$k = 3 \quad z = \sqrt[4]{2}Cis(\frac{19\pi}{12})$

h. Find the square roots of $6 + 8i$

$$z = (6+8i)^{\frac{1}{2}} \approx (10Cis(0.464+2\pi k))^{\frac{1}{2}} = \sqrt{10}Cis(\frac{0.464+2\pi k}{2})$$

$k = 0 \quad z \approx \sqrt{10}Cis(0.232)$

$k = 1 \quad z \approx \sqrt{10}Cis(3.37)$

Polynomials with Real Coefficients

If $f(x) = a_n x^n + a_{n-1} x^{n-1} + \cdots + a_1 x + a_0 = 0$ is a polynomial with **Real** coefficients and degree $n \geq 2$ then if $z = a + bi$ is a root of this polynomial, then $\overline{z} = a - bi$ is also a root.

20. Given that a certain polynomial equation with real coefficients of the 3rd degree has -2 and $3 - 2i$ as solutions.
    a. The 3rd solution is: $\underline{3 + 2i}$
    b. The equation, factorized is: $\underline{(z + 2)(z - (3 - 2i))(z - (3 + 2i)) = 0}$
    c. Expand the equation written in b. $\underline{z^3 - 4z^2 + z + 26 = 0}$

21. Given that a certain polynomial equation with real coefficients of the 3rd degree has 2 and $1 + i$ as solutions.
    a. The 3rd solution is: $\underline{1 - i}$
    d. The equation, factorized is: $\underline{(z - 2)(z - (1 + i))(z - (1 - i)) = 0}$
    e. Expand the equation written in b. $\underline{z^3 - 4z^2 + 6z - 4 = 0}$

22. Given that a certain polynomial equation with real coefficients of the 3rd degree has -5, and i as solutions.
    a. The 3rd solution is: $\underline{-i}$
    b. The equation, factorized is: $\underline{(z + 2)(z - i)(z + i)) = 0}$
    c. Expand the equation written in b. $\underline{z^3 - 2z^2 + z - 2 = 0}$

23. Solve the equation $x^2 + 2x + 2 = 0$. Write the factorized equation.
    $x = -1 + i, -1 - i$ $\qquad (x - (-1 + i))(x - (-1 - i)) = 0$

24. Solve the equation $x^2 - 2x + 5 = 0$. Write the factorized equation.
    $x = 1 + 2i, 1 - 2i$ $\qquad (x - (1 + 2i))(x - (1 - 2i)) = 0$

25. Solve the equation $(z^2 + 2)(x + 5) = 0$. Write the factorized equation.
    $x = -5, \sqrt{2}i, -\sqrt{2}i$ $\qquad (x + 5)(x - \sqrt{2}i)(x + \sqrt{2}i) = 0$

26. Solve the equation $x^3 - 3x^2 + 7x - 5 = 0$. Write the factorized equation.
    $x = 1, 1 + 2i, 1 - 2i$ $\qquad (x - 1)(x - (1 - \sqrt{2}i))(x - (1 + \sqrt{2}i)) = 0$

27. Solve the equation $x^3 - 6x^2 + 13x - 10 = 0$. Write the factorized equation.
    $x = 2, 2 + i, 2 - i$ $\qquad (x - 2)(x - (2 - i))(x - (2 + i)) = 0$

28. Given that $3 + i$ a solution to the equation $x^3 - 5x^2 + 4x + 10 = 0$, find the other solutions $x = 3 - i, -1$

29. Given that i is a solution of the equation $x^4 - 2x^3 + 6x^2 - 2x + 5 = 0$, find all the other solutions. $x = -i, 1 + 2i, 1 - 2i$

30. **Remainder theorem:** If a polynomial is **divided** by a first degree Polynomial of the form $(x - a)$ then the remainder is **P(a)** In case the Remainder obtained is **zero** we say that the divisor is a **factor of the polynomial**

31. Find the remainder on dividing $x^{10} - x^9 + 2x + 1$ by $x - i$

    $R = P(i) = i^{10} - i^9 + 2i + 1 = i$

32. Find the remainder on dividing $x^3 - x + 1$ by $x - i - 1$.

    $R = P(1 + i) = (1+i)^3 - (1 + i) + 1 = i - 2$

431

1.11. – MATHEMATICAL INDUCTION

1. Mathematical induction is used to prove mathematical conjectures. After a conjecture is proved we take it as a **theorem** and use it in other proofs.
2. The process takes place in <u>4</u> steps.

Prove by induction:

1. $1 + 2 + 3 + \ldots + n = \dfrac{n(n+1)}{2}$

   Step 1: <u>Check</u> that the statement is true for $n = 1$.
   $1 = 1$ yes

   Step 2: <u>Assume</u> that the statement is true for $n = k$.
   $1 + 2 + 3 + \ldots + k = \dfrac{k(k+1)}{2}$

   Step 3: <u>Check</u> that the statement is true for $n = k + 1$ using the assumption that it is true for $n = k$.

   $1 + 2 + 3 + \ldots + k + k + 1 = \dfrac{(k+1)(k+2)}{2}$

   $\dfrac{k(k+1)}{2} + k + 1 = \dfrac{(k+1)(k+2)}{2}$ using the assumption

   $\dfrac{k(k+1) + 2(k+1)}{2} = \dfrac{(k+1)(k+2)}{2}$ taking common factor $k + 1$ on LHS

   $\dfrac{(k+1)(k+2)}{2} = \dfrac{(k+1)(k+2)}{2}$ Proved

   Step 4: <u>Conclude</u> that since the conjecture is true for $n = 1$ and since it is true for $n = k + 1$ assuming it is true for $n = k$ it therefore must be true always.

2. $1^2 + 2^2 + 3^2 + \ldots + n^2 = \dfrac{n(n+1)(2n+1)}{6}$

   Step 1: <u>Check</u> that the statement is true for $n = 1$.
   $1 = 1$ yes

   Step 2: <u>Assume</u> that the statement is true for $n = k$.
   $1^2 + 2^2 + 3^2 + \ldots + k^2 = \dfrac{k(k+1)(2k+1)}{6}$

   Step 3: <u>Check</u> that the statement is true for $n = k + 1$ using the assumption that it is true for $n = k$.

   $1^2 + 2^2 + 3^2 + \ldots + k^2 + (k+1)^2 = \dfrac{(k+1)(k+2)(2(k+1)+1)}{6}$

   $\dfrac{k(k+1)(2k+1)}{6} + (k+1)^2 = \dfrac{(k+1)(k+2)(2(k+1)+1)}{6}$ using the assumption

   $\dfrac{k(k+1)(2k+1) + 6(k+1)^2}{6} = \dfrac{(k+1)(k+2)(2k+3)}{6}$ common factor $k + 1$ on LHS

432

$$\frac{(k+1)(2k^2+k+6k+6)}{6} = \frac{(k+1)(k+2)(2k+3)}{6}$$

$$\frac{(k+1)(k+2)(2k+3)}{6} = \frac{(k+1)(k+2)(2k+3)}{6} \text{ Proved}$$

Step 4: Conclude that since the conjecture is true for $n = 1$ and since it is true for $n = k + 1$ assuming it is true for $n = k$ it therefore must be true always.

3. $1 \cdot 2 + 2 \cdot 3 + 3 \cdot 4 + \ldots + n(n+1) = \dfrac{n(n+1)(n+2)}{3}$

Step 1: Check that the statement is true for $n = 1$.
$2 = 2$ yes

Step 2: Assume that the statement is true for $n = k$.
$$1 \cdot 2 + 2 \cdot 3 + 3 \cdot 4 + \ldots + k(k+1) = \frac{k(k+1)(k+2)}{3}$$

Step 3: Check that the statement is true for $n = k + 1$ using the assumption that it is true for n = k.

$$1 \cdot 2 + 2 \cdot 3 + 3 \cdot 4 + \ldots + k(k+1) + (k+1)(k+2) = \frac{(k+1)(k+2)(k+3)}{3}$$

$$\frac{k(k+1)(k+2)}{3} + (k+1)(k+2) = \frac{(k+1)(k+2)(k+3)}{3} \text{ using the assumption}$$

$$\frac{k(k+1)(k+2) + 3(k+1)(k+2)}{3} = \frac{(k+1)(k+2)(k+3)}{3}$$

$$\frac{(k+1)(k+2)(k+3)}{3} = \frac{(k+1)(k+2)(k+3)}{3} \text{ common factor } (k+1)(k+2) \text{ on LHS}$$

Step 4: Conclude that since the conjecture is true for $n = 1$ and since it is true for $n = k + 1$ assuming it is true for $n = k$ it therefore must be true always.

4. $n^3 + 1 > n^2$

Step 1: Check that the statement is true for $n = 1$.
$2 > 1$ yes

Step 2: Assume that the statement is true for $n = k$.
$k^3 + 1 > k^2$

Step 3: Check that the statement is true for $n = k + 1$ using the assumption that it is true for n = k.

$(k+1)^3 + 1 > (k+1)^2$

$k^3 + 3k^2 + 3k + 1 + 1 > k^2 + 2k + 1$, Eliminating $k^3 + 1$ from LHS and k^2 from RHS

$3k^2 + 3k + 1 > 2k + 1$, k is Natural, $3k > 2k$ and proof is complete.

Step 4: Conclude that since the conjecture is true for $n = 1$ and since it is true for $n = k + 1$ assuming it is true for $n = k$ it therefore must be true always.

5. $5^n - 3^n$ is divisible by 2 for any positive n.

Step 1: Check that the statement is true for $n = 1$.
   $5 - 3 = 2$, yes

Step 2: Assume that the statement is true for $n = k$.
   $5^k - 3^k = 2w, w \in \mathbb{Z}$

Step 3: Check that the statement is true for $n = k + 1$ using the assumption that it is true for n = k.

$5^{k+1} - 3^{k+1} =$

$5 \cdot 5^k - 3 \cdot 3^k =$

$2 \cdot 5^k + 3 \cdot 5^k - 3 \cdot 3^k =$

$2 \cdot 5^k + 3(5^k - 3^k) =$

$2 \cdot 5^k + 3(2w) =$

$2 \cdot (5^k + 3w)$

Step 4: Conclude that since the conjecture is true for $n = 1$ and since it is true for $n = k + 1$ assuming it is true for $n = k$ it therefore must be true always.

6. $7^n - 2^n$ is divisible by 5 for any positive n.

Step 1: Check that the statement is true for $n = 1$.
   $7 - 2 = 5$, yes

Step 2: Assume that the statement is true for $n = k$.
   $7^k - 2^k = 5w, w \in \mathbb{Z}$

Step 3: Check that the statement is true for $n = k + 1$ using the assumption that it is true for n = k.

$7^{k+1} - 2^{k+1} =$

$7 \cdot 7^k - 2 \cdot 2^k =$

$5 \cdot 7^k + 2 \cdot 7^k - 2 \cdot 2^k =$

$5 \cdot 7^k + 2(7^k - 2^k) =$

$5 \cdot 7^k + 2(5w) =$

$5 \cdot (7^k + 2w)$

Step 4: Conclude that since the conjecture is true for $n = 1$ and since it is true for $n = k + 1$ assuming it is true for $n = k$ it therefore must be true always.

CHAPTER 2 – FUNCTIONS

2.1. – INTRODUCTION TO FUNCTION

1. Write the definition of a function in your own words:
   A one to one or one to many relation between "things" (variables),

2. Write 2 examples of relations that <u>are</u> functions:
   Day of the week → color of my shirt
   Word → First letter of word
   Time → Temperature

3. Draw a sketch of the functions that describe those relations. Can you write the mathematical expression to describe them?
   Only the last example is "mathematical enough" to find an expression:
   $f(t) = A\sin(kt) + B$ (this will be discussed later). Approximate sketch can be:

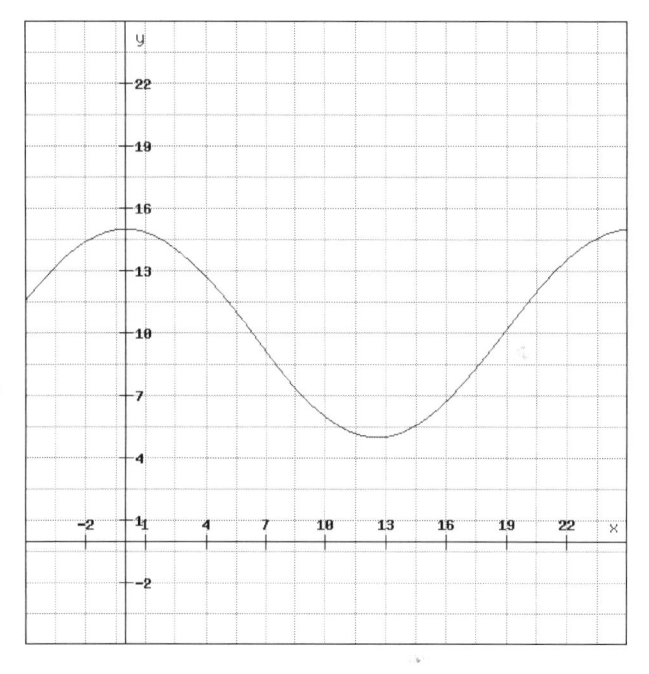

4. Write 2 examples of relations that <u>are not</u> functions:
   Name of person → Personal information   (one to many)
   Name of City → Names of habitants   (one to many)

5. Which one of the following graphs cannot represent function:

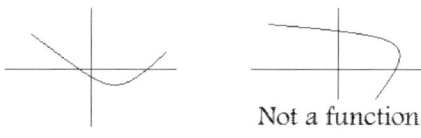

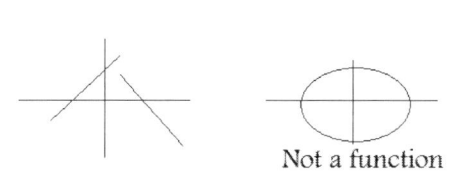

   Not a function

   Not a function

6. Draw an example of a curve that is not a function:

435

7. Draw an example of a curve that is a function:

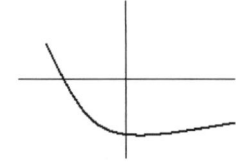

8. The domain of a function is the: <u>The set of allowed values of the independent variable ("what x can be")</u>
9. The Range of a function is the: <u>The set of allowed values of the dependent variable ("what y can be")</u>

10. Given the Height – age curve for a human.

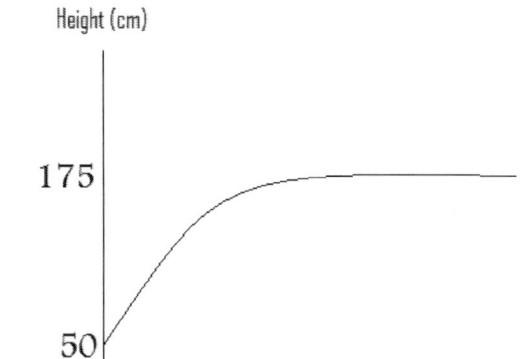

    a. Sketch an approximate graph:

    b. In your sketch Height(0) = <u>50cm</u>, it is the height of <u>a new born baby</u>

    c. In your sketch Height(t) = 100cm. Then t is: <u>2 years</u>

    d. State its domain: <u>$Age \ni [0, 80]$</u>

    e. State its range: <u>$Height \ni [50, 175]$</u>

11. Out of the following relations circle the ones that are functions:
    a. **<u>Person's name → Person's age</u>**
    b. **<u>City → Number of habitants</u>**
    c. City → Names of habitants
    d. **<u>Family → Home Address</u>**
    e. **<u>Satellite's name → Position of satellite</u>**
    f. **<u>Time → Position of object</u>**
    g. **<u>One → One</u>**
    h. One → Many
    i. **<u>Many → One</u>**

12. Given the following function that describes the temperature in C° as a function of time (t = 0 corresponds to midnight):

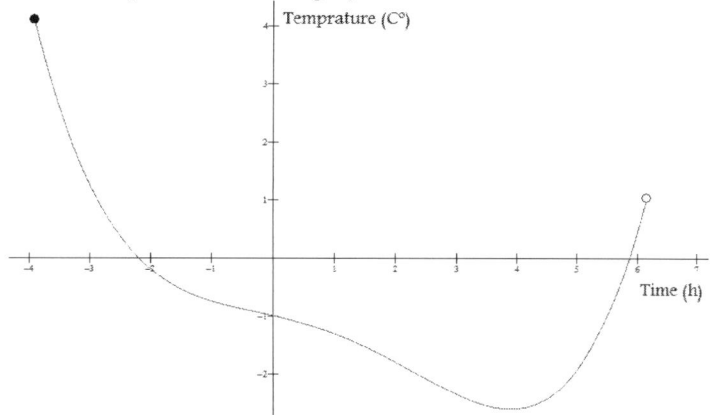

a. f(0) = −1
b. f(2) = −1.5 = f(5)
c. f(7) = out of domain
d. f(x) = 3, x = −3.7
e. f(x) = 0, x = −2.2, 5.8
f. f(x) = −2, x = 2.8, 4.7

g. State its domain: $x \in [-4, 6)$
h. State its range: $f(x) \in [-3, 4]$
i. Is this function one to one? One to many? Explain. No, Many to one

13. Given the function the describes the change in the benefit (%) given by a certain stock:

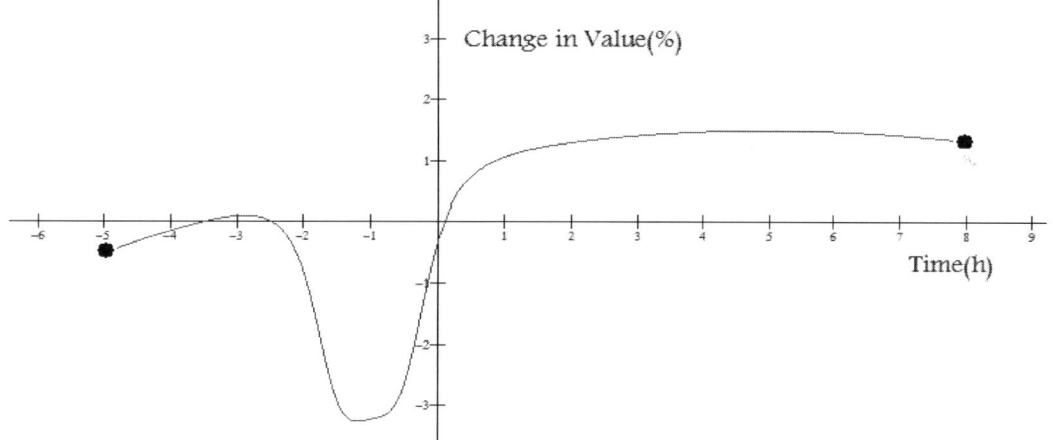

a. f(x) = 0, x = −2.5, −3.5, 0.2
b. f(0) = −0.5 = f(−2.2)
c. f(−5) = −0.6
d. f(1) = 1
e. f(−2) = −1 = f(−0.2)
f. f(3) = 1.4
g. f(x) = −2, x = −0.5, −1.5
h. Is f(−2) < 0 ? yes
i. Is f(−2) < f(−1) ? No
j. State its domain: $x \in [-5, 8]$

k. State its range: $f(x) \in [-3.2, 1.5]$
l. Where is the function increasing $x \in (-5, -3) \cup (-1.2, 5)$
m. Where is the function decreasing? $x \in (-3, -1.2) \cup (5, 8)$
n. Where is the function stationary? $x = -3, -1.2$
o. Is function one to one? One to many? No, it's many to one

437

14. Given the following function:

    Domain   Range
    -3 → -6
    -1 → -2
     0 →   0
     3 →   6
     5 → 10

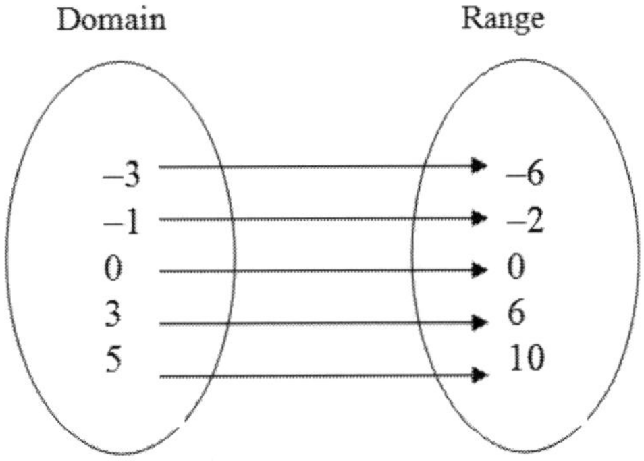

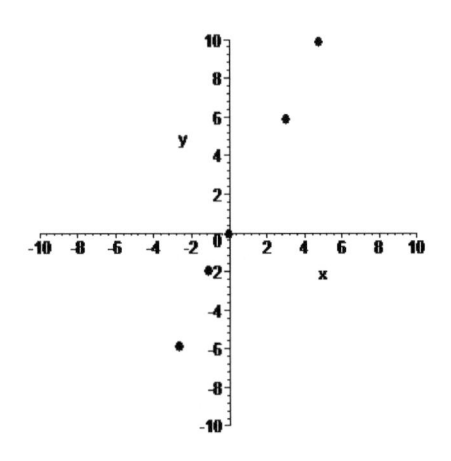

    a. The allowed values for the independent variable: $\{-3,-1,0,3,5\}$
    b. The allowed values for the dependent variable: $\{-6,-2,0,6,10\}$
    c. Sketch the function on the graph.
    d. A mathematical expression to express this function: $f(x) = 2x$

15. Given the following function:

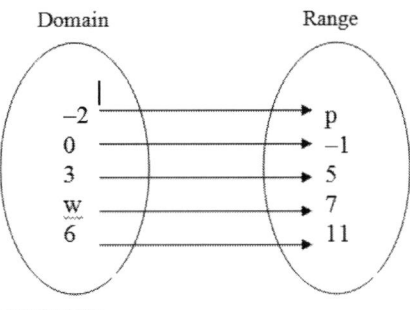

    a. A mathematical expression to express this function:
       $f(x) = 2x - 1$
    b. Find p. Find w. $p = -5$, $w = 4$

    Domain   Range
    -2 → p
     0 → -1
     3 → 5
     w → 7
     6 → 11

16. Use the graph of the gasoline consumption of a truck to answer:

    a. $f(0) = 0$
    b. $f(50) = 12.5$
    c. $f(5) = 2.5$
    d. For what values of x is $f(x) = 12$, $x = 33, 84, 116$ 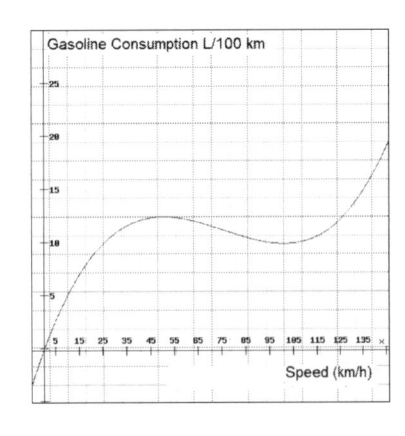
    e. Is $f(60) > f(70)$? Yes
    f. For what values of x is $f(x) > 15$? , $x > 135$
    g. At what positive speed is the consumption of gasoline minimum? 100
    h. Where is the function increasing? $x \in (0,50) \cup (100,145)$
    i. Where is the function decreasing? $x \in (50,100)$ $x \in (50,100)$
    j. Where is the function stationary? $x = 100$

17. Functions can be represented using: <u>Graphs</u> or <u>Expressions</u>

18. The following graph describes the concentration of a drug injected into the blood as a function of the time (in minutes) since the injection. $t=0$ corresponds to the time of injection.
    a. What is the concentration of the drug 4 hours after the injection? <u>4c</u>
    b. During what period of time is the concentration increasing? <u>$t \in (0, 2.2)$</u>
    c. After how long is the concentration maximum? <u>2.2 min</u>
    d. When is the concentration greater than 5c? <u>$t \in (1.2, 3.6)$</u>
    e. When is the concentration smaller than 2c? <u>$t \in (0,1) \cup (5.5, 16)$</u>
    f. State the domain and range of the function.
       Domain: <u>$t \in [0, 16]$</u>
       Range: <u>$f(t) \in [0, 11]$</u>

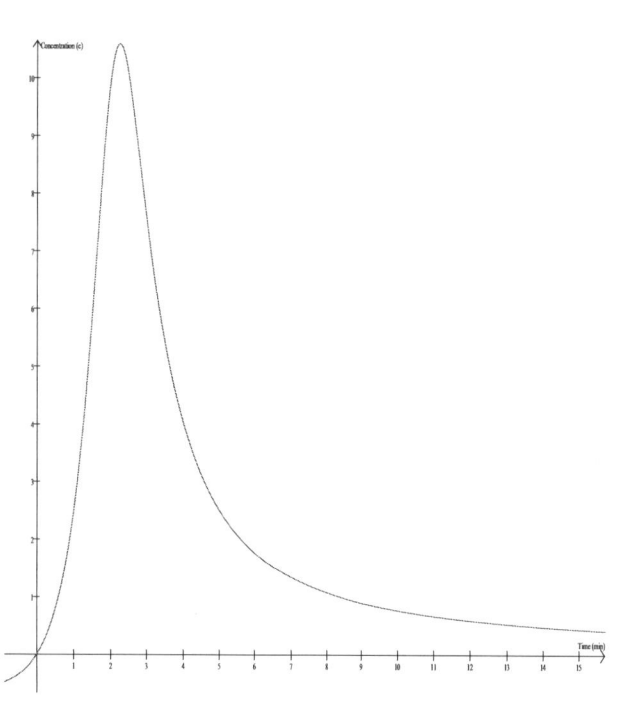

19. The graph below shows the temperature in C° on a particular day as a function of time since midnight.

    a. What was the temperature at 4:00 a.m.? <u>0.1</u>
    b. When was the temperature 0 degrees? <u>3:55 am, 7:55 am, 11:50 am</u>
    c. When was the temperature below freezing? (less than 0 degrees) <u>$t \in (11, 3:55) \cup (11:50, 16)$</u>
    d. When was the temperature increasing? <u>$t \in (11, 5:05) \cup (7:55, 10:35)$</u>
    e. State the domain and range of the function.
       Domain: <u>$t \in [11pm, 16pm]$</u> Range: <u>$f(t) \in [-5.5, 0.5]$</u>

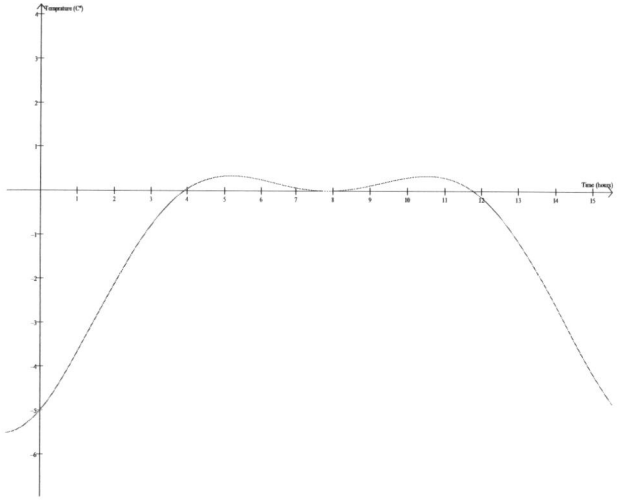

439

2.2. – LINEAR FUNCTIONS

1. Given the function: f(x) = –5

X	–5	–4	–3	–2	–1	0	1	2	3	4	5
f(x)	–5	–5	–5	–5	–5	–5	–5	–5	–5	–5	–5

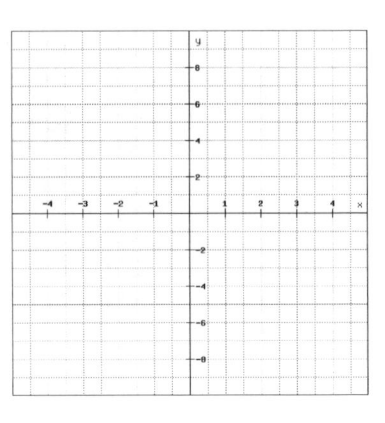

- Sketch the points of the chart on a graph (use a ruler).
- State the domain of the function: $x \in R$
- State the y intercept (sketched on the graph: (0, –5)
- State the x intercept: None
- The function is increasing on the interval: Never
- The function is decreasing on the interval: Never
- Sketch the function of the graph used for the points initially drawn
- State the range of the function: $f(x) \in \{-5\}$

2. Given the function: f(x) = x + 3

x	–5	–4	–3	–2	–1	0	1	2	3	4	5
f(x)	–2	–1	0	1	2	3	4	5	6	7	8

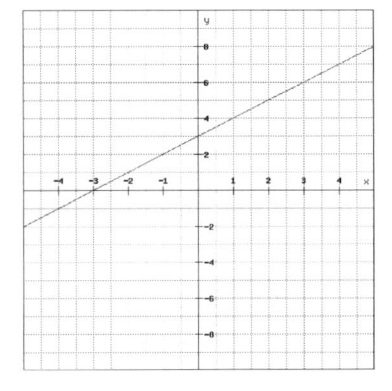

- Sketch the points of the chart on a graph (use a ruler).
- State the domain of the function: $x \in R$
- State the y intercept (sketched on the graph: (0, 3)
- State the x intercept: (–3,0)
- The function is increasing on the interval: $x \in R$
- The function is decreasing on the interval: Never
- Sketch the function of the graph used for the points initially drawn
- State the range of the function: $f(x) \in R$

3. Given the function: f(x) = –2x – 5

x	–5	–4	–3	–2	–1	0	1	2	3	4	5
f(x)	5	3	1	–1	–3	–5	–7	–9	–11	–13	–15

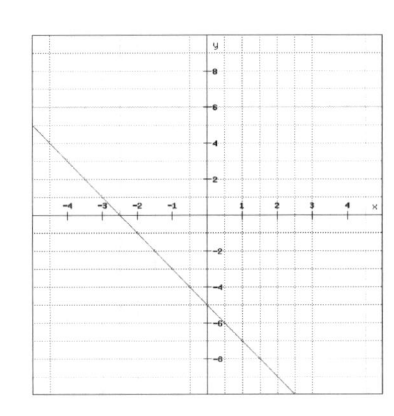

- Sketch the points of the chart on a graph (use a ruler).
- State the domain of the function: $x \in R$
- State the y intercept (sketched on the graph: (0, –5)
- State the x intercept: $\left(\dfrac{5}{2}, 0\right)$
- The function is increasing on the interval: Never
- The function is decreasing on the interval: $x \in R$
- Sketch the function of the graph used for the points initially drawn
- State the range of the function: $f(x) \in R$

4. Given the function: f(x) = 4x – 3

x	–5	–4	–3	–2	–1	0	1	2	3	4	5
f(x)	–23	–19	–15	–11	–7	–3	1	5	9	13	17

- Sketch the points of the chart on a graph (use a ruler).
- State the domain of the function: $x \in R$
- State the y intercept (sketched on the graph: (0, –3)
- State the x intercept: $\left(\dfrac{3}{4}, 0\right)$
- The function is increasing on the interval: $x \in R$
- The function is decreasing on the interval: Never
- Sketch the function of the graph used for the points initially drawn
- State the range of the function: $f(x) \in R$

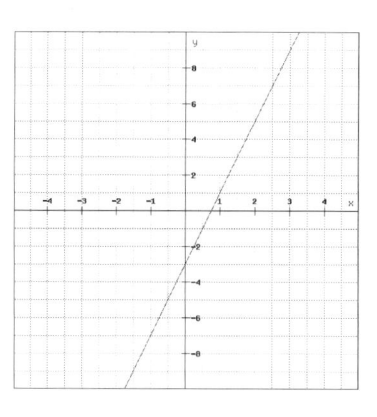

5. Given below are the equations for five different lines. Match the function with its graph.

Function	On the graph
f(x) = 20 + 2x	**B**
g(x) = 4x + 20	**C**
s(x) = –30 + 2x	**A**
a(x) = 60 – x	**D**
b(x) = – 2x + 60	**E**

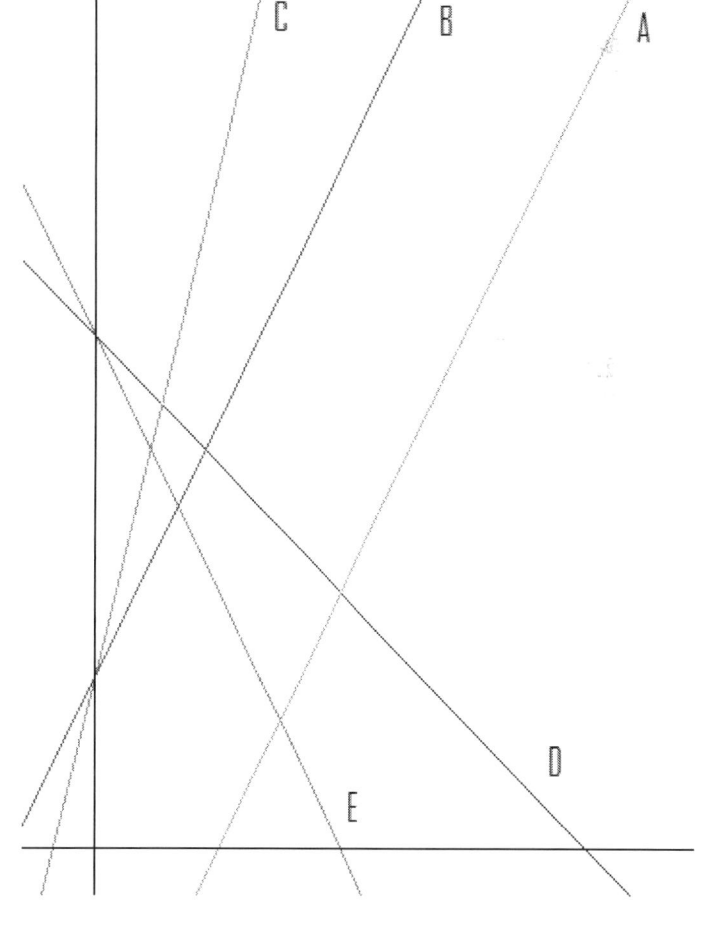

6. The general functions that describes a straight line is f(x) = mx + b
7. We know a function is a straight line because x is to the power of 1 only

441

8. The y–intercept (also called vertical intercept), tells us where the line crosses the y axis. The corresponding point is of the form (0 , b).
9. The x–intercept (also called horizontal intercept), tells us where the line crosses the x axis. The corresponding point is of the form (p , 0).
10. If m > 0, the line increases left to right. If m < 0 the line decreases left to right.
11. In case the line is horizontal m is zero and the line is of the form f(x) = b
12. The larger the value of m is, the steeper the graph of the line is.

13. Given the graph, write, the slope (m), b and the equation of the line:

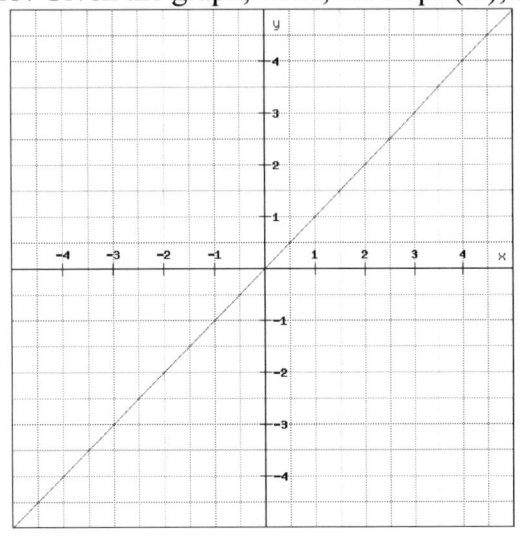

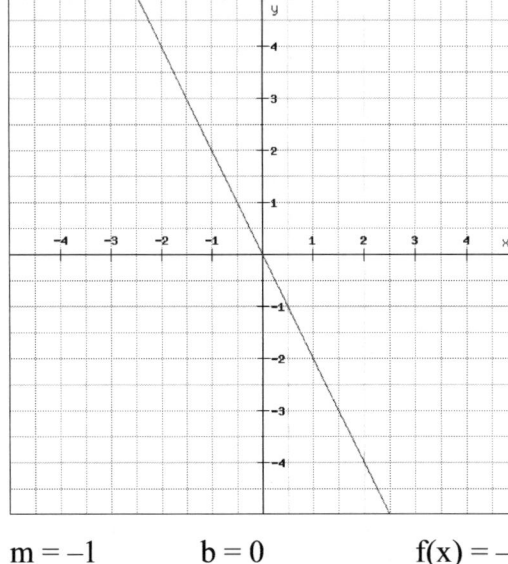

m = 1   b = 0   f(x) = x   m = –1   b = 0   f(x) = –x

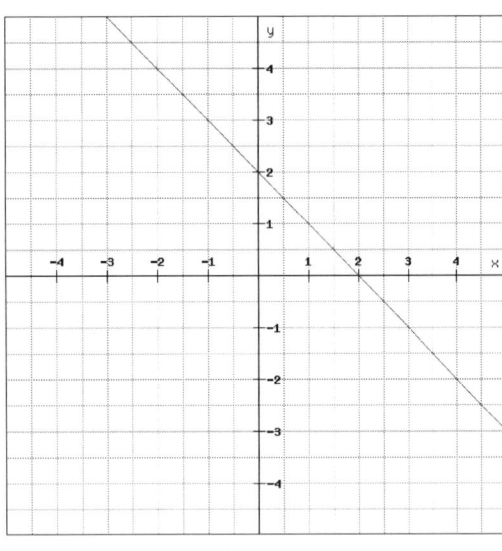

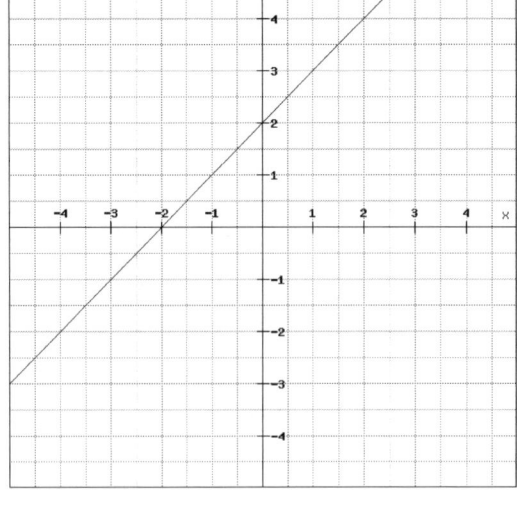

m = –1   b = 2   f(x) = –x + 2   m = 1   b = 2   f(x) = x + 2

442

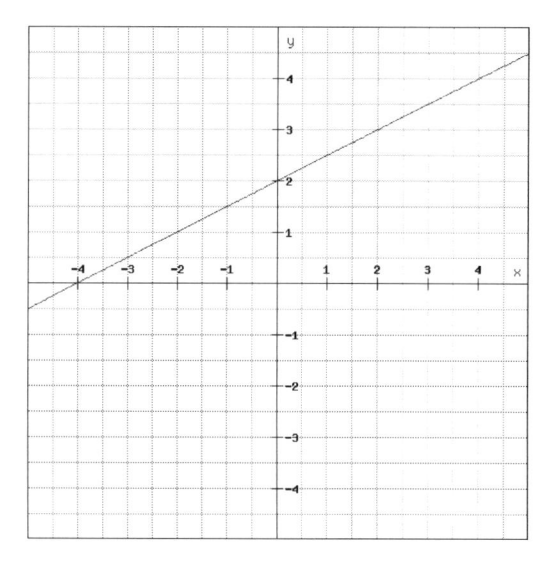

$m = \dfrac{1}{2}$ $b = 2$ $f(x) = \dfrac{1}{2}x + 2$

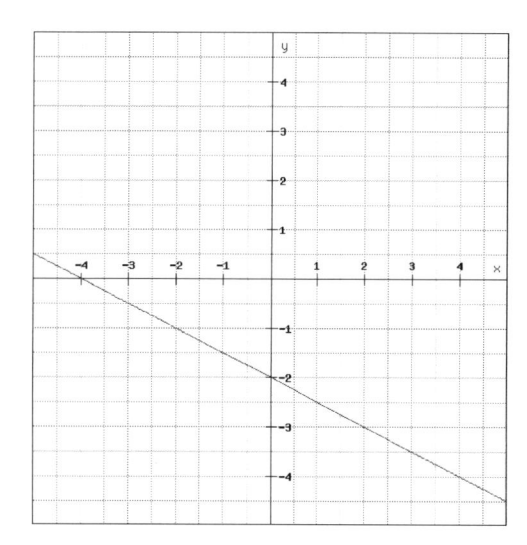

$m = -\dfrac{1}{2}$ $b = -2$ $f(x) = -\dfrac{1}{2}x - 2$

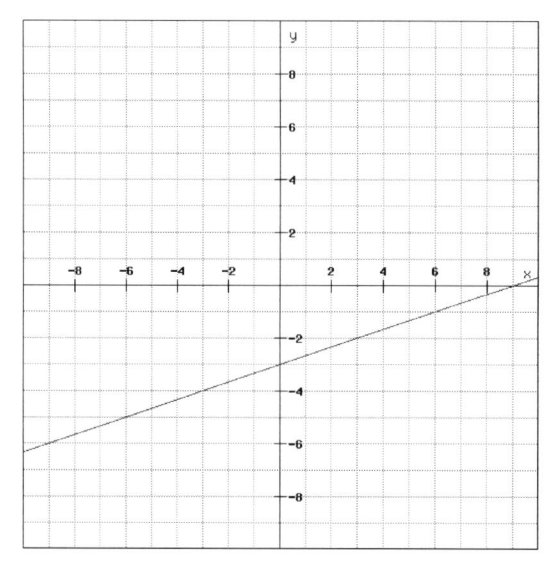

$m = \dfrac{1}{3}$ $b = -3$ $f(x) = \dfrac{1}{3}x - 3$

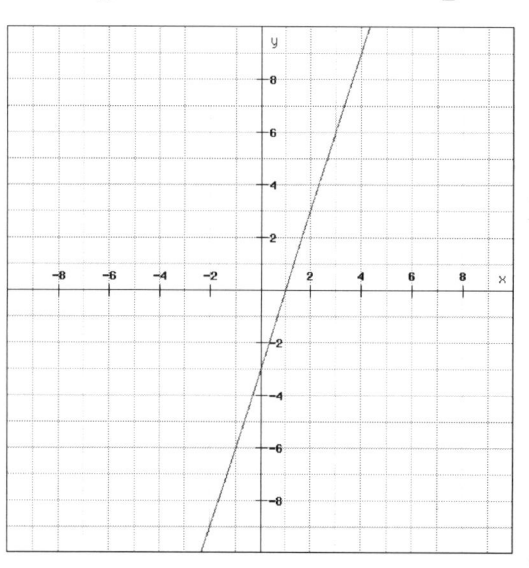

$m = 3$ $b = -3$ $f(x) = 3x - 3$

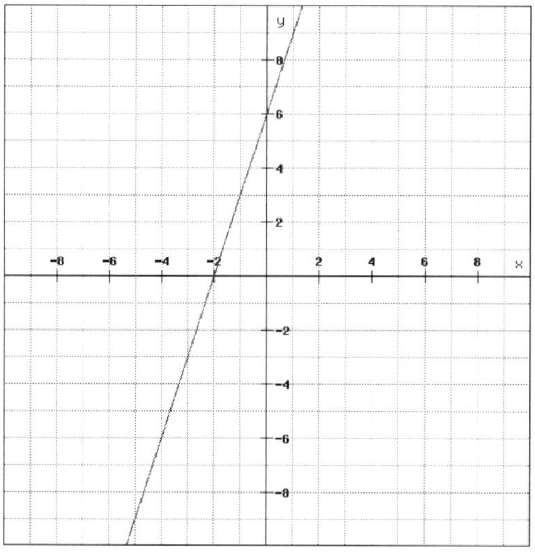

$m = 3$ $b = 6$ $f(x) = 3x + 6$

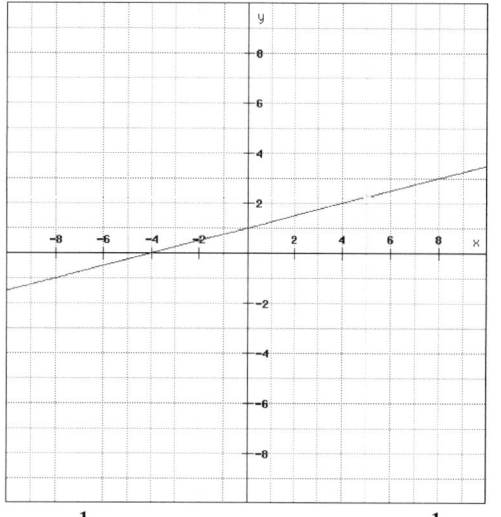

$m = \dfrac{1}{4}$ $b = 1$ $f(x) = \dfrac{1}{4}x + 1$

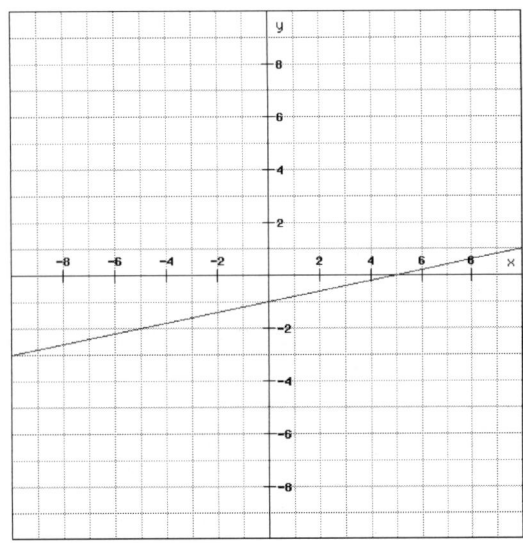

$m = \dfrac{1}{5}$ $b = -1$ $f(x) = \dfrac{1}{5}x - 1$

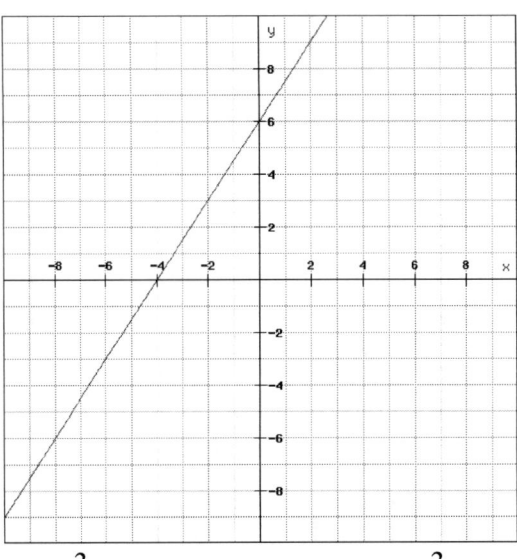

$m = \dfrac{3}{2}$ $b = 6$ $f(x) = \dfrac{3}{2}x + 6$

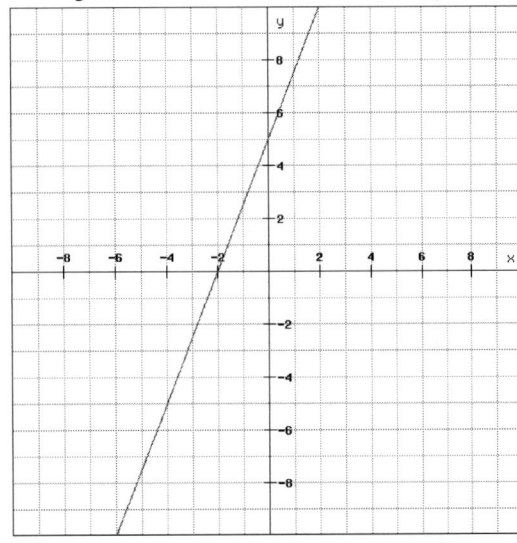

$m = \dfrac{5}{2}$ $b = 5$ $f(x) = \dfrac{5}{2}x + 5$

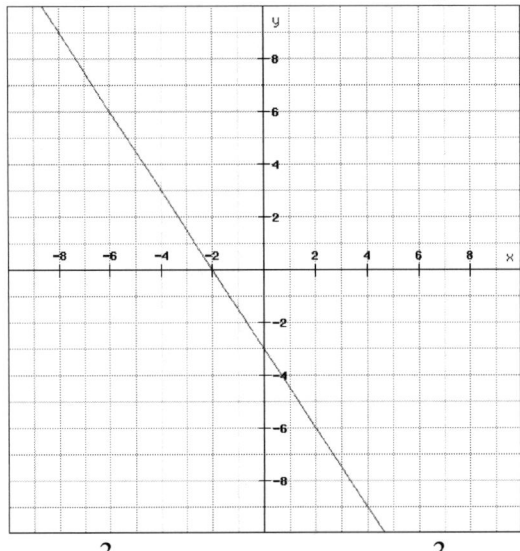

$m = -\dfrac{3}{2}$ $b = -3$ $f(x) = -\dfrac{3}{2}x - 3$

Analyze the following functions:

1. $f(x) = 1$

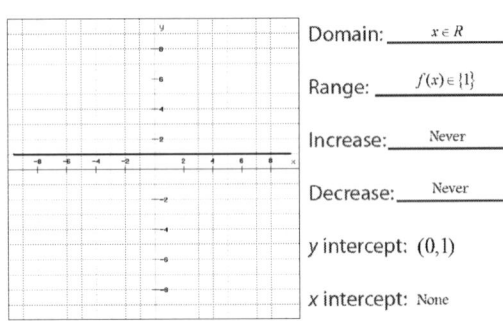

   Domain: $x \in R$
   Range: $f(x) \in \{1\}$
   Increase: Never
   Decrease: Never
   y intercept: $(0,1)$
   x intercept: None

2. $f(x) = 2$

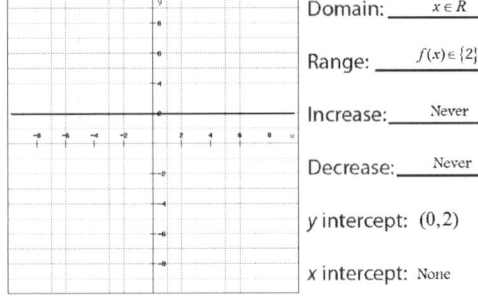

   Domain: $x \in R$
   Range: $f(x) \in \{2\}$
   Increase: Never
   Decrease: Never
   y intercept: $(0,2)$
   x intercept: None

444

3. f(x) = –1

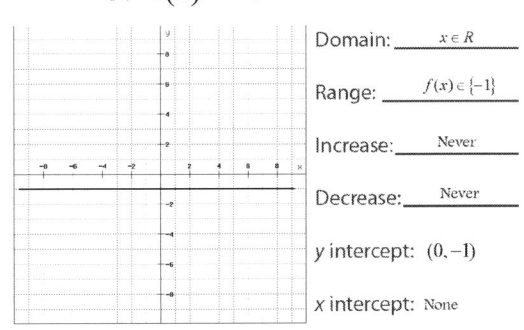

Domain: $x \in R$
Range: $f(x) \in \{-1\}$
Increase: Never
Decrease: Never
y intercept: (0, –1)
x intercept: None

4. f(x) = 0

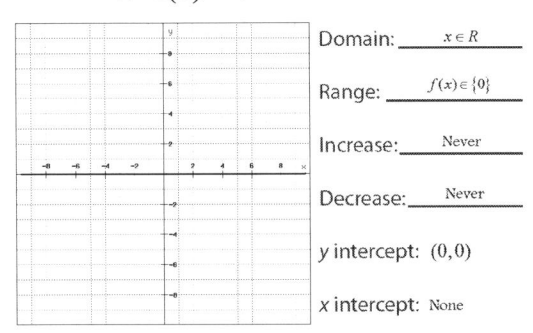

Domain: $x \in R$
Range: $f(x) \in \{0\}$
Increase: Never
Decrease: Never
y intercept: (0, 0)
x intercept: None

5. f(x) = x

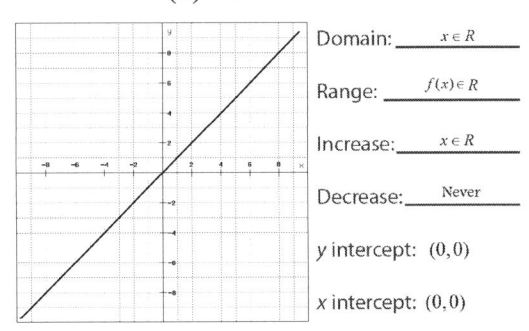

Domain: $x \in R$
Range: $f(x) \in R$
Increase: $x \in R$
Decrease: Never
y intercept: (0, 0)
x intercept: (0, 0)

6. f(x) = x+1

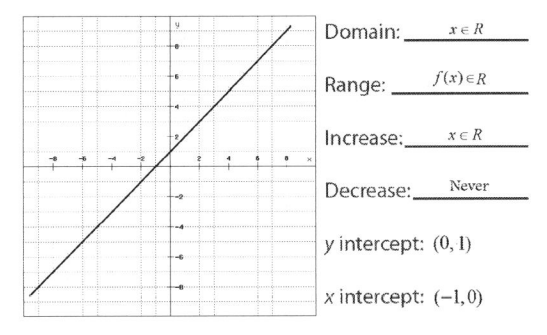

Domain: $x \in R$
Range: $f(x) \in R$
Increase: $x \in R$
Decrease: Never
y intercept: (0, 1)
x intercept: (–1, 0)

7. f(x) = –x

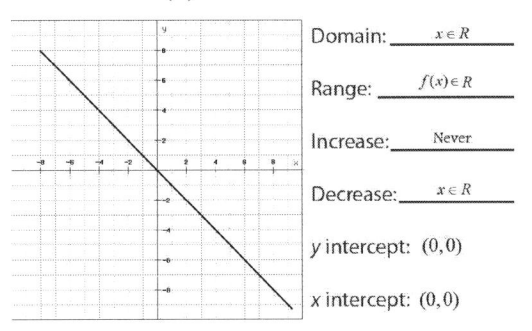

Domain: $x \in R$
Range: $f(x) \in R$
Increase: Never
Decrease: $x \in R$
y intercept: (0, 0)
x intercept: (0, 0)

8. f(x) = –x – 2

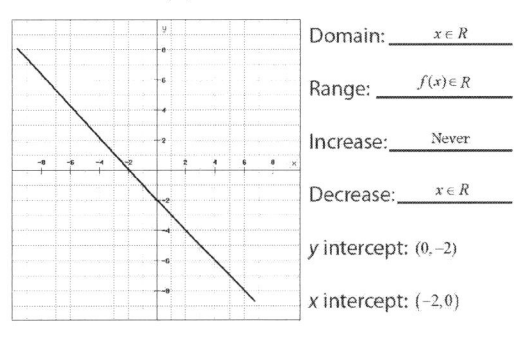

Domain: $x \in R$
Range: $f(x) \in R$
Increase: Never
Decrease: $x \in R$
y intercept: (0, –2)
x intercept: (–2, 0)

9. f(x) = 2x

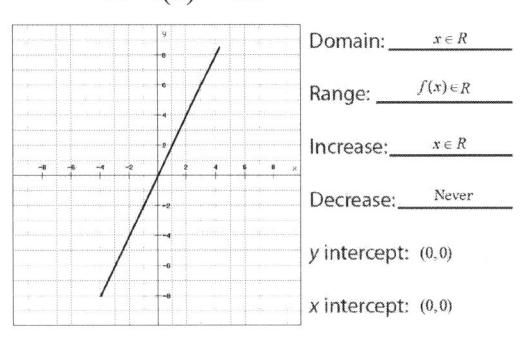

Domain: $x \in R$
Range: $f(x) \in R$
Increase: $x \in R$
Decrease: Never
y intercept: (0, 0)
x intercept: (0, 0)

10. f(x) = 3x – 5

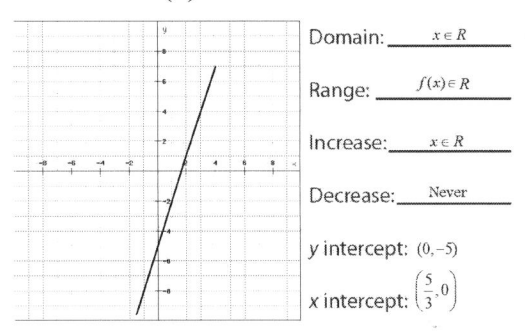

Domain: $x \in R$
Range: $f(x) \in R$
Increase: $x \in R$
Decrease: Never
y intercept: (0, –5)
x intercept: $\left(\frac{5}{3}, 0\right)$

11. f(x) = 3 – 2x

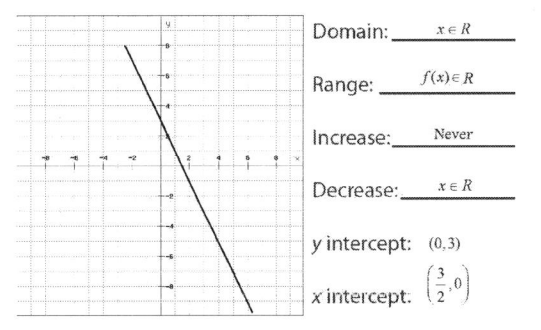

Domain: $x \in R$
Range: $f(x) \in R$
Increase: Never
Decrease: $x \in R$
y intercept: (0, 3)
x intercept: $\left(\frac{3}{2}, 0\right)$

12. f(x) = $\frac{x}{3}$

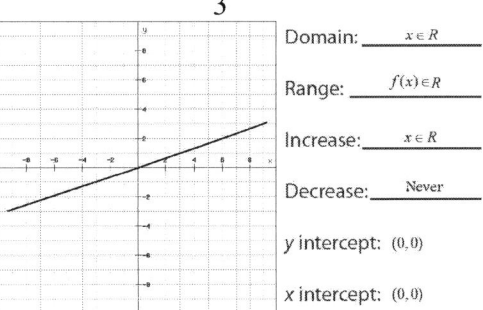

Domain: $x \in R$
Range: $f(x) \in R$
Increase: $x \in R$
Decrease: Never
y intercept: (0, 0)
x intercept: (0, 0)

13. $f(x) = 2x + 1$

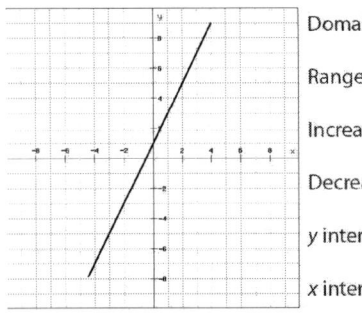

Domain: $x \in R$
Range: $f(x) \in R$
Increase: $x \in R$
Decrease: Never
y intercept: $(0,1)$
x intercept: $\left(-\frac{1}{2}, 0\right)$

14. $f(x) = 2x - 2$

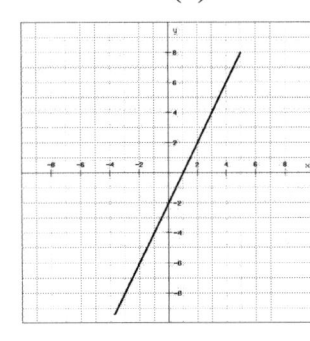

Domain: $x \in R$
Range: $f(x) \in R$
Increase: $x \in R$
Decrease: Never
y intercept: $(0,-2)$
x intercept: $(1,0)$

15. $f(x) = 3x + 5$

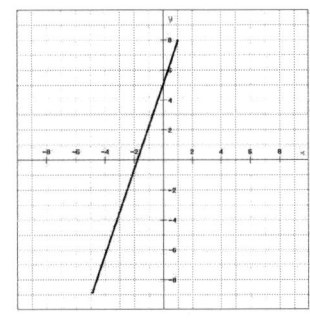

Domain: $x \in R$
Range: $f(x) \in R$
Increase: $x \in R$
Decrease: Never
y intercept: $(0,5)$
x intercept: $\left(-\frac{5}{3}, 0\right)$

16. $f(x) = \frac{x}{2} - 5$

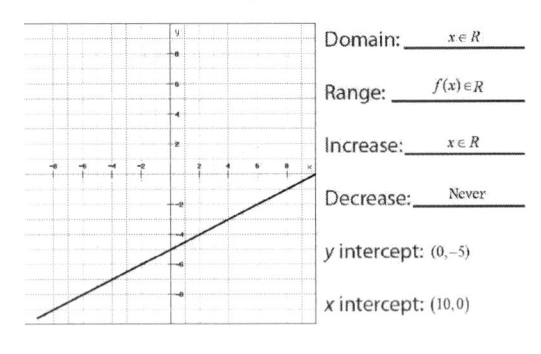

Domain: $x \in R$
Range: $f(x) \in R$
Increase: $x \in R$
Decrease: Never
y intercept: $(0,-5)$
x intercept: $(10,0)$

17. $f(x) = \frac{x}{4} + 6$

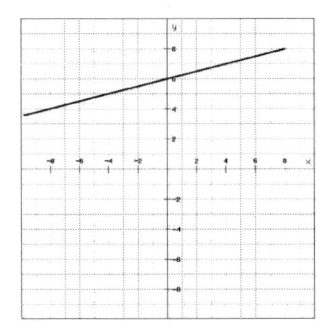

Domain: $x \in R$
Range: $f(x) \in R$
Increase: $x \in R$
Decrease: Never
y intercept: $(0,6)$
x intercept: $(-24,0)$

18. $f(x) = \frac{3}{2}x - 5$

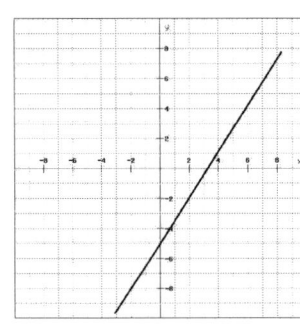

Domain: $x \in R$
Range: $f(x) \in R$
Increase: $x \in R$
Decrease: Never
y intercept: $(0,-5)$
x intercept: $\left(\frac{10}{3}, 0\right)$

19. $f(x) = -\frac{3}{2}x - \frac{3}{2}$

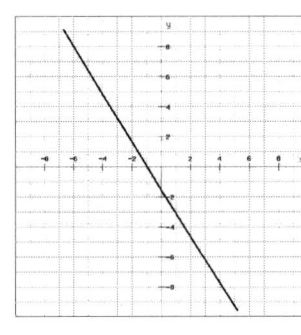

Domain: $x \in R$
Range: $f(x) \in R$
Increase: Never
Decrease: $x \in R$
y intercept: $\left(0, -\frac{3}{2}\right)$
x intercept: $(-1,0)$

20. $f(x) = -\frac{1}{2}x - \frac{3}{2}$

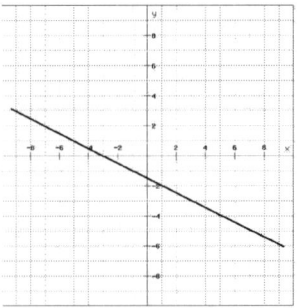

Domain: $x \in R$
Range: $f(x) \in R$
Increase: Never
Decrease: $x \in R$
y intercept: $\left(0, -\frac{3}{2}\right)$
x intercept: $(-3,0)$

21. $f(x) = \dfrac{7}{2}x - \dfrac{1}{4}$

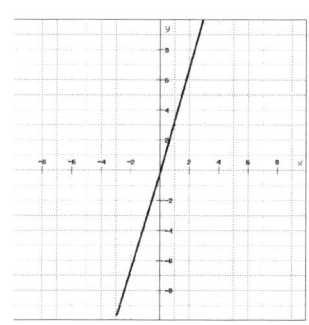

Domain: $x \in R$
Range: $f(x) \in R$
Increase: $x \in R$
Decrease: Never
y intercept: $\left(0, -\dfrac{1}{4}\right)$
x intercept: $\left(\dfrac{1}{14}, 0\right)$

22. $f(x) = -\dfrac{9}{5}x + \dfrac{8}{3}$

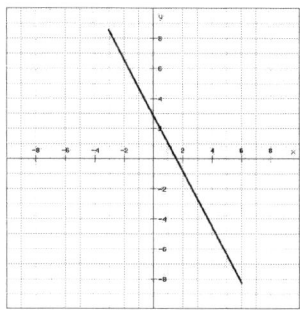

Domain: $x \in R$
Range: $f(x) \in R$
Increase: Never
Decrease: $x \in R$
y intercept: $\left(0, \dfrac{8}{3}\right)$
x intercept: $\left(\dfrac{40}{27}, 0\right)$

23. $3x + 2y = 2$

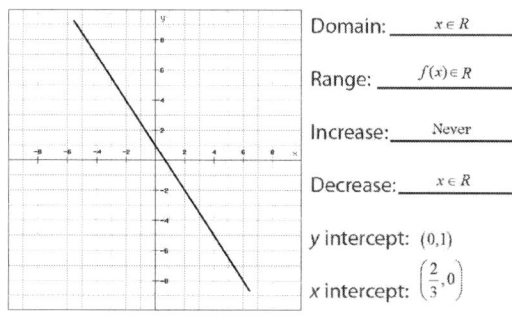

Domain: $x \in R$
Range: $f(x) \in R$
Increase: Never
Decrease: $x \in R$
y intercept: $(0, 1)$
x intercept: $\left(\dfrac{2}{3}, 0\right)$

24. $4x - 2y - 3 = 1$

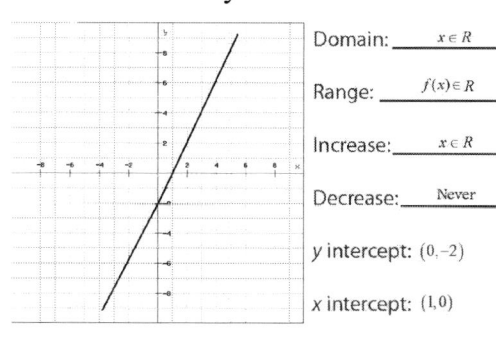

Domain: $x \in R$
Range: $f(x) \in R$
Increase: $x \in R$
Decrease: Never
y intercept: $(0, -2)$
x intercept: $(1, 0)$

25. $-2y + 3x = -5$

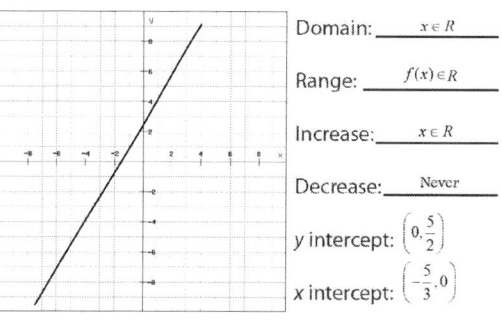

Domain: $x \in R$
Range: $f(x) \in R$
Increase: $x \in R$
Decrease: Never
y intercept: $\left(0, \dfrac{5}{2}\right)$
x intercept: $\left(-\dfrac{5}{3}, 0\right)$

26. $y - x = 2$

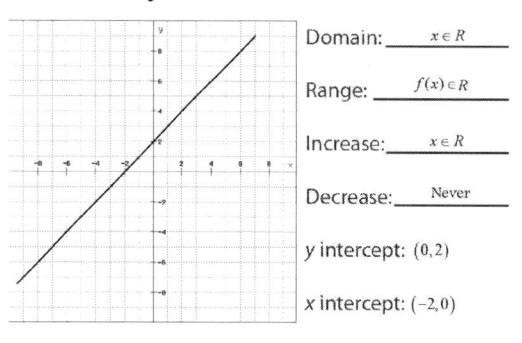

Domain: $x \in R$
Range: $f(x) \in R$
Increase: $x \in R$
Decrease: Never
y intercept: $(0, 2)$
x intercept: $(-2, 0)$

27. $y + 2x - 3 = 1$

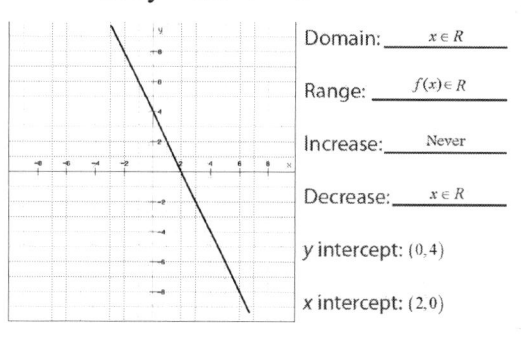

Domain: $x \in R$
Range: $f(x) \in R$
Increase: Never
Decrease: $x \in R$
y intercept: $(0, 4)$
x intercept: $(2, 0)$

28. $5y + 5x = 5$

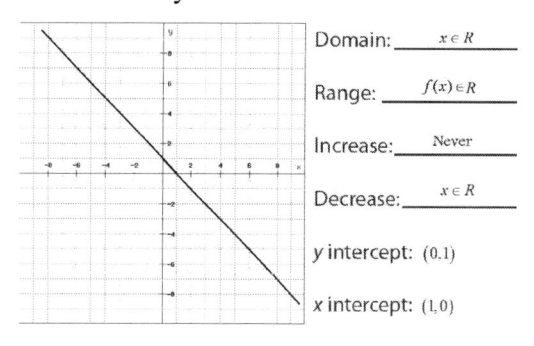

Domain: $x \in R$
Range: $f(x) \in R$
Increase: Never
Decrease: $x \in R$
y intercept: $(0, 1)$
x intercept: $(1, 0)$

29. $2x - 2y - 3 = 1$

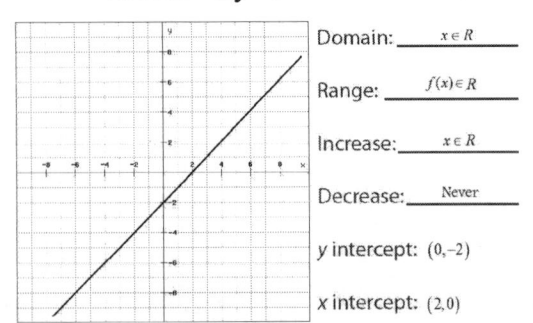

Domain: _____ $x \in R$ _____
Range: _____ $f(x) \in R$ _____
Increase: _____ $x \in R$ _____
Decrease: _____ Never _____
y intercept: $(0, -2)$
x intercept: $(2, 0)$

30. $x - 2y - 150 = 0$

Cannot be seen on this graph

Domain: _____ $x \in R$ _____
Range: _____ $f(x) \in R$ _____
Increase: _____ $x \in R$ _____
Decrease: _____ Never _____
y intercept: $(0, -75)$
x intercept: $(150, 0)$

31. the equation of the line that has a slope of 2 and passes through the point (2, 4) in the forms: $y = mx + b$ and $ax + by + c = 0$, $(a, b \in Z)$
    $y = 2x; 2x - y = 0$

32. the equation of the line that has a slope of $-\frac{1}{2}$ and passes through the point $(-2, -3)$ in the forms: $y = mx + b$ and $ax + by + c = 0$, $(a, b \in Z)$
    $y = \frac{1}{2}x - 2; x - 2y - 4 = 0$

33. the equation of the line that has a slope of $-\frac{5}{2}$ and passes through the point $(-1, 2)$ in the forms: $y = mx + b$ and $ax + by + c = 0$, $(a, b \in Z)$
    $y = -\frac{5}{2}x - \frac{1}{2}; 5x + 2y + 1 = 0$

34. The equation of the line that passes through the points (1, 1), (2, 4), indicate its y and x intercepts and sketch it. Write its equation in the forms: $y = mx + b$ and $ax + by + c = 0$, $(a, b \in Z)$
    $y = 3x - 2; 3x - y - 2 = 0$

35. The equation of the line that passes through the points $(-1, -5)$, $(4, 3)$, indicate its y and x intercepts and sketch it. Write its equation in the forms: $y = mx + b$ and $ax + by + c = 0$, $(a, b \in Z)$
    $y = \frac{8}{5}x - \frac{17}{5}; 8x - y - 17 = 0$

36. The equation of the line that passes through the points $(-5, 1)$, $(-2, 4)$, indicate its y and x intercepts, sketch it and write it in both forms $y = mx + b$ and $ax + by + c = 0$, $(a, b \in Z)$
    $y = x + 6; -x + y - 6 = 0$

37. The equation of the line that is parallel to the line $y = 5x - 2$ and passes through the point $(-2, -1)$. Write its equation in the forms: $y = mx + b$ and $ax + by + c = 0$, $(a, b \in Z)$
    $y = 5x + 9; -5x + y - 9 = 0$

448

38. The equation of the line that is parallel to the line y = –0.5x – 1 and passes through the point (–3, 6). Write its equation in the forms: y = mx + b and ax + by + c = 0, (a, b ∈ Z)
$$y = -\frac{1}{2}x + \frac{9}{2}; x + 2y - 9 = 0$$

39. the equation of the line with a slope of $-\frac{1}{5}$ that passes through the point (0,2). $y = -\frac{1}{5}x + 2; x + 5y - 10 = 0$

40. the equation of the lines with a slope: 1, 2, –3, –1, $-\frac{1}{2}, -\frac{1}{3}$, that passes through the point (0,0).
$$y = x; y = 2x; y = -3x; y = -x; y = -\frac{1}{2}x; y = -\frac{1}{3}x$$

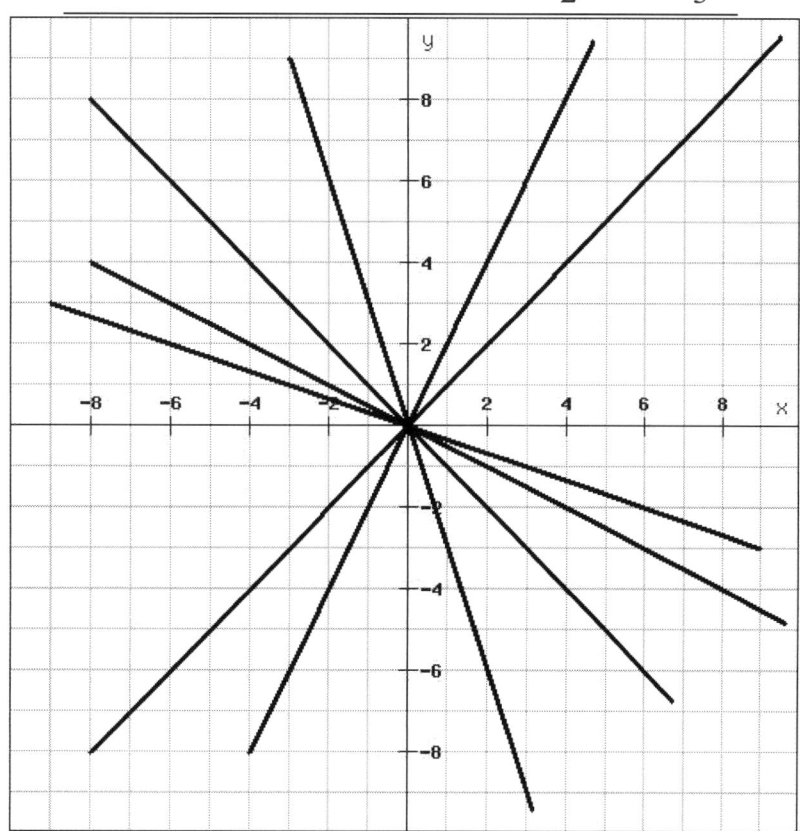

41. The equation of the line with a slope of –3 that passes through the point (0,–3). $y = -3x - 3$

42. The equation of the line with a slope of 2 that passes through the point (2,0) $y = 2x - 4$

43. The equation of the line with a slope of $-\frac{1}{2}$ that passes through the point (–2,0) $y = -\frac{1}{2}x - 1$

449

44. The equation of the line with a slope of 2 that passes through the point (–4,2)
    $y = 2x + 10$

45. The intersection between the lines f(x) = 2x – 3 and f(x) = –5x –2
    $2x - 3 = -5x - 2$; $x = \dfrac{1}{7}$; $\left(\dfrac{1}{7}, -\dfrac{19}{7}\right)$

46. The intersection between the lines f(x) = –12x – 13 and f(x) = 15x +20.
    $-12x - 13 = 15x + 20$; $x = -\dfrac{33}{27}$; $\left(-\dfrac{33}{27}, \dfrac{5}{3}\right)$

DISTANCE AND MIDPOINT BETWEEN 2 POINTS

47. Given the points (1, 2) and (5, 8). Find the distance between them. Find the midpoint.
    Distance $= \sqrt{16 + 36} = \sqrt{52}$; Midpoint $= (3, 5)$

48. Given the points (–3, 2) and (5, –6). Find the distance between them. Find the midpoint.
    Distance $= \sqrt{64 + 64} = \sqrt{128}$; Midpoint $= (1, -2)$

49. Given the points (–1, –6) and (–5, –1). Find the distance between them. Find the midpoint.
    Distance $= \sqrt{16 + 25} = \sqrt{41}$; Midpoint $= \left(-3, -\dfrac{7}{2}\right)$

PERPENDICULAR LINES (m m⊥ = –1)

50. Find the equation of a line perpendicular to the line y = 3x – 2 that passes through the point (3, 12). $y = -\dfrac{1}{3}x + 13$

51. Find all the lines perpendicular to the line y = –3x + 4. Fin the ones that passes through the point (–3, 1). $y = \dfrac{1}{3}x + 2$

52. Find a line perpendicular to the line $y = -\dfrac{2}{5}x + 1$ that passes through the point (–1, –7). $y = \dfrac{5}{2}x - \dfrac{9}{2}$

53. Given that the slope of one of the lines is 3 and that the lines are perpendicular, find the **exact** coordinates of the point of intersection of the two lines.
    Increasing line (plug (1,0): $y = 3x - 3$
    Decreasing line: $y = -\dfrac{1}{3}x + 2$
    Intersection: $3x - 3 = -\dfrac{1}{3}x + 2$; $x = \dfrac{3}{2}$; $\left(\dfrac{3}{2}, \dfrac{1}{2}\right)$

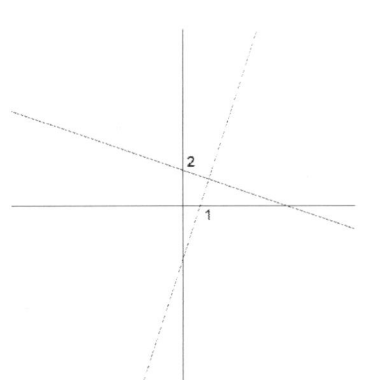

450

Application

1. The price of a new toy (in US$) is C(t) = 20 − 0.5t, t given in days.
   a. Sketch the corresponding graph.
   b. The initial price of the toy   20$
   c. The price of the toy after 10 days   15$
   d. The domain of the function, argument the answer, $t \in [0, 40]$, Price cannot be negative.
   e. The range of the function $C \in [0, 20]$
   f. The meaning of 0.5? units? What are they?
      0.5 $/day, it is reduction of the price per day

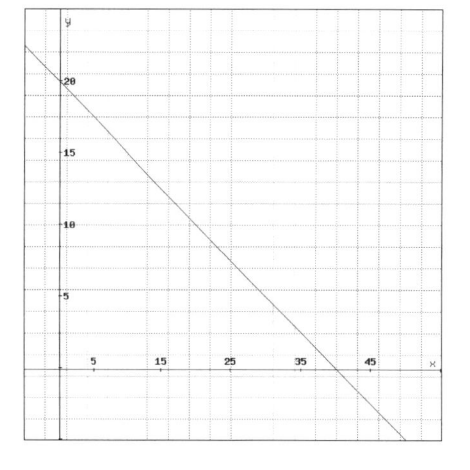

2. You need to rent a car for one day and to compare the charges of 3 different companies. Company I charges 20$ per day with additional cost of 0.20$ per mile. Company II charges 30$ per day with additional cost of 0.10$ per mile. Company III charges 70$ per day with no additional mileage charge.

   a. Write the cost function for each one of the companies.
      $C_I = 20 + 0.2x$
      $C_{II} = 30 + 0.1x$
      $C_{III} = 70$
   b. Sketch all 3 graphs on the same axes system.
   c. Comment on the circumstances in which renting a car from each one of the companies is best.
      The black line represent the cheapest price:

      It is important to find the intersection points between: lines I, II and lines II, III.
      I, II: (100, 40)
      II, III (400, 70)

      If we travel less (or equal) to 100 miles Company I is best.
      If we travel between 100 and 400 miles Company II is best (or equal).
      If we travel more (or equal) to 400 miles Company III is best.

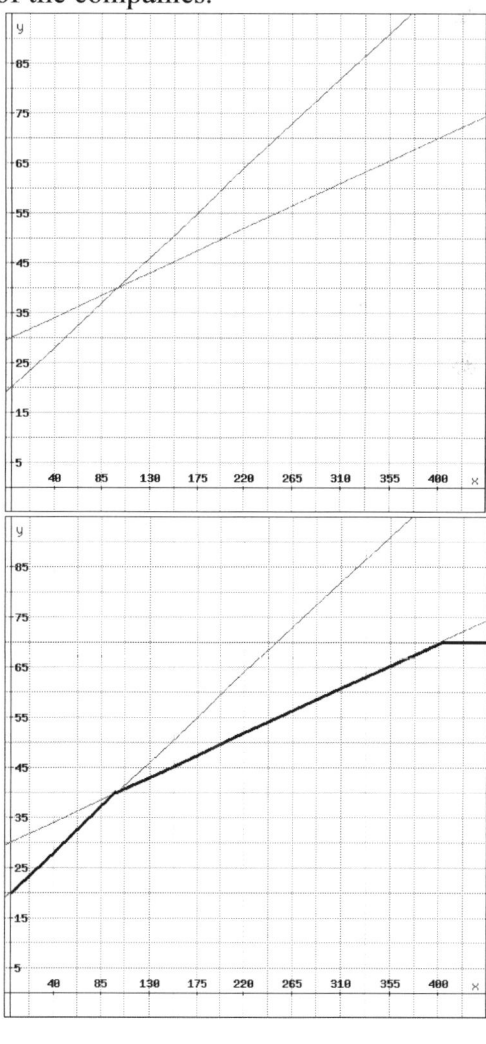

451

2.3. – QUADRATIC FUNCTIONS

1. Given the functions: $f(x) = x^2$, $g(x) = x^2 - 2$. Complete the following table:

x	−5	−4	−3	−2	−1	0	1	2	3	4	5	6
f(x)	25	16	9	4	1	0	1	4	9	16	25	36
g(x)	23	14	7	2	−1	−2	−1	2	7	14	23	34

- Sketch the points of the table on a graph (use a ruler).

- State the domain of the function: $x \in R$

- State the y intercept (sketched on the graph): $f(x):(0,0); g(x):(0,-2)$

- State the x intercept(s): $f(x):(0,0); g(x):(\sqrt{2},0),(-\sqrt{2},0)$

- Write in all possible forms:

  $f(x) = x^2$ $g(x) = x^2 - 2 = (x+\sqrt{2})(x-\sqrt{2})$

- Find the max/**min** point(s): $f(x):(0,0); g(x):(0,-2)$

- The function is increasing on the interval: $f(x): x \in (0,\infty); g(x): x \in (0,\infty)$

- The function is decreasing on the interval: $f(x): x \in (-\infty,0); g(x): x \in (-\infty,0)$

- State the range of the function: $f(x) \in [0,\infty); g(x) \in [-2,\infty)$

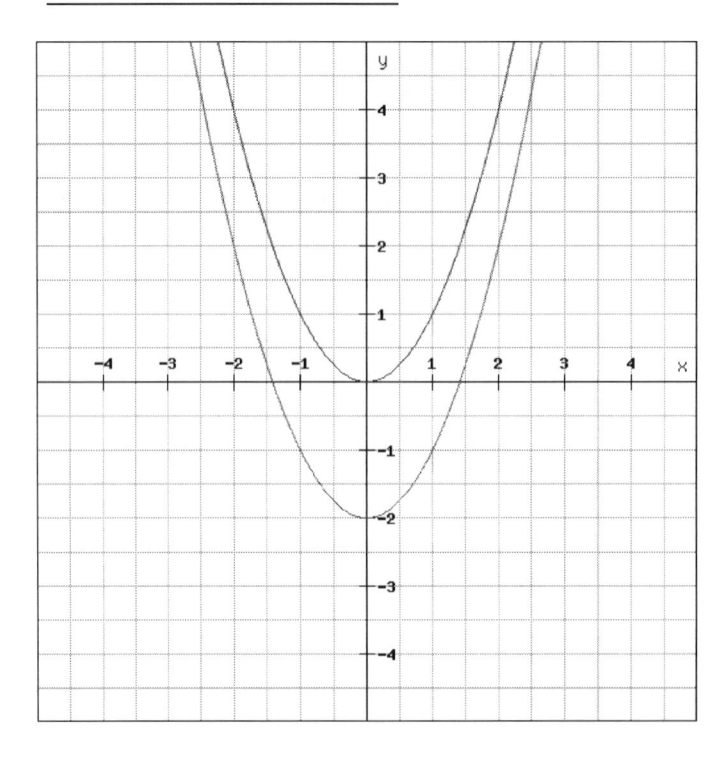

452

2. Given the functions: f(x) = (x − 2)², g(x) = (x + 3)² − 2. Complete the following table:

x	−5	−4	−3	−2	−1	0	1	2	3	4	5	6
f(x)	49	36	25	16	9	4	1	0	1	4	9	16
g(x)	2	−1	−2	−1	2	7	14	23	34	47	62	79

- State the domain of the function: $x \in R$

- State the y intercept (sketched on the graph): $f(x):(0,4); g(x):(0,7)$

- State the x intercept(s): $f(x):(2,0); g(x):(\sqrt{2}-3,0),(-\sqrt{2}-3,0)$

- Write in all possible forms:

$$f(x) = (x-2)^2 = x^2 - 4x + 4$$
$$g(x) = (x+3)^2 - 2 = (x-(\sqrt{2}-3))(x-(-\sqrt{2}-3)) = x^2 + 6x + 7$$

- Find the max/**min** point(s): $f(x):(2,0); g(x):(-3,-2)$

- The function is increasing on the interval: $f(x): x \in (2,\infty); g(x): x \in (-3,\infty)$

- The function is decreasing on the interval: $f(x): x \in (-\infty,2); g(x): x \in (-\infty,-3)$

- State the range of the function: $f(x) \in [0,\infty); g(x) \in [-2,\infty)$
- State its axes of symmetry: $f(x): x = 2; g(x): x = -3$

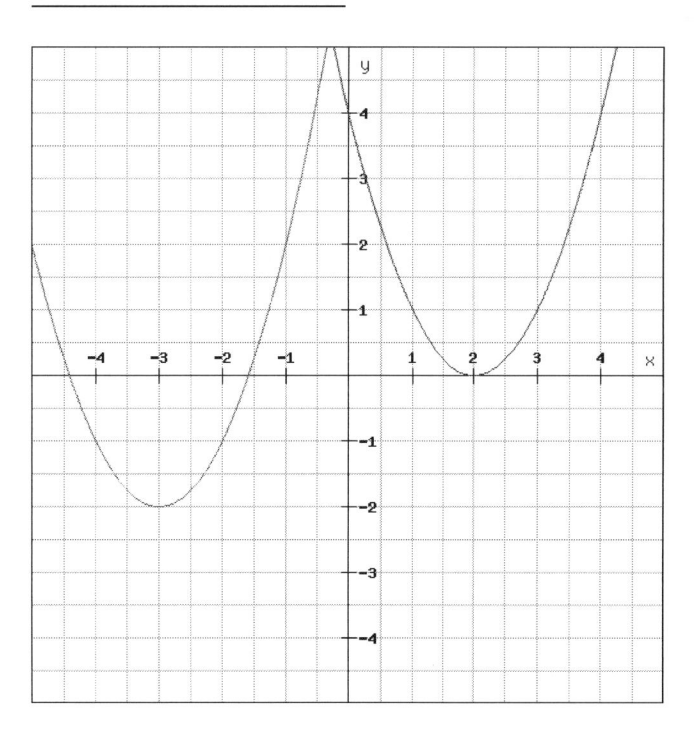

453

3. Given the function: f(x) = (x + 2)(x − 4), g(x) = 2(x + 2)(x − 4) Complete the following table:

x	−5	−4	−3	−2	−1	0	1	2	3	4	5	6
f(x)	27	16	7	0	−5	−8	−9	−8	−5	0	7	16
g(x)	54	32	14	0	−10	−16	−18	−16	−10	0	14	32

- State the domain of the function: $\underline{x \in R}$

- State the y intercept (sketched on the graph): $\underline{f(x):(0,-8); g(x):(0,-16)}$

- State the x intercept(s): $\underline{f(x):(-2,0),(4,0); g(x):(-2,0),(4,0)}$

- Write in all possible forms:

  $\underline{f(x) = (x+2)(x-4) = x^2 - 2x - 8 = (x-1)^2 - 9}$
  $\underline{g(x) = 2(x+2)(x-4) = 2x^2 - 4x - 16 = 2(x-1)^2 - 18}$

- Find the max/**min** point(s): $\underline{f(x):(1,-9); g(x):(1,-18)}$

- The function is increasing on the interval: $\underline{f(x): x \in (1,\infty); g(x): x \in (1,\infty)}$

- The function is decreasing on the interval: $\underline{f(x): x \in (-\infty,1); g(x): x \in (-\infty,1)}$

- State the range of the function: $\underline{f(x) \in [-9,\infty); g(x) \in [-18,\infty)}$

- State its axes of symmetry: $\underline{f(x): x=1; g(x): x=1}$

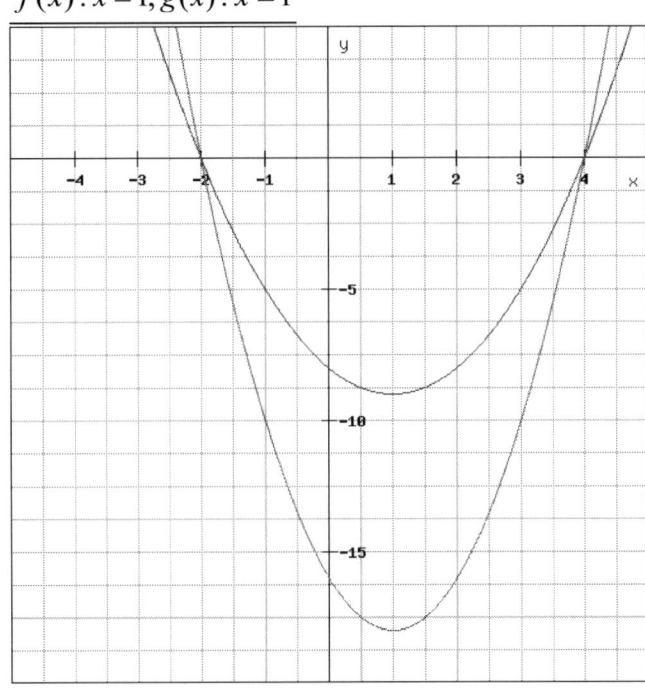

454

In general, a quadratic function f can be written in several different ways:

a. $f(x) = ax^2 + bx + c$ **standard form**, where a, b and c are constants
b. $f(x) = a(x-r)(x-s)$ **factored form**, where a, r and s are constants
c. $f(x) = a(x-h)^2 + k$ **vertex form**, where a, h and k are constants

Example:

Vertex form: $f(x) = 3(x-2)^2 - 3$
Partial factored form: $f(x) = 3(x-1)(x-3)$
Standard form: $f(x) = 3x^2 + 12x + 9$

Complete the sentences:

1. The graph of a quadratic function is called a <u>Parabola</u>

2. In factored form, the numbers r and s represent <u>the x–coordinates of the x intercepts</u> of f.

3. In vertex form, the point (h, k) is called the <u>vertex</u> of the parabola.
   The axis of symmetry of the parabola is the line <u>x = h</u>

4. The graph of the parabola opens upwards if <u>a > 0</u> and downwards if <u>a < 0</u>

5. In case $f(x) = x^2 + 1$, the function can be written in <u>1</u> form(s) only. Why?
   <u>No x intercepts so no factored form. Vertex and standard forms are identical.</u>

6. In case $f(x) = x^2 - 1$, the function can be written in <u>2</u> form(s) only. Show your answer: <u>Vertex and standard are identical.</u>

7. A parabola has its vertex at the point (2, 3) and goes through the point (6, 11). Find the expression of the function.

   $f(x) = a(x-2)^2 + 3; 11 = a(6-2)^2 + 3; a = \dfrac{1}{2}$

   $f(x) = \dfrac{1}{2}(x-2)^2 + 3$

8. A parabola has its vertex at the point (– 2, 4) and passes through the point (2, – 6). Find the expression of the function.

   $f(x) = a(x+2)^2 + 4; -6 = a(2+2)^2 + 4; a = -\dfrac{10}{16} = -\dfrac{5}{8}$

   $f(x) = -\dfrac{5}{8}(x+2)^2 + 4$

9. Write the analytical expression that corresponds the following functions in all possible forms, assume $a = 1$ or -1 in all cases:

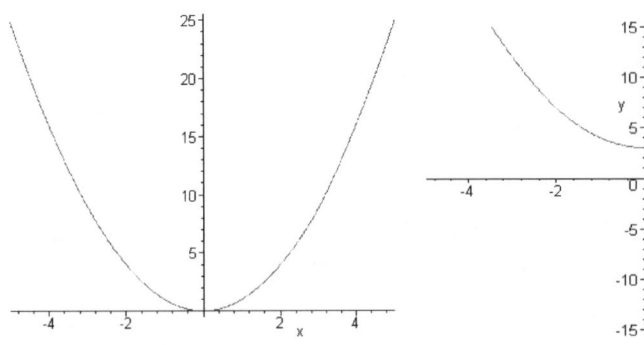

Range: $f(x) \in [0, \infty)$
Vertex form: $f(x) = x^2$
Factorized form: $f(x) = x^2$
Standard form: $f(x) = x^2$

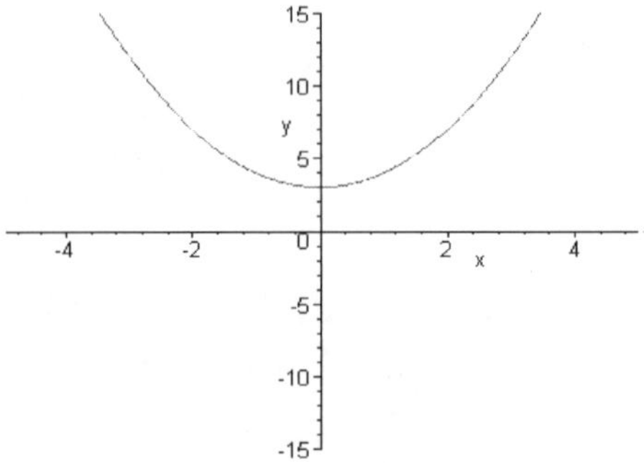

Range: $f(x) \in [3, \infty)$
Vertex form: $f(x) = x^2 + 3$
Factorized form: None
Standard form: $f(x) = x^2 + 3$

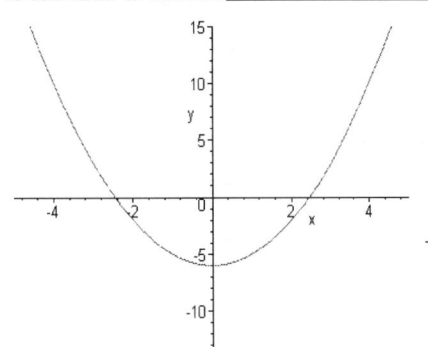

Range: $f(x) \in [-6, \infty)$
Vertex form: $f(x) = x^2 - 6$
Factorized form: $f(x) = (x - \sqrt{6})(x + \sqrt{6})$
Standard form: $f(x) = x^2 - 6$

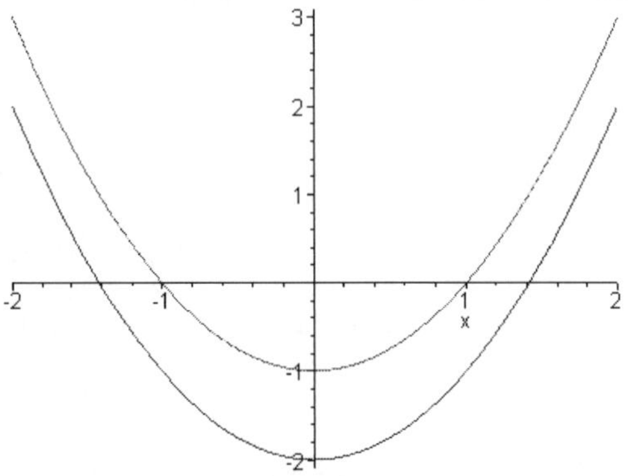

Range: $f(x) \in [-1, \infty)$; $f(x) \in [-2, \infty)$
Vertex form: $f(x) = x^2 - 1$; $f(x) = x^2 - 2$
Factorized form: $f(x) = (x-1)(x+1); f(x) = (x - \sqrt{2})(x + \sqrt{2})$
Standard form: $f(x) = x^2 - 1$; $f(x) = x^2 - 2$

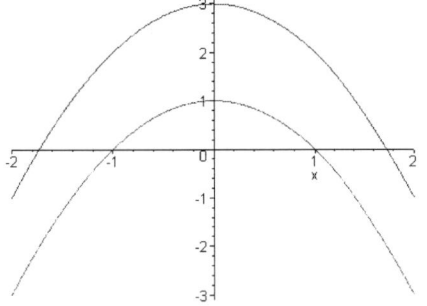

(upper curve)
Range: $f(x) \in (-\infty, 3]$
Vertex form: $f(x) = -x^2 + 3$
Factorized form: $f(x) = -(x - \sqrt{3})(x + \sqrt{3})$
Standard form: $f(x) = -x^2 + 3$

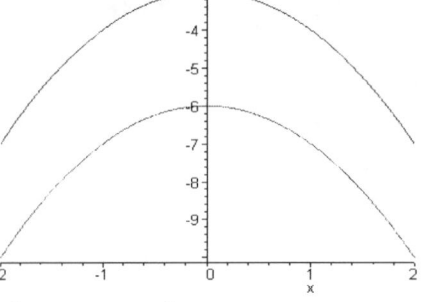

(upper curve)
Range: $f(x) \in (-\infty, -3]$
Vertex form: $f(x) = -x^2 - 3$
Factorized form: None
Standard form: $f(x) = -x^2 - 3$

10. Complete the tables:

Function	On the graph
$f(x) = x^2$	B
$f(x) = \dfrac{x^2}{2}$	C
$f(x) = \dfrac{x^2}{3}$	D
$f(x) = 2x^2$	A

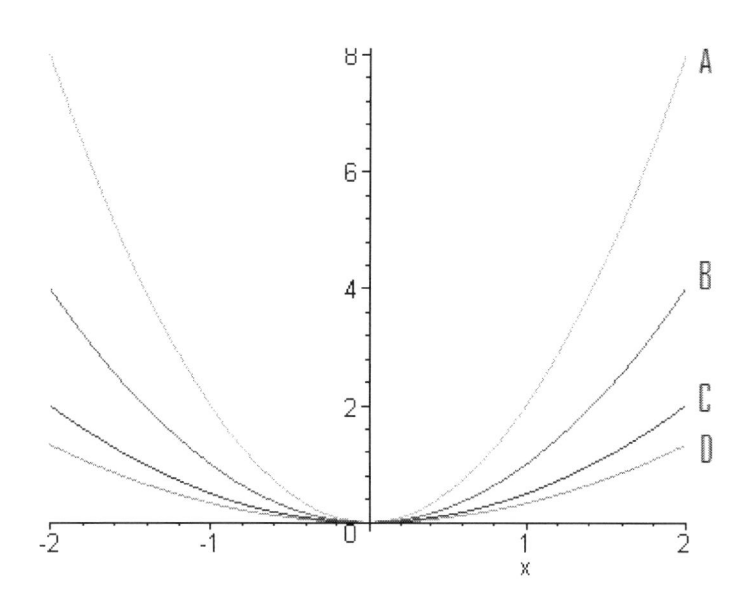

11. Complete the table:

Function	On the graph
$f(x) = x^2 + 2$	B
$f(x) = x^2 - 2$	C
$f(x) = x^2 - 3$	D
$f(x) = 2x^2 + 2$	A

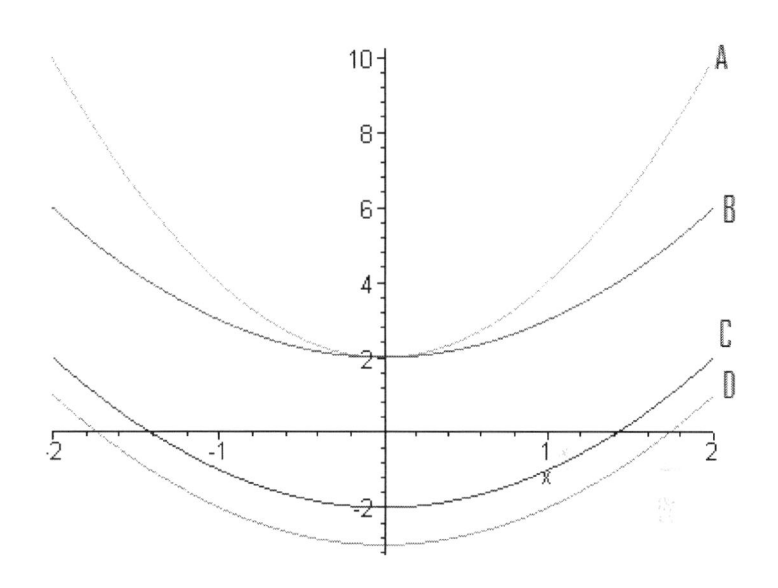

12. Complete the table:

Function	On the graph
$f(x) = -x^2 + 2$	C
$f(x) = x^2 - 4$	D
$f(x) = -x^2 + 3$	B
$f(x) = 2x^2 + 2$	A

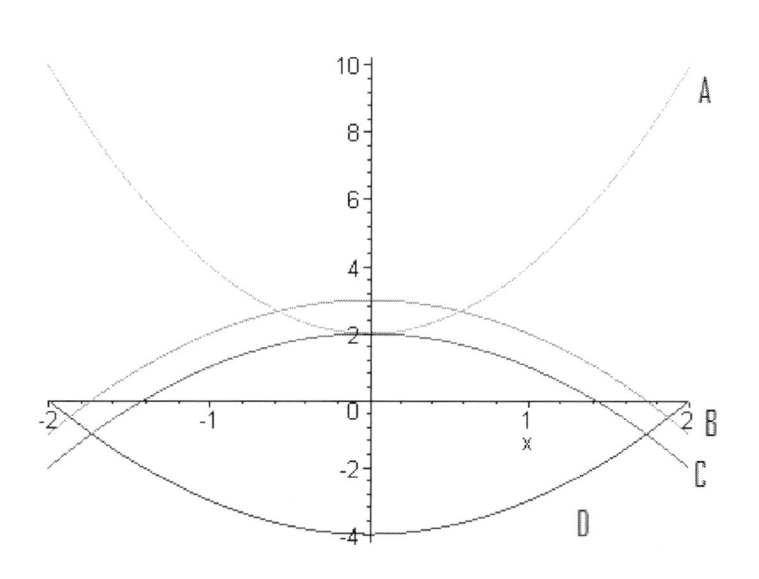

457

13. Write the expression of the function in all possible forms, indicate the range assume $a = 1$ or -1 in all cases. Use GDC to check your answer.

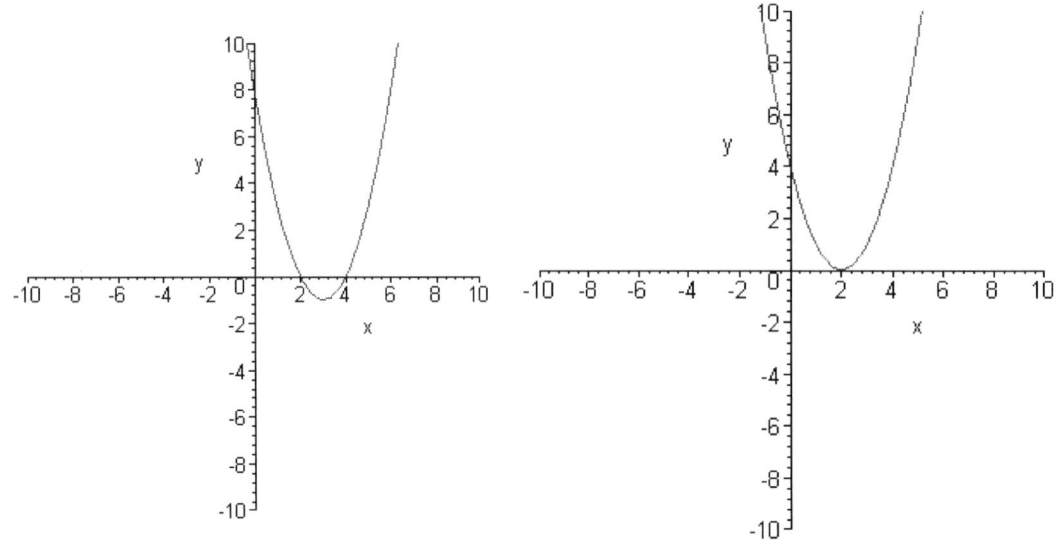

Range: $f(x) \in [-1, \infty)$
Vertex form: $f(x) = (x-3)^2 - 1$
Factorized form: $f(x) = (x-2)(x-4)$
Standard form: $f(x) = x^2 - 6x + 8$

Range: $f(x) \in [0, \infty)$
Vertex form: $f(x) = (x-2)^2$
Factorized form: $f(x) = (x-2)(x-2)$
Standard form: $f(x) = x^2 - 4x + 4$

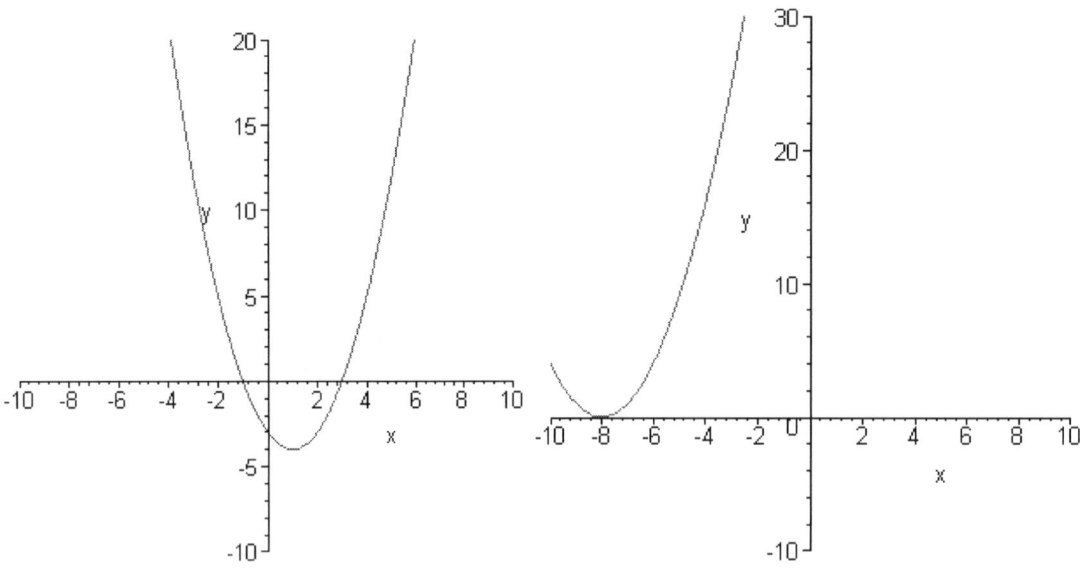

Range: $f(x) \in [-4, \infty)$
Vertex form: $f(x) = (x-1)^2 - 4$
Factorized form: $f(x) = (x+1)(x-3)$
Standard form: $f(x) = x^2 - 2x - 3$

Range: $f(x) \in [0, \infty)$
Vertex form: $f(x) = (x+8)^2$
Factorized form: $f(x) = (x+8)(x+8)$
Standard form: $f(x) = x^2 + 16x + 64$

Range: $f(x) \in [-4, \infty)$ Range: $f(x) \in [-16, \infty)$
Vertex form: $f(x) = x^2 - 4$ Vertex form: $f(x) = (x-2)^2 - 16$
Factorized form: $f(x) = (x+2)(x-2)$ Factorized form: $f(x) = (x+2)(x-6)$
Standard form: $f(x) = x^2 - 4$ Standard form: $f(x) = x^2 - 4x - 12$

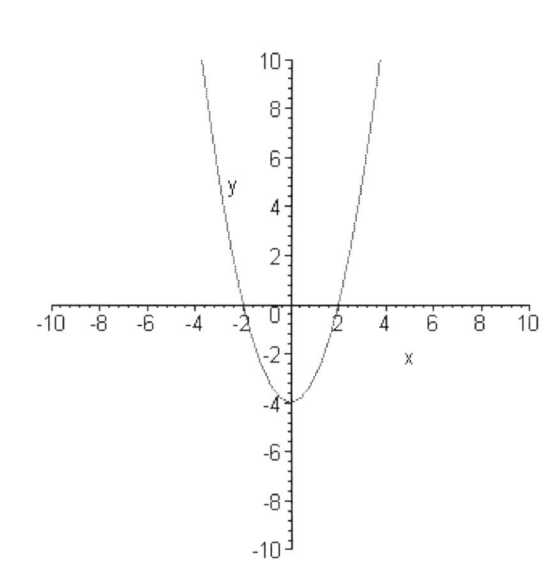

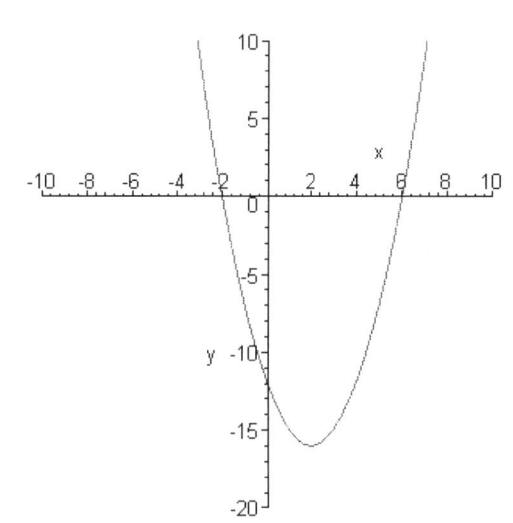

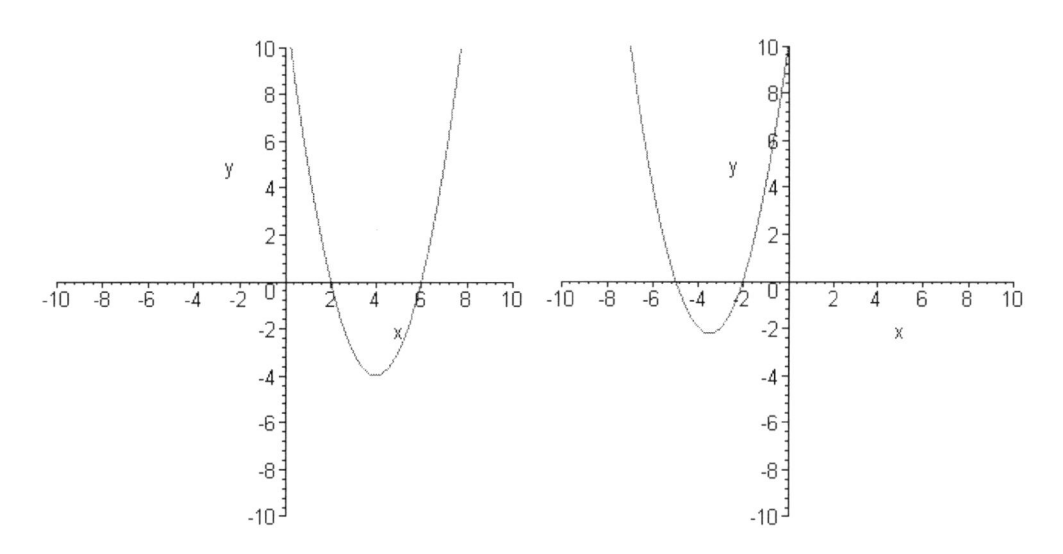

Range: $f(x) \in [-4, \infty)$ Range: $f(x) \in [-\frac{9}{4}, \infty)$
Vertex form: $f(x) = (x-4)^2 - 4$ Vertex form: $f(x) = \left(x+\frac{7}{2}\right)^2 - \frac{9}{4}$
Factorized form: $f(x) = (x-2)(x-6)$ Factorized form: $f(x) = (x+2)(x+5)$
Standard form: $f(x) = x^2 - 8x + 12$ Standard form: $f(x) = x^2 + 7x + 10$

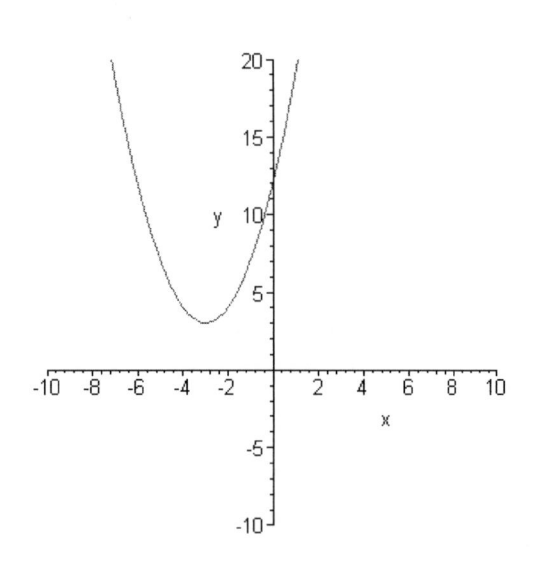

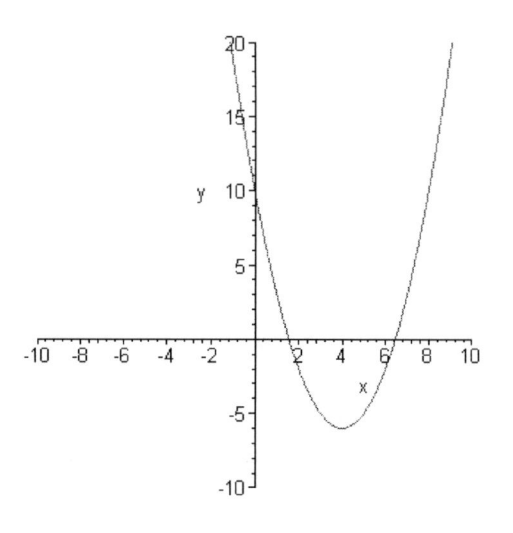

Range: $f(x) \in [3, \infty)$
Vertex form: $f(x) = (x+3)^2 + 3$
Factorized form: None
Standard form: $f(x) = x^2 + 6x + 12$

Range: $f(x) \in [-6, \infty)$
Vertex form: $f(x) = (x-4)^2 - 6$
Factorized form: $f(x) = (x - (\sqrt{6}+4))(x - (-\sqrt{6}+4))$
Standard form: $f(x) = x^2 - 8x + 10$

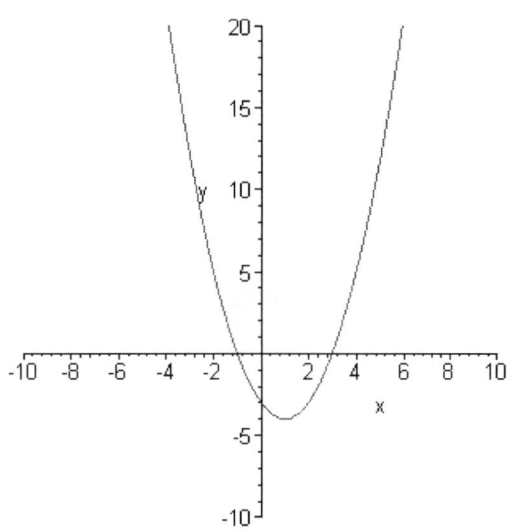

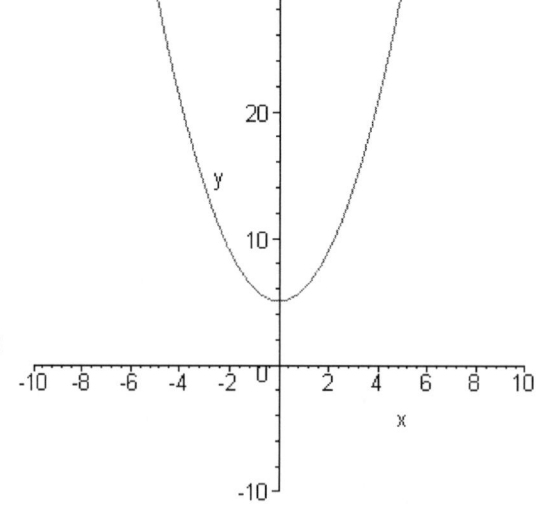

Range: $f(x) \in [-4, \infty)$
Vertex form: $f(x) = (x-1)^2 - 4$
Factorized form: $f(x) = (x-3)(x+1)$
Standard form: $f(x) = x^2 - 2x - 3$

Range: $f(x) \in [5, \infty)$
Vertex form: $f(x) = x^2 + 5$
Factorized form: None
Standard form: $f(x) = x^2 + 5$

460

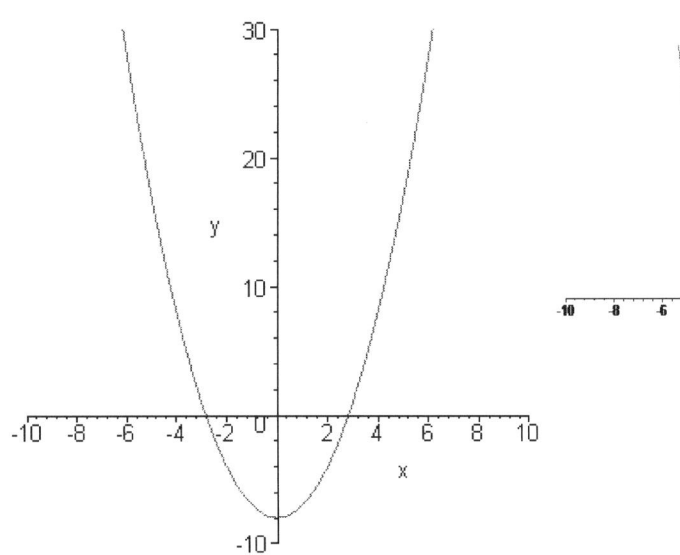

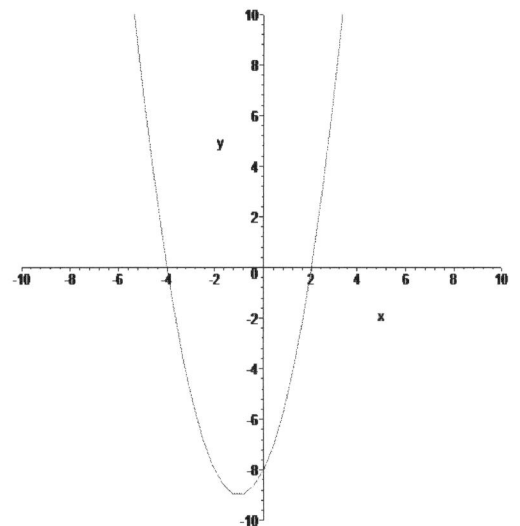

Range: $f(x) \in [-8, \infty)$
Vertex form: $f(x) = x^2 - 8$
Factorized form: $f(x) = (x - \sqrt{8})(x + \sqrt{8})$
Standard form: $f(x) = x^2 - 8$

Range: $f(x) \in [-9, \infty]$
Vertex form: $f(x) = (x+1)^2 - 9$
Factorized form: $f(x) = (x-2)(x+4)$
Standard form: $f(x) = x^2 + 2x - 8$

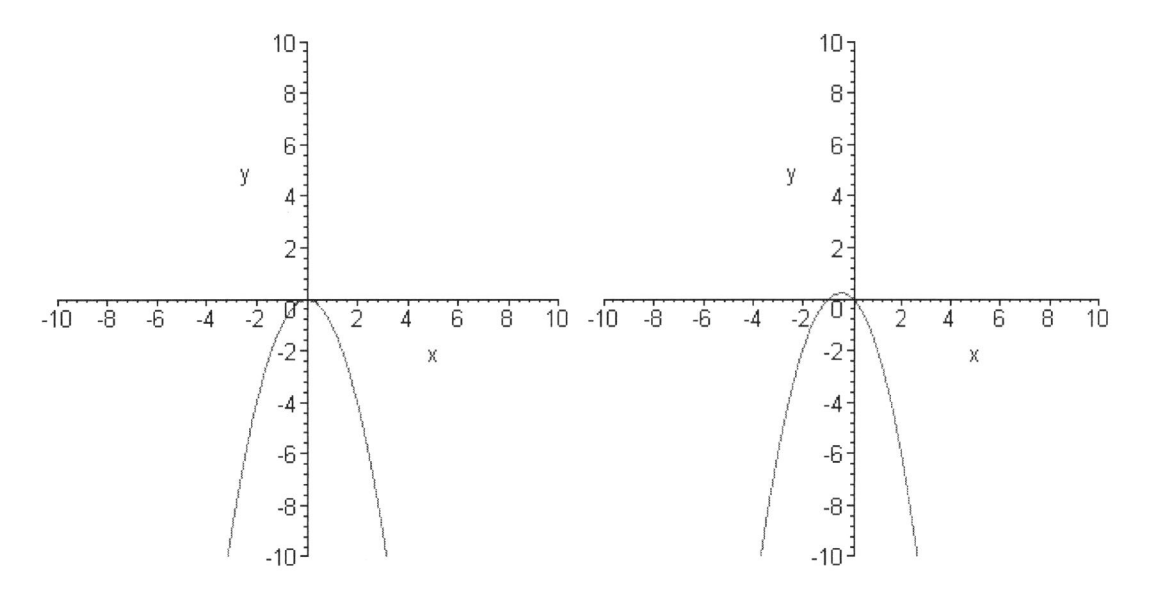

Range: $f(x) \in (-\infty, 0]$
Vertex form: $f(x) = -x^2$
Factorized form: $f(x) = -x^2$
Standard form: $f(x) = -x^2$

Range: $f(x) \in (-\infty, \frac{1}{4}]$
Vertex form: $f(x) = -\left(x + \frac{1}{2}\right)^2 + \frac{1}{4}$
Factorized form: $f(x) = -x(x+1)$
Standard form: $f(x) = -x^2 - x$

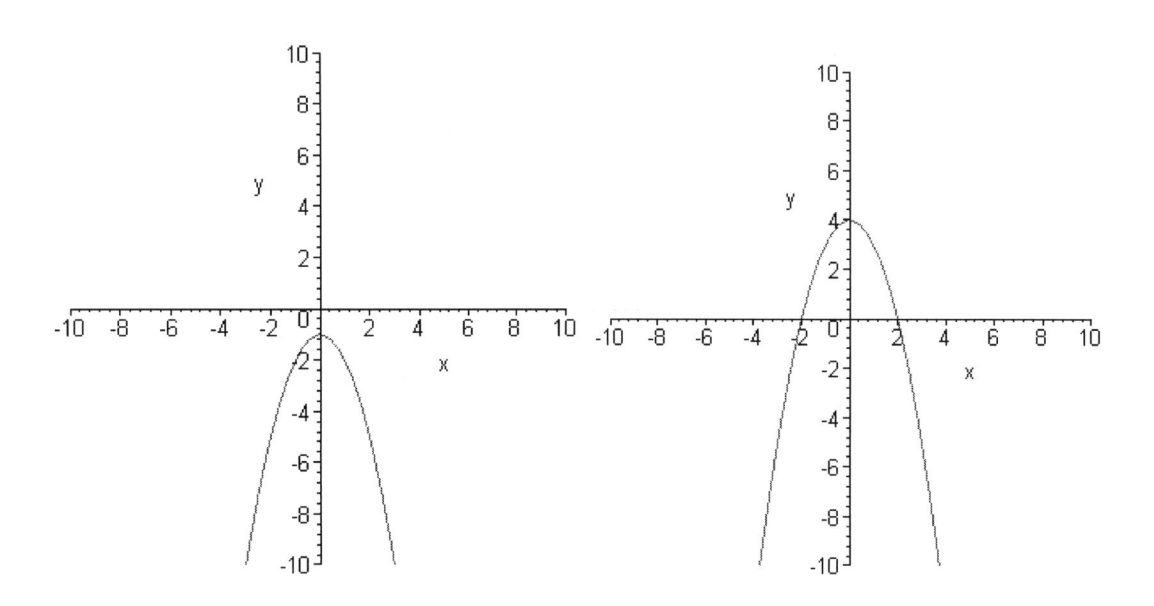

Range: $f(x)\in(-\infty,-1]$

Vertex form: $f(x)=-x^2-1$

Factorized form: None

Standard form: $f(x)=-x^2-1$

Range: $f(x)\in(-\infty,4]$

Vertex form: $f(x)=-x^2+4$

Factorized form: $f(x)=-(x-2)(x+2)$

Standard form: $f(x)=-x^2+4$

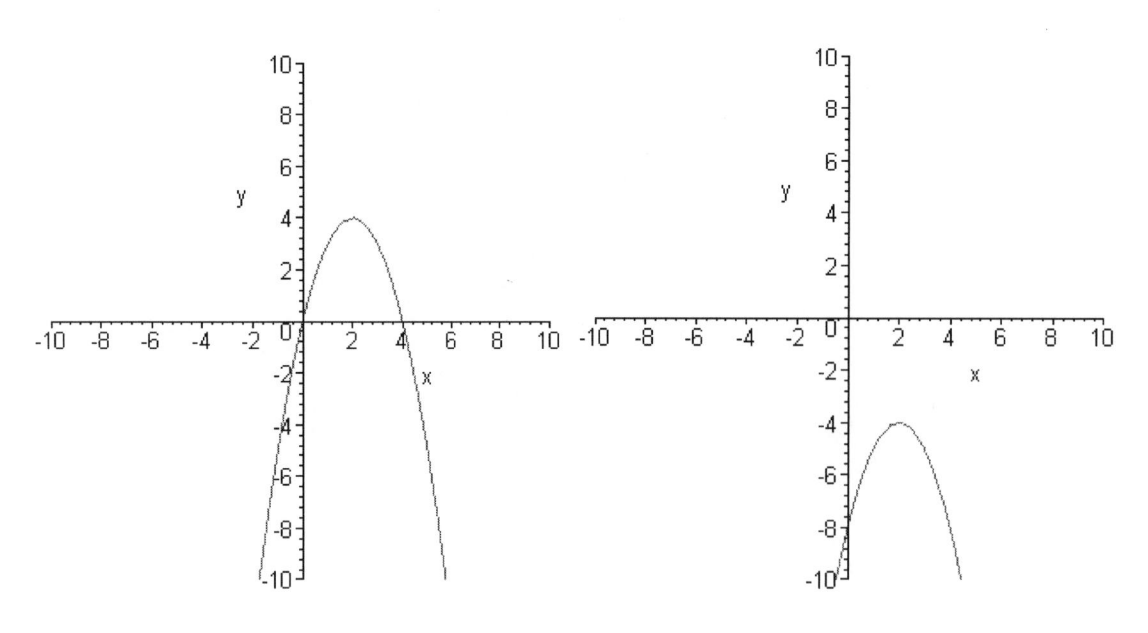

Range: $f(x)\in(-\infty,4]$

Vertex form: $f(x)=-(x-2)^2+4$

Factorized form: $f(x)=-x(x-4)$

Standard form: $f(x)=-x^2+4x$

Range: $f(x)\in(-\infty,-4]$

Vertex form: $f(x)=-(x-2)^2-4$

Factorized form: None

Standard form: $f(x)=-x^2+4x-8$

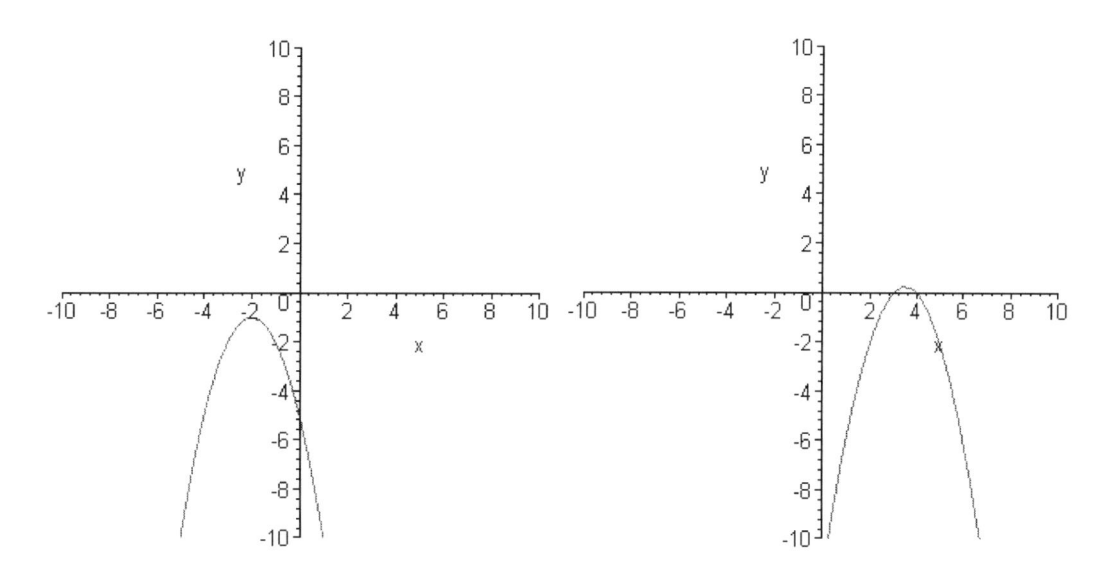

Range: $f(x) \in (-\infty, -1]$
Vertex form: $f(x) = -(x+2)^2 - 1$
Factorized form: None
Standard form: $f(x) = -x^2 - 4x - 5$

Range: $f(x) \in (-\infty, \frac{1}{4}]$
Vertex form: $f(x) = -\left(x - \frac{7}{2}\right)^2 + \frac{1}{4}$
Factorized form: $f(x) = -(x-3)(x-4)$
Standard form: $f(x) = -x^2 - 7x - 12$

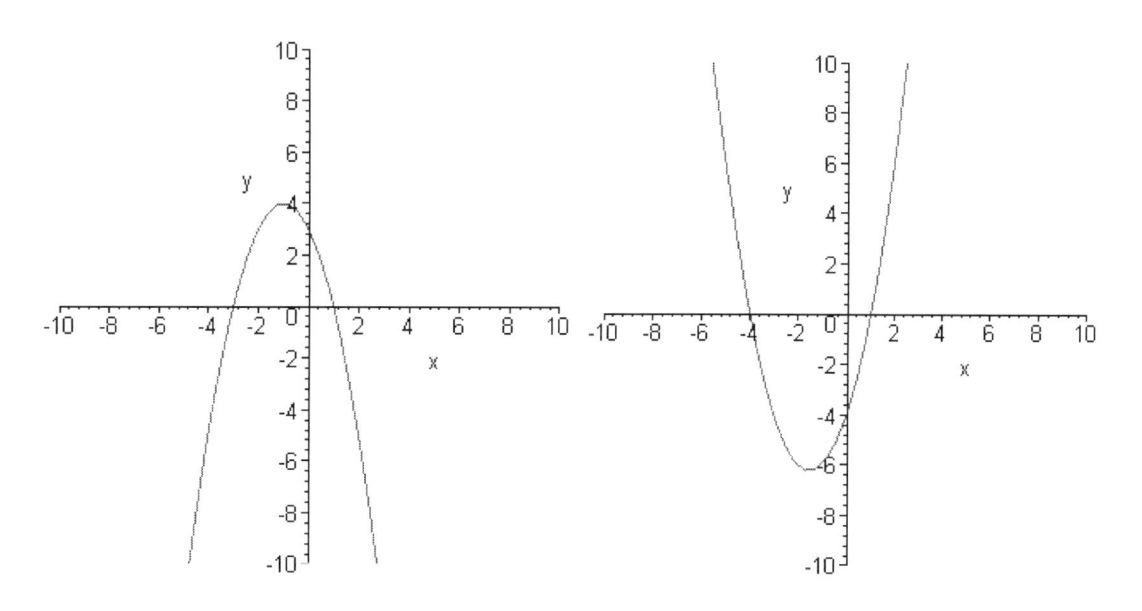

Range: $f(x) \in (-\infty, 4]$
Vertex form: $f(x) = -(x+1)^2 + 4$
Factorized form: $f(x) = -(x-1)(x+3)$
Standard form: $f(x) = -x^2 - 2x + 3$

Range: $f(x) \in [-\frac{25}{4}, \infty)$
Vertex form: $f(x) = \left(x + \frac{3}{2}\right)^2 - \frac{25}{4}$
Factorized form: $f(x) = (x-1)(x+4)$
Standard form: $f(x) = x^2 + 3x - 4$

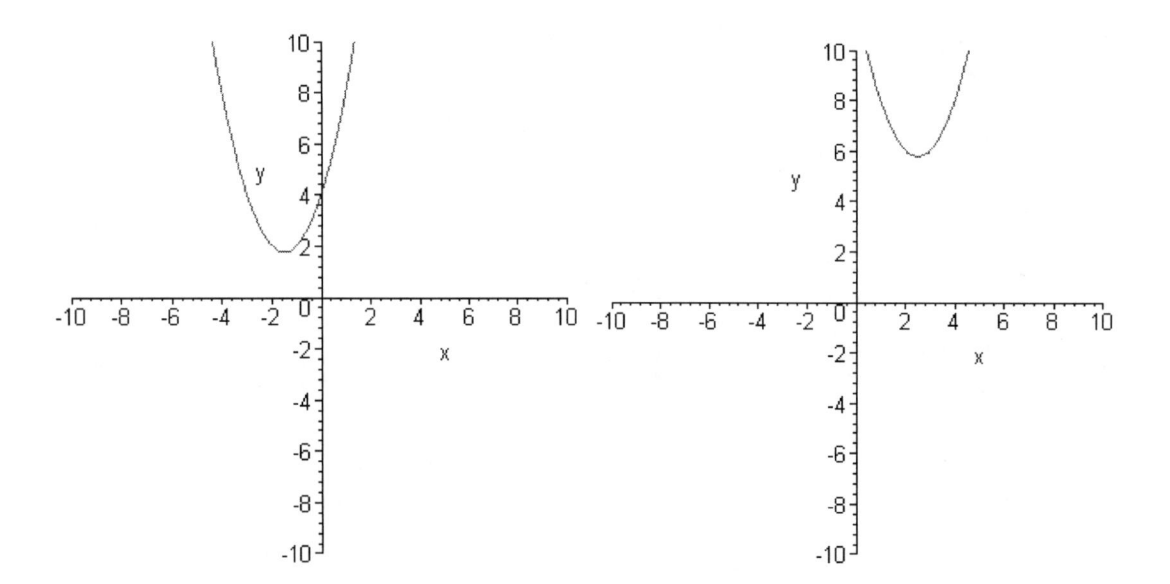

Range: $f(x) \in [\frac{7}{4}, \infty)$ 	 Range: $f(x) \in [\frac{23}{4}, \infty)$

Vertex form: $f(x) = \left(x+\frac{3}{2}\right)^2 + \frac{7}{4}$ 	 Vertex form: $f(x) = \left(x+\frac{5}{2}\right)^2 + \frac{23}{4}$

Factorized form: *None* 	 Factorized form: *None*

Standard form: $f(x) = x^2 + 3x + 4$ 	 Standard form: $f(x) = x^2 + 5x + 12$

14. Analyze the following functions:
    1. f(x) = –3

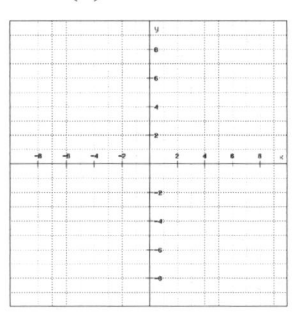

    $Vertex\ Form: None(Linear)$
    $Factorized\ Form: None(Linear)$
    $Domain: x \in R \quad Range: f(x) \in \{-3\}$
    $y\,int: (0,-3) \quad Vertex: None$
    $x\,int: None$
    $Increase: Never \quad Decrease: Never$

    2. f(x) = 5x

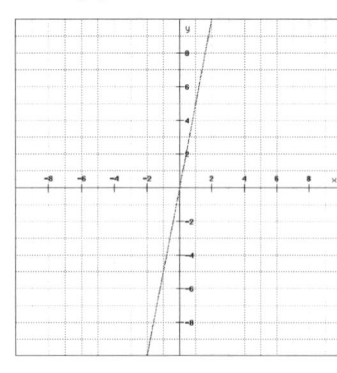

    $Vertex\ Form: None(Linear)$
    $Factorized\ Form: None(Linear)$
    $Domain: x \in R \quad Range: f(x) \in R$
    $y\,int: (0,0) \quad Vertex: None$
    $x\,int: (0,0)$
    $Increase: x \in R \quad Decrease: Never$

3. $f(x) = x^2 + 8x + 19$

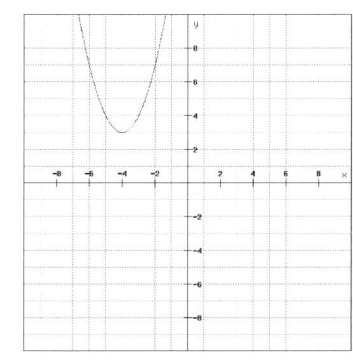

$Vertex\ Form: f(x) = (x+4)^2 + 3$
$Factorized\ Form: None$
$Domain: x \in R \quad Range: f(x) \in [3, \infty)$
$y\,int: (0, 19) \quad Vertex: (-4, 3)$
$x\,int: None$
$Increase: x \in (-4, \infty) \quad Decrease: x \in (-\infty, 4)$

4. $f(x) = 10x^2 - 8x - 2$

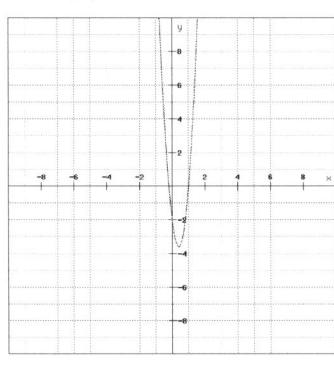

$Vertex\ Form: f(x) = 10\left(x - \dfrac{2}{5}\right)^2 - \dfrac{90}{25}$
$Factorized\ Form: f(x) = 10\left(x + \dfrac{1}{5}\right)(x-1)$
$Domain: x \in R \quad Range: f(x) \in [-\dfrac{90}{25}, \infty)$
$y\,int: (0, -2) \quad Vertex: (\dfrac{2}{5}, -\dfrac{90}{25})$
$x\,int: (-\dfrac{1}{5}, 0), (1, 0)$
$Increase: x \in (\dfrac{2}{5}, \infty) \quad Decrease: x \in (-\infty, \dfrac{2}{5})$

5. $f(x) = x^2 + 4x + 1$

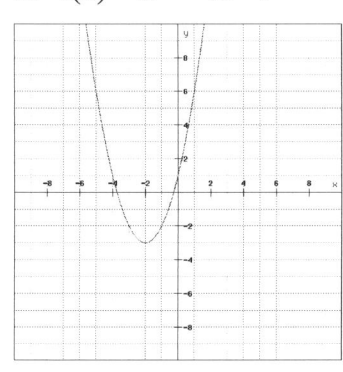

$Vertex\ Form: f(x) = (x+2)^2 - 3$
$Factorized\ Form: f(x) = \left(x - (\sqrt{3} - 2)\right)\left(x - (-\sqrt{3} - 2)\right)$
$Domain: x \in R \quad Range: f(x) \in [-3, \infty)$
$y\,int: (0, 1) \quad Vertex: (-2, -3)$
$x\,int: (\sqrt{3} - 2, 0), (-\sqrt{3} - 2, 0)$
$Increase: x \in (-2, \infty) \quad Decrease: x \in (-\infty, -2)$

6. $f(x) = 4x^2 - 14x + 6$

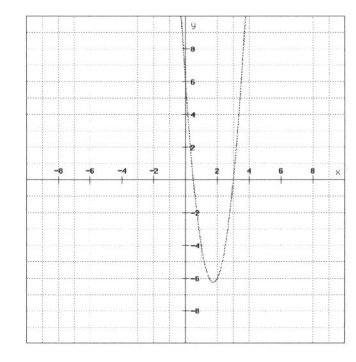

$Vertex\ Form: f(x) = 4\left(x - \dfrac{7}{4}\right)^2 - \dfrac{25}{4}$
$Factorized\ Form: f(x) = 2\left(x - \dfrac{1}{2}\right)(x - 3)$
$Domain: x \in R \quad Range: f(x) \in [-\dfrac{25}{4}, \infty)$
$y\,int: (0, 6) \quad Vertex: (\dfrac{7}{4}, -\dfrac{25}{4})$
$x\,int: (\dfrac{1}{2}, 0), (3, 0)$
$Increase: x \in (\dfrac{7}{4}, \infty) \quad Decrease: x \in (-\infty, \dfrac{7}{4})$

7. $f(x) = 2x^2 - 3x - 5$

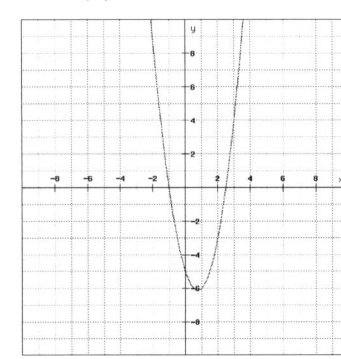

Vertex Form: $f(x) = 2\left(x - \dfrac{3}{4}\right)^2 - \dfrac{49}{8}$

Factorized Form: $f(x) = 2\left(x - \dfrac{5}{2}\right)(x+1)$

Domain: $x \in R$ Range: $f(x) \in [-\dfrac{49}{8}, \infty)$

$y$int: $(0,-5)$ Vertex: $(\dfrac{3}{4}, -\dfrac{49}{8})$

$x$int: $(\dfrac{5}{2}, 0), (-1, 0)$

Increase: $x \in (\dfrac{3}{4}, \infty)$ Decrease: $x \in (-\infty, \dfrac{3}{4})$

8. $f(x) = x^2 + 3x - 10$

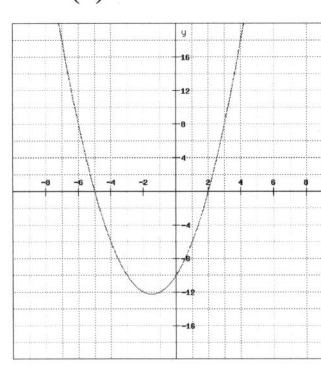

Vertex Form: $f(x) = \left(x + \dfrac{3}{2}\right)^2 - \dfrac{49}{4}$

Factorized Form: $f(x) = (x+5)(x-2)$

Domain: $x \in R$ Range: $f(x) \in [-\dfrac{49}{4}, \infty)$

$y$int: $(0,-10)$ Vertex: $(-\dfrac{3}{2}, -\dfrac{49}{4})$

$x$int: $(-5, 0), (2, 0)$

Increase: $x \in (-\dfrac{3}{2}, \infty)$ Decrease: $x \in (-\infty, -\dfrac{3}{2})$

9. $f(x) = x^2 + 7x - 1$

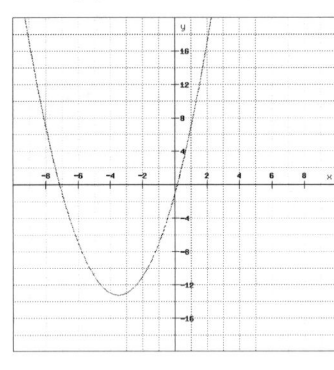

Vertex Form: $f(x) = \left(x + \dfrac{7}{2}\right)^2 - \dfrac{53}{4}$

Factorized Form: $f(x) = \left(x - \left(\sqrt{\dfrac{53}{5}} - \dfrac{7}{2}\right)\right)\left(x - \left(-\sqrt{\dfrac{53}{5}} - \dfrac{7}{2}\right)\right)$

Domain: $x \in R$ Range: $f(x) \in [-\dfrac{53}{4}, \infty)$

$y$int: $(0,-1)$ Vertex: $(-\dfrac{7}{2}, -\dfrac{53}{4})$

$x$int: $(\sqrt{\dfrac{53}{5}} - \dfrac{7}{2}, 0), (-\sqrt{\dfrac{53}{5}} - \dfrac{7}{2}, 0)$

Increase: $x \in (-\dfrac{7}{2}, \infty)$ Decrease: $x \in (-\infty, -\dfrac{7}{2})$

10. $f(x) = x^2 + 2x + 7$

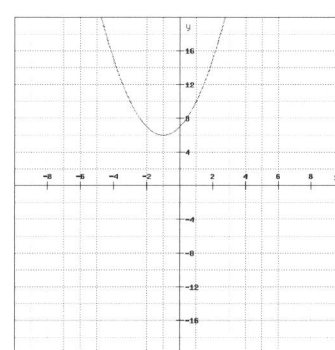

Vertex Form: $f(x) = (x+1)^2 + 6$
Factorized Form: None
Domain: $x \in R$ Range: $f(x) \in [6, \infty)$
y int: $(0, 7)$ Vertex: $(-1, 6)$
x int: None
Increase: $x \in (-1, \infty)$ Decrease: $x \in (-\infty, -1)$

11. $f(x) = x^2 + x - 1$

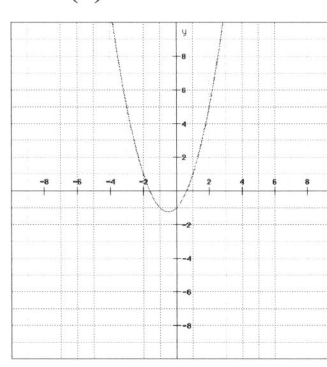

Vertex Form: $f(x) = \left(x + \dfrac{1}{2}\right)^2 - \dfrac{5}{4}$

Factorized Form: $f(x) = \left(x - \left(\sqrt{\dfrac{5}{4}} - \dfrac{1}{2}\right)\right)\left(x - \left(-\sqrt{\dfrac{5}{4}} - \dfrac{1}{2}\right)\right)$

Domain: $x \in R$ Range: $f(x) \in [-\dfrac{5}{4}, \infty)$

y int: $(0, -1)$ Vertex: $(-\dfrac{1}{2}, -\dfrac{5}{4})$

x int: $(\sqrt{\dfrac{5}{4}} - \dfrac{1}{2}, 0), (-\sqrt{\dfrac{5}{4}} - \dfrac{1}{2}, 0)$

Increase: $x \in (-\dfrac{1}{2}, \infty)$ Decrease: $x \in (-\infty, -\dfrac{1}{2})$

12. $f(x) = x^2 + 2x + 1$

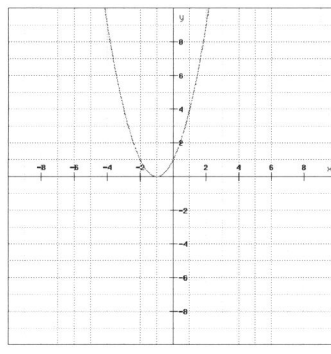

Vertex Form: $f(x) = (x+1)^2$
Factorized Form: $f(x) = (x+1)(x+1)$
Domain: $x \in R$ Range: $f(x) \in [0, \infty)$
y int: $(0, 1)$ Vertex: $(-1, 0)$
x int: $(-1, 0)$
Increase: $x \in (-1, \infty)$ Decrease: $x \in (-\infty, -1)$

13. $f(x) = x^2 + 1$

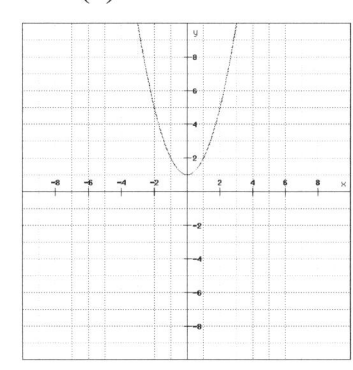

Vertex Form: $f(x) = x^2 + 1$
Factorized Form: None
Domain: $x \in R$ Range: $f(x) \in [1, \infty)$
y int: $(0, 1)$ Vertex: $(0, 1)$
x int: None
Increase: $x \in (0, \infty)$ Decrease: $x \in (-\infty, 0)$

14. $f(x) = x^2 - 1$

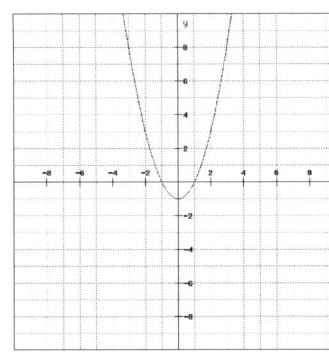

Vertex Form: $f(x) = x^2 - 1$
Factorized Form: $f(x) = (x+1)(x-1)$
Domain: $x \in R$ *Range*: $f(x) \in [-1, \infty)$
y int: $(0, -1)$ *Vertex*: $(0, -1)$
x int: $(-1, 0), (1, 0)$
Increase: $x \in (0, \infty)$ *Decrease*: $x \in (-\infty, 0)$

15. $f(x) = x^2 + 3x$

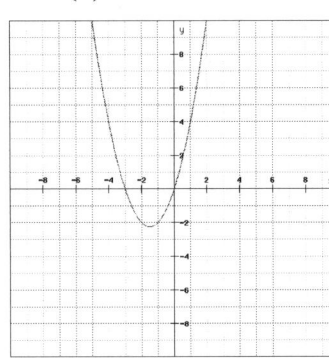

Vertex Form: $f(x) = \left(x + \dfrac{3}{2}\right)^2 - \dfrac{9}{4}$
Factorized Form: $f(x) = x(x+3)$
Domain: $x \in R$ *Range*: $f(x) \in [-\dfrac{9}{4}, \infty)$
y int: $(0, 0)$ *Vertex*: $(-\dfrac{3}{2}, -\dfrac{9}{4})$
x int: $(-3, 0), (0, 0)$
Increase: $x \in (-\dfrac{3}{2}, \infty)$ *Decrease*: $x \in (-\infty, -\dfrac{3}{2})$

16. $f(x) = x^2 + 5x$

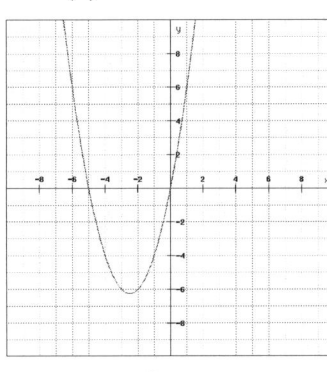

Vertex Form: $f(x) = \left(x + \dfrac{5}{2}\right)^2 - \dfrac{25}{4}$
Factorized Form: $f(x) = x(x+5)$
Domain: $x \in R$ *Range*: $f(x) \in [-\dfrac{25}{4}, \infty)$
y int: $(0, 0)$ *Vertex*: $(-\dfrac{5}{2}, -\dfrac{25}{4})$
x int: $(-5, 0), (0, 0)$
Increase: $x \in (-\dfrac{5}{2}, \infty)$ *Decrease*: $x \in (-\infty, -\dfrac{5}{2})$

17. $f(x) = x^2 - 3x$

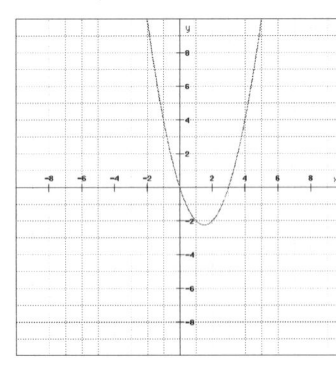

Vertex Form: $f(x) = \left(x - \dfrac{3}{2}\right)^2 - \dfrac{9}{4}$
Factorized Form: $f(x) = x(x-3)$
Domain: $x \in R$ *Range*: $f(x) \in [-\dfrac{9}{4}, \infty)$
y int: $(0, 0)$ *Vertex*: $(\dfrac{3}{2}, -\dfrac{9}{4})$
x int: $(0, 0), (3, 0)$
Increase: $x \in (\dfrac{3}{2}, \infty)$ *Decrease*: $x \in (-\infty, \dfrac{3}{2})$

18. f(x) = x² – 7x

Vertex Form: $f(x) = \left(x - \dfrac{7}{2}\right)^2 - \dfrac{49}{4}$

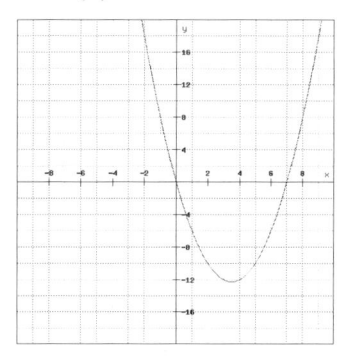

Factorized Form: $f(x) = x(x-7)$

Domain: $x \in R$ *Range*: $f(x) \in [-\dfrac{49}{4}, \infty)$

y int: $(0,0)$ *Vertex*: $(\dfrac{7}{2}, -\dfrac{49}{4})$

x int: $(0,0), (7,0)$

Increase: $x \in (\dfrac{7}{2}, \infty)$ *Decrease*: $x \in (-\infty, \dfrac{7}{2})$

19. f(x) = x² + 4x + 6

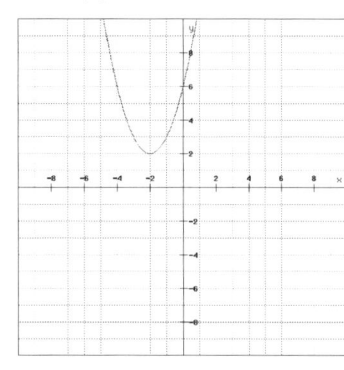

Vertex Form: $f(x) = (x+2)^2 + 2$

Factorized Form: None

Domain: $x \in R$ *Range*: $f(x) \in [2, \infty)$

y int: $(0,6)$ *Vertex*: $(-2, 2)$

x int: None

Increase: $x \in (-2, \infty)$ *Decrease*: $x \in (-\infty, -2)$

20. f(x) = –2x² – 16x – 29

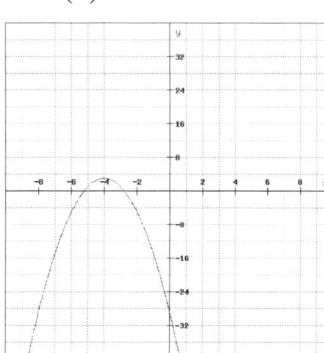

Vertex Form: $f(x) = -2(x+4)^2 + 3$

Factorized Form: $f(x) = -2\left(x - \left(\sqrt{\dfrac{3}{2}} - 2\right)\right)\left(x - \left(-\sqrt{\dfrac{3}{2}} - 2\right)\right)$

Domain: $x \in R$ *Range*: $f(x) \in (-\infty, 3]$

y int: $(0, -29)$ *Vertex*: $(-4, 3)$

x int: $(\sqrt{\dfrac{3}{2}} - 2, 0), (-\sqrt{\dfrac{3}{2}} - 2, 0)$

Increase: $x \in (-\infty, -4)$ *Decrease*: $x \in (-4, \infty)$

21. f(x) = x² – 6x + 4

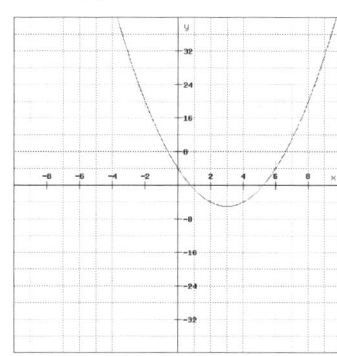

Vertex Form: $f(x) = (x-3)^2 - 5$

Factorized Form: $f(x) = \left(x - (\sqrt{5} + 3)\right)\left(x - (-\sqrt{5} + 3)\right)$

Domain: $x \in R$ *Range*: $f(x) \in [-5, \infty)$

y int: $(0, 4)$ *Vertex*: $(3, -5)$

x int: $(\sqrt{5} + 3, 0), (-\sqrt{5} + 3, 0)$

Increase: $x \in (3, \infty)$ *Decrease*: $x \in (-\infty, 3)$

22. $f(x) = x^2 - 7x + 2$

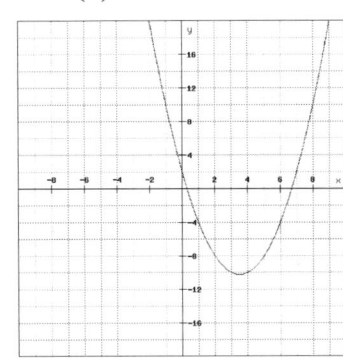

$Vertex\ Form: f(x) = \left(x - \frac{7}{2}\right)^2 - \frac{41}{4}$

$Factorized\ Form: f(x) = \left(x - \left(\sqrt{\frac{41}{4}} + \frac{7}{2}\right)\right)\left(x - \left(-\sqrt{\frac{41}{4}} + \frac{7}{2}\right)\right)$

$Domain: x \in R \quad Range: f(x) \in [-\frac{41}{4}, \infty)$

$y\,\text{int}: (0, 2) \quad Vertex: (\frac{7}{2}, -\frac{41}{4})$

$x\,\text{int}: (\sqrt{\frac{41}{4}} + \frac{7}{2}, 0), (-\sqrt{\frac{41}{4}} + \frac{7}{2}, 0)$

$Increase: x \in (\frac{7}{2}, \infty) \quad Decrease: x \in (-\infty, \frac{7}{2})$

23. $f(x) = x^2 + 3x + 10$

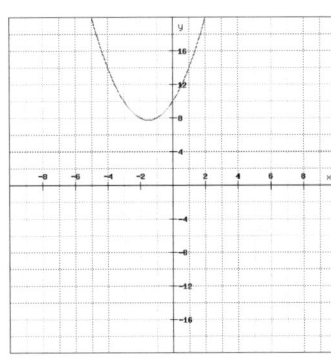

$Vertex\ Form: f(x) = \left(x + \frac{3}{2}\right)^2 + \frac{31}{4}$

$Factorized\ Form: None$

$Domain: x \in R \quad Range: f(x) \in [\frac{31}{4}, \infty)$

$y\,\text{int}: (0, 10) \quad Vertex: (-\frac{3}{2}, \frac{31}{4})$

$x\,\text{int}: None$

$Increase: x \in (-\frac{3}{2}, \infty) \quad Decrease: x \in (-\infty, -\frac{3}{2})$

24. $f(x) = x^2 + 5$

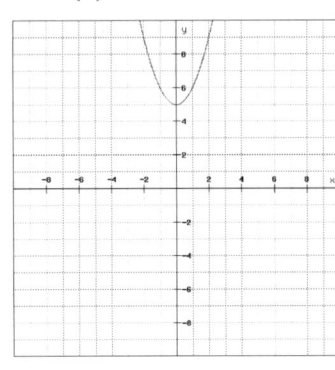

$Vertex\ Form: f(x) = x^2 + 5$

$Factorized\ Form: None$

$Domain: x \in R \quad Range: f(x) \in [5, \infty)$

$y\,\text{int}: (0, 5) \quad Vertex: (0, 5)$

$x\,\text{int}: None$

$Increase: x \in (0, \infty) \quad Decrease: x \in (-\infty, 0)$

25. $f(x) = x^2 - 3$

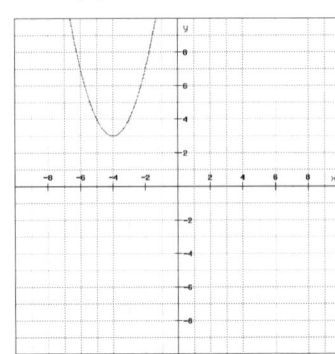

$Vertex\ Form: f(x) = x^2 - 3$

$Factorized\ Form: f(x) = (x + \sqrt{3})(x - \sqrt{3})$

$Domain: x \in R \quad Range: f(x) \in [-3, \infty)$

$y\,\text{int}: (0, -3) \quad Vertex: (0, -3)$

$x\,\text{int}: (-\sqrt{3}, 0), (\sqrt{3}, 0)$

$Increase: x \in (0, \infty) \quad Decrease: x \in (-\infty, 0)$

26. f(x) = x² − 7x

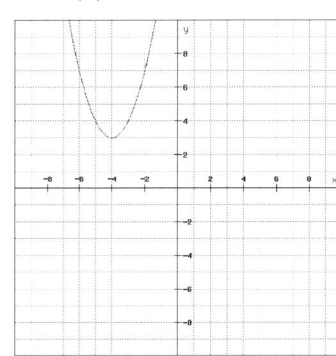

$Vertex\ Form: f(x) = \left(x - \frac{7}{2}\right)^2 - \frac{49}{4}$

$Factorized\ Form: f(x) = x(x-7)$

$Domain: x \in R \quad Range: f(x) \in [-\frac{49}{4}, \infty)$

$y\,\text{int}: (0,0) \quad Vertex: (\frac{7}{2}, -\frac{49}{4})$

$x\,\text{int}: (0,0), (7,0)$

$Increase: x \in (\frac{7}{2}, \infty) \quad Decrease: x \in (-\infty, \frac{7}{2})$

27. f(x) = x² + 3x − 5

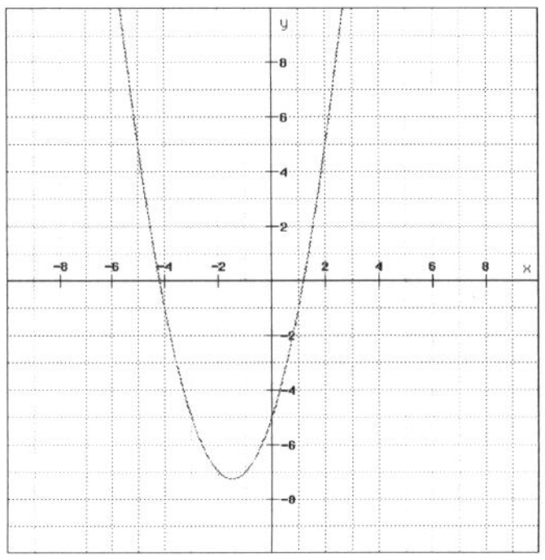

$Vertex\ Form: f(x) = \left(x + \frac{3}{2}\right)^2 - \frac{29}{4}$

$Factorized\ Form: f(x) = \left(x - \left(\sqrt{\frac{29}{4}} - \frac{3}{2}\right)\right)\left(x - \left(-\sqrt{\frac{29}{4}} - \frac{3}{2}\right)\right)$

$Domain: x \in R \quad Range: f(x) \in [-\frac{29}{4}, \infty)$

$y\,\text{int}: (0,-5) \quad Vertex: (-\frac{3}{2}, -\frac{29}{4})$

$x\,\text{int}: (\sqrt{\frac{29}{4}} - \frac{3}{2}, 0), (-\sqrt{\frac{29}{4}} - \frac{3}{2}, 0)$

$Increase: x \in (-\frac{3}{2}, \infty) \quad Decrease: x \in (-\infty, -\frac{3}{2})$

28. f(x) = 5x² − 3

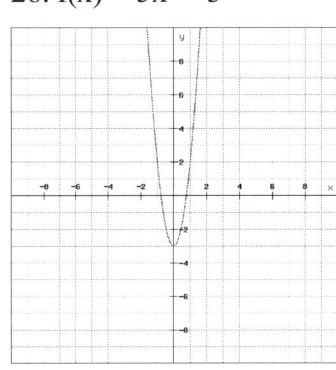

$Vertex\ Form: f(x) = 5x^2 - 3$

$Factorized\ Form: f(x) = 5\left(x - \sqrt{\frac{3}{5}}\right)\left(x + \sqrt{\frac{3}{5}}\right)$

$Domain: x \in R \quad Range: f(x) \in [-3, \infty)$

$y\,\text{int}: (0,-3) \quad Vertex: (0,-3)$

$x\,\text{int}: (-\sqrt{\frac{3}{5}}, 0), (\sqrt{\frac{3}{5}}, 0)$

$Increase: x \in (0, \infty) \quad Decrease: x \in (-\infty, 0)$

29. f(x) = 5x² − 10x

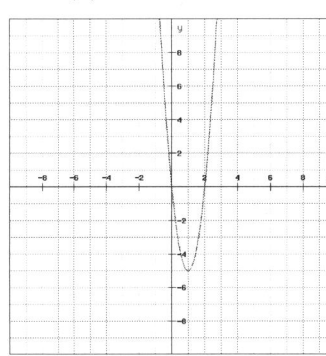

$Vertex\ Form: f(x) = 5(x-1)^2 - 5$

$Factorized\ Form: f(x) = 5x(x-2)$

$Domain: x \in R \quad Range: f(x) \in [-5, \infty)$

$y\,\text{int}: (0,0) \quad Vertex: (1,-5)$

$x\,\text{int}: (0,0), (2,0)$

$Increase: x \in (1, \infty) \quad Decrease: x \in (-\infty, 1)$

30. f(x) = –5x²

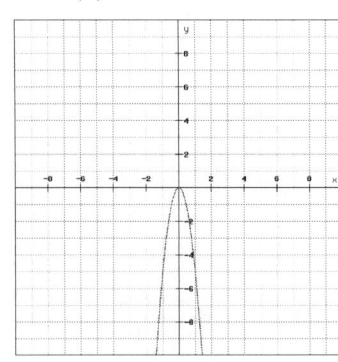

Vertex Form: $f(x) = -5x^2$
Factorized Form: $f(x) = -5x^2$
Domain: $x \in R$ Range: $f(x) \in (-\infty, 0]$
$y$int: $(0,0)$ Vertex: $(0,0)$
$x$int: $(0,0)$
Increase: $x \in (-\infty, 0)$ Decrease: $x \in (0, \infty)$

31. f(x) = –x² + 6x – 8

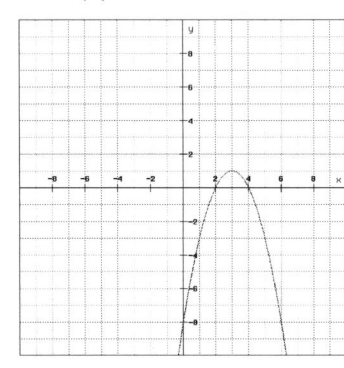

Vertex Form: $f(x) = -(x-3)^2 + 1$
Factorized Form: $f(x) = -(x-2)(x-4)$
Domain: $x \in R$ Range: $f(x) \in (-\infty, 1]$
$y$int: $(0,-8)$ Vertex: $(3,-1)$
$x$int: $(2,0), (4,0)$
Increase: $x \in (-\infty, 3)$ Decrease: $x \in (3, \infty)$

32. f(x) = –x² – 6x + 2

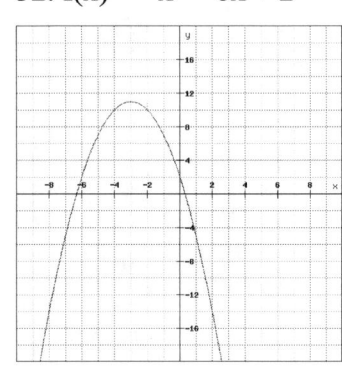

Vertex Form: $f(x) = -(x+3)^2 + 11$
Factorized Form: $f(x) = -\left(x - \left(\sqrt{11} - 3\right)\right)\left(x - \left(-\sqrt{11} - 3\right)\right)$
Domain: $x \in R$ Range: $f(x) \in (-\infty, 11]$
$y$int: $(0,2)$ Vertex: $(-3,11)$
$x$int: $(\sqrt{11} - 3, 0), (-\sqrt{11} - 3, 0)$
Increase: $x \in (-\infty, -3)$ Decrease: $x \in (-3, \infty)$

33. f(x) = –x² + x – 5

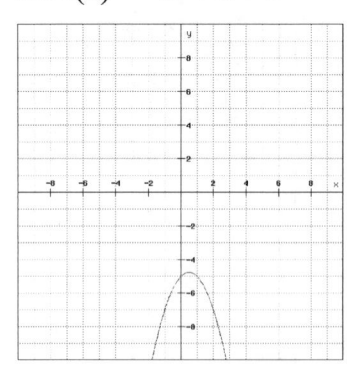

Vertex Form: $f(x) = -\left(x - \dfrac{1}{2}\right)^2 - \dfrac{19}{4}$
Factorized Form: None
Domain: $x \in R$ Range: $f(x) \in (-\infty, -\dfrac{19}{4}]$
$y$int: $(0,-5)$ Vertex: $(\dfrac{1}{2}, -\dfrac{19}{4})$
$x$int: None
Increase: $x \in (-\infty, \dfrac{1}{2})$ Decrease: $x \in (\dfrac{1}{2}, \infty)$

472

34. f(x) = –x² – 4x – 4

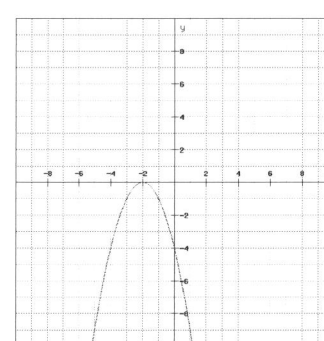

Vertex Form: $f(x) = -(x+2)^2$
Factorized Form: $f(x) = -(x+2)(x+2)$
Domain: $x \in R$ *Range*: $f(x) \in (-\infty, 0]$
y int: $(0, -4)$ *Vertex*: $(-2, 0)$
x int: $(-2, 0)$
Increase: $x \in (-\infty, -2)$ *Decrease*: $x \in (-2, \infty)$

35. f(x) = –x² + 3

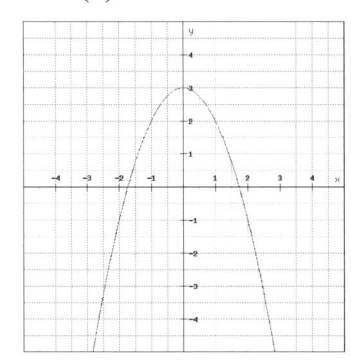

Vertex Form: $f(x) = -x^2 + 3$
Factorized Form: $f(x) = -(x+\sqrt{3})(x-\sqrt{3})$
Domain: $x \in R$ *Range*: $f(x) \in (-\infty, 3]$
y int: $(0, 3)$ *Vertex*: $(0, 3)$
x int: $(\sqrt{3}, 0), (-\sqrt{3}, 0)$
Increase: $x \in (-\infty, 0)$ *Decrease*: $x \in (0, \infty)$

36. f(x) = 3x²

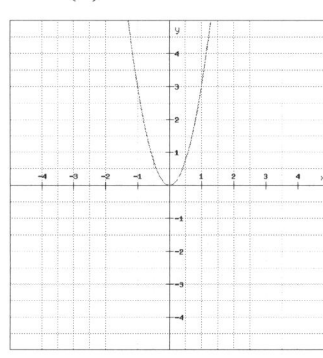

Vertex Form: $f(x) = 3x^2$
Factorized Form: $f(x) = 3x^2$
Domain: $x \in R$ *Range*: $f(x) \in [0, \infty)$
y int: $(0, 0)$ *Vertex*: $(0, 0)$
x int: $(0, 0)$
Increase: $x \in (0, \infty)$ *Decrease*: $x \in (-\infty, 0)$

37. f(x) = 2((x + 3)x + 4) = 2x² + 6x + 8 = 2(x² + 3x + 4)

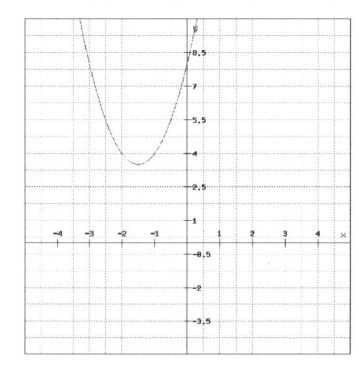

Vertex Form: $f(x) = 2\left(x + \dfrac{3}{2}\right)^2 + \dfrac{7}{2}$
Factorized Form: *None*
Domain: $x \in R$ *Range*: $f(x) \in [\dfrac{7}{2}, \infty)$
y int: $(0, 8)$ *Vertex*: $(-\dfrac{3}{2}, \dfrac{7}{2})$
x int: *None*
Increase: $x \in (-\dfrac{3}{2}, \infty)$ *Decrease*: $x \in (-\infty, -\dfrac{3}{2})$

38. $f(x) = \dfrac{2x - 4x^2}{2} = -2x^2 + x$ Vertex Form: $f(x) = -2\left(x - \dfrac{1}{4}\right)^2 + \dfrac{1}{8}$

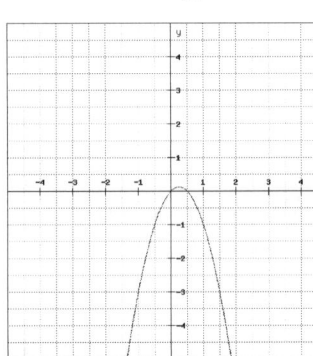

Factorized Form: $f(x) = -x(2x - 1)$

Domain: $x \in R$ Range: $f(x) \in (-\infty, \dfrac{1}{8}]$

y int: $(0,0)$ Vertex: $(\dfrac{1}{4}, \dfrac{1}{8})$

x int: $(0,0), (\dfrac{1}{2}, 0)$

Increase: $x \in (-\infty, \dfrac{1}{4})$ Decrease: $x \in (\dfrac{1}{4}, \infty)$

39. $f(x) = \dfrac{4x^2 + 8x}{4} - 2 = x^2 + 2x - 2$

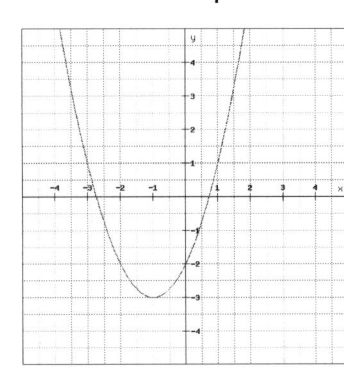

Vertex Form: $f(x) = (x + 1)^2 - 3$

Factorized Form: $f(x) = (x - (\sqrt{3} - 1))(x - (-\sqrt{3} - 1))$

Domain: $x \in R$ Range: $f(x) \in [-3, \infty)$

y int: $(0, -2)$ Vertex: $(-1, 3)$

x int: $(\sqrt{3} - 1, 0), (-\sqrt{3} - 1, 0)$

Increase: $x \in (-1, \infty)$ Decrease: $x \in (-\infty, -1)$

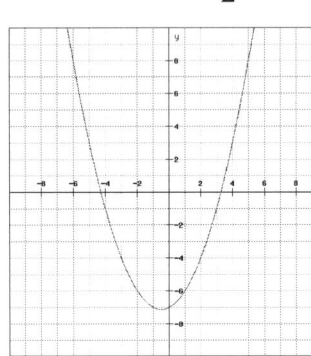

40. $f(x) = \dfrac{(x-3)(x+4)}{2} - 1 = \dfrac{1}{2}x^2 + \dfrac{1}{2}x - 7$

Vertex Form: $f(x) = \dfrac{1}{2}\left(x + \dfrac{1}{2}\right)^2 - \dfrac{57}{8}$

Factorized Form: $f(x) = \dfrac{1}{2}\left(x - \left(-\dfrac{1}{2} + \dfrac{\sqrt{57}}{2}\right)\right)\left(x - \left(-\dfrac{1}{2} - \dfrac{\sqrt{57}}{2}\right)\right)$

Domain: $x \in R$ Range: $f(x) \in [-1, \infty)$

y int: $(0, -7)$ Vertex: $(-\dfrac{1}{2}, -\dfrac{57}{8})$

x int: $(-\dfrac{1}{2} + \dfrac{\sqrt{57}}{2}, 0), (-\dfrac{1}{2} - \dfrac{\sqrt{57}}{2}, 0)$

Increase: $x \in (-\dfrac{1}{2}, \infty)$ Decrease: $x \in (-\infty, -\dfrac{1}{2})$

41. Vertex of $y = 7(x + 3)^2 + 4$? (–3, 4), its axes of symmetry: x = –3

42. Vertex of $y = -2(x - 4)^2 + 2$? (4, 2), its axes of symmetry: x = 4

43. The graph of the relation $x = -5(y + 2)^2 + 6$ opens to the left.

44. b = 16, x = 4

45. When a quadratic function can be written as a perfect square on the graph it means that its vertex is on the x axis and it has a single x intercept.

474

46. The zeros: x = 0, x = 2, axis of symmetry x = 1

47. The roots: $x = -\dfrac{6}{5}, x = 12,$ axis of symmetry: $x = \dfrac{27}{5}$

48. The quadratic equation is used to find the zeros (x intercepts) of the quadratic function. in case this equation has no solutions it means the quadratic function is completely above or below the x axis and the value of $b^2 - 4ac$ is negative. In case $b^2 - 4ac$ is positive the quadratic function will have 2 zeros (2 x intercepts) and lastly if $b^2 - 4ac$ is zero the quadratic function will have 1 zero.

    If $b^2 - 4ac > 0$ there are 2 zeros (2 x intercepts) Example: $f(x) = x^2 - 10x + 2$

    If $b^2 - 4ac = 0$ there are 1 zero (1 x intercept) Example: $f(x) = x^2 - 6x + 9$

    If $b^2 - 4ac < 0$ there are no zeros (no x intercepts) Example: $f(x) = x^2 + 4x + 1$

49. What values of b make the relation $y = 6x^2 + bx + 5$ have no zeros?

    $Discri\min ant = b^2 - 120 < 0; b \in (-\sqrt{120}, \sqrt{120})$

50. Under what conditions will the parabola with equation $y = a(x - h)^2 + k$ have two x–intercepts? $k < 0$

51. $y = -1.7(x + 13.2)^2 - 3.1$ Opens down, vertex below x axes so no zeros

52. A parabola has its vertex in the third quadrant and opens down. A possible value for $b^2 - 4ac$ can be -4

53. The equation, $f(x) = -2(x + 2)^2 + 3$

54. The equation $f(x) = \dfrac{1}{2}(x + 2)^2 - 3$

55. Give the relation $y = -4(x - 2)^2 + 7$, state its axis of symmetry: x = 2

56. The vertex of the relation $y = -(x - 3)(x + 1)$.

    Maximum: (1, 4), axis of symmetry x = 1

57. The parabola $y = 4(x - 2)^2 - 7$ is the image parabola.

Inequalities of the 2nd degree – use a graph to solve

1. $x^2 > 0$ $x \in \Re, x \neq 0$ $x^2 < 0$ No Solution

2. $x^2 + 1 > 0$ $x \in \Re$ $x^2 + 1 < 0$ No Solution

3. $x^2 - 1 > 0$ $x \in (-\infty, -1) \cup (1, \infty)$ $x^2 - 1 < 0$ $x \in (-1, 1)$

4. $x^2 - 3 \geq 0$ $x \in (-\infty, -\sqrt{3}] \cup [\sqrt{3}, \infty)$ $x^2 - 3 \leq 0$ $x \in [-\sqrt{3}, \sqrt{3}]$

5. $x^2 - 3x > 0$ $x \in (-\infty, 0) \cup (3, \infty)$ $x^2 - 3x < 0$ $x \in (0, 3)$

6. $2x^2 + 4 > 0$ $x \in \Re$ $2x^2 + 4 < 0$ No Solution

7. $x^2 - 3x + 2 > 0$ $x \in (-\infty, 1) \cup (2, \infty)$ $x^2 - 3x + 2 < 0$ $x \in (1, 2)$

8. $x^2 + 2x - 3 > 0$ $x \in (-\infty, -3) \cup (1, \infty)$ $x^2 + 2x - 3 < 0$ $x \in (-3, 1)$

9. $2x^2 + 8x - 10 > 0$ $x \in (-\infty, -5) \cup (1, \infty)$ $2x^2 + 8x - 10 < 0$ $x \in (-5, 1)$

10. $x^2 - 2x + 1 > 0$ $x \in \Re, x \neq 1$ $2x^2 + 2x \leq 0$ $x \in (-1, 0)$

11. $x^2 + 11x + 10 > 0$ $x \in (-\infty, -10) \cup (-1, \infty)$ $2x^2 + 3x + 1 < 0$ $x \in (-\frac{1}{2}, -1)$

Applications

1. The height of a ball kicked upwards is given by $h(t) = 40t - 16t^2$ meters, $t \in [0, 2.5]$ where t is measured in seconds.

   a. The corresponding function, label the axes.

   b. Calculate h(1) and give a practical interpretation to your answer.

   h(1) = 24m, the height of the ball after 1 second.

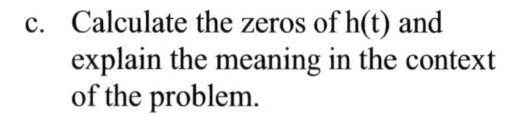

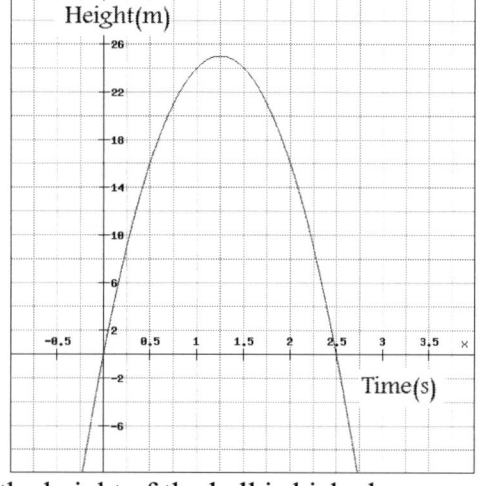

   c. Calculate the zeros of h(t) and explain the meaning in the context of the problem.

   t = 0s, t = 2.5s, the instants in which the height of the ball is kicked. Right in the beginning and after it fell back.

   d. Solve the equation h(t) = 10 and explain the meaning of the solutions in the context of the problem.

   $h(t) = 40t - 16t^2 = 10$;   t ≈ 0.28s, t ≈ 2.22s the instants in which the height of the ball is 10m once on the way up and once on the way down.

   The maximum height of the ball and the instant in which it reaches it.

   The vertex of the parabola is (1.25, 25) so the maximum height is 25m

2. The width of a rectangle is three times is length, its area is 243 m². Find its perimeter.

   $x \cdot 3x = 243; x = 9; Perimeter = 18 + 54 = 72m$

476

3. Find 2 consecutive even numbers that when their sum is squared 100 is obtained.

   $(2x+2)^2 = 100; x = 4$ The numbers are 4 and 6

4. The efficiency of an engine as a function of the concentration of a certain chemical component is given by f(x) = –0.5x² + x, 0 ≤ x ≤ 2.

   a. Sketch the function in its domain.

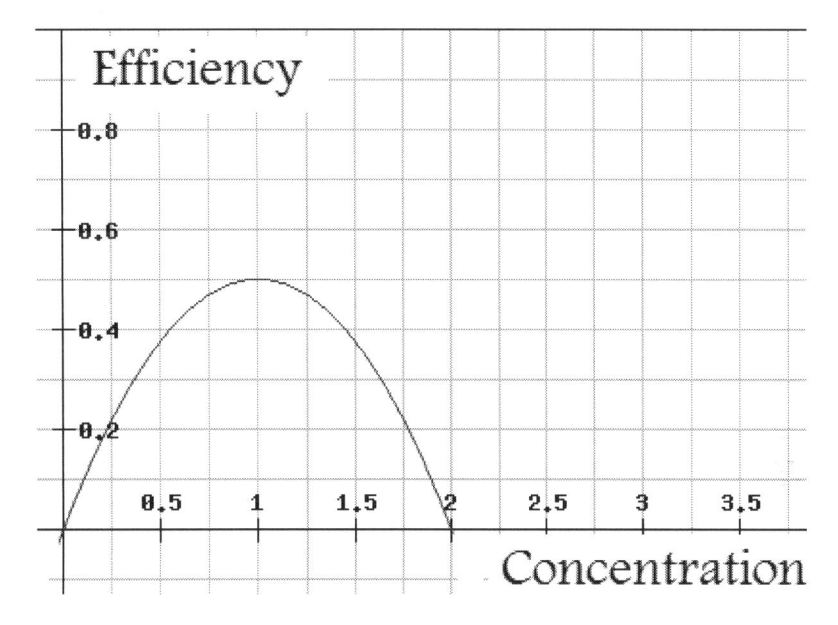

   b. Find the concentration of the chemical for which the efficiency is maximized. What is the efficiency in this case?

   The vertex of the parabola is (1, 0.5) so the concentration required is 1 and the efficiency is 0.5

5. A hundred meters of fencing is available to enclose a rectangular field along side of a River, What dimensions will produce the maximum area that can be enclosed?

   A(x) = x(100 – 2x)

   Parabola whose maximum is

   (25, 1250) so the dimensions are:

   25m width and 50m length

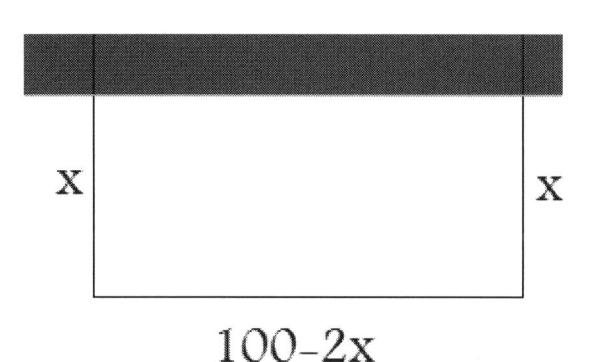

477

2.4. – TRANSLATIONS AND REFLECTIONS

Vertical translation: f(x) → f(x) + a
1. $f(x)+1 = x^2 +1$, Vertical translation 1 unit up.
2. $f(x)-3 = (x+1)^2 -3$, Vertical translation 3 units down.

Horizontal Translation (f(x) → f(x + b)):
3. $f(x-3) = (x-3)^2$, Horizontal translation 3 units to the right.
4. $f(x+1) = -(x+1)^2 +2$, Horizontal translation 1 unit to the left.
5. $f(x+3) = (x+3)^2$, Horizontal translation 3 units to the left.
6. $f(x-3)+5 = (x-1)^2 +4$, Horizontal translation 3 units to the right and vertical translation 5 units up.

Horizontal and Vertical translation: f(x) → f(x + b) + a
7. $f(x-3)+1 = (x-3)^2 +1$, Horizontal translation 3 units to the right and vertical translation 1 unit up.
8. $f(x+2)-3 = -(x+2)^2 -2$, Horizontal translation 2 units to the right and vertical translation 3 units down.

Vertical Dilation (change of amplitude): f(x) → pf(x)
9. $2f(x) = 2x^2$, vertical dilation, factor 2, attention that points located on x axis are fixed, the distance of all other points from x axis is multiplied by 2
10. $\frac{1}{3}f(x) = -\frac{1}{3}x^2 +2$, vertical dilation, factor $\frac{1}{3}$, attention that points located on x axis are fixed, the <u>distance</u> of all other points from x axis is multiplied by $\frac{1}{3}$
11. $f(x-3) = (x-3)^2$ Horizontal translation 3 units to the right
    $3f(x-3) = 3(x-3)^2$ Vertical dilation, factor 3
    $3f(x-3)-4 = 3(x-3)^2 -4$ Vertical translation 4 units down.

Horizontal Dilation (change of scale): $f(x) \to f(\frac{1}{b}x)$

12. $f(2x) = (2x)^2 = 4x^2$, Horizontal dilation factor $\frac{1}{2}$.
13. $f\left(\frac{1}{3}x\right) = \left(\frac{1}{3}x+1\right)^2 = \left(\frac{x+3}{3}\right)^2 = \frac{1}{9}(x+3)^2$, Horizontal dilation factor 3.
    attention that points located on y axis are fixed, the distance of all other points from y axis is multiplied by 3
14. $\frac{1}{3}f(2x) = \frac{1}{3}(2x)^2 +2 = \frac{4}{3}x^2 +2$, Horizontal dilation factor $\frac{1}{2}$. Attention that points located on y axis are fixed, the distance of all other points from y axis is multiplied by 3, then vertical dilation, factor $\frac{1}{3}$, attention that points located on x axis are fixed, the <u>distance</u> of all other points from x axis is multiplied by $\frac{1}{3}$

Reflections about x axis: f(x) → –f(x)

15. $-f(x) = -(x-2)^2$, Reflection about the x axis, attention that points located on x axis are fixed, for all other points y changes to –y.

16. $f(3x) = (3x-4)^2 = \left(3\left(x-\frac{4}{3}\right)\right)^2 = 9\left(x-\frac{4}{3}\right)^2$, Horizontal dilation factor $\frac{1}{3}$, attention that all points on the y axis are fixed, the distance of all other points from the y axis is multiplied by $\frac{1}{3}$.

$-f(3x) = -9\left(x-\frac{4}{3}\right)^2$ Reflection about the x axis, attention that points located on x axis are fixed, for all other points y changes to –y.

Reflections about y axis: f(x) → f(–x)

17. $f(-x) = -2x - 4$, Reflection about the y axis, attention that points located on y axis are fixed, for all other points x changes to –x.

18. $f(-x) = (-x+2)^2 - 7 = (x-2)^2 - 7$, Reflection about the y axis, attention that points located on y axis are fixed, for all other points x changes to –x.

$-f(-x) = -\left((-x+2)^2 - 7\right) = -(x-2)^2 + 7$, Reflection about the x axis, attention that points located on x axis are fixed, for all other points y changes to –y.

Exercises:

1. Consider the function f(x) = x²

   a. Write the expression of the function

   g(x) = f(x) + 2 = $\underline{f(x) + 2 = x^2 + 2}$

   b. This is a <u>vertical</u> translation 2 up

   c. Sketch both functions on the same graph.

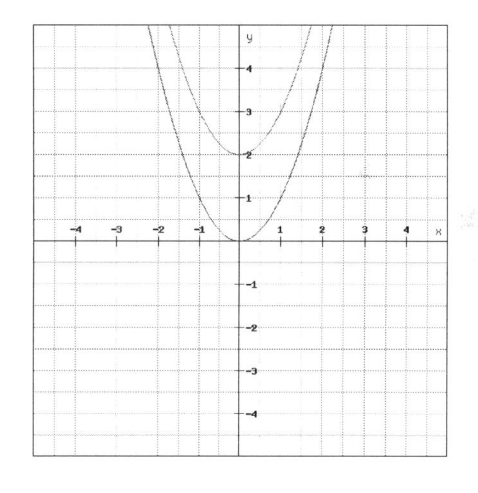

2. Consider the function f(x) = (x – 2)(x + 3)

   a. Write the expression of the function

   g(x) = $\underline{f(x) - 3 = (x-2)(x+3) - 3}$

   b. This is a <u>vertical</u> translation 3 down.

   c. Sketch functions on the same graph.

479

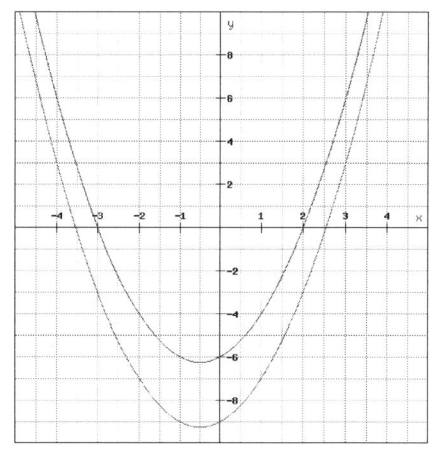

3. Consider the function f(x) = $-2x^2$

   a. Write the expression of the function

      g(x) = $f(x+1) - 5 = -2(x+1)^2 - 5$

   b. This is a <u>vertical</u> translation 5 down and a <u>Horizontal</u> translation 1 left

   c. Sketch both functions on the same graph.

4. Consider the function f(x) = $2(x-3)^2$

   a. Write the expression of the function
      g(x) = $-f(x) = -2(x-3)^2$

   b. This is a <u>reflection</u> about the <u>x axis</u>

   c. Sketch both functions on the same graph.

5. Consider the function f(x) = $(x+2)^2 - 1$

   a. Write the expression of the function

      g(x) = $f(-x) = (-x+2)^2 - 1 = (x-2)^2 - 1$

   b. This is a <u>reflection</u> about the <u>y axis</u>

   c. Sketch both functions on the same graph.

6. Consider the function f(x) = $-(x-2)^2 + 5$

   a. Write the expression of the function
      g(x) = $3f(x) = -3(x-2)^2 + 15$

   b. This is a <u>vertical dilation</u> with scale factor <u>3</u>

   c. Sketch both functions on the same graph.

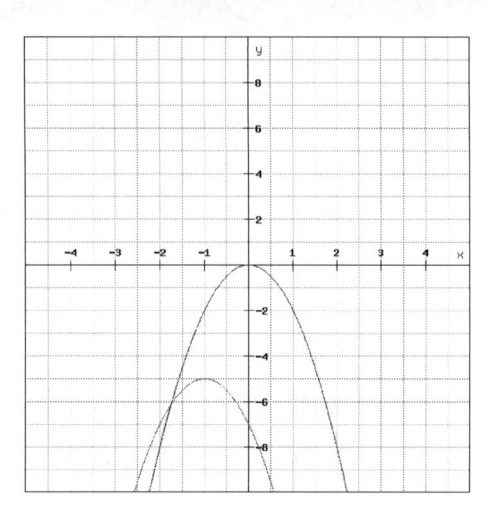

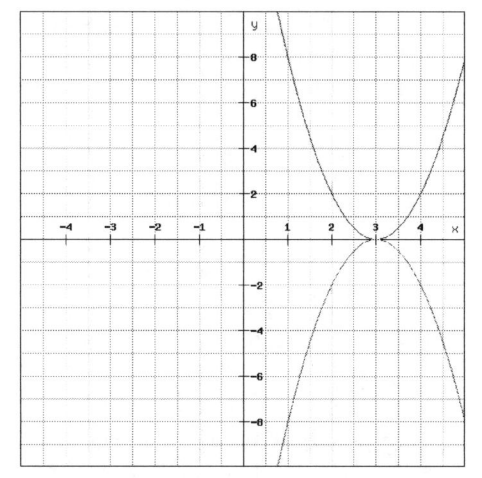

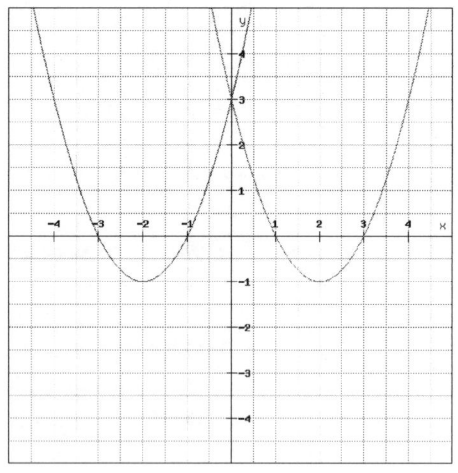

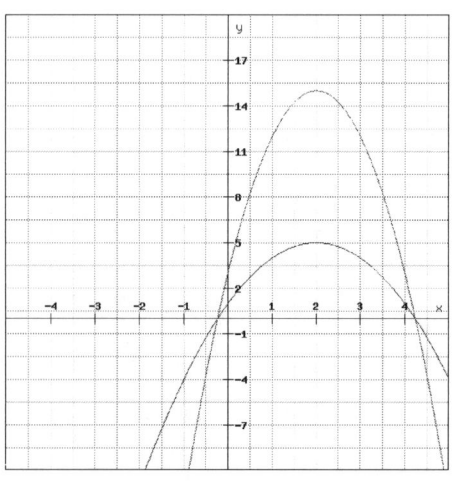

7. Consider the function $f(x) = (x - 5)^2 + 2$

   a. Write the expression of the function

   $g(x) =$

   $f(\frac{x}{2}) = (\frac{x}{2} - 5)^2 + 2 = (\frac{x-10}{2})^2 = \frac{1}{4}(x-10)^2 + 2$

   b. This is a horizontal dilation with scale factor 2

   c. Sketch both functions on the same graph.

8. Consider the function $f(x) = x^2 - 6$

   a. Write the expression of the function

   $g(x) = -f(3x) = -((3x)^2 - 6) = -9x^2 + 6$

   d. This is a <u>horizontal dilation</u> with scale factor $\frac{1}{3}$ and a <u>reflection about the x axis.</u>

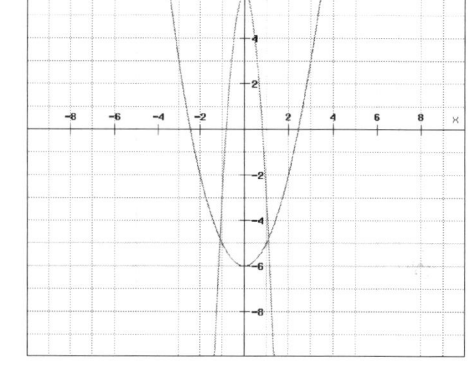

   b. Sketch both functions on the same graph.

9. $f(x) = \frac{x}{x^2 + 1}$ shifted 2 positions up and 3 left. $f(x+3) + 2 = \frac{x+3}{(x+3)^2 + 1} + 2$

10. $f(x) = \frac{x-1}{x^3 + 1}$ shifted 5 positions down and 4 right. $f(x-4) - 5 = \frac{x-5}{(x-4)^3 + 1} - 5$

11. $f(x) = \frac{x}{x^2 + 1}$ dilated vertically 3 times. $3f(x) = \frac{3x}{x^2 + 1}$

12. $f(x) = \frac{x+1}{x^2 + 1}$ dilated horizontally 3 times, shifted 2 positions to the right and 1 up. $f(\frac{x-2}{3}) + 1 \frac{(\frac{x-2}{3} + 1)}{(\frac{x-2}{3})^2 + 1} + 1$

13. $f(x) = x^2$ is transformed to $g(x) = (x - 2)^2 + 5$. Write the sequence of transformations applied.
    - Shifted 2 positions to the right $(x - 2)^2$
    - Shifted 5 positions up $(x - 2)^2 + 5$

14. f(x) = x² is transformed to g(x) = 2(x + 1)² + 5. Write the sequence of transformations applied.
    - Shifted 1 position to the left   (x + 1)²
    - Vertical dilation factor 2   2(x + 1)²
    - Shifted 5 positions up   2(x + 1)² + 5

15. f(x) = –x² is transformed to g(x) = (x – 1)² – 5. Write the sequence of transformations applied.
    - Shifted 1 position to the right   –(x – 1)²
    - Reflection about the x axis   (x – 1)²
    - Shifted 5 positions down   (x – 1)² – 5

16. The function f(x) = (x – 7)² is transformed to g(x) = –6(x + 3)² – 2. Write the sequence of transformations applied.
    - Shifted 10 position to the right   (x + 3)²
    - Reflection about the x axis   –(x + 3)²
    - Vertical dilation factor 6   –6(x + 3)²
    - Shifted 2 positions down   –6(x + 3)² – 2

17. f(x) = x², f(–x) = (-x)² = x². Is f(x) = f(–x)? <u>Yes</u>

18. f(x) = x³, f(–x) = (-x)³ = -x³. Is f(x) = f(–x)? <u>No</u>

19. f(x) = x⁴, f(–x) = (-x)⁴ = x⁴. Is f(x) = –f(–x)? <u>Yes</u>

20. f(x) = $\dfrac{1-x^2}{x^2+1}$, f(–x) = $\dfrac{1-(-x)^2}{(-x)^2+1} = \dfrac{1-x^2}{x^2+1}$. Is f(x) = f(–x) ? <u>Yes</u>

21. Given f(x) = $\dfrac{x^3}{x^2+1}$, f(–x) = $\dfrac{(-x)^3}{(-x)^2+1} = \dfrac{-x^3}{x^2+1}$ Is f(x) = –f(–x)? <u>Yes</u>

22. Given f(x) = $(x-3)^2$, f(–x) = $(-x-3)^2 = (x+3)^2$. Is f(x) = f(–x)? <u>Yes,</u> f(x) = –f(–x) ? <u>No</u>

23. Functions in which f(x) = f(–x) are called <u>even</u>. The graphical meaning is that <u>the function f(x) is symmetrical with respect to the y axis.</u>

24. Functions in which f(x) = –f(–x) are called <u>odd</u>. The graphical meaning is that <u>the function f(x) is symmetrical with respect to the origin.</u>

2.5. – ABSOLUTE VALUE FUNCTIONS

1. Given the function: f(x) = |x| (absolute value of x) Complete the following table:

x	−5	−4	−3	−2	−1	0	1	2	3	4	5
f(x)	5	4	3	2	1	0	1	2	3	4	5

- Domain of the function: $x \in R$
- y intercept (sketched on the graph): $(0,0)$
- x intercept(s): $(0,0)$
- Other forms: $f(x) = |x| = \begin{cases} -x & x \leq 0 \\ x & x > 0 \end{cases}$
- max/**min** point(s): $(0,0)$
- Increasing on the interval: $x \in (0, \infty)$
- Decreasing on the interval: $x \in (-\infty, 0)$
- Range of the function: $f(x) \in [0, \infty)$

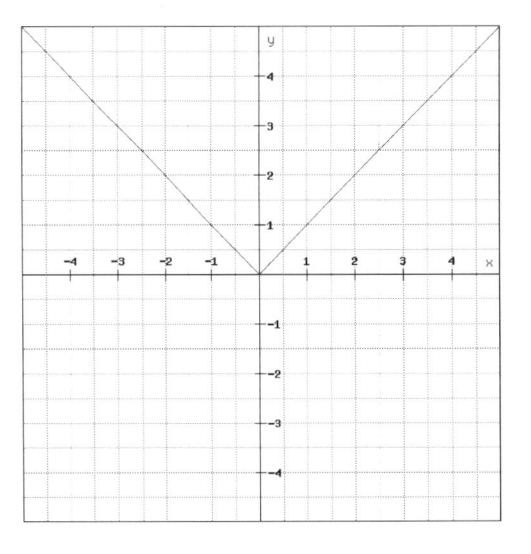

2. Given the function: f(x) = |x + 1| Complete the following table:

x	−5	−4	−3	−2	−1	0	1	2	3	4	5
f(x)	4	3	2	1	0	1	2	3	4	5	6

- Domain of the function: $x \in R$
- y intercept (sketched on the graph): $(0,1)$
- x intercept(s): $(-1,0)$
- Other forms: $f(x) = |x+1| = \begin{cases} -x-1 & x \leq -1 \\ x+1 & x > -1 \end{cases}$
- max/**min** point(s): $(-1,0)$
- Increasing on the interval: $x \in (-1, \infty)$
- Decreasing on the interval: $x \in (-\infty, -1)$
- Range of the function: $f(x) \in [0, \infty)$

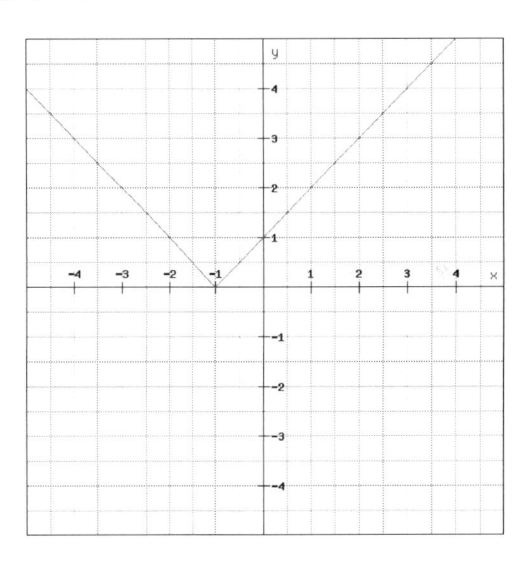

3. Given the function: f(x) = |3x – 2| Complete the following table:

x	−5	−4	−3	−2	−1	0	1	2	3	4	5
f(x)	17	14	11	8	5	2	1	4	7	10	13

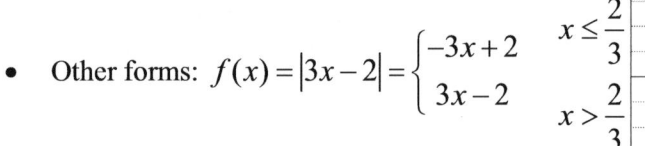

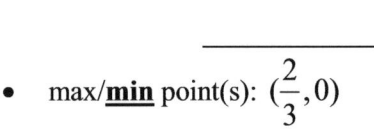

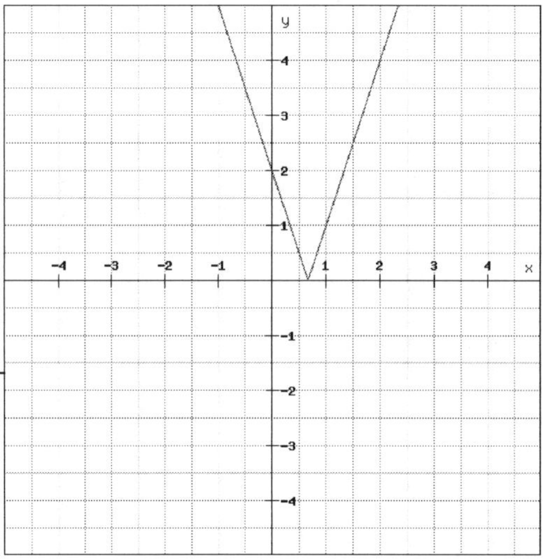

- Domain of the function: $x \in R$
- y intercept (sketched on the graph): $(0, 2)$
- x intercept(s): $(\frac{2}{3}, 0)$
- Other forms: $f(x) = |3x - 2| = \begin{cases} -3x + 2 & x \leq \frac{2}{3} \\ 3x - 2 & x > \frac{2}{3} \end{cases}$
- max/**min** point(s): $(\frac{2}{3}, 0)$
- Increasing on the interval: $x \in (\frac{2}{3}, \infty)$
- Decreasing on the interval: $x \in (-\infty, \frac{2}{3})$
- Range of the function: $f(x) \in [0, \infty)$

4. Given the function: f(x) = |x − 4| − 3   Complete the following table:

x	−5	−4	−3	−2	−1	0	1	2	3	4	5
f(x)	6	5	4	3	2	1	0	-1	-2	-3	-2

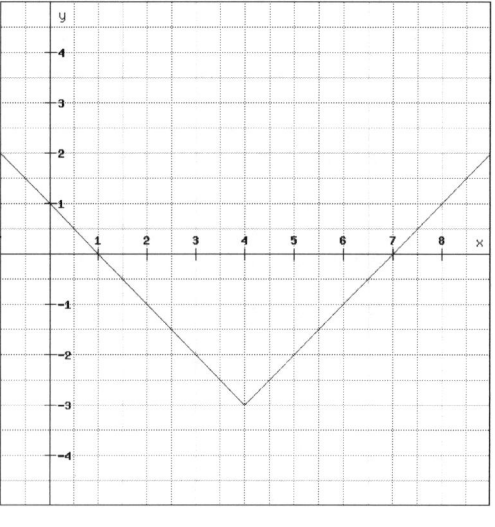

- Domain of the function: $x \in R$
- y intercept (sketched on the graph): $(0, 1)$
- x intercept(s): $(1, 0), (7, 0)$
- Other forms: $f(x) = |x - 4| - 3 = \begin{cases} -x + 1 & x \leq 4 \\ x - 7 & x > 4 \end{cases}$
- max/**min** point(s): $(4, -3)$
- Increasing on the interval: $x \in (4, \infty)$
- Decreasing on the interval: $x \in (-\infty, 4)$
- Range of the function: $f(x) \in [-3, \infty)$

5. Given the function: f(x) = |2x² − x| Complete the following table:

x	−5	−4	−3	−2	−1	0	1	2	3	4	5
f(x)	55	36	21	10	3	0	1	6	15	28	45

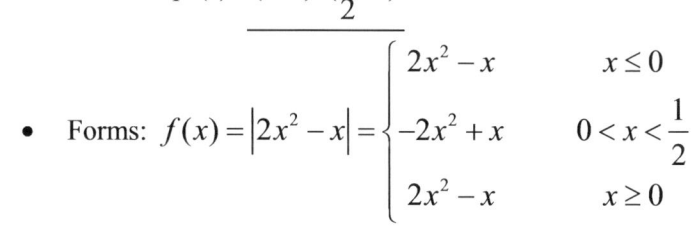

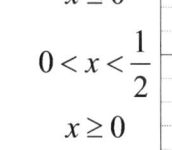

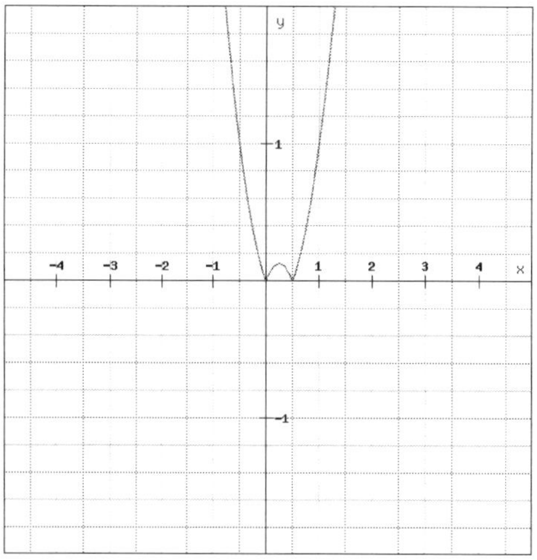

- Domain of the function: $x \in R$
- y intercept (sketched on the graph): $(0,0)$
- x intercept(s): $(0,0), (\frac{1}{2}, 0)$
- Forms: $f(x) = |2x^2 - x| = \begin{cases} 2x^2 - x & x \leq 0 \\ -2x^2 + x & 0 < x < \frac{1}{2} \\ 2x^2 - x & x \geq 0 \end{cases}$
- Min: $(\frac{1}{2}, 0), (0,0)$ Max: $(\frac{1}{4}, \frac{1}{8})$
- Increasing on the interval: $x \in (0, \frac{1}{4}) \cup (\frac{1}{2}, \infty)$
- Decreasing on the interval: $x \in (-\infty, 0) \cup (\frac{1}{4}, \frac{1}{2})$
- Range of the function: $f(x) \in [0, \infty)$

6. Given the graph, complete the table below:

Function	On the graph
$f(x) = |x+1|$	D
$f(x) = -|x-3| - 2$	A
$f(x) = |2x - 2|$	E
$f(x) = |x - 2| - 2$	B
$f(x) = |x + 3.5| + 3$	F
$-f(x) = |x + 3|$	G
$f(x) = |x - 2|$	C

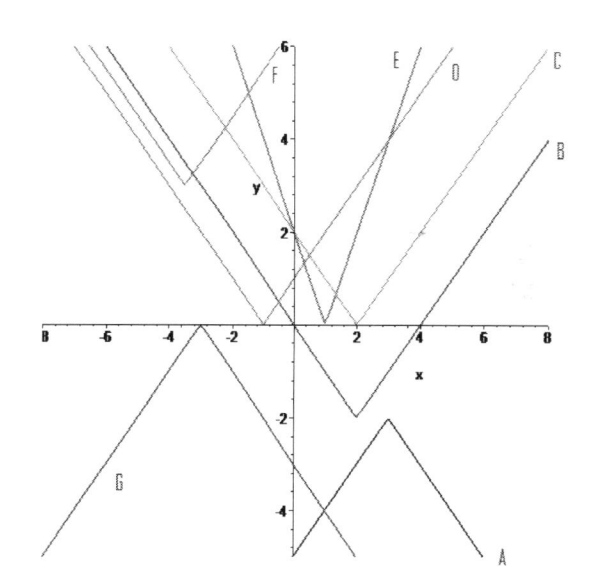

7. Given the function f(x) = |x|
   a. Translated 2 positions up.
      $f(x) + 2 = |x| + 2$
   b. Translated 2 positions left. $f(x+2) = |x+2|$
   c. Translated 4 positions up and 3 right. $f(x-3) + 4 = |x-3| + 4$

9. Given the function f(x) = |−3x − 2|
   a. Translated 1 positions up. $f(x) + 1 = |-3x - 2| + 1$
   b. Translated 3 positions left. $f(x+3) = |-3(x+3) - 2| = |-3x - 11|$
   c. Translated 6 positions up and 13 right.
      $f(x-13) + 6 = |-3(x-13) - 2| + 6 = |-3x + 37| + 6$

485

Analyze the following functions:

1. f(x) =|5|

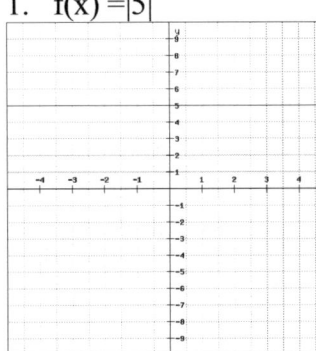

    Hybrid Form: *None*
    Domain: $x \in R$ *Range*: $f(x) \in \{5\}$
    y int: $(0,5)$ *Max/Min*: *None*
    x int: *None*
    Increase: *Never*   *Decrease*: *Never*

2. f(x) =|−3|

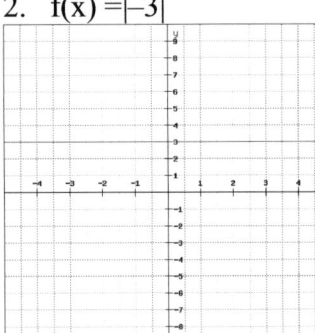

    Hybrid Form: *None*
    Domain: $x \in R$ *Range*: $f(x) \in \{3\}$
    y int: $(0,3)$ *Max/Min*: *None*
    x int: *None*
    Increase: *Never*   *Decrease*: *Never*

3. f(x) =|5x|

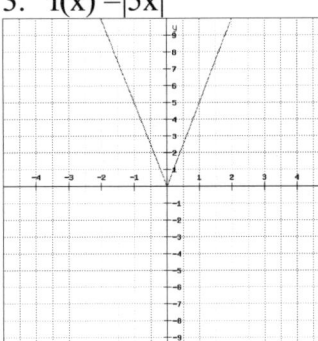

    Hybrid Form: $f(x) = \begin{cases} -5x & x \leq 0 \\ 5x & x > 0 \end{cases}$
    Domain: $x \in R$ *Range*: $f(x) \in [0, \infty)$
    y int: $(0,0)$ *Min*: $(0,0)$
    x int: $(0,0)$
    Increase: $x \in (0, \infty)$ *Decrease*: $x \in (-\infty, 0)$

4. f(x) =|5x+1|

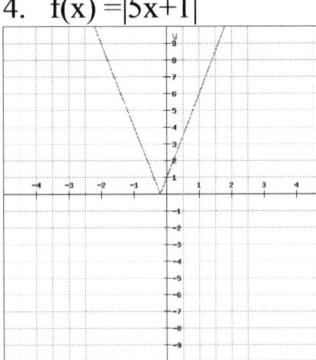

    Hybrid Form: $f(x) = \begin{cases} -5x-1 & x \leq -\dfrac{1}{5} \\ 5x+1 & x > -\dfrac{1}{5} \end{cases}$
    Domain: $x \in R$ *Range*: $f(x) \in [0, \infty)$
    y int: $(0,1)$ *Min*: $(-\dfrac{1}{5}, 0)$
    x int: $(-\dfrac{1}{5}, 0)$
    Increase: $x \in (-\dfrac{1}{5}, \infty)$ *Decrease*: $x \in (-\infty, -\dfrac{1}{5})$

5. f(x) = |−2x| + 1

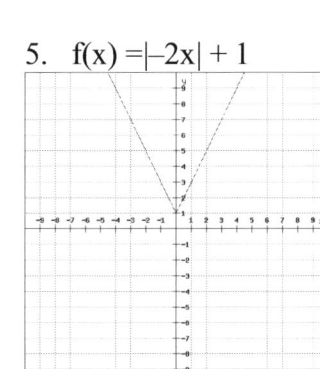

Hybrid Form: $f(x) = \begin{cases} -2x+1 & x \leq 0 \\ 2x+1 & x > 0 \end{cases}$

Domain: $x \in R$ Range: $f(x) \in [1, \infty)$

y int: $(0,1)$ Min: $(0,1)$

x int: None

Increase: $x \in (0, \infty)$ Decrease: $x \in (-\infty, 0)$

6. f(x) = |−2x − 3|

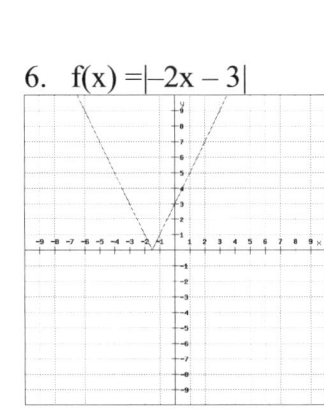

Hybrid Form: $f(x) = \begin{cases} -2x-3 & x \leq -\frac{3}{2} \\ 2x+3 & x > -\frac{3}{2} \end{cases}$

Domain: $x \in R$ Range: $f(x) \in [0, \infty)$

y int: $(0,3)$ Min: $(-\frac{3}{2}, 0)$

x int: $(-\frac{3}{2}, 0)$

Increase: $x \in (-\frac{3}{2}, \infty)$ Decrease: $x \in (-\infty, -\frac{3}{2})$

7. f(x) = |−2x + 3| − 2

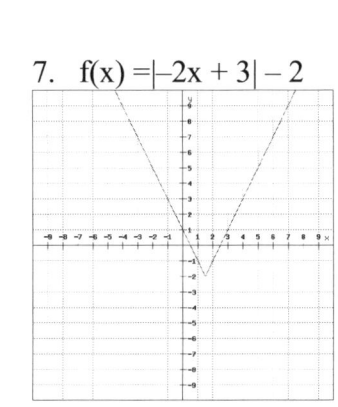

Hybrid Form: $f(x) = \begin{cases} -2x+1 & x \leq \frac{3}{2} \\ 2x-5 & x > \frac{3}{2} \end{cases}$

Domain: $x \in R$ Range: $f(x) \in [-2, \infty)$

y int: $(0,3)$ Min: $(-\frac{3}{2}, 0)$

x int: $(\frac{5}{2}, 0), (\frac{1}{2}, 0)$

Increase: $x \in (\frac{3}{2}, \infty)$ Decrease: $x \in (-\infty, \frac{3}{2})$

8. f(x) = |x|² + 2|x|

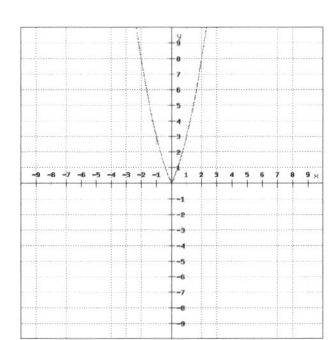

Hybrid Form: $f(x) = \begin{cases} x^2 - 2x & x \leq 0 \\ x^2 + 2x & x > 0 \end{cases}$

Domain: $x \in R$ Range: $f(x) \in [0, \infty)$

y int: $(0,0)$ Min: $(0,0)$

x int: $(0,0)$

Increase: $x \in (0, \infty)$ Decrease: $x \in (-\infty, 0)$

9. $f(x) = |x|^2 + 7|x| - 1$

Hybrid Form: $f(x) = \begin{cases} x^2 - 7x - 1 & x \leq 0 \\ x^2 + 7x - 1 & x > 0 \end{cases}$

Domain: $x \in R$ Range: $f(x) \in [-1, \infty)$

y int: $(0, -1)$ Min: $(0, -1)$

x int: $(\frac{7 - \sqrt{53}}{2}, 0), (\frac{-7 + \sqrt{53}}{2}, 0)$

Increase: $x \in (0, \infty)$ Decrease: $x \in (-\infty, 0)$

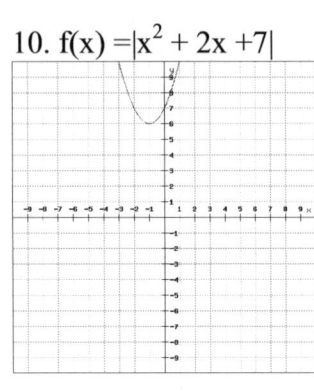

10. $f(x) = |x^2 + 2x + 7|$

Hybrid Form: No Need

Domain: $x \in R$ Range: $f(x) \in [6, \infty)$

y int: $(0, 7)$ Min: $(-1, 6)$

x int: None

Increase: $x \in (-1, \infty)$ Decrease: $x \in (-\infty, -1)$

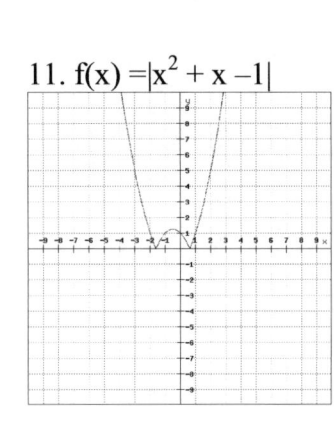

11. $f(x) = |x^2 + x - 1|$

Hybrid Form: $f(x) = \begin{cases} x^2 + x - 1 & x \leq \frac{-1 - \sqrt{5}}{2} \\ -x^2 - x + 1 & \frac{-1 - \sqrt{5}}{2} < x < \frac{-1 + \sqrt{5}}{2} \\ x^2 + x - 1 & x \geq \frac{-1 + \sqrt{5}}{2} \end{cases}$

Domain: $x \in R$ Range: $f(x) \in [0, \infty)$

y int: $(0, 1)$ Min: $(\frac{-1 - \sqrt{5}}{2}, 0), (\frac{-1 + \sqrt{5}}{2}, 0)$, Max: $(-\frac{1}{2}, \frac{5}{4})$

x int: $(\frac{-1 - \sqrt{5}}{2}, 0), (\frac{-1 + \sqrt{5}}{2}, 0)$

Increase: $x \in (\frac{-1 - \sqrt{5}}{2}, -\frac{1}{2}) \cup (\frac{-1 + \sqrt{5}}{2}, \infty)$

Decrease: $x \in (-\infty, \frac{-1 - \sqrt{5}}{2}) \cup (-\frac{1}{2}, \frac{-1 + \sqrt{5}}{2})$

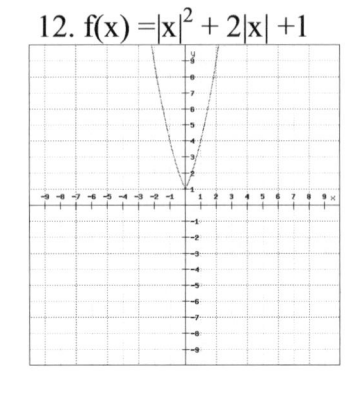

12. $f(x) = |x|^2 + 2|x| + 1$

Hybrid Form: $f(x) = \begin{cases} x^2 - 2x + 1 & x \leq 0 \\ x^2 + 2x + 1 & x > 0 \end{cases}$

Domain: $x \in R$ Range: $f(x) \in [1, \infty)$

y int: $(0, 1)$ Min: $(0, 1)$

x int: None

Increase: $x \in (0, \infty)$ Decrease: $x \in (-\infty, 0)$

488

13. $f(x) = |x^2 + 1| + 2 = x^2 + 3$

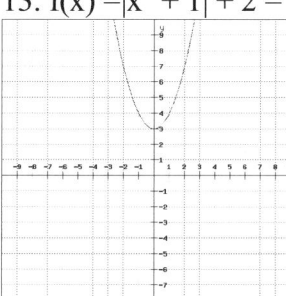

Hybrid Form: No Need

Domain: $x \in R$ *Range*: $f(x) \in [3, \infty)$

y int: $(0, 3)$ *Min*: $(0, 3)$

x int: *None*

Increase: $x \in (0, \infty)$ *Decrease*: $x \in (-\infty, 0)$

14. $f(x) = |x|^2 - 1$

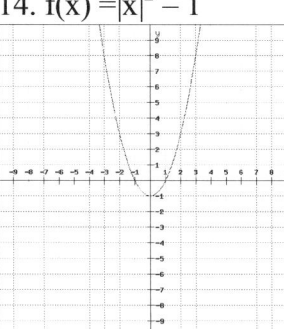

Hybrid Form: No Need

Domain: $x \in R$ *Range*: $f(x) \in [1, \infty)$

y int: $(0, -1)$ *Min*: $(0, -1)$

x int: $(1, 0), (-1, 0)$

Increase: $x \in (0, \infty)$ *Decrease*: $x \in (-\infty, 0)$

15. $f(x) = |x^2 - 2|$

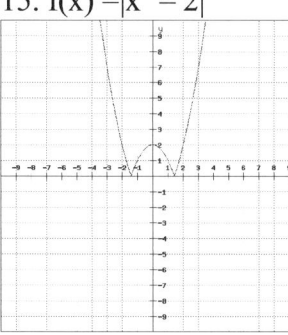

Hybrid Form: $f(x) = \begin{cases} x^2 - 2 & x \leq -\sqrt{2} \\ -x^2 + 2 & -\sqrt{2} < x < \sqrt{2} \\ x^2 - 2 & x \geq \sqrt{2} \end{cases}$

Domain: $x \in R$ *Range*: $f(x) \in [0, \infty)$

y int: $(0, 1)$ *Min*: $(-\sqrt{2}, 0), (\sqrt{2}, 0)$, *Max*: $(0, 2)$

x int: $(\sqrt{2}, 0), (-\sqrt{2}, 0)$

Increase: $x \in (-\sqrt{2}, 0) \cup (\sqrt{2}, \infty)$

Decrease: $x \in (-\infty, -\sqrt{2}) \cup (0, \sqrt{2})$

16. $f(x) = |x^2 - 2x|$

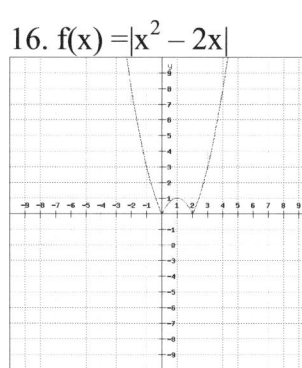

Hybrid Form: $f(x) = \begin{cases} x^2 - 2x & x \leq 0 \\ -x^2 + 2x & 0 < x < 2 \\ x^2 - 2x & x \geq 2 \end{cases}$

Domain: $x \in R$ *Range*: $f(x) \in [0, \infty)$

y int: $(0, 0)$ *Min*: $(0, 0), (2, 0)$, *Max*: $(1, 1)$

x int: $(0, 0), (-2, 0)$

Increase: $x \in (0, 1) \cup (2, \infty)$

Decrease: $x \in (-\infty, 0) \cup (1, 2)$

17. $f(x) = |5x^2 - 10x| - 2$

$Hybrid\ Form: f(x) = \begin{cases} 5x^2 - 10x - 2 & x \leq 0 \\ -5x^2 + 10x - 2 & 0 < x < 2 \\ 5x^2 - 10x - 2 & x \geq 2 \end{cases}$

$Domain: x \in R \quad Range: f(x) \in [-2, \infty)$

$y\,int: (0, -2) \quad Min: (0, -2), (2, -2), Max: (1, 3)$

$x\,int: (\frac{5+\sqrt{35}}{5}, 0), (\frac{5-\sqrt{15}}{5}, 0), (\frac{5+\sqrt{15}}{5}, 0)$

$Increase: x \in (0, 1) \cup (2, \infty)$

$Decrease: x \in (-\infty, 0) \cup (1, 2)$

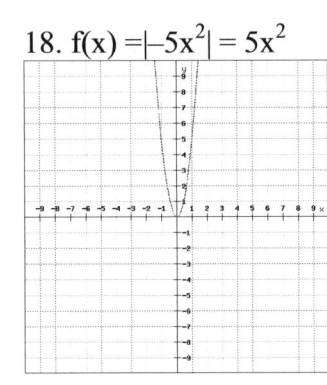

18. $f(x) = |-5x^2| = 5x^2$

$Hybrid\ Form: No\ Need$

$Domain: x \in R \quad Range: f(x) \in [0, \infty)$

$y\,int: (0, 0) \quad Min: (0, 0)$

$x\,int: (0, 0)$

$Increase: x \in (0, \infty) \quad Decrease: x \in (-\infty, 0)$

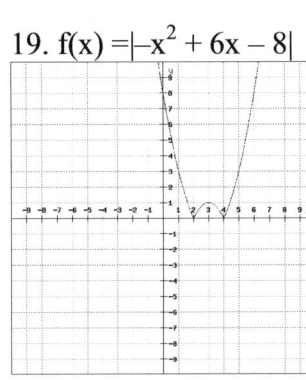

19. $f(x) = |-x^2 + 6x - 8|$

$Hybrid\ Form: f(x) = \begin{cases} x^2 - 6x + 8 & x \leq 2 \\ -x^2 + 6x - 8 & 2 < x < 4 \\ x^2 - 6x + 8 & x \geq 4 \end{cases}$

$Domain: x \in R \quad Range: f(x) \in [0, \infty)$

$y\,int: (0, 8) \quad Min: (2, 0), (4, 0), Max: (3, 1)$

$x\,int: (2, 0), (4, 0)$

$Increase: x \in (2, 3) \cup (4, \infty)$

$Decrease: x \in (-\infty, 2) \cup (3, 4)$

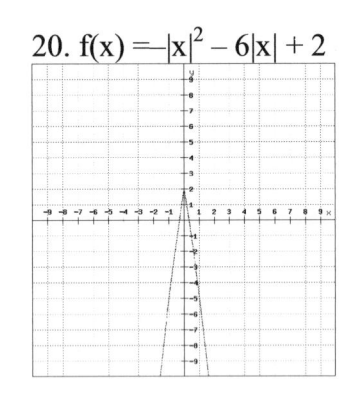

20. $f(x) = -|x|^2 - 6|x| + 2$

$Hybrid\ Form: f(x) = \begin{cases} -x^2 + 6x + 2 & x \leq 0 \\ -x^2 - 6x + 2 & x > 0 \end{cases}$

$Domain: x \in R \quad Range: f(x) \in (-\infty, 2]$

$y\,int: (0, 2) \quad Max: (0, 2)$

$x\,int: (-3 + \sqrt{11}, 0), (3 - \sqrt{11}, 0)$

$Increase: x \in (-\infty, 0) \quad Decrease: x \in (0, \infty)$

21. $f(x) = |-x^2 + x - 5|$

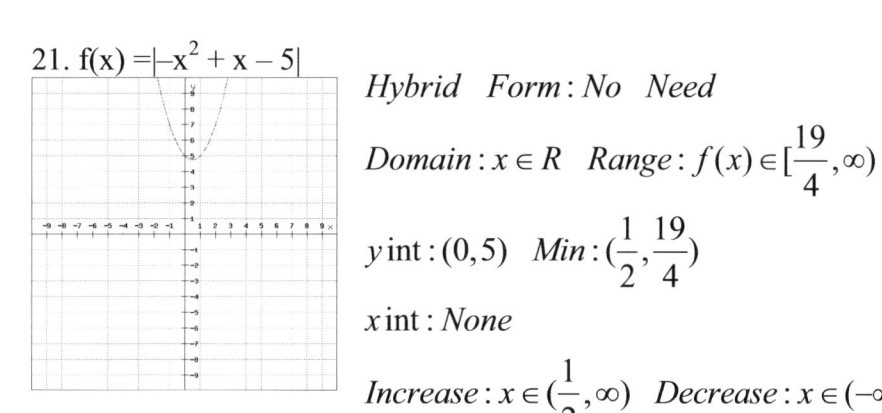

Hybrid Form: No Need

Domain: $x \in R$ *Range*: $f(x) \in [\frac{19}{4}, \infty)$

y int: $(0, 5)$ *Min*: $(\frac{1}{2}, \frac{19}{4})$

x int: *None*

Increase: $x \in (\frac{1}{2}, \infty)$ *Decrease*: $x \in (-\infty, \frac{1}{2})$

22. $f(x) = |-x^2 - 4x - 4|$

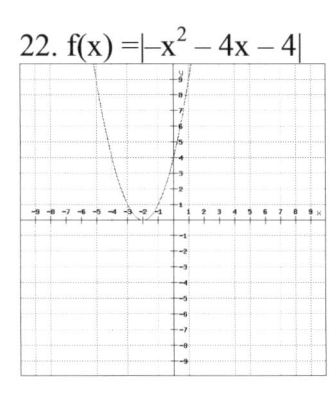

Hybrid Form: No Need

Domain: $x \in R$ *Range*: $f(x) \in [0, \infty)$

y int: $(0, 4)$ *Min*: $(-2, 0)$

x int: $(-2, 0)$

Increase: $x \in (-2, \infty)$ *Decrease*: $x \in (-\infty, -2)$

23. $f(x) = |-x^2 + 3|$

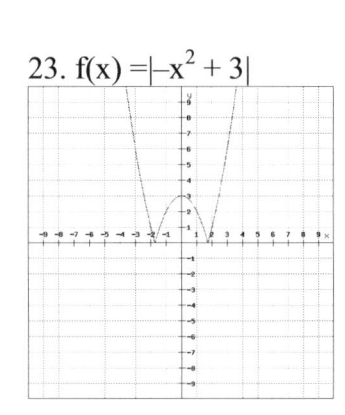

Hybrid Form: $f(x) = \begin{cases} x^2 - 3 & x \leq -\sqrt{3} \\ -x^2 + 3 & -\sqrt{3} < x < \sqrt{3} \\ x^2 - 3 & x \geq \sqrt{3} \end{cases}$

Domain: $x \in R$ *Range*: $f(x) \in [0, \infty)$

y int: $(0, 3)$ *Min*: $(-\sqrt{3}, 0), (\sqrt{3}, 0)$, *Max*: $(0, 3)$

x int: $(-\sqrt{3}, 0), (\sqrt{3}, 0)$

Increase: $x \in (-\sqrt{3}, 0) \cup (\sqrt{3}, \infty)$

Decrease: $x \in (-\infty, -\sqrt{3}) \cup (0, \sqrt{3})$

24. $f(x) = |x| - |x|^2$

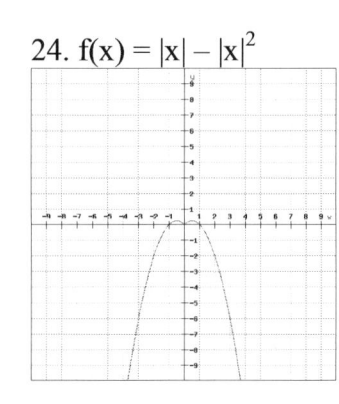

Hybrid Form: $f(x) = \begin{cases} -x^2 - x & x \leq 0 \\ -x^2 + x & x > 0 \end{cases}$

Domain: $x \in R$ *Range*: $f(x) \in (-\infty, \frac{1}{4}]$

y int: $(0, 0)$ *Min*: $(0, 0)$, *Max*: $(-\frac{1}{2}, \frac{1}{4}), (\frac{1}{2}, \frac{1}{4})$

x int: $(0, 0), (1, 0), (-1, 0)$

Increase: $x \in (-\infty, -\frac{1}{2}) \cup (0, \frac{1}{2})$

Decrease: $x \in (-\frac{1}{2}, 0) \cup (\frac{1}{2}, \infty)$

25. f(x) = |x − 6| − 2

Hybrid Form: $f(x) = \begin{cases} -x+4 & x \leq 6 \\ x-8 & x > 6 \end{cases}$

Domain: $x \in R$ Range: $f(x) \in [-2, \infty)$

y int: $(0, 4)$ Min: $(6, 2)$

x int: $(4, 0), (8, 0)$

Increase: $x \in (6, \infty)$ Decrease: $x \in (-\infty, 6)$

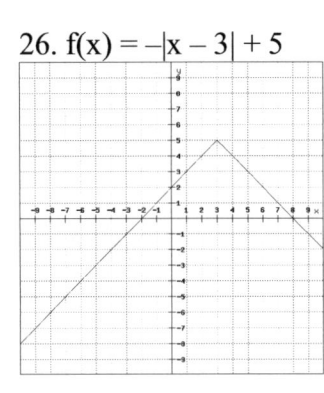

26. f(x) = −|x − 3| + 5

Hybrid Form: $f(x) = \begin{cases} x+2 & x \leq 3 \\ -x+8 & x > 3 \end{cases}$

Domain: $x \in R$ Range: $f(x) \in (-\infty, 5]$

y int: $(0, 2)$ Max: $(3, 5)$

x int: $(-2, 0), (8, 0)$

Increase: $x \in (-\infty, 3)$ Decrease: $x \in (3, \infty)$

27. f(x) = |5x² − 3|

Hybrid Form: $f(x) = \begin{cases} 5x^2 - 3 & x \leq -\sqrt{\frac{3}{5}} \\ -5x^2 + 3 & -\sqrt{\frac{3}{5}} < x < \sqrt{\frac{3}{5}} \\ 5x^2 - 3 & x \geq \sqrt{\frac{3}{5}} \end{cases}$

Domain: $x \in R$ Range: $f(x) \in [0, \infty)$

y int: $(0, 3)$ Min: $(-\sqrt{\frac{3}{5}}, 0), (\sqrt{\frac{3}{5}}, 0)$, Max: $(0, 3)$

x int: $(-\sqrt{\frac{3}{5}}, 0), (\sqrt{\frac{3}{5}}, 0)$

Increase: $x \in (-\sqrt{\frac{3}{5}}, 0) \cup (\sqrt{\frac{3}{5}}, \infty)$

Decrease: $x \in (-\infty, -\sqrt{\frac{3}{5}}) \cup (0, \sqrt{\frac{3}{5}})$

28. f(x) = |3x²| + 1

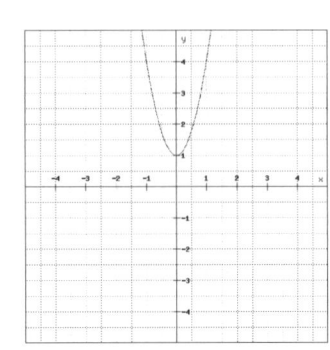

Hybrid Form: No Need

Domain: $x \in R$ Range: $f(x) \in [1, \infty)$

y int: $(0, 1)$ Min: $(0, 1)$

x int: None

Increase: $x \in (0, \infty)$ Decrease: $x \in (-\infty, 0)$

29. f(x) = |x² + 3x + 4|

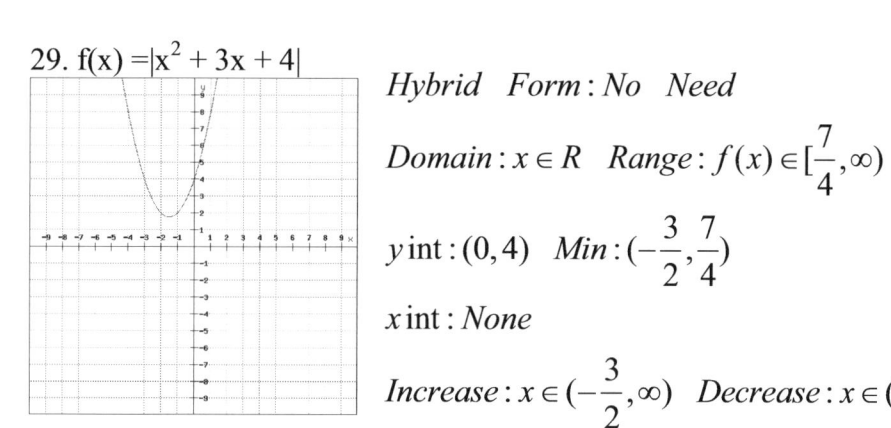

Hybrid Form: No Need

Domain: $x \in R$ *Range*: $f(x) \in [\frac{7}{4}, \infty)$

y int: $(0, 4)$ *Min*: $(-\frac{3}{2}, \frac{7}{4})$

x int: *None*

Increase: $x \in (-\frac{3}{2}, \infty)$ *Decrease*: $x \in (-\infty, -\frac{3}{2})$

30. f(x) = –|x – 5|

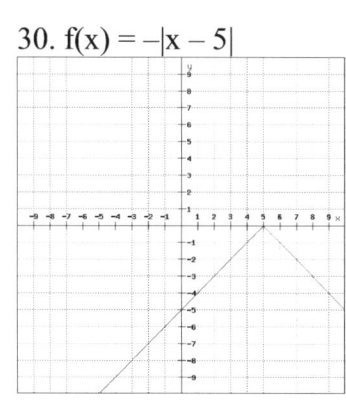

Hybrid Form: $f(x) = \begin{cases} x - 5 & x \leq 5 \\ -x + 5 & x > 5 \end{cases}$

Domain: $x \in R$ *Range*: $f(x) \in (-\infty, 0]$

y int: $(0, -5)$ *Max*: $(5, 0)$

x int: $(5, 0)$

Increase: $x \in (-\infty, 5)$ *Decrease*: $x \in (5, \infty)$

31. f(x) = |–4x + 3| + 3

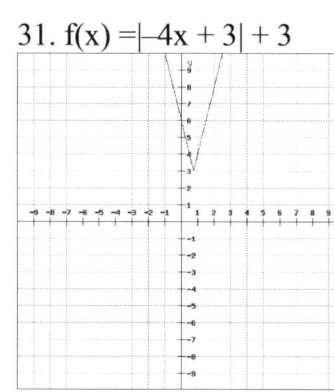

Hybrid Form: $f(x) = \begin{cases} -4x + 6 & x \leq \frac{3}{4} \\ 4x & x > \frac{3}{4} \end{cases}$

Domain: $x \in R$ *Range*: $f(x) \in [3, \infty)$

y int: $(0, 6)$ *Min*: $(\frac{3}{4}, 3)$

x int: *None*

Increase: $x \in (\frac{3}{4}, \infty)$ *Decrease*: $x \in (-\infty, \frac{3}{4})$

32. f(x) = |–12x – 13|

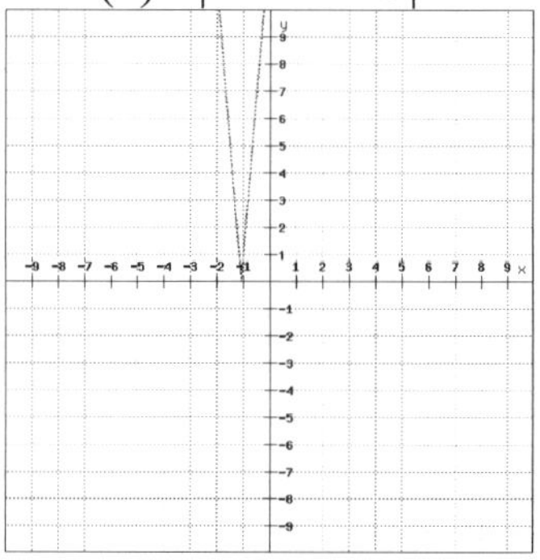

Hybrid Form: $f(x) = \begin{cases} -12x - 13 & x \leq -\frac{13}{12} \\ 12x + 13 & x > -\frac{13}{12} \end{cases}$

Domain: $x \in R$ *Range*: $f(x) \in [0, \infty)$

y int: $(0, 13)$ *Min*: $(-\frac{13}{12}, 0)$

x int: $(-\frac{13}{12}, 0)$

Increase: $x \in (-\frac{13}{12}, \infty)$ *Decrease*: $x \in (-\infty, -\frac{13}{12})$

33. f(x) = |x + 3| + |x + 2|

$$Hybrid\ \ Form: f(x) = \begin{cases} -2x-5 & x \leq -3 \\ 1 & -3 < x < -2 \\ 2x+5 & x \geq -2 \end{cases}$$

$Domain: x \in R \quad Range: f(x) \in [1, \infty)$

$y\,int: (0,5) \quad Min: f(-3 \leq x \leq -2) = 1$

$x\,int: None$

$Increase: x \in (-\infty, -3) \quad Decrease: x \in (-2, \infty)$

34. f(x) = |−2x − 2| − |2x − 1|

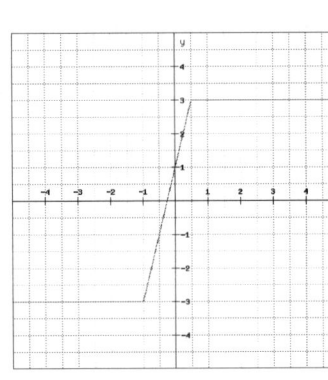

$$Hybrid\ \ Form: f(x) = \begin{cases} -3 & x \leq -1 \\ 4x+1 & -1 < x < \frac{1}{2} \\ 3 & x \geq \frac{1}{2} \end{cases}$$

$Domain: x \in R \quad Range: f(x) \in [-3, 3]$

$y\,int: (0,1) \quad Min: f(-\infty \leq x \leq -2) = -3, Max: f(\frac{1}{2} \leq x \leq \infty) = 3$

$x\,int: (-\frac{1}{4}, 0)$

$Increase: x \in (-1, \frac{1}{2}) \quad Decrease: Never$

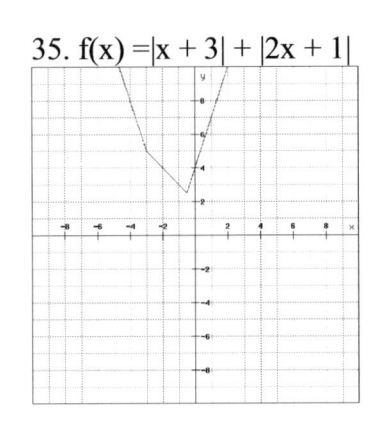

35. f(x) = |x + 3| + |2x + 1|

$$Hybrid\ \ Form: f(x) = \begin{cases} -3x-4 & x \leq -3 \\ -x+2 & -3 < x < -\frac{1}{2} \\ 3x+4 & x \geq -\frac{1}{2} \end{cases}$$

$Domain: x \in R \quad Range: f(x) \in [\frac{5}{2}, \infty)$

$y\,int: (0,4) \quad Min: (-\frac{1}{2}, \frac{5}{2})$

$x\,int: None$

$Increase: x \in (-\frac{1}{2}, \infty) \quad Decrease: x \in (-\infty, -\frac{1}{2})$

36. f(x) = |−2x + 4| − |3x + 2|

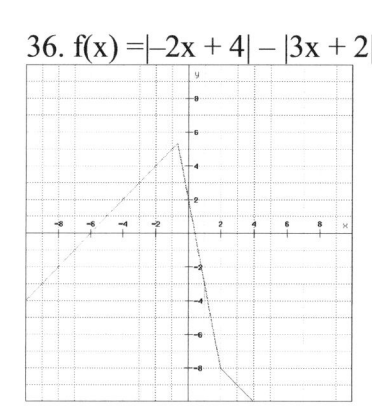

$$Hybrid\ Form: f(x) = \begin{cases} x+6 & x \leq -\frac{2}{3} \\ -5x+2 & -\frac{2}{3} < x < 2 \\ -x-6 & x \geq 2 \end{cases}$$

$Domain: x \in R$ $Range: f(x) \in (-\infty, \frac{16}{3}]$

$y\,int: (0,2)$ $Max: (-\frac{2}{3}, \frac{16}{3})$

$x\,int: (-6,0), (\frac{2}{5}, 0)$

$Increase: x \in (-\infty, -\frac{2}{3})$ $Decrease: x \in (-\frac{2}{3}, \infty)$

37. f(x) = |3x − 4| + |2x − 2|

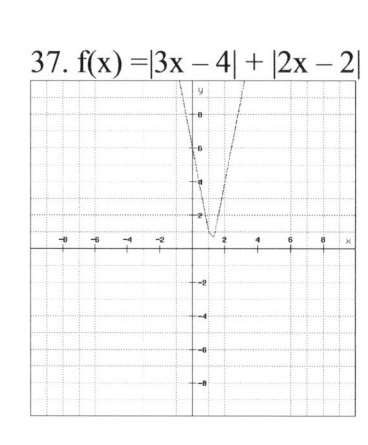

$$Hybrid\ Form: f(x) = \begin{cases} -5x+6 & x \leq 1 \\ -x+2 & 1 < x < \frac{4}{3} \\ 5x-6 & x \geq \frac{4}{3} \end{cases}$$

$Domain: x \in R$ $Range: f(x) \in [\frac{2}{3}, \infty)$

$y\,int: (0,2)$ $Max: (\frac{4}{3}, \frac{2}{3})$

$x\,int: None$

$Increase: x \in (-\infty, \frac{4}{3})$ $Decrease: x \in (-\infty, \frac{4}{3})$

38. f(x) = |x + 1||x + 2| = |x² + 3x + 2|

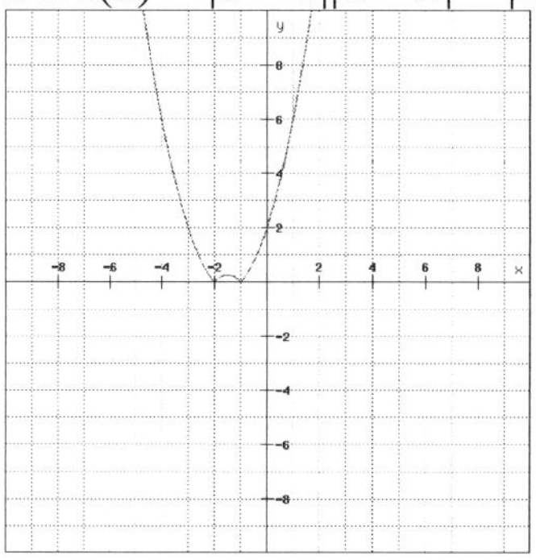

$$Hybrid\ Form: f(x) = \begin{cases} x^2+3x+2 & x \leq -2 \\ -x^2-3x-2 & -2 < x < -1 \\ x^2+3x+2 & x \geq -1 \end{cases}$$

$Domain: x \in R$ $Range: f(x) \in [0, \infty)$

$y\,int: (0,2)$ $Min: (-2,0), (-1,0), Max: (-\frac{3}{2}, \frac{1}{4})$

$x\,int: (-2,0), (-1,0)$

$Increase: x \in (-2, -\frac{3}{2}) \cup (-1, \infty)$

$Decrease: x \in (-\infty, -2) \cup (-\frac{3}{2}, -1)$

39. $f(x) = -|x+1||x+2| = -|x^2 + 3x + 2|$ (Reflection about x axis of previous function)

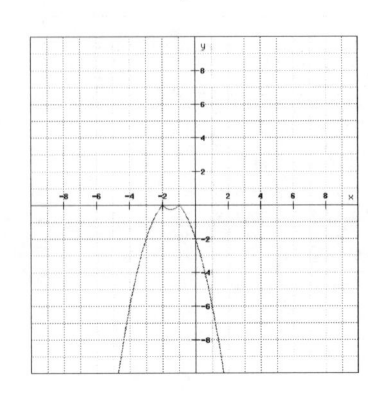

$$Hybrid\ Form: f(x) = \begin{cases} -x^2 - 3x - 2 & x \leq -2 \\ x^2 + 3x + 2 & -2 < x < -1 \\ -x^2 - 3x - 2 & x \geq -1 \end{cases}$$

$Domain: x \in R \quad Range: f(x) \in (-\infty, 0]$

$y\,int: (0,-2) \quad Max: (-2,0), (-1,0), Min: (-\frac{3}{2}, \frac{1}{4})$

$x\,int: (-2,0), (-1,0)$

$Increase: x \in (-\infty, -2) \cup (-\frac{3}{2}, -1)$

$Decrease: x \in (-2, -\frac{3}{2}) \cup (-1, \infty)$

2.6. – RATIONAL FUNCTIONS

1. Given the functions: $f(x) = \dfrac{1}{x}$, $g(x) = \dfrac{2}{x}$, Complete the following table:

x	−10	−2	−1	−0.5	−0.1	−0.01	0	0.01	0.1	1	2	10
f(x)	−0.1	−0.5	−1	−2	−10	−100	D.E	100	10	1	0.5	0.1
g(x)	−0.2	−1	−2	−4	−20	−200	D.E	200	20	2	1	0.2

- Sketch the points of the table on a graph (use a ruler).
- State the domain of the function: $x \in (-\infty, 0) \cup (0, \infty)$

- State the *y* intercept (sketched on the graph: <u>None</u>
- State the *x* intercept(s): <u>None</u>
- The corresponding limits and the equation of the vertical asymptote:
  $Lim_{x \to 0^-}(f(x)) = -\infty$ $Lim_{x \to 0^+}(f(x)) = \infty$ $V.Asymptote: x = 0$
  $Lim_{x \to 0^-}(g(x)) = -\infty$ $Lim_{x \to 0^+}(g(x)) = \infty$ $V.Asymptote: x = 0$

- The corresponding limits and the equation of the horizontal asymptote:
  $Lim_{x \to -\infty}(f(x)) = 0$ $Lim_{x \to \infty}(f(x)) = 0$ $H.Asymptote: y = 0$
  $Lim_{x \to -\infty}(g(x)) = 0$ $Lim_{x \to \infty}(g(x)) = 0$ $H.Asymptote: y = 0$

- Function is increasing on the interval: <u>Never,</u> decreasing: $x \in (-\infty, 0) \cup (0, \infty)$
  Find the max/min point(s): <u>None</u>
- State the range of the function: $f(x) \in (-\infty, 0) \cup (0, \infty)$ $g(x) \in (-\infty, 0) \cup (0, \infty)$

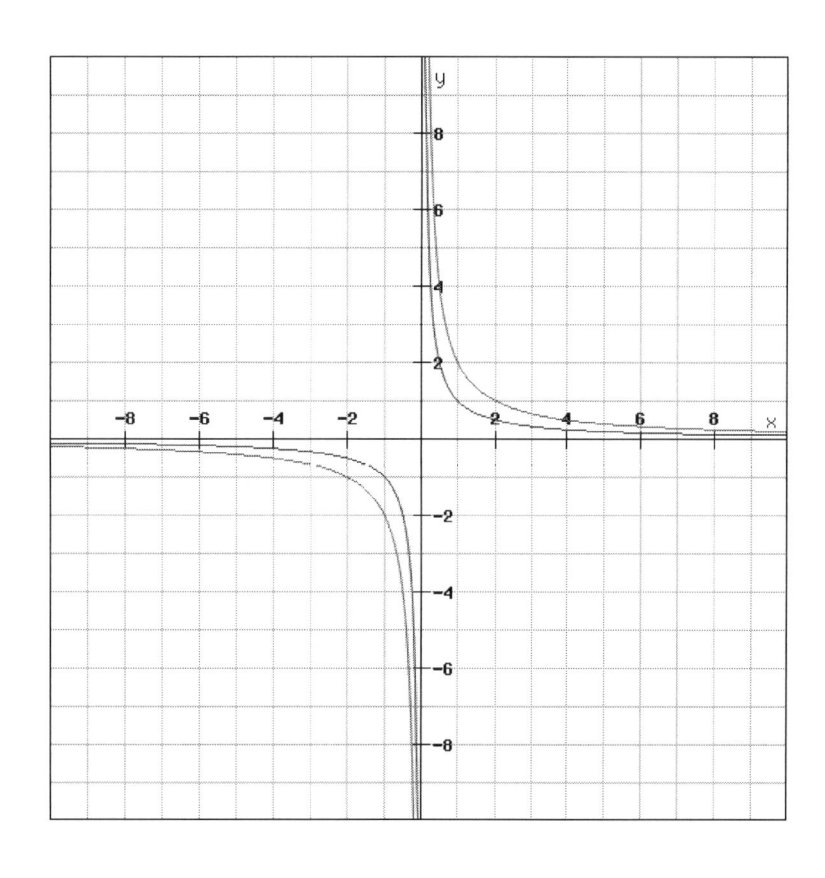

2. Given the functions: $f(x) = -3\dfrac{1}{x}$, $g(x) = \dfrac{-2}{x}$, Complete the following table:

x	−10	−2	−1	−0.5	−0.1	−0.01	0	0.01	0.1	1	2	10
f(x)	0.3	1.5	3	6	30	300	D.E	−300	−30	−3	−1.5	−0.3
g(x)	0.2	1	2	4	20	200	D.E	−200	−20	−2	−1	−0.2

- Sketch the points of the table on a graph (use a ruler).
- State the domain of the function: $x \in (-\infty, 0) \cup (0, \infty)$
- State the y intercept (sketched on the graph: <u>None</u>
- State the x intercept(s): <u>None</u>
- The corresponding limits and the equation of the vertical asymptote:
  $\lim_{x \to 0^-}(f(x)) = -\infty$ $\lim_{x \to 0^+}(f(x)) = \infty$ V.Asymptote: $x = 0$
  $\lim_{x \to 0^-}(g(x)) = -\infty$ $\lim_{x \to 0^+}(g(x)) = \infty$ V.Asymptote: $x = 0$

- The corresponding limits and the equation of the horizontal asymptote:
  $\lim_{x \to -\infty}(f(x)) = 0$ $\lim_{x \to \infty}(f(x)) = 0$ H.Asymptote: $y = 0$
  $\lim_{x \to -\infty}(g(x)) = 0$ $\lim_{x \to \infty}(g(x)) = 0$ H.Asymptote: $y = 0$

- Function is increasing on the interval: $x \in (-\infty, 0) \cup (0, \infty)$, decreasing: <u>Never</u>
- Find the max/min point(s): <u>None</u>
- State the range of the function: $f(x) \in (-\infty, 0) \cup (0, \infty)$ $g(x) \in (-\infty, 0) \cup (0, \infty)$

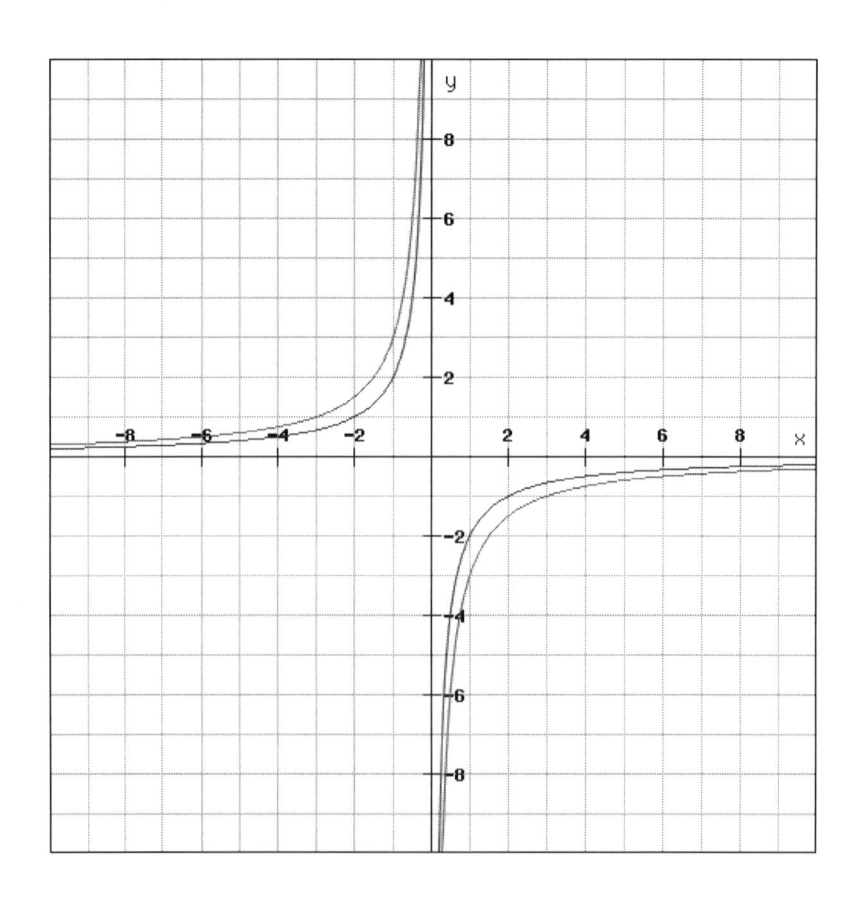

3. Given the functions: $f(x) = \dfrac{1}{x} + 2$, $g(x) = \dfrac{2}{x} - 3$, Complete the following table:

x	−10	−2	−1	−0.5	−0.1	−0.01	0	0.01	0.1	1	2	10
f(x)	1.9	1.5	1	0	−8	−98	D.E	102	12	3	2.5	2.1
g(x)	−3.2	−4	−5	−7	−23	−203	D.E	197	17	−1	−2	−2.8

- Sketch the points of the table on a graph (use a ruler).
- State the domain of the function: $x \in (-\infty, 0) \cup (0, \infty)$
- State the y intercept (sketched on the graph: <u>None</u>
- State the x intercept(s): $f(x): (-\dfrac{1}{2}, 0)$ $g(x): (\dfrac{2}{3}, 0)$
- The corresponding limits and the equation of the vertical asymptote: $x = 0$
  $\lim_{x \to 0^-}(f(x)) = -\infty$ $\lim_{x \to 0^+}(f(x)) = \infty$ V.Asymptote: $x = 0$
  $\lim_{x \to 0^-}(g(x)) = -\infty$ $\lim_{x \to 0^+}(g(x)) = \infty$ V.Asymptote: $x = 0$
- The corresponding limits and the equation of the horizontal asymptote:
  $\lim_{x \to -\infty}(f(x)) = 2$ $\lim_{x \to \infty}(f(x)) = 2$ H.Asymptote: $y = 2$
  $\lim_{x \to -\infty}(g(x)) = -3$ $\lim_{x \to \infty}(g(x)) = -3$ H.Asymptote: $y = -3$
- Function is increasing on the interval: <u>Never,</u> decreasing: $x \in (-\infty, 0) \cup (0, \infty)$
  Find the max/min point(s): <u>None</u>
- State the range of the function:
  $f(x) \in (-\infty, 2) \cup (2, \infty)$ $g(x) \in (-\infty, -3) \cup (-3, \infty)$

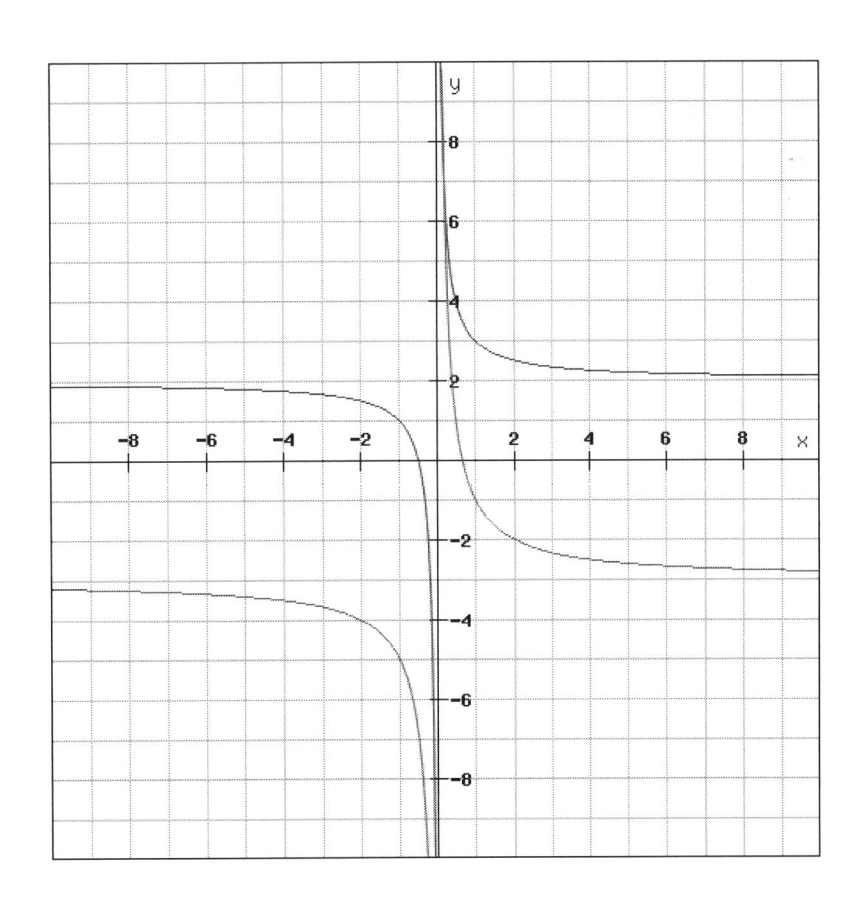

4. Given the functions: $f(x) = \dfrac{1}{x+2}$, $g(x) = \dfrac{-2}{x-4}$, Complete the following table values:

x	−10	−2.1	−2.01	−2	−1.99	−1.9	0	1	3.9	3.99	4	4.01	100
f(x)	$-\dfrac{1}{8}$	-10	-100	D.E	100	10	0.5	$\dfrac{1}{3}$	Approaching 0				
g(x)	Approaching 0						0.5	$\dfrac{2}{3}$	20	200	D.E	200	≈0

- Sketch the points of the table on a graph (use a ruler).
- State the domain of the function: $f(x): x \in (-\infty, -2) \cup (-2, \infty)$
  $g(x): x \in (-\infty, 4) \cup (4, \infty)$

- State the y intercept (sketched on the graph: $f(x): (0, \dfrac{1}{2})$ $g(x): (0, \dfrac{1}{2})$

- State the x intercept(s): None
- The corresponding limits and the equation of the vertical asymptote:
  $Lim_{x \to -2^-}(f(x)) = -\infty$ $Lim_{x \to -2^+}(f(x)) = \infty$ V.Asymptote: $x = -2$
  $Lim_{x \to 4^-}(g(x)) = -\infty$ $Lim_{x \to 4^+}(g(x)) = \infty$ V.Asymptote: $x = 4$

- The corresponding limits and the equation of the horizontal asymptote:
  $Lim_{x \to -\infty}(f(x)) = 0$ $Lim_{x \to \infty}(f(x)) = 0$ H.Asymptote: $y = 0$
  $Lim_{x \to -\infty}(g(x)) = 0$ $Lim_{x \to \infty}(g(x)) = 0$ H.Asymptote: $y = 0$

- Function is increasing on the interval: Never, decreasing:
  $f(x): x \in (-\infty, -2) \cup (-2, \infty)$
  $g(x): x \in (-\infty, 4) \cup (4, \infty)$

- Find the max/min point(s): None
- State the range of the function: $f(x) \in (-\infty, 0) \cup (0, \infty)$ $g(x) \in (-\infty, 0) \cup (0, \infty)$

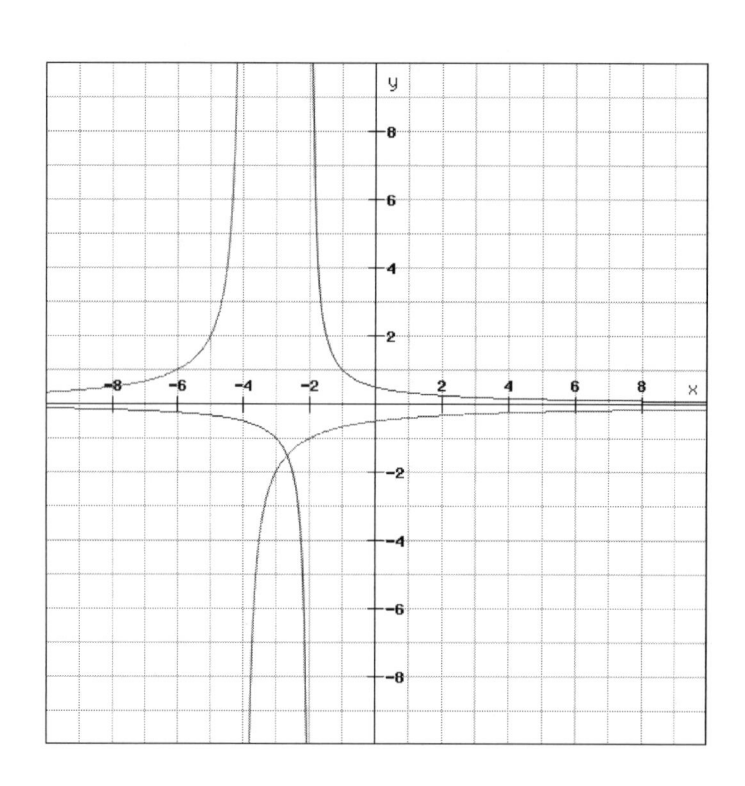

5. Given the functions: $f(x) = \dfrac{1}{x-3} + 2$, $g(x) = \dfrac{4}{x-5} - 2$, Complete the following table:

x	−10	0	2.9	2.99	3	3.01	3.1	4.9	4.99	5	5.01	5.1	10
f(x)	$\dfrac{25}{13}$	$\dfrac{5}{3}$	-8	-98	D.E	102	12	\multicolumn{5}{c	}{Approaching 2}
g(x)	\multicolumn{5}{c	}{Approaching -2}			-42	-402	D.E	398	38	0

- Sketch the points of the table on a graph (use a ruler).
- State the domain of the function: $f(x): x \in (-\infty, 3) \cup (3, \infty)$
  $g(x): x \in (-\infty, 5) \cup (5, \infty)$
- State the y intercept (sketched on the graph): $f(x): (0, \dfrac{5}{3})$ $g(x): (0, -\dfrac{14}{5})$
- State the x intercept(s): $f(x): (\dfrac{5}{2}, 0)$ $g(x): (7, 0)$
- The corresponding limits and the equation of the vertical asymptote:
  $Lim_{x \to 3^-}(f(x)) = -\infty$ $Lim_{x \to 3^+}(f(x)) = \infty$ V.Asymptote: $x = 3$
  $Lim_{x \to 5^-}(g(x)) = -\infty$ $Lim_{x \to 5^+}(g(x)) = \infty$ V.Asymptote: $x = 5$
- The corresponding limits and the equation of the horizontal asymptote:
  $Lim_{x \to -\infty}(f(x)) = 2$ $Lim_{x \to \infty}(f(x)) = 2$ H.Asymptote: $y = 2$
  $Lim_{x \to -\infty}(g(x)) = -2$ $Lim_{x \to \infty}(g(x)) = -2$ H.Asymptote: $y = -2$
- Function is increasing on the interval: Never, decreasing:
  $f(x): x \in (-\infty, 3) \cup (3, \infty)$
  $g(x): x \in (-\infty, 5) \cup (5, \infty)$
- Find the max/min point(s): None
- State the range of the function:
  $f(x) \in (-\infty, 2) \cup (2, \infty)$ $g(x) \in (-\infty, -2) \cup (-2, \infty)$

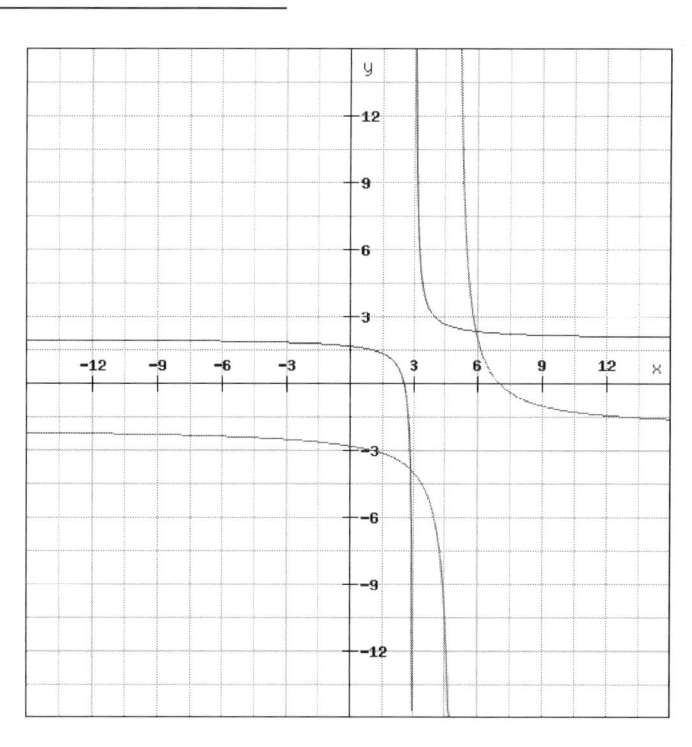

6. Given the function $f(x) = \dfrac{1}{x}$ Write the same function translated:

   a. 2 positions up: $f(x)+2 = \dfrac{1}{x}+2$ \qquad 2 positions left: $f(x+2) = \dfrac{1}{x+2}$

   b. 4 positions up and 3 right: $f(x-3)+4 = \dfrac{1}{x-3}+4$

7. Given the function $f(x) = \dfrac{3}{x}$

   a. 3 positions down: $f(x)-3 = \dfrac{3}{x}-3$ \qquad 5 positions right: $f(x-5) = \dfrac{3}{x-5}$

   b. 0.5 positions up and $\dfrac{3}{7}$ right: $f(x-\dfrac{3}{7})+\dfrac{1}{2} = \dfrac{3}{\left(x-\dfrac{3}{7}\right)}+\dfrac{1}{2}$

8. Given the function $f(x) = \dfrac{-3}{x}+1$

   a. 6 positions down: $f(x)-6 = \dfrac{-3}{x}-5$ \qquad 5 positions left: $f(x+5) = \dfrac{-3}{x+5}+1$

   b. 12 positions up and 10 right: $f(x-10)+12 = \dfrac{-3}{x-10}+12$

   c. Write in different forms: $f(x) = \dfrac{-3}{x}+1 = \dfrac{x-3}{x}$

9. Given the function $f(x) = \dfrac{7}{2x}+5$

   a. 1 positions down: $f(x)-1 = \dfrac{7}{2x}+4$ 7 positions right: $f(x-7) = \dfrac{7}{2(x-7)}+5$

   b. 2 positions up and 1 left: $f(x+1)+2 = \dfrac{7}{2(x+1)}+7$

   c. Write in different forms: $f(x) = \dfrac{7}{2x}+4 = \dfrac{8x+7}{2x}$

10. Given the function $f(x) = \dfrac{2x+3}{2x+6}$

    a. State its domain: $\underline{f(x): x \in (-\infty,-3)\cup(-3,\infty)}$

    b. Write in different forms:
    $f(x) = \dfrac{2x+3+(3-3)}{2x+6} = \dfrac{-6}{2x+6}+1$

    c. This is a Rational function as can be seen from rewriting or sketching.

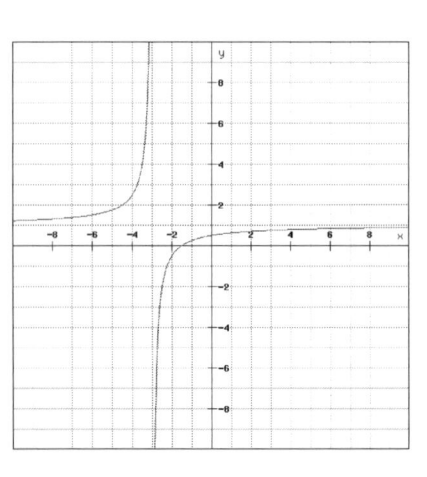

502

Analyze the following functions:

1. $f(x) = \dfrac{1}{2x}$

   $H.Asymptote: y = 0$ $Domain: x \in (-\infty, 0) \cup (0, \infty)$
   $Lim_{x \to -\infty}(f(x)) = 0$ $Range: f(x) \in (-\infty, 0) \cup (0, \infty)$
   $Lim_{x \to \infty}(f(x)) = 0$ $Increases: Never$
   $V.Asymptote: x = 0$ $Decreases: x \in (-\infty, 0) \cup (0, \infty)$
   $Lim_{x \to 0^-}(f(x)) = -\infty$ $x \; Intercept: None$
   $Lim_{x \to 0^+}(f(x)) = \infty$ $y \; Intercept: None$

2. $f(x) = -2\dfrac{1}{x}$

   $H.Asymptote: y = 0$ $Domain: x \in (-\infty, 0) \cup (0, \infty)$
   $Lim_{x \to -\infty}(f(x)) = 0$ $Range: f(x) \in (-\infty, 0) \cup (0, \infty)$
   $Lim_{x \to \infty}(f(x)) = 0$ $Increases: x \in (-\infty, 0) \cup (0, \infty)$
   $V.Asymptote: x = 0$ $Decreases: Never$
   $Lim_{x \to 0^-}(f(x)) = \infty$ $x \; Intercept: None$
   $Lim_{x \to 0^+}(f(x)) = -\infty$ $y \; Intercept: None$

3. $f(x) = \dfrac{1}{2+x}$

   $H.Asymptote: y = 0$ $Domain: x \in (-\infty, -2) \cup (-2, \infty)$
   $Lim_{x \to -\infty}(f(x)) = 0$ $Range: f(x) \in (-\infty, 0) \cup (0, \infty)$
   $Lim_{x \to \infty}(f(x)) = 0$ $Increases: Never$
   $V.Asymptote: x = -2$ $Decreases: x \in (-\infty, -2) \cup (-2, \infty)$
   $Lim_{x \to -2^-}(f(x)) = -\infty$ $x \; Intercept: None$
   $Lim_{x \to -2^+}(f(x)) = \infty$ $y \; Intercept: (0, \dfrac{1}{2})$

4. $f(x) = \dfrac{1}{1-x}$

   $H.Asymptote: y = 0$ $Domain: x \in (-\infty, 1) \cup (1, \infty)$
   $Lim_{x \to -\infty}(f(x)) = 0$ $Range: f(x) \in (-\infty, 0) \cup (0, \infty)$
   $Lim_{x \to \infty}(f(x)) = 0$ $Increases: x \in (-\infty, 1) \cup (1, \infty)$
   $V.Asymptote: x = 0$ $Decreases: Never$
   $Lim_{x \to 1^-}(f(x)) = \infty$ $x \; Intercept: None$
   $Lim_{x \to 1^+}(f(x)) = -\infty$ $y \; Intercept: (0, 1)$

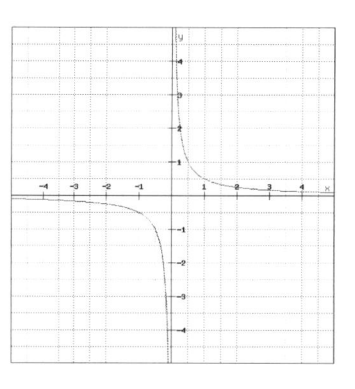

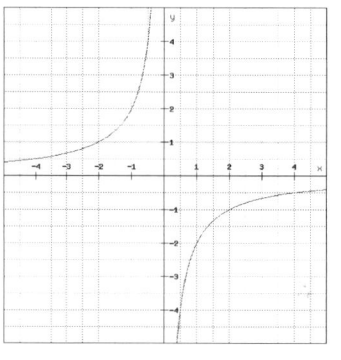

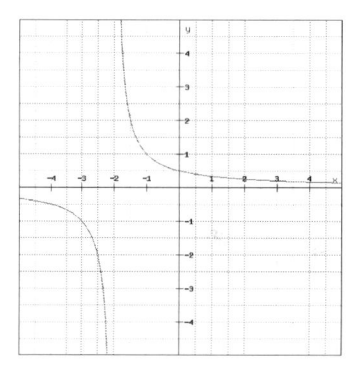

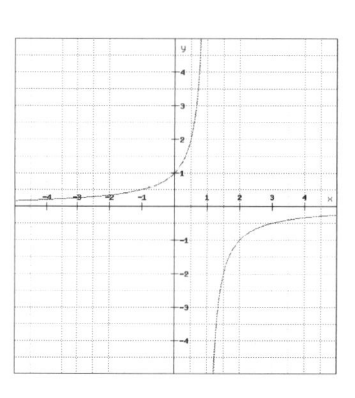

5. $f(x) = -\dfrac{2}{x+1}$

$H.Asymptote: y = 0$ $Domain: x \in (-\infty, -1) \cup (-1, \infty)$
$Lim_{x \to -\infty}(f(x)) = 0$ $Range: f(x) \in (-\infty, 0) \cup (0, \infty)$
$Lim_{x \to \infty}(f(x)) = 0$ $Increases: x \in (-\infty, -1) \cup (-1, \infty)$
$V.Asymptote: x = 0$ $Decreases: Never$
$Lim_{x \to -1^-}(f(x)) = \infty$ $x\ Intercept: None$
$Lim_{x \to -1^+}(f(x)) = -\infty$ $y\ Intercept: (0, -2)$

6. $f(x) = \dfrac{5}{2x} + 1$

$H.Asymptote: y = 1$ $Domain: x \in (-\infty, 0) \cup (0, \infty)$
$Lim_{x \to -\infty}(f(x)) = 1$ $Range: f(x) \in (-\infty, 1) \cup (1, \infty)$
$Lim_{x \to \infty}(f(x)) = 1$ $Increases: Never$
$V.Asymptote: x = 0$ $Decreases: x \in (-\infty, 0) \cup (0, \infty)$
$Lim_{x \to 0^-}(f(x)) = -\infty$ $x\ Intercept: (-\dfrac{2}{5}, 0)$
$Lim_{x \to 0^+}(f(x)) = \infty$ $y\ Intercept: None$

7. $f(x) = -\dfrac{2x}{x+1} = -2\dfrac{x+1-1}{x+1} = \dfrac{2}{x+1} - 2$

$H.Asymptote: y = -2$ $Domain: x \in (-\infty, -1) \cup (-1, \infty)$
$Lim_{x \to -\infty}(f(x)) = -2$ $Range: f(x) \in (-\infty, -2) \cup (-2, \infty)$
$Lim_{x \to \infty}(f(x)) = -2$ $Increases: x \in (-\infty, -1) \cup (-1, \infty)$
$V.Asymptote: x = 0$ $Decreases: Never$
$Lim_{x \to -1^-}(f(x)) = -\infty$ $x\ Intercept: (0, 0)$
$Lim_{x \to -1^+}(f(x)) = \infty$ $y\ Intercept: (0, 0)$

8. $f(x) = \dfrac{2-x}{x+3} = \dfrac{2-(x+3)+3}{x+3} = \dfrac{5}{x+3} - 1$

$H.Asymptote: y = -1$ $Domain: x \in (-\infty, -3) \cup (-3, \infty)$
$Lim_{x \to -\infty}(f(x)) = -1$ $Range: f(x) \in (-\infty, -1) \cup (-1, \infty)$
$Lim_{x \to \infty}(f(x)) = -1$ $Increases: Never$
$V.Asymptote: x = -3$ $Decreases: x \in (-\infty, -3) \cup (-3, \infty)$
$Lim_{x \to -3^-}(f(x)) = -\infty$ $x\ Intercept: (2, 0)$
$Lim_{x \to -3^+}(f(x)) = \infty$ $y\ Intercept: (0, \dfrac{2}{3})$

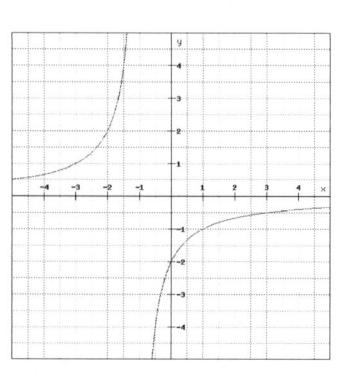

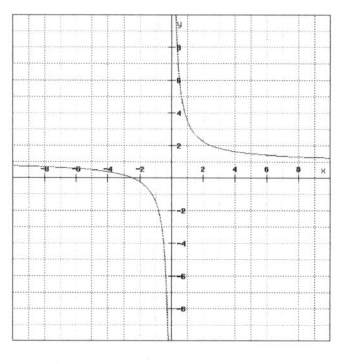

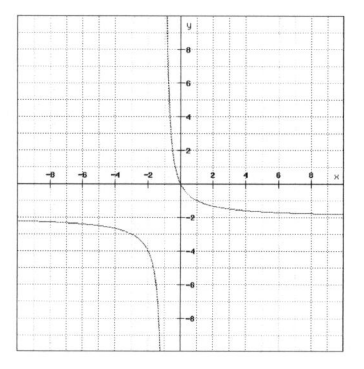

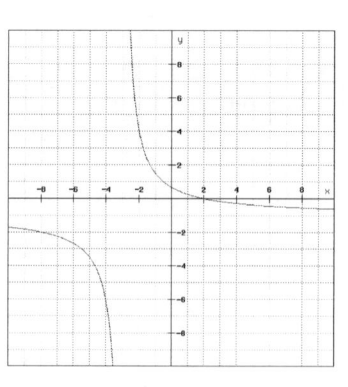

9. $f(x) = \dfrac{2}{7-x} + 4$

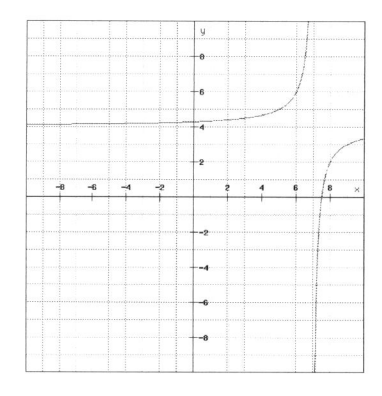

H.Asymptote: $y = 4$ Domain: $x \in (-\infty, 7) \cup (7, \infty)$
$Lim_{x \to -\infty}(f(x)) = 4$ Range: $f(x) \in (-\infty, 4) \cup (4, \infty)$
$Lim_{x \to \infty}(f(x)) = 4$ Increases: $x \in (-\infty, 7) \cup (7, \infty)$
V.Asymptote: $x = 7$ Decreases: Never
$Lim_{x \to 7^-}(f(x)) = \infty$ x Intercept: $(\dfrac{15}{2}, 0)$
$Lim_{x \to 7^+}(f(x)) = -\infty$ y Intercept: $(0, \dfrac{30}{7})$

10. $f(x) = \dfrac{3x+3}{2x-1} = \dfrac{9}{4x-2} + \dfrac{3}{2}$

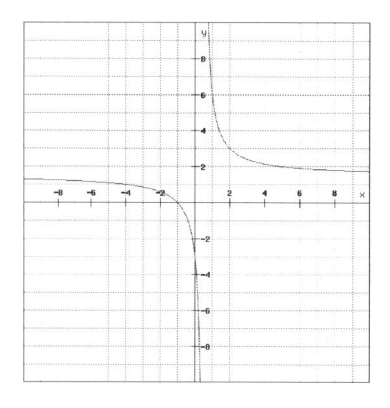

H.Asymptote: $y = \dfrac{3}{2}$ Domain: $x \in (-\infty, \dfrac{1}{2}) \cup (\dfrac{1}{2}, \infty)$
$Lim_{x \to -\infty}(f(x)) = \dfrac{3}{2}$ Range: $f(x) \in (-\infty, \dfrac{3}{2}) \cup (\dfrac{3}{2}, \infty)$
$Lim_{x \to \infty}(f(x)) = \dfrac{3}{2}$ Increases: Never
V.Asymptote: $x = \dfrac{1}{2}$ Decreases: $x \in (-\infty, \dfrac{1}{2}) \cup (\dfrac{1}{2}, \infty)$
$Lim_{x \to (\frac{1}{2})^-}(f(x)) = -\infty$ x Intercept: $(-1, 0)$
$Lim_{x \to (\frac{1}{2})^+}(f(x)) = \infty$ y Intercept: $(0, -3)$

11. $f(x) = -\dfrac{4}{x+4} - 2$

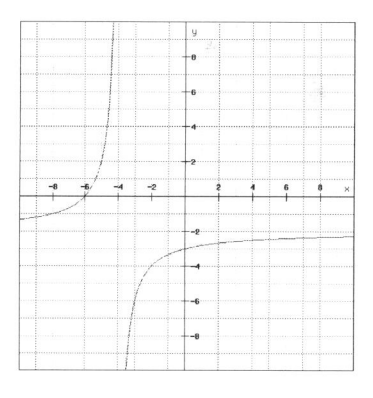

H.Asymptote: $y = -2$ Domain: $x \in (-\infty, -4) \cup (-4, \infty)$
$Lim_{x \to -\infty}(f(x)) = -2$ Range: $f(x) \in (-\infty, -2) \cup (-2, \infty)$
$Lim_{x \to \infty}(f(x)) = -2$ Increases: $x \in (-\infty, -4) \cup (-4, \infty)$
V.Asymptote: $x = -4$ Decreases: Never
$Lim_{x \to -4^-}(f(x)) = \infty$ x Intercept: $(-6, 0)$
$Lim_{x \to -4^+}(f(x)) = -\infty$ y Intercept: $(0, -3)$

12. $f(x) = \dfrac{x^2 - 2x}{x-2} = \dfrac{x(x-2)}{x-2} \approx x$

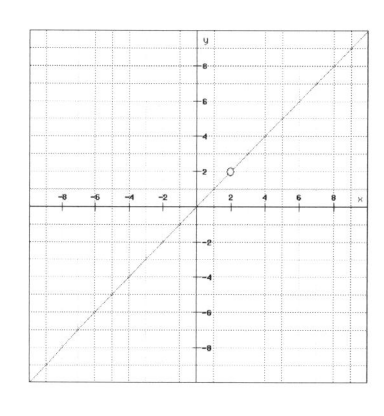

H.Asymptote: None   Domain: $x \in \mathbb{R}$
Range: $f(x) \in (-\infty, 2) \cup (2, \infty)$
Increases: $x \in (-\infty, 2) \cup (2, \infty)$
V.Asymptote: None   Decreases: Never
x Intercept: $(0, 0)$
y Intercept: $(0, 0)$

505

13. $f(x) = \dfrac{8x+3}{4x-2} = \dfrac{2(4x-2)+4+3}{4x-2} = \dfrac{7}{4x-2} + 2$

H.Asymptote: $y = 2$ Domain: $x \in (-\infty, \tfrac{1}{2}) \cup (\tfrac{1}{2}, \infty)$

$Lim_{x \to -\infty}(f(x)) = 2$ Range: $f(x) \in (-\infty, 2) \cup (2, \infty)$

$Lim_{x \to \infty}(f(x)) = 2$ Increases: Never

V.Asymptote: $x = \dfrac{1}{2}$ Decreases: $x \in (-\infty, \tfrac{1}{2}) \cup (\tfrac{1}{2}, \infty)$

$Lim_{x \to (\tfrac{1}{2})^-}(f(x)) = -\infty$ x Intercept: $(-\tfrac{3}{8}, 0)$

$Lim_{x \to (\tfrac{1}{2})^+}(f(x)) = \infty$ y Intercept: $(0, -\tfrac{3}{2})$

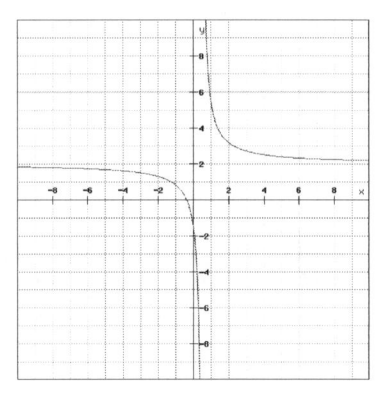

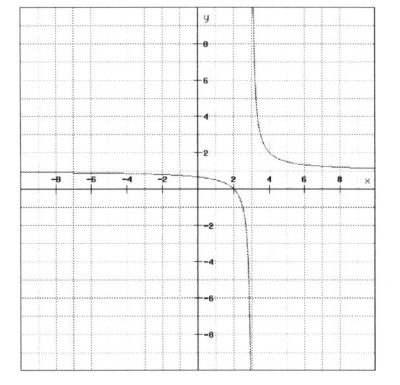

14. $f(x) = \dfrac{x-2}{x-3} = \dfrac{x-3+1}{x-3} = \dfrac{1}{x-3} + 1$

H.Asymptote: $y = 1$ Domain: $x \in (-\infty, 3) \cup (3, \infty)$

$Lim_{x \to -\infty}(f(x)) = 1$ Range: $f(x) \in (-\infty, 1) \cup (1, \infty)$

$Lim_{x \to \infty}(f(x)) = 1$ Increases: Never

V.Asymptote: $x = 3$ Decreases: $x \in (-\infty, 3) \cup (3, \infty)$

$Lim_{x \to 3^-}(f(x)) = -\infty$ x Intercept: $(2, 0)$

$Lim_{x \to 3^+}(f(x)) = \infty$ y Intercept: $(0, \tfrac{2}{3})$

15. $f(x) = \dfrac{3x-5}{4x+3} = \dfrac{\tfrac{3}{4}(4x+3) - \tfrac{9}{4} + 5}{4x+3} = \dfrac{-\tfrac{9}{4}+5}{4x+3} + 3 = \dfrac{\left(\tfrac{11}{4}\right)}{4x+3} + 3$

H.Asymptote: $y = 3$ Domain: $x \in (-\infty, -\tfrac{3}{4}) \cup (-\tfrac{3}{4}, \infty)$

$Lim_{x \to -\infty}(f(x)) = 3$ Range: $f(x) \in (-\infty, 3) \cup (3, \infty)$

$Lim_{x \to \infty}(f(x)) = 3$ Increases: Never

V.Asymptote: $x = -\dfrac{3}{4}$ Decreases: $x \in (-\infty, -\tfrac{3}{4}) \cup (-\tfrac{3}{4}, \infty)$

$Lim_{x \to \left(-\tfrac{3}{4}\right)^-}(f(x)) = -\infty$ x Intercept: $(-\tfrac{47}{48}, 0)$

$Lim_{x \to \left(-\tfrac{3}{4}\right)^+}(f(x)) = \infty$ y Intercept: $(0, \tfrac{47}{12})$

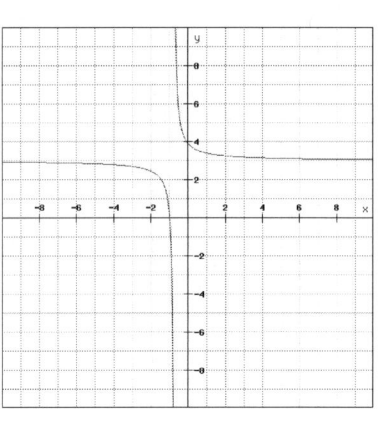

16. $f(x) = \dfrac{6}{4x+3} - 5$

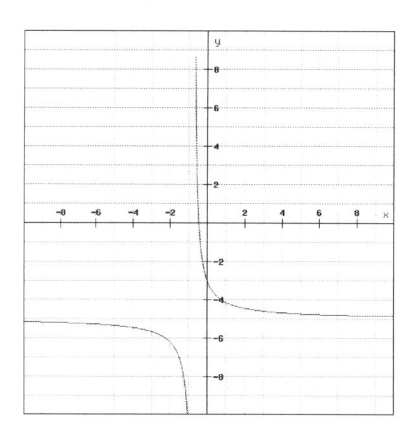

$H.Asymptote: y = -5$ $Domain: x \in (-\infty, -\dfrac{3}{4}) \cup (-\dfrac{3}{4}, \infty)$

$Lim_{x \to -\infty}(f(x)) = -5$ $Range: f(x) \in (-\infty, -5) \cup (-5, \infty)$

$Lim_{x \to \infty}(f(x)) = -5$ $Increases: Never$

$V.Asymptote: x = -\dfrac{3}{4}$ $Decreases: x \in (-\infty, -\dfrac{3}{4}) \cup (-\dfrac{3}{4}, \infty)$

$Lim_{x \to \left(-\frac{3}{4}\right)^-}(f(x)) = -\infty$ $x\ Intercept: (-\dfrac{9}{20}, 0)$

$Lim_{x \to \left(-\frac{3}{4}\right)^+}(f(x)) = \infty$ $y\ Intercept: (0, -3)$

17. $f(x) = \dfrac{3x - x^2}{x - 3} = \dfrac{x(3-x)}{x-3} \approx -x$

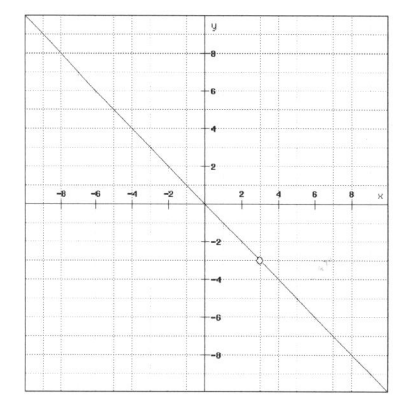

$H.Asymptote: None$ $Domain: x \in \mathbb{R}$

$Range: f(x) \in (-\infty, -3) \cup (-3, \infty)$

$Increases: Never$

$V.Asymptote: None$ $Decreases: x \in (-\infty, 2) \cup (2, \infty)$

$x\ Intercept: (0, 0)$

$y\ Intercept: (0, 0)$

18. $f(x) = \dfrac{3x - 2}{x - 3} = \dfrac{3(x-3) + 9 - 2}{x - 3} = \dfrac{7}{x-3} + 3$

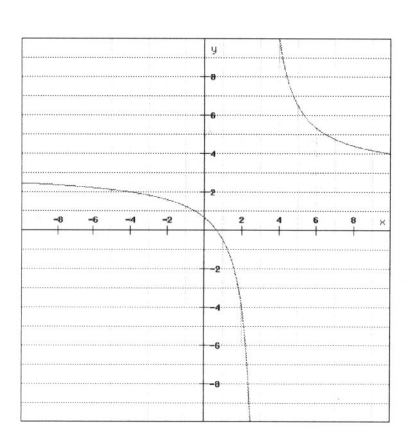

$H.Asymptote: y = 3$ $Domain: x \in (-\infty, 3) \cup (3, \infty)$

$Lim_{x \to -\infty}(f(x)) = 3$ $Range: f(x) \in (-\infty, 3) \cup (3, \infty)$

$Lim_{x \to \infty}(f(x)) = 3$ $Increases: Never$

$V.Asymptote: x = 3$ $Decreases: x \in (-\infty, 3) \cup (3, \infty)$

$Lim_{x \to 3^-}(f(x)) = -\infty$ $x\ Intercept: (\dfrac{2}{3}, 0)$

$Lim_{x \to 3^+}(f(x)) = \infty$ $y\ Intercept: (0, -\dfrac{1}{3})$

507

19. $f(x) = \dfrac{4x-1}{-2x-3} = \dfrac{-2(-2x-3)-6-1}{-2x-3} = \dfrac{-7}{-2x-3} - 2 = \dfrac{7}{2x+3} - 2$

H.Asymptote: $y = -2$ Domain: $x \in (-\infty, -\dfrac{3}{2}) \cup (-\dfrac{3}{2}, \infty)$

$Lim_{x \to -\infty}(f(x)) = -2$ Range: $f(x) \in (-\infty, -2) \cup (-2, \infty)$

$Lim_{x \to \infty}(f(x)) = -2$ Increases: Never

V.Asymptote: $x = -\dfrac{3}{2}$ Decreases: $x \in (-\infty, -\dfrac{3}{2}) \cup (-\dfrac{3}{2}, \infty)$

$Lim_{x \to \left(-\frac{3}{2}\right)^-}(f(x)) = -\infty$ x Intercept: $(\dfrac{1}{4}, 0)$

$Lim_{x \to \left(-\frac{3}{2}\right)^+}(f(x)) = \infty$ y Intercept: $(0, \dfrac{1}{3})$

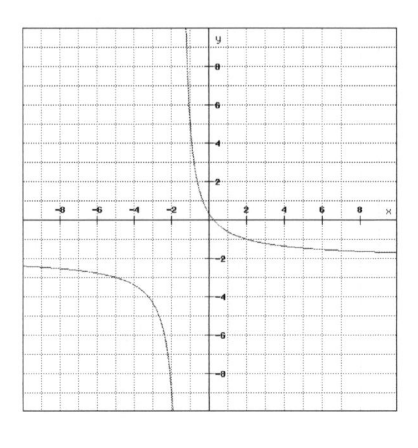

20. $f(x) = \dfrac{4x}{8x-5} = \dfrac{\frac{1}{2}(8x-5) + \frac{5}{2}}{8x-5} = \dfrac{\left(\frac{5}{2}\right)}{8x-5} + \dfrac{1}{2}$

H.Asymptote: $y = \dfrac{1}{2}$ Domain: $x \in (-\infty, \dfrac{5}{8}) \cup (\dfrac{5}{8}, \infty)$

$Lim_{x \to -\infty}(f(x)) = \dfrac{1}{2}$ Range: $f(x) \in (-\infty, \dfrac{1}{2}) \cup (\dfrac{1}{2}, \infty)$

$Lim_{x \to \infty}(f(x)) = \dfrac{1}{2}$ Increases: Never

V.Asymptote: $x = \dfrac{5}{8}$ Decreases: $x \in (-\infty, -\dfrac{3}{2}) \cup (-\dfrac{3}{2}, \infty)$

$Lim_{x \to \left(\frac{5}{8}\right)^-}(f(x)) = -\infty$ x Intercept: $(0, 0)$

$Lim_{x \to \left(\frac{5}{8}\right)^+}(f(x)) = \infty$ y Intercept: $(0, 0)$

21. $f(x) = \dfrac{x^2+4x+3}{x+1} + 3 = \dfrac{(x+1)(x+3)}{x+1} + 3 \approx x + 6$

H.Asymptote: None Domain: $x \in \mathbb{R}$

Range: $f(x) \in (-\infty, -1) \cup (-1, \infty)$

Increases: $x \in (-\infty, -1) \cup (-1, \infty)$

V.Asymptote: None Decreases: Never

x Intercept: $(0, 6)$

y Intercept: $(-6, 0)$

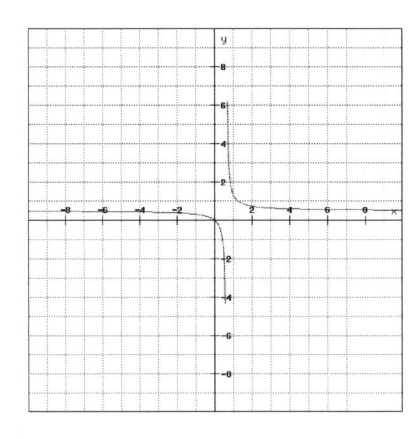

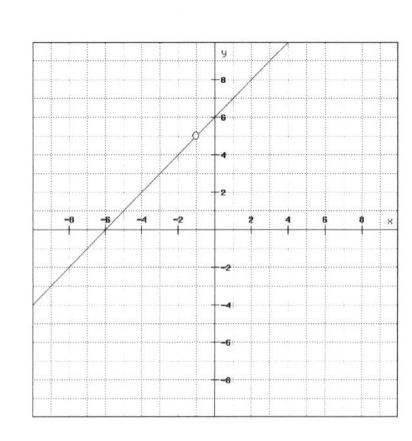

508

22. $f(x) = \dfrac{4x+3}{5x+3} = \dfrac{\frac{4}{5}(5x+3) - \frac{12}{5} + 3}{5x+3} = \dfrac{\left(\frac{3}{5}\right)}{5x+3} + \dfrac{4}{5}$

H. Asymptote: $y = \dfrac{4}{5}$ Domain: $x \in (-\infty, -\dfrac{3}{5}) \cup (-\dfrac{3}{5}, \infty)$

$Lim_{x \to -\infty}(f(x)) = \dfrac{4}{5}$ Range: $f(x) \in (-\infty, \dfrac{4}{5}) \cup (\dfrac{4}{5}, \infty)$

$Lim_{x \to \infty}(f(x)) = \dfrac{4}{5}$ Increases: Never

V. Asymptote: $x = -\dfrac{3}{5}$ Decreases: $x \in (-\infty, -\dfrac{3}{5}) \cup (-\dfrac{3}{5}, \infty)$

$Lim_{x \to \left(-\frac{3}{5}\right)^-}(f(x)) = -\infty$ x Intercept: $(-\dfrac{3}{4}, 0)$

$Lim_{x \to \left(-\frac{3}{5}\right)^+}(f(x)) = \infty$ y Intercept: $(0, 1)$

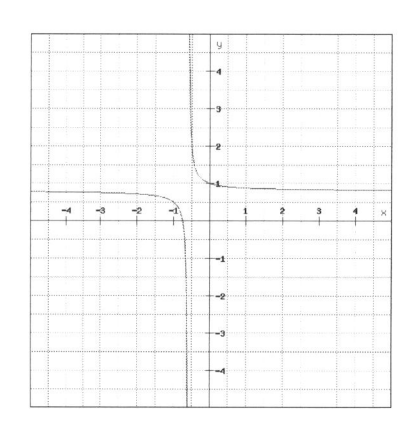

23. On making a certain product there is a fixed cost of 2 Euros and a variable cost per product. The variable cost is 60 Euros for 1 product, 30 Euros for 2 products, 20 Euros for 3 products etc.
    a. The cost of making a product in case 4 products are made is <u>15 euros</u>
    b. Write a function for the cost of a product. $f(x) = \dfrac{60}{x} + 2, x \in [1, \infty)$
    c. Sketch the function obtained on a graph, label the graph.
    d. The cost of a product in case a large number of products is made <u>approaches 2</u>.

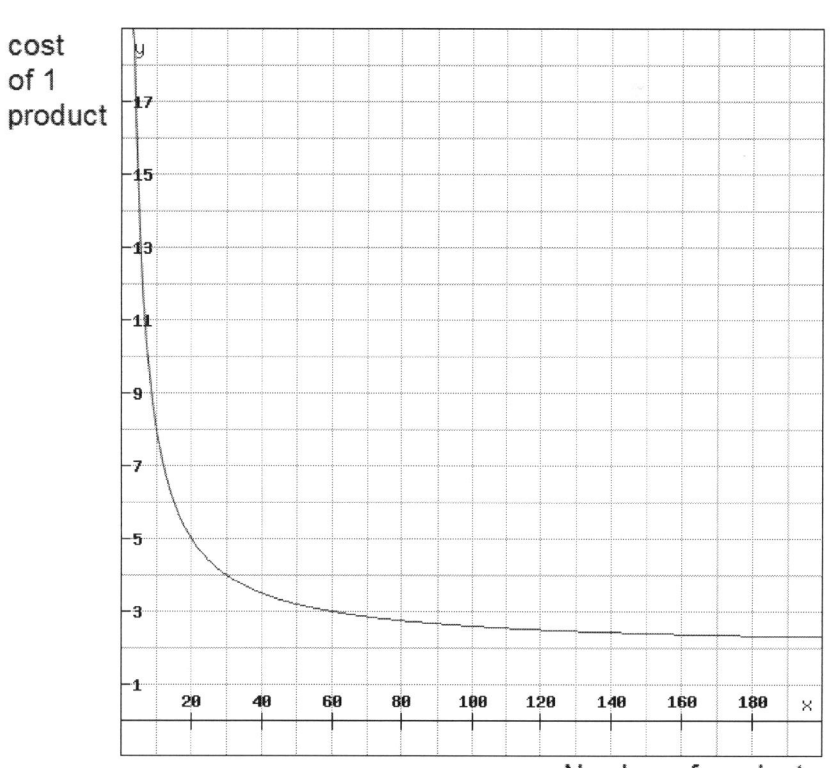

cost of 1 product

Number of products

509

24. The cost per unit C(x) to produce x units of a product is given by $C(x) = \dfrac{300}{x+10}$

   a. The cost per unit when 180 units are produced is $C(180) = \dfrac{300}{190}\$$
   b. If the cost per unit is $1.50, how many units have been produced?
   $1.5 = \dfrac{300}{x+10}; x = 190 \, products$

25. In the following formula, S(x) is the minimum number of hours of studying required to attain a test score of x $S(x) = \dfrac{0.32x}{100.5 - x}$

   a. The hours of study needed to score 85: $S(85) = \dfrac{0.32 \cdot 85}{100.5 - 85} \approx 1.75h$
   b. The score in case you study 8 hours: $8 = \dfrac{0.32 \cdot x}{100.5 - x}; x = 96$
   c. The number of hours of study needed to score 100:
   $S(100) = \dfrac{0.32 \cdot 100}{100.5 - 100} = 64h$
   d. The domain of the function: $x \in (0, 100)$
   e. Sketch the function in the domain found.

Number of hours

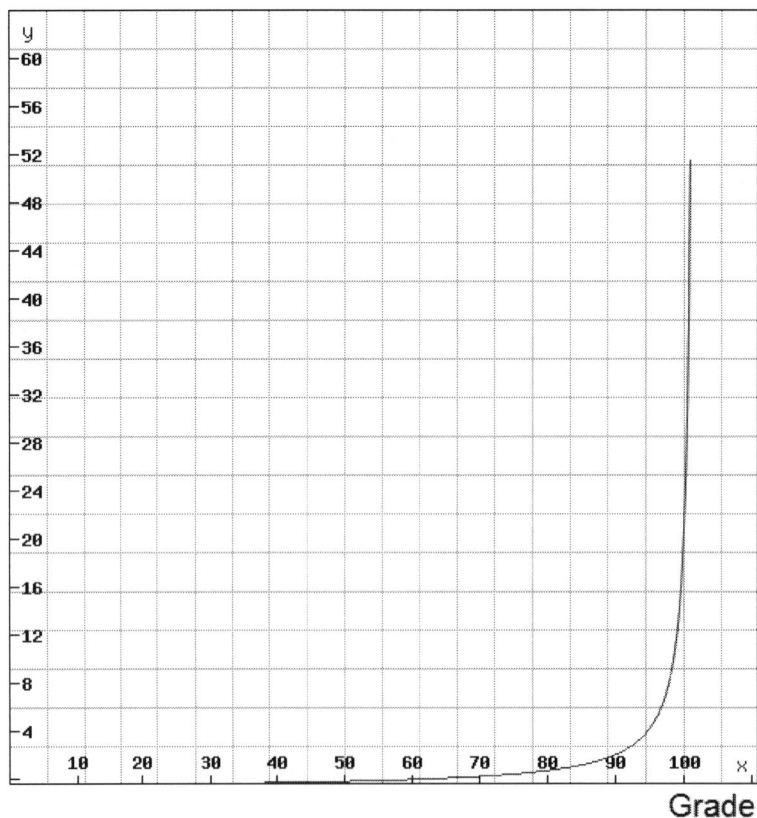

Grade

2.7. – EXPONENTIAL FUNCTIONS

1. Given the functions: $f(x) = 2^x$, $g(x) = 3^x$, Complete the following chart:

x	−5	−4	−3	−2	−1	0	1	2	3	4	5	6
f(x)	$\frac{1}{32}$	$\frac{1}{16}$	$\frac{1}{8}$	$\frac{1}{4}$	$\frac{1}{2}$	1	2	4	8	16	32	64
g(x)	$\frac{1}{243}$	$\frac{1}{81}$	$\frac{1}{27}$	$\frac{1}{9}$	$\frac{1}{3}$	1	3	9	27	81	243	729

- Domain of the functions: $x \in R$
- y intercept: $f(x):(0,1); g(x):(0,1)$
- x intercept(s): None
- The equation of the horizontal asymptotes: y = 0 (in both cases)
- Increasing: $x \in R$; Decreasing: Never
- max/min point(s): None, always increasing
- The range of the function:
  $f(x) \in (0,\infty); g(x) \in (0,\infty)$

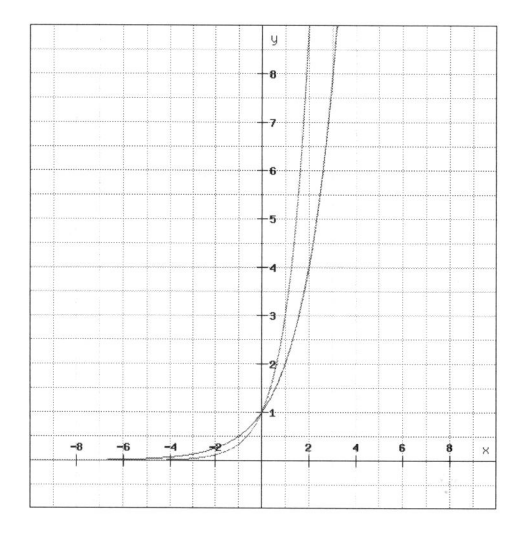

2. Given the functions: $f(x) = 2^{-x}$, $g(x) = 3^{-x}$, Complete the following chart:

x	−5	−4	−3	−2	−1	0	1	2	3	4	5	6
f(x)	32	16	8	4	2	1	$\frac{1}{2}$	$\frac{1}{4}$	$\frac{1}{8}$	$\frac{1}{16}$	$\frac{1}{32}$	$\frac{1}{64}$
g(x)	243	81	27	9	3	1	$\frac{1}{3}$	$\frac{1}{9}$	$\frac{1}{27}$	$\frac{1}{81}$	$\frac{1}{243}$	$\frac{1}{729}$

- Domain of the functions: $x \in R$
- y intercept: $f(x):(0,1); g(x):(0,1)$
- x intercept(s): None
- The equation of the horizontal asymptote: y = 0 (in both cases)
- Increasing: Never; Decreasing: $x \in R$
- max/min point(s): None, always decreasing
- The range of the function:
  $f(x) \in (0,\infty); g(x) \in (0,\infty)$
- Write in more forms: $f(x) = 2^{-x} = \left(\frac{1}{2}\right)^x = \frac{1}{2^x}$

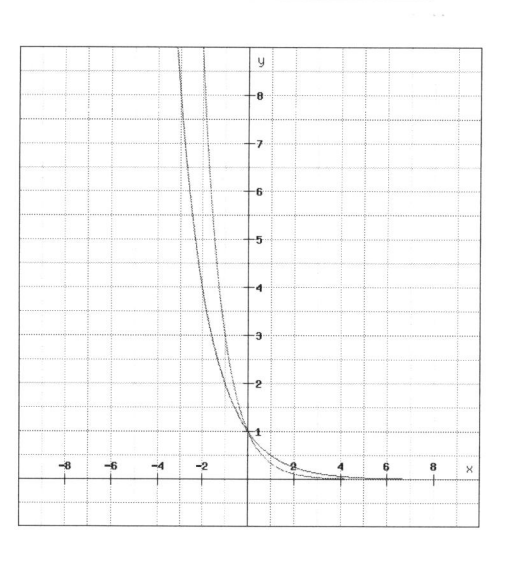

3. Given the functions: f(x) = –2^x, g(x) = –3^x, Complete the following chart:

x	–5	–4	–3	–2	–1	0	1	2	3	4	5	6
f(x)		–32	–16	–8	–4	–2	–1	$-\dfrac{1}{2}$	$-\dfrac{1}{4}$	$-\dfrac{1}{8}$	$-\dfrac{1}{16}$	$-\dfrac{1}{32}$	$-\dfrac{1}{64}$
g(x)	–243	–81	–27	–9	–3	–1	$-\dfrac{1}{3}$	$-\dfrac{1}{9}$	$-\dfrac{1}{27}$	$-\dfrac{1}{81}$	$-\dfrac{1}{243}$	$-\dfrac{1}{729}$

- Domain of the function: $x \in R$
- y intercept: $f(x):(0,-1); g(x):(0,-1)$
- x intercept(s): None
- The equation of the horizontal asymptote: y = 0 (in both cases)
- Increasing: Never; Decreasing: $x \in R$
- max/min point(s): None, always decreasing
- The range of the function:
  $f(x) \in (-\infty, 0); g(x) \in (-\infty, 0)$
- Write in more forms: None

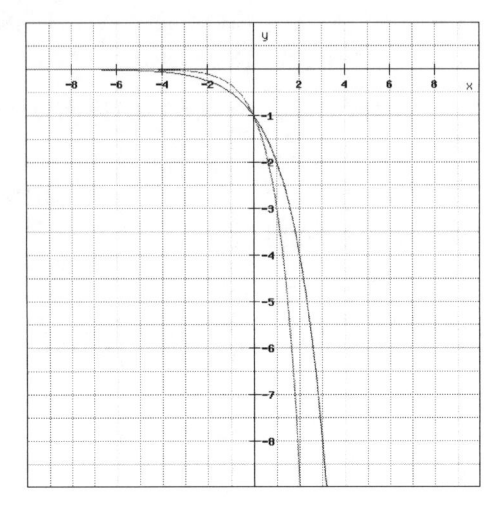

4. Given the functions: f(x) = –2^(–x), g(x) = –3^(–x), Complete the following chart:

x	–5	–4	–3	–2	–1	0	1	2	3	4	5	6
f(x)	–32	–16	–8	–4	–2	–1	$-\dfrac{1}{2}$	$-\dfrac{1}{4}$	$-\dfrac{1}{8}$	$-\dfrac{1}{16}$	$-\dfrac{1}{32}$	$-\dfrac{1}{64}$
g(x)	–243	–81	–27	–9	–3	–1	$-\dfrac{1}{3}$	$-\dfrac{1}{9}$	$-\dfrac{1}{27}$	$-\dfrac{1}{81}$	$-\dfrac{1}{243}$	$-\dfrac{1}{729}$

- The domain of the function: $x \in R$
- y intercept: $f(x):(0,-1); g(x):(0,-1)$
- x intercept(s): None
- The equation of the horizontal asymptote: y = 0 (in both cases)
- Increasing: $x \in R$, Decreasing: Never
- max/min point(s): None, always increasing
- The range of the function:
  $f(x) \in (-\infty, 0); g(x) \in (-\infty, 0)$
- Write in more forms: $f(x) = -2^{-x} = -\left(\dfrac{1}{2}\right)^x = \dfrac{-1}{2^x}$

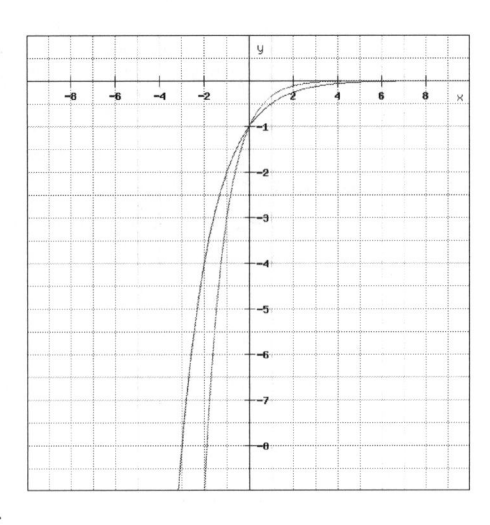

5. Given the function: $f(x) = -5 \times 4^{-2x} + 1$, Complete the following chart:

x	−5	−4	−3	−2	−1	0	1	2	3	4	5
f(x)	$-5 \cdot 4^{10}+1$	$-5 \cdot 4^8+1$	$-5 \cdot 4^6+1$	$-5 \cdot 4^4+1$	-79	-4	$\frac{11}{16}$	$\frac{-5}{4^4}+1$	$\frac{-5}{4^6}+1$	$\frac{-5}{4^8}+1$	$\frac{-5}{4^4}+1$

- State the domain of the function: $x \in R$
- y intercept: $(0, -4)$
- x intercept(s): $(\frac{\ln(5)}{4\ln(2)}, 0)$
- The equation of horizontal asymptote: $y = 1$
- Increasing: $x \in R$; Decreasing: Never
- max/min point(s): None, always increasing
- The range of the function: $f(x) \in (-\infty, 1)$
- Write in more forms:
$$f(x) = -5 \times 4^{-2x} + 1 = \frac{-5}{4^{2x}} + 1 = \frac{-5}{16^x} + 1$$

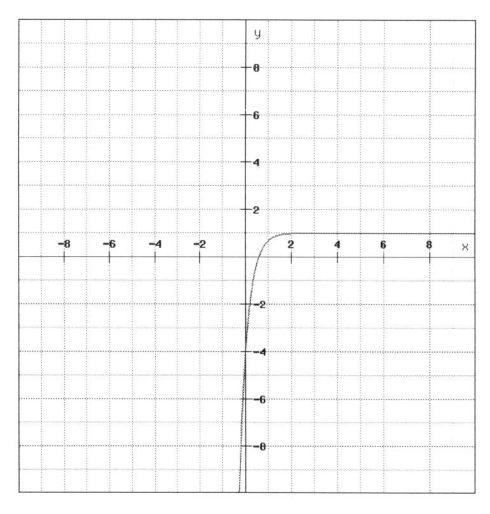

6. Given the graph of the function $f(x) = \left(\frac{1}{2}\right)^x = (2^{-1})^x = 2^{-x}$ sketch, on the same set of axes, the graphs of the functions:

$$g(x) = \left(\frac{1}{2}\right)^{x-2} = (2^{-1})^{x-2} = 2^{2-x} = 4 \cdot 2^{-x}$$

$$d(x) = \left(\frac{1}{2}\right)^x - 2 = 2^{-x} - 2$$

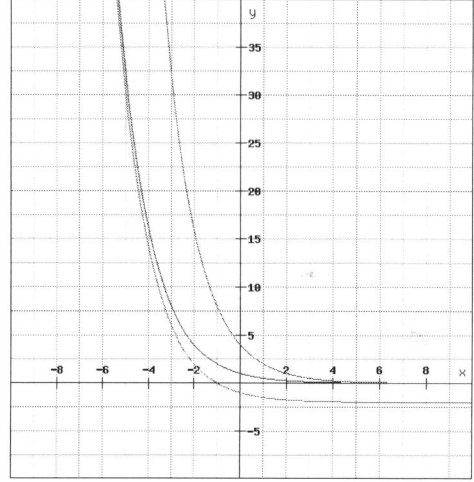

7. Given the graph, complete the table below:

Function	On the graph
$f(x) = 5 \times 2^x$	E
$f(x) = 2 + 2 \times 3^{-x}$	B
$f(x) = 3 \times 3^{-x} + 1$	A
$f(x) = (1.3)^x$	C
$f(x) = -e^x$	F
$f(x) = 3^x$	D
$f(x) = -3 \times 2^x + 1$	G

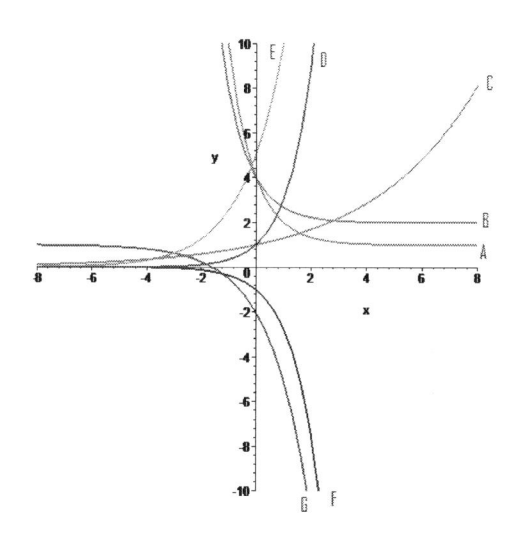

8. Given the function f(x) = e^x
   a. Function translated 2 positions up $f(x) = e^x + 2$
   b. Function translated 2 positions left. $f(x) = e^{x+2}$
   c. Function translated 4 positions up and 3 right. $f(x) = e^{x-3} + 4$ 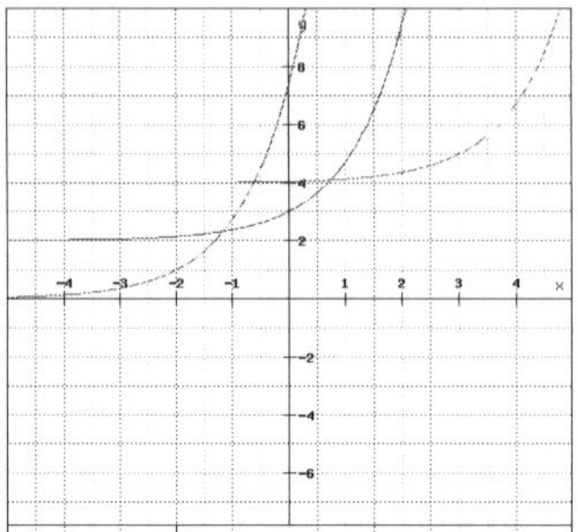
9. Given the function f(x) = $-3 \times 6^{-2x} + 1$

   a. Function translated 2 positions up. $f(x) = -3 \times 6^{-2x} + 3$
   b. Function translated 2 positions left. $f(x) = -3 \times 6^{-2(x+2)} + 1$
   c. Function translated 4 positions up and 3 right.
      $f(x) = -3 \times 6^{-2(x-3)} + 5$

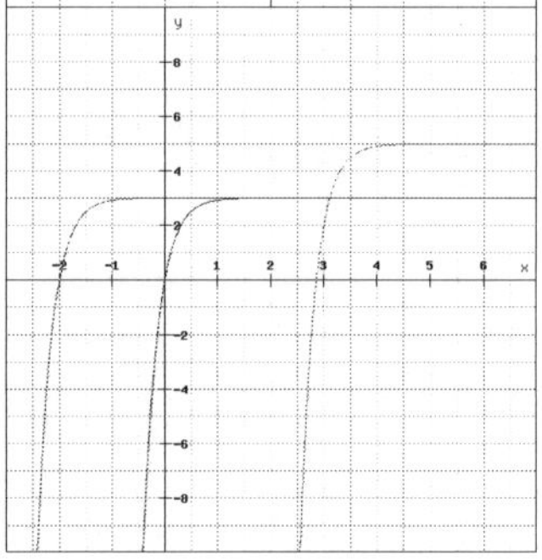

Analyze the functions:

1. $f(x) = 4^x$

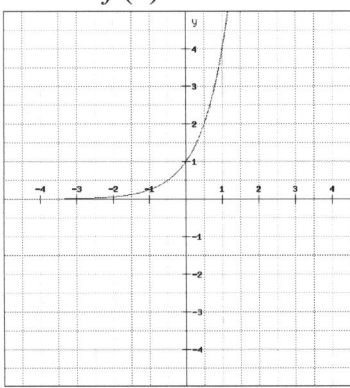

$Domain: x \in R$ $Horizontal\ Asymptote: y = 0$
$Range: f(x) \in (0, \infty)$ $Lim_{x \to -\infty}(f(x)) = 0$
$Increase: x \in R$ $Lim_{x \to \infty}(f(x)) = \infty$
$Decrease: Never$ $Vertical\ Asymptote: None$
$y\ int: (0,1)$ $x\ int: None$

2. $f(x) = -3^x$

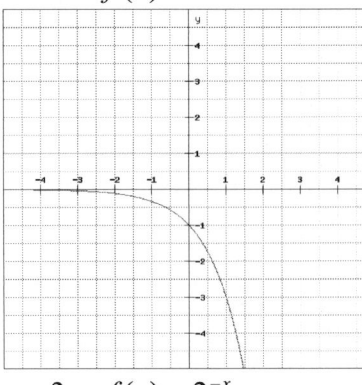

$Domain: x \in R$ $Horizontal\ Asymptote: y = 0$
$Range: f(x) \in (-\infty, 0)$ $Lim_{x \to -\infty}(f(x)) = 0$
$Increase: Never$ $Lim_{x \to \infty}(f(x)) = -\infty$
$Decrease: x \in R$ $Vertical\ Asymptote: None$
$y\ int: (0,-1)$ $x\ int: None$

3. $f(x) = 2^{-x}$

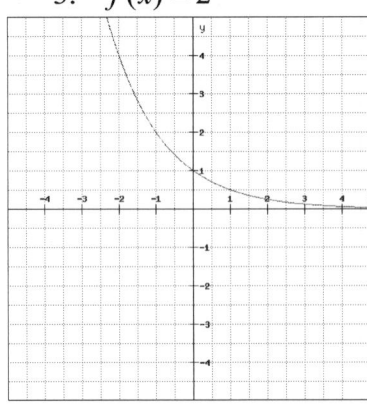

$Domain: x \in R$ $Horizontal\ Asymptote: y = 0$
$Range: f(x) \in (0, \infty)$ $Lim_{x \to -\infty}(f(x)) = \infty$
$Increase: Never$ $Lim_{x \to \infty}(f(x)) = 0$
$Decrease: x \in R$ $Vertical\ Asymptote: None$
$y\ int: (0,1)$ $x\ int: None$

4. $f(x) = -2^{-x}$

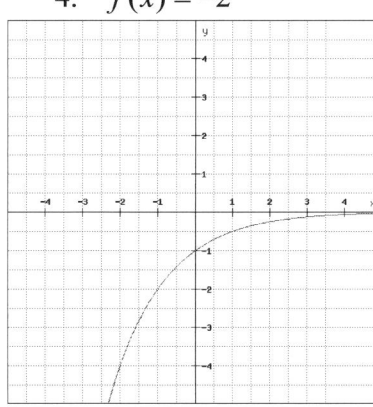

Domain: $x \in R$ Horizontal Asymptote: $y = 0$
Range: $f(x) \in (-\infty, 0)$ $Lim_{x \to -\infty}(f(x)) = -\infty$
Increase: $x \in R$ $Lim_{x \to \infty}(f(x)) = 0$
Decrease: Never   Vertical Asymptote: None
y int: $(0, -1)$ x int: None

5. $f(x) = \left(\dfrac{1}{4}\right)^x$

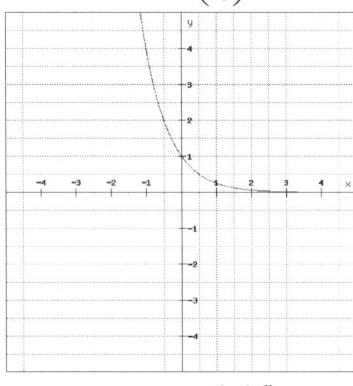

Domain: $x \in R$ Horizontal Asymptote: $y = 0$
Range: $f(x) \in (0, \infty)$ $Lim_{x \to -\infty}(f(x)) = \infty$
Increase: Never $Lim_{x \to \infty}(f(x)) = 0$
Decrease: $x \in R$ Vertical Asymptote: None
y int: $(0, 1)$ x int: None

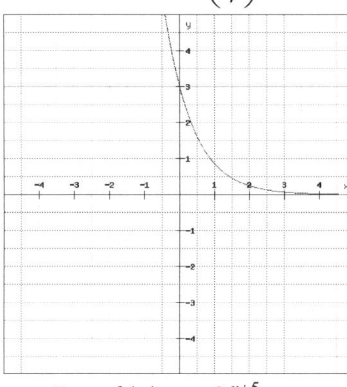

6. $f(x) = 3\left(\dfrac{2}{7}\right)^x$

Domain: $x \in R$ Horizontal Asymptote: $y = 0$
Range: $f(x) \in (0, \infty)$ $Lim_{x \to -\infty}(f(x)) = \infty$
Increase: Never $Lim_{x \to \infty}(f(x)) = 0$
Decrease: $x \in R$ Vertical Asymptote: None
y int: $(0, 3)$ x int: None

7. $f(x) = -2^{x+5}$

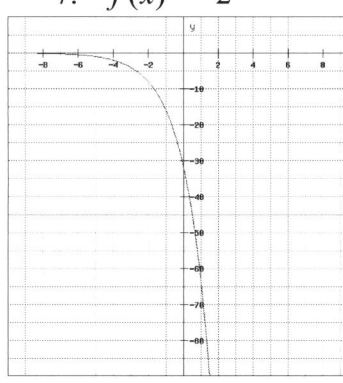

Domain: $x \in R$ Horizontal Asymptote: $y = 0$
Range: $f(x) \in (-\infty, 0)$ $Lim_{x \to -\infty}(f(x)) = 0$
Increase: Never $Lim_{x \to \infty}(f(x)) = -\infty$
Decrease: $x \in R$ Vertical Asymptote: None
y int: $(0, -32)$ x int: None

8. $f(x) = \left(\dfrac{2}{3}\right)^x$

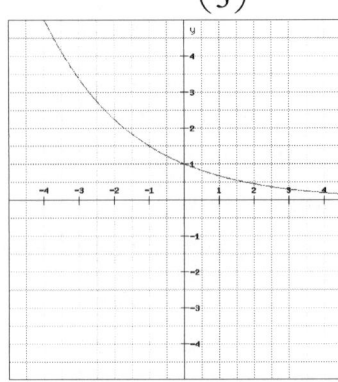

Domain: $x \in R$ Horizontal Asymptote: $y = 0$
Range: $f(x) \in (0, \infty)$ $Lim_{x \to -\infty}(f(x)) = \infty$
Increase: Never $Lim_{x \to \infty}(f(x)) = 0$
Decrease: $x \in R$ Vertical Asymptote: None
$y$int: $(0, 1)$ $x$int: None

9. $f(x) = 3 \cdot 7^{x-4}$

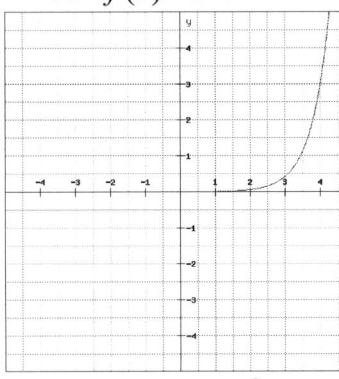

Domain: $x \in R$ Horizontal Asymptote: $y = 0$
Range: $f(x) \in (0, \infty)$ $Lim_{x \to -\infty}(f(x)) = 0$
Increase: $x \in R$ $Lim_{x \to \infty}(f(x)) = \infty$
Decrease: Never   Vertical Asymptote: None
$y$int: $(0, \dfrac{3}{7^4})$ $x$int: None

10. $f(x) = -7^{x-2} + 2$

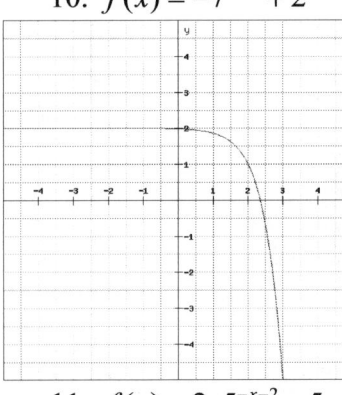

Domain: $x \in R$ Horizontal Asymptote: $y = 2$
Range: $f(x) \in (-\infty, 2)$ $Lim_{x \to -\infty}(f(x)) = 2$
Increase: Never $Lim_{x \to \infty}(f(x)) = -\infty$
Decrease: $x \in R$ Vertical Asymptote: None
$y$int: $(0, \dfrac{97}{49})$ $x$int: $(\approx 2.36, 0)$

11. $f(x) = 2 \cdot 5^{-x-2} - 5$

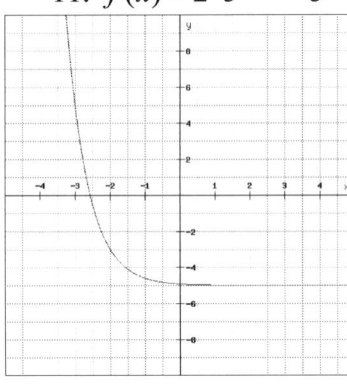

Domain: $x \in R$ Horizontal Asymptote: $y = -5$
Range: $f(x) \in (-5, \infty)$ $Lim_{x \to -\infty}(f(x)) = \infty$
Increase: Never $Lim_{x \to \infty}(f(x)) = -5$
Decrease: $x \in R$ Vertical Asymptote: None
$y$int: $(0, -\dfrac{123}{25})$ $x$int: $(\approx -2.57, 0)$

12. $f(x) = -3^{-x-3} + 4$

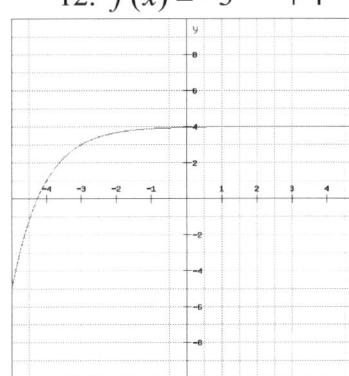

Domain: $x \in R$ Horizontal Asymptote: $y = -5$
Range: $f(x) \in (-\infty, 4)$ $Lim_{x \to -\infty}(f(x)) = -\infty$
Increase: $x \in R$ $Lim_{x \to \infty}(f(x)) = 4$
Decrease: Never   Vertical Asymptote: None
y int: $(0, \frac{107}{27})$ x int: $(\approx -4.26, 0)$

13. $f(x) = -e^x$

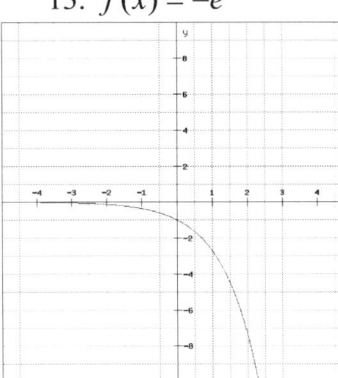

Domain: $x \in R$ Horizontal Asymptote: $y = 0$
Range: $f(x) \in (-\infty, 0)$ $Lim_{x \to -\infty}(f(x)) = 0$
Increase: Never $Lim_{x \to \infty}(f(x)) = -\infty$
Decrease: $x \in R$ Vertical Asymptote: None
y int: $(0, -1)$ x int: None

14. $f(x) = e^{x+2}$

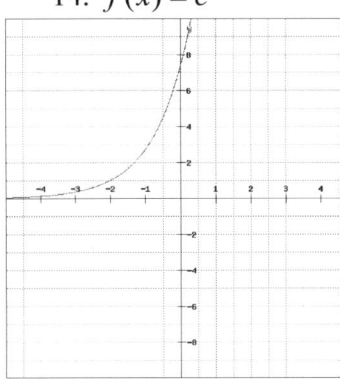

Domain: $x \in R$ Horizontal Asymptote: $y = 0$
Range: $f(x) \in (0, \infty)$ $Lim_{x \to -\infty}(f(x)) = 0$
Increase: $x \in R$ $Lim_{x \to \infty}(f(x)) = \infty$
Decrease: Never   Vertical Asymptote: None
y int: $(0, e^2)$ x int: None

15. $f(x) = -e^x + 4$

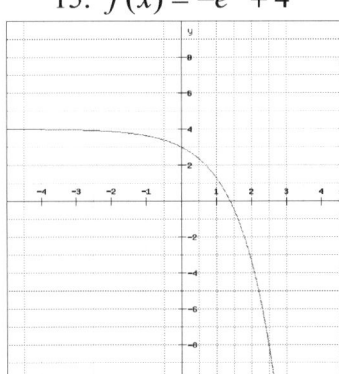

Domain: $x \in R$ Horizontal Asymptote: $y = 4$
Range: $f(x) \in (-\infty, 4)$ $Lim_{x \to -\infty}(f(x)) = 4$
Increase: Never $Lim_{x \to \infty}(f(x)) = -\infty$
Decrease: $x \in R$ Vertical Asymptote: None
y int: $(0, 3)$ x int: $(\ln(4), 0)$

16. $f(x) = 0.1e^{x+1} + 2$

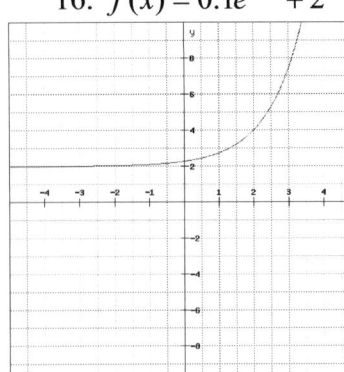

$Domain: x \in R$ $Horizontal\ Asymptote: y = 2$
$Range: f(x) \in (2, \infty)$ $Lim_{x \to -\infty}(f(x)) = 2$
$Increase: x \in R$ $Lim_{x \to \infty}(f(x)) = \infty$
$Decrease: Never$ $Vertical\ Asymptote: None$
$y\operatorname{int}: (0, 0.1e + 2)$ $x\operatorname{int}: None$

17. $f(x) = 2e^{2x+1} - 4$

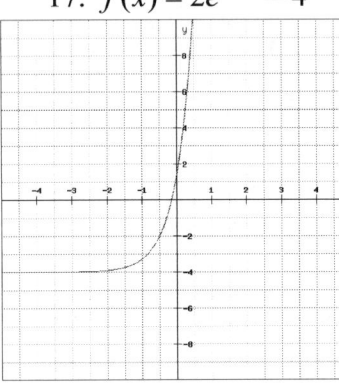

$Domain: x \in R$ $Horizontal\ Asymptote: y = -4$
$Range: f(x) \in (-4, \infty)$ $Lim_{x \to -\infty}(f(x)) = -4$
$Increase: x \in R$ $Lim_{x \to \infty}(f(x)) = \infty$
$Decrease: Never$ $Vertical\ Asymptote: None$
$y\operatorname{int}: (0, 2e - 4)$ $x\operatorname{int}: None$

18. $f(x) = -2 \cdot 6^{x-2} - 1$

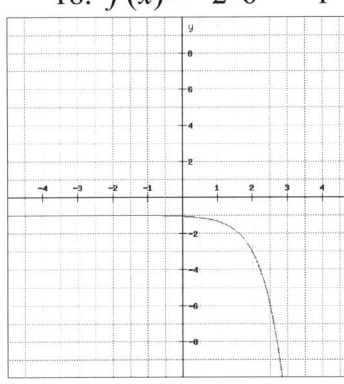

$Domain: x \in R$ $Horizontal\ Asymptote: y = -1$
$Range: f(x) \in (-\infty, -1)$ $Lim_{x \to -\infty}(f(x)) = -1$
$Increase: Never$ $Lim_{x \to \infty}(f(x)) = -\infty$
$Decrease: x \in R$ $Vertical\ Asymptote: None$
$y\operatorname{int}: (0, -\frac{19}{18})$ $x\operatorname{int}: None$

19. $f(x) = 2 \cdot 3^{x-2} - 5$

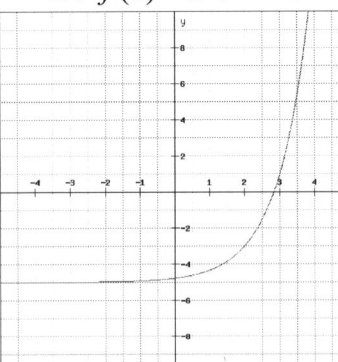

$Domain: x \in R$ $Horizontal\ Asymptote: y = -5$
$Range: f(x) \in (-5, \infty)$ $Lim_{x \to -\infty}(f(x)) = -5$
$Increase: x \in R$ $Lim_{x \to \infty}(f(x)) = \infty$
$Decrease: Never$ $Vertical\ Asymptote: None$
$y\operatorname{int}: (0, -\frac{43}{9})$ $x\operatorname{int}: (\approx -0.153, 0)$

20. $f(x) = 7 \cdot 5^{x-2} + 2$

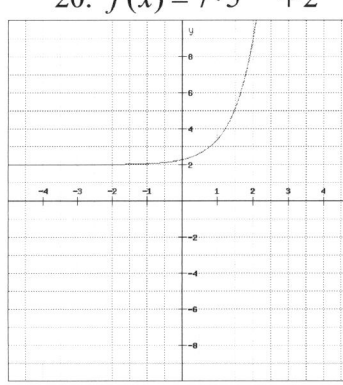

$Domain: x \in R$ $Horizontal\ Asymptote: y = 2$
$Range: f(x) \in (2, \infty)$ $Lim_{x \to -\infty}(f(x)) = 2$
$Increase: x \in R$ $Lim_{x \to \infty}(f(x)) = \infty$
$Decrease: Never$ $Vertical\ Asymptote: None$
$y\,int: (0, \frac{57}{25})$ $x\,int: None$

21. $f(x) = -2 \cdot 3^{-2x+1} + 4$

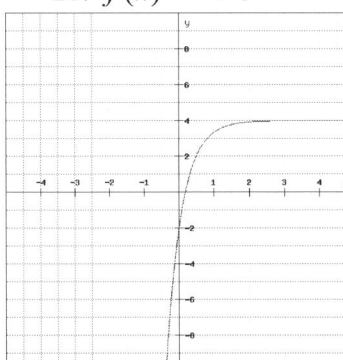

$Domain: x \in R$ $Horizontal\ Asymptote: y = -5$
$Range: f(x) \in (-\infty, 4)$ $Lim_{x \to -\infty}(f(x)) = -\infty$
$Increase: x \in R$ $Lim_{x \to \infty}(f(x)) = 4$
$Decrease: Never$ $Vertical\ Asymptote: None$
$y\,int: (0, -2)$ $x\,int: (\approx 0.185, 0)$

Applications

1. The population of a rapidly-growing country starts at 4 million and increases by 10% each year.
    a. Complete the table below:

t(years)	P, population (in millions)	ΔP, increase in population (in millions)
0	4	0.4
1	4.4	0.44
2	4.84	0.484
3	5.324	0.5324
4	5.8564	0.58564

   b. Do you identify a pattern? Can you write a general expression of the population (P) as a function of the time (t)?

   $P(t) = 4 \cdot (1.10)^t$

   c. Sketch its graph:

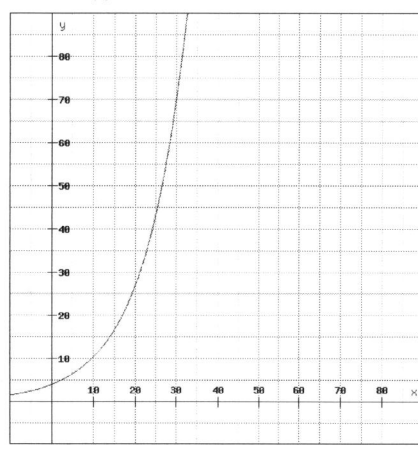

519

2. A chemical reaction starts with 200 grams of radioactive substance that decays by 20% per year.

   a. First, complete the table below.

t (years)	0	1	2	3	4
Q (grams)	200	160	128	102.4	81.92

   b. Find the expression of the function A(t), A the amount of substance and t the time in years.

   $$A(t) = 200 \cdot (0.8)^t$$

   c. Sketch its graph.

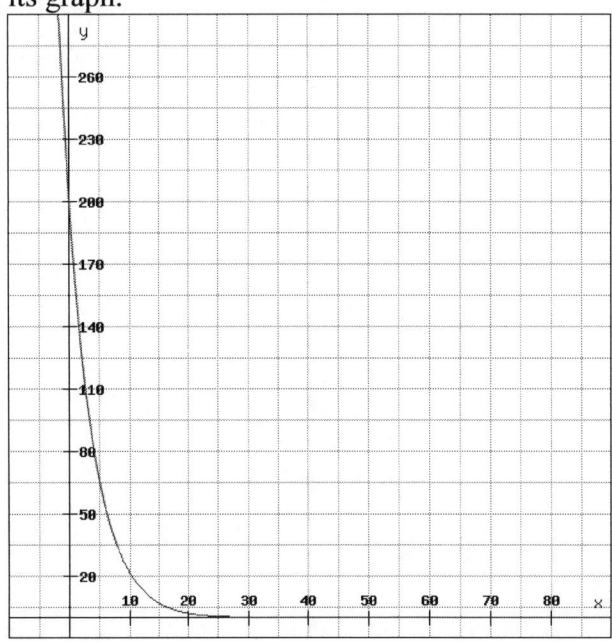

3. Suppose you invest 10000$ in the year 2000 and the investment earns 5.5% annually.

   a. Find the expression of the function A(t), A the amount of money and t the time in years.

   $$A(t) = 10000 \cdot (1.055)^t$$

   b. What will be the investment worth in 2010, 2020, 2030?

   $$A(t) = 10000 \cdot (1.055)^{10} \approx 1.71 \cdot 10^4 \$$$

   $$A(t) = 10000 \cdot (1.055)^{20} \approx 2.92 \cdot 10^4 \$$$

   $$A(t) = 10000 \cdot (1.055)^{30} \approx 4.99 \cdot 10^4 \$$$

2.8. – LOGARITHMIC FUNCTIONS

1. Given the functions: f(x) = log$_2$(x), g(x) = log$_3$(x), Complete the following table:

x	−5	−1	−0.1	0	0.0001	0.001	0.1	1	2	16	81	1024
f(x)	D.E.	D.E.	D.E.	D.E.	≈ −13	≈ −10	≈ −3	0	1	4	≈ 6	10
g(x)	D.E.	D.E.	D.E.	D.E.	≈ −8	≈ −6	≈ −2	0	≈ 0.6	≈ 3	4	≈ 6

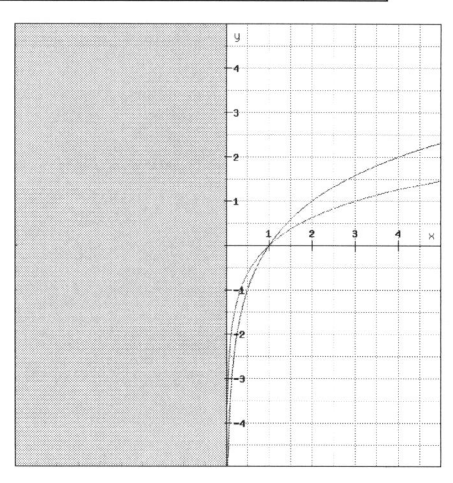

- The domain of the functions: $x \in (0, \infty)$
- y intercept: None
- x intercept(s): (1, 0)
- The corresponding limits and the equation of the vertical asymptote: (identical for f(x) and g(x))
  $Lim_{x \to 0^+}(f(x)) = -\infty$ $Asymptote: x = 0$
- The corresponding limits and the equation of the horizontal asymptote: None
- Increasing: $x \in (0, \infty)$, decreasing: Never
- max/min point(s): None
- Range : $f(x) \in (-\infty, \infty), g(x) \in (-\infty, \infty)$

2. Given the functions: f(x) = log$_1$(x), g(x) = log$_{-2}$(x), Complete the following table:

x	−5	−1	−0.1	0	0.0001	0.001	0.1	1	2	16	81	1024
f(x)	D.E.	D.E.	D.E.	D.E.	D.E.	D.E.	D.E.	Not Unique	D.E.	D.E.	D.E.	D.E.
g(x)	D.E.	D.E.	D.E.	D.E.	D.E.	D.E.	D.E.	0	D.E.	D.E.	D.E.	D.E.

Conclusion: The base of the logarithm must be positive and different than 1.

3. Given the functions: f(x) = log$_e$(x), g(x) = log(x), Complete the following table:

x	−5	−1	−0.1	0	0.0001	0.001	0.1	1	2	16	81	1024
f(x)	D.E.	D.E.	D.E.	D.E.	−4	−3	−1	0	≈ 0.3	≈1.2	≈2	≈3
g(x)	D.E.	D.E.	D.E.	D.E.	≈−9	≈−7	≈−2	0	≈0.7	≈3	≈4	≈7

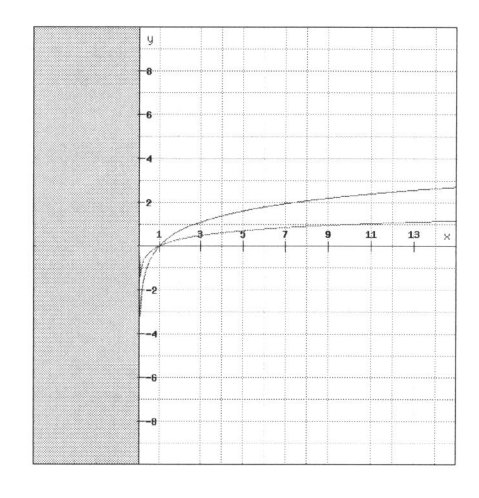

- The domain of the function: $x \in (0, \infty)$
- y intercept: None
- x intercept(s): (1, 0)
- The corresponding limits and the equation of the vertical asymptote:
  $Lim_{x \to 0^+}(f(x)) = -\infty$ $Asymptote: x = 0$
  $Lim_{x \to 0^+}(g(x)) = -\infty$ $Asymptote: x = 0$
- The corresponding limits and the equation of the horizontal asymptote: None
- Increasing: $x \in (0, \infty)$, decreasing: Never
- max/min point(s): None
- Range: $f(x) \in (-\infty, \infty), g(x) \in (-\infty, \infty)$

4. Given the functions: f(x) = log₄(x) + 4, g(x) = log₃(x) − 3, Complete the following table:

x	−5	−1	−0.1	0	0.0001	0.001	0.1	1	2	16	81	1024
f(x)	D.E.	D.E.	D.E.	D.E.	−2.6	−1	≈2	4	4.5	6	≈7	9
g(x)	D.E.	D.E.	D.E.	D.E.	≈−11	≈−9	≈−5	−3	≈−2	≈−0.5	1	≈3

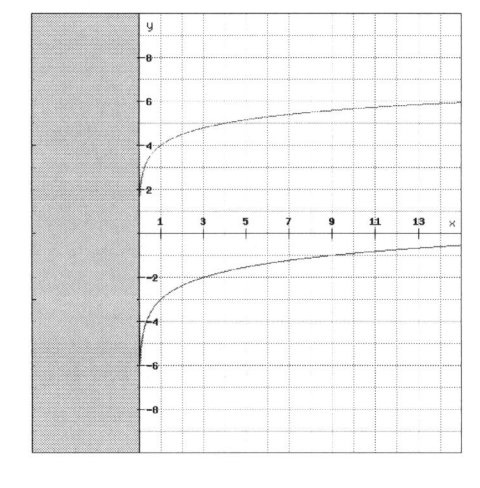

- The domain of the function: $x \in (0, \infty)$
- y intercept: None
- x intercept(s): $f(x): (\frac{1}{256}, 0), g(x): (27, 0)$
- The corresponding limits and the equation of the vertical asymptote:
  $Lim_{x \to 0^+}(f(x)) = -\infty$ Asymptote: $x = 0$
  $Lim_{x \to 0^+}(g(x)) = -\infty$ Asymptote: $x = 0$
- The corresponding limits and the equation of the horizontal asymptote: None
- Increasing: $x \in (0, \infty)$, decreasing: Never
- max/min point(s): None
- The range of the function: $f(x) \in (-\infty, \infty), g(x) \in (-\infty, \infty)$

5. Given the functions: f(x) = log₂(x − 2), g(x) = log₃(x + 4), Complete the following table:

x	−5	−1	−0.1	0	0.0001	0.001	0.1	1	2	16	81	1024
f(x)	D.E.	D.E.	D.E.	D.E.	D.E.	D.E.	D.E.	D.E.	D.E.	≈3.8	≈6	≈10
g(x)	D.E.	D.E.	D.E.	D.E.	D.E.	D.E.	D.E.	D.E.	D.E.	≈3	≈4	≈6

- The domain of the function: $f(x): x \in (2, \infty), g(x): x \in (-4, \infty)$
- y intercept (sketched on the graph:
  $f(x): None, g(x): x \in (0, \log_3(4))$
- x intercept(s): $f(x): (3, 0), g(x): (-3, 0)$
- Write the corresponding limits and the equation of the vertical asymptote:
  $Lim_{x \to 2^+}(f(x)) = -\infty$ Asymptote: $x = 2$
  $Lim_{x \to -4^+}(g(x)) = -\infty$ Asymptote: $x = -4$
- The corresponding limits and the equation of the horizontal asymptote: None
- Increasing: $f(x): x \in (2, \infty), g(x): x \in (-4, \infty)$, decreasing: Never
- max/min point(s): None
- The range of the function: $f(x) \in (-\infty, \infty), g(x) \in (-\infty, \infty)$

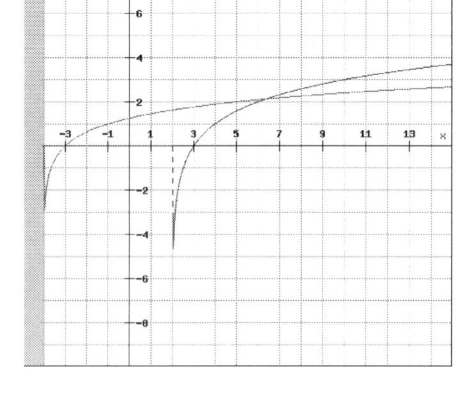

6. Given the functions: f(x) = log₂(2x − 5) + 1, g(x) = log₃(3x + 2) − 5, Complete the following table:

- The domain of the function: $f(x): x \in (\frac{5}{2}, \infty), g(x): x \in (-\frac{2}{3}, \infty)$

- y intercept (sketched on the graph:
  $f(x): None, g(x): x \in (0, \log_3(2) - 5)$

- x intercept(s): $f(x): (\frac{21}{4}, 0), g(x): (\frac{241}{3}, 0)$

- The corresponding limits and the equation of the vertical asymptote:

  $Lim_{x \to (\frac{5}{2})^+} (f(x)) = -\infty$ Asymptote: $x = \frac{5}{2}$

  $Lim_{x \to (-\frac{2}{3})^+} (g(x)) = -\infty$ Asymptote: $x = -\frac{2}{3}$

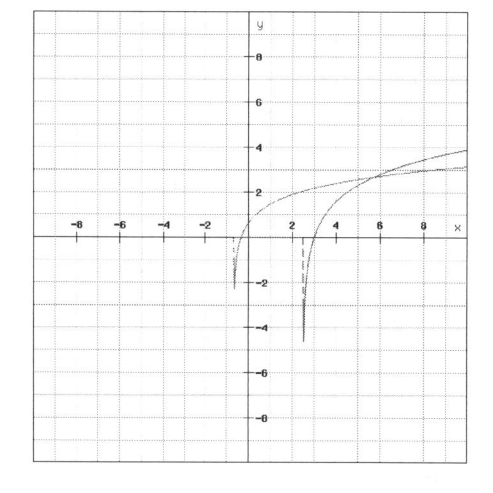

- The corresponding limits and the equation of the horizontal asymptote: None

- Increasing: $f(x): x \in (\frac{5}{2}, \infty), g(x): x \in (-\frac{2}{3}, \infty)$, decreasing: Never

- max/min point(s): None
- The range of the function: $f(x) \in (-\infty, \infty), g(x) \in (-\infty, \infty)$

7. Given the graph, complete the table below:

Function	On the graph
$f(x) = 2\ln(-x)$	G
$f(x) = \ln(x+2) + 1$	B
$f(x) = 2\ln(3-x)$	F
$f(x) = \ln(2x-1)$	C
$f(x) = -\ln(x+4)$	E
$f(x) = -\ln(2x-3)$	D
$f(x) = \ln(x-2) + 3$	A

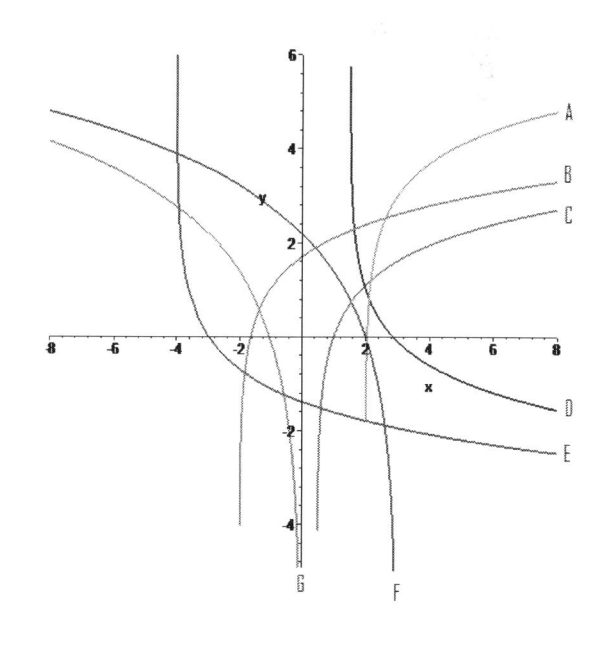

523

8. Given the function f(x) = Ln(x)
   a. Function translated 2 positions up
      $f(x) + 2 = \ln(x) + 2$
   b. The function translated 2 positions left.
      $f(x+2) = \ln(x+2)$
   c. The function translated 4 positions up and 3 right.
      $f(x-3) + 4 = \ln(x-3) + 4$
   d. Sketch all 3 functions

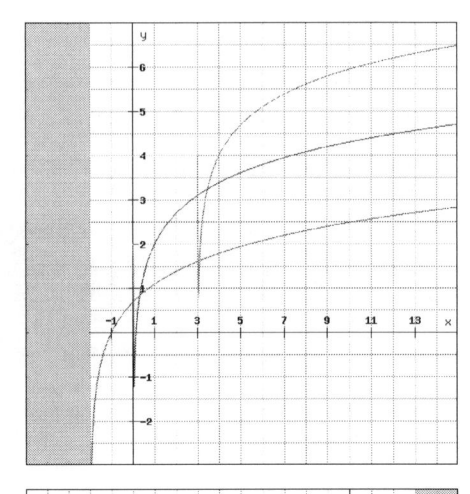

9. Given the function f(x) = –Log₃(–2x)

   a. The function translated 2 positions up.
      $f(x) + 2 = -\log_3(-2x) + 2$
   b. The function translated 2 positions left.
      $f(x+2) = -\log_3(-2(x+2))$
   c. The function translated 4 positions up and 3 right.
      $f(x-3) + 4 = -\log_3(-2(x-3)) + 4$
   d. Sketch all 3 functions

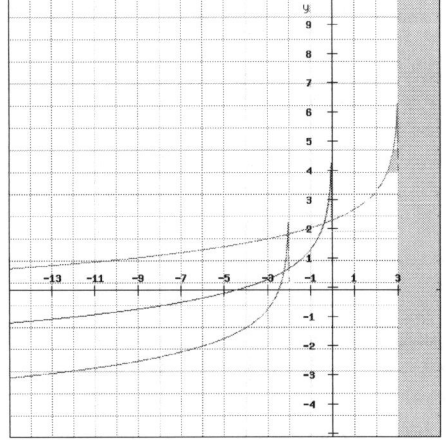

Analyze the following functions:

1. f(x) = log(x) – 2
   Domain: $x \in (0, \infty)$ Horizontal Asymptote: None
   Range: $f(x) \in (-\infty, \infty)$ $\lim_{x \to -\infty}(f(x)) = D.E.$
   Increase: $x \in (0, \infty)$ $\lim_{x \to \infty}(f(x)) = \infty$
   Decrease: Never   Vertical Asymptote: $x = 0$
   y int: None $\lim_{x \to 0^+}(f(x)) = -\infty$
   x int: $(100, 0)$ $\lim_{x \to 0}(f(x)) = D.E$

2. f(x) = log(x–1)
   Domain: $x \in (1, \infty)$ Horizontal Asymptote: None
   Range: $f(x) \in (-\infty, \infty)$ $\lim_{x \to -\infty}(f(x)) = D.E$
   Increase: $x \in (1, \infty)$ $\lim_{x \to \infty}(f(x)) = \infty$
   Decrease: Never   Vertical Asymptote: $x = 1$
   y int: None $\lim_{x \to 1^-}(f(x)) = D.E.$
   x int: $(2, 0)$ $\lim_{x \to 1^+}(f(x)) = -\infty$

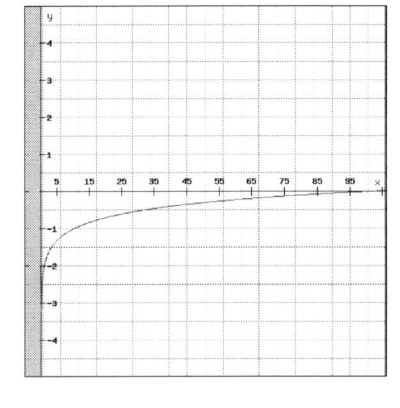

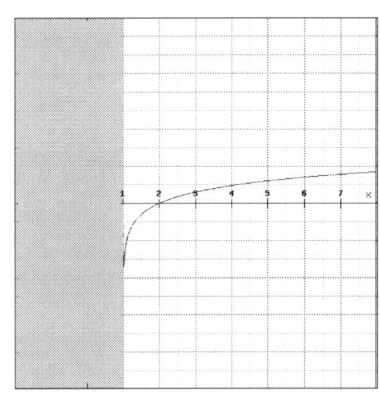

3. $f(x) = \log(x^2)$
Domain: $x \in (-\infty, 0) \cup (0, \infty)$ Horizontal Asymptote: None
Range: $f(x) \in (-\infty, \infty)$ $Lim_{x \to -\infty}(f(x)) = \infty$
Increase: $x \in (0, \infty)$ $Lim_{x \to \infty}(f(x)) = \infty$
Decrease: $x \in (-\infty, 0)$ Vertical Asymptote: $x = 0$
y int: None $Lim_{x \to 0^+}(f(x)) = -\infty$
x int: $(1, 0), (-1, 0)$ $Lim_{x \to 0^-}(f(x)) = -\infty$

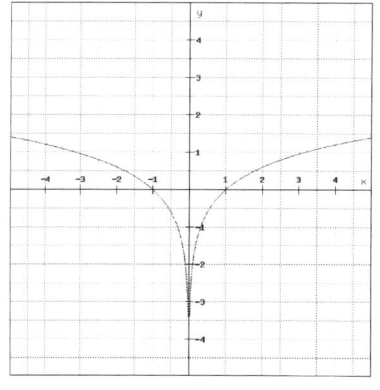

4. $f(x) = -\log(5 - x)$
Domain: $x \in (-\infty, 5)$ Horizontal Asymptote: None
Range: $f(x) \in (-\infty, \infty)$ $Lim_{x \to -\infty}(f(x)) = -\infty$
Increase: $x \in (-\infty, 5)$ $Lim_{x \to \infty}(f(x)) = D.E$
Decrease: Never   Vertical Asymptote: $x = 5$
y int: $(0, log(5))$ $Lim_{x \to 5^+}(f(x)) = D.E.$
x int: $(4, 0)$ $Lim_{x \to 5^-}(f(x)) = \infty$

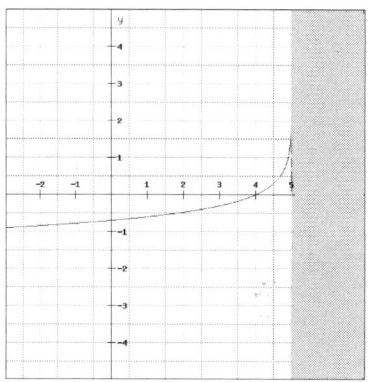

5. $f(x) = \log(x - 3) + 5$
Domain: $x \in (3, \infty)$ Horizontal Asymptote: None
Range: $f(x) \in (-\infty, \infty)$ $Lim_{x \to -\infty}(f(x)) = D.E$
Increase: $x \in (3, \infty)$ $Lim_{x \to \infty}(f(x)) = \infty$
Decrease: Never   Vertical Asymptote: $x = 3$
y int: None $Lim_{x \to 3^-}(f(x)) = D.E.$
x int: $(10^{-5} + 3, 0)$ $Lim_{x \to 3^+}(f(x)) = -\infty$

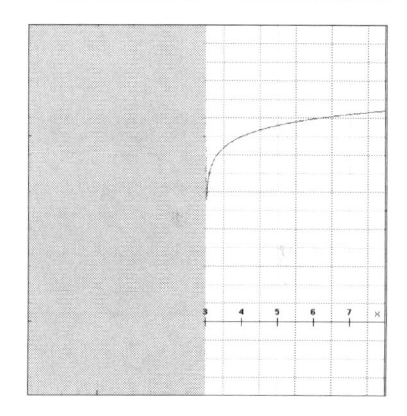

6. $f(x) = \log(-x + 3) - 2$
Domain: $x \in (-\infty, 3)$ Horizontal Asymptote: None
Range: $f(x) \in (-\infty, \infty)$ $Lim_{x \to -\infty}(f(x)) = \infty$
Increase: $x \in (-\infty, 3)$ $Lim_{x \to \infty}(f(x)) = D.E$
Decrease: Never   Vertical Asymptote: $x = 3$
y int: $(0, log(3) - 2)$ $Lim_{x \to 3^+}(f(x)) = D.E.$
x int: $(-97, 0)$ $Lim_{x \to 3^-}(f(x)) = -\infty$

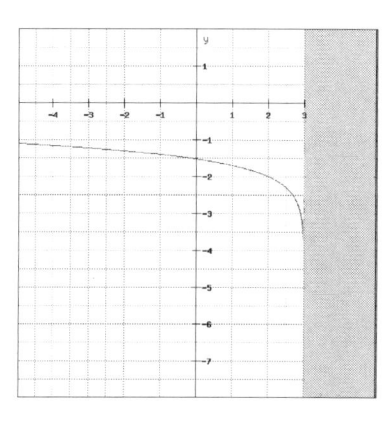

7. f(x) = –log(x) – 5

Domain: $x \in (0, \infty)$ Horizontal Asymptote: None

Range: $f(x) \in (-\infty, \infty)$ $Lim_{x \to -\infty}(f(x)) = D.E.$

Increase: Never $Lim_{x \to \infty}(f(x)) = -\infty$

Decrease: $x \in (0, \infty)$ Vertical Asymptote: $x = 0$

y int: None $Lim_{x \to 0^+}(f(x)) = \infty$

x int: $(\frac{1}{100000}, 0)$ $Lim_{x \to 0^-}(f(x)) = D.E$

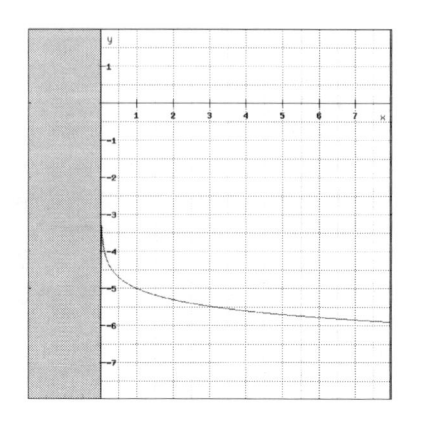

8. f(x) = log(2x)

Domain: $x \in (0, \infty)$ Horizontal Asymptote: None

Range: $f(x) \in (-\infty, \infty)$ $Lim_{x \to -\infty}(f(x)) = D.E.$

Increase: $x \in (0, \infty)$ $Lim_{x \to \infty}(f(x)) = \infty$

Decrease: Never   Vertical Asymptote: $x = 0$

y int: None $Lim_{x \to 0^+}(f(x)) = -\infty$

x int: $(\frac{1}{2}, 0)$ $Lim_{x \to 0^-}(f(x)) = D.E$

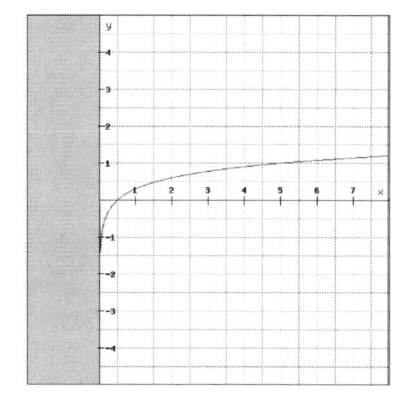

9. f(x) = –log(–2x + 3)

Domain: $x \in (-\infty, \frac{3}{2})$ Horizontal Asymptote: None

Range: $f(x) \in (-\infty, \infty)$ $Lim_{x \to -\infty}(f(x)) = -\infty$

Increase: $x \in (-\infty, \frac{3}{2})$ $Lim_{x \to \infty}(f(x)) = D.E$

Decrease: Never   Vertical Asymptote: $x = \frac{3}{2}$

y int: $(0, -log(3))$ $Lim_{x \to (\frac{3}{2})^+}(f(x)) = D.E.$

x int: $(1, 0)$ $Lim_{x \to (\frac{3}{2})^-}(f(x)) = \infty$

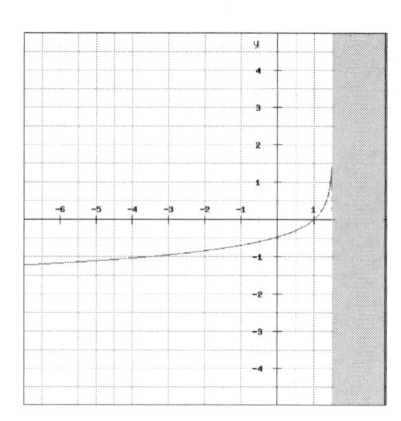

10. f(x) = log(2x – 3) – 1

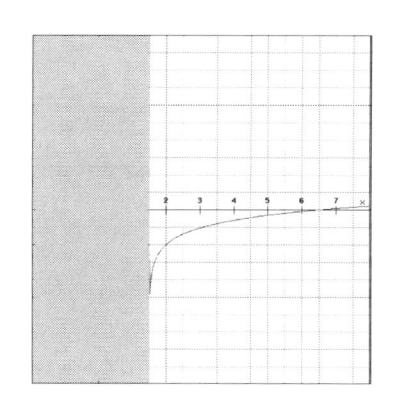

$Domain: x \in (\frac{3}{2}, \infty)$ Horizontal Asymptote: None

$Range: f(x) \in (-\infty, \infty)$ $Lim_{x \to -\infty}(f(x)) = D.E.$

$Increase: x \in (\frac{3}{2}, \infty)$ $Lim_{x \to \infty}(f(x)) = \infty$

$Decrease: Never$ $Vertical\ Asymptote: x = \frac{3}{2}$

$y\,int: None$ $Lim_{x \to \left(\frac{3}{2}\right)^+}(f(x)) = -\infty$

$x\,int: (\frac{13}{2}, 0)$ $Lim_{x \to \left(\frac{3}{2}\right)^-}(f(x)) = D.E$

11. f(x) = log(3x – 5) – 6

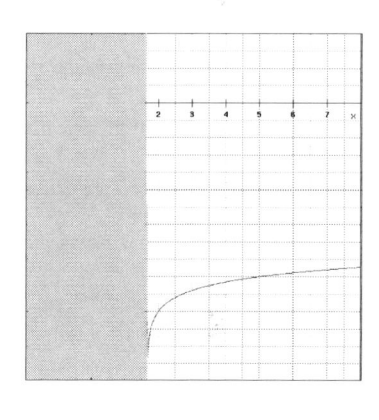

$Domain: x \in (\frac{5}{3}, \infty)$ Horizontal Asymptote: None

$Range: f(x) \in (-\infty, \infty)$ $Lim_{x \to -\infty}(f(x)) = D.E.$

$Increase: x \in (\frac{5}{3}, \infty)$ $Lim_{x \to \infty}(f(x)) = \infty$

$Decrease: Never$ $Vertical\ Asymptote: x = \frac{5}{3}$

$y\,int: None$ $Lim_{x \to \left(\frac{5}{3}\right)^+}(f(x)) = -\infty$

$x\,int: (\frac{1000005}{3}, 0)$ $Lim_{x \to \left(\frac{5}{3}\right)^-}(f(x)) = D.E$

12. $f(x) = -\log(x^2) + 5$

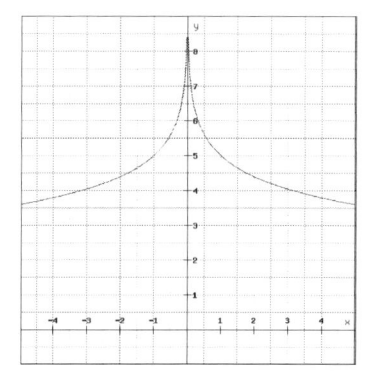

$Domain: x \in (-\infty, 0) \cup (0, \infty)$ Horizontal Asymptote: None

$Range: f(x) \in (-\infty, \infty)$ $Lim_{x \to -\infty}(f(x)) = -\infty$

$Increase: x \in (0, \infty)$ $Lim_{x \to \infty}(f(x)) = -\infty$

$Decrease: x \in (-\infty, 0)$ $Vertical\ Asymptote: x = 0$

$y\,int: None$ $Lim_{x \to 0^+}(f(x)) = \infty$

$x\,int: (10^5, 0), (-10^5, 0)$ $Lim_{x \to 0^-}(f(x)) = \infty$

527

13. $f(x) = \log(x^2) - 3$ 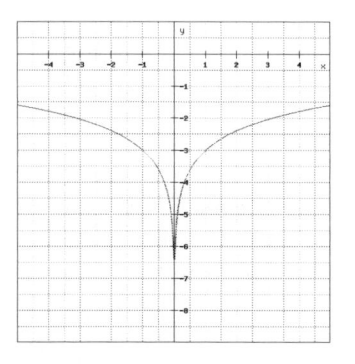
Domain: $x \in (-\infty, 0) \cup (0, \infty)$ Horizontal Asymptote: None
Range: $f(x) \in (-\infty, \infty)$ $Lim_{x \to -\infty}(f(x)) = \infty$
Increase: $x \in (0, \infty)$ $Lim_{x \to \infty}(f(x)) = \infty$
Decrease: $x \in (-\infty, 0)$ Vertical Asymptote: $x = 0$
y int: None $Lim_{x \to 0^+}(f(x)) = -\infty$
x int: $(1000, 0), (-1000, 0)$ $Lim_{x \to 0^-}(f(x)) = -\infty$

14. $f(x) = -\log(|x|) - 3$ 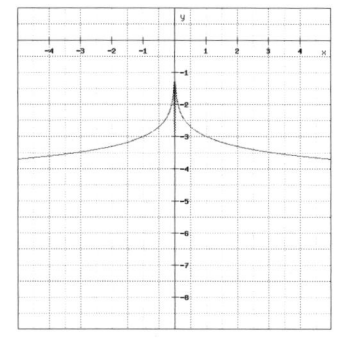
Domain: $x \in (-\infty, 0) \cup (0, \infty)$ Horizontal Asymptote: None
Range: $f(x) \in (-\infty, \infty)$ $Lim_{x \to -\infty}(f(x)) = -\infty$
Increase: $x \in (0, \infty)$ $Lim_{x \to \infty}(f(x)) = -\infty$
Decrease: $x \in (-\infty, 0)$ Vertical Asymptote: $x = 0$
y int: None $Lim_{x \to 0^+}(f(x)) = \infty$
x int: $(-10^{-3}, 0), (10^{-3}, 0)$ $Lim_{x \to 0^-}(f(x)) = \infty$

15. $f(x) = \log(|x - 2|)$ 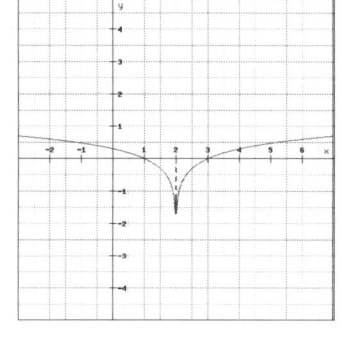
Domain: $x \in (-\infty, 2) \cup (2, \infty)$ Horizontal Asymptote: None
Range: $f(x) \in (-\infty, \infty)$ $Lim_{x \to -\infty}(f(x)) = \infty$
Increase: $x \in (2, \infty)$ $Lim_{x \to \infty}(f(x)) = \infty$
Decrease: $x \in (-\infty, 2)$ Vertical Asymptote: $x = 2$
y int: $(0, \log(2))$ $Lim_{x \to 2^+}(f(x)) = -\infty$
x int: $(3, 0), (1, 0)$ $Lim_{x \to 2^-}(f(x)) = -\infty$

16. $f(x) = \log(|x + 2|) - 5$ 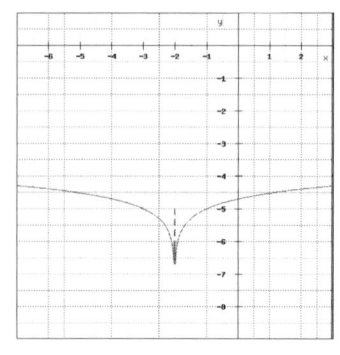
Domain: $x \in (-\infty, -2) \cup (-2, \infty)$ Horizontal Asymptote: None
Range: $f(x) \in (-\infty, \infty)$ $Lim_{x \to -\infty}(f(x)) = \infty$
Increase: $x \in (-2, \infty)$ $Lim_{x \to \infty}(f(x)) = \infty$
Decrease: $x \in (-\infty, -2)$ Vertical Asymptote: $x = -2$
y int: $(0, \log(2) - 5)$ $Lim_{x \to -2^+}(f(x)) = -\infty$
x int: $(-10^5 - 2, 0), (10^5 - 2, 0)$ $Lim_{x \to -2^-}(f(x)) = -\infty$

17. $f(x) = -\log(|x+6|) - 3$ 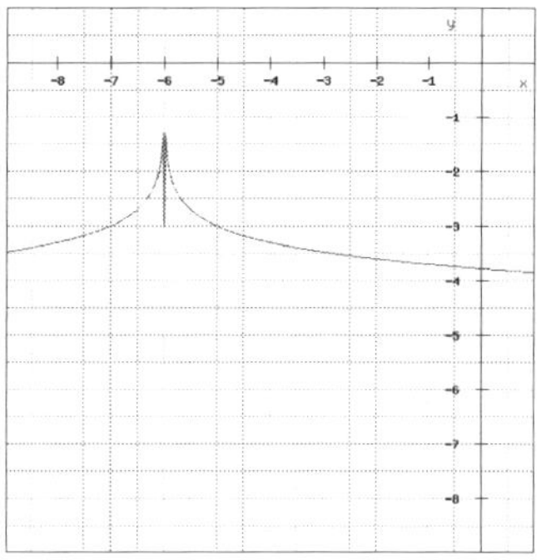
$Domain: x \in (-\infty, -6) \cup (-6, \infty)$ $Horizontal\ Asymptote: None$
$Range: f(x) \in (-\infty, \infty)$ $Lim_{x \to -\infty}(f(x)) = -\infty$
$Increase: x \in (-6, \infty)$ $Lim_{x \to \infty}(f(x)) = -\infty$
$Decrease: x \in (-\infty, -6)$ $Vertical\ Asymptote: x = -6$
$y\,int: (0, -\log(6) - 3)$ $Lim_{x \to -6^+}(f(x)) = \infty$
$x\,int: (10^{-3} - 6, 0), (-10^{-3} - 6, 0)$ $Lim_{x \to -6^-}(f(x)) = \infty$

18. $f(x) = \ln(x) - 3$ 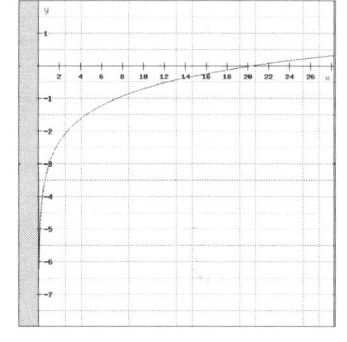
$Domain: x \in (0, \infty)$ $Horizontal\ Asymptote: None$
$Range: f(x) \in (-\infty, \infty)$ $Lim_{x \to -\infty}(f(x)) = D.E.$
$Increase: x \in (0, \infty)$ $Lim_{x \to \infty}(f(x)) = \infty$
$Decrease: Never$ $Vertical\ Asymptote: x = 0$
$y\,int: None$ $Lim_{x \to 0^+}(f(x)) = -\infty$
$x\,int: (e^3, 0)$ $Lim_{x \to 0^-}(f(x)) = D.E$

19. $f(x) = \log(x) - 3$ 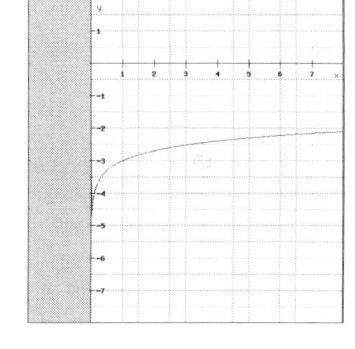
$Domain: x \in (0, \infty)$ $Horizontal\ Asymptote: None$
$Range: f(x) \in (-\infty, \infty)$ $Lim_{x \to -\infty}(f(x)) = D.E.$
$Increase: x \in (0, \infty)$ $Lim_{x \to \infty}(f(x)) = \infty$
$Decrease: Never$ $Vertical\ Asymptote: x = 0$
$y\,int: None$ $Lim_{x \to 0^+}(f(x)) = -\infty$
$x\,int: (1000, 0)$ $Lim_{x \to 0^-}(f(x)) = D.E$

20. $f(x) = \ln(x) - 2$ 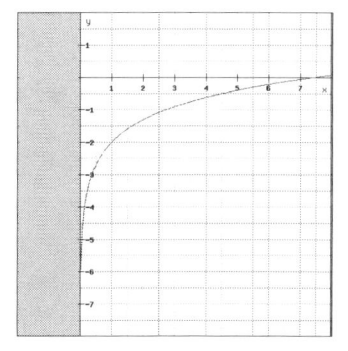
$Domain: x \in (0, \infty)$ $Horizontal\ Asymptote: None$
$Range: f(x) \in (-\infty, \infty)$ $Lim_{x \to -\infty}(f(x)) = D.E.$
$Increase: x \in (0, \infty)$ $Lim_{x \to \infty}(f(x)) = \infty$
$Decrease: Never$ $Vertical\ Asymptote: x = 0$
$y\,int: None$ $Lim_{x \to 0^+}(f(x)) = -\infty$
$x\,int: (e^2, 0)$ $Lim_{x \to 0^-}(f(x)) = D.E$

21. f(x) = ln(–x–1)
Domain: $x \in (-\infty, -1)$
Range: $f(x) \in (-\infty, \infty)$
Increase: Never
Decrease: $x \in (-\infty, -1)$
y int: None
x int: $(-2, 0)$
Horizontal Asymptote: None
$Lim_{x \to -\infty}(f(x)) = \infty$
$Lim_{x \to \infty}(f(x)) = D.E$
Vertical Asymptote: $x = -1$
$Lim_{x \to -1^+}(f(x)) = D.E.$
$Lim_{x \to -1^-}(f(x)) = -\infty$

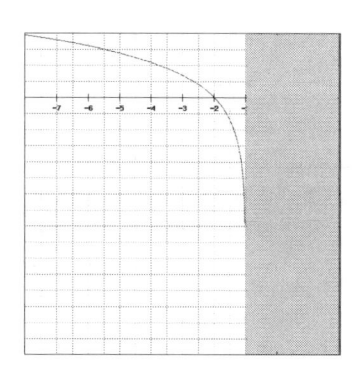

22. f(x) = log₂(2 – x)
Domain: $x \in (-\infty, 2)$
Range: $f(x) \in (-\infty, \infty)$
Increase: Never
Decrease: $x \in (-\infty, 2)$
y int: $(0, 1)$
x int: $(1, 0)$
Horizontal Asymptote: None
$Lim_{x \to -\infty}(f(x)) = \infty$
$Lim_{x \to \infty}(f(x)) = D.E$
Vertical Asymptote: $x = 2$
$Lim_{x \to 2^+}(f(x)) = D.E.$
$Lim_{x \to 2^-}(f(x)) = -\infty$

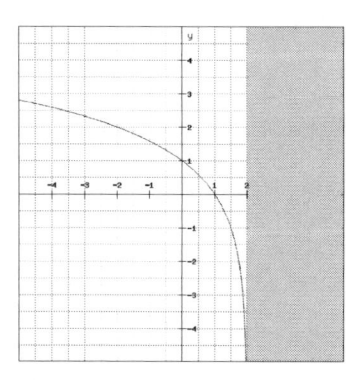

23. f(x) = –ln(x+5)
Domain: $x \in (-5, \infty)$
Range: $f(x) \in (-\infty, \infty)$
Increase: Never
Decrease: $x \in (-5, \infty)$
y int: $(0, -\ln(5))$
x int: $(-4, 0)$
Horizontal Asymptote: None
$Lim_{x \to -\infty}(f(x)) = D.E.$
$Lim_{x \to \infty}(f(x)) = -\infty$
Vertical Asymptote: $x = -5$
$Lim_{x \to -5^+}(f(x)) = \infty$
$Lim_{x \to -5^-}(f(x)) = D.E$

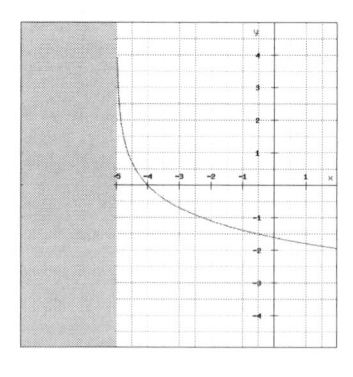

24. f(x) = log₃(4 – 2x) + 1
Domain: $x \in (-\infty, 2)$
Range: $f(x) \in (-\infty, \infty)$
Increase: Never
Decrease: $x \in (-\infty, 2)$
y int: $(0, \log_3(4) + 1)$
x int: $(\frac{11}{6}, 0)$
Horizontal Asymptote: None
$Lim_{x \to -\infty}(f(x)) = \infty$
$Lim_{x \to \infty}(f(x)) = D.E$
Vertical Asymptote: $x = 2$
$Lim_{x \to 2^+}(f(x)) = D.E.$
$Lim_{x \to 2^-}(f(x)) = -\infty$

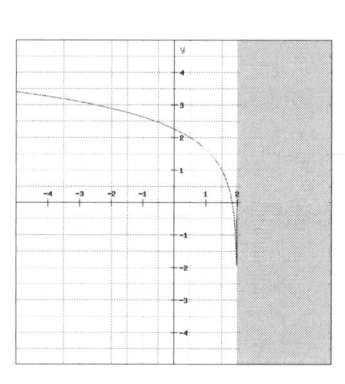

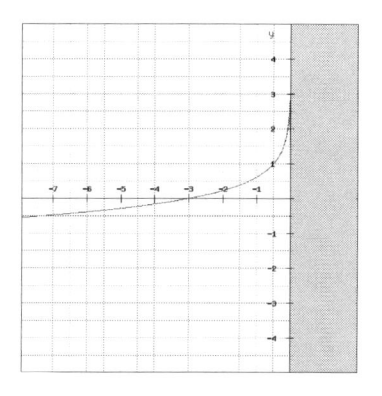

25. f(x) = ln(2 − 2x) − 3
$Domain: x \in (-\infty, 1)$ $Horizontal\ Asymptote: None$
$Range: f(x) \in (-\infty, \infty)$ $Lim_{x \to -\infty}(f(x)) = \infty$
$Increase: Never$ $Lim_{x \to \infty}(f(x)) = D.E$
$Decrease: x \in (-\infty, 1)$ $Vertical\ Asymptote: x = 2$
$y\,int: (0, \ln(2) - 3)$ $Lim_{x \to 1^+}(f(x)) = D.E.$
$x\,int: (\dfrac{2-e^3}{2}, 0)$ $Lim_{x \to 1^-}(f(x)) = -\infty$

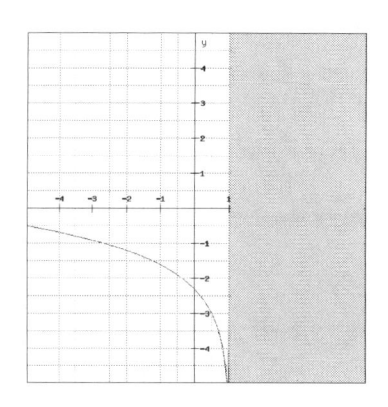

26. f(x) = −ln(x) − 5
$Domain: x \in (0, \infty)$ $Horizontal\ Asymptote: None$
$Range: f(x) \in (-\infty, \infty)$ $Lim_{x \to -\infty}(f(x)) = D.E.$
$Increase: Never$ $Lim_{x \to \infty}(f(x)) = -\infty$
$Decrease: x \in (0, \infty)$ $Vertical\ Asymptote: x = 0$
$y\,int: None$ $Lim_{x \to 0^+}(f(x)) = \infty$
$x\,int: (e^{-5}, 0)$ $Lim_{x \to 0^-}(f(x)) = D.E$

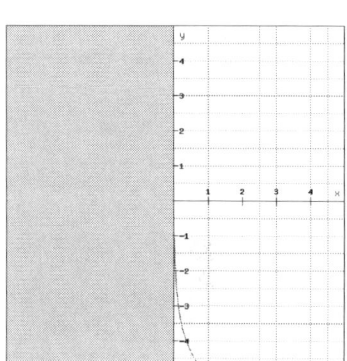

27. f(x) = log$_4$(2x)
$Domain: x \in (0, \infty)$ $Horizontal\ Asymptote: None$
$Range: f(x) \in (-\infty, \infty)$ $Lim_{x \to -\infty}(f(x)) = D.E.$
$Increase: x \in (0, \infty)$ $Lim_{x \to \infty}(f(x)) = \infty$
$Decrease: Never$ $Vertical\ Asymptote: x = 0$
$y\,int: None$ $Lim_{x \to 0^+}(f(x)) = -\infty$
$x\,int: (\dfrac{1}{2}, 0)$ $Lim_{x \to 0^-}(f(x)) = D.E$

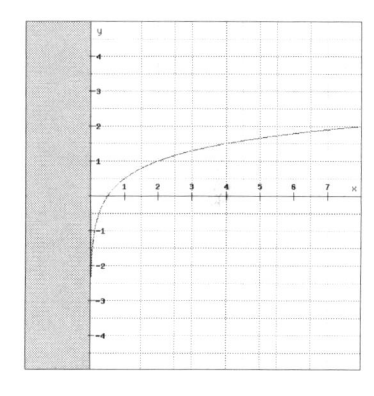

28. f(x) = −log$_6$(−2x) + 1
$Domain: x \in (-\infty, 0)$ $Horizontal\ Asymptote: None$
$Range: f(x) \in (-\infty, \infty)$ $Lim_{x \to -\infty}(f(x)) = -\infty$
$Increase: x \in (-\infty, 0)$ $Lim_{x \to \infty}(f(x)) = D.E$
$Decrease: Never$ $Vertical\ Asymptote: x = 0$
$y\,int: None$ $Lim_{x \to 0^+}(f(x)) = D.E.$
$x\,int: (-3, 0)$ $Lim_{x \to 0^-}(f(x)) = \infty$

29. $f(x) = \ln(-2x - 3) - 1$

Domain: $x \in (-\infty, -\frac{3}{2})$ Horizontal Asymptote: None

Range: $f(x) \in (-\infty, \infty)$ $\lim_{x \to -\infty}(f(x)) = \infty$

Increase: Never $\lim_{x \to \infty}(f(x)) = D.E$

Decrease: $x \in (-\infty, -\frac{3}{2})$ Vertical Asymptote: $x = -\frac{3}{2}$

y int: None $\lim_{x \to \left(-\frac{3}{2}\right)^+}(f(x)) = D.E.$

x int: $(\frac{e+3}{-2}, 0)$ $\lim_{x \to \left(-\frac{3}{2}\right)^-}(f(x)) = -\infty$

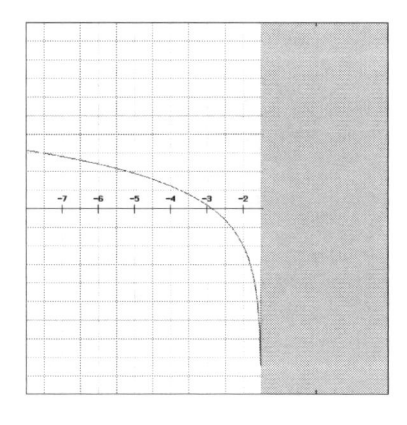

30. $f(x) = -\log(10x - 5) - 1$

Domain: $x \in (\frac{1}{2}, \infty)$ Horizontal Asymptote: None

Range: $f(x) \in (-\infty, \infty)$ $\lim_{x \to -\infty}(f(x)) = D.E.$

Increase: Never $\lim_{x \to \infty}(f(x)) = -\infty$

Decrease: $x \in (\frac{1}{2}, \infty)$ Vertical Asymptote: $x = \frac{1}{2}$

y int: None $\lim_{x \to \left(\frac{1}{2}\right)^+}(f(x)) = \infty$

x int: $(\frac{51}{100}, 0)$ $\lim_{x \to \left(\frac{1}{2}\right)^-}(f(x)) = D.E$

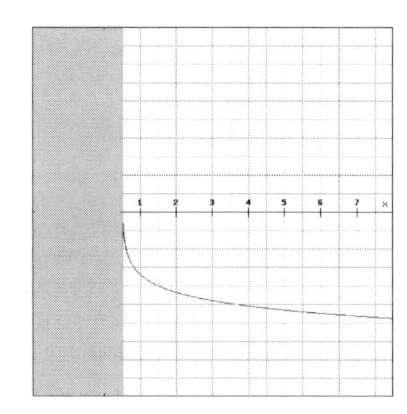

31. $f(x) = \ln(x^2) + 1$

Domain: $x \neq 0$ Horizontal Asymptote: None

Range: $f(x) \in (-\infty, \infty)$ $\lim_{x \to -\infty}(f(x)) = \infty$

Increase: $x \in (0, \infty)$ $\lim_{x \to \infty}(f(x)) = \infty$

Decrease: $x \in (-\infty, 0)$ Vertical Asymptote: $x = 0$

y int: None $\lim_{x \to 0^+}(f(x)) = -\infty$

x int: $(e^{-1}, 0), (-e^{-1}, 0)$ $\lim_{x \to 0}(f(x)) = -\infty$

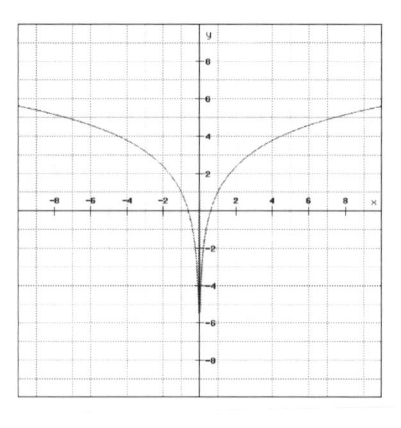

32. f(x) = −ln(|x|) + 1 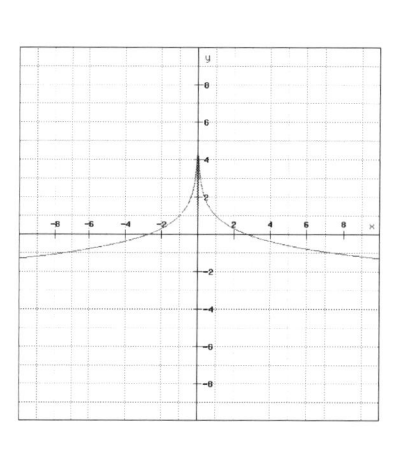
Domain: $x \neq 0$ Horizontal Asymptote: None
Range: $f(x) \in (-\infty, \infty)$ $\lim_{x \to -\infty}(f(x)) = -\infty$
Increase: $x \in (-\infty, 0)$ $\lim_{x \to \infty}(f(x)) = -\infty$
Decrease: $x \in (0, \infty)$ Vertical Asymptote: $x = 0$
y int: None $\lim_{x \to 0^+}(f(x)) = \infty$
x int: $(e, 0), (-e, 0)$ $\lim_{x \to 0^-}(f(x)) = \infty$

33. f(x) = ln(|x − 2|) 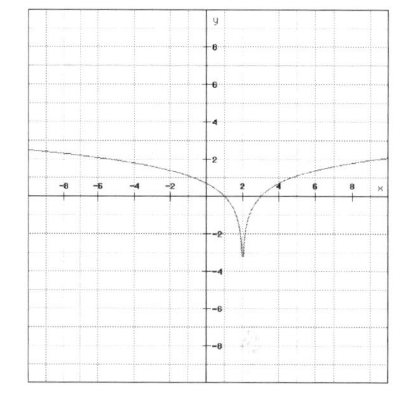
Domain: $x \neq 2$ Horizontal Asymptote: None
Range: $f(x) \in (-\infty, \infty)$ $\lim_{x \to -\infty}(f(x)) = \infty$
Increase: $x \in (2, \infty)$ $\lim_{x \to \infty}(f(x)) = \infty$
Decrease: $x \in (-\infty, 2)$ Vertical Asymptote: $x = 2$
y int: $(0, \ln(2))$ $\lim_{x \to 2^+}(f(x)) = -\infty$
x int: $(1, 0), (3, 0)$ $\lim_{x \to 2^-}(f(x)) = -\infty$

34. The population of a city increases by 5% every year. Find the number of years it will take it to double. $2N = N(1.05)^t$; $t = \dfrac{\ln(2)}{\ln(1.05)} \approx 14.2\, years$

35. The population of a city increases by k% every year; find the time it will take it to triple in terms of k. $3N = N(1 + \dfrac{k}{100})^t$; $t = \dfrac{\ln(3)}{\ln(1 + \dfrac{k}{100})}$

36. The population of a city increases by k% every month; find k in case the population grew by 50% after 3 years.
$1.5N = N(1 + \dfrac{k}{100})^{36}$; $k = 100\left(\sqrt[36]{1.5} - 1\right) \approx 1.13$
No need to use logarithms in this case!

37. The PH level in a substance is given by: $PH = -\log(H^+)$, where H^+ is the concentration of hydrogen ions (only proton) in moles/litter.
   a. Given that the PH level of different substances complete the following table:

   b. People who have cancer have about a 100 times more acid blood than normal blood, find their level of PH.

Substance	PH Level	Concentration of Hydrogen ions
Battery Acid	0	$0 = -\log(H^+); H^+ = 1$ mol/litter
Lemon Juice	2	$2 = -\log(H^+); H^+ = 0.01$ mol/litter
Mile	6	$6 = -\log(H^+); H^+ = 10^{-6}$ mol/litter
Pure Water	7	$7 = -\log(H^+); H^+ = 10^{-7}$ mol/litter
Human Blood	7.4	$7.4 = -\log(H^+); H^+ = 10^{-7.4}$ mol/litter
Great salt lake	10	$10 = -\log(H^+); H^+ = 10^{-10}$ mol/litter
Liquid drain cleaner	14	$14 = -\log(H^+); H^+ = 10^{-14}$ mol/litter

$PH = -\log(H^+); PH = -\log(100 \cdot 10^{-7.4}) = -\log(10^{-5.4}) = -5.4$

533

38. Richter scale for measuring earthquake strength as felt in a particular place (M) can be approximated by $M = \log(x)$
    a. Given that in a certain location A the Richter scale measure M was 5 and in location B the Richter scale measure M was 6. Find how much stronger was the earthquake in location B?
    $5 = \log(x_A) \Leftrightarrow x_A = 10^5, 6 = \log(x_B) \Leftrightarrow x_B = 10^6$, so 10 times stronger.
    b. Given that in a certain location A the Richter scale measure was 5 and in location B the earthquake was 3 times as strong, what was the Richter scale measure in location B?
    $5 = \log(x_A), M_B = \log(3x_A) = \log(3) + \log(x_A) \approx 5.48$

39. The Weber – Fechner law can be approximated by: $S = k\log_{10} I$, where I is the intensity of light and S is the sensation of brightness.

    a. This law means that:
    Big changes in the Intensity will cause <u>small</u> changes in the sensation.

    b. The change needed in the intensity that will double the sensation of brightness.
    $S = k\log(I); 2S = 2k\log(I) = k\log(I^2)$, so the intensity has to be squared for the sensation of brightness to double.

40. Decibels (DB) are used for measuring the volume of sound. They are given by: $I = 10\log(P/P_0)$ where P_0 is the minimum intensity of sound detected by the human ear.
    a. What is the threshold in DB of the human ear?
    $I = 10\log(\frac{P_0}{P_0}) = 0 DB$
    b. In normal conversation 60 DB will be measured. Express P in terms of P_0. How many times louder is this than the threshold?
    $60 = 10\log(\frac{P_{conversation}}{P_0}) \Leftrightarrow P_{conversation} = 10^6 P_0$, so a million times louder
    c. In a rock concert 120 DB will be measured. Express P in terms of P_0. How many times louder is this than a normal conversation?
    $120 = 10\log(\frac{P}{P_0}) \Leftrightarrow P = 10^{12} P_0 = 10^6 P_{conversation}$, so a million times louder
    d. Find the number of DB of a sound twice is strong as the threshold.
    $I = 10\log(\frac{2P_0}{P_0}) = 10\log(2) \approx 3.01 DB$

2.9 – RADICAL FUCNTIONS

1. Given the functions: $f(x) = \sqrt{x}$, $g(x) = -\sqrt{x}$, Complete the following table:

x	–2	–1	0	1	2	3	4	5	6	7	8	9
f(x)	D.E.	D.E.	0	1	$\sqrt{2}$	$\sqrt{3}$	2	$\sqrt{5}$	$\sqrt{6}$	$\sqrt{7}$	$\sqrt{8}$	3
g(x)	D.E.	D.E.	0	–1	$-\sqrt{2}$	$-\sqrt{3}$	–2	$-\sqrt{5}$	$-\sqrt{6}$	$-\sqrt{7}$	$-\sqrt{8}$	–3

- Sketch the points of the table on a graph.
- State the domain of the functions: $x \in [0, \infty)$
- State the y intercepts: $(0,0)$
- State the x intercept(s): $(0,0)$
- Write the corresponding limits and the equation of the vertical asymptote:
  $Lim_{x \to 0^-}(f(x)) = D.E.; f(0) = 0; Lim_{x \to 0^+}(f(x)) = 0$ Asymptote: None
  $Lim_{x \to 0^-}(g(x)) = D.E.; g(0) = 0; Lim_{x \to 0^+}(g(x)) = 0$ Asymptote: None
- Write the corresponding limits and the equation of the horizontal asymptote:
  $Lim_{x \to -\infty}(f(x)) = D.E.; Lim_{x \to \infty}(f(x)) = \infty$ Asymptote: None
  $Lim_{x \to -\infty}(g(x)) = D.E.; Lim_{x \to \infty}(g(x)) = -\infty$ Asymptote: None
- Function is increasing on the interval: $f(x): x \in (0, \infty), g(x): Never$ decreasing on the interval: $f(x): Never, g(x): x \in (0, \infty)$
- Find the max/min point(s): $f(x): \min(0,0), g(x): \max(0,0)$
- State the range of the function: $f(x) \in [0, \infty), g(x) \in (-\infty, 0]$

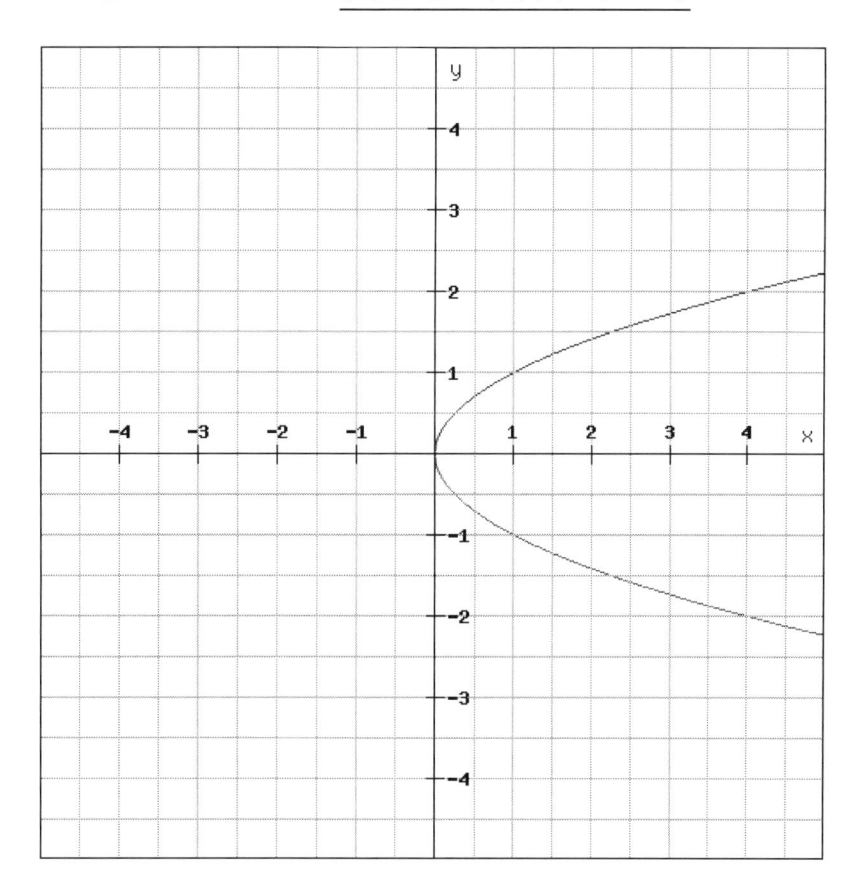

2. Given the functions: $f(x) = \sqrt{-x+1}$, $g(x) = -\sqrt{x-3}$, Complete the table:

x	-2	-1	0	1	2	3	4	5	6	7	8	9
f(x)	$\sqrt{3}$	$\sqrt{2}$	1	0	D.E.	D.E.	D.E.	D.E.	D.E.	D.E.	D.E.	D.E.
g(x)	D.E.	D.E.	D.E.	D.E.	D.E.	0	-1	$-\sqrt{2}$	$-\sqrt{3}$	-2	$-\sqrt{5}$	$-\sqrt{6}$

- Sketch the points of the table on a graph.
- State the domain of the function: $f(x): x \in (-\infty, 1], g(x): x \in [3, \infty)$
- State the y intercept (sketched on the graph: $f(x): (0,1), g(x): None$
- State the x intercept(s): $f(x): (1,0), g(x): (3,0)$
- Write the corresponding limits and the equation of the vertical asymptote:
  $Lim_{x \to 1^-}(f(x)) = 0; f(1) = 0; Lim_{x \to 1^+}(f(x)) = D.E.$ Asymptote: None
  $Lim_{x \to 3^-}(g(x)) = D.E.; g(3) = 0; Lim_{x \to 3^+}(g(x)) = 0$ Asymptote: None
- Write the corresponding limits and the equation of the horizontal asymptote:
  $Lim_{x \to -\infty}(f(x)) = \infty; Lim_{x \to \infty}(f(x)) = D.E.$ Asymptote: None
  $Lim_{x \to -\infty}(g(x)) = D.E.; Lim_{x \to \infty}(g(x)) = -\infty$ Asymptote: None
- Function is increasing on the interval: $f(x): Never, g(x): Never$ decreasing on the interval: $f(x): x \in (-\infty, 1), g(x): x \in (3, \infty)$
- Find the max/min point(s): $f(x): min(1,0), g(x): max(3,0)$
- State the range of the function: $f(x) \in [0, \infty), g(x) \in (-\infty, 0]$

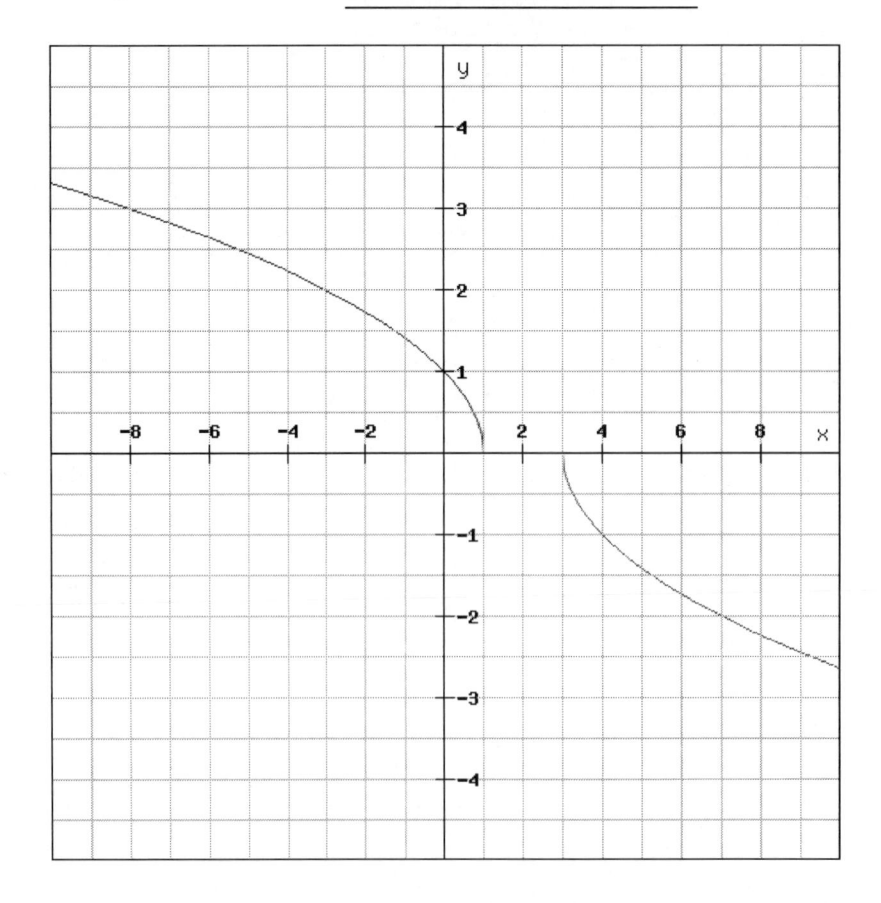

3. Given the functions: $f(x) = \sqrt{x+1} + 3$, $g(x) = -\sqrt{x-3} - 6$. Complete the table:

x	−2	−1	0	1	2	3	4	5	6	7	8	9
f(x)	D.E.	3	4	$\sqrt{2}+3$	$\sqrt{3}+3$	5	$\sqrt{5}+3$	$\sqrt{6}+3$	$\sqrt{7}+3$	$\sqrt{8}+3$	6	$\sqrt{10}+3$
g(x)	D.E.	D.E.	D.E.	D.E.	D.E.	−6	−7	$-\sqrt{2}-6$	$-\sqrt{3}-6$	−8	$-\sqrt{5}-6$	$-\sqrt{6}-6$

- Sketch the points of the table on a graph.
- State the domain of the function: $f(x): x \in [-1, \infty), g(x): x \in [3, \infty)$
- State the y intercept (sketched on the graph: $f(x): (0, 4), g(x): None$
- State the x intercept(s): $f(x): None, g(x): None$
- Write the corresponding limits and the equation of the vertical asymptote:
  $Lim_{x \to -1^-}(f(x)) = D.E.; f(-1) = 3; Lim_{x \to 1^+}(f(x)) = 3$ Asymptote: None
  $Lim_{x \to 3^-}(g(x)) = D.E.; g(3) = -6; Lim_{x \to 3^+}(g(x)) = -6$ Asymptote: None
- Write the corresponding limits and the equation of the horizontal asymptote:
  $Lim_{x \to -\infty}(f(x)) = D.E.; Lim_{x \to \infty}(f(x)) = \infty$ Asymptote: None
  $Lim_{x \to -\infty}(g(x)) = D.E.; Lim_{x \to \infty}(g(x)) = -\infty$ Asymptote: None
- Function is increasing on the interval: $f(x): x \in (-1, \infty), g(x): Never$ decreasing on the interval: $f(x): Never, g(x): x \in (3, \infty)$
- Find the max/min point(s): $f(x): min(-1, 3), g(x): max(-3, -6)$
- State the range of the function: $f(x) \in [3, \infty), g(x) \in (-\infty, -6]$

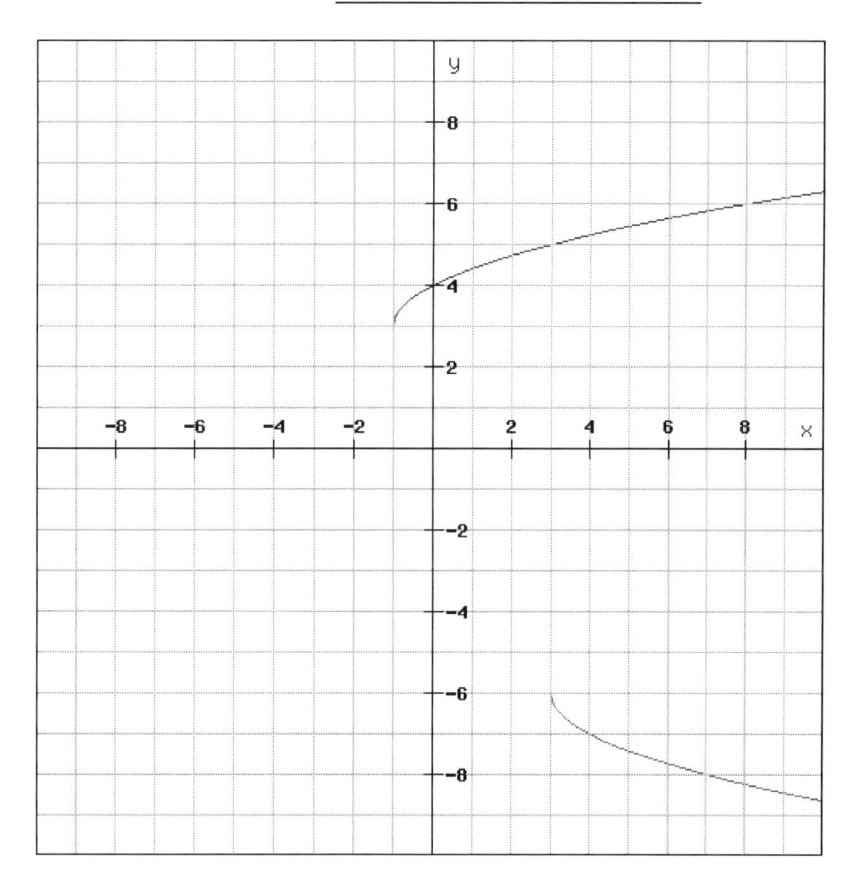

4. Given the graph, complete the table below:

Function	On the graph
$f(x) = 3\sqrt{x-2} - 3$	B
$f(x) = \sqrt{3x+2}$	A
$f(x) = \sqrt{-2x+1}$	I
$f(x) = \sqrt{x+1}$	C
$f(x) = \sqrt{-x-2}$	H
$f(x) = 2 - \sqrt{x-2}$	D
$f(x) = -2\sqrt{x-1}$	F
$f(x) = -1 - \sqrt{-x+4}$	G
$f(x) = -\sqrt{2x-5} - 1$	E

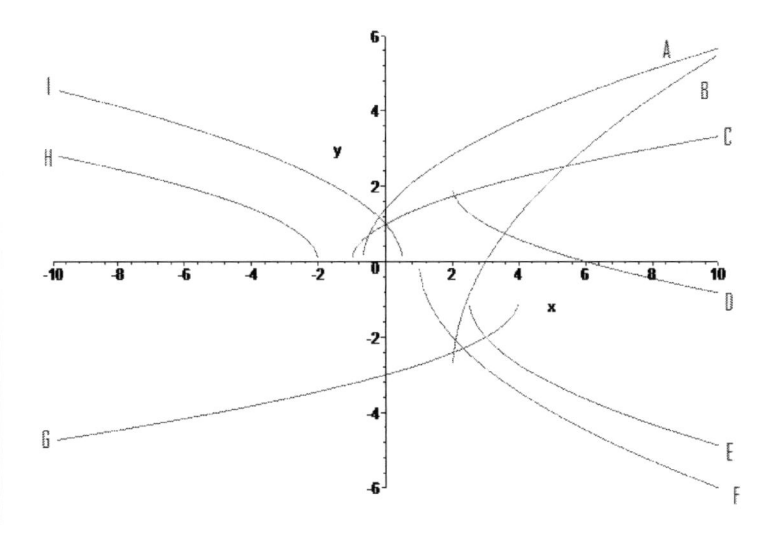

5. Given the function $f(x) = \sqrt{x}$

   a. The function translated 2 positions up. $f(x) + 2 = \sqrt{x} + 2$

   b. The function translated 2 positions left. $f(x+2) = \sqrt{x+2}$

   c. The function translated 4 positions up and 3 right. $f(x-3) + 4 = \sqrt{x-3} + 4$

   d. Sketch the 3 functions:

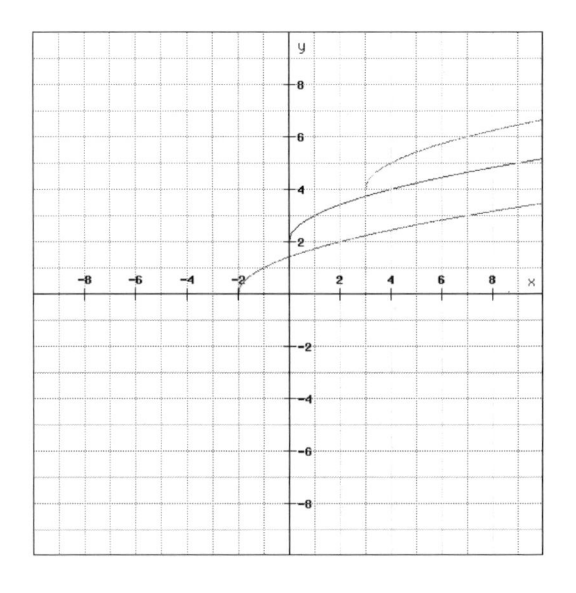

6. Given the function $f(x) = 4\sqrt{-2x+1}$

   a. The function translated 2 positions up. $f(x) + 2 = 4\sqrt{-2x+1} + 2$

   b. The function translated 2 positions left. $f(x+2) = 4\sqrt{-2(x+2)+1}$

   c. The function translated 4 positions up and 3 right. $f(x-3) + 4 = 4\sqrt{-2(x-3)+1} + 4$

   e. Sketch the 3 functions:

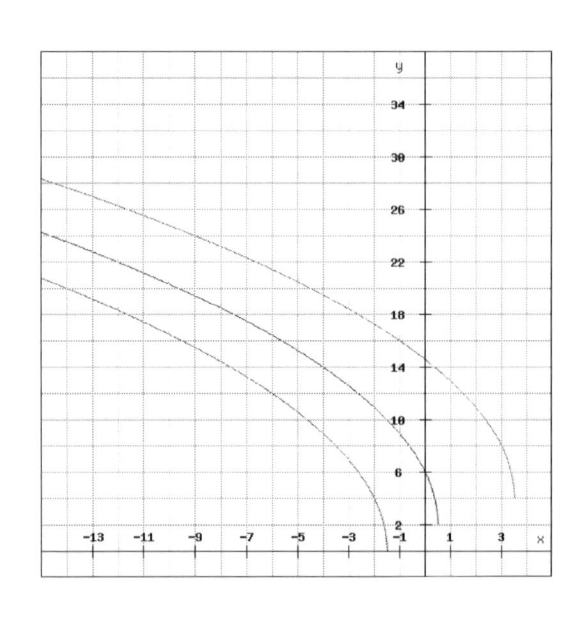

538

Analyze the following functions:

1. f(x) = $\sqrt{x+3}$

Domain: $x \in [-3, \infty)$ Horizontal Asymptote: None
Range: $f(x) \in [0, \infty)$ $Lim_{x \to -\infty}(f(x)) = D.E.$
Increase: $x \in (-3, \infty)$ $Lim_{x \to \infty}(f(x)) = \infty$
Decrease: Never   y int: $(0, \sqrt{3})$
Min: $(-3, 0)$ x int: $(-3, 0)$

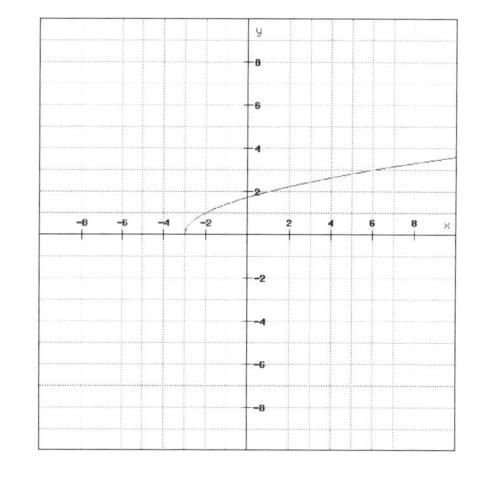

2. f(x) = $3\sqrt{x-2}$

Domain: $x \in [2, \infty)$ Horizontal Asymptote: None
Range: $f(x) \in [0, \infty)$ $Lim_{x \to -\infty}(f(x)) = D.E.$
Increase: $x \in (2, \infty)$ $Lim_{x \to \infty}(f(x)) = \infty$
Decrease: Never   y int: None
Min: $(2, 0)$ x int: $(2, 0)$

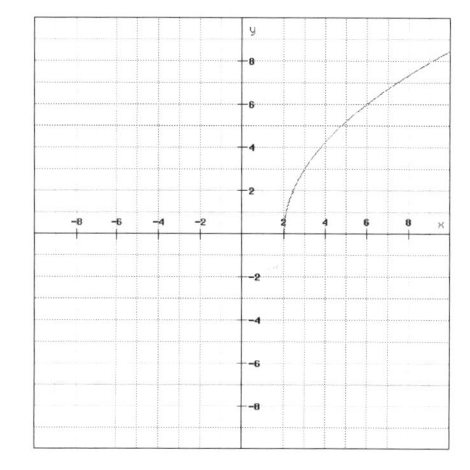

3. f(x) = $\sqrt{5x+6}$

Domain: $x \in [-\frac{6}{5}, \infty)$ Horizontal Asymptote: None
Range: $f(x) \in [0, \infty)$ $Lim_{x \to -\infty}(f(x)) = D.E.$
Increase: $x \in (-\frac{6}{5}, \infty)$ $Lim_{x \to \infty}(f(x)) = \infty$
Decrease: Never   y int: $(0, 6)$
Min: $(-\frac{6}{5}, 0)$ x int: $(-\frac{6}{5}, 0)$

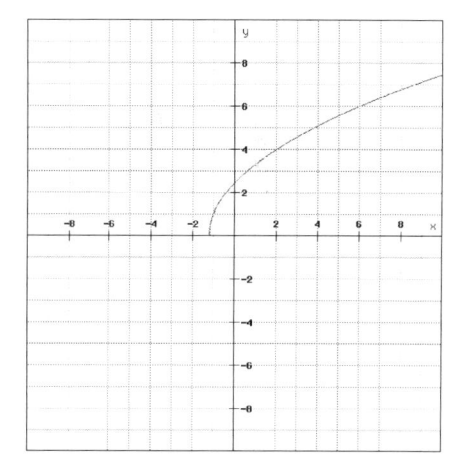

4. f(x) = $2\sqrt{-4x-2}$

Domain: $x \in (-\infty, -\frac{1}{2}]$ Horizontal Asymptote: None
Range: $f(x) \in [0, \infty)$ $Lim_{x \to -\infty}(f(x)) = \infty$
Increase: Never $Lim_{x \to \infty}(f(x)) = D.E.$
Decrease: $x \in (-\infty, -\frac{1}{2})$ y int: None
Min: $(-\frac{1}{2}, 0)$ x int: $(-\frac{1}{2}, 0)$

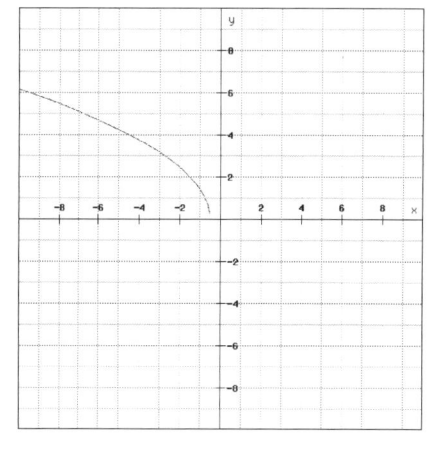

539

5. $f(x) = -\sqrt{x-3}$

   $Domain: x \in [3, \infty)$ $Horizontal\ Asymptote: None$
   $Range: f(x) \in (-\infty, 0]$ $Lim_{x \to -\infty}(f(x)) = D.E.$
   $Increase: Never$ $Lim_{x \to \infty}(f(x)) = -\infty$
   $Decrease: x \in (3, \infty)$ $y\ int: None$
   $Max: (3, 0)$ $x\ int: (3, 0)$

6. $f(x) = \sqrt{2x-5}$

   $Domain: x \in [\frac{5}{2}, \infty)$ $Horizontal\ Asymptote: None$
   $Range: f(x) \in [0, \infty)$ $Lim_{x \to -\infty}(f(x)) = D.E.$
   $Increase: x \in (\frac{5}{2}, \infty)$ $Lim_{x \to \infty}(f(x)) = \infty$
   $Decrease: Never$ $y\ int: None$
   $Min: (\frac{5}{2}, 0)$ $x\ int: (\frac{5}{2}, 0)$

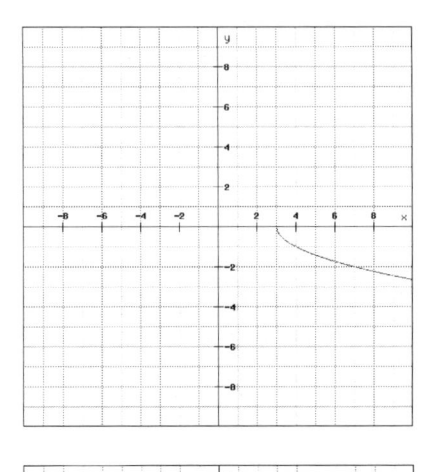

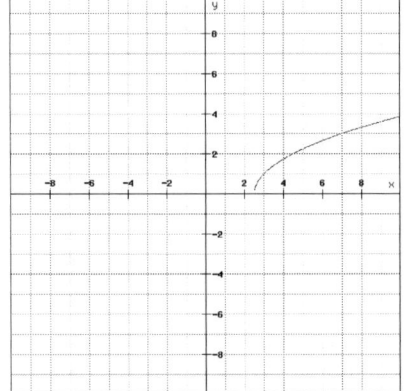

7. $f(x) = 2\sqrt{-3x-2}$

   $Domain: x \in (-\infty, -\frac{3}{2}]$ $Horizontal\ Asymptote: None$
   $Range: f(x) \in [0, \infty)$ $Lim_{x \to -\infty}(f(x)) = \infty$
   $Increase: Never$ $Lim_{x \to \infty}(f(x)) = D.E.$
   $Decrease: x \in (-\infty, -\frac{3}{2})$ $y\ int: None$
   $Min: (-\frac{1}{2}, 0)$ $x\ int: (-\frac{1}{2}, 0)$

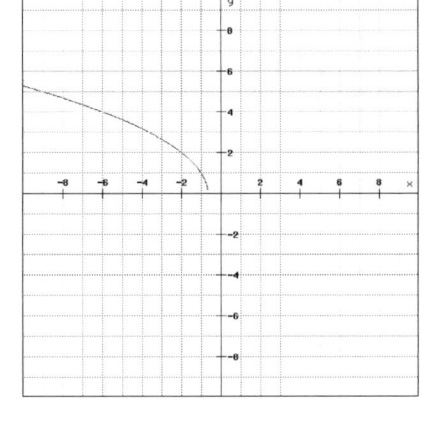

8. $f(x) = \sqrt{x-5} + 6$

   $Domain: x \in [5, \infty)$ $Horizontal\ Asymptote: None$
   $Range: f(x) \in [6, \infty)$ $Lim_{x \to -\infty}(f(x)) = D.E.$
   $Increase: x \in (5, \infty)$ $Lim_{x \to \infty}(f(x)) = \infty$
   $Decrease: Never$ $y\ int: None$
   $Min: (5, 6)$ $x\ int: None$

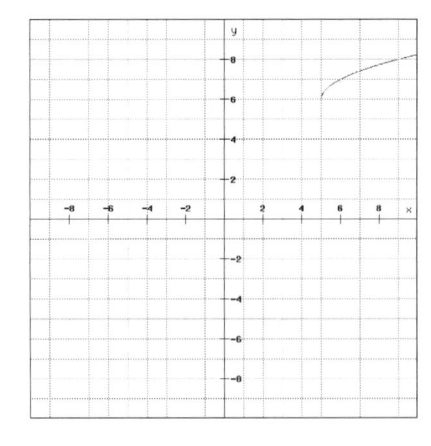

9. f(x) = $\sqrt{-x+3} - 8$

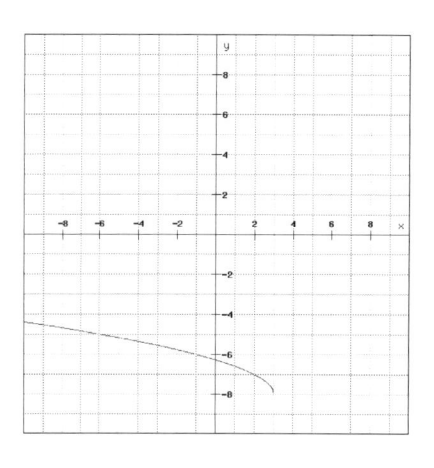

Domain: $x \in (-\infty, 3]$ *Horizontal Asymptote*: *None*
Range: $f(x) \in [-8, \infty)$ $Lim_{x \to -\infty}(f(x)) = \infty$
Increase: *Never* $Lim_{x \to \infty}(f(x)) = D.E.$
Decrease: $x \in (-\infty, 3)$ $y\,int: (0, \sqrt{3} - 8)$
Min: $(3, -8)$ $x\,int: (-61, 0)$

10. f(x) = $\sqrt{4x+3} + 4$

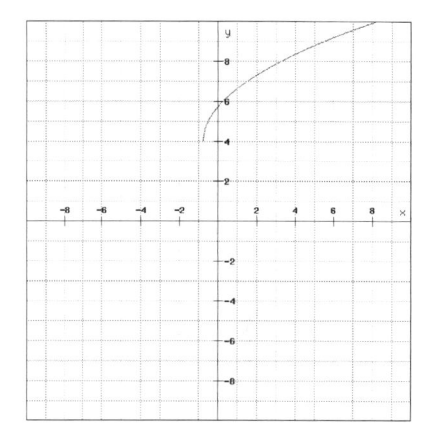

Domain: $x \in [-\frac{3}{4}, \infty)$ *Horizontal Asymptote*: *None*
Range: $f(x) \in [4, \infty)$ $Lim_{x \to -\infty}(f(x)) = D.E.$
Increase: $x \in (-\frac{3}{4}, \infty)$ $Lim_{x \to \infty}(f(x)) = \infty$
Decrease: *Never* $y\,int: (0, \sqrt{3} + 4)$
Min: $(-\frac{3}{4}, 4)$ $x\,int$: *None*

11. f(x) = $\sqrt{x-6} - 2$

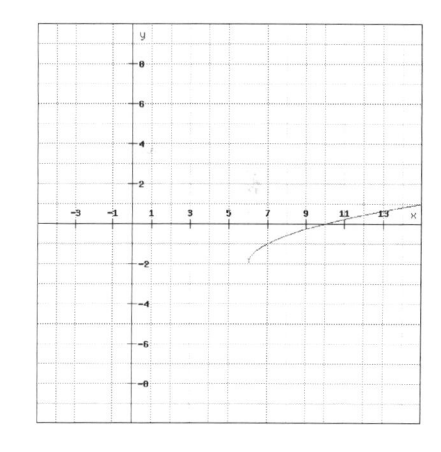

Domain: $x \in [6, \infty)$ *Horizontal Asymptote*: *None*
Range: $f(x) \in [-2, \infty)$ $Lim_{x \to -\infty}(f(x)) = D.E.$
Increase: $x \in (6, \infty)$ $Lim_{x \to \infty}(f(x)) = \infty$
Decrease: *Never* $y\,int$: *None*
Min: $(6, 2)$ $x\,int: (10, 0)$

12. f(x) = $5\sqrt{x} - 5$

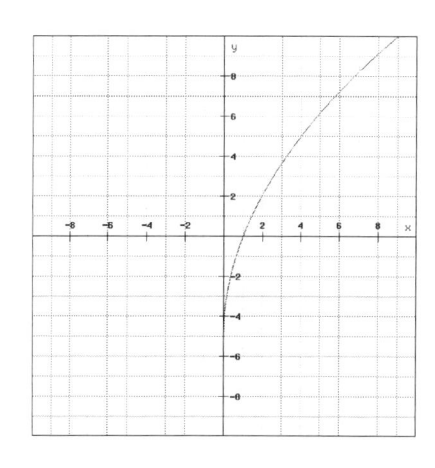

Domain: $x \in [0, \infty)$ *Horizontal Asymptote*: *None*
Range: $f(x) \in [-5, \infty)$ $Lim_{x \to -\infty}(f(x)) = D.E.$
Increase: $x \in (0, \infty)$ $Lim_{x \to \infty}(f(x)) = \infty$
Decrease: *Never* $y\,int: (0, -5)$
Min: $(0, -5)$ $x\,int: (1, 0)$

13. $f(x) = -\sqrt{-x-3} - 1$

Domain: $x \in (-\infty, -3]$ Horizontal Asymptote: None
Range: $f(x) \in (-\infty, -1]$ $Lim_{x \to -\infty}(f(x)) = -\infty$
Increase: $x \in (-\infty, -3)$ $Lim_{x \to \infty}(f(x)) = D.E.$
Decrease: Never $y$int: None
Max: $(-3, -1)$ $x$int: None

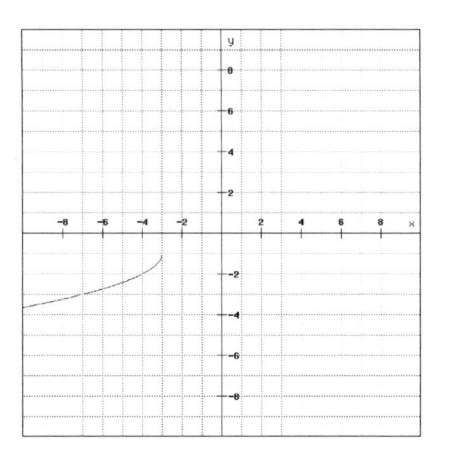

14. $f(x) = -2\sqrt{x} + 9$

Domain: $x \in [0, \infty)$ Horizontal Asymptote: None
Range: $f(x) \in (-\infty, 9]$ $Lim_{x \to -\infty}(f(x)) = D.E.$
Increase: Never $Lim_{x \to \infty}(f(x)) = -\infty$
Decrease: $x \in (0, \infty)$ $y$int: $(0, 9)$
Max: $(0, 9)$ $x$int: $(\frac{81}{4}, 0)$

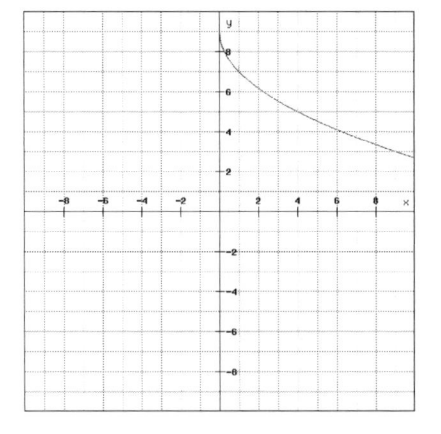

15. $f(x) = \left|\sqrt{x+3}\right| = \sqrt{x+3}$

Domain: $x \in [-3, \infty)$ Horizontal Asymptote: None
Range: $f(x) \in [0, \infty)$ $Lim_{x \to -\infty}(f(x)) = D.E.$
Increase: $x \in (-3, \infty)$ $Lim_{x \to \infty}(f(x)) = \infty$
Decrease: Never $y$int: $(0, \sqrt{3})$
Min: $(-3, 0)$ $x$int: $(-3, 0)$

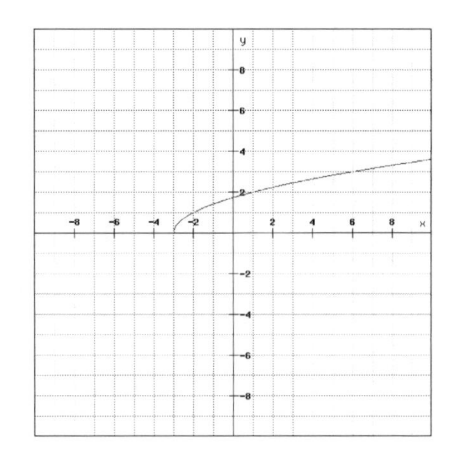

16. $f(x) = \left|-\sqrt{x-2}\right| = \sqrt{x-2}$

Domain: $x \in [2, \infty)$ Horizontal Asymptote: None
Range: $f(x) \in [0, \infty)$ $Lim_{x \to -\infty}(f(x)) = D.E.$
Increase: $x \in (2, \infty)$ $Lim_{x \to \infty}(f(x)) = \infty$
Decrease: Never $y$int: None
Min: $(2, 0)$ $x$int: $(2, 0)$

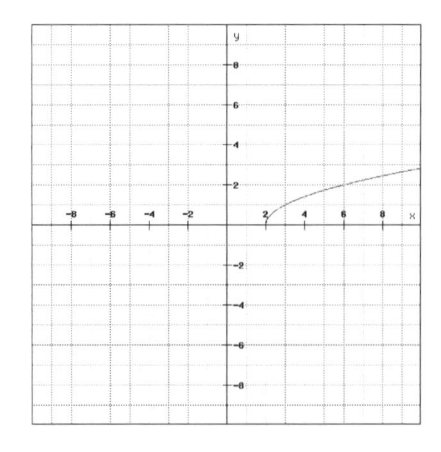

17. $f(x) = \left|\sqrt{x+3} - 2\right| = \begin{cases} -\sqrt{x+3} + 2 & -3 \leq x \leq 1 \\ \sqrt{x+3} - 2 & x > 1 \end{cases}$

Domain: $x \in [-3, \infty)$ Horizontal Asymptote: None
Range: $f(x) \in [0, \infty)$ $Lim_{x \to -\infty}(f(x)) = D.E.$
Increase: $x \in (1, \infty)$ $Lim_{x \to \infty}(f(x)) = \infty$
Decrease: $x \in (-3, 1)$ y int: $(0, 2 - \sqrt{3})$
Min: $(1, 0)$ x int: $(1, 0)$

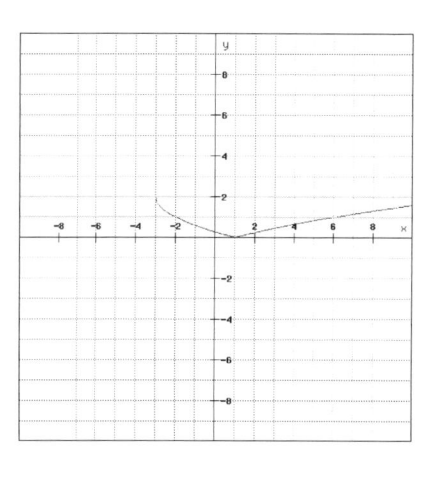

18. $f(x) = \sqrt{|x| + 3} - 2 = \begin{cases} \sqrt{-x+3} - 2 & x \leq 0 \\ \sqrt{x+3} - 2 & x > 0 \end{cases}$

Domain: $x \in (-\infty, \infty)$ Horizontal Asymptote: None
Range: $f(x) \in [1 - \sqrt{3}, \infty)$ $Lim_{x \to -\infty}(f(x)) = \infty$
Increase: $x \in (0, \infty)$ $Lim_{x \to \infty}(f(x)) = \infty$
Decrease: $x \in (-\infty, 0)$ y int: $(0, \sqrt{3} - 2)$
Min: $(0, \sqrt{3} - 2)$ x int: $(1, 0), (-1, 0)$

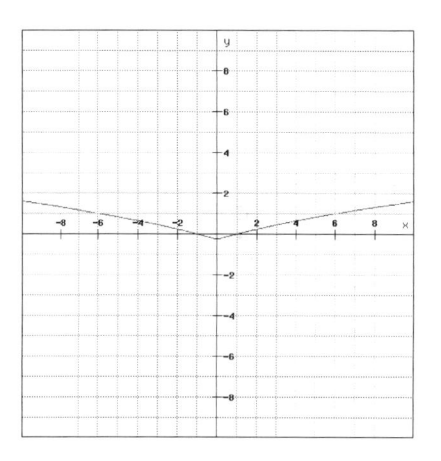

19. $f(x) = \sqrt{|x| - 1} - 2 = \begin{cases} \sqrt{-x-1} - 2 & x \leq -1 \\ \sqrt{x-1} - 2 & x \geq 1 \end{cases}$

Domain: $x \in (-\infty, -1] \cup [1, \infty)$ Horizontal Asymptote: None
Range: $f(x) \in [-2, \infty)$ $Lim_{x \to -\infty}(f(x)) = \infty$
Increase: $x \in (1, \infty)$ $Lim_{x \to \infty}(f(x)) = \infty$
Decrease: $x \in (-\infty, -1)$ y int: None
Min: $(1, -2), (-1, -2)$ x int: $(5, 0), (-5, 0)$

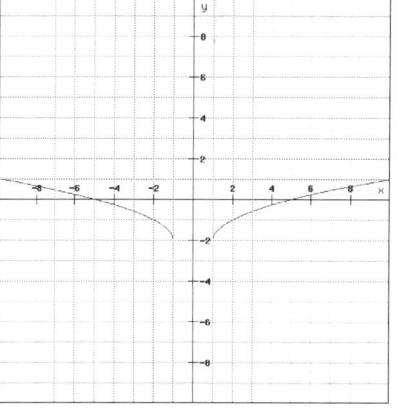

2.10. – HYBRID (OR PIECEWISE) FUNCTIONS

Analyze the following functions:

2. $f(x) = \begin{cases} -x & x < 0 \\ x & 0 \leq x \end{cases}$

Domain: $x \in (-\infty, \infty)$ H. Asymptote: None
Range: $f(x) \in [0, \infty)$ $Lim_{x \to -\infty}(f(x)) = \infty$
Increase: $x \in (0, \infty)$ $Lim_{x \to \infty}(f(x)) = \infty$
Decrease: $x \in (-\infty, 0)$ V. Asymptote: None
Min: $(0, 0)$ x int: $(0, 0)$, y int: $(0, 0)$

3. $f(x) = \begin{cases} -x & x < 2 \\ x & 2 \leq x \end{cases}$

Domain: $x \in (-\infty, \infty)$ H. Asymptote: None
Range: $f(x) \in (-2, \infty)$ $Lim_{x \to -\infty}(f(x)) = \infty$
Increase: $x \in (2, \infty)$ $Lim_{x \to \infty}(f(x)) = \infty$
Decrease: $x \in (-\infty, 2)$ V. Asymptote: None
Min: None x int: $(0, 0)$, y int: $(0, 0)$

4. $f(x) = \begin{cases} 3 & x < -3 \\ x^2 & -3 \leq x \end{cases}$

Domain: $x \in (-\infty, \infty)$ H. Asymptote: None
Range: $f(x) \in [0, \infty)$ $Lim_{x \to -\infty}(f(x)) = \infty$
Increase: $x \in (0, \infty)$ $Lim_{x \to \infty}(f(x)) = 3$
Decrease: $x \in (-3, 0)$ V. Asymptote: None
Min: $(0, 0)$ x int: $(0, 0)$, y int: $(0, 0)$

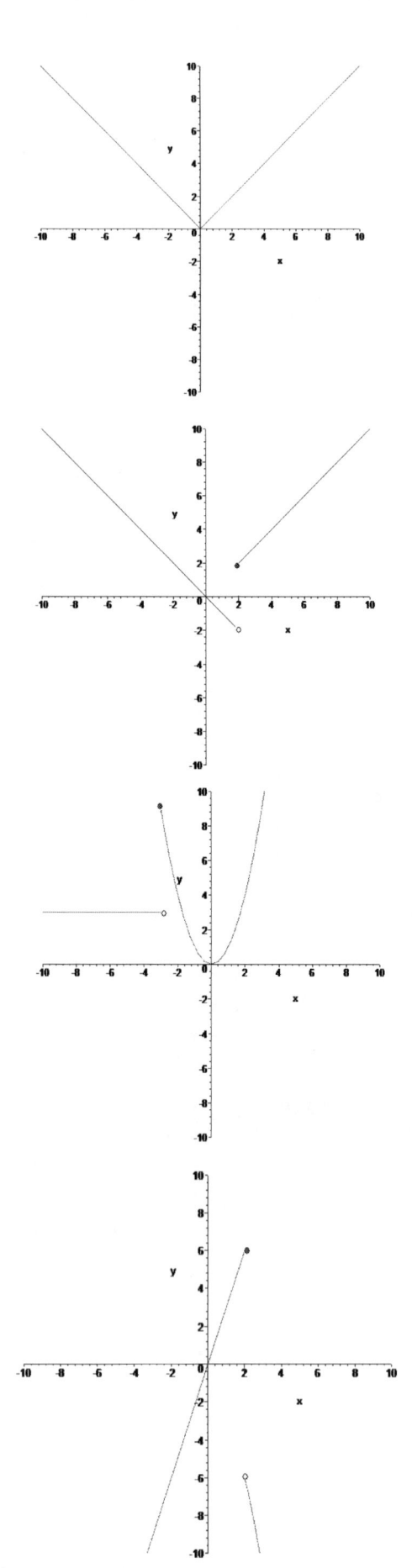

5. $f(x) = \begin{cases} 3x & x \leq 2 \\ -x^2 - 2 & 2 < x \end{cases}$

Domain: $x \in (-\infty, \infty)$ H. Asymptote: None
Range: $f(x) \in (-\infty, 6]$ $Lim_{x \to -\infty}(f(x)) = -\infty$
Increase: $x \in (-\infty, 2)$ $Lim_{x \to \infty}(f(x)) = -\infty$
Decrease: $x \in (2, \infty)$ V. Asymptote: None
Max: $(2, 6)$ x int: $(0, 0)$, y int: $(0, 0)$

6. $f(x) = \begin{cases} e^x & x \leq 2 \\ -(x-2)^2 & 2 < x \end{cases}$

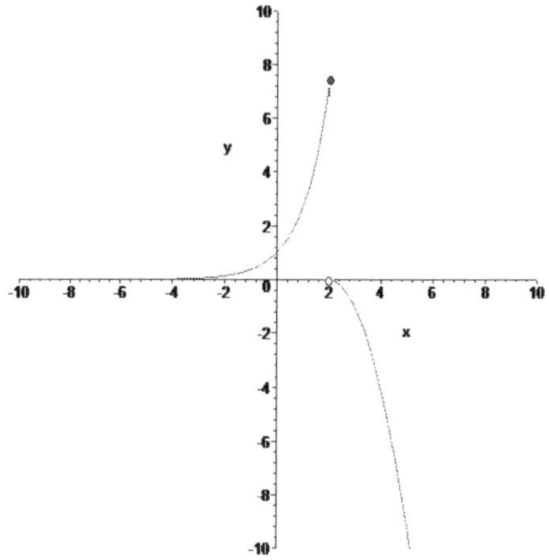

Domain: $x \in (-\infty, \infty)$ H. Asymptote: $y = 0$
Range: $f(x) \in (-\infty, 0) \cup (0, e^2]$ $Lim_{x \to -\infty}(f(x)) = 0$
Increase: $x \in (-\infty, 2)$ $Lim_{x \to \infty}(f(x)) = -\infty$
Decrease: $x \in (2, \infty)$ V. Asymptote: None
Max: $(2, e^2)$ x int: None, y int: $(0, 1)$

7. $f(x) = \begin{cases} -2^x & x \leq -3 \\ (x+1)^2 - 2 & -3 < x \end{cases}$

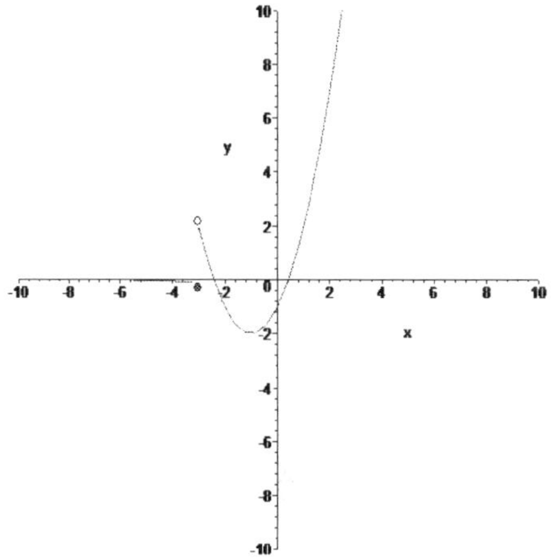

Domain: $x \in (-\infty, \infty)$ H. Asymptote: $y = 0$
Range: $f(x) \in [-2, \infty)$ $Lim_{x \to -\infty}(f(x)) = 0$
Increase: $x \in (-1, \infty)$ $Lim_{x \to \infty}(f(x)) = \infty$
Decrease: $x \in (-\infty, -3) \cup (-3, -1)$ V. Asymptote: None
Min: $(-1, -2)$ y int: $(0, -1)$
x int: $(\sqrt{2} - 1, 0), (-\sqrt{2} - 1, 0)$

8. $f(x) = \begin{cases} x & x < 2 \\ x^2 - 1 & 2 \leq x \end{cases}$

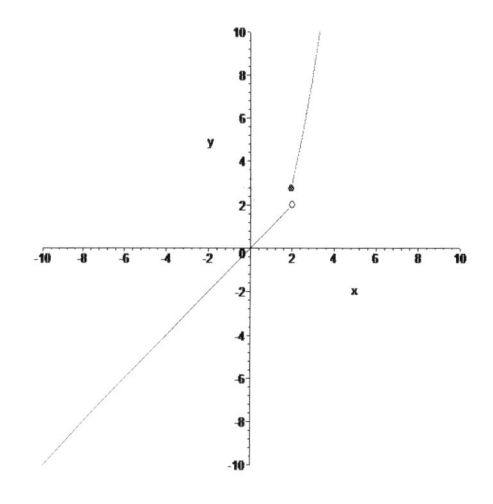

Domain: $x \in (-\infty, \infty)$ H. Asymptote: Non
Range: $f(x) \in (-\infty, 2) \cup [3, \infty)$ $Lim_{x \to -\infty}(f(x)) = -\infty$
Increase: $x \in (-\infty, 2) \cup (2, \infty)$ $Lim_{x \to \infty}(f(x)) = \infty$
Decrease: Never   V. Asymptote: None
Min / Max: None y int: $(0, 0)$, x int: $(0, 0)$

9. $f(x) = \begin{cases} -x^2 + 3 & x < -2 \\ x^2 - 1 & -2 \leq x \end{cases}$

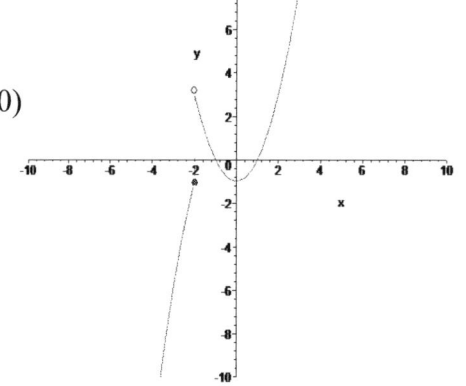

Domain: $x \in (-\infty, \infty)$ H. Asymptote: None
Range: $f(x) \in (-\infty, \infty)$ $Lim_{x \to -\infty}(f(x)) = -\infty$
Increase: $x \in (-\infty, -2) \cup (0, \infty)$ $Lim_{x \to \infty}(f(x)) = \infty$
Decrease: $x \in (-2, 0)$ V. Asymptote: None
Min: $(0, 1)$ y int: $(0, -1)$, x int: $(-1, 0), (1, 0)$

10. $f(x) = \begin{cases} -2x^2 + 47 & x < -5 \\ x + 2 & -5 \leq x \end{cases}$

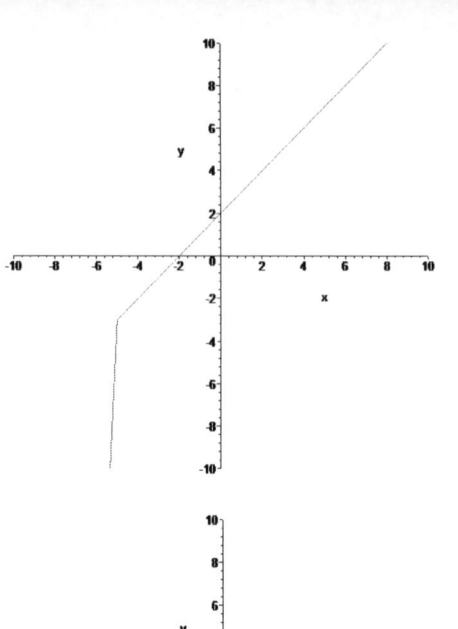

Domain: $x \in (-\infty, \infty)$ H. Asymptote: None
Range: $f(x) \in (-\infty, \infty)$ $Lim_{x \to -\infty}(f(x)) = -\infty$
Increase: $x \in (-\infty, \infty)$ $Lim_{x \to \infty}(f(x)) = \infty$
Decrease: Never   V. Asymptote: None
Min/Max: None y int: $(0, 2)$, x int: $(-2, 0)$

11. $f(x) = \begin{cases} x & x < 3 \\ \ln(x) & 3 < x \end{cases}$

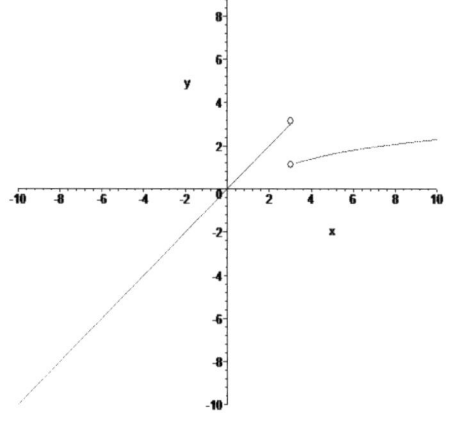

Domain: $x \in (-\infty, 3) \cup (3, \infty)$ H. Asymptote: None
Range: $f(x) \in (-\infty, \infty)$ $Lim_{x \to -\infty}(f(x)) = -\infty$
Increase: $x \in (-\infty, 3) \cup (3, \infty)$ $Lim_{x \to \infty}(f(x)) = \infty$
Decrease: Never   V. Asymptote: None
Min/Max: None y int: $(0, 0)$, x int: $(0, 0)$

12. $f(x) = \begin{cases} x - \dfrac{8}{3} & x < 3 \\ \dfrac{1}{x} & 3 \leq x \end{cases}$

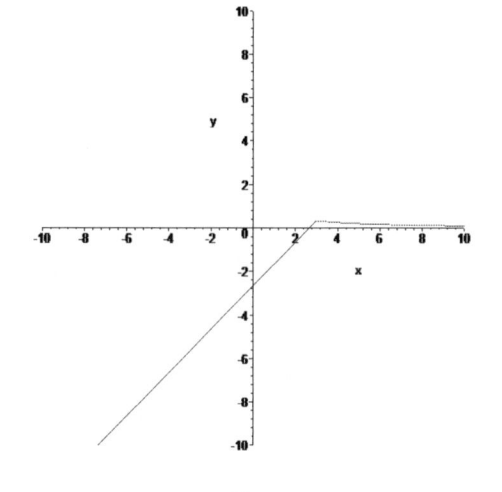

Domain: $x \in (-\infty, \infty)$ H. Asymptote: $y = 0$
Range: $f(x) \in (-\infty, \dfrac{1}{3}]$ $Lim_{x \to -\infty}(f(x)) = -\infty$
Increase: $x \in (-\infty, \dfrac{1}{3})$ $Lim_{x \to \infty}(f(x)) = 0$
Decrease: $x \in (\dfrac{1}{3}, \infty)$ V. Asymptote: None
Max: $(3, \dfrac{1}{3})$ y int: $(0, -\dfrac{8}{3})$, x int: $(\dfrac{8}{3}, 0)$

13. $f(x) = \begin{cases} \dfrac{1}{x+1} & x \leq 2 \\ \dfrac{1}{x} & 2 < x \end{cases}$

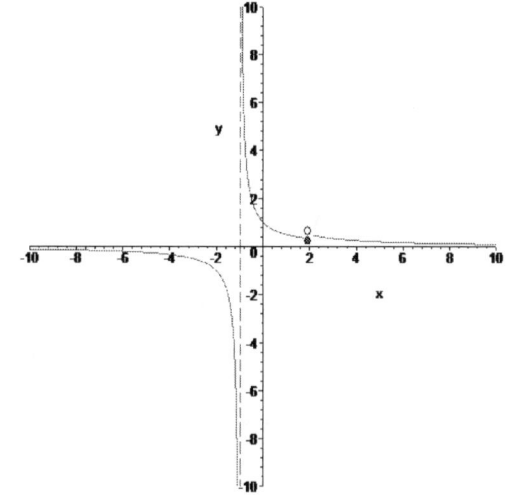

Domain: $x \in (-\infty, -1) \cup (-1, \infty)$ Max: None
Range: $f(x) \in (-\infty, 0) \cup (0, \infty)$ y int: None,
Increase: Never x int: None
Decrease: $x \in (-\infty, -1) \cup (-1, 2) \cup (2, \infty)$
V. Asymptote: $x = -1$ H. Asymptote: $y = 0$
$Lim_{x \to -1^-}(f(x)) = -\infty$ $Lim_{x \to -\infty}(f(x)) = 0$
$Lim_{x \to -1^+}(f(x)) = \infty$ $Lim_{x \to \infty}(f(x)) = 0$

546

14. $f(x) = \begin{cases} \dfrac{1}{x+1} & x < \dfrac{-1}{2} \\ \dfrac{1}{x} & \dfrac{-1}{2} < x \end{cases}$

Domain: $x \in (-\infty, -1) \cup (-1, 0) \cup (0, \infty)$

Range: $f(x) \in (-\infty, \infty)$ y int: None

Increase: Never x int: None

Decrease: $x \in (-\infty, -1) \cup (-1, 0) \cup (0, \infty)$

V. Asymptote: $x = 0, x = -1$ H. Asymptote: $y = 0$

$Lim_{x \to -1^-}(f(x)) = -\infty$ $Lim_{x \to -\infty}(f(x)) = 0$

$Lim_{x \to -1^+}(f(x)) = \infty$ $Lim_{x \to \infty}(f(x)) = 0$

$Lim_{x \to 0^-}(f(x)) = -\infty$ Max: None

$Lim_{x \to 0^+}(f(x)) = \infty$

15. $f(x) = \begin{cases} \dfrac{1}{x-2} + 2 & x < 3 \\ \ln(x) & 3 \leq x \end{cases}$

Domain: $x \in (-\infty, 2) \cup (2, \infty)$ Max: None

Range: $f(x) \in (-\infty, \infty)$ y int: $(0, \dfrac{3}{2})$

Increase: $x \in (3, \infty)$ x int: $(\dfrac{3}{2}, 0)$

Decrease: $x \in (-\infty, 2) \cup (2, 3)$

V. Asymptote: $x = 2$ H. Asymptote: $y = 2$

$Lim_{x \to 2^-}(f(x)) = -\infty$ $Lim_{x \to -\infty}(f(x)) = 2$

$Lim_{x \to 2^+}(f(x)) = \infty$ $Lim_{x \to \infty}(f(x)) = \infty$

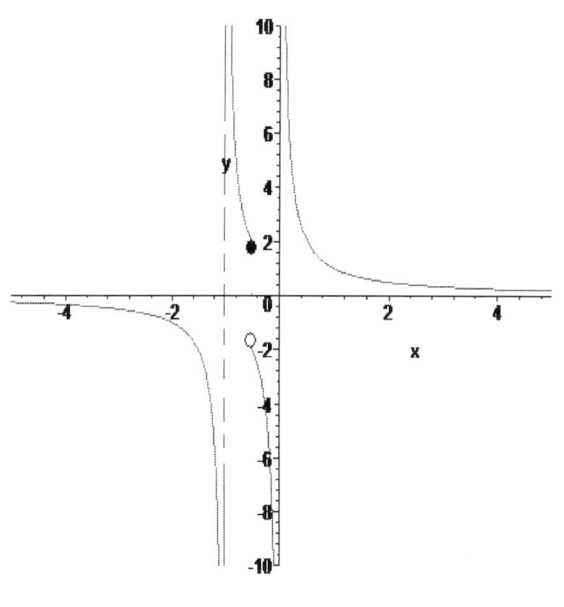

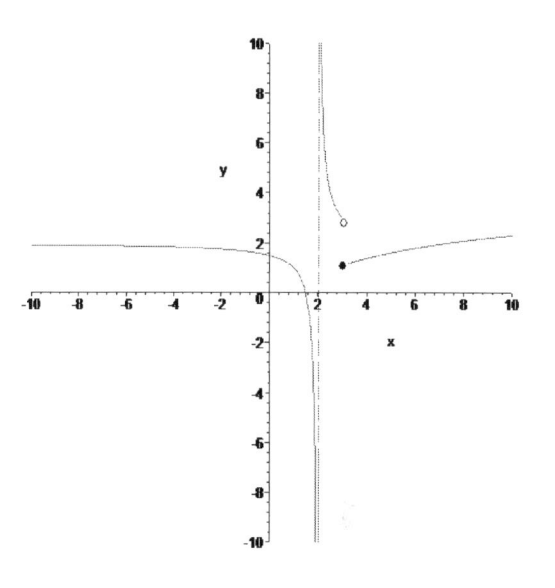

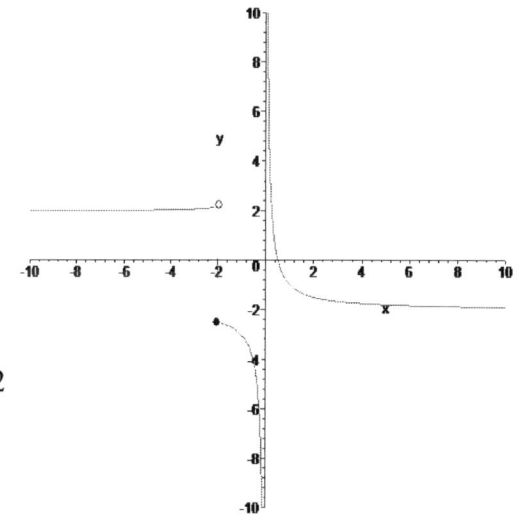

16. $f(x) = \begin{cases} e^x + 2 & x < -2 \\ \dfrac{1}{x} - 2 & -2 \leq x \end{cases}$

Domain: $x \in (-\infty, 0) \cup (0, \infty)$ Max: None

Range: $f(x) \in (-\infty, -\dfrac{5}{2}] \cup (-2, \infty)$ y int: None

Increase: $x \in (-\infty, -2)$ x int: $(\dfrac{1}{2}, 0)$

Decrease: $x \in (-2, 0) \cup (0, \infty)$

V. Asymptote: $x = 0$ H. Asymptote: $y = -2, y = 2$

$Lim_{x \to 0^-}(f(x)) = -\infty$ $Lim_{x \to -\infty}(f(x)) = 2$

$Lim_{x \to 0^+}(f(x)) = \infty$ $Lim_{x \to \infty}(f(x)) = -2$

17. $f(x) = \begin{cases} e^{(-x)} - 2 & x < 1 \\ \dfrac{1}{x-2} + 1 & 1 \leq x \end{cases}$

Domain: $x \in (-\infty, 2) \cup (2, \infty)$ Max: None
Range: $f(x) \in (-\infty, \infty)$ y int: $(0, -1)$
Increase: Never x int: $(1, 0), (-\ln(2), 0)$
Decrease: $x \in (-\infty, 1) \cup (1, 2) \cup (2, \infty)$
V. Asymptote: $x = 2$ H. Asymptote: $y = 1$
$\text{Lim}_{x \to 2^-}(f(x)) = -\infty$ $\text{Lim}_{x \to -\infty}(f(x)) = \infty$
$\text{Lim}_{x \to 2^+}(f(x)) = \infty$ $\text{Lim}_{x \to \infty}(f(x)) = 1$

18. $f(x) = \begin{cases} -x^2 - 2 & x < 1 \\ \dfrac{1}{-3+x} & 1 \leq x \end{cases}$

Domain: $x \in (-\infty, 3) \cup (3, \infty)$ Max: None
Range: $f(x) \in (-\infty, -\dfrac{1}{2}] \cup (0, \infty)$ y int: $(0, -2)$
Increase: $x \in (-\infty, 0)$ x int: None
Decrease: $x \in (0, 1) \cup (1, 3) \cup (3, \infty)$
V. Asymptote: $x = 3$ H. Asymptote: $y = 0$
$\text{Lim}_{x \to 3^-}(f(x)) = -\infty$ $\text{Lim}_{x \to -\infty}(f(x)) = -\infty$
$\text{Lim}_{x \to 3^+}(f(x)) = \infty$ $\text{Lim}_{x \to \infty}(f(x)) = 0$

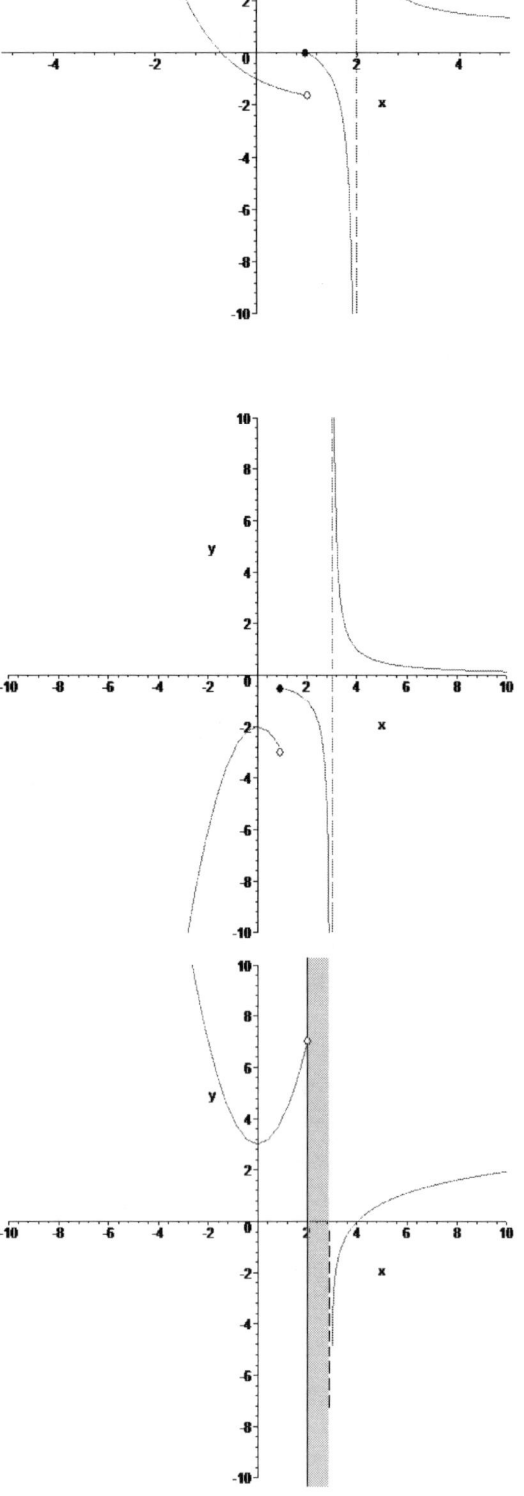

19. $f(x) = \begin{cases} x^2 + 3 & x < 2 \\ \ln(-3 + x) & 2 \leq x \end{cases}$

Domain: $x \in (-\infty, 2) \cup (3, \infty)$ Min: $(0, 3)$
Range: $f(x) \in (-\infty, \infty)$ y int: $(0, 3)$
Increase: $x \in (0, 2) \cup (3, \infty)$ x int: $(4, 0)$
Decrease: $x \in (-\infty, 0)$
V. Asymptote: $x = 3$ H. Asymptote: None
$\text{Lim}_{x \to 3^-}(f(x)) = D.E.$ $\text{Lim}_{x \to -\infty}(f(x)) = \infty$
$\text{Lim}_{x \to 3^+}(f(x)) = -\infty$ $\text{Lim}_{x \to \infty}(f(x)) = \infty$

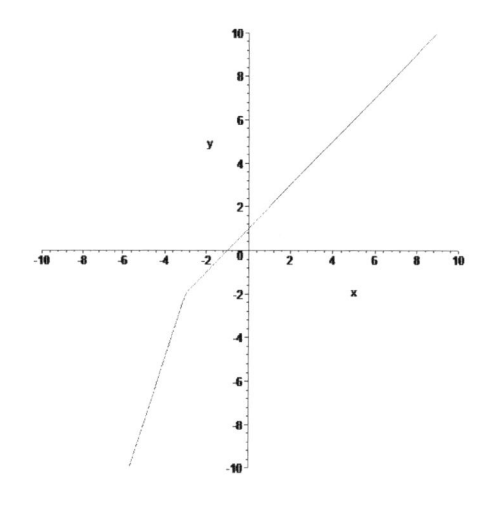

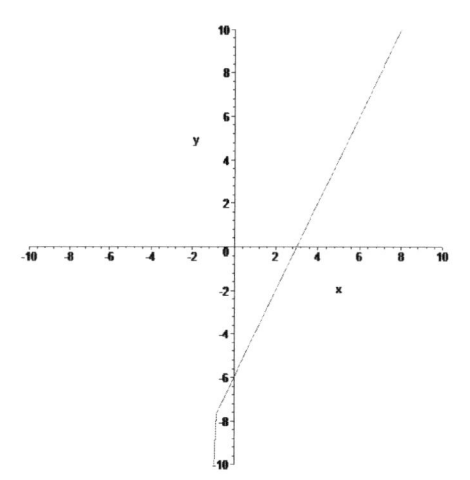

20. $f(x) = \begin{cases} x^2 + 3 & x < 2 \\ \ln(3+x) & 2 \leq x \end{cases}$

Domain: $x \in (-\infty, \infty)$ Min: $(0, 3)$
Range: $f(x) \in [\ln(5), \infty)$ y int: $(0, 3)$
Increase: $x \in (0, 2) \cup (2, \infty)$ x int: None
Decrease: $x \in (-\infty, 0)$
V. Asymptote: None H. Asymptote: None
$Lim_{x \to -\infty}(f(x)) = \infty$ $Lim_{x \to \infty}(f(x)) = \infty$

21. $f(x) = \begin{cases} 3x - 2 & x < 0 \\ \ln(3+x) - 1 & 0 \leq x \end{cases}$

Domain: $x \in (-\infty, \infty)$ Min: None
Range: $f(x) \in (-\infty, -2) \cup [\ln(3) - 1, \infty)$
Increase: $x \in (-\infty, 0) \cup (0, \infty)$ x int: None
Decrease: Never y int: $(0, \ln(3) - 1)$
V. Asymptote: None H. Asymptote: None
$Lim_{x \to -\infty}(f(x)) = -\infty$ $Lim_{x \to \infty}(f(x)) = \infty$

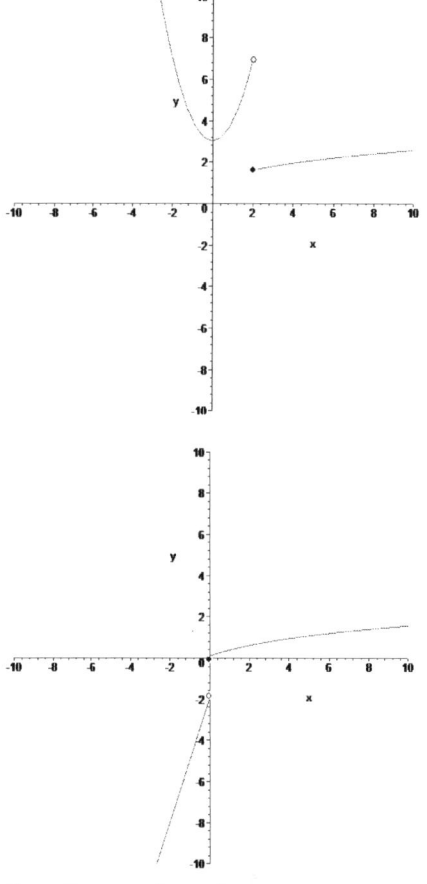

Value(s) of *a* for which the following functions are continuous, function analyzed:

22. $f(x) = \begin{cases} ax + 7 & x < -3 \\ x + 1 & -3 \leq x \end{cases}$

$Lim_{x \to -3^-}(f(x)) = 7 - 3a; Lim_{x \to -3^+}(f(x)) = -2; f(-3) = -2$
$7 - 3a = -2; a = 3$

Domain: $x \in (-\infty, \infty)$ Min/Max: None
Range: $f(x) \in (-\infty, \infty)$ y int: $(0, 1)$
Increase: $x \in (-\infty, \infty)$ x int: $(-1, 0)$
Decrease: Never
V. Asymptote: None H. Asymptote: None
$Lim_{x \to -\infty}(f(x)) = -\infty$ $Lim_{x \to \infty}(f(x)) = \infty$

23. $f(x) = \begin{cases} ax^2 + 7 & x < -1 \\ 2x - 6 & -1 \leq x \end{cases}$

$Lim_{x \to -1^-}(f(x)) = a + 7; Lim_{x \to -1^+}(f(x)) = -8; f(-1) = -8$
$a + 7 = -8; a = -15$

Domain: $x \in (-\infty, \infty)$ Min/Max: None
Range: $f(x) \in (-\infty, \infty)$ y int: $(0, -6)$
Increase: $x \in (-\infty, \infty)$ x int: $(3, 0)$
Decrease: Never
V. Asymptote: None H. Asymptote: None
$Lim_{x \to -\infty}(f(x)) = -\infty$ $Lim_{x \to \infty}(f(x)) = \infty$

24. $f(x) = \begin{cases} x^2 + a & x < -1 \\ 2x - 6 & -1 \leq x \end{cases}$

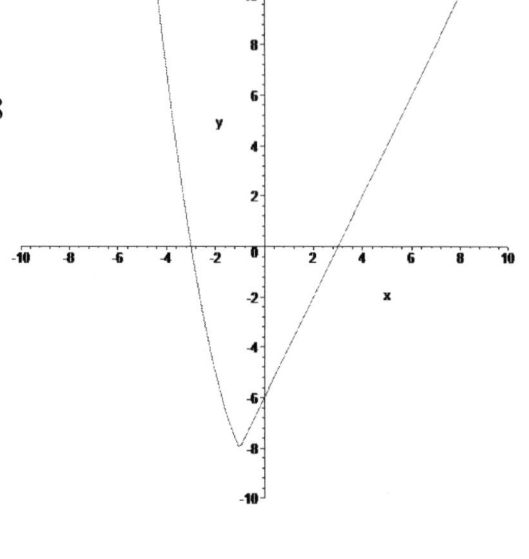

$Lim_{x \to -1^-}(f(x)) = a+1; Lim_{x \to -1^+}(f(x)) = -8; f(-1) = -8$
$a+1 = -8; a = -9$

Domain: $x \in (-\infty, \infty)$ Min: $(-1, -8)$
Range: $f(x) \in (-\infty, \infty)$ $y$int: $(0, -6)$
Increase: $x \in (-\infty, \infty)$ $x$int: $(3, 0), (-3, 0)$
Decrease: Never
V. Asymptote: None   H. Asymptote: None
$Lim_{x \to -\infty}(f(x)) = \infty$ $Lim_{x \to \infty}(f(x)) = \infty$

25. $f(x) = \begin{cases} -x^2 + 2 & x < 3 \\ 2x^2 - a & -3 \leq x \end{cases}$

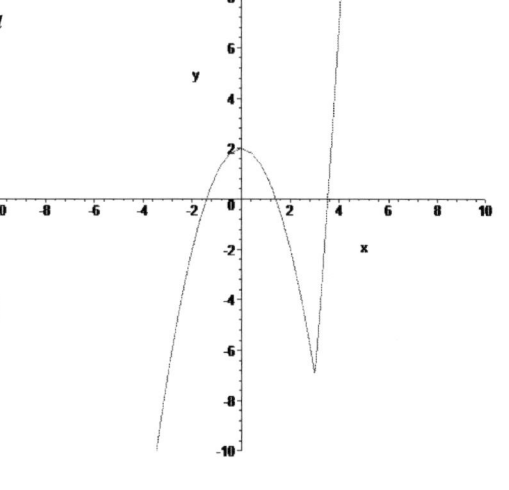

$Lim_{x \to 3^-}(f(x)) = -7; Lim_{x \to 3^+}(f(x)) = 18 - a; f(3) = 18 - a$
$-7 = 18 - a; a = 25$

Domain: $x \in (-\infty, \infty)$ Min: $(3, -7)$
Range: $f(x) \in (-\infty, \infty)$ $y$int: $(0, 2)$
Increase: $x \in (-\infty, 0) \cup (3, \infty)$ Max: $(0, 2)$
Decrease: $x \in (0, 3)$ $x$int: $(\sqrt{2}, 0), (-\sqrt{2}, 0), (\sqrt{\frac{25}{2}}, 0)$
V. Asymptote: None   H. Asymptote: None
$Lim_{x \to -\infty}(f(x)) = -\infty$ $Lim_{x \to \infty}(f(x)) = \infty$

Analyze the following functions:

26. $f(x) = \begin{cases} \sqrt{x} - 1 & x < 2 \\ \dfrac{2}{x} + 1 & 2 \leq x \end{cases}$

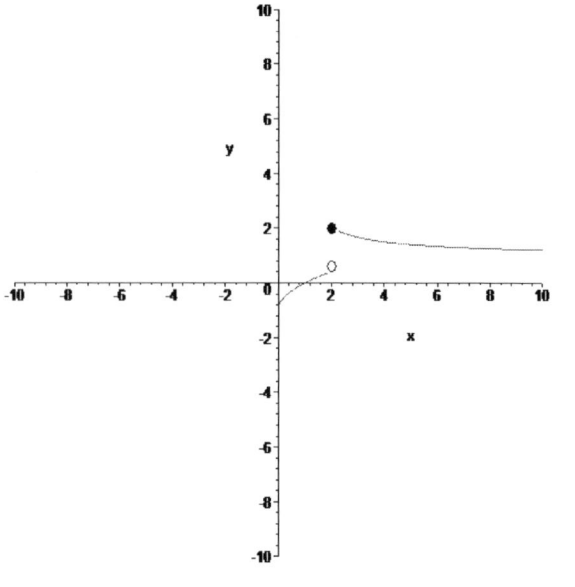

Domain: $x \in [0, \infty)$ Min: $(0, -1)$
Range: $f(x) \in (-1, \sqrt{2} - 1) \cup (1, 2]$
Increase: $x \in (-1, 2)$ $x$int: $(1, 0)$
Decrease: $x \in (2, \infty)$ $y$int: $(0, -1)$
V. Asymptote: None   H. Asymptote: $y = 1$
$Lim_{x \to 0^-}(f(x)) = D.E$ $Lim_{x \to \infty}(f(x)) = 1$
$Lim_{x \to 0^+}(f(x)) = -1$ $Lim_{x \to -\infty}(f(x)) = D.E$

27. $f(x) = \begin{cases} \sqrt{x+2} - 2 & x < 7 \\ \dfrac{16}{x+1} - 1 & 7 \leq x \end{cases}$

Domain: $x \in [-2, \infty)$ Max: $(7, 1)$
Range: $f(x) \in [-2, 1]$
Increase: $x \in (-2, 7)$ x int: $(2, 0), (15, 0)$
Decrease: $x \in (7, \infty)$ y int: $(0, \sqrt{2} - 2)$
V. Asymptote: None   H. Asymptote: $y = -1$
$Lim_{x \to -2^-}(f(x)) = D.E$ $Lim_{x \to \infty}(f(x)) = -1$
$Lim_{x \to -2^+}(f(x)) = -2$ $Lim_{x \to -\infty}(f(x)) = D.E$

28.
   a. $c = 1$ c. $d = 2, g = -7$
   b. $a = -1, b = 3$ d. $h = 3, k = 2$

29. $f(x) = \begin{cases} -1 & x \leq 5 \\ 1 & 5 < x \text{ and } x < 6 \\ 2 & 6 \leq x \end{cases}$

Domain: $x \in (-\infty, \infty)$ Max: none
Range: $f(x) \in \{-1, 1, 2\}$
Increase: Never x int: None
Decrease: Never y int: $(0, -1)$
V. Asymptote: None   H. Asymptote: None

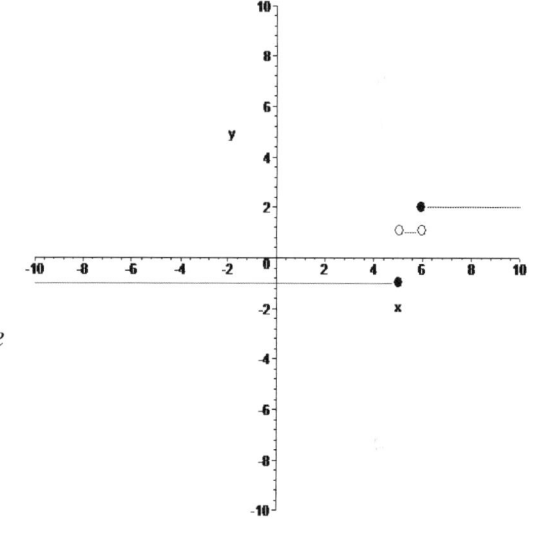

30. $f(x) = \begin{cases} 2x + 7 & x < -6 \\ x + 1 & -6 \leq x \text{ and } x < 2 \\ x^2 & 2 \leq x \end{cases}$

Domain: $x \in (-\infty, \infty)$ Max: None
Range: $f(x) \in (-\infty, 3) \cup [4, \infty)$
Increase: $x \in (-\infty, 2)$ x int: $(-1, 0)$
Decrease: $x \in (2, \infty)$ y int: $(0, 1)$
V. Asymptote: None   H. Asymptote: None
$Lim_{x \to \infty}(f(x)) = \infty$ $Lim_{x \to -\infty}(f(x)) = \infty$

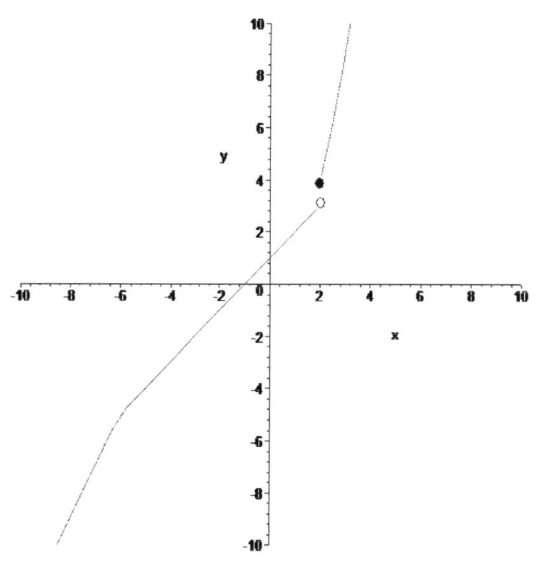

551

31. $f(x) = \begin{cases} -(3+x)^2 & x < -2 \\ x^2 - 5 & -2 \le x \text{ and } x < 1 \\ -2x - 5 & 1 \le x \end{cases}$

Domain: $x \in (-\infty, \infty)$ Max: $(-3, 0)$
Range: $f(x) \in (-\infty, 0]$ Min: $(0, -5)$
Increase: $x \in (-\infty, -3) \cup (0, 1)$ x int: $(-3, 0)$
Decrease: $x \in (-3, 0) \cup (1, \infty)$ y int: $(0, -5)$
V. Asymptote: None H. Asymptote: None
$Lim_{x \to \infty}(f(x)) = -\infty$ $Lim_{x \to -\infty}(f(x)) = -\infty$

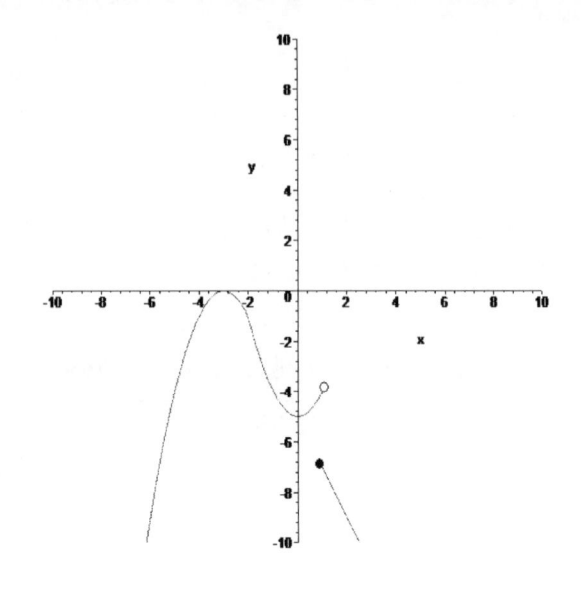

32. $f(x) = \begin{cases} 2x & x \le -3 \\ (x+2)^2 & -3 < x \text{ and } x \le 0 \\ \ln(x) & 0 < x \end{cases}$

Domain: $x \in (-\infty, \infty)$ Max: $(-3, 0)$
Range: $f(x) \in (-\infty, \infty)$ x int: $(-3, 0)$
Increase: $x \in (-\infty, -3) \cup (-2, 0) \cup (0, \infty)$
Decrease: $x \in (-3, 2)$ y int: $(0, 4)$
V. Asymptote: $x = 0$ H. Asymptote: None
$Lim_{x \to 0^-}(f(x)) = 4$ $Lim_{x \to -\infty}(f(x)) = -\infty$
$Lim_{x \to 0^+}(f(x)) = -\infty$ $Lim_{x \to \infty}(f(x)) = \infty$

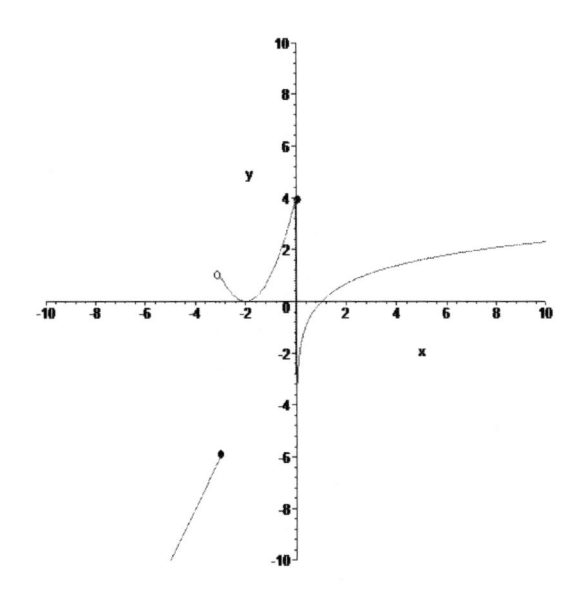

33. $f(x) = \begin{cases} -2x + 1 & x \le 2 \\ e^x & 2 < x \text{ and } x < 4 \\ \dfrac{1}{x} & 4 < x \end{cases}$

Domain: $x \in (-\infty, \infty)$ Max: None
Range: $f(x) \in [-3, \infty)$ x int: $(\dfrac{1}{2}, 0)$
Increase: $x \in (2, 4)$ y int: $(0, 1)$
Decrease: $x \in (-\infty, 2) \cup (4, \infty)$
V. Asymptote: None H. Asymptote: $y = 0$
$Lim_{x \to -\infty}(f(x)) = \infty$ $Lim_{x \to \infty}(f(x)) = 0$

552

34. $f(x) = \begin{cases} x & x \leq -2 \\ -3x - 2 & -2 < x \text{ and } x < 0 \\ \ln(2x+1) - 1 & 0 \leq x \end{cases}$

Domain: $x \in (-\infty, \infty)$ Max: None

Range: $f(x) \in (-\infty, \infty)$ x int: $(-\frac{2}{3}, 0), (\frac{e-1}{2}, 0)$

Increase: $x \in (-\infty, -2) \cup (0, \infty)$ y int: $(0, -1)$

Decrease: $x \in (-2, 0)$

V. Asymptote: None   H. Asymptote: None

$Lim_{x \to -\infty}(f(x)) = -\infty$ $Lim_{x \to \infty}(f(x)) = \infty$

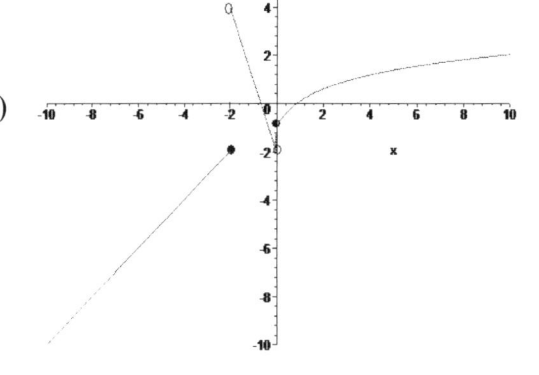

Value(s) of *a* for which the following functions are continuous, analyze the function:

35. $f(x) = \begin{cases} \sqrt{x+1} & x < 2 \\ \dfrac{a}{x+1} - 1 & 2 \leq x \end{cases}$

$Lim_{x \to 2^-}(f(x)) = \sqrt{3}; Lim_{x \to 2^+}(f(x)) = \dfrac{a}{3} - 1; f(2) = \dfrac{a}{3} - 1$

$\dfrac{a}{3} - 1 = \sqrt{3}; a = 3(1 + \sqrt{3})$

Domain: $x \in (-1, \infty)$ Max: $(2, \sqrt{3})$

Range: $f(x) \in (-1, \sqrt{3}]$ y int: $(0, 1)$

Increase: $x \in (-1, 2)$ x int: $(-1, 0), (2 + 3\sqrt{3}, 0)$

Decrease: $x \in (2, \infty)$

V. Asymptote: None   H. Asymptote: $y = -1$

$Lim_{x \to -\infty}(f(x)) = D.E.$ $Lim_{x \to \infty}(f(x)) = -1$

36. $f(x) = \begin{cases} \ln(x) + 1 & x < 1 \\ \dfrac{a}{2x+1} - 3 & 1 \leq x \end{cases}$

$Lim_{x \to 1^-}(f(x)) = 1; Lim_{x \to 1^+}(f(x)) = \dfrac{a}{3} - 3; f(1) = \dfrac{a}{3} - 3$

$\dfrac{a}{3} - 3 = 1; a = 12$

Domain: $x \in (0, \infty)$ Max: $(1, 1)$

Range: $f(x) \in (-\infty, 1]$ y int: None

Increase: $x \in (0, 1)$ x int: $(\dfrac{1}{e}, 0), (\dfrac{3}{2}, 0)$

Decrease: $x \in (1, \infty)$

V. Asymptote: $x = 0$ H. Asymptote: $y = -3$

$Lim_{x \to 0^-}(f(x)) = D.E.$ $Lim_{x \to \infty}(f(x)) = -3$

$Lim_{x \to 0^+}(f(x)) = -\infty$ $Lim_{x \to -\infty}(f(x)) = D.E.$

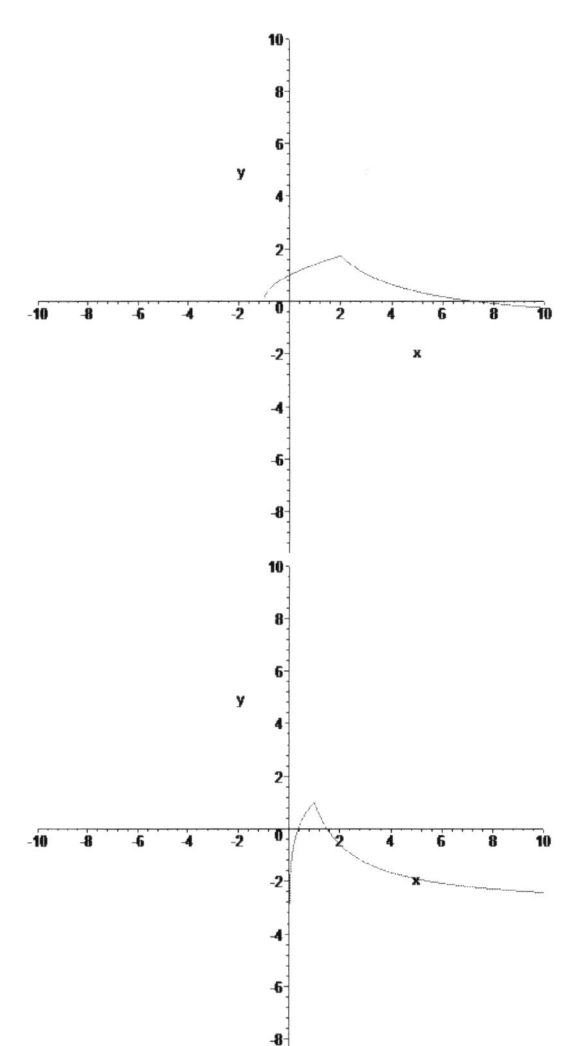

37. $f(x) = \begin{cases} x^2 & x < -2 \\ \dfrac{a}{x+3} - 3 & -2 \leq x \end{cases}$

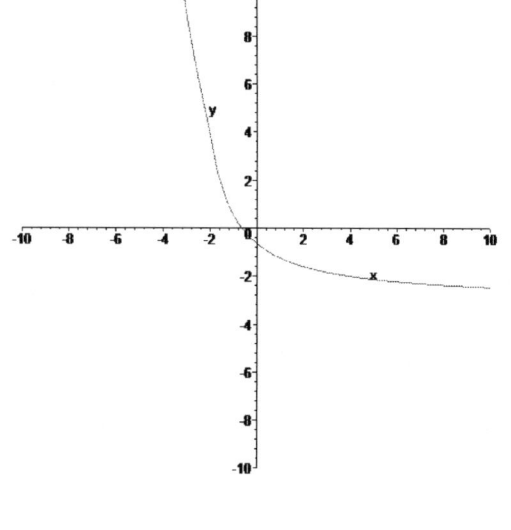

$Lim_{x \to -2^-}(f(x)) = 4; Lim_{x \to -2^+}(f(x)) = a - 3; f(-2) = a - 3$
$a - 3 = 4; a = 7$

Domain: $x \in (-\infty, \infty)$ Max: None

Range: $f(x) \in (-3, \infty)$ y int: $(0, -\dfrac{2}{3})$

Increase: Never x int: $(-\dfrac{2}{3}, 0)$

Decrease: $x \in (-\infty, \infty)$

V. Asymptote: None   H. Asymptote: $y = -3$

$Lim_{x \to -\infty}(f(x)) = \infty$ $Lim_{x \to \infty}(f(x)) = -3$

38. $f(x) = \begin{cases} x^2 & x < -2 \\ \sqrt{x+3} - a & -2 \leq x \end{cases}$

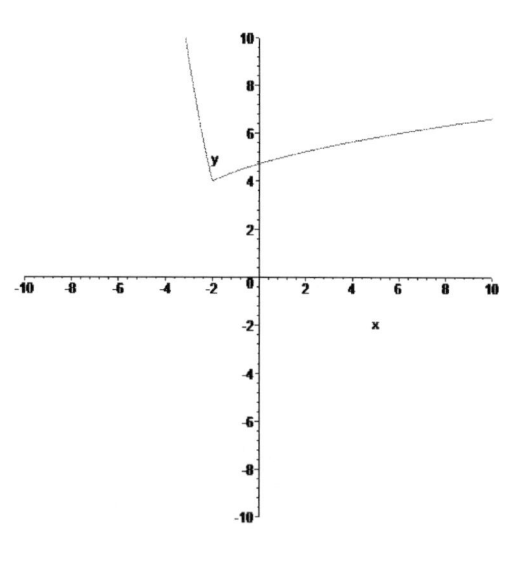

$Lim_{x \to -2^-}(f(x)) = 4; Lim_{x \to -2^+}(f(x)) = 1 - a; f(-2) = 1 - a$
$1 - a = 4; a = -3$

Domain: $x \in (-\infty, \infty)$ Min: $(-2, 4)$

Range: $f(x) \in [4, \infty)$ y int: $(0, \sqrt{3} + 3)$

Increase: $x \in (-2, \infty)$ x int: None

Decrease: $x \in (-\infty, -2)$

V. Asymptote: None   H. Asymptote: None

$Lim_{x \to -\infty}(f(x)) = \infty$ $Lim_{x \to \infty}(f(x)) = \infty$

Analyze the following functions:

39. $f(x) = \begin{cases} -x + 1 & x < 0 \\ x & 0 \leq x \end{cases}$

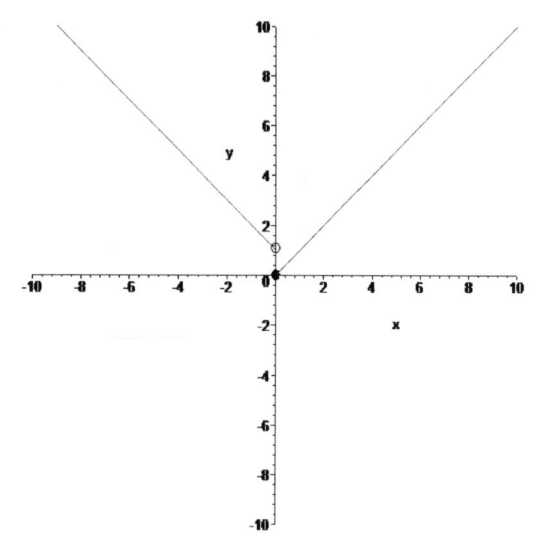

Domain: $x \in (-\infty, \infty)$ Min: $(0, 0)$

Range: $f(x) \in [0, \infty)$ y int: $(0, 0)$

Increase: $x \in (0, \infty)$ x int: $(0, 0)$

Decrease: $x \in (-\infty, 0)$

V. Asymptote: None   H. Asymptote: None

$Lim_{x \to -\infty}(f(x)) = \infty$ $Lim_{x \to \infty}(f(x)) = \infty$

554

40. $f(x) = \begin{cases} -2x+2 & x < 1 \\ \dfrac{1}{x} & 1 \leq x \end{cases}$

Domain: $x \in (-\infty, \infty)$ *Min*: None
Range: $f(x) \in (0, \infty)$ y int: $(0, 2)$
Increase: Never x int: None
Decrease: $x \in (-\infty, 1) \cup (1, \infty)$
V. Asymptote: None   *H. Asymptote*: $y = 0$
$Lim_{x \to -\infty}(f(x)) = \infty$ $Lim_{x \to \infty}(f(x)) = 0$

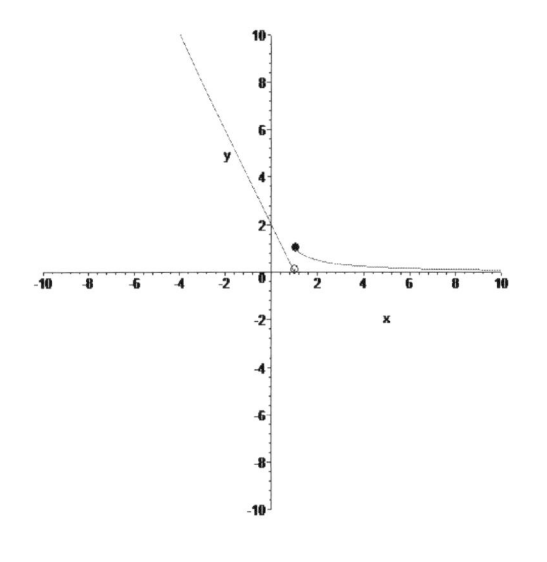

41. $f(x) = \begin{cases} x^2 - 2 & x < -3 \\ \dfrac{1}{x+1} & -3 \leq x \end{cases}$

Domain: $x \in (-\infty, -1) \cup (-1, \infty)$ *Min*: None
Range: $f(x) \in (-\infty, -\dfrac{1}{2}] \cup (0, \infty)$ y int: $(0, 1)$
Increase: Never x int: None
Decrease: $x \in (-\infty, -3) \cup (-3, -1) \cup (-1, \infty)$
V. Asymptote: $x = -1$ *H. Asymptote*: $y = 0$
$Lim_{x \to -1^-}(f(x)) = -\infty$ $Lim_{x \to -\infty}(f(x)) = \infty$
$Lim_{x \to -1^+}(f(x)) = \infty$ $Lim_{x \to \infty}(f(x)) = 0$

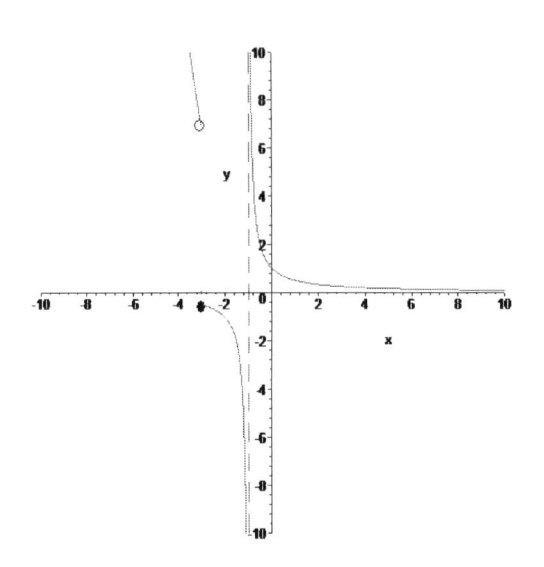

42. $f(x) = \begin{cases} x^2 - 2 & x < 2 \\ \ln(x) & 2 \leq x \end{cases}$

Domain: $x \in (-\infty, \infty)$ *Min*: None
Range: $f(x) \in [-2, \infty)$ y int: $(0, -2)$
Increase: $x \in (0, 2) \cup (2, \infty)$ x int: $(-\sqrt{2}, 0), (\sqrt{2}, 0)$
Decrease: $x \in (-\infty, 0)$
V. Asymptote: None   *H. Asymptote*: None
$Lim_{x \to -\infty}(f(x)) = \infty$ $Lim_{x \to \infty}(f(x)) = \infty$

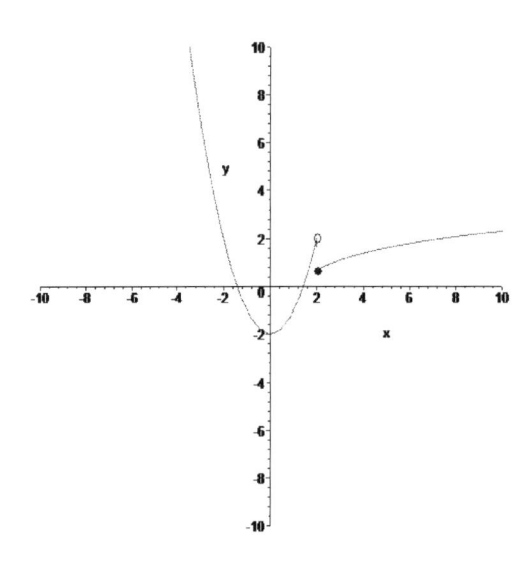

43. Find the value of a that will make f(x) continuous:

$$f(x) = \begin{cases} 2x^2 - 5 & x < 2 \\ a & 2 \leq x \end{cases}$$

$Lim_{x \to 2^-}(f(x)) = 3; Lim_{x \to 2^+}(f(x)) = a; f(2) = a; 3 = a$

Domain: $x \in (-\infty, \infty)$ Min: $(0,0)$
Range: $f(x) \in [-5, \infty)$ y int: $(0,0)$
Increase: $x \in (0,2)$ x int: $(\pm\sqrt{\frac{5}{2}}, 0)$
Decrease: $x \in (-\infty, 0)$
V. Asymptote: None   H. Asymptote: None
$Lim_{x \to -\infty}(f(x)) = \infty$ $Lim_{x \to \infty}(f(x)) = 3$

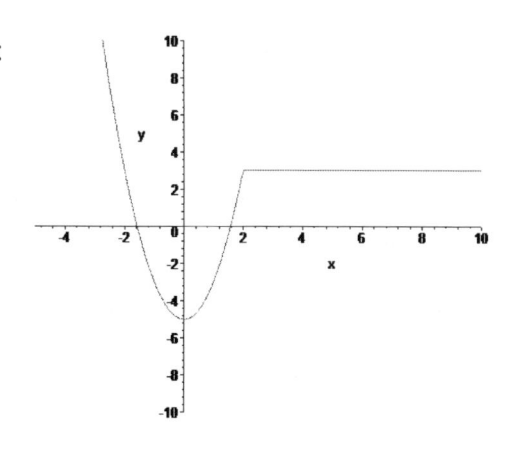

44. $f(x) = \begin{cases} \ln(x+1) & x < 2 \\ -x^2 & 2 \leq x \end{cases}$

Domain: $x \in (-1, \infty)$ Min: None
Range: $f(x) \in (-\infty, \ln(3))$ y int: $(0,0)$
Increase: $x \in (-1, 2)$ x int: $(0,0)$
Decrease: $x \in (2, -\infty)$
V. Asymptote: $x = -1$ H. Asymptote: None
$Lim_{x \to -1^-}(f(x)) = D.E.$ $Lim_{x \to -\infty}(f(x)) = D.E.$
$Lim_{x \to -1^+}(f(x)) = -\infty$ $Lim_{x \to \infty}(f(x)) = -\infty$

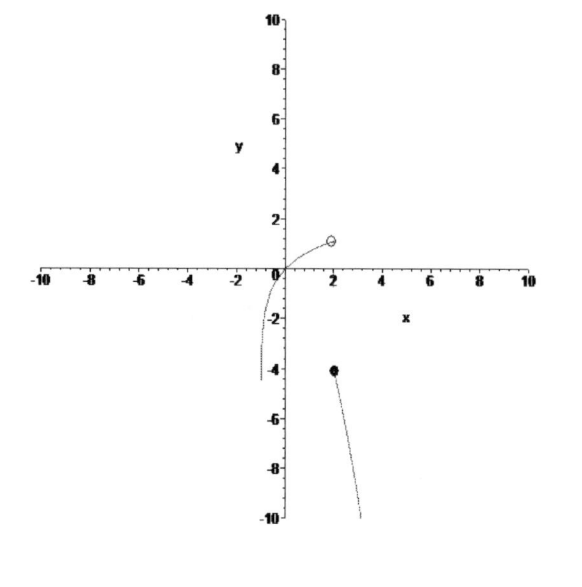

45. $f(x) = \begin{cases} \ln(x-1) & x < 2 \\ (x-2)^2 & 2 \leq x \end{cases}$

Domain: $x \in (1, \infty)$ Min: None
Range: $f(x) \in (-\infty, \infty)$ y int: None
Increase: $x \in (-1, \infty)$ x int: $(2, 0)$
Decrease: Never
V. Asymptote: $x = 1$ H. Asymptote: None
$Lim_{x \to 1^-}(f(x)) = D.E.$ $Lim_{x \to -\infty}(f(x)) = D.E.$
$Lim_{x \to 1^+}(f(x)) = -\infty$ $Lim_{x \to \infty}(f(x)) = \infty$

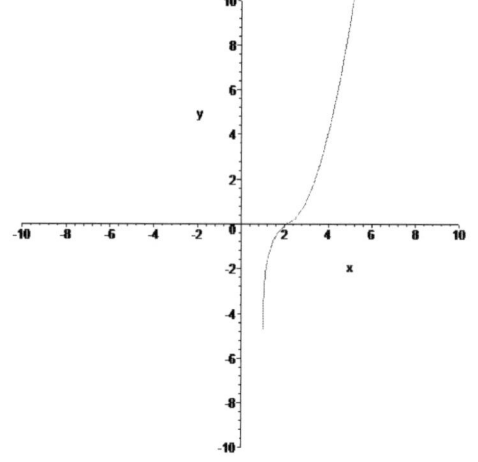

46. The value of a that will make f(x) continuous:

$$f(x) = \begin{cases} x^2 + a & x \leq 1 \\ (x-3)^2 & 1 < x \end{cases}$$

$Lim_{x \to 1^-}(f(x)) = 1 + a; Lim_{x \to 1^+}(f(x)) = 4; f(1) = 1 + a$
$1 + a = 4; a = 3$

556

47. $f(x) = \begin{cases} 1 & x < 0 \\ x & 0 \leq x \text{ and } x < 2 \\ -(x-3)^2 & 2 \leq x \end{cases}$

Domain: $x \in (-\infty, \infty)$ Max: $(3,0)$
Range: $f(x) \in (-\infty, 2)$ y int: $(0,0)$
Increase: $x \in (0,2) \cup (2,3)$ x int: $(0,0), (3,0)$
Decrease: $x \in (3, \infty)$
V. Asymptote: None   H. Asymptote: None
$Lim_{x \to -\infty}(f(x)) = 1$ $Lim_{x \to \infty}(f(x)) = -\infty$

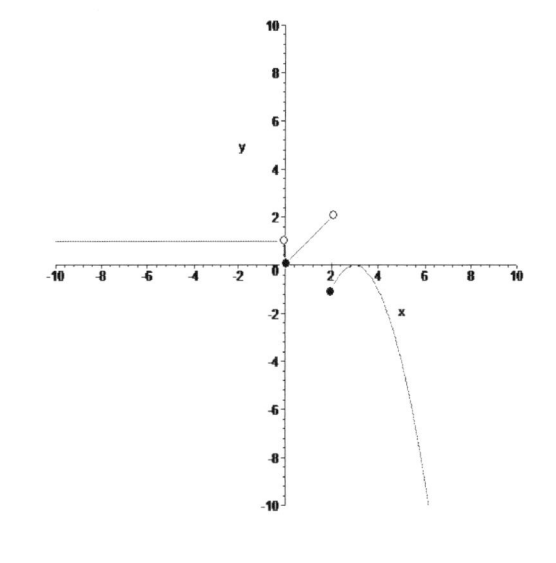

48. $f(x) = \begin{cases} -2x & x < -1 \\ x^2 & -1 \leq x \text{ and } x < 3 \\ (x+1)^2 & 3 \leq x \end{cases}$

Domain: $x \in (-\infty, \infty)$ Min: $(0,0)$
Range: $f(x) \in [0, \infty)$ y int: $(0,0)$
Increase: $x \in (0,3) \cup (3, \infty)$ x int: $(0,0)$
Decrease: $x \in (-\infty, -1) \cup (-1, 0)$
V. Asymptote: None   H. Asymptote: None
$Lim_{x \to -\infty}(f(x)) = \infty$ $Lim_{x \to \infty}(f(x)) = \infty$

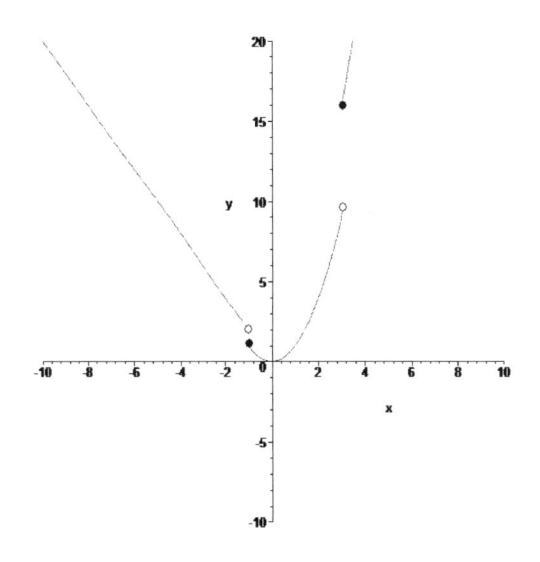

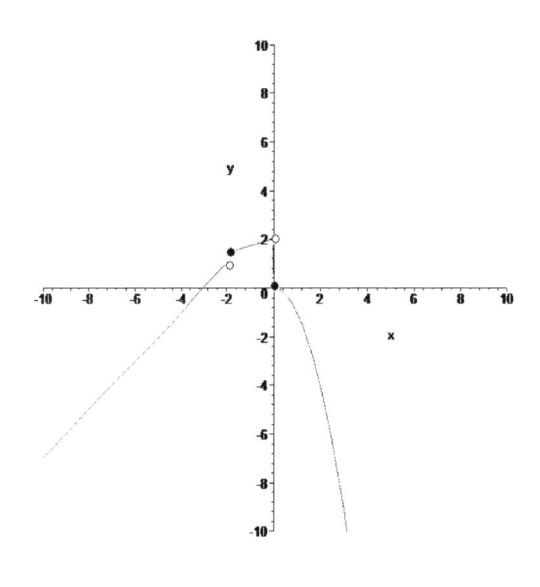

49. $f(x) = \begin{cases} x+3 & x < -2 \\ \sqrt{x+4} & -2 \leq x \text{ and } x < 0 \\ -x^2 & 0 \leq x \end{cases}$

Domain: $x \in (-\infty, \infty)$ Min: None
Range: $f(x) \in (-\infty, 1) \cup [\sqrt{2}, 2)$ y int: $(0,0)$
Increase: $x \in (-\infty, -2) \cup (-2, 0)$ x int: $(0,0), (-3, 0)$
Decrease: $x \in (0, \infty)$
V. Asymptote: None   H. Asymptote: None
$Lim_{x \to -\infty}(f(x)) = -\infty$ $Lim_{x \to \infty}(f(x)) = -\infty$

50. $f(x) = \begin{cases} -3x-1 & x < 0 \\ \ln(x-1) & 0 \leq x \text{ and } x < 4 \\ \sqrt{x} & 4 \leq x \end{cases}$

Domain: $x \in (-\infty, 0) \cup (1, \infty)$ Min: None
Range: $f(x) \in (-\infty, \infty)$ $y$int: None
Increase: $x \in (1, 4) \cup (4, \infty)$ $x$int: $(2, 0), (-\frac{1}{3}, 0)$
Decrease: $x \in (-\infty, 0)$
V. Asymptote: $x = 1$ H. Asymptote: None
$Lim_{x \to 1^-}(f(x)) = D.E.$ $Lim_{x \to -\infty}(f(x)) = \infty$
$Lim_{x \to 1^+}(f(x)) = -\infty$ $Lim_{x \to \infty}(f(x)) = \infty$

51. $f(x) = \begin{cases} e^x & x < -1 \\ -x^2 & -1 \leq x \text{ and } x < 2 \\ e^{(-x)} & 2 \leq x \end{cases}$

Domain: $x \in (-\infty, \infty)$ Max: $(0, 0)$
Range: $f(x) \in (-4, e^{-1})$ $y$int: $(0, 0)$
Increase: $x \in (-\infty, -1) \cup (-1, 0)$ $x$int: $(0, 0)$
Decrease: $x \in (0, 2) \cup (2, \infty)$
V. Asymptote: None   H. Asymptote: $y = 0$
$Lim_{x \to -\infty}(f(x)) = 0$ $Lim_{x \to \infty}(f(x)) = 0$

52. $f(x) = \begin{cases} -(x+2)^2 & x < 0 \\ 3^{(-x)} & 0 \leq x \text{ and } x < 3 \\ x-6 & 3 \leq x \end{cases}$

Domain: $x \in (-\infty, \infty)$ Max: $(-2, 0)$
Range: $f(x) \in (-\infty, \infty)$ $y$int: $(0, 1)$
Increase: $x \in (-\infty, -2) \cup (3, \infty)$ $x$int: $(-2, 0), (6, 0)$
Decrease: $x \in (-2, 0) \cup (0, 3)$
V. Asymptote: None   H. Asymptote: None
$Lim_{x \to -\infty}(f(x)) = -\infty$ $Lim_{x \to \infty}(f(x)) = \infty$

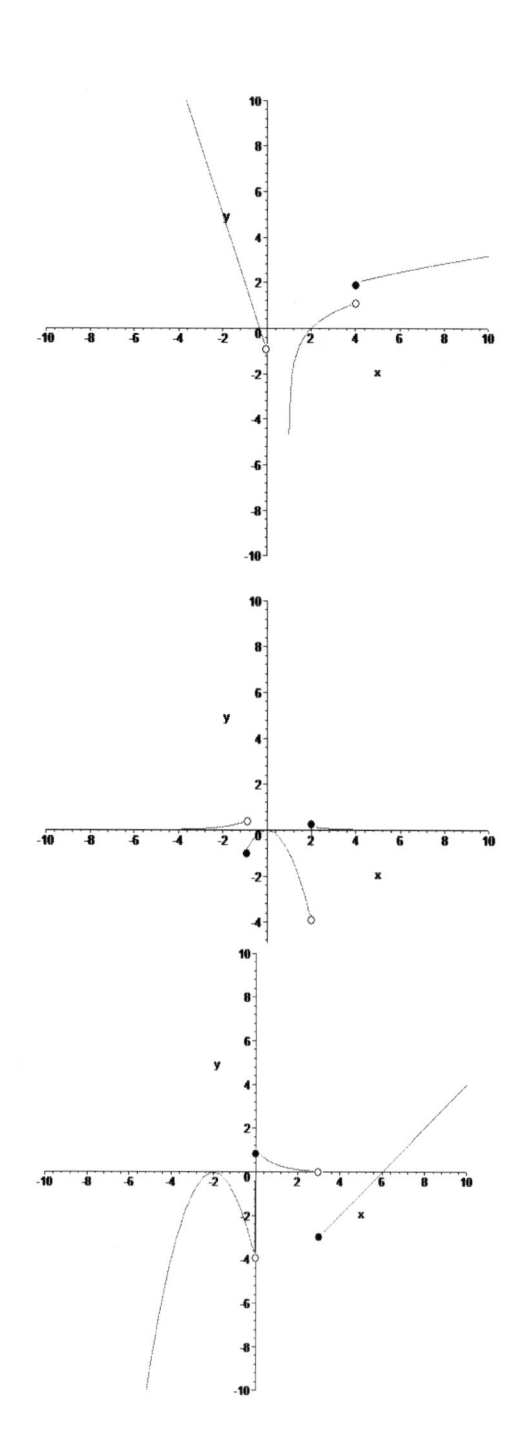

53. $f(x) = \begin{cases} x^2 - 1 & x < 0 \\ 2^x & 0 \leq x \text{ and } x < 3 \\ \dfrac{1}{x-6} & 3 \leq x \end{cases}$

Domain: $x \in (-\infty, 6) \cup (6, \infty)$ Max: None
Range: $f(x) \in (-\infty, \infty)$ y int: $(0,1)$
Increase: $x \in (0,3)$ x int: $(-1,0)$
Decrease: $x \in (-\infty, 0) \cup (3,6) \cup (6, \infty)$
V. Asymptote: $x = 6$ H. Asymptote: $y = 0$
$Lim_{x \to 6^-}(f(x)) = -\infty$ $Lim_{x \to -\infty}(f(x)) = \infty$
$Lim_{x \to 6^+}(f(x)) = \infty$ $Lim_{x \to \infty}(f(x)) = 0$

54. $f(x) = \begin{cases} \dfrac{1}{x} & x < -1 \\ e^x & -1 \leq x \text{ and } x < 2 \\ \ln(x) & 2 \leq x \end{cases}$

Domain: $x \in (-\infty, \infty)$ Max: None
Range: $f(x) \in (-1, 0) \cup [e^{-1}, \infty)$ y int: $(0,1)$
Increase: $x \in (-1, 2) \cup (2, \infty)$ x int: None
Decrease: $x \in (-\infty, -1)$
V. Asymptote: None   H. Asymptote: $y = 0$
$Lim_{x \to -\infty}(f(x)) = 0$ $Lim_{x \to \infty}(f(x)) = \infty$

55. $f(x) = \begin{cases} \dfrac{1}{x+3} & x < -2 \\ \sqrt{x+2} & -2 \leq x \text{ and } x < 0 \\ \ln(x) & 0 \leq x \end{cases}$

Domain: $x \in (-\infty, -3) \cup (-3, 0) \cup (0, \infty)$ Max: None
Range: $f(x) \in (-\infty, \infty)$ y int: None
Increase: $x \in (-2, 0) \cup (0, \infty)$ x int: $(1, 0)$
Decrease: $x \in (-\infty, -3) \cup (-3, -2)$
V. Asymptote: $x = -3$ H. Asymptote: $y = 0$
$Lim_{x \to -3^-}(f(x)) = -\infty$ $Lim_{x \to -\infty}(f(x)) = 0$
$Lim_{x \to -3^+}(f(x)) = \infty$ $Lim_{x \to \infty}(f(x)) = \infty$

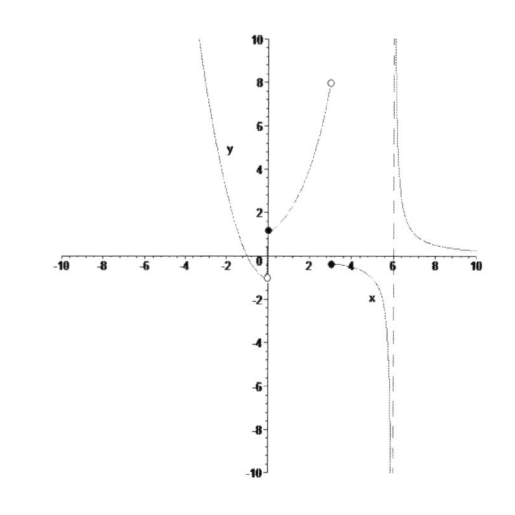

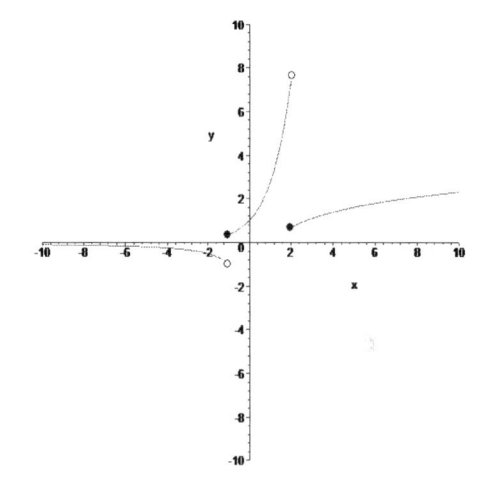

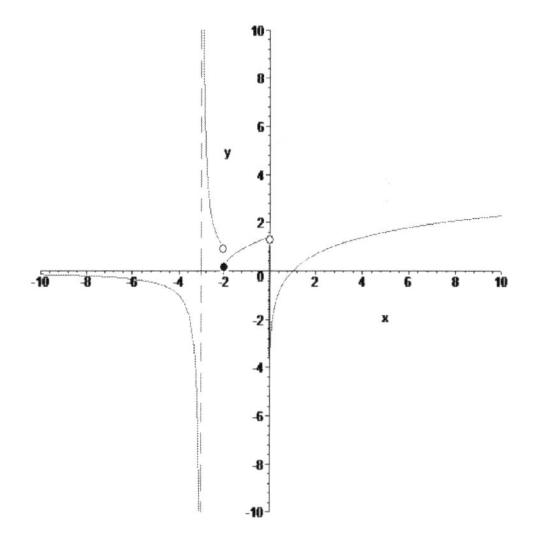

2.11. – COMPOSITE FUNCTIONS

1. Given The functions $f(x) = x + 4$ and $g(x) = 2x^2$, find
   a. $f(g(x)) = 2x^2 + 4$ $g(f(x)) = 2(x+4)^2$
   b. $f(f(x)) = x + 8$ $g(g(x)) = 2(2x^2)^2$
   c. $f(g(f(x)x)) = 2x^2(x+4)^2 + 4$ $g(f(g(x))) = 2(2x^2 + 4)^2$

2. Given The functions $f(x) = 2x^3 + x$ and $g(x) = Ln(x + 1)$, find
   a. $f(g(x)) = 2(Ln(x+1))^3 + Ln(x+1)$ $g(f(x)) = Ln(2x^3 + x + 1)$
   b. $f(f(x)) = 2(2x^3 + x)^3 + 2x^3 + x$ $g(g(x)) = Ln(Ln(x + 1) + 1)$,
   c. $f(g(f(x)x)) = 2(Ln(x(2x^3 + x + 1)))^3 + Ln(x(2x^3 + x) + 1)$
      $g(f(g(x))) = Ln(2(Ln(x+1))^3 + Ln(x+1) + 1)$

3. Given The functions $f(x) = \sqrt{x+1}$ and $g(x) = 3^x - 2$, find
   a. $f(g(x)) = \sqrt{3^x - 1}$ $g(f(x)) = 3^{\sqrt{x+1}} - 2$
   b. $f(f(x)) = \sqrt{\sqrt{x+1} + 1}$ $g(g(x)) = 3^{(3^x-2)} - 2$
   c. $f(g(f(x)x)) = \sqrt{\left(3^{x\sqrt{x+1}} - 1\right)}$ $g(f(g(x))) = 3^{\sqrt{3^x-1}} - 2$

4. Given The functions $f(x) = \dfrac{2}{x^2 + 1}$ and $g(x) = Sin(x + 1)$, find
   a. $f(g(x)) = \dfrac{2}{(Sin(x+1))^2 + 1}$ $g(f(x)) = Sin\left(\dfrac{2}{x^2+1} + 1\right)$
   b. $f(f(x)) = \dfrac{2}{\left(\dfrac{2}{x^2+1}\right)^2 + 1}$ $g(g(x)) = Sin(Sin(x+1) + 1)$
   c. $f(g(f(x)x)) = \dfrac{2}{\left(Sin\left(\dfrac{2x}{x^2+1} + 1\right)\right)^2 + 1}$ $g(f(g(x))) = Sin\left(\dfrac{2}{(Sin(x+1))^2 + 1} + 1\right)$

5. Given The functions $f(x) = \dfrac{1}{x}$ and $g(x) = x^2$, find
   a. $f(g(x)) = \dfrac{1}{x^2}$ $g(f(x)) = \dfrac{1}{x^2}$
   b. $f(f(x)) = x$ $g(g(x)) = x^4$
   c. $f(g(f(x)x)) = 1$ $g(f(g(x))) = \dfrac{1}{x^4}$

6. In general, is $f(g(x)) = g(f(x))$? No, but in some particular cases yes like in part a.

7. The functions $f(x) = x$ and $g(x) = x^2$, $s(x) = sin(x^2 + 3)$, $a(x) = Ln(\dfrac{1}{x})$ find
   a. $f(g(x)) = x^2$ $g(f(x)) = x^2$
   b. $f(s(x)) = sin(x^2 + 3)$ $s(f(x)) = sin(x^2 + 3)$
   c. $f(a(x)) = Ln(\dfrac{1}{x})$ $a(f(x)) = Ln(\dfrac{1}{x})$
   d. What is your conclusion? The function $f(x) = x$ is called the identity function since, as can be seen, it does not cause changes when composed with other functions.

2.12. – INVERSE FUCNTIONS

1. Given The functions $f(x) = x + 4$ and $g(x) = x - 4$, find

   a. $f(g(x)) = x$ $g(f(x)) = x$

2. Given The functions $f(x) = 2x^3$ and $g(x) = \sqrt[3]{\frac{x}{2}}$, find

   a. $f(g(x)) = x$ $g(f(x)) = x$

3. What is your conclusion? $g(x)$ and $f(x)$ are inverse functions (of each other) and as can be seen $f(f^{-1}(x)) = x$

4. Given The function $f(x) = \sqrt{x+1}$, find $f^{-1}(x)$

   Using $f(f^{-1}(x)) = x$ $\sqrt{f^{-1}(x)+1} = x$ so $f^{-1}(x) = x^2 - 1$

5. Given The function $f(x) = \dfrac{2x-3}{x+5}$, find $f^{-1}(x)$. Using $f(f^{-1}(x)) = x$

   $\dfrac{2f^{-1}(x)-3}{f^{-1}(x)+5} = x$; $2f^{-1}(x)-3 = x\left(f^{-1}(x)+5\right)$; $f^{-1}(x) = \dfrac{5x+3}{2-x}$

6. Given The function $f(x) = 2^{3x-5} + 3$, find $f^{-1}(x)$. Using $f(f^{-1}(x)) = x$

   $2^{3f^{-1}(x)-5} + 3 = x$; $f^{-1}(x) = \dfrac{\ln(x-3)}{3\ln(2)} + \dfrac{5}{3}$

7. Given The function $f(x) = e^{\sqrt{x-2}} + 5$, find $f^{-1}(x)$. Using $f(f^{-1}(x)) = x$

   $e^{\sqrt{f^{-1}(x)-2}} + 5 = x$; $f^{-1}(x) = \left(\ln(x-5)\right)^2 + 2$

8. Given The function $f(x) = Ln(x^2 + 2) + 3$, find $f^{-1}(x)$. Using $f(f^{-1}(x)) = x$

   $Ln\left(\left(f^{-1}(x)\right)^2 + 2\right) + 3 = x$; $f^{-1}(x) = \sqrt{e^{x-3} - 2}$

9. Given The function $f(x) = Log_2(2x - 3)$, find $f^{-1}(1)$. Using $f(f^{-1}(x)) = x$

   $Log_2\left(2f^{-1}(x) - 3\right) = x$; $f^{-1}(x) = \dfrac{2^x + 3}{2}$; $f^{-1}(1) = \dfrac{5}{2}$ or

   $Log_2(2x-3) = 1$; $x = \dfrac{5}{2}$ (numerical so no need to find inverse function)

10. Given The function $f(x) = (2x - 4)^2$, find $f^{-1}(0)$

    $\left(2f^{-1}(x) - 4\right)^2 = x$; $f^{-1}(x) = \dfrac{\sqrt{x}+4}{2}$; $f^{-1}(0) = 2$ or

    $(2x-4)^2 = 0$; $x = 2$ (numerical so no need to find inverse function)

11. Given The function f(x) = x² + 2x, find f⁻¹(x)

$$\left(f^{-1}(x)\right)^2 + 2f^{-1}(x) = x \ ; \ \left(f^{-1}(x)+1\right)^2 - 1 = x \ ; \ f^{-1}(x) = \sqrt{x+1} - 1$$

12. Given the function, sketch the inverse function/curve:

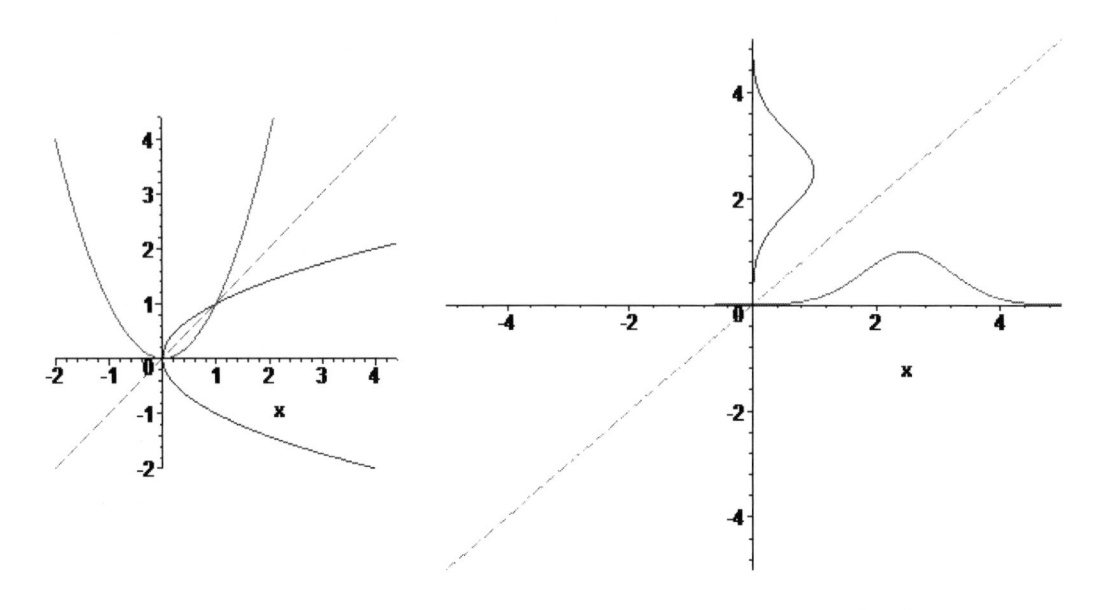

13. Given the function, sketch the inverse function/curve: **In the first case, identical!!**

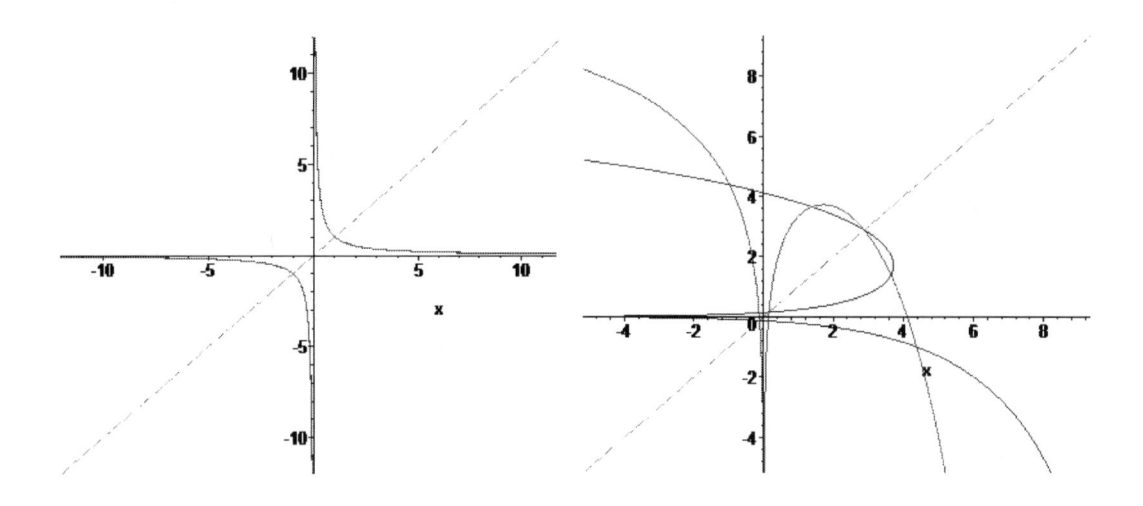

14. Graphically, the inverse function is a <u>reflection about the line y = x</u>.

15. (**T**/F) In case the inverse curve is not a function, the inverse function is not well defined.

CHAPTER 3 – TRIGONOMETRIC FUNCTIONS

3.1. – DEGREES AND RADIANS

. If we go back to the definition of an angle in a circle it is the following:

$X = \dfrac{\text{Length of Arc}}{\text{Radius}}$, In case that S is the entire circle we obtain:

$X = \dfrac{S}{R} = \dfrac{Length-of-circumfernece}{Radius-of-circumfernece} = 6.2831... = 2\pi$

So what we see is that the angle of the entire circle is approximately 6.28 or exactly 2π.

That means: $2\pi_{rad} = 360°$; $1° = \dfrac{2\pi}{360} rad \approx 0.017_{rad}$; $1_{rad} = \left(\dfrac{360}{2\pi}\right)° \approx 57.3°$

Exercises:

1. Complete the table:

Degrees	360°	–180°	90°	45°	22.5°
Radians	2π	$-\pi$	$\dfrac{\pi}{2}$	$\dfrac{\pi}{4}$	$\dfrac{\pi}{8}$

2. Complete the table:

Degrees	0°	30°	60°	–120°	150°
Radians	0	$\dfrac{\pi}{6}$	$\dfrac{\pi}{3}$	$-\dfrac{2\pi}{3}$	$\dfrac{5\pi}{6}$

3. Complete the table:

Degrees	315°	–225°	135°	330°	420°
Radians	$\dfrac{7\pi}{4}$	$-\dfrac{5\pi}{4}$	$\dfrac{3\pi}{4}$	$\dfrac{11\pi}{6}$	$\dfrac{7\pi}{3}$

4. Complete the table:

Degrees	54°	–18°	–36°	15°	75°
Radians	$\dfrac{3\pi}{10}$	$\dfrac{\pi}{10}$	$-\dfrac{\pi}{5}$	$\dfrac{\pi}{12}$	$\dfrac{5\pi}{12}$

5. Complete the table:

Degrees	10°	–9°	12°	3°	7.5°
Radians	$\dfrac{\pi}{18}$	$-\dfrac{\pi}{20}$	$\dfrac{\pi}{15}$	$\dfrac{\pi}{60}$	$\dfrac{\pi}{24}$

6. Complete the table:

Degrees	5°	1°	–10°	660°	540°
Radians	$\dfrac{\pi}{36}$	$\dfrac{\pi}{180}$	$-\dfrac{\pi}{18}$	$\dfrac{11\pi}{3}$	3π

7. Complete the table:

Degrees	180°	18°	−300°	$\dfrac{2160°}{7}$	792°
Radians	π	$\dfrac{\pi}{10}$	$-\dfrac{5\pi}{3}$	$\dfrac{12\pi}{7}$	$\dfrac{22\pi}{5}$

8. Complete the table:

Degrees	$\dfrac{180}{\pi}$	$2.4 \cdot \dfrac{180}{\pi}$	$3.5 \cdot \dfrac{180}{\pi}$	$-\dfrac{360}{\pi}$	$-3.1 \cdot \dfrac{180}{\pi}$
Radians	1	2.4	3.5	−2	−3.1

9. Given the following circles, find θ or L in each one of the cases (in degrees and radians):

$\theta = \dfrac{6}{2} = 3\,Rad = \left(\dfrac{540}{\pi}\right)^{\circ}$

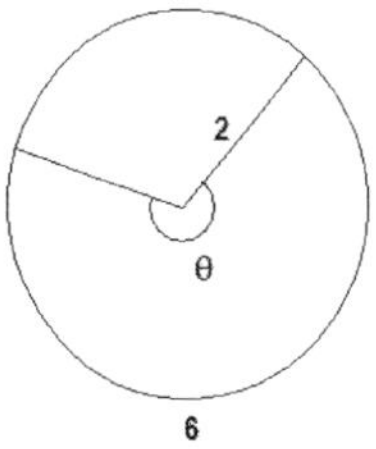

$\theta = \dfrac{2}{3}\,Rad = \left(\dfrac{120}{\pi}\right)^{\circ}$

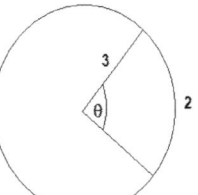

$L = \dfrac{2\pi}{3} \cdot 3 = 2\pi$

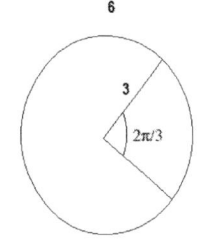

$L = \dfrac{7\pi}{18} \cdot 3 = \dfrac{7\pi}{6}$

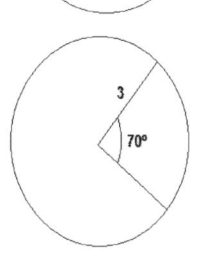

10. The length of the perimeter of a circle with radius r is $2\pi r$. The length of the arc that corresponds an angle x° is $\dfrac{x°}{360} 2\pi r$. In case the angle x is measured in radians it would be $\dfrac{x}{2\pi} 2\pi r = xr$

11. The area of a circle with radius r is πr^2 The area of the sector that corresponds an angle x° is $\dfrac{x°}{360} \pi r^2$ In case the angle x is measured in radians it would be $\dfrac{x}{2\pi} \pi r^2 = \dfrac{x}{2} r^2$

12. Given the circle with r = 2cm : 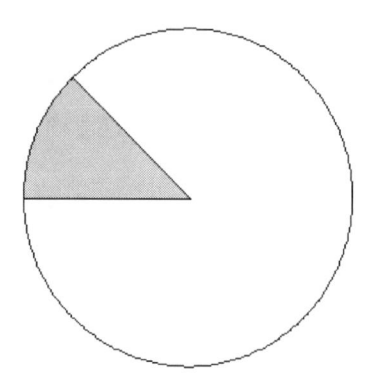
    a. Show the arc corresponding an angle of 45°.
    b. Calculate its length. $L = \dfrac{\pi}{4} 2 = \dfrac{\pi}{2} cm$
    c. Shade the corresponding sector area.
    d. Calculate it. $A = \dfrac{\pi}{8} 2^2 = \dfrac{\pi}{4} cm^2$

13. Given the circle with r = 3.2m:
    a. Show Shade the arc corresponding an angle of 20°.
    b. Calculate its length.
    $$L = \frac{\pi}{9} \cdot 3.2 = \frac{3.2\pi}{9} m$$
    c. Shade the corresponding sector area.
    d. Calculate it.
    $$A = \frac{\pi}{18}(3.2)^2 \approx 1.79 m^2$$

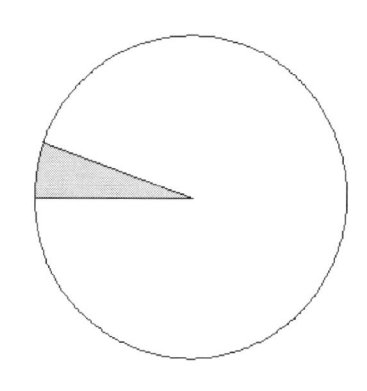

14. Given the circle with r = 3.2m:
    a. Show Shade the arc corresponding an angle of $\frac{\pi}{10} rad$.
    b. Calculate its length.
    $$L = \frac{\pi}{10} \cdot 3.2 = 0.32\pi \ m$$
    c. Shade the corresponding sector area.
    d. Calculate it.
    $$A = \frac{\pi}{20}(3.2)^2 \approx 1.61 m^2$$

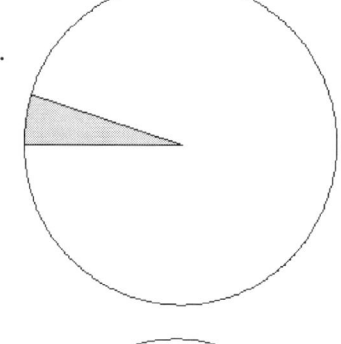

15. Given the circle with r = 3.2m:
    a. Show Shade the arc corresponding an angle of 1 radian.
    b. Calculate its length.
    $$L = 1 \cdot 3.2 = 3.2 m$$
    c. Shade the corresponding sector area.
    d. Calculate it.
    $$A = \frac{1}{2}(3.2)^2 \approx 5.12 m^2$$

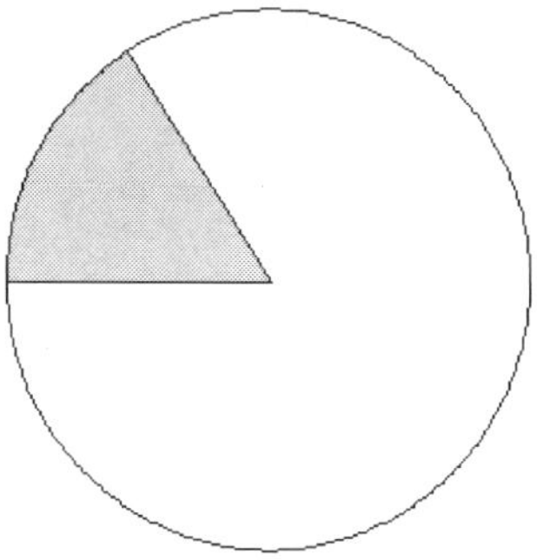

16. Given the following concentric circles with radii 3 cm and 5 cm correspondingly. Calculate the shaded area.
    $$A = \pi 5^2 - \pi 3^2 = 16\pi cm^2$$

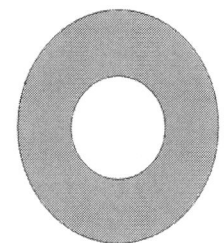

17. Given the following concentric circles with radii 10m and 14m correspondingly. Calculate the shaded area.
    $$A = \frac{40}{360}\left(\pi(14)^2 - \pi(10)^2\right) = \frac{32\pi}{3} cm^2$$

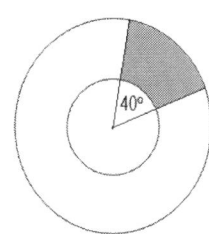

3.2. – TRIGONOMETRIC FUNCTIONS

Definition of Sin(x):
As can be deduced from the unit circle in the <u>first</u> and <u>second</u> quadrants the Sin(x) function is <u>positive</u>, while in the <u>third</u> and <u>forth</u> quadrants it is <u>negative</u>.

Definition of Cos(x):
As can be deduced from the unit circle in the <u>first</u> and <u>forth</u> quadrants the Cos(x) function is <u>positive</u>, while in the <u>second</u> and <u>third</u> quadrants it is <u>negative</u>

Exercises:
In each one of the cases sketch the unit circle and the corresponding angle and then find the corresponding value:

1. $Sin(0°) = 0$
2. $Cos(0_{rad}) = 1$
3. $Sin(0_{rad}) = 0$
4. $Cos(0°) = 1$
5. $Sin(90°) = 1$
6. $Cos(\pi_{rad}) = -1$
7. $Sin(3\pi/4\ _{rad}) = \dfrac{1}{\sqrt{2}}$
8. $Cos(225°) = -\dfrac{1}{\sqrt{2}}$
9. $Sin(225°) = -\dfrac{1}{\sqrt{2}}$
10. $Cos(4\pi/3\ _{rad}) = -\dfrac{1}{2}$
11. $Sin(4\pi/3\ _{rad}) = -\dfrac{\sqrt{3}}{2}$
12. $Cos(210°) = -\dfrac{\sqrt{3}}{2}$
13. $Sin(210°) = -\dfrac{1}{2}$
14. $Sin(3\pi/4\ _{rad}) = \dfrac{1}{\sqrt{2}}$
15. $Cos(225°) = -\dfrac{1}{\sqrt{2}}$
16. $Sin(-225°) = \dfrac{1}{\sqrt{2}}$
17. $Cos(4\pi/3\ _{rad}) = -\dfrac{1}{2}$
18. $Sin(4\pi/3\ _{rad}) = -\dfrac{\sqrt{3}}{2}$
19. $Cos(210°) = -\dfrac{\sqrt{3}}{2}$
20. $Sin(-210°) = \dfrac{1}{2}$
21. $Sin(-\pi_{rad}) = 0$
22. $Cos(90°) = 0$
23. $Sin(270°) = -1$
24. $Cos(\pi/2_{rad}) = 0$
25. $Sin(3\pi/2_{rad}) = -1$
26. $Cos(270°) = 0$
27. $Sin(360°) = 0$
28. $Cos(-\pi/2_{rad}) = 0$
29. $Sin(2\pi_{rad}) = 0$
30. $Cos(180°) = -1$
31. $Sin(180°) = 0$
32. $Cos(\pi/3_{rad}) = \dfrac{1}{2}$
33. $Sin(\pi/4_{rad}) = \dfrac{1}{\sqrt{2}}$
34. $Cos(-45°) = \dfrac{1}{\sqrt{2}}$
35. $Sin(3\pi/2\ _{rad}) = -1$
36. $Cos(-2\pi/3\ _{rad}) = -\dfrac{1}{2}$
37. $Sin(2\pi/3\ _{rad}) = \dfrac{\sqrt{3}}{2}$
38. $Cos(3\pi/4\ _{rad}) = -\dfrac{1}{\sqrt{2}}$
39. $Cos(300°) = \dfrac{1}{2}$
40. $Sin(300°) = -\dfrac{\sqrt{3}}{2}$

41. $\cos(2\pi_{rad}) = 1$
42. $\sin(2\pi_{rad}) = 0$
43. $\sin(330°) = -\dfrac{1}{2}$
44. $\cos(390°) = \dfrac{\sqrt{3}}{2}$
45. $\cos(135°) = -\dfrac{1}{\sqrt{2}}$
46. $\sin(135°) = \dfrac{1}{\sqrt{2}}$
47. $\sin(45°) = \dfrac{1}{\sqrt{2}}$
48. $\cos(-3\pi/2_{rad}) = 0$
49. $\cos(70°) \approx 0.342$
50. $\cos(130°) \approx -0.642$
51. $\cos(1°) \approx 0.999$
52. $\cos(3_{rad}) \approx -0.990$
53. $\sin(1_{rad}) \approx 0.841$
54. $\cos(\Pi/5_{rad}) \approx 0.809$
55. $\sin(2\Pi/7_{rad}) \approx 0.782$

An angle between 0° and 360° different than the first one.

56. $\sin(25°) = \sin(155°)$
57. $\sin(145°) = \sin(35°)$
58. $\sin(70°) = \sin(110°)$
59. $\sin(-20°) = \sin(200°)$
60. $\sin(-30°) = \sin(210°)$
61. $\sin(225°) = \sin(315°)$
62. $\sin(250°) = \sin(290°)$
63. $\cos(250°) = \cos(110°)$
64. $\cos(350°) = \cos(10°)$
65. $\cos(450°) = \cos(90°)$
66. $\cos(-250°) = \cos(250°)$
67. $\cos(-50°) = \cos(50°)$
68. $\cos(-73°) = \cos(73°)$

Definitions of Tan(x), Cot(x), Sec(x) Cosec(x)

$$Tan(x) = \left(\dfrac{Sin(x)}{Cos(x)}\right), Cos(x) \neq 0 \qquad Cot(x) = \left(\dfrac{Cos(x)}{Sin(x)}\right), Sin(x) \neq 0$$

$$Sec(x) = \left(\dfrac{1}{Cos(x)}\right), Cos(x) \neq 0 \qquad Csc(x) = \left(\dfrac{1}{Sin(x)}\right), Sin(x) \neq 0$$

In Consequence:
Tan(x) = tg(x) is positive in the 1st and 3rd quadrants and negative in the 2nd and 4th quadrants. Cotg(x) = Cot(x) = Cotan(x) is positive in the 1st and 3rd quadrants and negative in the 2nd and 4th quadrants.

69. The following trigonometric functions in terms of a and b:
    a. $Sin(\theta) = b \quad Cos(\theta) = a$
    b. $Sin(\theta + 360°) = b$
    c. $Sin(\theta + 180°) = -b$
    d. $Sin(180° - \theta) = b$
    e. $Cos(180° - \theta) = -a$
    f. $Sin(360° - \theta) = -b$
    g. $Cos(360° - \theta) = a$
    h. $Sin(90° - \theta) = a$
    i. $Cos(90° - \theta) = b$
    j. $Tan(\theta) = \dfrac{b}{a}$
    k. $Cotan(\theta) = \dfrac{a}{b}$
    l. $Sec(\theta) = \dfrac{1}{a}$
    m. $Csc(\theta) = \dfrac{1}{b}$
    n. $Tan(\theta + 180°) = \dfrac{b}{a}$
    o. $Tan(\theta + 90°) = \dfrac{Sin(\theta + 90°)}{Cos(\theta + 90°)} = \dfrac{a}{-b}$
    p. $Cos(270° - \theta) = -b$
    q. $Sin(270° + \theta) = -a$

Complete the following table:

Angle in degrees	Angle in Radians	Sin(x)	Cos(x)	Tan(x)	Cot(x)	Sec(x)	Csc(x)
0	0	0	1	0	D.E.	1	D.E.
30°	$\dfrac{\pi}{6}$	$\dfrac{1}{2}$	$\dfrac{\sqrt{3}}{2}$	$\dfrac{1}{\sqrt{3}}$	$\sqrt{3}$	$\dfrac{2}{\sqrt{3}}$	2
45°	$\dfrac{\pi}{4}$	$\dfrac{1}{\sqrt{2}}$	$\dfrac{1}{\sqrt{2}}$	1	1	$\sqrt{2}$	$\sqrt{2}$
60°	$\dfrac{\pi}{3}$	$\dfrac{\sqrt{3}}{2}$	$\dfrac{1}{2}$	$\sqrt{3}$	$\dfrac{1}{\sqrt{3}}$	2	$\dfrac{2}{\sqrt{3}}$
90°	$\dfrac{\pi}{2}$	1	0	D.E.	0	D.E.	1
120°	$\dfrac{2\pi}{3}$	$\dfrac{\sqrt{3}}{2}$	$-\dfrac{1}{2}$	$-\sqrt{3}$	$-\dfrac{1}{\sqrt{3}}$	-2	$\dfrac{2}{\sqrt{3}}$
135°	$\dfrac{3\pi}{4}$	$\dfrac{1}{\sqrt{2}}$	$-\dfrac{1}{\sqrt{2}}$	-1	-1	$-\sqrt{2}$	$\sqrt{2}$
150°	$\dfrac{5\pi}{6}$	$\dfrac{1}{2}$	$-\dfrac{\sqrt{3}}{2}$	$-\dfrac{1}{\sqrt{3}}$	$-\sqrt{3}$	$-\dfrac{2}{\sqrt{3}}$	2
180°	π	0	-1	0	D.E.	-1	D.E.
210°	$\dfrac{7\pi}{6}$	$-\dfrac{1}{2}$	$-\dfrac{\sqrt{3}}{2}$	$\dfrac{1}{\sqrt{3}}$	$\sqrt{3}$	$-\dfrac{2}{\sqrt{3}}$	-2
225°	$\dfrac{5\pi}{4}$	$-\dfrac{1}{\sqrt{2}}$	$-\dfrac{1}{\sqrt{2}}$	1	1	$-\sqrt{2}$	$-\sqrt{2}$
240°	$\dfrac{4\pi}{3}$	$-\dfrac{\sqrt{3}}{2}$	$-\dfrac{1}{2}$	$\sqrt{3}$	$\dfrac{1}{\sqrt{3}}$	-2	$-\dfrac{2}{\sqrt{3}}$
270°	$\dfrac{3\pi}{2}$	-1	0	D.E.	0	D.E.	-1
300°	$\dfrac{5\pi}{3}$	$-\dfrac{\sqrt{3}}{2}$	$\dfrac{1}{2}$	$-\sqrt{3}$	$-\dfrac{1}{\sqrt{3}}$	2	$-\dfrac{2}{\sqrt{3}}$
315°	$\dfrac{7\pi}{4}$	$-\dfrac{1}{\sqrt{2}}$	$\dfrac{1}{\sqrt{2}}$	-1	-1	$\sqrt{2}$	$-\sqrt{2}$
330°	$\dfrac{11\pi}{6}$	$-\dfrac{1}{2}$	$\dfrac{\sqrt{3}}{2}$	$-\dfrac{1}{\sqrt{3}}$	$-\sqrt{3}$	$\dfrac{2}{\sqrt{3}}$	-2
360°	2π	0	1	0	D.E.	1	D.E.
390°	$\dfrac{13\pi}{6}$	$\dfrac{1}{2}$	$\dfrac{\sqrt{3}}{2}$	$\dfrac{1}{\sqrt{3}}$	$\sqrt{3}$	$\dfrac{2}{\sqrt{3}}$	2

Exercises:

1. Given that $\sin(x) = \dfrac{2}{7}$ and $0 < x < \dfrac{\pi}{2}$, find:

   a. $\cos(x) = \dfrac{\sqrt{45}}{7}$

   b. $\tan(x) = \dfrac{2}{\sqrt{45}}$

   c. $\cot(x) = \dfrac{\sqrt{45}}{2}$

   d. $\csc(x) = \dfrac{7}{2}$

   e. $\sin(2x) = \dfrac{4\sqrt{45}}{49}$

   f. $\cos(2x) = \dfrac{51}{49}$

   g. $\sin(3x) = \dfrac{262}{343}$

   h. $\cos(3x) = \dfrac{99\sqrt{5}}{343}$

   i. $\sin(\pi - x) = \dfrac{2}{7}$

   j. $\cos(\pi - x) = -\dfrac{\sqrt{45}}{7}$

   k. $\sin(2\pi - x) = -\dfrac{2}{7}$

   l. $\cos(2\pi - x) = \dfrac{\sqrt{45}}{7}$

   m. $\sin(x + \dfrac{\pi}{2}) = \dfrac{\sqrt{45}}{7}$

2. Given that $\cos(x) = -\dfrac{1}{6}$ and $\pi < x < \dfrac{3\pi}{2}$, find:

   a. $\sin(x) = -\dfrac{\sqrt{35}}{6}$

   b. $\tan(x) = \sqrt{35}$

   c. $\cot(x) = \dfrac{1}{\sqrt{35}}$

   d. $\csc(x) = -\dfrac{6}{\sqrt{35}}$

   e. $\sin(2x) = \dfrac{\sqrt{35}}{18}$

   f. $\cos(2x) = -\dfrac{17}{18}$

   g. $\sin(4x) = -\dfrac{17\sqrt{35}}{162}$

   h. $\cos(4x) = \dfrac{127}{162}$

   i. $\sin(\pi - x) = -\dfrac{\sqrt{35}}{6}$

   j. $\cos(\pi - x) = \dfrac{1}{6}$

   k. $\sin(2\pi - x) = \dfrac{\sqrt{35}}{6}$

   l. $\cos(2\pi - x) = -\dfrac{1}{6}$

   m. $\cos(x + \dfrac{\pi}{2}) = \dfrac{\sqrt{35}}{6}$

3. Given that $\tan(x) = 3$ and $\pi < x < 2\pi$, so x is in the 3rd quadrant. find:

   a. $\cos(x) = -\dfrac{\sqrt{10}}{10}$

   b. $\tan(x) = 3$

   c. $\cot(x) = \dfrac{1}{3}$

   d. $\csc(x) = \dfrac{10}{3\sqrt{10}}$

   e. $\tan(2x) = -\dfrac{3}{4}$

   f. $\sin(3x) = -\dfrac{9\sqrt{10}}{50}$

   g. $\cos(3x) = -\dfrac{13\sqrt{10}}{50}$

   h. $\sin(\pi - x) = \dfrac{3\sqrt{10}}{10}$

   i. $\cos(\pi - x) = \dfrac{\sqrt{10}}{10}$

   j. $\sin(2\pi - x) = -\dfrac{3\sqrt{10}}{10}$

   k. $\cos(2\pi - x) = -\dfrac{\sqrt{10}}{10}$

   l. $\sin(x + \dfrac{\pi}{2}) = -\dfrac{\sqrt{10}}{10}$

3.3. – TRIGONOMETRIC IDENTITIES

1. $\sin(\theta)\sec(\theta)\cot(\theta) = 1$

   $\sin(\theta)\dfrac{1}{\cos(\theta)}\dfrac{\cos(\theta)}{\sin(\theta)} = 1$

   $1 = 1$

2. $\dfrac{\sin(\theta)}{\csc(\theta)} = (\sin(\theta))^2$

   $\dfrac{\sin(\theta)}{\left(\dfrac{1}{\sin(\theta)}\right)} = (\sin(\theta))^2$

   $(\sin(\theta))^2 = (\sin(\theta))^2$

3. $\sin(\theta)\tan(\theta) + \cos(\theta) = \sec(\theta)$

   $\sin(\theta)\dfrac{\sin(\theta)}{\cos(\theta)} + \cos(\theta) = \sec(\theta)$

   $\dfrac{(\sin(\theta))^2 + (\cos(\theta))^2}{\cos(\theta)} = \sec(\theta)$

   $\dfrac{1}{\cos(\theta)} = \sec(\theta)$

4. $\sec(\theta) = \tan(\theta)\csc(\theta)$

   $\sec(\theta) = \dfrac{\sin(\theta)}{\cos(\theta)\sin(\theta)}$

   $\sec(\theta) = \sec(\theta)$

5. $(\tan(\theta))^2 + 1 = (\sec(\theta))^2$

   $\dfrac{(\sin(\theta))^2}{(\cos(\theta))^2} + 1 = (\sec(\theta))^2$

   $\dfrac{(\sin(\theta))^2 + (\cos(\theta))^2}{(\cos(\theta))^2} = (\sec(\theta))^2$

   $(\sec(\theta))^2 = (\sec(\theta))^2$

6. $\dfrac{\sec(\theta)}{\csc(\theta)} = \tan(\theta)$

   $\left(\dfrac{\dfrac{1}{\cos(\theta)}}{\dfrac{1}{\sin(\theta)}}\right) = \tan(\theta)$

   $\dfrac{\sin(\theta)}{\cos(\theta)} = \tan(\theta)$

7. $(\sec(\theta))^2 - (\tan(\theta))^2 = 1$

   $\dfrac{1}{(\cos(\theta))^2} - \dfrac{(\sin(\theta))^2}{(\cos(\theta))^2} = 1$

   $\dfrac{1 - (\sin(\theta))^2}{(\cos(\theta))^2} = 1$

   $\dfrac{(\cos(\theta))^2}{(\cos(\theta))^2} = 1$

   $1 = 1$

8. $\dfrac{\tan(\theta) - \cot(\theta)}{\tan(\theta) + \cot(\theta)} = (\sin(\theta))^2 - (\cos(\theta))^2$

   $\dfrac{\left(\dfrac{\sin(\theta)}{\cos(\theta)} - \dfrac{\cos(\theta)}{\sin(\theta)}\right)}{\left(\dfrac{\sin(\theta)}{\cos(\theta)} + \dfrac{\cos(\theta)}{\sin(\theta)}\right)} = (\sin(\theta))^2 - (\cos(\theta))^2$

   $\dfrac{\left(\dfrac{(\sin(\theta))^2 - (\sin(\theta))^2}{\cos(\theta)\sin(\theta)}\right)}{\left(\dfrac{(\sin(\theta))^2 + (\sin(\theta))^2}{\cos(\theta)\sin(\theta)}\right)} = (\sin(\theta))^2 - (\cos(\theta))^2$

   $\dfrac{\left(\dfrac{(\sin(\theta))^2 - (\sin(\theta))^2}{\cos(\theta)\sin(\theta)}\right)}{\left(\dfrac{1}{\cos(\theta)\sin(\theta)}\right)} = (\sin(\theta))^2 - (\cos(\theta))^2$

   $(\sin(\theta))^2 - (\cos(\theta))^2 = (\sin(\theta))^2 - (\cos(\theta))^2$

9. $\dfrac{\sin(\theta)\cos(\theta)}{(\cos(\theta))^2 - (\sin(\theta))^2} = \dfrac{\tan(\theta)}{1 - (\tan(\theta))^2}$

   Dividing numerator and denominator of LHS by $(\cos(\theta))^2$

   $\dfrac{\tan(\theta)}{1 - (\tan(\theta))^2} = \dfrac{\tan(\theta)}{1 - (\tan(\theta))^2}$

570

10. $\dfrac{1+\tan(\theta)}{1-\tan(\theta)} = \dfrac{1+\cot(\theta)}{\cot(\theta)-1}$

$\dfrac{\left(1+\dfrac{\sin(\theta)}{\cos(\theta)}\right)}{\left(1-\dfrac{\sin(\theta)}{\cos(\theta)}\right)} = \dfrac{1+\cot(\theta)}{\cot(\theta)-1}$

$\dfrac{\left(\dfrac{\cos(\theta)+\sin(\theta)}{\cos(\theta)}\right)}{\left(\dfrac{\cos(\theta)-\sin(\theta)}{\cos(\theta)}\right)} = \dfrac{1+\cot(\theta)}{\cot(\theta)-1}$

$\dfrac{\cos(\theta)+\sin(\theta)}{\cos(\theta)-\sin(\theta)} = \dfrac{1+\cot(\theta)}{\cot(\theta)-1}$

$\dfrac{1+\cot(\theta)}{\cot(\theta)-1} = \dfrac{1+\cot(\theta)}{\cot(\theta)-1}$

In last step numerator and denominator are divided by $\sin(\theta)$

11. $\dfrac{1-\sin(\theta)}{1+\sin(\theta)} = (\sec(\theta)-\tan(\theta))^2$

$\left(\dfrac{1-\sin(\theta)}{1+\sin(\theta)}\right)\cdot\left(\dfrac{1-\sin(\theta)}{1-\sin(\theta)}\right) = (\sec(\theta)-\tan(\theta))^2$

$\left(\dfrac{1-2\sin(\theta)+(\sin(\theta))^2}{1-(\sin(\theta))^2}\right) = (\sec(\theta)-\tan(\theta))^2$

$\left(\dfrac{1-2\sin(\theta)+(\sin(\theta))^2}{(\cos(\theta))^2}\right) = (\sec(\theta)-\tan(\theta))^2$

$\dfrac{1}{(\cos(\theta))^2} - \dfrac{2\sin(\theta)}{(\cos(\theta))^2} + \dfrac{(\sin(\theta))^2}{(\cos(\theta))^2} = RHS$

$\sec(\theta) - 2\tan(\theta)\sec(\theta) + (\tan(\theta))^2 = RHS$

$(\sec(\theta)-\tan(\theta))^2 = (\sec(\theta)-\tan(\theta))^2$

12. $\dfrac{1-\cos(\theta)}{1+\cos(\theta)} = (\csc(\theta)-\cot(\theta))^2$

$\left(\dfrac{1-\cos(\theta)}{1+\cos(\theta)}\right)\cdot\left(\dfrac{1-\cos(\theta)}{1-\cos(\theta)}\right) = (\csc(\theta)-\cot(\theta))^2$

$\left(\dfrac{1-2\cos(\theta)+(\cos(\theta))^2}{1-(\cos(\theta))^2}\right) = (\csc(\theta)-\cot(\theta))^2$

$\left(\dfrac{1-2\cos(\theta)+(\cos(\theta))^2}{(\sin(\theta))^2}\right) = (\csc(\theta)-\cot(\theta))^2$

$\dfrac{1}{(\sin(\theta))^2} - \dfrac{2\cos(\theta)}{(\sin(\theta))^2} + \dfrac{(\cos(\theta))^2}{(\sin(\theta))^2} = RHS$

$\csc(\theta) - 2\cot(\theta)\csc(\theta) + (\cot(\theta))^2 = RHS$

$(\csc(\theta)-\cot(\theta))^2 = (\csc(\theta)-\cot(\theta))^2$

13. $\dfrac{1+\sin(\theta)}{1-\sin(\theta)} - \dfrac{1-\sin(\theta)}{1+\sin(\theta)} = 4\tan(\theta)\sec(\theta)$

$\dfrac{(1+\sin(\theta))^2 - (1-\sin(\theta))^2}{(1-\sin(\theta))(1+\sin(\theta))} = 4\tan(\theta)\sec(\theta)$

$\dfrac{4\sin(\theta)}{1-(\sin(\theta))^2} = 4\tan(\theta)\sec(\theta)$

$\dfrac{4\sin(\theta)}{(\cos(\theta))^2} = 4\tan(\theta)\sec(\theta)$

$4\tan(\theta)\sec(\theta) = 4\tan(\theta)\sec(\theta)$

14. $\dfrac{\tan(x)+\tan(y)}{\cot(x)+\cot(y)} = \tan(x)\tan(y)$

$\dfrac{\left(\dfrac{\sin(x)}{\cos(x)}+\dfrac{\sin(y)}{\cos(y)}\right)}{\left(\dfrac{\cos(x)}{\sin(x)}+\dfrac{\cos(y)}{\sin(y)}\right)} = \tan(x)\tan(y)$

$\dfrac{\left(\dfrac{\sin(x)\cos(y)+\cos(x)\sin(y)}{\cos(x)\cos(y)}\right)}{\left(\dfrac{\sin(y)\cos(x)+\cos(y)\sin(x)}{\sin(x)\sin(y)}\right)} = \tan(x)\tan(y)$

$\dfrac{\sin(x)\sin(y)}{\cos(x)\cos(y)} = \tan(x)\tan(y)$

571

15. $\sin(\theta)\tan(\theta) + \cos(\theta) = \sec(\theta)$

$\sin(\theta)\dfrac{\sin(\theta)}{\cos(\theta)} + \cos(\theta) = \sec(\theta)$

$\dfrac{(\sin(\theta))^2 + (\cos(\theta))^2}{\cos(\theta)} = \sec(\theta)$

$\dfrac{1}{\cos(\theta)} = \sec(\theta)$

16. $(\sin(x))^2 - (\sin(y))^2 = (\cos(y))^2 - (\cos(x))^2$

$\quad 1 - (\cos(x))^2 - \left(1 - (\cos(y))^2\right) = (\cos(y))^2 - (\cos(x))^2$

$\quad (\cos(y))^2 - (\cos(x))^2 = (\cos(y))^2 - (\cos(x))^2$

17. $(\sin(x))^4 - (\cos(x))^4 = 2(\sin(x))^2 - 1$

$\quad \left((\sin(x))^2 - (\cos(x))^2\right)\left((\sin(x))^2 + (\cos(x))^2\right) = 2(\sin(x))^2 - 1$

$\quad (\sin(x))^2 - (\cos(x))^2 = 2(\sin(x))^2 - 1$

$\quad (\sin(x))^2 - (1 - (\sin(x))^2) = 2(\sin(x))^2 - 1$

$\quad 2(\sin(x))^2 - 1 = 2(\sin(x))^2 - 1$

18. $\dfrac{1}{1-\sin(\theta)} + \dfrac{1}{1+\sin(\theta)} = 2(\sec(\theta))^2$

$\dfrac{1+\sin(\theta) + 1 - \sin(\theta)}{(1-\sin(\theta))(1+\sin(\theta))} = 2(\sec(\theta))^2$

$\dfrac{2}{1-(\sin(\theta))^2} = 2(\sec(\theta))^2$

$\dfrac{2}{(\cos(\theta))^2} = 2(\sec(\theta))^2$

$2(\sec(\theta))^2 = 2(\sec(\theta))^2$

19. $3(\sin(x))^2 + 4(\cos(x))^2 = 3 + (\cos(x))^2$

$\quad 3(\sin(x))^2 + 4(\cos(x))^2 = 3 + (\cos(x))^2$

$\quad 3\left((\sin(x))^2 + (\cos(x))^2\right) + (\cos(x))^2 = 3 + (\cos(x))^2$

$\quad 3 + (\cos(x))^2 = 3 + (\cos(x))^2$

3.4. – TRIGONOMETRIC FUNCTIONS

1. Write next to each one of the functions if it's periodic or not. Determine the period of the periodic ones.
   a. No   b. Yes   c. Yes   d. Yes
2. Given the function f(x) = Sin(x), g(x) = Cos(x), Complete the following table:

x°	0	15	30	45	60	75	90	105	120	135	150	165	180
Rad	0	$\frac{\pi}{12}$	$\frac{\pi}{6}$	$\frac{\pi}{4}$	$\frac{\pi}{3}$	$\frac{5\pi}{12}$	$\frac{\pi}{2}$	$\frac{7\pi}{12}$	$\frac{2\pi}{3}$	$\frac{3\pi}{4}$	$\frac{5\pi}{6}$	$\frac{11\pi}{12}$	π
f(x)	0	≈0.259	$\frac{1}{2}$	$\frac{1}{\sqrt{2}}$	$\frac{\sqrt{3}}{2}$	≈0.966	1	$\frac{\sqrt{3}}{2}$	$\frac{\sqrt{3}}{2}$	$\frac{1}{\sqrt{2}}$	$\frac{1}{2}$	≈0.259	0
g(x)	1	$\frac{\sqrt{3}}{2}$	$\frac{\sqrt{3}}{2}$	$\frac{1}{\sqrt{2}}$	$\frac{1}{2}$	≈0.259	0	≈−0.259	$-\frac{1}{2}$	$-\frac{1}{\sqrt{2}}$	$-\frac{\sqrt{3}}{2}$	≈−0.966	−1

195	210	225	240	255
$\frac{13\pi}{12}$	$\frac{7\pi}{6}$	$\frac{5\pi}{4}$	$\frac{4\pi}{3}$	$\frac{17\pi}{12}$
≈−0.259	$-\frac{1}{2}$	$-\frac{1}{\sqrt{2}}$	$-\frac{\sqrt{3}}{2}$	≈−0.966
≈−0.966	$-\frac{\sqrt{3}}{2}$	$-\frac{1}{\sqrt{2}}$	$-\frac{1}{2}$	≈−0.259

- The domain of the function: $x \in R$
- The y intercept: $f(x): (0,0); g(x): (0,1)$
- The x intercept(s): $f(x): (0+\pi k, 0); g(x): (\frac{\pi}{2}+\pi k, 0), k \in \mathbb{Z}$
- The corresponding limits and the equation of the vertical asymptote: None
- The corresponding limits and the equation of the horizontal asymptote: None
- Increasing:
  $f(x): x \in (-\frac{\pi}{2}, \frac{\pi}{2}); g(x): x \in (\pi, 2\pi)$, and in the corresponding intervals
- Decreasing:
  $f(x): x \in (\frac{\pi}{2}, \frac{3\pi}{2}); g(x): x \in (0, \pi)$, and in the corresponding intervals
- Max: $f(x): x \in (\frac{\pi}{2}+2\pi k, 1); g(x): x \in (2\pi k, 1), k \in \mathbb{Z}$

  Min: $f(x): x \in (-\frac{\pi}{2}+2\pi k, -1); g(x): x \in (\pi+2\pi k, -1), k \in \mathbb{Z}$
- State the range of the function: $f(x) \in [-1,1]; g(x) \in [-1,1]$

3. Given the function f(x) = Sin(x)
    a. The function translated 2 positions up. f(x) + 2 = Sin(x) + 2
    b. The function translated 3 positions left. f(x + 3) = Sin(x + 3)
    c. The function translated 3 positions left and 1 up. f(x + 3) + 1 = Sin(x + 3) + 1
    d. The function translated 4 positions right and 1 up. f(x − 4) + 1 = Sin(x − 4) + 1
    e. Change the function so that the period would be 2. $f(x) = Sin(\pi x)$

    f. The period is 3 and the amplitude 2. $f(x) = 2Sin(\frac{2\pi}{3}x)$

    g. The period would is π and the amplitude 4. $f(x) = 4Sin(2x)$

    h. The period is $\frac{\pi}{3}$ and the amplitude k. $f(x) = kSin(6x)$

    i. The period would be 6, the amplitude 3, then shift the function 2 positions right and 1 down. $f(x) = 3Sin\left(\frac{\pi}{3}(x-2)\right) - 1$

    j. The period would be $\frac{\pi}{3}$, the amplitude 1.3, then shift the function 4 positions left and 2 down. $f(x) = 1.3Sin(6(x+4)) - 2$

    k. The period would be $\frac{\pi}{5}$, the amplitude 4, then shift the function π positions left and 5 down. $f(x) = 4Sin(10(x+\pi)) - 5$

4. Given the function f(x) = 3Sin(5(x − 2)) + 3
    a. Amplitude = 5
    b. Period = $\frac{2\pi}{5}$
    c. Horizontal Translation = 2 Right (from sin(5x))
    d. Vertical Translation: 3 up (midline: y = 3)

5. Given the function f(x) = −5Cos(3x − 2) − 3.4 = −5Cos(3(x − $\frac{2}{3}$)) − 3.4
    a. Amplitude = 5
    b. Period = $\frac{2\pi}{3}$
    a. Horizontal Translation = $\frac{2}{3}$ Right (from cos(3x))
    c. Vertical Translation (midline) = 3.4 down (midline: y = −3.4)

6. Given the function $f(x) = 2.4\sin(\pi x - \frac{\pi}{2}) - 3 = 2.4\sin(\pi(x - \frac{1}{2})) - 3$
   a. Amplitude = 2.4
   b. Period = 2
   a. Horizontal Translation = $\frac{1}{2}$ Right (from $\sin(\pi x)$)
   c. Vertical Translation (midline) = 3 down (midline: y = –3)

7. Given the function $f(x) = 4 - (2.4)\cos(2\pi x - \frac{\pi}{3}) = -(2.4)\cos(2\pi(x - \frac{1}{6})) + 4$
   a. Amplitude = 4
   b. Period = 1
   c. Horizontal Translation = $\frac{1}{6}$ Right (from $\cos(2\pi x)$)
   d. Vertical Translation (midline) = 4 up (midline: y = 4)

8. Given the function $f(x) = 1 + 4\sin(\frac{\pi}{3}x - 3) = 4\sin(\frac{\pi}{3}(x - \frac{9}{\pi})) + 1$
   a. Amplitude = 4
   b. Period = 6
   c. Horizontal Translation = $\frac{9}{\pi}$ Right (from $\sin(\frac{\pi}{3}x)$)
   d. Vertical Translation (midline) = 1 up (midline: y = 1)

9. Given the function $f(x) = -\sin(\frac{\pi}{5}x - 1) + 1 = -\sin(\frac{\pi}{5}(x - \frac{5}{\pi})) + 1$
   a. Amplitude = 1
   b. Period = 10
   c. Horizontal Translation = $\frac{5}{\pi}$ Right (from $\sin(\frac{\pi}{5}x)$)
   d. Vertical Translation (midline) = 1 up (midline: y = 1)

10. Given the function $f(x) = 4 - 3\cos(3x°)$
    a. Amplitude = 3
    b. Period = 120°
    c. Horizontal Translation = 0
    d. Vertical Translation: 4 up
    e. Midline: y = 4

11. Given the function $f(x) = -\sin(\frac{x°}{10}) + 1$
    a. Amplitude = 1
    b. Period = 3600°
    c. Horizontal Translation = 0
    d. Vertical Translation: 1 up
    e. Midline: y = 1

12. Given the graph, complete: 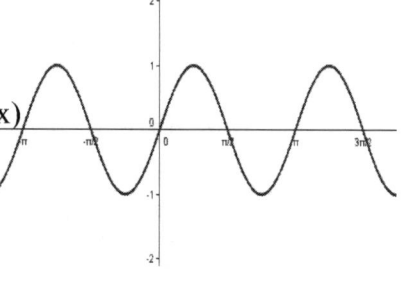
    a. Amplitude = 1
    b. Period = π
    c. Horizontal Translation: Depends, from sin(x) or cos(x)
    d. Midline: y = 0
    e. $f(x) = Sin(2x) = Cos\left(2\left(x - \frac{\pi}{4}\right)\right)$
    f. Range: $f(x) \in [-1, 1]$

13. Given the graph, complete: 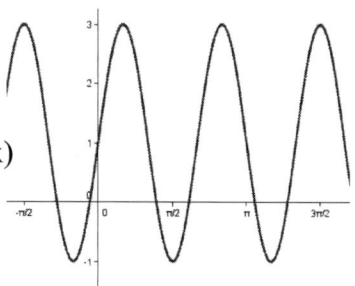
    a. Amplitude = 2
    b. Period = $\frac{2\pi}{3}$
    c. Horizontal Translation: Depends, from sin(x) or cos(x)
    d. Midline: y = 1
    e. $f(x) = 2Sin(\frac{3}{2\pi}x) + 1 = 2Cos\left(3\left(x - \frac{\pi}{6}\right)\right) + 1$
    f. Range: $f(x) \in [-1, 3]$

14. Given the graph, complete: 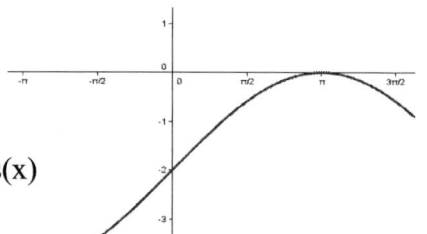
    a. Amplitude = 2
    b. Period = 4π
    c. Horizontal Translation: Depends, from sin(x) or cos(x)
    d. Midline: y = –2
    e. $f(x) = 2Sin(\frac{1}{2}x) - 2 = 2Cos\left(\frac{1}{2}(x - \pi)\right) - 2$
    f. Range: $f(x) \in [-4, 0]$

15. Given the graph, complete: 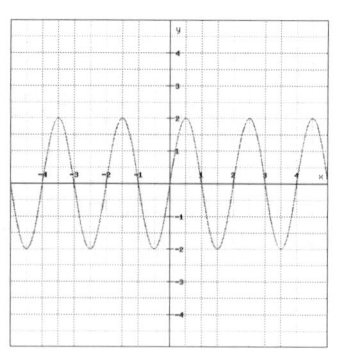
    a. Amplitude = 2
    b. Period = 2
    c. Horizontal Translation: Depends, from sin(x) or cos(x)
    d. Midline: y = 0
    e. $f(x) = 2Sin(\pi x) = 2Cos\left(\pi\left(x - \frac{1}{2}\right)\right)$
    f. Range: $f(x) \in [-2, 2]$

16. Given the graph, complete: 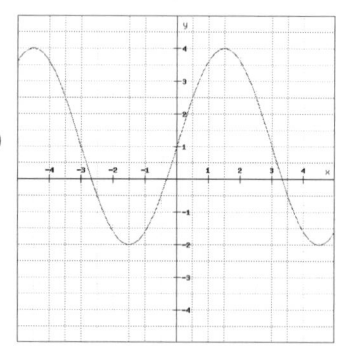
    a. Amplitude = 3
    b. Period = 6
    c. Horizontal Translation: Depends, from sin(x) or cos(x)
    d. Midline: y = 1
    e. $f(x) = 3Sin(\frac{\pi}{3}x) + 1 = 3Cos\left(\frac{\pi}{3}\left(x - \frac{3}{2}\right)\right) + 1$
    f. Range: $f(x) \in [-2, 4]$

17. Given the graph, complete: 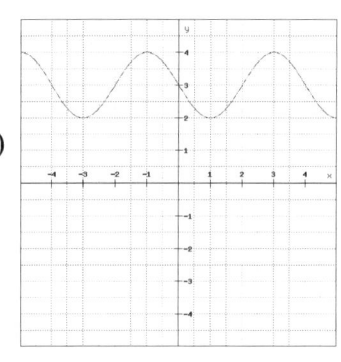
    a. Amplitude = 1
    b. Period = 4
    c. Horizontal Translation: Depends, from sin(x) or cos(x)
    d. Midline: y = 3
    e. $f(x) = -Sin(\frac{\pi}{2}x) + 3 = Cos\left(\frac{\pi}{2}(x+1)\right) + 3$
    f. Range: $f(x) \in [2, 4]$

18. Given the graph, complete: 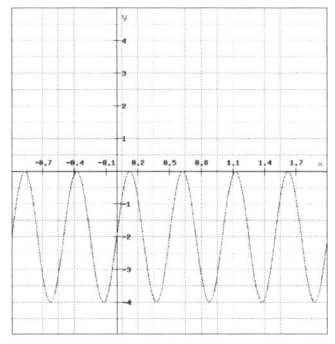
    a. Amplitude = 2
    b. Period = 0.5
    c. Horizontal Translation: Depends, from sin(x) or cos(x)
    d. Midline: y = −2
    e. $f(x) = 2Sin(4\pi x) - 2 = 2Cos\left(4\pi\left(x - \frac{1}{8}\right)\right) - 2$
    f. Range: $f(x) \in [-4, 0]$

19. Given the graph, complete: 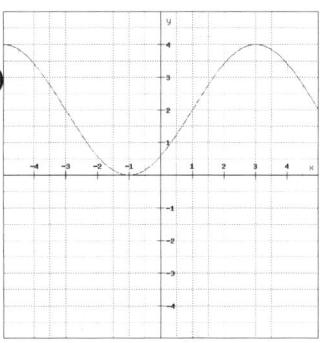
    a. Amplitude = 2
    b. Period = 8
    c. Horizontal Translation = Depends, from sin(x) or cos(x)
    d. Midline: y = 2
    e. $f(x) = 2Sin\left(\frac{\pi}{4}(x-1)\right) + 2 = 2Cos\left(\frac{\pi}{4}(x-3)\right) + 2$
    f. Range: $f(x) \in [0, 4]$

20. Given the graph, complete: 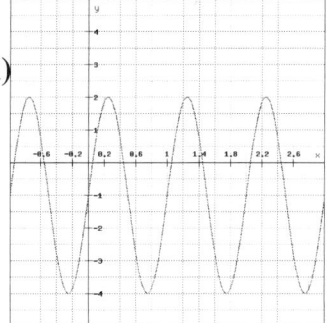
    a. Amplitude = 3
    b. Period = 1
    c. Horizontal Translation = Depends, from sin(x) or cos(x)
    d. Midline: y = −1
    e. $f(x) = 3Sin(2\pi x) - 1 = 3Cos\left(2\pi\left(x - \frac{1}{4}\right)\right) - 1$
    f. Range: $f(x) \in [-4, 2]$

21. Given the graph, complete: 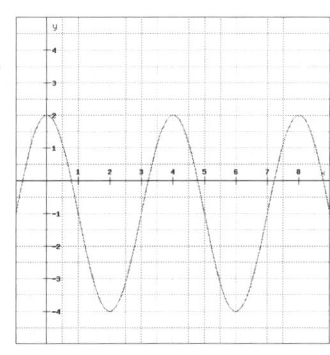
    a. Amplitude = 3
    b. Period = 4
    c. Horizontal Translation: Depends, from sin(x) or cos(x)
    d. Midline: y = −1
    e. $f(x) = 3Sin\left(\frac{\pi}{2}(x+1)\right) - 1 = 3Cos\left(\frac{\pi}{2}x\right) - 1$
    f. Range: $f(x) \in [-4, 2]$

22. Given the graph, complete:
    a. Amplitude = 5
    b. Period = 2
    c. Horizontal Translation: Depends, from sin(x) or cos(x)
    d. Midline: y = –1
    e. $f(x) = 5Sin\left(\pi\left(x-\frac{1}{2}\right)\right) - 1 = 5Cos(\pi(x-1)) - 1 = -5Cos(\pi x) - 1$
    f. Range: $f(x) \in [-6, 4]$

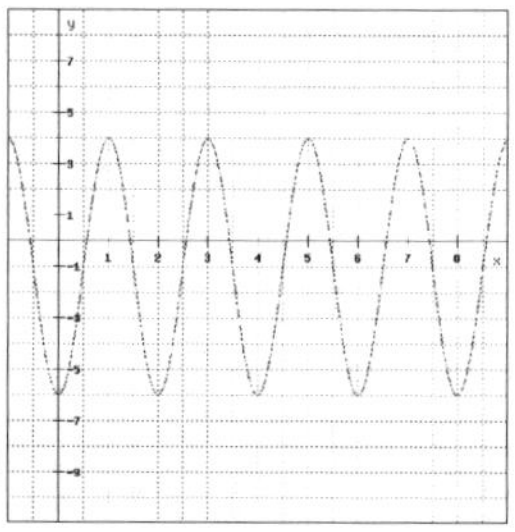

23. Given the graph, complete:
    a. Amplitude = 4
    b. Period = 2
    c. Horizontal Translation: Depends, from sin(x) or cos(x)
    d. Midline: y = –3
    e. $f(x) = 4Sin(\pi(x-1)) - 3 = 4Cos\left(\pi\left(x-\frac{3}{2}\right)\right) - 3 = -4Sin(\pi x) - 3$
    f. Range: $f(x) \in [-7, 1]$

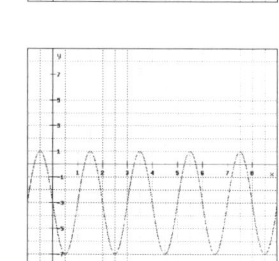

24. Given the function f(x) = 3 – 2Cos(πx – $\frac{\pi}{2}$) = 3 – 2Cos(π(x – $\frac{1}{2}$))

    a. Amplitude = 2
    b. Period = 2
    c. Horizontal Translation: $\frac{1}{2}$ right
       (from cos(π x)
    d. Vertical Translation: 3 up
    e. Midline: y = 3
    f. Range: $f(x) \in [1, 5]$

    g. 2 periods of the function:

    Max: (0.75, 5), (3.5, 5)
    Min: (0.5, 1), (2.5, 1)

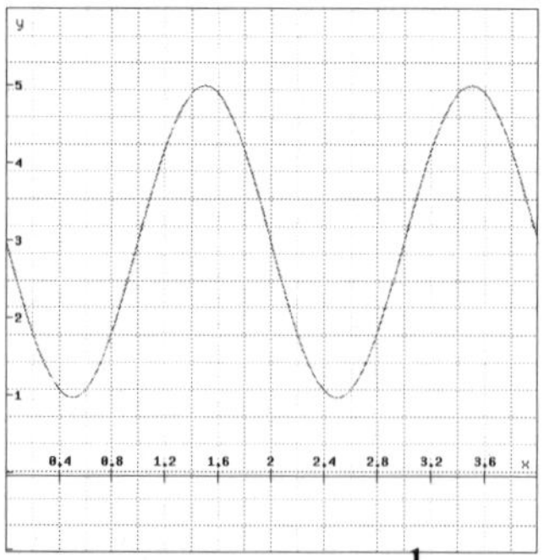

25. Given the function f(x) = –2Sin(πx – $\frac{\pi}{2}$) + 1 = –2Sin(π(x – $\frac{1}{2}$)) + 1

    a. Amplitude = 2
    b. Period = 2
    c. Horizontal Translation: $\frac{1}{2}$ right
       (from sin(π x)
    d. Vertical Translation: 1 up
    e. Midline: y = 1
    f. Range: $f(x) \in [-1, 3]$

    g. 2 periods of the function:

    Max: (0, 3), (2, 3), (4, 3)
    Min: (1, -1), (3, -1)

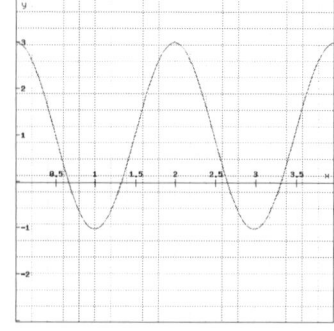

26. Given the function f(x) = Tan(x), Complete the following table:

x°	0	15	30	45	60	75	90	105	120	135	150	165	180
Rad	0	$\frac{\pi}{12}$	$\frac{\pi}{6}$	$\frac{\pi}{4}$	$\frac{\pi}{3}$	$\frac{5\pi}{12}$	$\frac{\pi}{2}$	$\frac{7\pi}{12}$	$\frac{2\pi}{3}$	$\frac{3\pi}{4}$	$\frac{5\pi}{6}$	$\frac{11\pi}{12}$	π
f(x)	0	≈0.268	$\frac{1}{\sqrt{3}}$	1	$\sqrt{3}$	≈3.73	D.E.	≈−3.73	$-\sqrt{3}$	−1	$-\frac{1}{\sqrt{3}}$	≈−0.268	0

195	210	225	240	255
$\frac{13\pi}{12}$	$\frac{7\pi}{6}$	$\frac{5\pi}{4}$	$\frac{4\pi}{3}$	$\frac{17\pi}{12}$
≈0.268	$\frac{1}{\sqrt{3}}$	1	$\sqrt{3}$	≈3.73

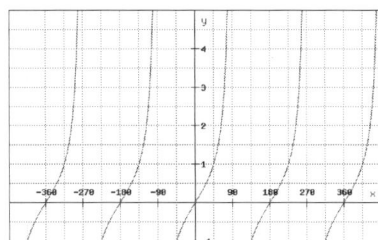

- State the domain of the function: $x \notin (\frac{\pi}{2} + \pi k), k \in \mathbb{Z}$
- State the y intercept: $f(x): (0,0)$
- State the x intercept(s): $f(x): (0 + \pi k, 0), k \in \mathbb{Z}$
- The corresponding limits and equation of vertical asymptotes: $x = \frac{\pi}{2} + \pi k, k \in \mathbb{Z}$
- The corresponding limits and the equation of the horizontal asymptote: None
- Increasing on the interval: $x \notin (\frac{\pi}{2} + \pi k), k \in \mathbb{Z}$, decreasing on the interval: None
- Find the max/min point(s): None
- State the range of the function: $f(x) \in (-\infty, \infty)$

27. Given the function f(x) = Tan(x)
    a. The function translated 2 positions up. f(x) + 2 = Tan(x) +2
    b. The function translated 3 positions left. f(x + 3) = Tan(x + 3)
    c. The function translated 3 positions left and 1 up. f(x + 3) + 1 = Tan(x + 3) + 1
    d. The function translated 4 positions right and 1 up. f(x − 4) + 1 = Tan(x − 4) + 1
    e. Period is 2. $f(x) = \tan(\frac{\pi}{2} x)$
    f. Period is 3 and the amplitude 2. $g(x) = \tan(\frac{\pi}{2} x)$. Tan has no amplitude!
    g. The period is π. $g(x) = \tan(x)$
    h. The period is $\frac{\pi}{3}$. $g(x) = \tan(3x)$
    i. The period is 6, 2 positions right and 1 down. $g(x) = \tan\left(\frac{\pi}{6}(x-2)\right) - 1$
    j. The period is $\frac{\pi}{3}$, 4 positions left and 2 down. $g(x) = \tan(3(x+4)) - 2$
    k. The period is $\frac{\pi}{5}$, π positions left and 5 down. $f(x) = \tan(4(x+\pi)) - 5$

579

28. Given the graph, complete:
    a. Amplitude = None
    b. Period = π
    c. Horizontal Translation: None
    d. Midline: y = 0
    e. $f(x) = \tan(x)$
    f. Range: $f(x): x \in (-\infty, \infty)$

29. Given the graph, complete:
    a. Amplitude = None
    b. Period = $\dfrac{\pi}{3}$
    c. Horizontal Translation: None
    d. Midline: y = 0
    e. $f(x) = \tan(3x)$
    f. Range: $f(x): x \in (-\infty, \infty)$

30. Given the graph, complete:
    a. Amplitude = None
    b. Period = 2
    c. Horizontal Translation: None
    d. Midline: y = 0
    e. $f(x) = \tan(\dfrac{\pi}{2}x)$
    f. Range: $f(x): x \in (-\infty, \infty)$

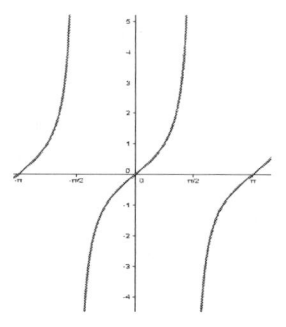

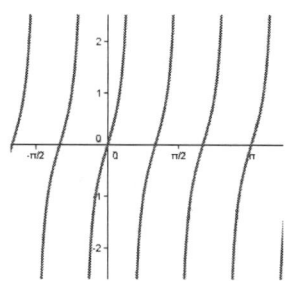

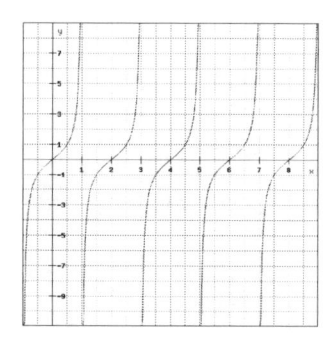

3.5. – SINE AND COSINE RULE

The sine rule: For any triangle, given the sides a, b and c and their corresponding opposite angles, A, B and C:

$$\frac{Sin(A)}{a} = \frac{Sin(B)}{b} = \frac{Sin(C)}{c}$$

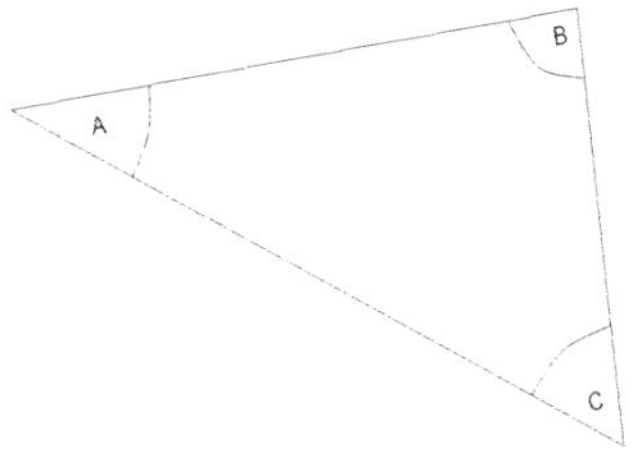

How many equations are written above? 3

$$\frac{Sin(A)}{a} = \frac{Sin(B)}{b} \; ; \; \frac{Sin(A)}{a} = \frac{Sin(C)}{c} \; ; \; \frac{Sin(B)}{b} = \frac{Sin(C)}{c}$$

$$c^2 = a^2 + b^2 - 2ab\cos(C)$$

Given the following triangle:
  a. Find AD in terms of AC and the angle C. $AD = AC\sin(C)$
  b. Find the Area of the triangle in terms of BC, AC and the angle C.

  $$S_{ABC} = \frac{BC \cdot AC \sin(C)}{2}$$

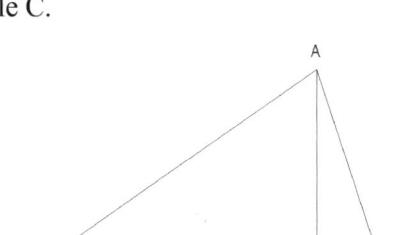

  c. Conclusion: **Area of any triangle is given by half of the product of 2 of its sides multiplied by the sine of the angle between those sides**

  $$S_{ABC} = \frac{a \cdot b \sin(\alpha)}{2}$$

Exercises

1. Sketch a triangle with angles: 20°, 80°, C and sides 10, b, c. Write the Sine and Cosine rule for this triangle.

$$\frac{Sin(20°)}{10} = \frac{Sin(80°)}{b} = \frac{Sin(80°)}{c}$$

$$10^2 = b^2 + c^2 - 2bc\cos(20°)$$
$$b^2 = 10^2 + c^2 - 20c\cos(80°)$$
$$c^2 = 10^2 + b^2 - 20b\cos(80°)$$

2. Find all the missing sides, angles and area of the triangles below. If there is more than one set of solutions, try to find them all.

$$12^2 = 8^2 + 10^2 - 2 \cdot 8 \cdot 10 \cos(G)$$
$$G \approx 82.8°$$
$$10^2 = 8^2 + 12^2 - 2 \cdot 8 \cdot 12 \cos(S)$$
$$S \approx 55.8°$$
$$M = 180° - 82.8° - 55.8° = 41.4°$$

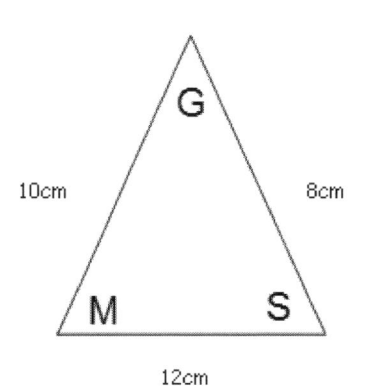

581

$$Area = \frac{10 \cdot 12 \cdot \sin(41.4°)}{2} \approx 36.7 cm^2$$

$x^2 = 11^2 + 10^2 - 2 \cdot 11 \cdot 10 \cos(30)$

$x \approx 5.52 cm$

$11^2 = (5.52)^2 + 10^2 - 2 \cdot 11 \cdot 10 \cos(G)$

$G \approx 87.5°$

$M = 180° - 30° - 87.5° = 62.5°$

$$Area = \frac{10 \cdot 11 \cdot \sin(30°)}{2} \approx 27.5 cm^2$$

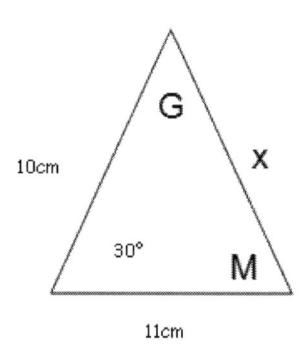

Conclusion: The cosine rule must be used in the following cases:
  I. <u>All sides are known and no angle</u>
  II. <u>2 sides are know and only the angle between them</u>

3. Find all the sides, angles and the area of the following triangles:
Ambiguous Case (2 possible solutions)

$6^2 = 8^2 + x^2 - 2 \cdot x \cdot 8 \cos(40°)$

$x_1 \approx 3.04 cm$; $x_2 \approx 9.22 cm$

$8^2 = 6^2 + 3.04^2 - 2 \cdot 3.04 \cdot 8 \cos(G)$

$G_1 \approx 121°$

$M_1 = 180° - 121° - 40° = 19°$

$8^2 = 6^2 + 9.22^2 - 2 \cdot 9.22 \cdot 8 \cos(G)$

$G_2 \approx 59.0°$

$M_2 = 180° - 59° - 40° = 81°$

$$Area_1 = \frac{6 \cdot 8 \cdot \sin(19°)}{2} \approx 7.81 cm^2 \quad Area_2 = \frac{6 \cdot 8 \cdot \sin(81°)}{2} \approx 23.7 cm^2$$

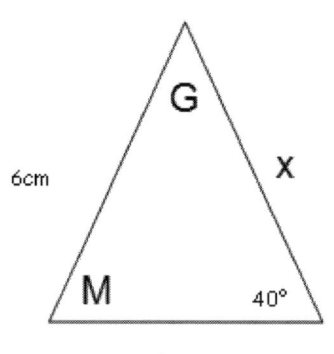

$$\frac{\sin(20°)}{10} = \frac{\sin(G)}{15}$$

$G_1 \approx 30.9°$; $G_2 \approx 141°$

$M_1 = 180° - 30.9° - 20° = 129.1°$

$M_2 = 180° - 141° - 20° = 19°$

$x_1^2 = 10^2 + 15^2 - 2 \cdot 10 \cdot 15 \cos(129.1°)$

$x_1 \approx 22.7 cm$

$x_2^2 = 10^2 + 15^2 - 2 \cdot 10 \cdot 15 \cos(19°)$

$x_2 \approx 6.43 cm$

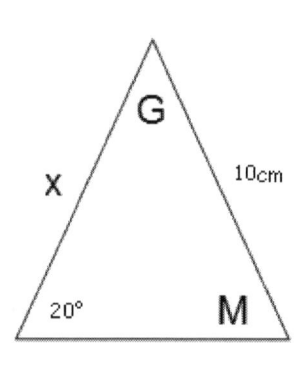

$$Area_1 = \frac{15 \cdot 22.7 \cdot \sin(20°)}{2} \approx 58.2 cm^2 \quad Area_2 = \frac{15 \cdot 6.43 \cdot \sin(20°)}{2} \approx 16.5 cm^2$$

Conclusion: The ambiguous case appears when 2 sides are known and the angle opposite to the shorter of those sides

4. Find all the sides, angles and the area of the following triangles:
$M = 180° - 20° - 50° = 110°$

$$\frac{\sin(110°)}{15} = \frac{\sin(20°)}{x} \quad ; x \approx 5.45 cm$$

$$\frac{\sin(110°)}{15} = \frac{\sin(50)}{y} \quad ; y \approx 12.2 cm$$

$$Area = \frac{15 \cdot 5.45 \cdot \sin(50°)}{2} \approx 31.3 cm^2$$

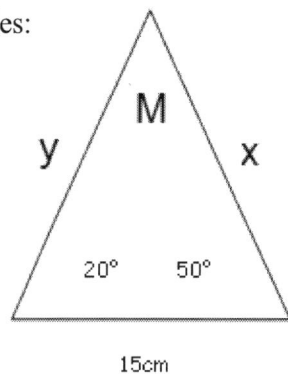

5. Find all the sides, angles and the area of the triangle:
This triangle can have any size as only angles are given

6. Find all the sides, angles and the area of the triangle:

Ambiguous Case (2 possible solutions)
$5^2 = 9^2 + x^2 - 2 \cdot x \cdot 9 \cos(20°)$

$x_1 \approx 4.52 cm$

$x_2 \approx 12.4 cm$

$$\frac{\sin(20°)}{5} = \frac{\sin(G)}{9}$$

$G_1 \approx 28.6°$

$G_2 \approx 180 - 28.6° = 151°$

$M_1 = 180° - 20° - 28.6° = 131°$

$M_2 = 180° - 20° - 151.4° = 8.6°$

$$Area_1 = \frac{9 \cdot 5 \cdot \sin(131°)}{2} \approx 44.0 cm^2$$

$$Area_2 = \frac{9 \cdot 5 \cdot \sin(8.6°)}{2} \approx 6.73 cm^2$$

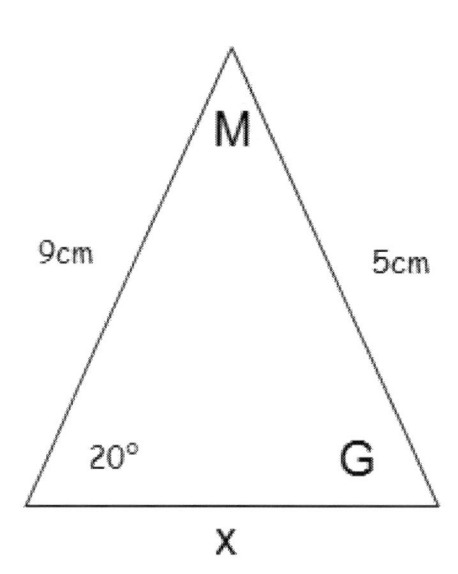

7. Find all the sides, angles and the area of the triangle:

   This triangle cannot exist as the sum 5 + 6 is smaller than 13

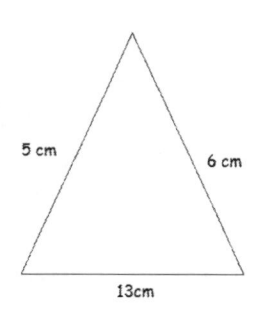

8. Find all the sides, angles and the area of the triangle:
   $$\frac{\sin(50°)}{15} = \frac{\sin(G)}{12}$$
   $G \approx 37.8°$
   $M = 180° - 37.8° - 50° = 92.2°$
   $x^2 = 12^2 + 15^2 - 2 \cdot 12 \cdot 15 \cos(92.2°)$
   $x \approx 19.6 cm$
   $$Area = \frac{15 \cdot 12 \cdot \sin(50°)}{2} \approx 48.2 cm^2$$

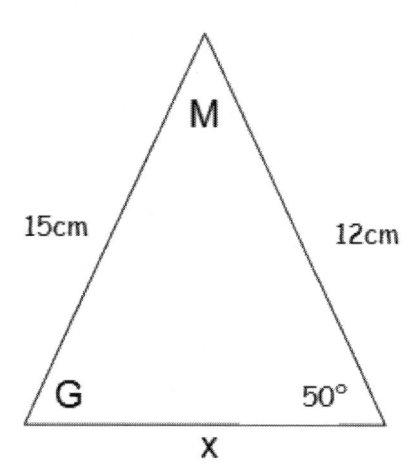

9. Find all the sides, angles and the area of the triangle:
   $x^2 = 12^2 + 8^2 - 2 \cdot 12 \cdot 8 \cos(40°)$
   $x \approx 7.81 cm$
   $$\frac{7.81}{Sin(40°)} = \frac{8}{Sin(G)}$$
   $G \approx 41.2°$
   $M = 180° - 41.2° - 40° = 98.8°$
   $$Area = \frac{8 \cdot 12 \cdot \sin(40°)}{2} \approx 30.9 cm^2$$

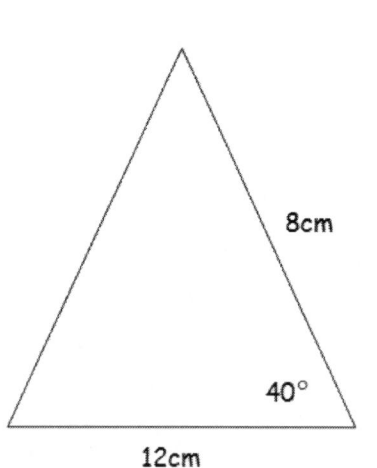

10. Find all the sides, angles and the area of the triangle:
    $x^2 = 13^2 + 6^2 - 2 \cdot 13 \cdot 6 \cos(20°)$
    $x \approx 7.64 cm$
    $$\frac{7.64}{Sin(20°)} = \frac{6}{Sin(G)}$$
    $G \approx 15.6°$
    $M = 180° - 15.6° - 40° = 134.4°$
    $$Area = \frac{6 \cdot 13 \cdot \sin(20°)}{2} \approx 13.3 cm^2$$

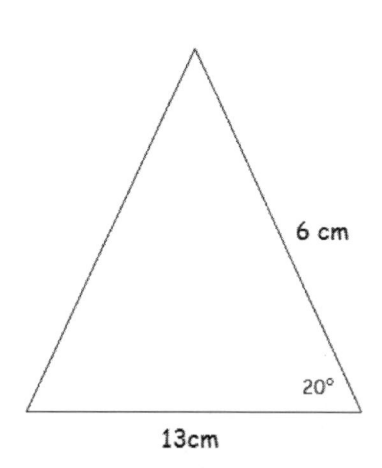

11. Can you identify how many triangles (not to scale) you could draw using the given information? In which example could you find the ambiguous case? Sketch (to scale as possible) both triangles in that case.

a. Ambiguous case – 2 triangles

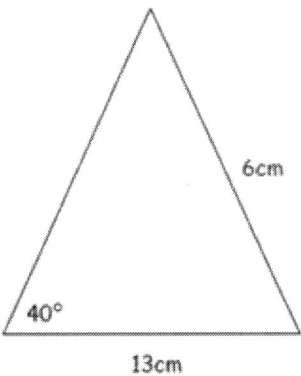

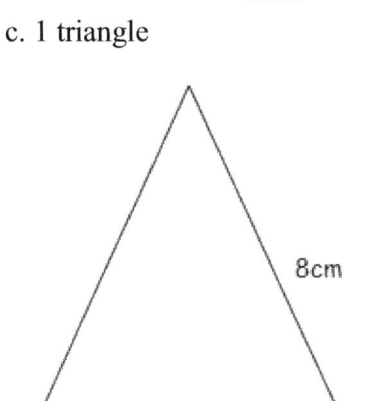

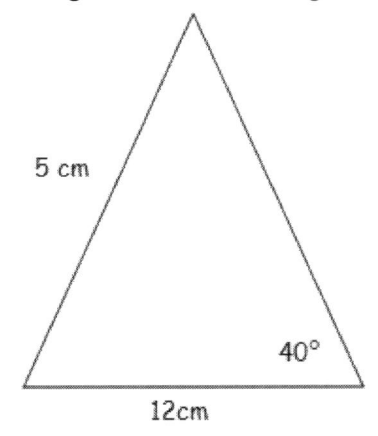

  6cm, 40°, 13cm

b. 1 triangle

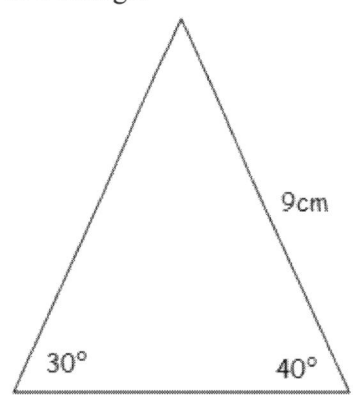

  9cm, 30°, 40°

c. 1 triangle

  8cm, 40°, 12cm

d. Triangle cannot exist

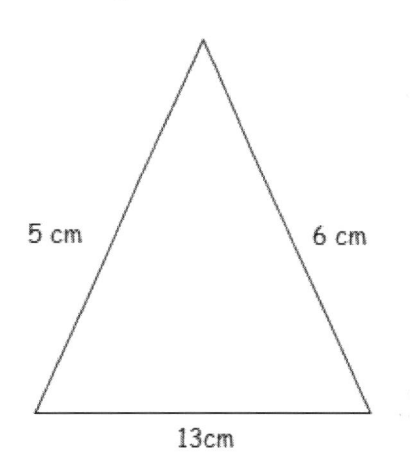

  5 cm, 6 cm, 13cm

e. Ambiguous case – 2 triangles

  5 cm, 40°, 12cm

f. 1 triangle

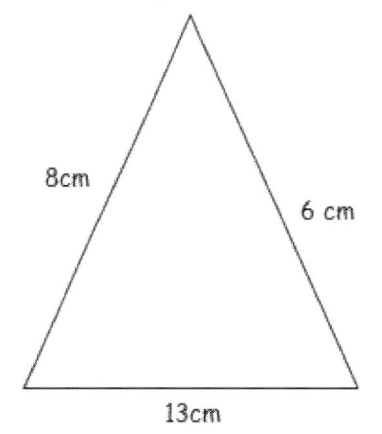

  8cm, 6 cm, 13cm

585

3.6. – TRIGONOMETRIC RATIOS

Exercises:

1. Find x and y in the following cases:

    a.
    $$\sin(25°) = \frac{5}{y}$$
    $$y \approx 11.8$$
    $$\tan(25°) = \frac{5}{x}$$
    $$x \approx 10.7$$

    b.
    $$\sin(20°) = \frac{y}{8}$$
    $$y \approx 2.74$$
    $$\cos(20°) = \frac{x}{8}$$
    $$x \approx 7.52$$

2. The Triangle in the diagram (not to scale) is <u>not</u> right angled, find x and y.

    $$Y^2 = 40^2 + 10^2 - 2 \cdot 40 \cdot 10 \cos(35)$$
    $$Y \approx 32.3$$
    $$\frac{10}{Sin(x)} = \frac{32.3}{Sin(35)}$$
    $$x \approx 10.2°$$

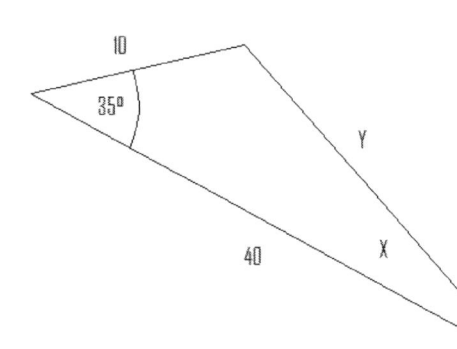

3. The shade formed by building is 100m long. The depression angle of the light as it approaches the ground is 40°.
    a. Sketch a diagram that describes the situation.
    b. Find the height of the building.

    $$\tan(40°) = \frac{h}{100}$$
    $$h \approx 83.9m$$

586

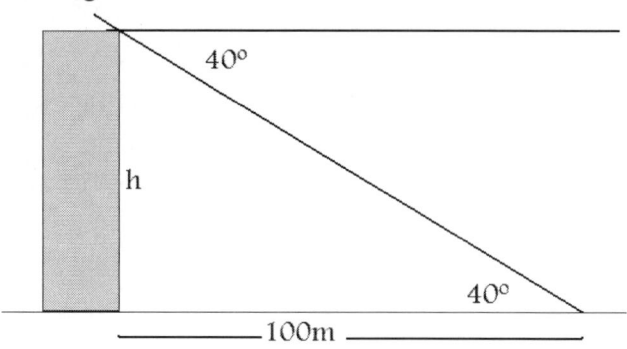

4. The height of building is 120m. The depression angle of the light as it approaches the ground is 30°.
   a. Sketch a diagram that describes the situation.
   b. Find the length of the shade on the ground.

$$\tan(30°) = \frac{120}{L}$$
$$L = 120 \cdot \sqrt{3}\,m$$

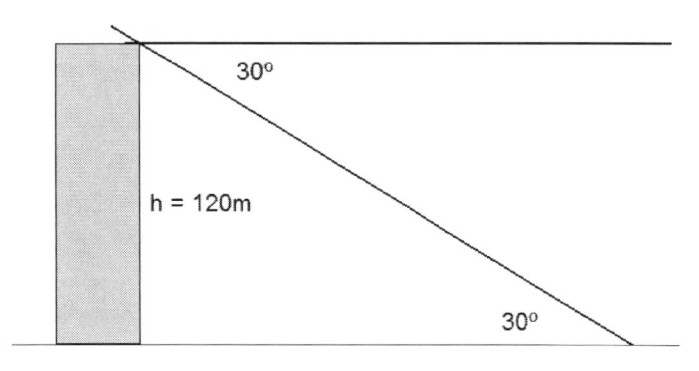

h = 120m

5. In its search for food the 1.5m tall lion is observing a certain prey located 2 m above the ground. The lion's head forms an angle of 12° as he looks at his prey.
   a. Sketch a diagram that describes the situation.
   b. Find the distance from the lion's mouth to its prey.

$$\sin(12°) = \frac{0.5}{L}$$
$$L = 2.40\,m$$

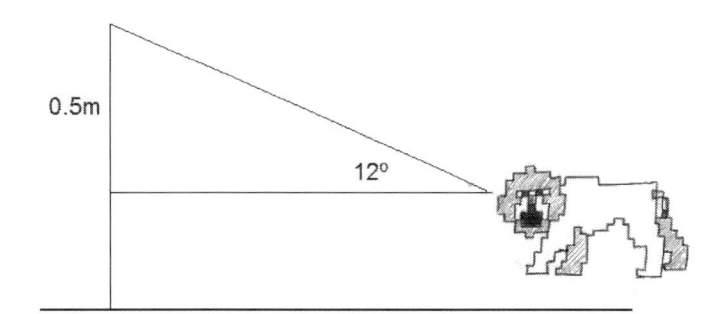

0.5m

12°

6. Measuring the height and distance of objects:

   x = 20°. AB = 4m, y = 18°. Find AD, AC, CD.

$$\tan(20°) = \frac{h}{AD}\ ;\tan(18°) = \frac{h}{AD+4}$$
$$x \approx 33.3m \quad h \approx 12.1m$$

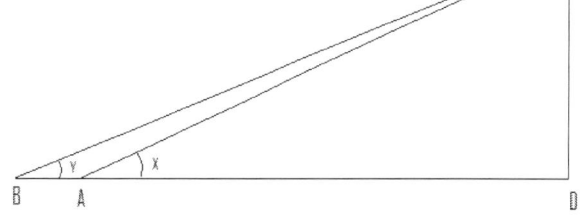

587

3.7. – INVERSE TRIGONOMETRIC FUNCTIONS

Give your answer(s) in radians and degrees, use a calculator if necessary:

1. $\text{Arcsin}(0) = 0 = 0°$
2. $\text{Arcos}(0) = \dfrac{\pi}{2} = 90°$
3. $\text{Arcsin}(1) = \dfrac{\pi}{2} = 90°$
4. $\text{Arcos}(2) = $ D.E.
5. $\text{Arcsin}(0.5) = \dfrac{\pi}{6} = 30°$
6. $\text{Arcos}(-0.5) = -\dfrac{\pi}{3} = -60°$
7. $\text{Arcsin}(\dfrac{\sqrt{3}}{2}) = \dfrac{\pi}{3} = 60°$
8. $\text{Arcos}(-\dfrac{\sqrt{3}}{2}) = -\dfrac{\pi}{6} = -30°$
9. $\text{Arcsin}(\dfrac{\sqrt{2}}{2}) = \dfrac{\pi}{4} = 45°$
10. $\text{Arcos}(-\dfrac{\sqrt{2}}{2}) = \dfrac{\pi}{4} = 45°$
11. $\text{Arcsin}(\dfrac{\sqrt{2}}{2}) = \dfrac{\pi}{4} = 45°$
12. $\text{Arcsin}(-1) = -\dfrac{\pi}{2} = -90°$
13. $\text{Arcos}(-1) = \pi = 180°$
14. $\text{Arcsin}(0.2) \approx 0.201 \approx 11.5°$
15. $\text{Arcos}(-0.4) \approx 1.98 \approx 114°$
16. $\text{Arcsin}(1/5) \approx 0.201 \approx 11.5°$
17. $\text{Arcos}(-5) = $ D.E.
18. $\text{Arcsin}(0.9) \approx 1.12 \approx 65.2°$
19. $\text{Arcsin}(-2.4) = $ D.E.
20. $\text{Arcos}(0.05) \approx 1.52 \approx 87.1°$
21. $\text{Arctan}(-5) \approx -1.37 \approx -78.7°$
22. $\text{Arctan}(1) = \dfrac{\pi}{4} = 45°$
23. $\text{Arctan}(-2.4) \approx -1.18 \approx -67.4°$
24. $\text{Arctan}(\dfrac{1}{\sqrt{3}}) = \dfrac{\pi}{6} = 30°$
25. $\text{Arctan}(-\sqrt{3}) = -\dfrac{\pi}{3} = -60°$
26. $\text{Arctan}(\sqrt{3}) = \dfrac{\pi}{3} = 60°$
27. $\text{Arctan}(-1) = -\dfrac{\pi}{4} = -45°$

Evaluate:

28. $\text{Arcsin}\left(\dfrac{-1}{2}\right) = -\dfrac{\pi}{6} = -30°$
29. $\text{Arccos}\left(\dfrac{\sqrt{3}}{2}\right) = \dfrac{\pi}{6} = 30°$
30. $\text{Arctan}(0) = 0 = 0°$
31. $\cos\left(\arcsin\left(\dfrac{\sqrt{3}}{2}\right)\right) = \cos(60°) = \dfrac{1}{2}$
32. $\cos\left(\arcsin\left(\dfrac{2}{5}\right)\right) = \sqrt{1 - \sin^2\left(\arcsin\left(\dfrac{2}{5}\right)\right)} = \sqrt{\dfrac{1}{5}}$
33. $\sin\left(\arcsin\left(\dfrac{\pi}{5}\right)\right) = \dfrac{\pi}{5}$
34. $\csc\left(\arcsin\left(-\dfrac{2}{7}\right)\right) = -\dfrac{7}{2}$
35. $\cos\left(\arctan\left(\dfrac{3}{4}\right)\right) = \dfrac{1}{\sqrt{1 + \tan^2\left(\arctan\left(\dfrac{3}{4}\right)\right)}} = \dfrac{4}{5}$
36. $\csc\left(\arccos\left(\dfrac{2\sqrt{5}}{5}\right)\right) = \dfrac{1}{\sin\left(\arccos\left(\dfrac{2\sqrt{5}}{5}\right)\right)}$
$= \dfrac{1}{\sqrt{1 - \cos^2\left(\arccos\left(\dfrac{2\sqrt{5}}{5}\right)\right)}} = \sqrt{5}$

3.8. – TRIGONOMETRIC EQUATIONS

1. $\sin(x) = 1$
   Degrees: $x_1 = 90° + 360°k, k \in \mathbb{Z}$
   Radians: $x_1 = \frac{\pi}{2} + 2\pi k, k \in \mathbb{Z}$

2. $\cos(x) = \frac{1}{2}$
   Degrees: $x_1 = 60° + 360°k, k \in \mathbb{Z}$ $\qquad x_2 = 300° + 360°k, k \in \mathbb{Z}$
   Radians: $x_1 = \frac{\pi}{3} + 2\pi k, k \in \mathbb{Z}$ $\qquad x_2 = \frac{5\pi}{3} + 2\pi k, k \in \mathbb{Z}$

3. Conclusion, In general trigonometric equations have <u>infinite</u> solutions.

4. $\cos(x) = -2$, No solution

5. Solve: $\sin(3x) = \frac{1}{2}$, $0 \leq x \leq 2\pi$

   $3x_1 = \frac{\pi}{6} + 2\pi k, k \in \mathbb{Z}$, $x_1 = \frac{\pi}{18} + \frac{2\pi}{3}k, k \in \mathbb{Z}$, $x_{1a} = \frac{\pi}{18}$, $x_{1b} = \frac{13\pi}{18}$ $x_{1c} = \frac{25\pi}{18}$

   $3x_2 = \frac{5\pi}{6} + 2\pi k, k \in \mathbb{Z}$, $x_2 = \frac{5\pi}{18} + \frac{2\pi}{3}k, k \in \mathbb{Z}$, $x_{2a} = \frac{5\pi}{18}$, $x_{2b} = \frac{17\pi}{18}$ $x_{2c} = \frac{30\pi}{18}$

   6 Solutions in total.

6. $\cos(2x - \frac{\pi}{4}) = -1$, $0 \leq x \leq 2\pi$

   $2x - \frac{\pi}{4} = \pi + 2\pi k, k \in \mathbb{Z}$, $x = \frac{5\pi}{8} + \pi k, k \in \mathbb{Z}$, $x_1 = \frac{5\pi}{8}$, $x_2 = \frac{13\pi}{8}$ $x_3 = \frac{21\pi}{8}$

   3 Solutions in total.

7. $\sin(2x° - 100°) = -\frac{\sqrt{3}}{2}$, $0 \leq x \leq 360°$

   $2x_1° - 100 = 240° + 360°k, k \in \mathbb{Z}$, $x_1° = 170° + 180°k, k \in \mathbb{Z}$, $x_{1a} = 170°$, $x_{2b} = 350°$
   $2x_1° - 100 = 300° + 360°k, k \in \mathbb{Z}$, $x_2° = 200° + 180°k, k \in \mathbb{Z}$, $x_{2a} = 200°$ $x_{2b} = 20°$

   4 Solutions in total.

8. $\cos(\frac{\pi}{3}x) = -\frac{1}{2}$, $2\pi \leq x \leq 4\pi$

   $\frac{\pi}{3}x_1 = \frac{2\pi}{3} + 2\pi k, k \in \mathbb{Z}$, $x_1 = 2 + 6k, k \in \mathbb{Z}$, $x_{1a} = 8$

   $\frac{\pi}{3}x_2 = \frac{4\pi}{3} + 2\pi k, k \in \mathbb{Z}$, $x_2 = 4 + 6k, k \in \mathbb{Z}$, $x_{2a} = 10$

   2 Solutions in total.

9. $\sin(\frac{\pi}{4}x) = 2$, $2\pi \leq x \leq 4\pi$

   No solution.

589

10. $\sin(2x) = \dfrac{1}{3}$, $0 \leq x \leq 2\pi$

$2x_1 \approx 0.340 + 2\pi k, k \in \mathbb{Z}$, $x_1 \approx 0.170 + \pi k, k \in \mathbb{Z}$, $x_{1a} \approx 0.170$ $x_{1b} \approx 3.31$

$2x_2 \approx 2.80 + 2\pi k, k \in \mathbb{Z}$, $x_2 \approx 1.40 + \pi k, k \in \mathbb{Z}$, $x_{2a} \approx 1.40$ $x_{1b} \approx 4.54$

4 Solutions in total.

11. $\sin(\dfrac{3\pi}{7}x) = -\dfrac{1}{2}$, $0 \leq x \leq 2\pi$

$\dfrac{3\pi}{7}x_1 = \dfrac{7\pi}{6} + 2\pi k, k \in \mathbb{Z}$, $x_1 = \dfrac{49}{18} + \dfrac{14}{3}k, k \in \mathbb{Z}$, $x_1 = \dfrac{49}{18}$

$\dfrac{3\pi}{7}x_2 = \dfrac{11\pi}{6} + 2\pi k, k \in \mathbb{Z}$, $x_2 = \dfrac{77}{18} + \dfrac{14}{3}k, k \in \mathbb{Z}$, $x_2 = \dfrac{77}{18}$

2 Solutions in total.

12. $\sin(\dfrac{\pi}{4}x - \dfrac{\pi}{2}) = -\dfrac{1}{2}$

$\dfrac{\pi}{4}x_1 - \dfrac{\pi}{2} = \dfrac{7\pi}{6} + 2\pi k, k \in \mathbb{Z}$, $x_1 = \dfrac{20}{3} + 8k, k \in \mathbb{Z}$

$\dfrac{\pi}{4}x_2 - \dfrac{\pi}{2} = \dfrac{11\pi}{6} + 2\pi k, k \in \mathbb{Z}$, $x_2 = \dfrac{22}{3} + 8k, k \in \mathbb{Z}$

This is the general solution; infinite solutions exist for the different values of k.

13. $\cos(\dfrac{\pi}{5}x) = -\dfrac{1}{\sqrt{2}}$

$\dfrac{\pi}{5}x_1 = \dfrac{3\pi}{4} + 2\pi k, k \in \mathbb{Z}$, $x_1 = \dfrac{15}{4} + 10k, k \in \mathbb{Z}$

$\dfrac{\pi}{5}x_2 = \dfrac{5\pi}{4} + 2\pi k, k \in \mathbb{Z}$, $x_2 = \dfrac{25}{4} + 10k, k \in \mathbb{Z}$

This is the general solution; infinite solutions exist for the different values of k.

14. $2\cos(\dfrac{1}{5}x) = 1$, Rewriting: $\cos(\dfrac{1}{5}x) = \dfrac{1}{2}$

$\dfrac{1}{5}x_1 = \dfrac{\pi}{3} + 2\pi k, k \in \mathbb{Z}$, $x_1 = \dfrac{15\pi}{3} + 10\pi k, k \in \mathbb{Z}$

$\dfrac{1}{5}x_2 = \dfrac{5\pi}{3} + 2\pi k, k \in \mathbb{Z}$, $x_2 = \dfrac{25\pi}{3} + 10\pi k, k \in \mathbb{Z}$

This is the general solution; infinite solutions exist for the different values of k.

15. $4\sin(3x° - 5°) = -\dfrac{2}{5}$, Rewriting: $\sin(3x° - 5°) = -\dfrac{1}{10}$,

$3x_1° - 5° \approx 5.74° + 360°k, k \in \mathbb{Z}$, $x_1° \approx 3.58° + 120°k, k \in \mathbb{Z}$

$3x_2° - 5° \approx 174° + 360°k, k \in \mathbb{Z}$, $x_2° \approx 58.1° + 120°k, k \in \mathbb{Z}$

This is the general solution; infinite solutions exist for the different values of k.

16. $\sin(4x° + 20°) = \dfrac{1}{\sqrt{2}}$

   $4x_1° + 20° = 45° + 360°k, k \in \mathbb{Z}, \quad x_1° = 6.25° + 90°k, k \in \mathbb{Z}$
   $4x_2° + 20° = 135° + 360°k, k \in \mathbb{Z}, \quad x_2° = 28.75° + 90°k, k \in \mathbb{Z}$
   This is the general solution; infinite solutions exist for the different values of k.

17. $-\tan(\pi x) = \dfrac{1}{\sqrt{3}}, 0 \leq x \leq 2\pi, \tan(\pi x) = -\dfrac{1}{\sqrt{3}},$

   $\pi x = \dfrac{5\pi}{6} + \pi k, k \in \mathbb{Z}, \quad x = \dfrac{5}{6} + k, k \in \mathbb{Z}, x = \dfrac{5}{6}, \dfrac{11}{6}, \dfrac{17}{6}, \dfrac{23}{6}, \dfrac{29}{6}, \dfrac{35}{6}$
   6 Solutions in total.

18. $\tan(\dfrac{2\pi}{7} x) = \dfrac{1}{\sqrt{3}}$

   $\dfrac{2\pi}{7}x = \dfrac{\pi}{6} + \pi k, k \in \mathbb{Z}, \quad x = \dfrac{7}{12} + \dfrac{7}{2}k, k \in \mathbb{Z}$
   This is the general solution; infinite solutions exist for the different values of k.

19. $\tan(2x°) = 5, 0 \leq x \leq 360°$
   $2x° \approx 78.7 + 180°k, k \in \mathbb{Z}, \quad x° = 39.3° + 90°k, k \in \mathbb{Z}$
   This is the general solution; infinite solutions exist for the different values of k.

20. $\tan(2x°) = -1$
   $2x° = 135° + 180°k, k \in \mathbb{Z}, \quad x_1° = 67.5° + 90°k, k \in \mathbb{Z}$
   This is the general solution; infinite solutions exist for the different values of k.

21. $\tan(3x) = \sqrt{3}$

   $3x = \dfrac{\pi}{3} + \pi k, k \in \mathbb{Z}, \quad x = \dfrac{\pi}{9} + \dfrac{\pi}{3}k, k \in \mathbb{Z}$
   This is the general solution; infinite solutions exist for the different values of k.

22. $\tan(2x - \dfrac{\pi}{3}) = 1$

   $2x - \dfrac{\pi}{3} = \dfrac{\pi}{4} + \pi k, k \in \mathbb{Z}, \quad x = \dfrac{7\pi}{24} + \dfrac{\pi}{2}k, k \in \mathbb{Z}$
   This is the general solution; infinite solutions exist for the different values of k.

23. $\sin(x)\cos(x) + 2\cos(x) = 0$, Rewriting: $\cos(x)(\sin(x) + 2) = 0$

   $\cos(x) = 0; x = \dfrac{\pi}{2} + \pi k, k \in \mathbb{Z}$ Or $\sin(x) = -2;$ No Solution

   This is the general solution; infinite solutions exist for the different values of k

24. $(\cos(x))^2 + \cos(x) = 0$, Rewriting: $\cos(x)(\cos(x) + 1) = 0$

   $\cos(x) = 0; x = \dfrac{\pi}{2} + \pi k, k \in \mathbb{Z}$ Or $\cos(x) = -1; x = \pi + \pi k, k \in \mathbb{Z}$

   This is the general solution; infinite solutions exist for the different values of k

25. tan(x)sin(2x) + sin(x)cos(x) = 0, Rewriting:
$$\frac{\sin(x)}{\cos(x)} \cdot 2\sin(x)\cos(x) - \sin(x)\cos(x) = 0; 2(\sin(x))^2 - \sin(x)\cos(x) = 0$$
$$\sin(x)(2\sin(x) - \cos(x)) = 0$$
$$\sin(x) = 0 \Rightarrow x = \pi k, k \in \mathbb{Z}$$
$$2\sin(x) - \cos(x) = 0 \Rightarrow \tan(x) = \frac{1}{2} \Rightarrow x \approx 0.464 + \pi k, k \in \mathbb{Z}$$

This is the general solution; infinite solutions exist for the different values of k

26. $(\cos(x))^2 + \cos(x) - 2 = 0$, making $\cos(x) = z$:
$$z^2 + z - 2 = 0; \quad (z+2)(z-1) = 0; \quad z = -2, 1$$
$$\cos(x) = -2, \text{No Solution}$$
$$\cos(x) = 1, x = 0 + 2\pi k, k \in \mathbb{Z}$$

This is the general solution; infinite solutions exist for the different values of k

27. $2(\sin(x))^2 + \sin(x) - 1 = 0$, making $\sin(x) = z$:
$$2z^2 + z - 1 = 0; \quad (2z-1)(z+1) = 0; \quad z = -1, \frac{1}{2}$$
$$\sin(x) = -1, x = \pi + 2\pi k, k \in \mathbb{Z}$$
$$\sin(x) = \frac{1}{2}, x_1 = \frac{\pi}{6} + 2\pi k, k \in \mathbb{Z}, x_2 = \frac{5\pi}{6} + 2\pi k, k \in \mathbb{Z}$$

This is the general solution; infinite solutions exist for the different values of k

28. $2(\sin(x))^2 - 7\sin(x) + 6 = 0$, making $\sin(x) = z$:
$$2z^2 - 7z + 6 = 0; \quad (2z-3)(z-2) = 0; \quad z = \frac{3}{2}, 2$$
$$\sin(x) = \frac{3}{2}, \text{No Solution}; \sin(x) = 2, \text{No Solution};$$

29. $2(\tan(x))^2 - 6\tan(x) + 4 = 0$, making $\tan(x) = z$:
$$2z^2 - 6z + 4 = 0; \quad (2z-4)(z-1) = 0; \quad z = 2, 1$$
$$\tan(x) = 2, x \approx 1.11 + \pi k, k \in \mathbb{Z}$$
$$\tan(x) = 1, x = \frac{\pi}{4} + \pi k, k \in \mathbb{Z}$$

3.9. – 3D GEOMETRY

1. Sketch each one of the solids and fill the blanks.
    a. Cuboid   Volume = abc Surface Area = $2(ab+ac+bc)$
    a, b and c the sides of the cuboid.
    b. Right pyramid   Volume = $\dfrac{A_{base} h}{3}$ Surface Area = $A_{base} + L(LateralArea)$
    a and h the side of the base and the height of the pyramid.
    c. Right prism   Volume = $A_{base} h$ Surface Area = $2A_{base} + L(LateralArea)$
    d. Right cone   Volume = $\dfrac{\pi r^2 h}{3}$ Surface Area = $\pi(r^2 + rh)$
    e. Cylinder   Volume = $\pi r^2 h$ Surface Area = $2\pi r^2 + 2\pi rh$
    f. Sphere   Volume = $\dfrac{4}{3}\pi r^3$ Surface Area = $4\pi r^2$
    g. Hemisphere   Volume = $\dfrac{2}{3}\pi r^3$ Surface Area = $2\pi r^2$

2. In the design process of a certain lamp the following diagram is obtained. Assuming the sun is directly above the lamp and length of the shadow on the ground is 2.5 meters.
    a. Find the angle between the lamp and the ground. $\cos(x) = \left(\dfrac{2.5}{3}\right)$
    $x \approx 33.6°$ 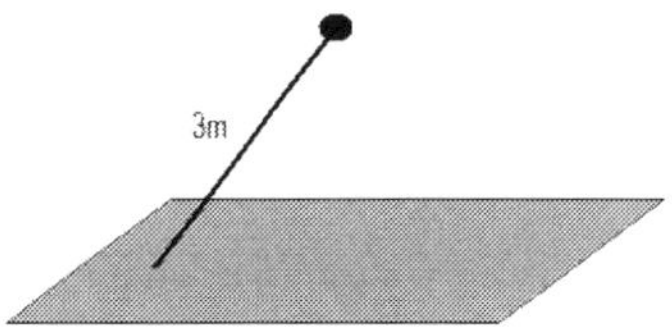
    b. Find the height of the lamp above the ground.
    $\sin(33.6) = \left(\dfrac{h}{3}\right)$
    $h \approx 1.66m$

3. Given the following diagram (not to scale): ABCD is a rectangle AB = 20 cm, BC = 12 cm, EA = BF = 14 cm. EM = 5 cm.
    a. Find the angle between NB and the base ABCD.
    First find DB = $\sqrt{544}$ cm, ND = 9 cm, then working in triangle NBD:
    $\tan(\alpha) = \left(\dfrac{ND}{DB}\right) = \left(\dfrac{9}{\sqrt{544}}\right)$
    $\alpha \approx 21.1°$ 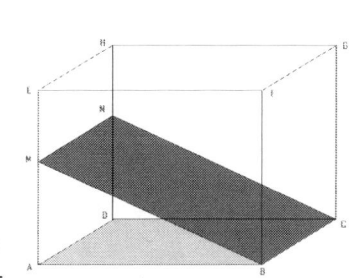
    b. Find the length of the segment MC. $\sqrt{544}$
    c. Find the area of MNBC $A = BC \cdot BM = 12 \cdot \sqrt{481} cm^2$
    d. Find the volume of the cuboid. $V = 20 \cdot 12 \cdot 14 = 3360 cm^3$
    e. Find the surface area of the cuboid. $S = 2(20 \cdot 12 + 20 \cdot 14 + 12 \cdot 14) = 1376 cm^2$

2. Given the following diagram (not to scale): ABCD is a square AB = 10 cm. CG = BF = 12 cm. M is the midpoint of DB.

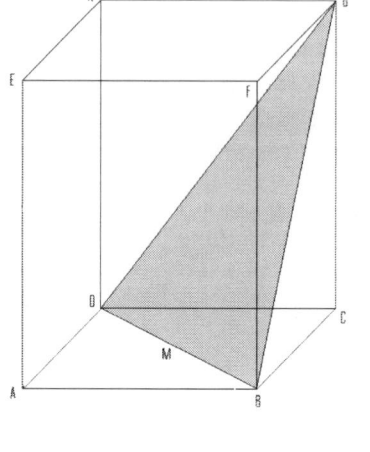

   a. Find the length DB. $DB = \sqrt{200}\,cm$

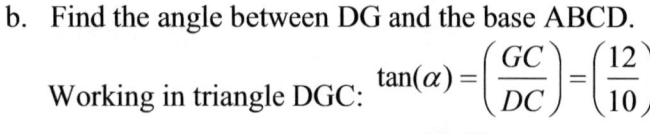

   b. Find the angle between DG and the base ABCD.

   Working in triangle DGC: $\tan(\alpha) = \left(\dfrac{GC}{DC}\right) = \left(\dfrac{12}{10}\right)$

   $\alpha \approx 50.2°$

   c. Find the angle between GM and the base ABCD.

   Working in triangle GMC:

   $\tan(\beta) = \left(\dfrac{GC}{CM}\right) = \left(\dfrac{12}{\left(\dfrac{\sqrt{200}}{2}\right)}\right)$

   $\beta \approx 59.5°$

   d. Find the area of BDG. First we find MG working in triangle MGC:

   $MG = \sqrt{12^2 + \left(\dfrac{\sqrt{200}}{2}\right)^2} = \sqrt{194}$

   Then:

   $A_{BDG} = \dfrac{DG \cdot MG}{2} = \dfrac{\left(\dfrac{\sqrt{200}}{2}\right)\sqrt{194}}{2} = 5\sqrt{97}\,cm^2$

3. In the design process of a modern building a sphere of 5m radius is put on top a cylinder with a radius twice as big. The height of the building is 30m.

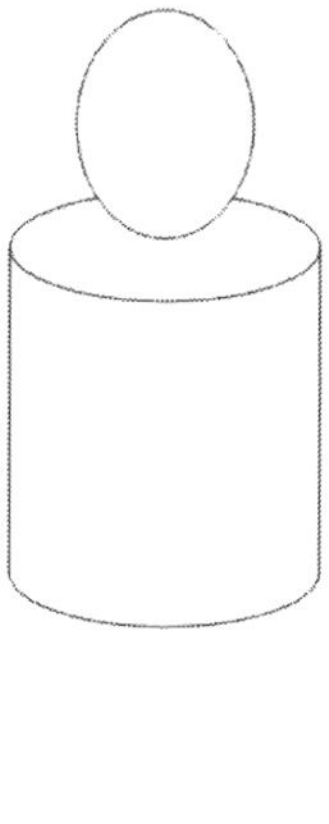

   a. Find the volume of the sphere. $V = \dfrac{4}{3}\pi 5^3 = \dfrac{500\pi}{3}\,cm^3$

   b. Find the height of the cylinder. $h = 30 - 10 = 20\,m$

   c. Find the volume of the building. $V = \dfrac{500\pi}{3} + 2000\pi\,cm^3$

   d. Find the surface area of the building that that is exposed to fresh air.
   $A = A_{sphere} + A_{cylinderTop} + A_{cylinderSide} = 100\pi + 100\pi + 400\pi = 600\pi\,cm^2$

4. Given the following right prism. AB = 12cm, AE = 15cm.

   a. The length of AD.

   In triangle ADE:
   $$\cos(30°) = \left(\frac{AD}{AE}\right) = \left(\frac{AD}{15}\right)$$
   $$AD = \frac{15\sqrt{3}}{2} \approx 13.0$$

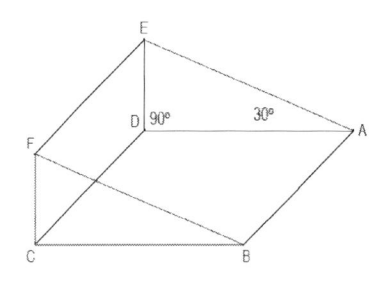

   b. The length of ED.

   In triangle ADE: $\sin(30°) = \left(\frac{DE}{AE}\right) = \left(\frac{DE}{15}\right); DE = 7.5 cm$

   c. The length of AF.
   In triangle ACD:
   $$AC^2 = AD^2 + CD^2; AC^2 = \left(\frac{15\sqrt{3}}{2}\right)^2 + (12)^2; AC = \sqrt{\frac{1251}{4}} \approx 17.7 cm$$

   In triangle ACF:
   $$AF^2 = CF^2 + AC^2; AF^2 = (7.5)^2 + \left(\sqrt{\frac{1251}{4}}\right)^2; AF = 3\sqrt{41} \approx 19.2 cm$$

   d. The angle FAB. $\tan(\delta) = \left(\frac{FB}{BA}\right) = \left(\frac{15}{12}\right); \delta \approx 51.3°$

   e. The surface area of the prism.
   $$A = 2A_{triangle} + A_{base} + A_{top} + A_{back} = \frac{450\sqrt{3}}{8} + 90\sqrt{3} + 180 + 90 = 270 + \frac{585\sqrt{3}}{4} \approx 523 cm^2$$

5. An old tower is made of a cone put on top of a cylinder. The radius of both is 5m. The height of the cylinder is 10m. The height of the cone is 60% of the cylinder's height.

   a. Find the height of the tower.
   $h = 10 + 6 = 16m$

   b. Find the volume of the tower.
   $$V = V_{cone} + V_{cylinder} = \frac{150\pi}{3} + 250\pi = 300\pi \ cm^3$$

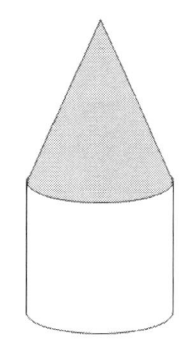

6. Given the following diagram (not to scale): ABCD is a rectangle AB = 9 cm. BC = 7 cm. EF = 10 cm is the height of the right pyramid.

   a. The length AE. $AE = \dfrac{\sqrt{112}}{2} cm$

   b. The length AF. $AF = \sqrt{\left(\dfrac{\sqrt{112}}{2}\right)^2 + (10)^2} = \sqrt{128} cm$

   c. The angle between AF and the base ABCD.
   $$\tan(\alpha) = \left(\dfrac{EF}{AE}\right) = \left(\dfrac{10}{\left(\dfrac{\sqrt{112}}{2}\right)}\right); \alpha \approx 62.1°$$

   d. The length MF.
   $$MF = \sqrt{EM^2 + EF^2} = \sqrt{(4.5)^2 + (10)^2} = \dfrac{\sqrt{481}}{2} \approx 11.0 cm$$

   e. The angle between MF and the base ABCD.
   $$\tan(\beta) = \left(\dfrac{EF}{EM}\right) = \left(\dfrac{10}{4.5}\right); \beta \approx 65.8°$$

   f. The area of FBC. $A_{FBC} = \dfrac{\left(7 \cdot \dfrac{\sqrt{481}}{2}\right)}{2} = \dfrac{7\sqrt{481}}{4} \approx 38.4 cm^2$

   g. Find the volume of the pyramid. $V = \dfrac{7 \cdot 9 \cdot 10}{3} = 210 cm^3$

   h. Find the surface area of the pyramid.

   $$S_{pyramid} = 2A_{FBC} + 2A_{ABF} + A_{ABCD} \approx 76.8 + 91.4 + 63 \approx 231 cm^2$$

Made in the USA
San Bernardino, CA
05 October 2016